EYEWITNESS TRAVEL

AUSTRALIA

**Darwin and
the Top End**
Pages 270–281

**Northern and
Outback Queensland**
Pages 252–261

**South of
Townsville**
Pages 238–251

Brisbane
Pages 222–237

Sydney
Pages 64–159

**The Blue Mountains
and Beyond**
Pages 168–185

**The South Coast and
Snowy Mountains**
Pages 186–193

• Cairns

QUEENSLAND

• Brisbane

NEW
SOUTH
WALES

• Port Augusta

• Adelaide

CANBERRA
AND ACT •

• Sydney

VICTORIA

• Melbourne

TASMANIA

• Hobart

Tasmania
Pages 456–475

Canberra and ACT
Pages 194–211

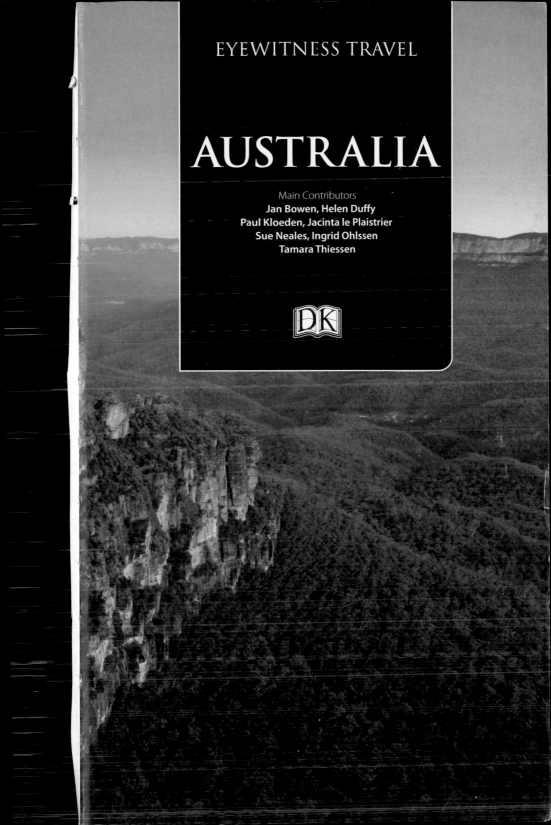

EYEWITNESS TRAVEL

AUSTRALIA

Main Contributors
Jan Bowen, Helen Duffy
Paul Kloeden, Jacinta le Plaistrier
Sue Neales, Ingrid Ohlssen
Tamara Thiessen

DK

LONDON, NEW YORK,
MELBOURNE, MUNICH AND DELHI
www.dk.com

Produced by Duncan Baird Publishers London, England

Managing Editor Zoë Ross

Managing Art Editors Vanessa Marsh (with Clare Sullivan and Virginia Walters)

Editor Rebecca Miles

Commissioning Designer Jill Mumford

Designers Dawn Davis-Cook, Lucy Parissi

Consultant Helen Duffy
Main Contributors Jan Bowen, Helen Duffy, Paul Kloeden,
Jacinta le Plaistrier, Sue Neales, Ingrid Ohlssen, Tamara Thiessen.

Photographers Max Alexander, Alan Keohane, Dave King, Rob Reichenfeld, Peter Wilson.

Illustrators Richard Bonson, Jo Cameron, Stephen Conlin, Eugene Fleury,
Chris Forsey, Steve Gyapay, Toni Hargreaves, Chris Orr, Robbie Polley, Kevin Robinson,
Peter Ross, John Woodcock.

Printed and bound in China

First American Edition 1998

15 16 17 18 10 9 8 7 6 5 4 3 2 1

Published in the United States by DK Publishing
345 Hudson Street, New York, New York 10014

Reprinted with revisions
1999, 2000, 2001, 2002, 2003, 2005, 2006, 2008, 2010, 2012, 2014, 2016

Copyright 1998, 2016 © Dorling Kindersley Limited, London
A Penguin Random House company

ISSN 1542-1554
ISBN 978 1 46543 956 7

MIX
Paper from
responsible sources
FSC
www.fsc.org   FSC™ C018179

The information in this
DK Eyewitness Travel Guide is checked regularly.
Every effort has been made to ensure that this book is as up-to-date as possible
at the time of going to press. Some details, however, such as telephone numbers,
opening hours, prices, gallery hanging arrangements and travel information are
liable to change. The publishers cannot accept responsibility for any consequences
arising from the use of this book, nor for any material on third party websites, and
cannot guarantee that any website address in this book will be a suitable source of
travel information. We value the views and suggestions of our readers very highly.
Please write to: Publisher, DK Eyewitness Travel Guides, Dorling Kindersley,
80 Strand, London, WC2R 0RL, UK, or email: travelguides@dk.com.

Front cover main image: Uluru in the Uluru-Kata Tjuṯa National Park, Northern Territory

◀ Sunset at the magnificent Three Sisters, in the Blue Mountains National Park, New South Wales

Contents

Giraffe in Sydney's Taronga Zoo

Sydney

Ben Boyd National Park on the south coast of New South Wales

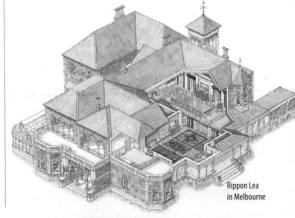
Rippon Lea in Melbourne

HOW TO USE THIS GUIDE

This guide helps you to get the most from your visit to Australia. *Introducing Australia* maps the whole country and sets it in its historical and cultural context. The 17 regional chapters, including *Sydney*, describe important sights with maps, pictures and illustrations, as well as introductory features on subjects of regional interest. Suggestions on restaurants, accommodation, shopping and entertainment are in *Travellers' Needs*. The *Survival Guide* has tips on getting around the country. The cities of Sydney, Melbourne and Brisbane also have their own *Practical Information* sections.

Sydney

The centre of Sydney has been divided into four sightseeing areas. Each area has its own chapter which opens with a list of the sights described. All the sights are numbered and plotted on an *Area Map*. Information on each sight is easy to locate within the chapter as it follows the numerical order on the map.

Sights at a Glance lists the chapter's sights by category: Historic Streets and Buildings, Museums and Galleries, Parks and Gardens etc.

All pages relating to Sydney have orange thumb tabs.

1 Area Map
Sights are numbered on a map. Sights in the city centre are also shown on the Sydney Street Finder (*see pp152–9*). Melbourne also has its own Street Finder (*see pp418–25*).

A locator map shows where you are in relation to other areas of the city centre.

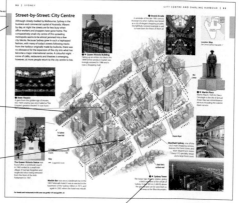

2 Street-by-Street Map
This gives a bird's-eye view of the heart of each sightseeing area.

A suggested route for a walk covers the more interesting streets in the area.

Stars indicate sights that no visitor should miss.

3 Detailed Information on each Sight
All the sights in Sydney are described individually. Useful addresses, telephone numbers, opening hours and other practical information are provided for each entry. The key to all the symbols used in the information block is shown on the back flap.

1 Introduction
The landscape, history and character of each region is described here, showing how the area has developed over the centuries and what it offers to the visitor today.

Australia Area by Area
Apart from Sydney, Australia has been divided into seven chapters. Within the chapters the regions are further divided into 16 areas. The most interesting towns and places to visit are numbered on an *Regional Map* at the beginning of each chapter.

Each area of Australia can be identified quickly by its own colour coding, which is shown on the inside front cover.

2 Regional Map
This shows the main road network and gives an illustrated overview of the whole area. All interesting places to visit are numbered and there are also useful tips on getting around the region.

3 Detailed Information
All the important towns and other places to visit are described individually. They are listed in order, following the numbering on the *Regional Map*. Within each town or city, there is detailed information on important buildings and other sights.

For all the top sights, a visitors' checklist provides the practical information needed to plan your visit.

4 Australia's Top Sights
Historic buildings are dissected to reveal their interiors; museums and galleries have colour-coded floorplans; the national parks have maps showing facilities and trails. Major towns have maps, with sights picked out and described.

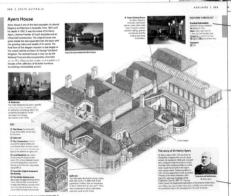

Story boxes explore specific subjects further.

INTRODUCING AUSTRALIA

DISCOVERING AUSTRALIA

The following tours have been designed to take in as many of Australia's highlights as possible. In a country as large as Australia, some long-distance travel is inevitable and driving times may be longer than readers are used to. However, the itineraries endeavour to keep travel distances realistic. To begin with there are three two-day city tours, covering Sydney, Melbourne and Perth. The itineraries for Sydney and Melbourne can easily be combined by anyone travelling between the two. Extra suggestions are provided for those who wish to extend their visit, or take in other nearby sights. The city tours are followed by 14 days on the East Coast, five days in the Red Centre and ten days on the West Coast. These tours can be combined with trips to southern and northern Australia. Pick, combine and follow your favourite tours, or simply dip in and out and be inspired.

10 Days on the West Coast – Perth to Exmouth

- Explore the boutiques and restaurants of colourful **Northbridge** in Perth.
- Wonder at the mysterious landscape of the Pinnacles in **Nambung National Park**.
- Discover all about the local shipwrecks at **Geraldton's** WA Museum.
- Peer into **Hamelin Pool** and learn about million-year-old stromatolites.
- Snorkel on Ningaloo Reef in the **Cape Range National Park**.
- Swim with whale sharks off the coast of **Exmouth**.

0 kilometres   300

0 miles   300

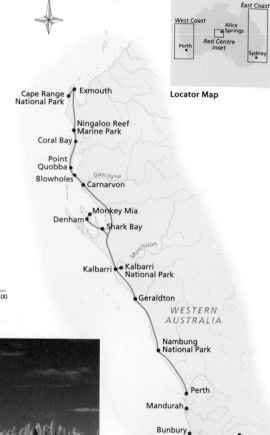

Locator Map

Western Australia map labels: Exmouth, Cape Range National Park, Ningaloo Reef Marine Park, Coral Bay, Point Quobba Blowholes, Gascoyne, Carnarvon, Monkey Mia, Denham, Shark Bay, Murchison, Kalbarri, Kalbarri National Park, Geraldton, WESTERN AUSTRALIA, Nambung National Park, Perth, Mandurah, Bunbury, Busselton, Katanning

Locator map labels: East Coast, West Coast, Alice Springs, Perth, Red Centre inset, Sydney

The Pinnacles
This extraordinary landscape of limestone pillars can be found in Nambung National Park, on the western coast of Australia.

◄ View of Sydney, New South Wales by Thomas Baines (1820–1875)

Key

— East Coast Tour
— Red Centre Tour
— West Coast Tour

0 kilometres   200
0 miles   200

5 Days in the Red Centre

- Find yourself a long way from anywhere in **Alice Springs** and visit the excellent galleries in town.

- Enjoy a spectacular sunset at **Uluṟu-Kata Tjuṯa National Park**. Try to capture Uluṟu's famous colour changes with your camera.

- Walk around the base of **Uluṟu**, marvelling at the colours and textures of the great rock.

- Embark on the Valley of the Winds walk at **Kata-Tjuṯa** and stroll among the giant boulders.

Byron Bay Lighthouse This iconic structure was erected on the easternmost point of the Australian mainland in 1901.

14 Days on the East Coast – Sydney to Cairns

- Tour the **Sydney Opera House** or admire it from aboard a ferry from **Circular Quay**.

- Visit one of **Sydney's beaches** and embark on a clifftop walk.

- Lounge on the beautiful beaches of the East Coast, such as **Byron Bay** and **Port Macquarie**.

- Wander around laid-back **Brisbane** and picnic in the Botanic Garden.

- Look for platypuses in **Eungella National Park**.

- Visit **Townsville's** aquarium and tour nearby **Magnetic Island**.

- Set off from **Cairns** to dive on the spectacular **Great Barrier Reef**.

2 Days in Sydney

This vibrant, beautiful city boasts museums, galleries and world-class restaurants, as well as iconic landmarks and tempting beaches.

- **Arriving** Sydney Airport, located about 10 km (6 miles) south of the city, is the main gateway. To reach the centre you can take a bus, train or taxi.

- **Moving on** The drive from Sydney to Melbourne takes just under 9 hours; the flight time is 1 hour and 35 minutes. If you have a lot of time on your hands, you could also catch a train. To reach Canberra from Sydney will take about 3 hours by car, just under an hour by plane, and just over 4 hours by train.

Day 1

Morning A couple of days in this city give you enough time to take in the main sights. On your first morning, visit the **Art Gallery of New South Wales** *(pp114–17)*; don't miss the Aboriginal and Torres Strait Islander art on display. Next, wander down through the **Royal Botanic Gardens** *(pp110–11)*, a peaceful oasis containing a vast variety of plants and trees. Continue past the Sydney Opera House, to **Circular Quay** *(pp78–89)*. There are several lunch spots here, especially in The Rocks and beyond the Overseas Passenger Terminal.

Dome of the Queen Victoria Building

Afternoon Tour the **Sydney Opera House** *(pp88–9)* or visit the **Museum of Contemporary Art** *(p82)*, where you can enjoy a breathtaking view from the café. If you are feeling active, walk over the **Sydney Harbour Bridge** *(pp84–5)* or challenge yourself to the Bridge Climb. Explore **The Rocks** *(pp80–81)* and stay in the area for dinner.

Day 2

Morning Take a ferry from Circular Quay to one of the many harbour bays, coves and beach areas around Sydney *(pp148–9)*. Consider a trip to **Manly** *(p130)*, where you can swim in the sea, relax in a café or learn to surf. Then, either take the ferry back or walk to Spit Bridge before jumping on a bus to **Sydney Town Hall** *(p97)*.

Afternoon If you're a keen shopper, head to George Street and visit the **Queen Victoria Building** *(p94)*, as well as the **Westfield Sydney** *(p93)* shopping centre, home to big department stores such as David Jones and Myer.

If relaxing in leafy surroundings is more appealing, flop on the grass in **Hyde Park** *(p97)* after checking out the Anzac Memorial, or walk down to **Darling Harbour** *(pp100–101)*. Relax with a cup of tea in the tranquillity of the **Chinese Garden** *(pp102–3)*, then visit the excellent interactive **Powerhouse Museum** *(pp106–7)*. For dinner, choose somewhere in **Chinatown** *(p103)* or, if you feel like treating yourself, admire the view from the restaurant in **Sydney Tower** *(p95)*. If you find you've still got energy to burn, head over to **Darlinghurst** *(pp120–29)* to check out Sydney's small bar scene, before walking down the infamous King's Cross strip.

> **To extend your trip...**
> Spend a day lounging on world-famous **Bondi Beach** *(p131)*; alternatively, walk from Bondi to **Coogee** *(p149)* along the clifftop. If beach life doesn't appeal, head to the **Blue Mountains** *(pp170–73)* for a couple of days, or spend a day tasting wines in the splendid **Hunter Valley** *(pp178–9)*. There is also the option of driving from Sydney to the capital city of **Canberra** *(pp194–209)*, in the Australian Capital Territory.

2 Days in Melbourne

Considered the most European of Australia's cities, Melbourne offers many gardens and parks to relax in, fascinating cultural events and some excellent tourist sights.

- **Arriving** Melbourne has two airports: Tullamarine and Avalon. Tullamarine is the main hub. To reach the city from Tullamarine, take the SkyBus or a taxi; the airport bus meets all flights from Avalon.

The iconic Sydney Opera House and Circular Quay

Statue of Charles La Trobe in Melbourne's State Library of Victoria

Day 1

Morning Join a walking tour of Melbourne's laneways and **arcades** (pp392–3), and discover cafés, boutiques and colourful street art. There is usually the option to include lunch in the tour; if not, just stop somewhere along the way that takes your fancy.

Afternoon Visit the **Ian Potter Centre: National Gallery of Victoria** (closed Mon; p407, which has an excellent collection of Australian art, or spend some time at the nearby **Immigration Museum** (p392), where you can learn more about the varied communities that make up modern Melbourne. It may well be raining by now, so jump on the free **City Circle Tram** (p116) as it travels around the Central Business District. In the evening, explore the suburb of **Fitzroy** (p400) and stop for dinner in Gertrude Street.

Day 2

Morning Head to the **Queen Victoria Market** (closed Mon & Wed; p390), and sample some of the delicious foods on offer. If the weather's nice, buy some picnic provisions and make your way to the **Royal Botanic Gardens** (pp402–3) for lunch.

Afternoon Stop in at the **Old Melbourne Gaol** (pp398–9), where Ned Kelly was hanged and where his death mask can still be seen, and learn more about the justice handed out here. Ned Kelly's armour is kept at the **State Library of Victoria**

(p389). Those travelling with children may prefer to head to the **Melbourne Museum** (p399) with its wonderful Forest Gallery and dinosaur skeletons. In the evening, tuck into an Italian meal on **Lygon Street** (p399).

To extend your trip...

Arrange a day trip south of Melbourne to see the penguins at **Phillip Island** (p446) or to the **Yarra Valley** (p447) to taste Victoria's famous wines. If you have more time, consider driving the **Great Ocean Road** (pp432–3) to **Adelaide** (pp344–53) or jumping on a ferry to explore **Tasmania** (pp456–75).

2 Days in Perth

This relaxed city is almost as close to Southeast Asia as it is to Sydney. Those in search of culture, beaches, interesting day trips and a laid-back atmosphere won't be disappointed.

- **Arriving** Perth Airport has an international and a domestic terminal. The Connect shuttle bus will drop you off at your accommodation in Perth or Fremantle; alternatively, you can take a taxi or a bus to the city centre.

Day 1

Morning Wander through **Central Perth** (pp306–9), exploring its arcades and malls, then head down to the Swan River to see the **Swan Bells** (p309). From here, make your way to **Kings Park** (p310), where you can take a guided walk, enjoy the view and have lunch.

Afternoon Double back through the city to the **Perth Cultural Centre** (p308), where you'll find the Art Gallery of Western Australia (closed Tue), the Perth Institute of Contemporary Art (PICA; closed Mon) and the Western Australian

Museum – Perth. Spend the evening in lively **Northbridge** (p308), where there is a range of restaurants and bars.

Day 2

Morning Explore the port city of **Fremantle** (pp314–15). Wander the streets admiring the 19th-century architecture and stopping in any shops or galleries that catch your eye. Don't miss Fremantle's oldest building, the **Round House** (p314). Alternatively, jump on a ferry to **Rottnest Island** (pp312–13), where you can hire a bike, look for quokkas, see the sights and take advantage of the beautiful white-sand beaches.

Afternoon If you've spent the morning on Rottnest Island, be sure to spend at least some time in Fremantle, admiring the city's historic buildings before finding somewhere to enjoy an evening meal. Take in a tour of **Fremantle Prison** (p315) and visit the **Shipwreck Galleries** of the **Western Australian Museum** (p314).

To extend your trip...

Visit Perth's **Sunset Coast** (pp310–11), where you can enjoy places like **Cottesloe Beach**, with its relaxed atmosphere and attractive beaches. Or head out to the **Swan Valley** wineries (p310).

The Bell Tower: Home of the Swan Bells, by the Swan River in Perth

14 Days on the East Coast – Sydney to Cairns

- **Airports** Arrive at Sydney Airport and depart from Cairns Airport.
- **Transport** A car is essential for this trip, although it is possible to take buses up the coast and amend and extend the itinerary as necessary.
- **Booking ahead** If planning a tour to Fraser Island and/or the Whitsunday Islands, consider arranging this in advance.

Days 1 and 2: Sydney
See the city itinerary on pages 12–13.

Day 3: Newcastle
Leave the busy streets of Sydney behind and head north, to the quieter, more down-to-earth city of **Newcastle** *(p177)*. Once there, visit the excellent **Newcastle Region Art Gallery** (closed Mon) to see its remarkable collection of Australian art, then make your way to the restored **Fort Scratchley** (closed Tue), where you can learn about what took place in this town during World War II.

Day 4: Port Macquarie
From Newcastle, continue north along the Pacific Highway to **Port Macquarie**

The pedestrian Goodwill Bridge in Brisbane, leading to the Queensland Cultural Precinct

(p183), a popular holiday destination with some attractive beaches. En route, you could leave the main road to visit **Crowdy Bay National Park** *(p182)*, where fishing is a popular activity.

Day 5: Coffs Harbour
The journey north to **Coffs Harbour** *(p182)* will take you past a number of lovely sandy beaches, including **Nambucca Heads** *(p183)* and the surf spot of **Third Headland Beach** *(p182)*. Coffs Harbour itself is one of the most popular tourist destinations in New South Wales and has lots of activities available, including horseriding, diving and surfing.

Days 6 and 7: Byron Bay
Travel through quaint **Grafton** *(p182)* on your way north and

stop for a walk along the river or, in season (Oct), to admire the jacaranda trees in bloom. **Byron Bay** *(p183)*, the easternmost point on the Australian mainland, draws backpackers, holidaymakers and people on weekend trips to the beach. Spend an afternoon admiring the views, relaxing on the golden sand, swimming in the sea and trying your hand at a range of watersports.

Days 8 and 9: Brisbane
Cross into Queensland and pass through a series of small surf communities until you reach **Surfers Paradise Beach** *(p243)*. If you enjoy pulsating nightlife, then consider extending your stay here. When you reach **Brisbane** *(pp222–37)*, be sure to visit the **City Botanic Gardens** *(pp228–9)* and the **Queensland Cultural Precinct** *(pp232–3)*, where you'll find the Queensland Museum & Science Centre, the Queensland Art Gallery (QAG) and the Gallery of Modern Art (GOMA). A popular trip outside the city centre is to the **Lone Pine Koala Sanctuary** *(p234)*, where you can enjoy a cuddle with one of these irresistible critters.

Day 10: Hervey Bay
The Sunshine Coast stretches north of Brisbane as far as **Noosa** *(p243)*. On your way there, you may want to stop at **Australia Zoo** *(p242)*, made famous by the late Steve Irwin.

Whale-watching boat returning to Hervey Bay Marina, Queensland

For practical information on travelling around Australia see pp556–63

The golden sands and clear waters of idyllic Magnetic Island

Most people come to **Hervey Bay** (p245) to travel on to Fraser Island, but if time is limited, note that it's possible to see whales from here too (Aug–Oct). Take the passenger ferry to **Fraser Island** (p246), the world's largest sand island, for a quick visit.

> **To extend your trip...**
> Organize a day trip to Fraser Island from Hervey Bay, either joining an organized tour or hiring a 4WD. Alternatively, travel further up the coast and embark on a boat trip around the **Whitsunday Islands** (p250).

Day 11: Rockhampton
This section of the journey will take you through the attractive town of **Bundaberg** (p245), home of Australia's most

Mount Hypipamee crater, Atherton Tableland

famous rum, before you reach **Rockhampton** (p248), a pleasant town with a number of heritage buildings from the 19th century. This is a good place to break your journey north. Visit the **Aboriginal Dreamtime Cultural Centre** (closed Sat & Sun), then stop by the spire marking the fact that the Tropic of Capricorn runs through the town. If you have time to spare, visit the caves at **Mount Etna National Park** (p248), 25 km (15 miles) north of town. This is where the endangered ghost bat nests.

Day 12: Mackay and Eungella National Park
The next stretch of highway is mostly uninteresting until you reach the town of **Mackay** (p250), where you can admire a number of Art Deco buildings and enjoy a little beach time. From Mackay, travel west to **Eungella National Park** (p250) and engage in some platypus spotting (dusk and dawn are the best times for this activity).

Day 13: Townsville and Magnetic Island
Townsville (p251) is Queensland's second-largest city, and there's an excellent aquarium here, **Reef HQ** (p251), as well as a number of museums. Most people, however, choose to press on to **Magnetic Island** (p251) and stay there. Enjoy the beaches and good walking opportunities, or organize a tour of the island by 4WD.

> **To extend your trip...**
> If you're an experienced scuba diver, head to nearby **Ayr** (p250), the jumping-off point for the SS *Yongala* wreck dive.

Day 14: North via the Atherton Tableland to Cairns
Continue to drive up the coast until you reach the town of Innisfail, then make your way inland to the **Atherton Tableland** (p259). Stop in this incredibly fertile farming area to enjoy the temperate climate and the beautiful scenery and to buy locally grown fruit and vegetables from numerous roadside stalls. Drop back down to the coast into **Cairns** (p258), where you can visit the **Flecker Botanic Gardens**, and consider taking part in some of the many activities on offer. There are a number of restaurants here, or buy some street food at the night market.

> **To extend your trip...**
> Stay in Cairns for a few extra days and explore the **Great Barrier Reef** (pp216–21). If snorkelling and diving are not for you, take the Kuranda Scenic Railway north to **Kuranda** (p258). There is also the option to head north to visit **Port Douglas** (p257), **Daintree National Park** (p257) and **Cape Tribulation** (p257).

5 Days in the Red Centre

- **Airports** Alice Springs Airport is 15 km (9 miles) out of town. The Alice Wanderer Airport Transfers Shuttle meets flights, or you can take a taxi to your hotel.

- **Transport** A car is essential for this trip. It can be picked up and dropped off in Alice Springs.

- **Booking ahead** When visiting Uluru, be sure to book your accommodation at Yulara well in advance.

Day 1: Alice Springs

This circular tour begins and ends in **Alice Springs** (pp286–7). There are several art galleries to visit here, as well as a number of sights to suit most interests. Those keen to find out more about the local fauna should head to the **Alice Springs Desert Park**; history buffs can pay a visit to the **Telegraph Station Historical Reserve** and the **Royal Flying Doctor Service Visitor Centre** (pm only Sun).

Day 2: Uluru-Kata Tjuta National Park

The drive from Alice Springs to **Uluru-Kata Tjuta National Park** (pp290–93) is a long one. Most people take the Stuart and Lassiter highways, but there are also some 4WD routes. En route, don't confuse Mount Conner for your first glance of Uluru. Check into your accommodation, then drive out to see Uluru at sunset.

Day 3: Uluru (Ayers Rock)

Make your way to **Uluru** (p292) and consider following one of the walking trails, such as the Base Walk, which should take about 3 to 4 hours. Don't forget to visit the **Uluru-Kata Tjuta Cultural Centre** (p293) while you're here to learn more about the park and the area's history.

Day 4: Kata Tjuta (The Olgas)

Consider visiting Uluru again, then travel on to **Kata Tjuta** (pp292–3), formerly known as The Olgas. There are a couple of walking trails here, the shorter Walpa Gorge Walk and the Valley of the Winds Walk, which takes about 3 hours. If you can, stay to see the sunset.

Day 5: Alice Springs

This is another long day of driving, so stop at one of the roadhouses along the way, then relax and wash the red dust off you in Alice Springs (see Day 1).

To extend your trip...
Drive to **Kings Canyon** (p289) and embark on the 6-km (4-mile) Rim Walk. The scenery is breathtaking, but be sure to walk early in the morning or in the afternoon rather than in the heat of the day. It is also possible to arrange a one-way car rental from Alice Springs, and drive either south, towards **Adelaide** (pp348–53), or north, to **Darwin** (pp274–7) and **Kakadu National Park** (pp280–81).

Entrance to Alice Springs Desert Park, in the Northern Territory

10 Days on the West Coast – Perth to Exmouth

- **Airports** Arrive and depart from Perth Airport.

- **Transport** A one-way hire car is essential for this trip, and a domestic flight required from Exmouth to Perth

- **Booking ahead** If you want to stay at Monkey Mia, book your accommodation well in advance.

Days 1 and 2: Perth

See the city itinerary on p13.

To extend your trip...
Head south for a few days to visit the wineries in **Margaret River** (pp318–19), climb the **Gloucester Tree** (p319) and explore the Timber Towns, such as **Pemberton** (p319) and **Manjimup** (p319).

Day 3: Nambung National Park

The Pinnacles, a landscape of limestone columns that formed underground and were revealed by the winds, is the main attraction in **Nambung National Park** (p328). Drive along the 3-km (2-mile) Pinnacles Drive, taking the time to get out of your car and wander around.

The distinctive shape of Uluru (Ayers Rock), in Uluru-Kata Tjuta National Park

For practical information on travelling around Australia see pp556–63

Erupting geyser at the Blowholes, north of Carnarvon

Day 4: Kalbarri via Geraldton
On your journey north, stop in **Geraldton** *(pp328–9)* to visit the **WA Museum – Geraldton**, which features an excellent gallery dedicated to the area's shipwrecks. From here, continue on to Kalbarri.

Day 5: Kalbarri National Park
Kalbarri National Park *(p329)* can be explored either on foot or by bicycle. In addition to beautiful beaches, it offers a series of vertiginous cliffs, gorges and lookouts. It's also possible to join a canoe tour down the Murchison River.

Day 6: Monkey Mia
Leave the Northwest Coastal Highway and head for Denham. Stop at **Shark Bay World Heritage and Marine Park** *(pp330–31)* to admire the ancient stromatolites of **Hamelin Pool** and visit nearby **Shell Beach** to see how shells were once used as building material. You can either choose to base yourself in **Denham** *(p330)* or, if you're not an early riser, press on to Monkey Mia.

Day 7: Carnarvon and the Blowholes
Get up early to witness the 8am dolphin-feeding session at the small beach of **Monkey Mia** *(p331)*, then head back the way you came to rejoin the highway and drive to **Carnarvon** *(p329)*, where you can take a tour of one of the fruit plantations. In the afternoon, drive the 70 km (43 miles) to see the **Blowholes** *(p329)*. If you're camping and don't mind roughing it a little, Point Quobba is a lovely spot to spend the night.

Day 8: Ningaloo Reef Marine Park
A great spot to experience **Ningaloo Reef Marine Park** *(p332)* is the small seaside town of Coral Bay, since its still waters allow snorkellers to enjoy the reef from close to the shore. It's also possible to fish, dive and whale-watch here in season.

> **To extend your trip...**
> There are a number of station stays in this area, so consider spending a couple of nights experiencing life in the Outback.

Days 9 and 10: Exmouth and the Cape Range National Park
There is not much to see in **Exmouth** *(p332)* itself, so head instead to one of the nearby beaches or go straight to the **Cape Range National Park** *(p332)*, where you can do some walking or take advantage of the superb snorkelling. If you enjoy camping, consider staying overnight in the park, but be aware that facilities are limited. At present only a handful of pitches can be booked in advance; the rest are allocated on a first-come-first-served basis at the entrance gate to the park. Spend the morning in the park, then make your way to the airport for the flight back to Perth.

> **To extend your trip...**
> In season (Mar–May), arrange to go swimming or **snorkelling with whale sharks** *(p332)*. You could also consider carrying on north to **Broome** *(p334)* or **Darwin** *(pp2/4–7)*, or driving west to visit **Karijini National Park** *(p333)*.

Cliffs in Kalbarri National Park, Western Australia

Putting Australia on the Map

Australia lies in the southern hemisphere and
covers 7,692,024 sq km (2,969,907 sq miles) of land.
A continent, it is bordered by the Pacific Ocean to
the east and the Indian Ocean to the west. More than
80 per cent of its 23 million people reside along the
coastline with its more hospitable climate. The
capital, Canberra, is in the Australian Capital
Territory (ACT), but the most populous city
is Sydney. Tasmania, an island state,
lies 240 km (150 miles) off the
southern tip of the
country, across the
Bass Strait.

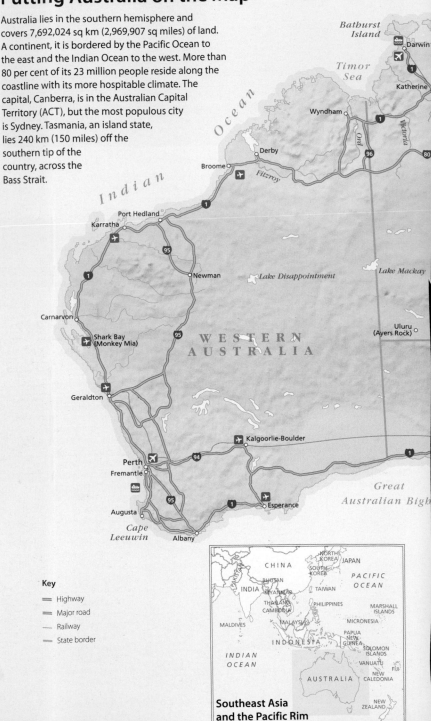

Key

=== Highway

=== Major road

— Railway

— State border

**Southeast Asia
and the Pacific Rim**

A PORTRAIT OF AUSTRALIA

Australia is the world's oldest continent, inhabited for more than 60,000 years by Aborigines. It was settled by the British during their maritime heyday, in 1788, and since then has transformed from a colonial outpost into a nation with a population of more than 23 million people. For visitors, its ancient, worn landscape contrasts with the vitality and youthful energy of its inhabitants.

Covering an area as large as the United States of America or the entire European continent, Australia's landscape is highly diverse, encompassing the dry Outback, the high plateaus of the Great Dividing Range, the lush woods of Tasmania, the rainforests and coral reefs of the tropical north and almost 36,000 km (22,300 miles) of mainland coastline. The Great Dividing Range forms a spine down eastern Australia, from Queensland to Victoria, separating the fertile coastal strip from the dry and dusty interior.

Dominating the vegetation is the eucalypt, known as the "gum tree", of which there are some 500 varieties.

Australian trees shed their bark rather than their leaves, the native flowers have no smell and, with the exception of the wattle, bloom only briefly.

Australia has a unique collection of fauna. Most are marsupials, such as the emblematic kangaroo and koala. The platypus and echidna are among the few living representatives in the world of mammals that both lay eggs and suckle their young. The dingo, brought to Australia by the Aborigines, is considered the country's native dog.

Australia's antiquity is nowhere more evident than in the vast inland area known as the Outback.

Sydney Opera House, jutting into Sydney Harbour

◄ The spectacular Twelve Apostles rock formation in Port Campbell National Park, Western Victoria

Ancient, eroded landscape of the Olgas, part of Uluru-Kata Tjuta National Park in the Northern Territory

Once a huge inland sea, its later aridity preserved the remains of the creatures that once inhabited the area. Some fossils found in Western Australia are 350 million years old – the oldest forms of life known on earth.

The Aborigines

The indigenous inhabitants of Australia, the Aborigines and Torres Strait Islanders, today constitute 3 per cent of the national population. Their rights and social status are gradually being improved.

The early days of European colonialism proved disastrous for the Aborigines. Thousands were killed in hostilities or by

Aboriginal Australian

unfamiliar diseases. During the 1850s, many Aborigines were confined to purpose-built reserves in a misguided attempt to overcome widespread poverty. Since the 1950s there have been serious efforts to redress this lack of understanding. Conditions are improving, but even today, in almost every aspect of life, including health care, education and housing, Aborigines are worse off than other Australians. In 1992, a milestone occurred when the High Court overturned the doctrine of *terra nullius* – that Australia belonged to no one at the time of British settlement. The Native Title Act followed, which, in essence, states that where Aborigines could establish unbroken occupancy of an area, they could then claim that land as their own.

Almost all Australians support this reconciliation and are increasingly aware of the rich heritage of the Aborigines. The Aboriginal belief in the Dreamtime *(see pp34–5)* may never be completely assimilated into the Australian consciousness,

The kangaroo, a famous icon of Australia

but an understanding of ancestral beings is an invaluable guide to traditional lifestyles. Aboriginal painting is now respected as one of the world's most ancient art forms and modern Aboriginal art began to be taken seriously in the 1970s. Aboriginal writers have also come to the forefront of Australian literature. Younger Aborigines are beginning to capitalize on this new awareness to promote equal rights and, with Aboriginal cultural centres being set up throughout the country, it is unlikely that Australia will dismiss its native heritage again.

Society

Given Australia's size and the fact that early settlements were far apart, Australian society is remarkably homogeneous. Its citizens are fundamentally prosperous and the way of life in the major cities and towns is much the same however many miles divide them. It takes a keen ear to identify regional accents.

However, there is some difference in lifestyle between city dwellers and the country people. Almost 90 per cent of the population lives in the fast-paced cities along the coast and has little more than a passing familiarity with the Outback. The major cities preserve pockets of colonial heritage, but the overall impression is modern, with new buildings reflecting the country's youth. In contrast, the rural communities tend to be slow-moving and

A maker of fortified wine takes a sample from a barrel of port in the Barossa Valley, South Australia

conservative. For many years, Australia was said to have "ridden on the sheep's back", a reference to wool being the country's main money-earner. However, the wool industry is no longer dominant. Much of Australia's relatively sound economy is now achieved from coal, iron ore and wheat, and as the largest diamond producer in the world. Newer industries such as tourism and wine making are also increasingly important. Australians are generally friendly and relaxed, with a self-deprecating sense of humour. On the whole, Australia has a society without hierarchies, an attitude generally held to stem from its convict beginnings. Yet, contrary to widespread belief, very few Australians have true convict origins. Within only one generation of the arrival of the First Fleet in 1788, Australia had become a nation of immigrants.

Isolated Outback church in Silverton, New South Wales

Originally hailing almost entirely from the British Isles, today one in three Australians comes from elsewhere. Australia's liberal postwar immigration policies led to an influx of survivors from war-torn Europe, most notably Greeks, Italians, Poles and Germans.

The emphasis shifted towards the end of the twentieth century and today the majority of new immigrants hail from Southeast Asia. Although some racism does exist, this blend of nations has, on the whole, been a successful experiment and Australia is justifiably proud to have one of the most harmonious multicultural communities in the world.

Indonesian satay stall at Parap Market in Darwin in the Northern Territory

Politics

Since 1901, Australia has been a federation, with its central government based in the purpose-built national capital, Canberra. Each state also has its own government. The nation inherited the central parliamentary system from England, and there is a two-party system consisting of the left (Labor) and the right (a coalition of Liberal and National Parties). The prime minister is the head of federal government, while the heads of state governments are premiers. Australia is a self-governing member of the British Commonwealth and retains the British

monarch as its titular head of state. At present, the national representative of the monarch is the Governor-General, but the nation is involved in an ongoing debate about its future as a republic. There is opposition from those who argue that the system currently in place has led to one of the most stable societies in the world, while others believe that swearing allegiance to a British monarch has little meaning for the current population, many of whom are immigrants from other parts of the world. A referendum in November 1999 saw the monarchy retained with some 55 per cent of the votes.

The nation's character has always been shaped by its sparsely populated island location, far distant from its European roots and geographically closer to Southeast Asia.

The Parliamentary area next to Lake Burley Griffin in Canberra

Today there is a growing realization that the country must look to the Pacific region for its future. Closer ties with Asia, such as business transactions with Indonesia, China and Japan, are being developed.

Art and Culture

Blessed with a sunny climate and surrounded by the sea, outdoor leisure is high on the list of priorities for Australians – going to the beach is almost a national pastime. Australians are also mad about sport: football, cricket, rugby, tennis and golf are high on the national agenda.

Film poster of the Academy-Award winning *Shine*

Yet despite this reputation, Australians actually devote more of their time and money to artistic pursuits than they do to sporting ones, and as a result the national cultural scene is very vibrant. It is no accident that the Sydney Opera House is one of the country's most recognizable symbols. The nation is probably best known for its opera singers, among whom have been two of the all-time greats, Dame Nellie Melba and Dame Joan Sutherland. Opera Australia and the Australian Ballet, both based in Sydney, are acknowledged for

Australian Rules football match in Melbourne

their high standards. Every state also has its own thriving theatre company and symphony orchestra. Major art galleries abound throughout the country, from the many excellent state galleries exhibiting international works to a multitude of small private galleries exhibiting local and contemporary Australian and Aboriginal art.

The Australian film industry has also come into its own since the 1970s. The best-known Australian film is possibly *Crocodile Dundee* (1985), but productions such as *Shine* (1996), *Moulin Rouge!* (2001) and *Happy Feet* (2006) compete on equal terms with films from around the world and have won international film awards.

This is not to say that Australia's cultural pursuits are entirely high-brow. Low-budget television soap operas such as *Neighbours* have become high-earning exports. Rock bands such as AC/DC also have an international following.

In almost all aspects, it seems, Australia lives up to its nickname of "the lucky country" and it is hard to meet an Australian who is not thoroughly convinced that this young and vast nation is now the best country on earth.

Young boogie boarder

Australia's Landscape

Geological stability has been largely responsible for creating the landscape of the earth's oldest, flattest and driest inhabited continent. Eighty million years ago, Australia's last major bout of geological activity pushed up the Great Dividing Range, but since then the continent has slept. Mountains have been eroded down, making it difficult for rain clouds to develop. Deserts have formed in once lush areas and today more than 70 per cent of the continent is arid. However, with some of the oldest rocks on earth, its landscapes are anything but uniform, and include rainforests, tropical beaches, glacial landforms, striking coastlines and flood plains.

Australia's drift towards the equator has brought a northern monsoon climate, as in Kakadu National Park *(see pp280–81)*.

Cradle Mountain *(see p471)* in southwest Tasmania was created by geological upheaval, glaciation and erosion. Here jagged mountain ranges, ravines and glacial lakes have formed a landscape that is quite unique in Australia.

Kata Tjuṯa (The Olgas)

Geological remnants of an immense bed of sedimentary rock now almost covered by sand from erosion, Kata Tjuṯa's weathered domes may once have been a single dome many times the size of Uluṟu *(see pp290–93)*.

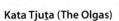

Western Plateau

Central Lowlands

Great Dividing Range

There are three main geological regions in Australia: the coastal plain including the Great Dividing Range; the Central Lowlands; and the Western Plateau. The Great Dividing Range is a relatively new feature in geological terms. It contains Australia's highest mountains, deep rivers, spectacular gorges and volcanic landforms. The Central Lowlands subsided when the continental margins on either side rose up – a result of rifting caused by continental drift. The Western Plateau contains many of Australia's large deserts and is composed of some of the most ancient rocks in the world.

The area to the east of Queensland was flooded at the end of the last Ice Age, creating ideal conditions for a coral reef. The Great Barrier Reef *(see pp216– 21)* now forms one of the world's most stunning sights.

The Nullarbor Plain *(see p371)* was created by the upthrust of an ancient sea floor. Today, sheer cliffs drop away from this desert landscape dotted with sinkholes and plunge into the sea below, creating one of Australia's most startling coastlines.

The Australian Continent

The Australian continent finally broke away from its last adjoining landmass, Antarctica, 40 million years ago and embarked on a long period of geographical isolation. During this time Australia's unique flora and fauna evolved and flourished *(see pp28–9)*. Aboriginal people lived undisturbed on this continent for at least 40,000 years, developing the land to their own needs, until the arrival of Europeans in 1770 *(see pp50–55)*.

Two hundred million years ago, the area of land that is now continental Australia was attached to the lower half of the earth's single landmass, Pangaea.

Between 200 and 65 million years ago, Pangaea separated to form two supercontinents, Gondwanaland in the south and Laurasia in the north.

Fifty million years ago, Gondwanaland had broken up into the various southern continents with only Antarctica and Australia still attached.

Today, the drifting of the continents continues and Australia is moving northwards towards the equator at the rate of 8 cm (3 in) a year.

Flora and Fauna

Forty million years of isolation from other major land masses have given Australia a collection of flora and fauna that is unique in the world. Low rainfall and poor soil has meant meagre food sources, and animals and plants have evolved some curious adaptations to help them cope. Surprisingly, these adverse conditions have also produced incredible biodiversity. Australia has more than 20,000 species of plants, and its rainforests are among the richest in the world in the number of species they support. Even its desert centre has 2,000 plant species and the world's greatest concentration of reptile species.

The platypus lives in an aquatic environment like a fish, suckles its young like a mammal, lays eggs and has the bill of a duck!

The lush rainforest is a haven for many endemic species of flora and fauna.

Epiphytes, ferns and vines abound around this rainforest creek.

At least 30 species of spinifex cover many of Australia's desert plains.

Rainforests

The east coast rainforests are among the most ancient ecosystems on earth. At least 18,000 plant species exist here. Some trees are more than 2,500 years old, and many are direct descendants of species from Gondwana *(see p27)*.

Arid Regions

The vast reaches of Australia's arid and semiarid regions teem with life. Desert plants and animals have developed unique and specific behavioural and physical features to maximize their survival chances in such harsh conditions.

The golden bowerbird of the rainforest builds spectacular bowers out of sticks as a platform for its mating displays. Some bowers reach well over 2 m (6.5 ft) in height.

The boab (baobab) tree sheds its leaves in the dry season to survive.

Spinifex grass, found across the desert, stores water and needs frequent exposure to fire to thrive.

The Wollemi pine was discovered in 1994 and caused a sensation. It belongs to a genus thought to have become extinct between 65 and 200 million years ago.

The thorny devil feeds only on ants and can consume more than 3,000 in one meal.

Mammals

Australian mammals are distinctive because the population is dominated by two groups that are rare or non-existent elsewhere. Monotremes, such as the platypus, are found only in Australia and New Guinea, and marsupials, represented by 180 species here, are scarce in other parts of the world. In contrast, placental mammals, highly successful on other continents, have been represented in Australia only by bats and rodents, and more recently by dingos. Mass extinctions of larger placentals occurred 20,000 years ago.

Red kangaroos are the most common of many species of this marsupial found in Australia.

The dingo was introduced into Australia by migrating humans c. 5,000 years ago.

Eucalypt trees provide food for possums and koalas.

Moist fern groundcover shelters a variety of small mammals and insects.

This coral garden is home to many molluscs, crustaceans and brightly coloured fish.

Open Woodland

The woodlands of the eastern seaboard, the southeast and southwest are known as the Australian bush. Eucalypt trees predominate in the hardy vegetation that has developed to survive fire, drought and poor-quality soil.

Koalas feed only on nutrient-poor eucalypt leaves, and have evolved low-energy lives to cope, such as sleeping for 20 hours a day.

Kookaburras are very efficient breeders: one of the young birds is kept on in the nest to look after the next batch of hatchlings, leaving both parents free to gather food.

Sealife

Australia's oceans are poor in nutrients but rich in the diversity of life they support. Complex ecosystems create beautiful underwater scenery, while the shores and islands are home to nesting seabirds and giant sea mammals.

Seagrass beds have high-saline conditions which attract many sea creatures. Shark Bay shelters the highest number of sea mammals in the world (see pp330–31).

The Australian sealion is one of two seal species unique to Australia. Its extended breeding cycle helps it contend with a poor food supply.

World Heritage Areas of Australia

UNESCO's World Heritage Convention was adopted in 1972 to protect areas of universal cultural and natural significance. Nineteen groups of sites in Australia are inscribed on the World Heritage List and include unusual landforms, ancient forests and areas of staggering biodiversity, as well as 12 historic convict sites and the Sydney Opera House. Several of the sites (including Kakadu National Park, Willandra Lakes, the Tasmanian wilderness and Uluṟu-Kata Tjuṯa National Park) are also listed for their Aboriginal cultural heritage.

Fossil sites in Riversleigh *(see p261)* and Naracoorte chart Australia's important evolutionary stages.

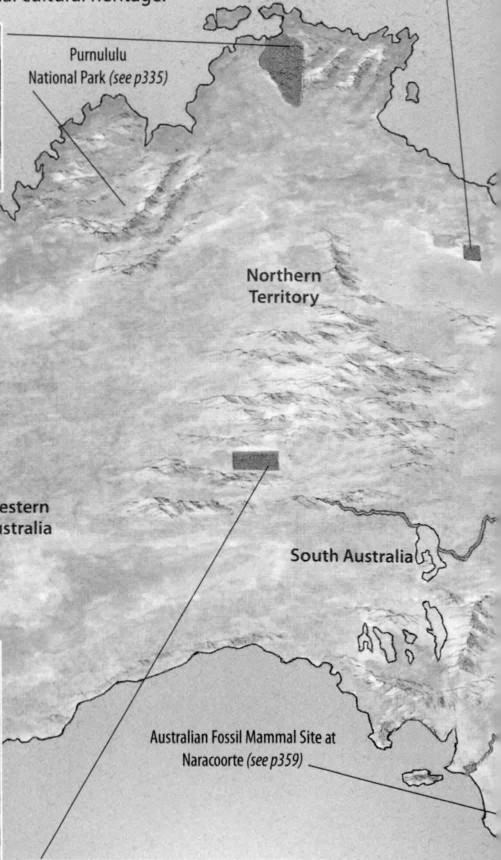

Purnululu
National Park *(see p335)*

Kakadu National Park is a landscape of wetlands and tropical splendour. Art sites document the interaction between Aborigines and the land *(see pp280–81)*.

The Ningaloo Coast
(see p332)

Northern Territory

Western Australia

South Australia

Australian Fossil Mammal Site at
Naracoorte *(see p359)*

Shark Bay is home to a vast colony of sea mammals. The bay's stromatolites (algae-covered rocks) are the oldest form of life known on earth *(see pp330–31)*.

Uluṟu-Kata Tjuṯa National Park contains two major Aboriginal sites *(see pp290–93)*. The world's largest monolith is an extraordinary geological phenomenon in the flat desert plains.

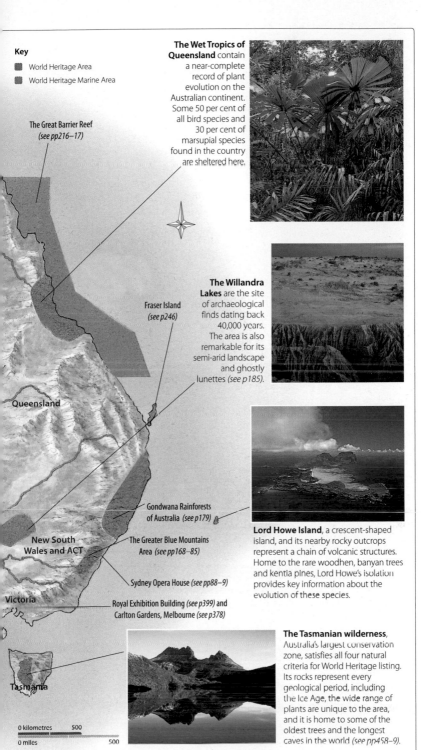

Key

World Heritage Area

World Heritage Marine Area

The Great Barrier Reef
(see pp216–17)

The Wet Tropics of Queensland contain a near-complete record of plant evolution on the Australian continent. Some 50 per cent of all bird species and 30 per cent of marsupial species found in the country are sheltered here.

Fraser Island
(see p246)

The Willandra Lakes are the site of archaeological finds dating back 40,000 years. The area is also remarkable for its semi-arid landscape and ghostly lunettes *(see p185)*.

Queensland

Gondwana Rainforests of Australia *(see p179)*

New South Wales and ACT

The Greater Blue Mountains Area *(see pp168–85)*

Sydney Opera House *(see pp88–9)*

Victoria

Royal Exhibition Building *(see p399)* and Carlton Gardens, Melbourne *(see p378)*

Lord Howe Island, a crescent-shaped island, and its nearby rocky outcrops represent a chain of volcanic structures. Home to the rare woodhen, banyan trees and kentia pines, Lord Howe's isolation provides key information about the evolution of these species.

Tasmania

0 kilometres   500

0 miles   500

The Tasmanian wilderness, Australia's largest conservation zone, satisfies all four natural criteria for World Heritage listing. Its rocks represent every geological period, including the Ice Age, the wide range of plants are unique to the area, and it is home to some of the oldest trees and the longest caves in the world *(see pp458–9)*.

The Australian Outback

The Outback is the heart of Australia and one of the most ancient landscapes in the world. It is extremely dry – rain may not fall for several years. Dramatic red rocks, ochre plains and purple mountains are framed by brilliant blue skies. Development is sparse: "towns" are often no more than a few buildings and facilities are basic. There may be hundreds of miles between one petrol station and another. The Outback isn't easy to explore, but it can be a rewarding experience. Make sure you are well equipped *(see p562)*, or take an organized tour.

Locator Map

🔲 *The Australian Outback*

Camels were brought to Australia in the 1870s from the Middle East, as a means of desert transport. The Outback is now home to the only wild camels in the world. Camel safaris for tourists are available in many places.

Saltbush, which gets its name from its ability to withstand saline conditions, is a typical form of vegetation.

Outback Life

The enduring image of Australia's Outback is red dust, solitary one-storey shacks and desert views as far as the eye can see. Although small areas of the Outback have seen towns spring up over the past 100 years, and many interstate roads are now suitable for most vehicles, this image remains true to life across vast stretches of the interior landscape. Most of the Outback remains pioneering country far removed from the modern nation.

Camping in the bush is one of the highlights of any trip into Australia's Outback, whether independently or with an organized tour. You will need a camping permit, a swag (canvas-covered bed roll), a mosquito net and a good camping stove to eat and sleep in relative comfort under the stars.

The film industry has long been a fan of the Outback's vast open spaces and dramatic colours. Films such as the 1994 comedy *The Adventures of Priscilla, Queen of the Desert* made spectacular use of the Red Centre's sparse and dusty landscape.

Australian "hotels" in Outback areas often operate only as public houses, re-named hotels to counteract Australia's once strict licensing laws.

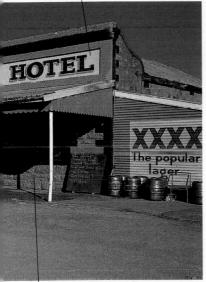

Pioneers and Explorers

Many European explorers, such as Edward Eyre and John Stuart, ventured into the Outback during the 19th century. The most infamous expedition was Robert O'Hara Burke's from Victoria to the Gulf of Carpentaria *(see p57)*. Ironically, it was the rescue missions due to his inexperience which brought about the pioneers' most significant investigations of Australia's interior.

Robert O'Hara Burke
1820–61

A solitary building set against vast areas of open desert landscape can be an evocative landmark in the Outback.

The Birdsville Races in Queensland are the biggest and best of the many horse races held in the Outback, where locals gather to bet and socialize.

Opal mining in towns such as Coober Pedy *(see p372)* is one source of the Outback's wealth. Tourists need a miner's permit, available from state tourist offices, to hunt for gems.

Aboriginal Culture

Far from being one homogeneous race, at the time of European settlement in the 18th century, the estimated 750,000 Aborigines in Australia had at least 300 different languages and a wide variety of lifestyles, depending on where they lived. The tribes of northern coastal areas, such as the Tiwis, had most contact with outsiders, especially from Indonesia, and their culture was quite different from the more isolated Pitjantjatjaras of Central Australia's deserts or the Kooris from the southeast. However, there were features common to Aboriginal life and these have passed down the centuries to present-day traditions.

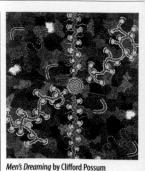

Men's Dreaming by Clifford Possum Tjapaltjarri

Aboriginal artifacts and tools, decorated in traditional ornate patterns

Traditional Aboriginal Lifestyles

For tens of thousands of years, the Aborigines were a race of hunters leading a nomadic existence. They made light-weight, versatile tools such as the boomerang, and built temporary mud dwellings. The extent of their wanderings differed from region to region. People who lived in areas with a plentiful supply of food and water were relatively more static than those in areas where such essentials were scarce.

Through living in small groups in a vast land, Aboriginal society came to be broken up into numerous clans separated by different languages and customs. Even people with a common language would live apart in extended family groups, consisting of a husband, wife, aunts, uncles and all their children to share the responsibilities of daily life. Groups would come together from time to time to conduct religious ceremonies, arrange marriages and settle inter-clan disputes. Trade was an important part of social life. Shell, ochre and wood were some of the goods exchanged along trade routes that criss-crossed the entire country.

The nomadic way of life largely ended when English settlers claimed vast tracts of land, but other aspects of traditional life have survived. In Aboriginal communities, senior members are still held in great respect, and are responsible for maintaining laws and meting out punishments to those who break them or divulge secrets of ancient rituals. Such rituals are part of the Aboriginal belief system called "Dreamtime".

The Dreamtime

The Dreamtime (or Dreaming) is the English term for the Aboriginal system of laws and beliefs. Its basis is a rich mythology about the earth's creation. "Creation ancestors" such as giant serpents are believed to have risen up from the earth's core and roamed the world, creating valleys, rivers and mountains. Other progenitors caused the rain and sun, and created the people and wildlife. Sites where ancestral beings are thought to have emerged from the earth are sacred and are still used as the locations for ceremonies and rituals today.

The belief in the Dreamtime is, in essence, a religious ideology for all Aborigines, whatever their tribe, and forms the basis of Aboriginal life. Every Aborgine is believed to

The Boomerang

Contrary to popular belief, not all boomerangs will return to the thrower. Originally, "boomerang" simply meant "throwing stick". They were used for hunting, fighting, making fire, stoking the coals when cooking and in traditional games. A hunter did not normally require a throwing stick to return since its purpose was to injure its target sufficiently to enable capture. Over time, intricate shapes were developed that allowed sticks to swirl in a large arc and return to the thrower. The returning boomerang is limited to games, killing birds and directing animals into traps. Light and thin, with a deep curvature, its ends are twisted in opposite directions. The lower surface is flat and the upper surface convex.

Aboriginal boomerang

have two souls – one mortal and one immortal, linked with their ancestral spirit (or totem). Each family clan is descended from the same ancestral being. These spirits provide protection: any misfortune is due to disgruntled forebears. As a consequence, some clan members have a responsibility for maintaining sacred sites. Anyone failing in these duties is severely punished.

Each Dreamtime story relates to a particular landscape; as one landscape connects with another, these stories form a "track". These "tracks" are called Songlines and criss-cross the Australian continent. Aborigines are able to connect with other tribes along these lines.

Aborigines painted with white paint to ward off evil spirits

Aboriginal Song and Dance

Aboriginal songs tell stories of Dreamtime ancestors and are intrinsically linked to the worship of spirits – the words of songs are often incomprehensible due to the secrecy of many ancestral stories. Simple instruments accompany the songs, including the didgeridoo, a 1-m- (3-ft-) long wind instrument with a deep sound.

Aborigines also use dance as a means of communicating with their ancestors. Aboriginal dance is experiencing a cultural renaissance, with new companies performing both traditional and new works.

Aboriginal Issues

Although few Aborigines now maintain a traditional nomadic lifestyle, the ceremonies, creation stories and art that make up their culture remain strong.

The right to own land has long been an issue for present-day Aborigines; they believe that they are responsible for caring for the land entrusted to them at birth. The Land Rights Act of 1976 has done much to improve these rights. The Act established Aboriginal Land Councils which negotiate between the government and Aborigines to claim land for its traditional owners (see pp62–3). Where Aboriginal rights have been established, that land cannot be altered in any way. In areas of large Aboriginal

Decorating bark with natural ochre stains

inhabitance, the government has also agreed that white law can exist alongside black law, which allows for justice against Aboriginal offenders to be meted out according to tribal law. In many cases, this law is harsh and savage, but it allows for Aborigines to live by their own belief system.

The revival of Aboriginal art was at the forefront of seeing Aboriginal culture in a more positive light by Australians. Aboriginal artists such as Emily Kame Kngwarreye combine traditional materials such as bark and ochre with acrylics and canvas, while telling Dreaming stories in a modern idiom.

Many Aborigines have now moved away from their traditional lifestyle and live within the major cities, but they remain distinctly Aboriginal and generally choose to live within Aboriginal communities. Within designated Aboriginal lands (see pp266–7), many still follow bush medical practices and perform traditional rituals.

It cannot be denied that Aborigines are still disadvantaged in comparison with the rest of Australians, particularly in terms of housing, health, employment and education. But the growing awareness of their culture and traditions is gradually leading to a more harmonious coexistence.

Aborigines performing a traditional dance at sunset

Aboriginal Art

As traditionally nomadic people with little interest in decorating their temporary dwellings, Aborigines often expressed their creativity on landscape features such as rocks and caves *(see pp51–2)*. Many art sites are thousands of years old, although they have often been re-painted over time to preserve the image. Rock art reflects daily Aboriginal life as well as religious beliefs. Some ancient sites contain representations of now extinct animals; others depict human figures with blue eyes, strange weapons and horses – evidently the arrival of Europeans. Aboriginal art is also seen in everyday objects – utensils and accessories such as belts and headbands.

Bark painting, such as this image of a fish, has disappeared from southern areas, but still flourishes in Arnhem Land and on Melville and Bathurst islands.

Cave rock was a popular "canvas" for traditional Aboriginal art, particularly when tribes took cover during the rainy season.

The outline style of rock engraving was developed most fully in the Sydney-Hawkesbury area, due to vast areas of soft Hawkesbury sandstone. More than 4,000 figures have been recorded, often gigantic in size – one whale engraving is more than 20 m (65 ft) long. Groups of engravings can cover more than 1 ha (2.5 acres).

Figures showing the human anatomy are often depicted in basic but exaggerated, stylized forms.

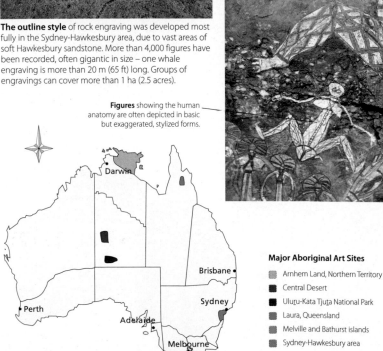

Darwin

Brisbane

Perth

Sydney

Adelaide

Melbourne

Hobart

Major Aboriginal Art Sites

- Arnhem Land, Northern Territory
- Central Desert
- Uluṟu-Kata Tjuṯa National Park
- Laura, Queensland
- Melville and Bathurst islands
- Sydney-Hawkesbury area

Quinkans are stick-like figures found in far north Queensland's Laura region. They represent spirits that are thought to emerge suddenly from rock crevices and startle people, to remind them that misbehaviour will bring swift retribution.

Burial poles are an example of how important decoration is to Aborigines, even to commemmorate death. These brightly coloured Tutini burial poles belong to the Tiwi people of Melville and Bathurst islands *(see p278)*.

The crocodile image personifies the force of nature, as well as symbolizing the relationship between humans and the natural environment. Both are common themes within Aboriginal art.

Bush Plum Dreaming (1991) by Clifford Possum Tjapaltjarri is a modern example of ancient Aboriginal techniques used by the Papunya tribe.

"X-ray art", such as this figure at Nourlangie Rock in Kakadu National Park *(see pp280–81)*, shows the internal and external anatomy of living subjects, including a range of animals.

Arnhem Land Rock Art

Arnhem Land is the 90,000-sq km (34,750-sq mile) Aboriginal territory which stretches from east of Darwin to the Gulf of Carpentaria (see pp266–7). Magnificent rock art "galleries" in this region date from 16,000 BC (see p51) – some of the oldest Aboriginal art in the country.

Totemic art at Uluru *(see pp290–93)* is thought to portray the beings in Aboriginal culture who are believed to have created the rock.

Australian Artists and Writers

The first Europeans to paint Australia were those who arrived on the *Endeavour (see pp54–5)*, but it was not until the prosperity generated by the 1850s gold rushes that art gained any public recognition. There had been colonial artists, of whom Conrad Martens (1801–78) was the best known, but in a country where survival was the most immediate problem, art was not a high priority. The first writings were also journals of early settlers; it was 100 years before Australia could claim the beginnings of a literary tradition, when Rolf Boldrewood (1826–1915) wrote *Robbery Under Arms* (1888), a heroic tale of the bush.

Sir Russell Drysdale

Artists

The so-called "Heidelberg School", named after an area around Melbourne, was the first distinctive Australian school of painting at the end of the 19th century. Its main-stays included Tom Roberts (1856–1931), Charles Conder (1868–1909), Frederick McCubbin (1855–1917) and Arthur Streeton (1867–1943). The group drew strongly on the *plein air* methods of the French Impressionists to capture the distinctive light and openness of the Australian landscape. Then, in the early 1900s, Hans Heysen captured the national imagination with his delicately coloured gum trees and his view of the Australian landscape. Sir Sidney

Nolan (1917–92), best known for his "Ned Kelly" series of the 1940s based on the country's most notorious bushranger *(see p398)*, also produced landscape paintings which propelled Australian art on to the international scene for the first time.

The best known of the talented Boyd family, Arthur Boyd (1920–99), is another great on the Australian art scene; his "Half-Caste Bride" series catapulted him into the art world in 1960.

Probably the greatest interpreter of Australia's Outback is Sir Russell Drysdale (1912–81), whose paintings depict the harshness of this landscape. Brett Whiteley (1939–92) is a more recent talent whose sensual work reflects his view of the world.

Winner of the Archibald Prize for portraiture, William Dobell (1899–1970) is often regarded as the figurehead of the Sydney Modernist movement. He achieved some level of notoriety when, in 1944, two fellow artists mounted a legal challenge to the granting of the Archibald for his portrait of Joshua Smith, claiming it was "not a portrait but a caricature". The action was unsuccessful, but all Dobell's further work generated publicity for the

wrong reasons. Possibly the most popularly recognized Australian artist is Ken Done. Often dismissed for blatant commercialism, his brilliantly coloured work has achieved sales of which most artists only dream.

The most significant collection of Australian art can be seen at Canberra's National Gallery *(see pp206–7)*.

Toberua (1994) by Ken Done

The Antipodeans

Formed in Melbourne in 1959, the Antipodeans consisted of seven of Australia's best-known modern artists, all born in the 1920s: Charles Blackman, Arthur Boyd, David Boyd, John Brack, Robert Dickerson, John Perceval and Clifton Pugh. The aim of the group was to support figurative painting rather than abstraction. The group denied that they were creating a national style and the name Antipodeans was adopted to avoid too narrow a focus on Australia, as the group aimed for international recognition at exhibitions in London. Ironically, it later came to apply to Australian art in general.

Kelly in Spring (1956), one of Sir Sidney Nolan's "Ned Kelly" series

Portrait of Miles Franklin by Marie McNiven

Writers

Much of Australian fiction is concerned with the difficulties Europeans experienced in a harsh land, or the relationship between white settlers and Aborigines. The themes can be traced back to an early Australian novelist, Henry Handel Richardson, the pseudonym of Ethel Richardson (1870–1946). Her trilogy, *The Fortunes of Richard Mahoney* (1929), was published to great acclaim, including a nomination for the Nobel Prize for Literature. Contemporary novelist David Malouf (born in 1934) continues to explore these issues in *Remembering Babylon* (1993), winner of the Prix Baudelaire, and *Conversations at Curlow Creek* (1996).

Film poster of *Schindler's List*, based on *Schindler's Ark*

Australia's most celebrated novelist is Patrick White (1912–90), who won the Nobel Prize in 1973 with *The Eye of the Storm*. White had made his mark in 1957 with *Voss*, the story of the explorer Ludwig Leichhardt. Two-time Booker Prize-winner Peter Carey (born in 1943) celebrated Australia's most famous bushranger in *The True History of the Kelly Gang* (2000).

Campaigner for women's suffrage, Louisa Lawson (1848–1920), is credited with Australia's first feminist journal, *Dawn*, written between 1888 and 1905. At the same time, another feminist, Miles Franklin (1879–1954), defied traditional women's roles of the time by pursuing an independent life in Australia, England and the USA. Her life was documented in several autobiographies, beginning with *My Brilliant Career* (1901).

For descriptions of pre- and postwar Sydney life in the slums, the novels of Ruth Park (born in 1922), such as *Harp in the South* (1948) and *Fence around the Cuckoo* (1992), are unbeatable. Novelist Thomas Keneally (born in 1935) won the 1982 Booker Prize with *Schindler's Ark*.

Aboriginal writer Sally Morgan (born in 1951) has put indigenous Australian writing on the map with her 1988 autobiography *My Place*.

Poets

Australia's early poets were mostly bush balladeers, articulating life in the Australian bush. "The Man from Snowy River" and "Clancy of the Overflow" by A B "Banjo" Paterson (1864–1941) are classics and have been immortalised in song and film. Writing from the late 1800s until his death in 1922,

Henry Lawson similarly wrote some enduring bush verse, but his poetry also had a more political edge. His first published poem in the *Bulletin* literary magazine in 1887 was the rallying "Song of the Republic". One of Australia's leading poets, Les Murray (1938–), is known as the "bush bard" for his writing on bush life.

Poets such as Judith Wright (1915–2000) and Oodgeroo Noonuccal (1920–93), have powerfully expressed the anguish of Aboriginal people.

Henry Lawson

Playwrights

Australia's most prolific contemporary playwright is David Williamson, born in 1942. A satirist exploring middle-class life and values, Williamson has been an international success and several of his plays, such as *Dead White Males* (1995), have been performed both in London and New York.

Ray Lawler gained renown in 1955 with *Summer of the Seventeenth Doll*, which challenged the deep-rooted Australian concept of male friendship. The play has been adapted as an opera, with music by Australian composer Richard Meale.

Other notable contemporary playwrights are Nick Enright, Stephen Sewell and Louis Nowra.

The Wines of Australia

Grapes and wine have been produced in Australia virtually since European settlement in 1788 *(see pp54–5)*. The first vineyards were planted in Sydney in 1791 and over the next 40 years vines were planted in the Hunter Valley (1827), the Barossa at Jacobs Creek (1847), the Yarra Valley (1930), and Adelaide (1937). John and Elizabeth Macarthur became Australia's first commercial wine producers with a small vintage in 1827 from their Sydney farm *(see p131)*. In the 1960s, with the introduction of international grape varieties, such as Chardonnay, small oak-barrel maturation and modern wine-making technology, the wine industry really developed. Since the 1990s Australia has earned an excellent reputation for high-quality wines and there are about 1,465 wineries operating today.

Locator Map
▨ *Major wine-producing regions of Australia*

0 kilometres 500
0 miles 500

Leeuwin Estate winery in Margaret River, Western Australia *(see pp318–19)* is one of the nation's largest producers of top-quality table wines, including Chardonnay and Cabernet Sauvignon.

41
42
● Perth
36
39
40
37
34
30
38
Adelaide 35

The Father of Australian Wine

James Busby is often regarded as the father of the Australian wine industry. Scottish-born, he arrived in Sydney in 1824. During the voyage to Australia he wrote the country's first wine book, detailing his experiences of French vineyards. He established a property at Kirkton in the Hunter Valley, New South Wales, and returned to Europe in 1831, collecting 570 vine cuttings from France and Spain. These were cultivated at Kirkton and at the Sydney and Adelaide Botanic Gardens. In 1833, having founded Australia's first wine-producing region, he emigrated to New Zealand.

James Busby

Mount Hurtle winery produces distinctive white table wines. It is located in one of South Australia's main wine regions, McLaren Vale *(see pp342–3)*.

Wine Regions of Australia

Since signing a trade agreement with the European Union, Australia has had to implement a new classification system for its wine-producing regions. The whole of Australia has 28 wine zones, which can be whole state (Tasmania) or parts of states (Western Victoria). Within these zones are 61 wine regions, such as the Barossa (see pp360–61), with the main ones listed below. Some of the up-and-coming areas in Australia are Mudgee and Orange (NSW), and Geelong (VIC).

① South Burnett
② Granite Belt
③ Hastings River
④ Hunter Valley
⑤ Mudgee
⑥ Orange
⑦ Cowra
⑧ Lachlan Valley
⑨ Canberra
⑩ Gundagai
⑪ Hilltops
⑫ Sydney
⑬ Shoalhaven
⑭ Riverina
⑮ Murray Darling

⑯ Swan Hill
⑰ Rutherglen Glenrowan King Valley
⑱ Yarra Valley
⑲ Mornington Peninsula
⑳ Geelong
㉑ Tasmania
㉒ Sunbury
㉓ Macedon
㉔ Pyrenees
㉕ Grampians
㉖ Coonawarra
㉗ Mount Benson
㉘ Padthaway
㉙ Langhorne Creek

㉚ McLaren Vale
㉛ Adelaide Hills
㉜ Eden Valley
㉝ Barossa
㉞ Clare Valley
㉟ Kangaroo Island
㊱ Esperance
㊲ Great Southern
㊳ Pemberton
㊴ Manjimup
㊵ Margaret River
㊶ Swan District
㊷ Perth Hills

Balmoral House is part of the Rosemount Estate in the Upper Hunter Valley (see pp166–7). The house gives its name to the winery's excellent Balmoral Shiraz.

Visiting a Winery

Wine tourism is increasingly popular in Australia and information and maps are readily available at information bureaux. Most wineries are open daily (but you should ring ahead to avoid disappointment) and if they charge for tastings it will be refunded against a purchase from the "cellar door". Winery restaurants are also popular and some have barbeques and entertainment for children while others have a wine-food paired menu. With strict drink-drive laws it may be better to take a guided tour – these can be by bus or limousine.

PIPERS BROOK VINEYARD
1988 CHARDONNAY
Tasmania

Pipers Brook in Tasmania was established in 1973 and is home to the acclaimed Kreglinger Wine Estates.

Surfing and Beach Culture

Australia is the quintessential home of beach culture, with the nation's beaches ranging from sweeping crescents with rolling waves to tiny, secluded coves. Almost all Australians live within a two-hour drive of the coast, and during the hot summers it is almost second nature to make for the water to cool off. The clichéd image of the sun-bronzed Australian is no longer the reality it once was thanks to increased sun protection awareness, but popular beaches are still packed with tanned bodies basking on golden sands or frolicking in deep blue waves. Fines levied for inappropriate behaviour mean that the atmosphere is calm and safe at all times. Surfing has always been a national sport, with regular carnivals and competitions held on the coastline. There are also opportunities for beginners to try their hand at this daring sport.

Baked-brown bodies and sun-bleached hair were once the epitome of beach culture.

Surf carnivals attract hundreds of spectators, who thrill to races, "iron man" competitions, dummy rescues and spectacular lifeboat displays.

Surfer in Action

Riding the waves is a serious business. Wetsuit-clad "surfies" study the surfing reports in the media and think nothing of travelling vast distances to reach a beach where the best waves are running.

Crouching down into the wave's crest increases stability on the board.

Where to Surf

The best surfing to be found in Australia is on the New South Wales coast (*see pp182–3*), the southern Queensland coast, especially the aptly named Surfer's Paradise and the Sunshine Coast (*pp242–3*) and the southern coastline of Western Australia (*pp316–17*). Tasmania also has some fine surfing beaches on its northwestern tip (*pp470–71*). Despite superb north Queensland beaches, the Great Barrier Reef stops the waves well before they reach the mainland. In summer, deadly marine stingers (box jellyfish) here make surf swimming impossible in many areas, unless there is a stinger-proof enclosure.

Surf lifesaving is an integral part of the Australian beach scene. Trained volunteer lifesavers, easily recognized by their red and yellow swimming caps, ensure that swimmers stay within flag-defined safe areas and are ready to spring into action if someone is in trouble.

Beach Activities

Australian beaches are not only the preserve of surfers. Winter temperatures are mild in most coastal areas, so many beach activities are enjoyed all year. Weekends see thousands of pleasure boats, from small runabouts to luxury yachts, competing in races or just out for a picnic in some sheltered cove. The sails of windsurfers create swirls of colour on gusty days. Kite-flying has become an art form, with the Festival of the Winds a September highlight at Sydney's Bondi Beach (see p44). Beach volleyball, once a knockabout game, is now a competitive sport.

Festival of the Winds

Takeaway snack food at the beach is an Australian tradition, since many sunlovers spend entire days by the ocean. Fish and chips, kebabs and burgers are on sale at beach cafés.

Surfboards, once made out of wood, are now built of light fibreglass, often in bright colours, improving speed and visibility.

Safety

Beaches are safe provided you follow a few guidelines:

· Always swim "between the flags".
· Don't swim alone.
· Note signs warning of strong currents, blue bottles or stingers.
· If you get into difficulty, do not wave but signal for help by raising one arm straight in the air.
· Use factor 50+ sunscreen and wear a shirt and hat.

The Australian crawl revolutionized swimming throughout the world in the 1880s. For most Australians, swimming is an everyday sport, learned at a very early age.

AUSTRALIA THROUGH THE YEAR

The seasons in Australia are the opposite of those in the northern hemisphere. In the southern half of the continent spring comes in September, summer is from December to February, autumn runs from March to May, while winter begins in June. In contrast, the tropical climate of the north coast is more clearly divided into wet and dry seasons, the former between November and April. Australia's vast interior has a typical desert climate – baking hot days and cool nights. The weather throughout Australia is reliable enough year-round to make outdoor events popular all over the country.

Spring

With the warm weather, the profusion of spring flowers brings gardens and national parks to life. Food, art and music festivals abound in cities. Footballers finish their seasons, cricketers warm up for summer matches and the horse-racing fraternity gets ready to place its bets.

Australian Football League Grand Final in September

September

Mudgee Wine Festival *(date varies)*. Includes bush dances as well as wine *(see p181)*.
Festival of the Winds *(Sun, date varies)*, Bondi Beach *(see p43)*. Multicultural kite-flying festival; music, dance.
Royal Melbourne Show *(last two weeks)*. Agricultural exhibitions, rides and displays.
Australian Football League Grand Final *(last Sat in Sep)*, Melbourne *(see p401)*.
Torres Strait Cultural Festival *(mid-Sep, even-numbered years)*, Thursday Island. The spiritual traditions of the Torres Strait Islanders are celebrated through dance, song and art.
Floriade *(mid-Sep–mid-Oct)*, Canberra. Magnificent flower festival in Commonwealth Park *(see p199)*.
Tulip Time Festival *(two weeks from mid-Sep)*, Bowral. The Corbett Gardens are carpeted with flowers *(see p190)*.
Carnival of Flowers *(date varies)*, Toowoomba. Popular floral festival including spectacular garden and flower displays *(see p244)*.

October

Melbourne Fringe Festival *(mid-Sep–early Oct, dates vary)*, The arts festival showcases hundreds of events, such as live performances, films, visual arts, multi-media exhibits and comedy shows.
Australian Rugby League Grand Final *(first Sun)*, Sydney. National event.

Floriade, the spring flower festival in Canberra

Melbourne International Arts Festival *(two weeks, mid-to late Oct)*, Dance, theatre, music and visual arts events.
Melbourne Marathon *(date varies)*. Fun run through the city.
Carlton Italian Festa *(Sun, date varies)*, Melbourne. Street carnival through the city's Italian district *(see p399)*.
Leura Garden Festival *(second–third weekends)*, Blue Mountains. Village fair and garden shows *(see p174)*.

Festival of the Winds, Australia's annual kite-flying festival

Rose and Rodeo Festival
(last weekend), Warwick.
Australia's oldest rodeo
attracts riders from all over
the world *(see p244)*.

Jacaranda Festival *(last week)*,
Grafton. Australia's oldest flower
festival features a Grand Float
procession through the town
(see p182).

Maldon Folk Festival *(late Oct/
early Nov, weekend before
Melbourne Cup)*. Folk music
concerts in this Victorian
country town.

The Melbourne Cup, Australia's annual
thoroughbred horse race

November
Sculpture by the Sea *(date varies,
around last week Oct/first week Nov)*,
Sydney. Great outdoor sculptures
can be seen at Bondi beach.

The High Country Festival
(late Oct–early Nov), Mansfield.
Horse races, parades, markets,
arts and cultural exhibitions.

Melbourne Cup *(first Tue)*.
Australia's most popular
horse race virtually brings
the nation to a halt.

Summer

The beginning of the school
holidays for Christmas marks
the start of the summer in
Australia and the festivities
continue until Australia Day
on 26 January. Summer also
brings a feast for sport lovers,
with tennis, surfing events
and a host of cricket matches.
Arts and music lovers make
the most of organized festivals.

Santa Claus celebrating Christmas on Bondi Beach, Sydney

December
Carols by Candlelight *(24 Dec)*,
Melbourne. Top musicians
unite with locals to celebrate
Christmas.

Christmas at Bondi Beach
(25 Dec). Holiday-makers hold
parties on the famous beach
(see p131).

Sydney to Hobart Yacht Race
(26 Dec). Sydney Harbour teems
with yachts setting off for
Hobart *(see p464–5)*.

Boxing Day Test Match *(26 Dec)*,
Melbourne.

New Year's Eve *(31 Dec)*, Sydney
Harbour. Street parties and
firework displays.

January
Hanging Rock Picnic Races
(1 Jan & 26 Jan). Premier country
horse racing event *(see p441)*.

Festival of Sydney *(second
week–end Jan)*. City throngs
during this cultural festival.

Australian Open *(last two
weeks)*, Melbourne. Australia's
popular Grand Slam tennis
tournament.

Country Music Festival *(last
two weeks)*, Tamworth. Australia's
main country music festival,
culminating in the Golden
Guitar Awards *(see p181)*.

Midsumma Festival *(mid-Jan–
first week Feb)*, Melbourne. This
annual Gay and Lesbian festival
includes street parades.

Tunarama Festival *(last
weekend)*, Port Lincoln. Tuna
tossing competitions and
fireworks *(see p370)*.

Australia Day Concert
(26 Jan), Sydney. This free
outdoor concert is part of the
celebrations for the birth of the
nation *(see p60)*.

Chinese New Year *(late Jan or
early Feb)*, Sydney and Melbourne.

Cricket Test Match, Sydney.

Fireworks in Sydney for the Australia
Day celebrations

February
Perth Festival *(three weeks
from mid-Feb)*. Australia's oldest
arts festival.

**Leeuwin Estate Winery Music
Concert** *(mid-Feb–Mar)*, Margaret
River. Concert attracting stars
(see p318).

Adelaide Fringe *(mid-Feb
–mid-Mar)*. Second-largest fringe
festival in the world.

Adelaide Festival *(late Feb–
mid-Mar)*. Multi-arts festival
held in even-numbered years.

Australian Grand Prix, held in Melbourne in March

Autumn

After the humidity of the summer, autumn brings fresh mornings and cooler days that are tailor-made for outdoor pursuits such as bushwalking, cycling and fishing, as well as outdoor festivals. There are numerous sporting and cultural events to tempt the visitor. Many of the country's wineries open their doors during the harvest season and hold gourmet food and wine events. Anzac Day (25 April) – the day in 1915 when Australian and New Zealand forces landed at Gallipoli – has been observed annually since 1916 and is a national holiday on which Australians commemorate their war dead.

March

Gay and Lesbian Mardi Gras Festival *(varies)*, Sydney. Flamboyant street parades and events.
Day on the Green *(weekends in Mar)*. Concerts at Rochford Winery in the Yarra Valley attracts international performers.
Begonia Festival *(first two weeks)*, Ballarat. Begonia displays in the Botanical Gardens *(see p439)*.
Moomba Festival *(second week)*, Melbourne. International aquatic events on the Yarra River *(see pp404–5)*.
Australian Formula One Grand Prix *(mid-Mar)*, Melbourne. Top Formula One drivers compete, while the city celebrates with street parties *(see p407)*.

St Patrick's Day Parade *(17 Mar or Sun before)*, Sydney. Pubs serve green beer and a flamboyant parade travels from Hyde Park.
International Flower and Garden Show *(late Mar–early Apr)*, Melbourne. Spectacular floral event held in the beautiful Exhibition Gardens *(see p399)*.

Yarra Valley wine

April

Melbourne International Comedy Festival *(end Mar–early Apr)*. Comedy acts from around the world perform indoors and out.
Royal Easter Show *(week preceding Good Fri)* Sydney. Agricultural shows, funfair rides, local arts and crafts displays and team games.

Rip Curl Pro Surfing Competition *(Easter weekend)*, Bells Beach. Pros and amateurs take part in this premier competition *(see p433)*.
Easter Fair *(Easter weekend)*, Maldon. An Easter parade and a colourful street carnival takes over this quaint country town *(see p436)*.
Bright Autumn Festival *(last week Apr–early May)*, Bright. Winery tours, art exhibitions and street parades *(see p451)*.
Anzac Day *(25 Apr)*. Australia's war dead and war veterans are honoured in remembrance services throughout the country.

May

Australian Celtic Festival *(first weekend)*, Glen Innes. Traditional Celtic events celebrate the town's British heritage *(see p180)*.
Message Sticks Festival *(mid-May)*, Sydney. A celebration of Aboriginal and Torres Strait Islander arts and culture, held at the Sydney Opera House.
Kernewek Lowender Cornish Festival *(mid- to late May)*, Little Cornwall. A biennial celebration of the area's Cornish heritage which began with the copper discoveries of the 1860s *(see p367)*.
Vivid Sydney *(late May–early Jun)*. Light installations and projections on landmark buildings.

Anzac Day ceremony along Canberra's Anzac Parade

Racing in Alice Springs' Camel Cup

Public Holidays

New Year's Day (1 Jan)

Australia Day (26 Jan, NSW;
1st Mon after 26 Jan, all
other states)

Good Friday (variable)

Easter Monday (variable)

Anzac Day (25 Apr)

Queen's Birthday (second
Mon in Jun)

Christmas Day (25 Dec)

Boxing Day (26 Dec)

Winter

Winter in the east can be cool enough to require warm jackets, and it is often icy in Victoria and Tasmania. Many festivals highlight the change of climate in celebration of freezing temperatures. Other events, such as film festivals, are arts-based and indoors. The warm rather than sweltering climate of the Outback in winter offers the opportunity for pleasurable outdoor events.

June
Three-Day Equestrian Event *(first weekend)*, Gawler. Spectacular riding skills are displayed at Australia's oldest equestrian event.
Sydney Film Festival *(two weeks mid-Jun)*. The latest blockbuster film releases are combined with retrospectives and showcases.
Laura Dance & Cultural Festival *(odd numbered years)*, Cape York. Celebration of Aboriginal culture.

July
Yulefest *(throughout Jun, Jul, Aug)*, Blue Mountains. Hotels, guesthouses and some restaurants celebrate a mid-winter "traditional Christmas" with log fires and all the usual yuletide trimmings.
Brass Monkey Festival *(throughout Jul)*, Stanthorpe. Inland Queensland turns the freezing winter temperatures into an opportunity for celebration *(see p244)*.
Alice Springs Show *(first weekend)*. Agricultural and historical displays are combined with arts, crafts and cookery demonstrations at this popular event.
Cairns Show *(mid-Jul)*. A cultural celebration of historical and contemporary life in the Australian tropics *(see p258)*.
Melbourne International Film Festival *(last week Jul–mid-Aug)*. The largest and most popular film festival.
Camel Cup *(mid-Jul)*, Alice Springs. Camel racing on the dry Todd River.

August
Almond Blossom Festival *(first week)*, Mount Lofty. Includes almond cracking.
City to Surf Race *(second Sun)*, Sydney. A 14-km (9-mile) fun run from the city centre (usually Hyde Park) to Bondi Beach.
Shinju Matsuri Festival *(last weekend–first week Sep)*, Broome. Pearl festival.
Melbourne Art Fair *(mid-Aug)*. Biennial modern art fair attracting both established and up-and-coming artists from all over the world. Works on display range from paintings to photographs, from sculptures to multimedia installations.
Mount Isa Rodeo *(mid-Aug)*. Largest rodeo *(see p261)*.
Henley-on-Todd Regatta *(third Sat)*, Alice Springs. Races in bottomless boats along the dry Todd River.
Open Garden Scheme *(Aug–May)*. The country's most magnificent private gardens open to the public *(see p378)*.

Dragon Boat race, part of the Shinju Matsuri in Broome

The Climate of Australia

This vast country experiences a variable climate. Three-quarters of its land is desert or scrub and has low, unreliable rainfall. The huge, dry interior is hot year-round during the day but can be very cold at night. The southern half of Australia, including Tasmania, has warm summers and mild winters. Further north, seasonal variations lessen and the Top End has just two seasons: the dry, and the wet, with its monsoon rains and occasional tropical cyclones.

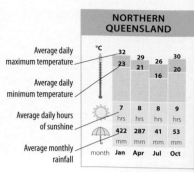

NORTHERN QUEENSLAND

Average daily maximum temperature

Average daily minimum temperature

Average daily hours of sunshine

Average monthly rainfall

°C	Jan	Apr	Jul	Oct
max	32	29	26	30
min	23	21	16	20
sunshine	7 hrs	8 hrs	8 hrs	9 hrs
rainfall	422 mm	287 mm	41 mm	53 mm

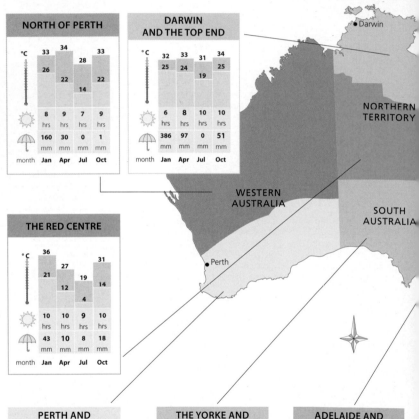

NORTH OF PERTH

°C	Jan	Apr	Jul	Oct
max	33	34	28	33
min	26	22	14	22
sunshine	8 hrs	9 hrs	7 hrs	9 hrs
rainfall	160 mm	30 mm	0 mm	1 mm

DARWIN AND THE TOP END

°C	Jan	Apr	Jul	Oct
max	32	33	31	34
min	25	24	19	25
sunshine	6 hrs	8 hrs	10 hrs	10 hrs
rainfall	386 mm	97 mm	0 mm	51 mm

THE RED CENTRE

°C	Jan	Apr	Jul	Oct
max	36	27	19	31
min	21	12	4	14
sunshine	10 hrs	10 hrs	9 hrs	10 hrs
rainfall	43 mm	10 mm	8 mm	18 mm

NORTHERN TERRITORY

WESTERN AUSTRALIA

SOUTH AUSTRALIA

Darwin

Perth

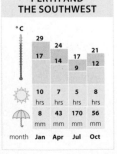

PERTH AND THE SOUTHWEST

°C	Jan	Apr	Jul	Oct
max	29	24	17	21
min	17	14	9	12
sunshine	10 hrs	7 hrs	5 hrs	8 hrs
rainfall	8 mm	43 mm	170 mm	56 mm

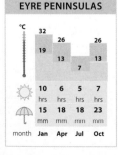

THE YORKE AND EYRE PENINSULAS

°C	Jan	Apr	Jul	Oct
max	32	26	13	26
min	19	13	7	13
sunshine	10 hrs	6 hrs	5 hrs	7 hrs
rainfall	15 mm	18 mm	18 mm	23 mm

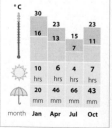

ADELAIDE AND THE SOUTHEAST

°C	Jan	Apr	Jul	Oct
max	30	23	15	23
min	16	13	7	11
sunshine	10 hrs	6 hrs	4 hrs	7 hrs
rainfall	20 mm	46 mm	66 mm	43 mm

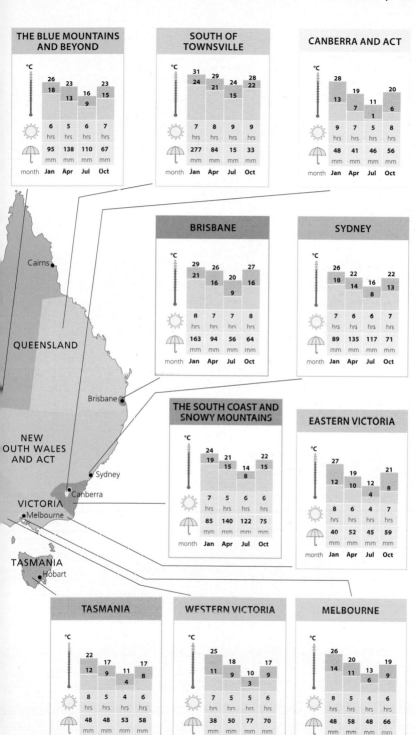

THE BLUE MOUNTAINS AND BEYOND

°C	Jan	Apr	Jul	Oct
high	26	23	16	23
low	18	13	9	15
hrs	6 hrs	5 hrs	6 hrs	7 hrs
mm	95 mm	138 mm	110 mm	67 mm
month	Jan	Apr	Jul	Oct

SOUTH OF TOWNSVILLE

°C	Jan	Apr	Jul	Oct
high	31	29	24	28
low	24	21	15	22
hrs	7 hrs	8 hrs	9 hrs	9 hrs
mm	277 mm	84 mm	15 mm	33 mm
month	Jan	Apr	Jul	Oct

CANBERRA AND ACT

°C	Jan	Apr	Jul	Oct
high	28	19	11	20
low	13	7	1	6
hrs	9 hrs	7 hrs	5 hrs	8 hrs
mm	48 mm	41 mm	46 mm	56 mm
month	Jan	Apr	Jul	Oct

Cairns

QUEENSLAND

Brisbane

NEW SOUTH WALES AND ACT

Sydney

Canberra

VICTORIA

Melbourne

TASMANIA

Hobart

BRISBANE

°C	Jan	Apr	Jul	Oct
high	29	26	20	27
low	21	16	9	16
hrs	8 hrs	7 hrs	7 hrs	8 hrs
mm	163 mm	94 mm	56 mm	64 mm
month	Jan	Apr	Jul	Oct

SYDNEY

°C	Jan	Apr	Jul	Oct
high	26	22	16	22
low	18	14	8	13
hrs	7 hrs	6 hrs	6 hrs	7 hrs
mm	89 mm	135 mm	117 mm	71 mm
month	Jan	Apr	Jul	Oct

THE SOUTH COAST AND SNOWY MOUNTAINS

°C	Jan	Apr	Jul	Oct
high	24	21	14	22
low	19	15	8	15
hrs	7 hrs	5 hrs	6 hrs	6 hrs
mm	85 mm	140 mm	122 mm	75 mm
month	Jan	Apr	Jul	Oct

EASTERN VICTORIA

°C	Jan	Apr	Jul	Oct
high	27	19	12	21
low	12	10	4	8
hrs	8 hrs	6 hrs	4 hrs	7 hrs
mm	40 mm	52 mm	45 mm	59 mm
month	Jan	Apr	Jul	Oct

TASMANIA

°C	Jan	Apr	Jul	Oct
high	22	17	11	17
low	12	9	4	8
hrs	8 hrs	5 hrs	4 hrs	6 hrs
mm	48 mm	48 mm	53 mm	58 mm
month	Jan	Apr	Jul	Oct

WESTERN VICTORIA

°C	Jan	Apr	Jul	Oct
high	25	18	10	17
low	11	9	3	9
hrs	7 hrs	5 hrs	5 hrs	6 hrs
mm	38 mm	50 mm	77 mm	70 mm
month	Jan	Apr	Jul	Oct

MELBOURNE

°C	Jan	Apr	Jul	Oct
high	26	20	13	19
low	14	11	6	9
hrs	8 hrs	5 hrs	4 hrs	6 hrs
mm	48 mm	58 mm	48 mm	66 mm
month	Jan	Apr	Jul	Oct

THE HISTORY OF AUSTRALIA

Australia is a young nation in an ancient land. It is a nation of immigrants, past and present, forced and free. The first European settlers occupied a harsh country; they explored it, exploited its mineral wealth and farmed it. In so doing, they suffered at the hands of nature, as well as enduring depressions and wars. Out of all this, however, has emerged a modern and cosmopolitan society.

The first rocks of the Australian landscape began to form some four-and-a-half billion years ago. Over time many older rocks were covered by more recent rocks, but in places such as the Pilbara region of Western Australia erosion has exposed a landscape 3,500 million years old (see pp334–5). About 500 million years ago Australia, together with South America, South Africa, India and the Antarctic, formed a supercontinent known as Gondwanaland. This landmass moved through a series of different climatic zones; today's desert interior was once a shallow sea (see pp26–7).

The First Immigrants

Australia was first settled by Aboriginal people who arrived by sea from Asia more than 60,000 years ago. On landing, they quickly adapted to the climatic and geographical conditions. Nomadic hunters and gatherers, the Aborigines moved with the seasons and spread across the continent, reaching Tasmania 35,000 years ago. They had few material possessions beyond the tools and weapons required for hunting and obtaining food. The early tools, known today as core tools, were very simple chopping implements, roughly formed by grinding stone. By 8,000 BC Aborigines had developed the sophisticated returning boomerang (see p34) and possibly the world's first barbed spear. So-called flaked tools of varying styles were in use 5,000 years later, finely made out of grained stones such as flint to create sharp cutting edges.

Beneath the apparently simple way of life, Aboriginal society was complex. It was based on a network of mainly nomadic bands, comprising between 50 and 100 people, bound by kin relationships, who lived according to strictly applied laws and customs. These laws and beliefs, including the spiritual significance of the land, were upheld through a tradition of song, dance and art (see pp34–7). With no centralized or formal system of government, individual groups were led by prominent, generally older men, who were held in great respect. Across the continent there were more than 200 languages spoken and approximately 800 dialects. In many respects, Aboriginal life was also very advanced: excavations at Lake Mungo provide fascinating evidence of ancient burial rituals, including what is

60,000 BC	50,000 BC	40,000 BC	30,000 BC	20,000 BC	10,000 BC

43,000–38,000 BC Tools found in a grave pit beside Nepean River are among the oldest firmly dated signs of human occupation in Australia

35,000 BC Aborigines reach Tasmania

Diprotodon 20,000 BC

13,000 End of Ice Age

170–60,000 BC Aborigines thought to have reached Australia

42,000 BC Aboriginal engravings at Olary, South Australia

25,000 BC Woman is cremated at Lake Mungo – the world's oldest known cremation

20,000 BC Humans live in the Blue Mountains despite Ice Age. Remains of the largest marsupial, Diprotodon, date back to this period

◀ *Desmond, A New South Wales Chief (about 1825) by Augustus Earle*

believed to be the world's oldest cremation 25,000 years ago *(see p185)*.

Theories of a Southern Land

In Europe, the existence of a southern land was the subject of debate for centuries. As early as the 5th century BC, with the European discovery of Australia some 2,000 years away, the mathematician Pythagoras speculated on the presence of southern lands necessary to counterbalance those in the northern hemisphere. In about AD 150, the ancient geographer Ptolemy of Alexandria continued this speculation by drawing a map showing a landmass enclosing the Atlantic and Indian oceans. Some scholars went so far as to suggest that it was inhabited by "antipodes", a race of men whose feet faced backwards. Religious scholar St Augustine (AD 354–430) declared categorically that the southern hemisphere contained no land; the contrary view was heretical. But not all men of religion agreed: the 1086 *Osma Beatus,* a series of maps illustrating the

Woodcut of an "antipodean man" (1493)

works of the monk Beatus, showed the hypothetical land as a populated region.

It was not until the 15th century, when Europe entered a golden age of exploration, that these theories were tested. Under the patronage of Prince Henry of Portugal (1394–1460), known as Henry the Navigator, Portuguese sailors crossed the equator for the first time in 1470. In 1488 they sailed around the southern tip of Africa, and by 1502 they claimed to have located a southern land while on a voyage to explore South America. The Italian navigator, Amerigo Vespucci, described it as Paradise, full of trees and colourful birds. The location of this land is not clear but it was definitely not Australia.

In 1519 another Portuguese expedition set off, under the command of Ferdinand Magellan, and was the first to circumnavigate the world. No drawings of the lands explored survive, but subsequent maps show Tierra del Fuego as the tip of a landmass south of the Americas. Between 1577 and 1580 the Englishman Sir Francis Drake also circumnavigated the world, but his maps indicate no such land. Meanwhile, maps prepared in Dieppe in France between 1540 and 1566 show a southern continent, Java la Grande, lying southeast of Indonesia.

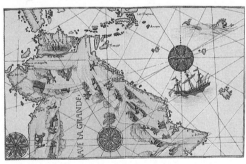

First known map of Australia known as the *Dauphin Chart*, 1530–36

5,000 BC Dingo is the first domesticated animal to reach Australia from Southeast Asia	**500 BC** Pythagoras speculates on existence of southern lands	**AD 150** Ptolemy believes the southern land encloses the Atlantic and Indian oceans	**450** Macrobius, in his *Dream of Scorpio*, envisages uninhabited southern land
5,000 BC	**1,000 BC**	**AD 1**	**1000**
		400 St Augustine declares south to be all ocean and rejects idea of antipodeans	**1086** Beatus, on his *Mappa mundi*, shows a southern land inhabited by a monster with one large foot

Copperplate print of a dingo

Abel Tasman's Dutch discovery ships

The Dutch Discovery

By the 17th century Portugal's power in Southeast Asia was beginning to wane, and Holland, with its control of the Dutch East Indies (Indonesia), was the new power and responsible for the European discovery of Australia.

Willem Jansz, captain of the ship *Duyfken*, was in search of New Guinea, a land thought to be rich in gold, when he sailed along the Cape York Peninsula in 1606. He found the coast inhospitable. In 1616 Dirk Hartog, commanding the *Eendracht*, was blown off course on his way to the East Indies. He landed on an island off Western Australia and nailed a pewter plate to a pole *(see p330)*.

Dutch navigator Abel Tasman charted large parts of Australia and New Zealand between 1642 and 1644, including Tasmania which he originally named Van Diemen's Land in honour of the Governor-General of the East Indies. It became Tasmania in 1855.

The Dutch continued to explore the country for 150 years, but although their discoveries were of geographic interest they did not result in any economic benefit.

The Forgotten Spaniard

Bronze relief of Luis Vaez de Torres

In 1606, the same year that Willem Jansz first set foot on Australian soil, Luis Vaez de Torres, a Spanish Admiral, led an expedition in search of "Terra Australis". He sailed through the strait which now bears his name between Australia and New Guinea *(see p256)*. His discovery, however, was inexplicably ignored for 150 years. He sent news of his exploration to King Felipe III of Spain from the Philippines but died shortly after. Perhaps his early death meant that the news was not disseminated and the significance of his maps not realized.

The First Englishman

The first Englishman to land on Australian soil was the privateer William Dampier in 1688. He published a book of his journey, *New Voyage Round the World*, in 1697. Britain gave him command of the *Roebuck*, in which he explored the northwest Australian coast in great detail. His ship sank on the return voyage. The crew survived but Dampier was court martialled for the mistreatment of his subordinates.

Portrait of William Dampier

1577–80 Sir Francis Drake circumnavigates the world but indicates no austral region beneath South America

Sir Francis Drake

Dampier's compass

1688 William Dampier lands on Australian soil

1300 Marco Polo describes a southern land which is later added to the imaginary Terra Australis on Renaissance maps

Hartog's plate

1616 Dirk Hartog sails from Amsterdam and lands on the western shore of Australia, nailing a pewter plate to a pole

1756 Final Dutch voyage of the *Buis* to Australia

1200	1400	1600

The Colonization of Australia

By the mid-18th century Britain had taken over as the world's main maritime power. In 1768 Captain James Cook set off to find Australia in the *Endeavour* and in 1770 King George III formally claimed possession of the east coast, named New South Wales. Overcrowding of jails and the loss of American colonies in the War of Independence led the British to establish a penal colony in the new land. The First Fleet, consisting of two men-of-war and nine transport ships, arrived in Sydney Cove on 26 January 1788. The initial settlement consisted of 750 convicts, approximately 210 marines and 40 women and children. Faced with great hardship, they survived in tents, eating local wildlife and rations from Britain.

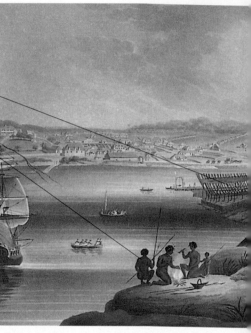

Captain James Cook *(c.1800)*
The English navigator charted eastern Australia for the first time between 1770 and 1771.

Boat building at the Government dockyard

Aborigines depicted observing the new white settlement.

Britain Takes Possession
In 1770 the Union Jack was raised on the east coast of Australia, and Britain finally claimed possession of this new-found land.

A View of Sydney Cove
This idyllic image, drawn by Edward Dayes and engraved by F Jukes in 1804, shows the Aboriginal peoples living peacefully within the infant colony alongside the flourishing maritime and agricultural industries. In reality, by the end of the 18th century they had been entirely ostracized from the life and prosperity of their native land. The first settlement was founded at Port Jackson, renamed Sydney Cove.

Sir Joseph Banks
Aboard the *Endeavour* with Captain Cook, botanist Joseph Banks was responsible for the proposal of Botany Bay as the first penal settlement.

First Fleet Ship
This painting by Francis Holman (c.1787) shows three views of the *Borrowdale*, one of the fleet's three commercial store ships.

Scrimshaw
Engraving bone or shell was a skilful way to pass time during long months spent at sea.

Buildings looked impressive but were poorly built.

Convict housing

Governor Phillip's House, Sydney
This grand colonial mansion, flanked by landscaped gardens, was home to Australia's first government.

Barracks housing NSW Rum Corps

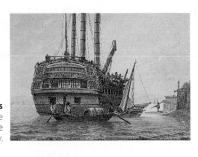

Prison Hulks
Old ships, unfit for naval service, were used as floating prisons to house convicts until the mid-19th century.

1768 Captain James Cook sets out from England for Tahiti on his ship, the *Endeavour*

1775 British overcrowding of jails and prison hulks

Aborigine Bennelong

1788 Aborigine Bennelong is captured and held for five months, then taken to England to meet King George III

1770 — 1780 — 1790

1770 Cook discovers the east coast of Australia and takes possession for Britain

1779 Botanist Joseph Banks recommends Botany Bay for penal settlement

Merino sheep

1797 John Macarthur introduces merino sheep from the Cape of Good Hope (*see p131*)

Exploring the Coastline

Once the survival of the first settlement was assured, both the government and the free settlers began to look beyond its confines. Faced with a vast, unknown continent and fuelled by desires for knowledge and wealth, they set out to explore the land. The 19th century was a period of exploration, discovery and settlement.

Between 1798 and 1799 the English midshipman Matthew Flinders and surgeon George Bass charted much of the Australian coastline south of Sydney. They also circumnavigated Tasmania, known at that time as Van Diemen's Land *(see p53)*.

John Batman and local Aboriginal chiefs

In 1801 Flinders was given command of the sloop *Investigator* and explored the entire Australian coastline, becoming the first man to successfully circumnavigate the whole continent.

William Wentworth and William Lawson forged a successful route across the Blue Mountains *(see pp172–3)*. In 1824 explorers Hamilton Hume and William Hovell opened up the continent further when they travelled overland from New South Wales to Port Phillip Bay, the present site of Melbourne.

Between 1828 and 1830 Charles Sturt, a former secretary to the New South Wales Governor, led two expeditions along Australia's inland river systems. On his first journey he discovered the Darling River. His second expedition began in Sydney and followed the Murray River to the sea in South Australia. This arduous task left Sturt, like many such explorers before and after him, suffering from ill health for the rest of his life.

Exploring the Interior

Inland New South Wales was opened up for settlement in 1813, when George Blaxland,

Sturt's party shown being attacked by Aborigines on their journey to the Murray River

New Colonies

Individual colonies began to emerge across the continent throughout the 19th century. First settled in 1804, Tasmania became a separate colony in 1825; in 1829 Western Australia became a colony with the establishment of Perth. Originally a colony of free settlers, a labour shortage led to the westward transportation of convicts.

In 1835 a farmer, John Batman, signed a contract with local Aborigines to acquire 250,000 ha (600,000 acres) of land where Melbourne now stands *(see p385)*. His action resulted in a rush for land in the area.

1798–9 Matthew Flinders and George Bass circumnavigate Tasmania

1808 Major Johnston leads an insurrection against rum being abolished as currency

1825 Van Diemen's Land (later Tasmania) becomes a separate colony

1840–41 Sheep farmer Edward John Eyre is the first European to cross the Nullarbor Plain

E J Eyre

1800   **1810**   **1820**   **1830**   **1840**

1801–3 Flinders circumnavigates Australia

1804 Hobart Town is established

1813 The first currency, the "holey dollar" and "dump", is introduced

Holey dollar and dump, made from Spanish coins

1833 Port Arthur opens as a penal establishment. It remains in use until 1877

1829 Western Australia is annexed, using convicts for cheap labour

A typical colonial house in Hobart Town (now Hobart), Tasmania, during its early days in 1856

The settlement was recognized in 1837, and the separate colony of Victoria was proclaimed in 1851, at the start of its gold rush (see pp58–9). Queensland became a separate colony in 1859. South Australia was established in 1836 as Australia's only convict-free colony. Based on a theory formulated by a group of English reformers, the colony was funded by land sales which paid for public works and the transportation of free labourers. It became a haven for religious dissenters, a tradition that still continues today.

Crossing the Continent

Edward John Eyre, a sheep farmer who arrived from England in 1833, was the first European to cross the Nullarbor Plain from Adelaide to Western Australia in 1840.

In 1859 the South Australian government, anxious to build an overland telegraph from Adelaide to the north coast, offered a reward to the first person to cross the continent from south to north. An expedition of 20 to 40 men and camels left Melbourne in 1860 under the command of police officer Robert O'Hara Burke and surveyor William Wills. Burke, Wills and two other men travelled from their base camp

The Rum Rebellion

In 1808, the military, under the command of Major George Johnston and John Macarthur (see p131), staged an insurrection known as the Rum Rebellion. At stake was the military's control of the profitable rum trade. Governor William Bligh (1754–1817), target of a mutiny when captain of the Bounty, was arrested after he tried to stop rum being used as currency. The military held power for 23 months until government was restored by Governor Lachlan Macquarie.

William Bligh

at Cooper Creek to the tidal mangroves of the Flinders River which they mistook for the ocean, before heading back south. They returned to the base camp only hours after the main party, who now believed them dead, had left. Burke and Wills died at the base camp from starvation and fatigue.

The crossing from south to north was finally completed by John McDouall Stuart in 1862. He returned to Adelaide sick with scurvy and almost blind.

The return of Burke and Wills to Cooper Creek in 1860

1850	1860	1870	1880	1890
1851 Gold discovered near Bathurst, New South Wales, and at Ballarat and Bendigo, Victoria (see pp58–9)	**1862** John Stuart is the first explorer to cross from south to north Australia	**1872** Overland telegraph from Adelaide to Darwin, via Alice Springs		**1899** Australians fight in the Boer War
		1873 Uluṟu (Ayers Rock) first sighted by Europeans		
1854 Eureka Stockade (see p58)	**1868** Last transportation of convicts to Australia arrive in Western Australia		**1880** Ned Kelly hanged (see p455)	
1853 Last convicts transported to Tasmania		**1876** Last full-blooded Tasmanian Aborigine, Trugaṉinī, dies (see p473)		

Death mask of Ned Kelly

The 1850s Gold Rush

Gold was discovered near Bathurst in New South Wales and at Ballarat and Bendigo in Victoria in 1851. Established towns were almost deserted as men from all over the country, together with immigrants from Europe and China, rushed to the gold fields. Some became extremely wealthy, while others returned empty-handed. By the 1880s, Australia was a prosperous country and cities were lined with ornate architecture, some of which was constructed by the last waves of convict labour. Despite gold found in Western Australia in the 1890s, however, the final decade of the 19th century was a period of depression, when wool prices fell, Victoria's land boom collapsed and the nation suffered a severe drought.

Edward Hargraves
In 1851 Hargraves made his name by discovering gold in Bathurst, New South Wales.

Panning dish

Lamp

Pick axe

Gold Mining Utensils
Mining for gold was initially an unskilled and laborious process that required only a few basic utensils. A panning dish to swill water, a pick axe to loosen rock and a miner's lamp were all that were needed to commence the search.

Digging for Gold
Edwin Stocqueler's painting Australian Gold Diggings *(1855) shows the varying methods of gold mining and the hard work put in by thousands of diggers in their quest for wealth. As men and their families came from all over the world to make their fortune, regions rich in gold, in particular Victoria, thrived. Previous wastelands were turned into tent settlements and gradually grew into impressive new cities.*

Eureka Stockade
In 1854 an insurrection took place just outside the town of Ballarat when miners rebelled against costly licences and burned them at a stockade (see p438).

Might versus Right *(c.1861)*
ST Gill's painting depicts the riots on the Lambing Flag gold fields in New South Wales in 1861. Chinese immigrants, who came to Australia in search of gold, were met with violent racism by European settlers who felt their wealth and position were in jeopardy.

Gold panning was the most popular extraction method.

Tent villages covered the Victoria landscape in the 1850s.

Prosperity in Bendigo
The buildings of Williamson Street in Bendigo *(see p436)* display the prosperity that resulted from gold finds in Victoria.

Chinese Miners' Medal
Racism against the Chinese eventually subsided. This medal was given by the Chinese to the district of Braidwood, Victoria, in 1881.

Miners wore hats and heavyweight trousers to protect them from the sun.

The sluice was a trough which trapped gold in its bars as water was flushed through.

Gold Prospecting Camel Team
Just as the gold finds dried up in Victoria, gold was discovered in Western Australia in the 1890s. Prospectors crossed the continent to continue their search.

Souvenir handkerchief of the Australian Federation

Federal Beginnings

Australia entered the 20th century on an optimistic note: the federation of its six colonies formed the Australian nation on 1 January 1901. Within the federation, there was one matter on which almost everyone agreed: Australia would remain "European" with strong ties to Britain. One of the first acts of the new parliament was to legislate the White Australia Policy. The Immigration Restriction Act required anyone wishing to emigrate to Australia to pass a dictation test in a European language. Unwanted

Labor government publicity poster

immigrants were tested in obscure languages such as Gaelic. Between 1901 and 1910 there were nine different governments led by five different prime ministers. None of the three major political groups, the Protectionists, the Free Traders and the Labor Party, had sufficient support to govern in its own right. By 1910, however, voters were offered a clear choice between two parties, Labor and Liberal. The Labor Party won a landslide victory and since then the Australian government has come solely from one of these two parties.

World War I

Enlisting poster

When Britain entered World War I in 1914, Australia followed to defend the "mother land". Most Australians supported the war, but they would not accept conscription or compulsory national service.

Australia paid a very high price for its allegiance, with 64 per cent of the 331,781 troops killed or wounded. Memorials to those who fought and died are found throughout the country, ranging from the simple to the impressive such as the Australian War Memorial in Canberra *(see pp204–5)*. World War I was a defining moment in Australia's history. Anzac Day, rather than Australia Day, is felt by many to be the true national day. It commemorates the landing of the Australian and New Zealand Army Corps at Gallipoli in Turkey on 25 April 1915, for their unsuccessful attempt to cross the

1901 The Commonwealth of Australia comes into being. The White Australia Policy becomes law with the passage of the Immigration Restriction Bill

Australia's national flag

1919 Postwar immigration includes the Big Brother movement, which welcomes adolescents

1921 Edith Cowan becomes the first woman MP in the country

1900	1905	1910	1915	1920

1902 Women's suffrage is granted in Australia

1912 Walter Burley Griffin is chosen to design Canberra *(see p195)*

1914–18 Australia takes part in World War I

QANTAS *Qantas logo*

1920 Qantas is formed as a local airline

Dardanelles and link up with the Russians. This was the first battle in which Australian soldiers fought as a national force and, although a failure, they gained a reputation for bravery and endurance. It is an event which many believe determined the Australian character and saw the real birth of the Australian nation.

Between the Wars

During the 1920s, Australia, boosted by the arrival of some 300,000 immigrants, entered a period of major development. In 1920 Qantas (Queensland and Northern Territory Aerial Service Ltd) was formed, which was to become the national airline, and made its first international flight in 1934. Building of the Sydney Harbour Bridge began in 1923 (see pp84–5). Australia's population reached 6 million in 1925, but this new optimism was not to last.

In 1929 Australia, along with much of the world, went into economic decline. Wool and wheat prices, the country's major export earners, fell dramatically. By 1931,

Celebrating the opening of Sydney Harbour Bridge

a third of the country was unemployed. People slept in tents in city parks; swagmen (workers with their possessions on their backs) appeared as men left cities in search of work in the country.

Prices began to increase again by 1933 and manufacturing revived. From 1934 to 1937 the economy improved and unemployment fell. The following year, however, Australia again faced the prospect of war.

World War II

Though World War II was initially a European war, Australians again fought in defence of freedom and the "mother land". However, when Japan entered the war, Australians felt for the first time that their national security was at risk. In 1942 Darwin, Broome and Townsville were bombed by the Japanese, the first act of war on Australian soil. The same year two Japanese midget submarines entered Sydney Harbour.

Britain asked for more Australian troops but for the first time they were refused: the men were needed in the Pacific. This was a

Swagmen during the Great Depression

1923 Vegemite first produced

Jar of Vegemite

1932 Sydney Harbour Bridge opens

1933 Western Australia produces a referendum in favour of secession from Britain, but parliament rejects it

1939–45 Australia takes part in World War II

1941 Australian War Memorial opens in Canberra

| 1925 | 1930 | 1935 | 1940 | 1945 |

1927 First federal parliament held in Canberra in temporary Parliament House

1929 The Great Depression hits Australia, bringing great hardship

1928 Royal Flying Doctor service starts

First Australian car

1948 Holden is the first car produced that is entirely made in Australia

major shift in Australian foreign policy away from Britain and towards the USA. Australians fought alongside the Americans in the Pacific and nearly 250,000 US troops spent time in Australia during the war. This led, in 1951, to the signing of Australia's first defence treaty with a foreign country: the ANZUS treaty between Australia, New Zealand and the United States.

Again, war affected most Australian communities and towns. Nearly one million of Australia's seven million population went to fight: 34,000 were killed and 180,000 wounded.

Poster promoting travel and tourism in 1950s Australia

Postwar Immigration

The proximity of the fighting in World War II left Australia feeling vulnerable. The future defence of the country was seen to be dependent upon a strong economy and a larger population.

The postwar immigration programme welcomed not only British immigrants but also Europeans. Almost two million immigrants arrived in Australia in the 20 years following World War II, 800,000 of whom were not British. In 1956, the status of "permanent resident" allowed non-Europeans to claim citizenship. In 1958, the dictation entry test was abolished. Yet until 1966 non-Europeans had to have 15 years' residence before gaining citizenship, as opposed to five years for Europeans.

The Menzies Era

From 1949 until 1966, Prime Minister Robert Menzies "reigned", winning eight con-secutive elections. The increasing population

British migrants arriving in Sydney in 1967 as part of the postwar wave of immigration

Mabo and Beyond

In 1982, Edward Koiki (Eddie) Mabo, a Torres Strait Islander, took action against the Queensland government claiming that his people had ancestral land rights. After a ten-year battle, the High Court ruled that Aborigines and Torres Strait Islanders may hold native title to land where there has been no loss of traditional connection. This ended the concept of *terra nullius* – that Australia belonged to no one when Europeans arrived there – and acknowledged that Aborigines held valid title to their land. Subsequent legislation has provided a framework for assessing such claims.

Edward Koiki Mabo

1955 Australian troops sent to Malaya

Neville Bonner

1971 Neville Bonner becomes Australia's first Aboriginal MP

1976 "Advance Australia Fair" becomes national anthem

1979 Severe droughts in the country last three years

1981 Preference given to immigrants with family members already in Australia. Increase in Asian immigration

1958 Immigration dictation test abolished

| 1955 | 1960 | 1965 | 1970 | 1975 | 1980 | 19 |

1965 Australian troops sent to Vietnam as part of their National Service

1967 Referendum on Aborigines ends legal discrimination

1973 Sydney Opera House opens (see pp88–9)

1983 Bob Hawke elected as prime minister

1986 Proclamation of Australia Act breaks legal ties with Britain

1956 Melbourne hosts the Olympic Games

1966–72 Demonstrations against the Vietnam War

Sydney Opera House

1983 America's Cup victory

Anti-Vietnam demonstrations as US President Johnson arrives in Australia

and international demand for Australian raw materials during this time provided a high standard of living. Menzies understood his people's desire for peace and prosperity, and gave Australians conservatism and stability. He did, however, also involve them in three more wars, in Korea (1950), Malaya (1955) and Vietnam (1965). Vietnam was the first time Australia fought in a war in which Britain was not also engaged.

Social Unrest and Change

Opposition to conscription and the Vietnam War increased in the late 1960s and led to major demonstrations. At the same time there was concern for issues such as Aboriginal land rights and free education. In 1967, a constitutional referendum was passed by 90.8 per cent of the voters, ending the ban on Aboriginal inclusion in the national census. It also gave power to the federal government to legislate for

Prime Minister Whitlam hands over Aboriginal land rights in 1975

Aborigines in all states, ending state discriminations.

In 1972, the Labor Party, under Edward Gough Whitlam, was elected on a platform of social reform. It abolished conscription, introduced free university education, lowered the voting age from 21 to 18 and gave some land rights to Aborigines. In 1974, an immigration policy without any racial discrimination was adopted.

The Changing Economy

In 1975, the Liberal leader Malcolm Fraser won the election. Subsequent governments, both Liberal under Fraser (1975–83) and Labor under Bob Hawke and Paul Keating (1983–96), were concerned with economic rather than social agendas. The boom of the 1980s was followed by recession in the 1990s. During this period Australia shifted its focus from Europe towards Asia. The election of Kevin Rudd as prime minister in 2007 marked a return to government for the Labor party after 11 years under Liberal leader John Howard. The new government's first act was a formal apology to indigenous Australians for the pain of past mistreatment. Rudd was toppled as Labor leader in 2010 by Julia Gillard, the country's first female prime minister. In 2013 the Liberals returned to power under Tony Abbott. However, he was toppled as Liberal leader by Malcolm Turnbull in 2015.

| 1988 Bicentenary new federal Parliament House opened in Canberra | 1991 Paul Keating elected as prime minister | 1992–3 High Court rules that Aborigines held valid claims to land | 1996 John Howard is elected as prime minister | 2000 Sydney hosts Olympic Games | 2006 Commonwealth Games held in Melbourne | 2007 Kevin Rudd elected prime minister | 2009 More than 170 killed and 1,800 homes destroyed in Victoria bushfires | 2010 Julia Gillard elected Australia's first female prime minister | 2010–11 Extensive flooding in Queensland, with 75 per cent of the state declared a disaster zone | 2011 Cadel Evans is the first Australian to win the Tour de France | 2012 Fourth coronial inquest into disappearance of Azaria Chamberlain rules a dingo took the baby from an Uluru camp site in 1980 | 2018 Gold Coast to host Commonwealth Games |

1990   1995   2000   2005   2010   2015   2020

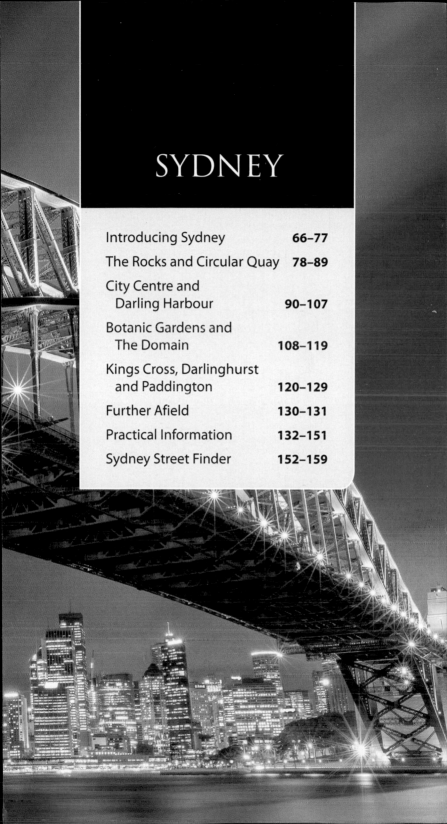

SYDNEY

Central Sydney

This guide divides the centre of Sydney into four distinct areas, and the majority of the city's main sights are contained in these districts. The Rocks and Circular Quay are the oldest part of inner Sydney. The City Centre is the central business district, and to its west lies Darling Harbour, which includes Sydney's well-known Chinatown. The Botanic Gardens and The Domain form a green oasis almost in the heart of the city. To the east are Kings Cross and Darlinghurst, the hub of café culture, and Paddington, an area that still retains its charming 19th-century character.

The Lord Nelson Brewery Hotel is a traditional pub in The Rocks (see p482), which first opened its doors in 1834. Its own specially brewed beers are available on tap.

Queen Victoria Building is a Romanesque former produce market, built in the 1890s. It forms part of a fine group of Victorian buildings in the City Centre (see p94). Now a shopping mall, it retains many of its original features, including its ornate roof statues.

◀ The Sydney Harbour Bridge, the central business district and the Opera House

Key

■ Major sight

□ Other buildings

0 metres 250
0 yards 250

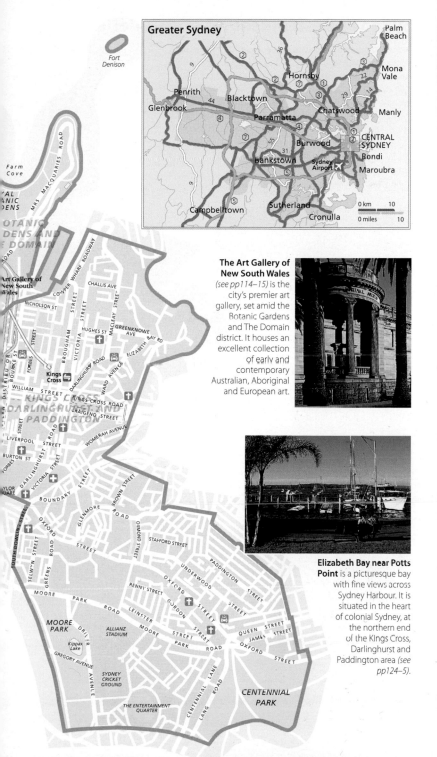

Greater Sydney

Fort
Denison

Palm
Beach

Mona
Vale

Hornsby

Penrith

Blacktown

Glenbrook

Parramatta

Chatswood

Manly

Burwood

CENTRAL
SYDNEY

bankstown

Sydney
Airport

Bondi

Maroubra

Campbelltown

Sutherland

Cronulla

0 km   10

0 miles   10

Farm
Cove

AL
NIC
ENS

OTANIC
DENS AND
E DOMAIN

Art Gallery of
New South
Wales

KINGS CROSS,
DARLINGHURST AND
PADDINGTON

Kings
Cross

MOORE
PARK

Kippax
Lake

ALLIANZ
STADIUM

SYDNEY
CRICKET
GROUND

THE ENTERTAINMENT
QUARTER

CENTENNIAL
PARK

**The Art Gallery of
New South Wales**
(see pp114–15) is the
city's premier art
gallery, set amid the
Botanic Gardens
and The Domain
district. It houses an
excellent collection
of early and
contemporary
Australian, Aboriginal
and European art.

**Elizabeth Bay near Potts
Point** is a picturesque bay
with fine views across
Sydney Harbour. It is
situated in the heart
of colonial Sydney, at
the northern end
of the Kings Cross,
Darlinghurst and
Paddington area *(see
pp124–5)*.

For additional map symbols *see back flap*

Sydney's Best: Museums and Galleries

Sydney is well endowed with museums and galleries, and, following the current appreciation of social history, much emphasis is placed on the lifestyles of past and present Sydneysiders. Small museums are also a feature of the Sydney scene, with a number of historic houses recalling the colonial days. Most of the major collections are housed in architecturally significant buildings – the Classical façade of the Art Gallery of NSW makes it a city landmark, while the MCA or Museum of Contemporary Art has given new life to a 1950s Art Deco-style building at Circular Quay.

The Museum of Sydney includes *The Edge of the Trees*, an interactive installation *(see p96)*.

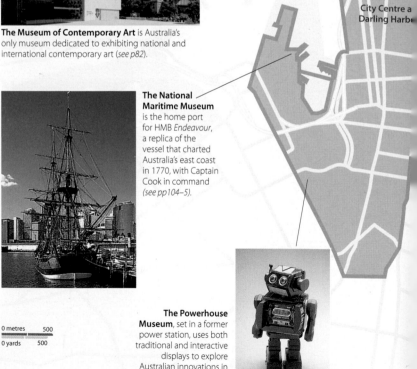

The Museum of Contemporary Art is Australia's only museum dedicated to exhibiting national and international contemporary art *(see p82)*.

The Rocks and Circular Quay

City Centre a Darling Harbo

The National Maritime Museum is the home port for HMB *Endeavour*, a replica of the vessel that charted Australia's east coast in 1770, with Captain Cook in command *(see pp104–5)*.

| 0 metres | 500 |
| 0 yards | 500 |

The Powerhouse Museum, set in a former power station, uses both traditional and interactive displays to explore Australian innovations in science and technology *(see pp106–7)*.

The Art Gallery of New South Wales includes colonial watercolours in its Australian collection, which, to avoid deterioration, are only shown for a few weeks each year. Charles Meere's *Australian Beach Pattern* (1940) is one of them *(see pp114–17)*.

Elizabeth Bay House is elegantly furnished to reflect the 1840s period, when the Colonial Secretary Alexander Macleay lived in the house that ultimately caused his bankruptcy *(see p124)*.

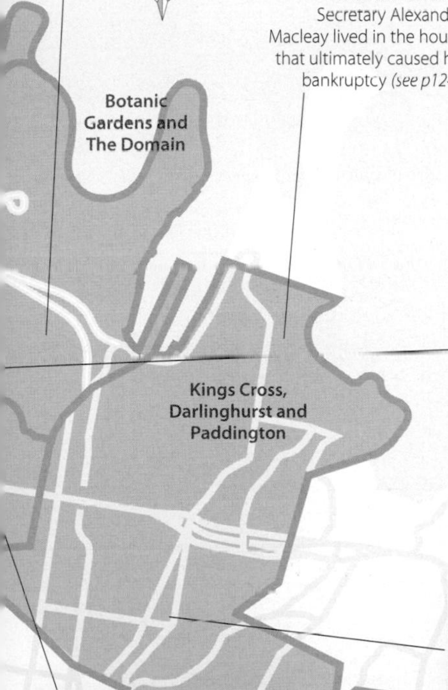

Botanic
Gardens and
The Domain

Kings Cross,
Darlinghurst and
Paddington

The Hyde Park Barracks were originally built by convicts for their own incarceration. They were later home to poor female immigrants. Exhibits recall the daily life of these occupants *(see p118)*.

The Sydney Jewish Museum documents the history of the city's Jewish community. Exhibits include reconstructed scenes, such as George Street in 1848, a Jewish business area *(see p125)*.

The Australian Museum is where visitors can discover the Earth's age, find out about meteorites, volcanic activity, mining and more with its stunning display of rocks and minerals *(see pp98–9)*.

Sydney's Best: Architecture

For such a young city, Sydney possesses a great diversity of architectural styles. They range from the simplicity of Francis Greenway's Georgian buildings *(see p177)* to Jørn Utzon's Expressionist Sydney Opera House *(see pp88–9)*. Practical colonial structures gave way to elaborate Victorian edifices such as Sydney Town Hall. The same passion for detail is seen in Paddington's terraces. Later, Federation warehouses and bungalows introduced a uniquely Australian style.

Colonial convict structures were simple with shingled roofs, based on the English homes of the first settlers. Cadman's Cottage is an example of this style *(see p82)*.

Contemporary architecture abounds in Sydney, including Governor Phillip Tower. The Museum of Sydney is at its base *(see p96)*.

The Rocks and Circular Quay

Colonial Georgian buildings include St James' Church *(see p119)*. Francis Greenway's design was adapted to suit the purposes of a church.

American Revivalism took up the 1890s vogue of arcades connecting many different streets. The Queen Victoria Building is a fine example *(see p94)*.

City Centre and Darling Harbour

Contemporary Expressionism's main emphasis is roof design and the silhouette. Innovations were made in sports stadiums and museums, such as the Australian National Maritime Museum *(see p104–5)*.

Victorian architecture abounds in the city. Sydney Town Hall includes a metal ceiling, installed for fear that the organ would vibrate a plaster one loose *(see p97)*.

| 0 metres | 500 |
| 0 yards | 500 |

Interwar Architecture encapsulates the spirit of Art Deco, as seen in the Anzac Memorial in Hyde Park *(see p97)*.

Modern Expressionism includes one of the world's greatest examples of 20th-century architecture. The construction of Jørn Utzon's Sydney Opera House began in 1959. Despite the architect's resignation in 1966, it was opened in 1973 (see pp88–9).

Early Colonial's first buildings, such as Hyde Park Barracks (see p118), were mainly built for the government.

Australian Regency was popular during the 1830s. The best-designed villas were the work of John Verge. The beautiful Elizabeth Bay House is considered his masterpiece (see p124).

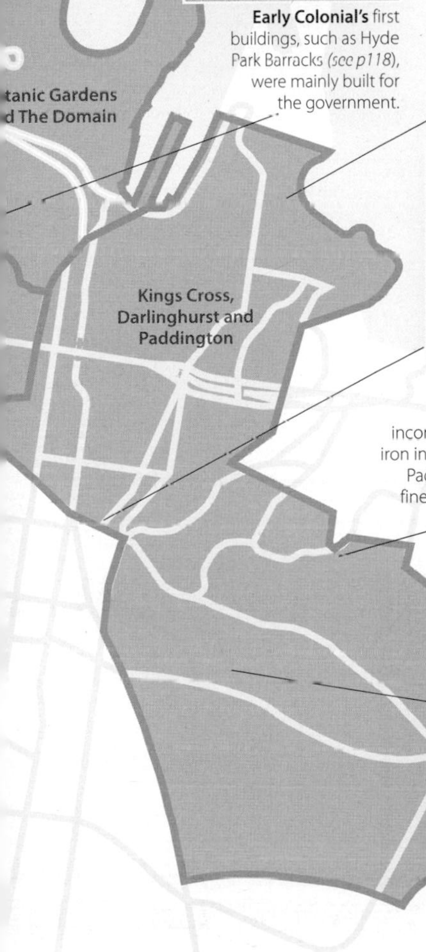

tanic Gardens
d The Domain

Kings Cross,
Darlinghurst and
Paddington

Colonial Grecian and Greek Revival were the most popular styles for public buildings designed during the 1820–50 period. The Darlinghurst Court House is a particularly fine example (see p125).

Victorian iron lace incorporated filigree of cast-iron in prefabricated patterns. Paddington's verandas are fine examples of this 1880s style (see pp126–7).

Colonial military buildings were both functional and ornate. Victoria Barracks, designed by engineers, is a fine example of a Georgian military compound (see p128).

Sydney's Best: Parks and Reserves

Sydney is almost completely surrounded by national parks and intact bushland. There are also a number of national parks and reserves within Greater Sydney itself. Here, the visitor can gain some idea of how the landscape looked before the arrival of European settlers. The city parks, too, are filled with plant and animal life. The more formal plantings of both native and exotic species are countered by the indigenous birds and animals that have adapted and made the urban environment their home. One of the highlights of a trip to Sydney is the huge variety of birds to be seen, from large birds of prey such as sea eagles and kites, to the shyer species such as wrens and tiny finches.

Garigal National Park is made up of rainforest and moist gullies, which provide shelter for superb lyrebirds and sugar gliders.

Lane Cove National Park is an open eucalypt forest dotted with grass trees, as well as fine stands of blue gums and apple gums. The rosella, a type of parrot, is common in the area.

North Arm Walk is covered in spring with grevilleas and flannel flowers blooming profusely.

Bicentennial Park is situated at Homebush Bay. The park features a mangrove habitat and attracts many water birds, including pelicans.

Hyde Park is situated on the edge of the city centre *(see p97)*. The park provides a peaceful respite from the hectic streets. The native iris is just one of the plants found in the lush gardens. The sacred ibis, a water bird, is often seen.

Middle Head and Obelisk Bay are dotted with gun emplacements, tunnels and bunkers built in the 1870s to protect Sydney from invasion. The superb fairy wren lives here, and water dragons can at times be seen basking on rocks.

North Head is covered with coastal heathland, with banksias, tea trees and casuarinas dominating the cliff tops. On the leeward side, moist forest surrounds tiny, secluded harbour beaches.

Grotto Point's paths, winding through the bush to the lighthouse, are lined with bottlebrushes, grevilleas and flannel flowers.

Bradleys Head is a nesting place for the ringtail possum. Noisy flocks of rainbow lorikeets are also often in residence. The views across the harbour to Sydney are spectacular.

South Head contains unique plant species such as the sundew.

Nielsen Park is inhabited by the kookaburra, easily identified by its call, which sounds like laughter.

The Domain features palms and Moreton Bay figs. The Australian magpie, with its black and white plumage, is a frequent visitor (see p113).

Moore Park is filled with huge Moreton Bay figs which provide an urban habitat for the flying fox.

Centennial Park contains open expanses and groves of paperbark and eucalypt trees, bringing sulphur-crested cockatoos en masse. The brushtail possum is a shy creature that comes out at night (see p129).

```
0 kilometres        4
0 miles        2
```

Garden Island to Farm Cove

Sydney's vast harbour, also named Port Jackson after a Secretary in the British Admiralty who promptly changed his name, is a drowned river valley which was transformed over millions of years. Its intricate coastal geography of headlands and secluded bays can sometimes confound even lifelong residents. This waterway was the lifeblood of the early colony, with the maritime industry a vital source of wealth and supply. The legacies of recessions and booms can be viewed along the shoreline: a representation of a nation where an estimated 80 per cent of the population cling to the coastal cities, especially in the east.

The city skyline is a result of random development. The 1960s' destruction of architectural history was halted, and towers now stand amid Victorian buildings.

Two harbour beacons, known as "wedding cakes" because of their three tiers, are solar powered and equipped with a fail-safe back-up service. There are around 350 buoys and beacons now in operation.

The barracks for the naval garrison date from 1888.

Garden Island marks a 1940s construction project with 12 ha (30 acres) reclaimed from the harbour.

Sailing on the harbour is a pastime not exclusively reserved for the rich elite. Of the several hundred thousand pleasure boats registered, some are available for hire while others take out groups of inexperienced sailors.

Mrs Macquaries Chair is a carved rock seat by Mrs Macquaries Road *(see p112)*. In the early days of the colony this was the site of a fruit and vegetable garden which was farmed until 1805.

| 0 metres | 250 |
| 0 yards | 250 |

The Andrew (Boy) Charlton Pool is a favourite bathing spot for inner-city residents, and is named after the 16-year old who won an Olympic gold medal in 1924. It was erected in 1963 on the Domain Baths' site, which had a grandstand for 1,700.

Woolloomooloo Finger Wharf was a disembarkation point when most travellers arrived by sea.

Locator Map
See Street Finder, map 2

Harry's Café de Wheels, a snack van, has been a Sydney culinary institution for more than 50 years. Photographs of celebrity customers are pinned to the van, attesting to its fame.

The Royal Botanic Gardens display both flowering and non-flowering plants. Here the first trees were planted by the new European colonists; some of these trees survive today *(see pp110–11).*

Farm Cove has long been a mooring place for visiting naval vessels. The land opposite, now the Botanic Gardens, has been continuously cultivated for over 200 years.

Sydney Cove to Walsh Bay

It is estimated that over 70 km (43 miles) of harbour foreshore have been lost as a result of the massive land reclamation projects carried out since the 1840s. That the 13 islands existing when the First Fleet arrived in 1788 have now been reduced to just eight is a startling indication of rapid and profound geographical transformation. Redevelopments around the Circular Quay and Walsh Bay area from the 1980s have opened up the waterfront for public use and enjoyment, acknowledging it as the city's greatest natural asset. Sydney's environmental and architectural aspirations recognize the need to integrate city and harbour.

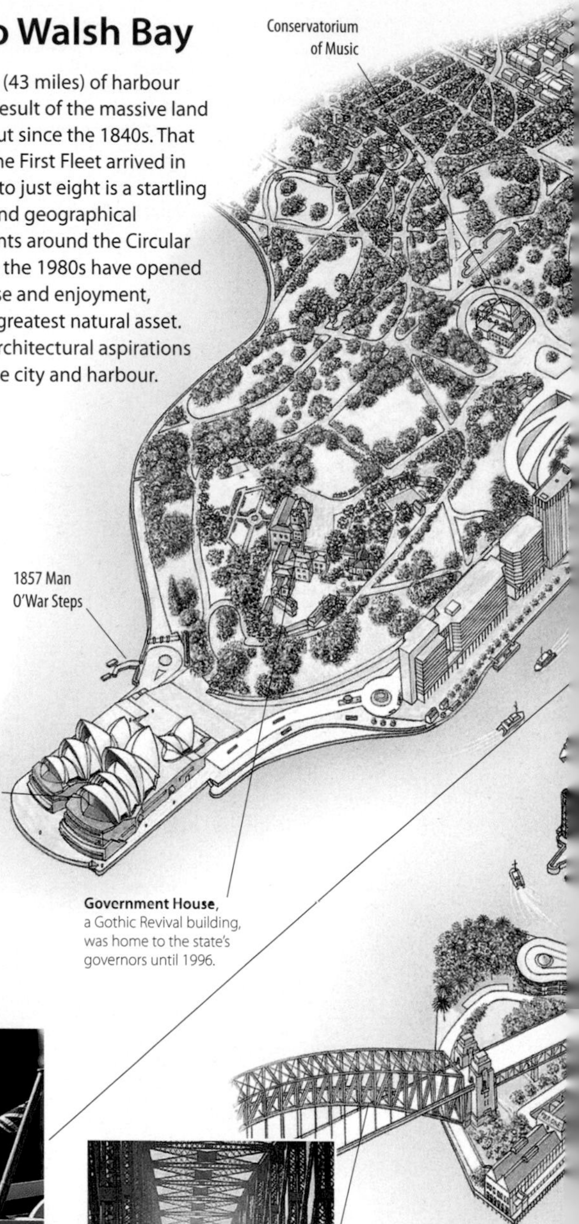

Conservatorium of Music

1857 Man O'War Steps

The Sydney Opera House was designed to take advantage of its spectacular setting. The roofs shine during the day and seem to glow at night. The building appears as a visionary landscape to the onlooker *(see pp88–9)*.

Government House, a Gothic Revival building, was home to the state's governors until 1996.

Harbour cruises regularly depart from Circular Quay, taking visitors out and about both during the day and in the evening. They are an incomparable way to see the city and its waterways.

| 0 metres | 250 |
| 0 yards | 250 |

The Sydney Harbour Bridge was also known as the "Iron Lung" at the time of its construction. During the Great Depression it provided on-site work for approximately 1,400, while others worked in specialist workshops *(see pp84–5)*.

The Rocks, settled by convicts and troops in 1788, is one of Sydney's oldest neighbourhoods. Rich in heritage, many of its old sandstone buildings have been restored and house speciality and craft shops.

Locator Map
See Street Finder, maps 1 & 2

The Tank Stream, the colony's first water supply, now runs underground and spills into the quay.

Cahill
Expressway

Circular Quay, originally and more accurately known as Semi-Circular Quay, was the last and arguably greatest convict-built structure. Tank Stream mudflats were filled in to shape the quay, and sandstone from The Rocks formed the sea wall.

The Wharf Theatre resides on a pier that took six years to build, mostly due to the diversion of labour and materials during World War I. The theatre was opened in 1984.

The wharves were completed in 1922.

Imports and exports to and from the city were stored in these wharves until 1977.

The wharves' design included a rat-proof sea wall around the port. This was an urgent response to the 1900 bubonic plague outbreak, attributed to rats on the wharves.

THE ROCKS AND CIRCULAR QUAY

Circular Quay, once known as Semi-Circular Quay, is often referred to as the "birthplace of Australia". It was here, in January 1788, that the First Fleet landed its human freight of convicts, soldiers and officials, and the new British colony of New South Wales was declared. Sydney Cove became a rallying point whenever a ship arrived bringing much-needed supplies from "home". Crowds still gather here whenever there is a national or civic celebration. The Quay and The Rocks are focal points for New Year's Eve festivities. Circular Quay was the setting for huge crowds when, in 1993, Sydney was awarded the year 2000 Olympic Games. The Rocks area offers visitors a taste of Sydney's past, but it is a far cry from the time, little more than 100 years ago, when most inhabitants lived in rat-infested slums, and gangs ruled its streets. Now scrubbed and polished, The Rocks forms part of the colourful promenade from the Sydney Harbour Bridge to the spectacular Sydney Opera House.

Sights at a Glance

Museums and Galleries
1. Susannah Place
2. Museum of Contemporary Art
4. Sailors' Home
5. The Rocks Discovery Museum
11. National Trust Centre
15. Justice and Police Museum

Theatres and Concert Halls
17. Sydney Opera House pp88–9

Historic Streets and Buildings
3. Cadman's Cottage
6. Campbell's Storehouses
7. Sydney Harbour Bridge pp84–5
8. Hero of Waterloo
10. Sydney Observatory
13. Macquarie Place
14. Customs House
16. Writers' Walk

Churches
9. Garrison Church
12. St Philip's Church

See also Street Finder, map 1

◀ Sydney's world-famous Opera House reflected in the harbour

For keys to symbols see back flap

Street-by-Street: The Rocks

Named for the rugged cliffs that were once its dominant feature, this area has played a vital role in Sydney's development. In 1788, the First Fleeters under Governor Phillip's command erected makeshift buildings here, with the convicts' hard labour used to establish more permanent structures in the form of rough-hewn streets. The Argyle Cut, a road carved through solid rock using just hammer and chisel, took 18 years to build, beginning in 1843. By 1900, The Rocks was overrun with disease; the street now known as Suez Canal was once Sewer's Canal. Today, the area is still rich in colonial history and colour.

❽ Hero of Waterloo
Lying beneath this historic pub is a tunnel originally used for smuggling.

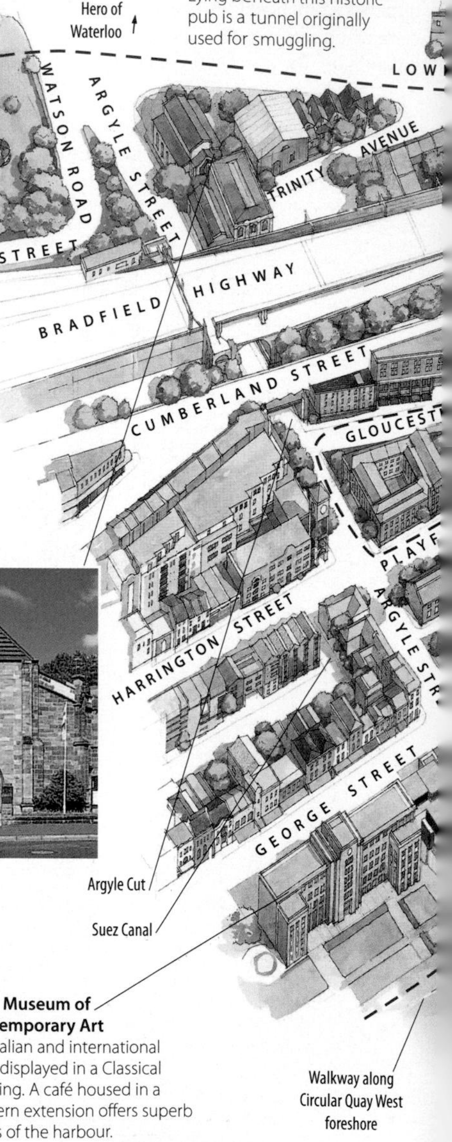

❿ ★ Sydney Observatory
The first European structure on this prominent site was a windmill. The present museum holds some of the earliest astronomical instruments brought to Australia.

❾ Garrison Church
Columns in this church are decorated with the insignia of British troops stationed here until 1870. Australia's first prime minister was educated next door.

Argyle Cut

Suez Canal

❷ ★ Museum of Contemporary Art
Australian and international art is displayed in a Classical building. A café housed in a modern extension offers superb views of the harbour.

Walkway along Circular Quay West foreshore

For hotels and restaurants in this area see pp482–3 and pp504–7

⑤ The Rocks Discovery Museum
Key episodes in The Rocks' history are illustrated by this museum's collection of maritime images and other artifacts.

Locator Map
See Central Sydney map pp66–7

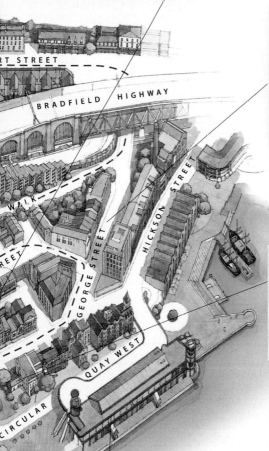

The Rocks Market is a hive of activity every weekend, offering an eclectic range of craft items and jewellery utilizing Australian icons from gum leaves to koalas *(see p137).*

❸ ★ Cadman's Cottage
John Cadman, government coxswain, resided in what was known as the Coxswain's Barracks with his family. His wife Elizabeth was also a significant figure, believed to be the first woman to vote in New South Wales, a right she insisted on.

The Overseas Passenger Terminal is where some of the world's luxury cruise liners berth during their stay in Sydney.

0 metres		100
0 yards		100

Key

— Suggested route

Old-fashioned Australian goods at the corner shop, Susannah Place

❶ Susannah Place

58–64 Gloucester St, The Rocks.
Map 1 B2. **Tel** (02) 9241 1893.
🚌 Sydney Explorer, 431, 432, 433, 434. 🚆 Circular Quay, Wynyard.
Open 2–5pm daily. **Closed** Good Fri, 25 Dec. 🔲 🖸 🖸 **sydneyliving museums.com.au**

This terrace of four brick and sandstone houses dating back to 1844 has a rare history of continuous domestic occupancy from the 1840s through to 1990. It is now a museum examining the living conditions of its former inhabitants. Rather than re-creating a single period, the museum retains the renovations carried out by different tenants.

Built for Edward and Mary Riley, who arrived from Ireland with their niece Susannah in 1838, these houses have basement kitchens and backyard outhouses. Piped water and sewerage were probably added by the mid-1850s.

The terrace escaped the wholesale demolitions that occurred after the outbreak of bubonic plague in 1900, as well as later clearings of land to make way for the Sydney Harbour Bridge (see pp84–5) and the Cahill Expressway. In the 1970s it was saved once again when the Builders Labourers' Federation imposed a "green ban" on The Rocks, temporarily halting all redevelopment work which was destructive to cultural heritage.

❷ Museum of Contemporary Art

Circular Quay West, The Rocks.
Map 1 B2. **Tel** (02) 9245 2400.
🚌 431, 432, 433, 434, Sydney Explorer. **Open** 10am–5pm daily (to 9pm Thu). **Closed** 25 Dec.
🖸 🖸 🖸 **mca.com.au**

When Sydney art collector John Power died in 1943, he left his entire collection and a financial bequest to the University of Sydney. In 1991 the collection, which by then included works by Hockney, Warhol, Lichtenstein and Christo was transferred to this 1950s Art Deco-style building at Circular Quay West. As well as showing its permanent collection, the museum hosts exhibitions by local and overseas artists. The MCA Store sells distinctive gifts by Australian designers.

❸ Cadman's Cottage

110 George St, The Rocks.
Map 1 B2. 🚌 431, 432, 433, 434.
Closed to the public.

Built in 1816 as barracks for the crews of the governor's boats, this sandstone cottage is Sydney's oldest surviving dwelling. Visitors can walk around the small, historic site, but cannot enter the building.

The cottage is named after John Cadman, a convict who was transported in 1798 for horse-stealing. By 1813, he was coxswain of a timber boat and later, coxswain of government craft. He was granted a full pardon and in 1827 he was made boat superintendent and moved to the four-room cottage that now bears his name.

Cadman married Elizabeth Mortimer in 1830, another ex-convict who was sentenced to seven years' transportation for the theft of one hairbrush. They lived in the cottage until 1845. Cadman's Cottage was built on the foreshore of Sydney Harbour. Now, as a result of successive land reclamations, it is set well back from the water's edge.

The Art Deco-style Museum of Contemporary Art, with the adjoining modern extension

❹ Sailors' Home

106 George St, The Rocks. **Map** 1 B2.
🚌 Sydney Explorer, 339, 340, 431,
432, 433, 434.

Built in 1864 as lodgings
for visiting sailors, the first
and second floors here were
dormitories, but these were
later divided into 56 cubicles
or "cabins" which were
arranged around open
galleries and lit by four
enormous skylights. At the
time it was built, the Sailors'
Home was a welcome
alternative to the many seedy
inns and brothels in the area,
saving sailors from the perils
of "crimping". "Crimps" would
tempt newly arrived men into
bars providing much sought-
after entertainment. While
drunk, the sailors would be
sold on to departing ships,
waking miles out at sea and
returning home in debt.

Sailors used the home until
1980. It is now home to the
highly-regarded Sailors' Thai
restaurant and noodle bar.

❺ The Rocks Discovery Museum

Kendall Lane, The Rocks. **Map** 1 B2.
Tel (02) 9240 8680. 🚌 Sydney
Explorer, 431, 432, 433, 434.
🚉 Circular Quay. **Open** 10am–5pm
daily. **Closed** Good Fri, 25 Dec. ♿
W therocks.com.au

This fascinating museum, in
a restored 1850s sandstone
coach house, is home to
a unique collection of
archaeological artifacts and
images that detail the story
of The Rocks from the pre-
European days to the present.
There are four permanent
exhibitions which are highly
interactive, making use of
touch screens and audio and
visual technology. Some of
the artifacts were found at
the archaeological site on
Cumberland Street.

The Rocks Discovery
Museum has been developed
in close consultation with
local Aboriginal groups, so
that their story of the area is
properly told.

Terrace restaurants at Campbell's Storehouses on the waterfront

❻ Campbell's Storehouses

7–27 Circular Quay West, The Rocks.
Map 1 B2. 🚌 Sydney Explorer, 431,
432, 433, 434. ♿

Robert Campbell, a prominent
Scottish merchant in the early
days of Sydney, purchased
this land on Sydney Cove in
1799. In 1802 he began
constructing a private wharf
and storehouses in which to
house the tea, sugar, spirits and
cloth he imported from India.
Campbell was the only
merchant operating in Australia
who managed to infiltrate the
monopoly held by the British
East India Company. The first
five sandstone bays were built
between 1839 and 1844. A
further seven bays were built
between 1854 and 1861. The
full row of storehouses were
finally completed in 1890,
including a brick upper storey.
Part of the old sea wall and 11
of the original stores are still
standing. The pulleys that were
used to raise cargo from the
wharf can be seen near the top
of the preserved buildings.

The area fell into disrepair
during the first half of the
20th century. However, in
the 1970s the Sydney Cove
Redevelopment Authority
finalized plans and began
renovating the site. Today the
bond stores contain a range of
fine restaurants catering to all
tastes, from contemporary
Australian to Chinese and
Italian. Their virtually
unimpeded views across
Circular Quay towards the
Sydney Opera House (see
pp88–9) and Sydney Harbour
Bridge (see pp84–5) make these
outdoor eating establishments
very popular with local business
people and tourists alike.

❼ Sydney Harbour Bridge

See pp84–5.

The historic Hero of Waterloo Inn, built in
the 19th century

❽ Hero of Waterloo

81 Lower Fort St, The Rocks. **Map** 1 A2.
Tel (02) 9252 4553. 🚌 431, 432, 433,
434. **Open** 10am–11:30pm Mon–Wed,
10am–midnight Thu–Sat, 10am–10pm
Sun. **Closed** Good Fri, 25 Dec.
♿ limited.

This picturesque old inn is
especially welcoming in the
winter with its log fires.

Built in 1844, this was a
favourite drinking place for the
nearby garrison's soldiers. Some
sea captains were said to use
the hotel to recruit. Patrons who
drank too much were pushed
into the cellars via a trapdoor.
Tunnels then led to the wharves
and on to waiting ships.

❼ Sydney Harbour Bridge

Completed in 1932, the construction of the Sydney Harbour Bridge was an economic feat, given the depressed times, as well as an engineering triumph. Prior to this, the only links between the city centre on the south side of the harbour and the residential north side were by ferry or a circuitous 20-km (12-mile) road route which involved five bridge crossings. The single-span arch bridge, colloquially known as the "Coathanger", took eight years to build, including the railway line. The bridge was manufactured in sections on the latter-day Luna Park site. Loans for the total cost of approximately 6.25 million old Australian pounds were eventually paid off in 1988.

The 1932 Opening
The ceremony was disrupted when zealous royalist Francis de Groot rode forward and cut the ribbon, in honour, he claimed, of King and Empire.

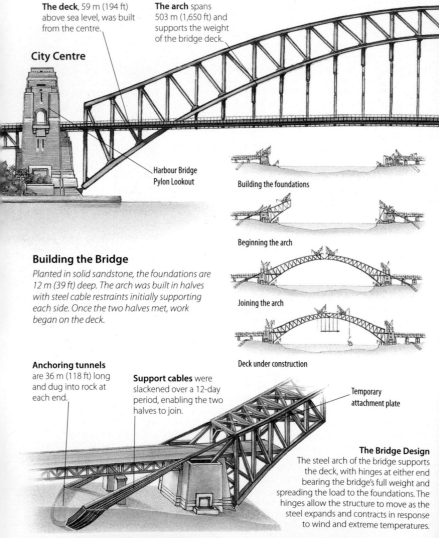

The deck, 59 m (194 ft) above sea level, was built from the centre.

The arch spans 503 m (1,650 ft) and supports the weight of the bridge deck.

City Centre

Harbour Bridge Pylon Lookout

Building the foundations

Beginning the arch

Building the Bridge

Planted in solid sandstone, the foundations are 12 m (39 ft) deep. The arch was built in halves with steel cable restraints initially supporting each side. Once the two halves met, work began on the deck.

Joining the arch

Deck under construction

Anchoring tunnels are 36 m (118 ft) long and dug into rock at each end.

Support cables were slackened over a 12-day period, enabling the two halves to join.

Temporary attachment plate

The Bridge Design
The steel arch of the bridge supports the deck, with hinges at either end bearing the bridge's full weight and spreading the load to the foundations. The hinges allow the structure to move as the steel expands and contracts in response to wind and extreme temperatures.

For hotels and restaurants in this area see pp482–3 and pp504–7

Bridge Climb
Thousands of people have enjoyed the spectacular bridge-top views after a 3.5-hour guided tour up ladders, catwalks and finally the upper arch of the bridge. A 2.5-hour "Express Climb" is also available.

VISITORS' CHECKLIST

Practical Information
3 Cumberland Street. **Map** 1 B1.
Bridge Climb: **Tel** (02) 82 74 7777.
Open Varies by season; call ahead.
Pylon Lookout: **Tel** (02) 9240 1100.
Open 10am–5pm daily.
Closed 25, 30, 31 Dec. 🅿 📷
Ⓦ bridgeclimb.com

Transport
🚌 All routes to The Rocks. 🚌
Circular Quay. 🚢 Circular Quay.

Over 150,000 vehicles
cross the bridge each day, about 15 times as many as in 1932.

Bridge Workers
The bridge was built by 1,400 workers, 16 of whom were killed in accidents during construction.

North Shore

Maintenance
Painting the bridge has become a metaphor for an endless task. Approximately 30,000 litres (6,593 gal) of paint are required for each coat, enough to cover an area equivalent to 60 soccer pitches.

The vertical hangers
support the slanting crossbeams which, in turn, carry the deck.

Father of the Bridge
Chief engineer Dr John Bradfield shakes the hand of the driver of the first train to cross the bridge. Over a 20-year period, Bradfield supervised all aspects of the bridge's design and construction. At the opening ceremony, the highway linking the harbour's south side and northern suburbs was named in his honour.

Paying the Toll
The initial toll of sixpence helped pay off the construction loan. The toll is now used for maintenance and to pay for the 1992 Sydney Harbour Tunnel.

A Flagpole on the Mudflats

The modest flagpole on Loftus Street, near Customs House, flies a flag, the Union Jack, on the spot where Australia's first ceremonial flag-raising took place. On 26 January 1788, Captain Arthur Phillip hoisted the flag to declare the foundation of the colony. A toast to the king was drunk and a musket volley fired. On this date each year, the country marks Australia Day with a national holiday *(see p45)*. In 1788, the flagpole was on the edge of mudflats on Sydney Cove. Today, due to land reclamations, it is set back from the water's edge.

The Founding of Australia by Algernon Talmage

9 Garrison Church

Cnr Argyle & Lower Fort sts, Millers Point. **Map** 1 A2. **Tel** (02) 9247 1071. 431, 433. **Open** 9am–6pm daily. **thegarrisonchurch.org.au**

Officially named the Holy Trinity Church, this was dubbed the Garrison Church because it was the colony's first military church.

Henry Ginn designed the church and, in 1840, the foundation stone was laid. In 1855, it was enlarged to hold up to 600 people. Regimental plaques hanging along interior walls recall the church's military associations. A museum contains Australian military and historical items.

Other features to look out for are the brilliantly coloured east window and the carved red cedar pulpit.

East window, Garrison Church

10 Sydney Observatory

Observatory Hill, Watson Rd, The Rocks. **Map** 1 A2. **Tel** (02) 9921 3485. Sydney Explorer, 343, 431, stop 22. **Open** 10am–5pm daily. Night viewings call to book. **Closed** 25 Dec. **sydneyobservatory.com.au**

In 1982 this domed building, which had been a centre for astronomical observation and research for almost 125 years, became the city's astronomy museum. It has interactive displays and games, along with night sky viewings; it is essential to book for these.

The building began life in the 1850s as a time-ball tower. At 1pm daily, the ball on top of the tower dropped to signal the correct time. At the same time, a cannon was fired at Fort Denison. This custom continues today *(see p112)*.

During the 1880s Sydney Observatory became known around the world when some of the first astronomical photographs of the southern sky were taken here. From 1890 to 1962 the observatory mapped some 750,000 stars as part of an international project that resulted in an atlas of the entire night sky.

11 National Trust Centre

Observatory Hill, Watson Rd, The Rocks. **Map** 1 A3. **Tel** (02) 9258 0123. Sydney Explorer, 343, 431, 432, 433, 434. **Open** 9am–5pm Tue–Fri. Gallery: **Open** 11am–5pm Tue–Sun. **Closed** pub hols. **nationaltrust.org.au**

The buildings that form the headquarters of the National Trust of Australia, date from 1815, when Governor Macquarie chose the site for a military hospital. Today they house a café, a National Trust shop and the S H Ervin Gallery, with changing exhibitions throughout the year, designed to explore the richness and diversity in Australian art.

12 St Philip's Church

3 York St (enter from Jamison St). **Map** 1 A3. **Tel** (02) 9247 1071. George St routes. **Open** 9am–5pm Mon–Fri. **Closed** 26 Jan. Phone first. 1pm Wed, 8am, 10am, 6:15pm Sun, 4pm 1st & 3rd Sun of month. **yorkstreetanglican.com**

The square tower of this Victorian Gothic church dwarfed by modern edifices was a local landmark when it was first built.

The original 1793 church burned down and was replaced in 1810. Construction of the current building, designed by Edmund Blacket, began in 1848. Work was disrupted in 1851, when the stonemasons left for the gold fields, but by 1856 the church was finally completed.

A peal of bells was donated in 1888 to mark Sydney's centenary, and they still announce the services each Sunday.

Interior and pipe organ of St Philip's Church

⑬ Macquarie Place

Map 1 B3. 🚍 Circular Quay routes.

Governor Macquarie created this park in 1810 on what was once the vegetable garden of the first Government House. The sandstone obelisk, designed by Francis Greenway *(see p177)*, was erected in 1818 to mark the starting point for all roads in the colony. The gas lamps recall the fact that this was also the site of the city's first street lamp in 1826.

Also in this area are the remains of the bow anchor and cannon from HMS *Sirius*, flagship of the First Fleet. The statue of Thomas Mort, a successful 19th-century industrialist, is today a marshalling place for the city's somewhat kamikaze bicycle couriers.

⑭ Customs House

31 Alfred St, Circular Quay.
Map 1 B3. **Tel** (02) 9242 8551.
🚍 Circular Quay routes. **Open** 8am–midnight Mon–Fri, 10am–midnight Sat, 11am–5pm Sun. 🚻 🖥 🚭
W sydneycustomshouse.com.au

Colonial architect James Barnet designed this 1885 sandstone Classical Revival building on the same site as a previous Customs House. Its recalls the bygone days when trading ships berthed at Circular Quay. The building stands near the mouth of Tank Stream, the fledgling colony's freshwater supply. Among its many fine features are tall veranda columns made out of polished granite, a finely sculpted coat of arms and an elaborate clock face, added in 1897, which features a pair of tridents and dolphins.

A complete refurbishment was completed in 2005. Facilities include a City Library with a reading room and exhibition space, and an open lounge area with an international newspaper and magazine salon, Internet access and bar. On the roof, Café Sydney offers great views.

Montage of criminal "mug shots", Justice and Police Museum

⑮ Justice and Police Museum

Cnr Albert & Phillip sts. **Map** 1 C3.
Tel (02) 9252 1144. 🚍 Circular Quay routes. **Open** 10am–5pm Sat & Sun (open daily in Jan). **Closed** Good Fri, 25 Dec. 🎫 🚫 🚻 limited.
W sydneylivingmuseums.com.au

The buildings housing this museum originally comprised the Water Police Court, designed by Edmund Blacket in 1856, the Water Police Station, designed by Alexander Dawson in 1858, and the Police Court, designed by James Barnet in 1885.

Here the rough-and-tumble underworld of quayside crime, from the petty to the violent, was dealt swift and, at times, harsh justice. The museum exhibits illustrate that turbulent period, as they re-create legal and criminal history.

Detail from Customs House

Formalities of the late-Victorian legal proceedings can be easily imagined in the fully restored courtroom. Menacing implements from knuckledusters to bludgeons are displayed as the macabre relics of notorious crimes. Other interesting aspects of policing, criminality and the legal system are highlighted in special changing exhibitions. The museum powerfully evokes the realities of Australian policing and justice.

⑯ Writers' Walk

Circular Quay. **Map** 1 C2.
🚍 Circular Quay routes.

This series of plaques is set in the pavement at regular intervals between East and West Circular Quay. It gives the visitor the chance to ponder the observations of famous Australian writers, both past and present, on their home country, as well as the musings of some noted literary visitors.

Each plaque is dedicated to a particular writer, consisting of a personal quotation and a brief biographical note. Australian writers in the series include the novelists Miles Franklin and Peter Carey, poets Oodgeroo Noonuccal and Judith Wright *(see pp38–9)*, humorists Barry Humphries and Clive James, and the influential feminist writer Germaine Greer. Among the international writers included who have visited Sydney are Mark Twain, Charles Darwin and Joseph Conrad.

Strolling along a section of the Writers' Walk at Circular Quay

⑰ Sydney Opera House

No other building on earth looks like the Sydney Opera House. Popularly known as the "Opera House" long before the building was complete, it is, in fact, a complex of theatres and halls linked beneath its famous shells. Its birth was long and complicated. Many of the construction problems had not been faced before, resulting in an architectural adventure which lasted 14 years. An appeal fund was set up, eventually raising A$900,000, while the Opera House Lottery raised the balance of the A$102 million final cost. Today it is the city's most popular tourist attraction, as well as one of the world's busiest performing arts centres.

★ **Dame Joan Sutherland Theatre**
This 1,507-seat theatre, mainly used for opera and ballet, has staged grand operas such as Verdi's *Aïda.*

Detail of The Possum Dreaming *(1988)*
The mural in the Dame Joan Sutherland Theatre foyer is by Michael Tjakamarra Nelson, an artist from the central Australian desert.

Opera House Walkway
Extensive public walkways around the building offer the visitor views from many different vantage points.

Northern Foyers
The Utzon Room and the large northern foyers of the Opera Theatre and Concert Hall have spectacular views over the harbour and can be hired for conferences, lunches, parties and weddings.

KEY

① **The Dame Joan Sutherland Theatre's** ceiling and walls are painted black to focus attention on the stage.

② **The Monumental Steps** and forecourt are used for outdoor performances.

③ **The Playhouse,** seating almost 400, is ideal for intimate productions, while also able to present plays with larger casts.

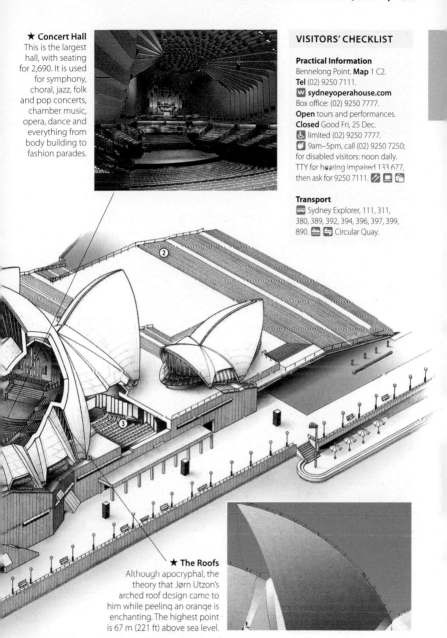

★ Concert Hall
This is the largest hall, with seating for 2,690. It is used for symphony, choral, jazz, folk and pop concerts, chamber music, opera, dance and everything from body building to fashion parades.

★ The Roofs
Although apocryphal, the theory that Jørn Utzon's arched roof design came to him while peeling an orange is enchanting. The highest point is 67 m (221 ft) above sea level.

Detail of Utzon's Tapestry *(2004)*
Jørn Utzon's original design for this Gobelin-style tapestry, which hangs floor to ceiling in the Utzon Room, was inspired by the music of Carl Philipp Emanuel Bach.

CITY CENTRE AND DARLING HARBOUR

George Street, Australia's first thoroughfare, was originally lined with mud and wattle huts, but following the gold rush shops and banks came to dominate the area. The city's first skyscraper, Culwulla Chambers, was completed in 1913. Hyde Park, on the edge of the city centre, was once a racecourse, attracting gambling taverns to Elizabeth Street. Today it provides a peaceful oasis, while the city's commercial centre is an area of department stores and arcades. The country's industrial age began in Darling Harbour in 1815 with the opening of a steam mill, but later the area became rundown. In the 1980s, it was the site of a massive urban redevelopment project. Today, Darling Harbour contains many fine museums and other attractions.

Sights at a Glance

Museums and Galleries
7 Museum of Sydney
10 *Australian Museum pp98–9*
15 *Australian National Maritime Museum pp104–5*
18 *Powerhouse Museum pp106–7*

Cathedrals and Synagogues
8 St Mary's Cathedral
11 Great Synagogue
13 St Andrew's Cathedral

Parks and Gardens
9 Hyde Park
17 Chinese Garden

Historic Streets and Buildings
1 Queen Victoria Building
3 Strand Arcade
4 Martin Place
5 *Sydney Tower p95*
6 Lands Department Building
12 Sydney Town Hall
20 Chinatown

Entertainment
2 State Theatre
14 Sea Life Sydney Aquarium, Wild Life Sydney Zoo and Madame Tussaud's
16 King Street Wharf

Markets
19 Paddy's Markets

See also Street Finder maps 1, 3 and 4

| 0 metres | 250 |
| 0 yards | 250 |

◄ Bird sculptures at the Harbourside Shopping Centre in Darling Harbour

For keys to symbols *see back flap*

Street-by-Street: City Centre

Although closely rivalled by Melbourne, Sydney is
the business and commercial capital of Australia.
Vibrant by day, at night the streets are far less busy
when office workers and shoppers have gone home.
The comparatively small city centre of this sprawling
metropolis seems to be almost jammed into a few
city blocks. Because Sydney grew in such a haphazard
fashion, with many of today's streets following tracks
from the harbour originally made by bullocks, there was
no allowance for the expansion of the city into what has
become a major international centre. A colourful night
scene of cafés, restaurants and theatres is emerging,
however, as more people return to the city centre to live.

❶ ★ Queen Victoria Building
Taking up an entire city block, this
1898 former produce market was
lovingly restored in 1986 and is
now a shopping mall.

❷ State Theatre
A gem from the golden age of movies,
this 1929 cinema was once hailed as "the
Empire's greatest theatre". It now hosts
live concerts too.

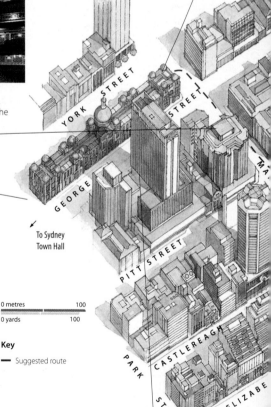

To Sydney
Town Hall

0 metres   100

0 yards   100

Key

— Suggested route

The Queen Victoria Statue was
found after a worldwide search
in 1983 ended in a small Irish
village. It had lain forgotten and
neglected since being removed
from the front of the Irish
Parliament in 1947.

Marble Bar was once a landmark bar in the
1893 Tattersalls hotel. It was re-erected in the
basement of the Sydney Hilton in 1973, and
again in 2005 when the hotel was rebuilt.

❸ Strand Arcade
A reminder of the late 19th century Victorian era when Sydney was famed as a city of elegant shopping arcades, this faithfully restored example is said to have been the finest of them all.

Locator Map
See Central Sydney map pp66–7

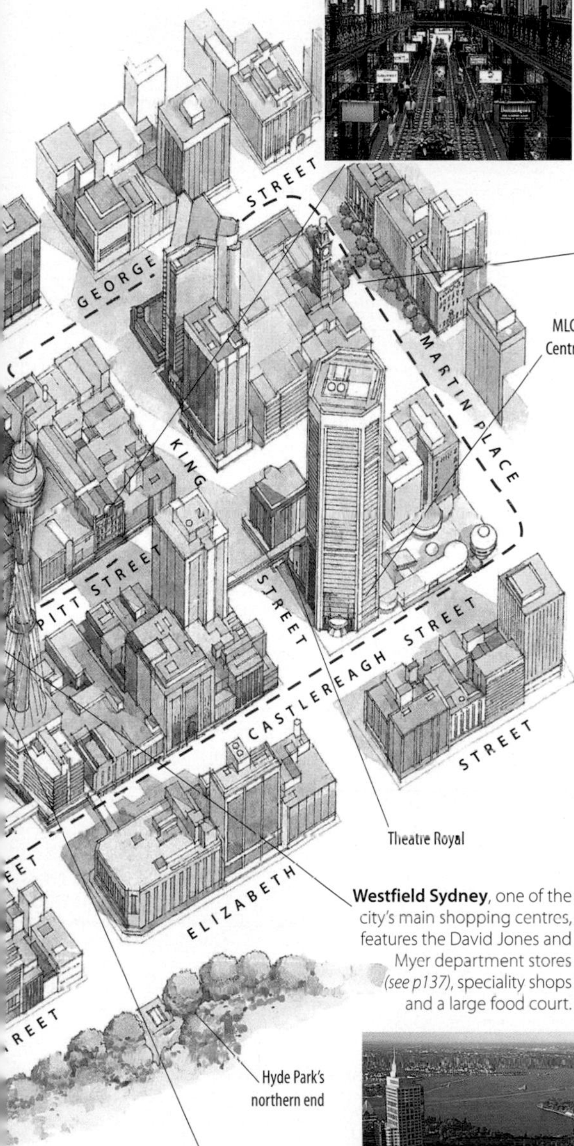

❹ ★ Martin Place
Martin Place's 1929 Art Deco Cenotaph is the site of annual Anzac Day war remembrance services including the solemn dawn service.

MLC Centre

Theatre Royal

Westfield Sydney, one of the city's main shopping centres, features the David Jones and Myer department stores *(see p137)*, speciality shops and a large food court.

Hyde Park's northern end

❺ ★ Sydney Tower
The tower tops the city skyline, giving a bird's eye view of the whole of Sydney. It rises 305 m (1,000 ft) above the ground and can be seen from as far away as the Blue Mountains.

❶ Queen Victoria Building

455 George St. **Map** 1 B5. **Tel** (02) 9265 6800. George St routes. **Open** 9am–6pm Mon–Wed, 9am–9pm Thu, 9am–6pm Fri & Sat, 11am–5pm Sun; 11am–5pm public hols. *See Shopping pp136–41.* **W** qvb.com.au

French designer Pierre Cardin called the Queen Victoria Building "the most beautiful shopping centre in the world". Yet this ornate Romanesque building, better known as the QVB, began life as the Sydney produce market. Completed to the design of City Architect George McRae in 1898, the dominant features are the central copper dome and the glass roof which lets in a flood of natural light.

The market closed at the end of World War I. By the 1950s, the building was threatened with demolition.

Ornately decorated Gothic foyer of the State Theatre

Refurbished at a cost of over A$75 million, the QVB reopened in 1986 as a shopping gallery with more than 190 shops. A wishing well incorporates a stone from Blarney Castle, a sculpture of Islay, Queen Victoria's dog and a statue of the queen herself.

Inside the QVB, suspended from the ceiling, is the Royal Clock. Designed in 1982 by Neil Glasser, it features part of Balmoral Castle above a copy of the four dials of Big Ben. Every hour, a fanfare is played with a parade depicting various English monarchs.

❷ State Theatre

49 Market St. **Map** 1 B5. **Tel** (02) 9373 6852. George St routes. Box office: **Open** 9am–5:30pm Mon–Fri. **Closed** Good Fri, 25 Dec. (bookings necessary). **W** statetheatre.com.au

When it opened in 1929, this cinema was hailed as the finest that local craftsmanship could achieve. The State Theatre is one of the best examples of ornate period cinemas in Australia.

Its Baroque style is evident in the foyer, with its high ceiling, mosaic floor, marble columns and statues. The auditorium is lit by a 20,000-piece chandelier. The beautiful Wurlitzer organ (under repair) rises from below stage before performances. The theatre is now one of the city's special events venues.

Roof detail, Queen Victoria Building

❸ Strand Arcade

412–414 George St. **Map** 1 B5. **Tel** (02) 9232 4199. George St routes. **Open** 9am–5:30pm Mon–Wed & Fri, 9am–9pm Thu, 9am–8pm Sat, 11am–4pm Sun. **Closed** 25, 26 Dec, some public hols. *See Shopping pp136–41.* **W** strandarcade.com.au

Victorian Sydney was a city of grand shopping arcades. The Strand, joining George and Pitt streets and designed by English

Pitt Street entrance to the majestic Strand Arcade

architect John Spencer, was the finest of all. Opened in April 1892, it was lit by natural light pouring through the glass roof and the chandeliers, each carrying 50 jets of gas as well as 50 lamps.

After a fire in 1976, the building was restored to its original Victorian splendour. Now visitors can enjoy its shopping and beautiful coffee shops.

❹ Martin Place

Map 1 B4. George St & Elizabeth St routes. Martin Place.

This plaza was opened in 1891 and made a traffic-free precinct in 1971. It is busiest at lunchtime as city workers enjoy their sandwiches while watching free entertainment in the amphitheatre near Castlereagh Street.

Every Anzac Day *(see p46)* the focus moves to the Cenotaph at the George Street end. Past and present service personnel attend a dawn service and wreath-laying ceremony, followed by a march past. The shrine, by Bertram MacKennal, was unveiled in 1929.

On the southern side of the Cenotaph is the façade of the Renaissance-style General Post Office, considered to be the finest building by James Barnet, colonial architect in 1866.

A stainless steel sculpture of upended cubes, the Dobell Memorial Sculpture, is a tribute to Australian artist William Dobell, created by Bert Flugelman in 1979.

❺ Sydney Tower

With a design capable of withstanding earthquakes and extreme wind, Sydney Tower was conceived as part of the original 1970s Centrepoint shopping centre, but was not completed until 1981. About one million people per year admire the stunning views. On the podium level, visitors enjoy a multimedia journey around Australia in the 4D Cinema Experience. Those with a head for heights can also venture outside the tower on a skywalk tour.

VISITORS' CHECKLIST

Practical Information
100 Market St. **Map** 1 B5. **Tel** 1800 614 069. **W** **sydneytowereye.com.au** **Open** May–Sep: 9am–9:30pm; Oct–Apr: 9am–10pm Last entry: 1 hr before closing. **Closed** 25 Dec.

Transport
Sydney Explorer, all city routes. Darling Harbour. St James, Martin Place, Town Hall.

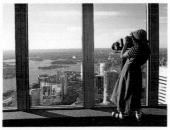

Sydney Tower Eye Observation Deck
Views from Level 4 stretch north to Pittwater, Botany Bay to the south, west to the Blue Mountains, and along the harbour out to the open sea.

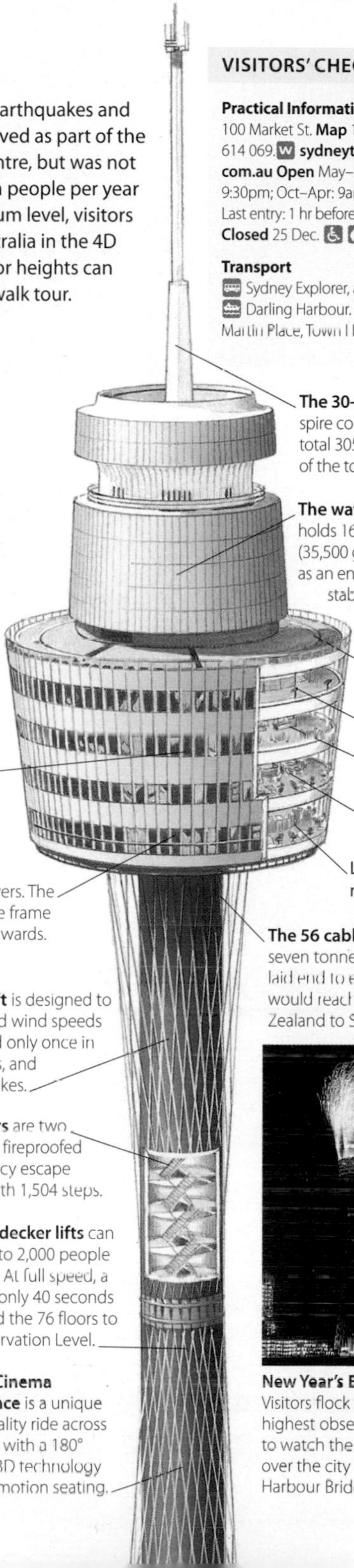

The 30-m (98-ft) spire completes the total 305 m (1,000 ft) of the tower's height.
The water tank holds 162,000 l (35,500 gal) and acts as an enormous stabilizer on very windy days.
Skywalk
Level 4: Sydney Tower Eye
Level 3: Private event space
Level 2: Buffet restaurant
Level 1: A la carte restaurant
The turret's nine levels, with room to hold almost 1,000 people at a time, include two revolving restaurants, a coffee shop and the Observation Level.
The windows comprise three layers. The outer has a gold dust coating. The frame design prevents panes falling outwards.
The 56 cables weigh seven tonnes each. If laid end to end, they would reach from New Zealand to Sydney.
The shaft is designed to withstand wind speeds expected only once in 500 years, and earthquakes.
The stairs are two separate, fireproofed emergency escape routes with 1,504 steps.
Double-decker lifts can carry up to 2,000 people per hour. At full speed, a lift takes only 40 seconds to ascend the 76 floors to the Observation Level.
The 4D Cinema Experience is a unique virtual reality ride across Australia, with a 180° cinema, 3D technology and real motion seating.

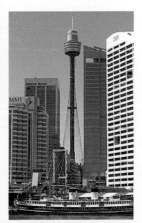

Construction of Turret
The nine turret levels were erected on the roof of the base building, then hoisted up the shaft using hydraulic jacks.

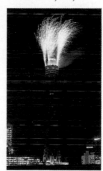

New Year's Eve
Visitors flock to Sydney's highest observation deck to watch the fireworks over the city and Harbour Bridge.

❻ Lands Department Building

23 Bridge St. **Map** 1 B3. 🚍 325, George St routes. **Open** only 2 weeks in the year. ♿

Designed by the colonial architect James Barnet, this three-storey Classical Revival sandstone edifice was built between 1877 and 1890. Pyrmont sandstone was used for the exterior, as it was for the GPO building.

All the decisions about the subdivision of much of rural eastern Australia were made in the offices within. Statues of explorers and legislators who "promoted settlement" fill 23 of the façade's 48 niches; the remainder are still empty. The luminaries include the explorers Hovell and Hume, Sir Thomas Mitchell, Blaxland, Lawson and Wentworth, Ludwig Leichhardt, Bass, Matthew Flinders and botanist Sir Joseph Banks.

The imposing sandstone edifice of the Lands Department Building

The Lookout on Level 3 of the Museum of Sydney

❼ Museum of Sydney

Cnr Phillip & Bridge sts. **Map** 1 B3. **Tel** (02) 9251 5988. 🚍 Circular Quay routes. **Open** 10am–5pm daily. **Closed** Good Fri, 25 Dec. 🎫 🍴 🎁 ♿ ✎ 📷
W sydneylivingmuseums.com.au/museum-of-sydney

Situated at the base of Governor Phillip Tower, the Museum of Sydney is a modern museum built on a historic site and details the history of Sydney from 1788 to the present. Its many attractions include the archaeological remains of the colony's first Government House, as well as exhibits that explore the evolution of Sydney over two centuries and honour the original Cadigal people.

Indigenous Peoples

This gallery explores the culture, history, continuity and place of Sydney's original inhabitants. The collectors' chests hold items of daily use such as flint and ochre. In the square outside the complex, the *Edge of the Trees* sculptural installation symbolizes the first contact between the Aborigines and Europeans. Inscribed in the wood are signatures of First Fleeters and names of botanical species in native languages and Latin.

History of Sydney

Outside the museum, a paving pattern outlines the site of the first Government House. The original foundations, below street level, can be seen through a window. A segment of wall has now been reconstructed using the original sandstone.

The Colony display on Level 2 focuses on Sydney during the critical decade of the 1840s: convict transportation ended, the town officially became a city and then suffered economic depression. On Level 3, 20th century Sydney is explored against a panorama of images.

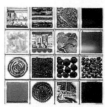

Display from Trade Exhibition on Level 2

❽ St Mary's Cathedral

St Marys Rd. **Map** 1 C5. **Tel** (02) 9220 0400. 🚍 Elizabeth St routes. **Open** 6:30am–6pm Mon–Fri, 6:30am–7pm Sat–Sun. ♿ with advance notice. 📷 by prior arrangement.
W stmaryscathedral.org.au

Although Catholics arrived with the First Fleet, the celebration of Mass was at first prohibited as it was feared priests would provoke civil strife among the colony's Irish Catholic population. It was not until 1820 that the first Catholic priests were officially appointed and services were permitted. In 1821, Governor Macquarie laid the foundation stone for St Mary's Chapel on the first land granted to the Catholic Church in Australia.

The initial section of this Gothic Revival-style cathedral was opened in 1882 and completed in 1928, but without the twin southern spires originally proposed by the architect William Wardell. By the entrance are statues of Australia's first cardinal, Moran, and Archbishop Kelly, who laid the stone for the final stage in 1913. They were sculpted by Bertram MacKennal, also responsible for the Martin Place Cenotaph *(see p93)*. The crypt's terrazzo mosaic floor took 15 years to complete.

❾ Hyde Park

Map 1 B5. Elizabeth St routes.

Hyde Park was named after its London equivalent by Governor Macquarie in 1810. The fence around the park marked the outskirts of the township. Once an exercise field for garrison troops, it later incorporated a racecourse and a cricket pitch. Though much smaller today than the original park, it is still a quiet haven in the middle of the bustling city centre, with many notable features.

The 30-m (98-ft) high Art Deco Anzac Memorial commemorates Australians who have died for their country. Opened in 1934 it now includes a military exhibition downstairs.

Sandringham Garden, filled with mauve wisteria, is a memorial to kings George V and George VI, opened by Queen Elizabeth II in 1954.

The bronze and granite Archibald Fountain commemorates the French and Australian World War I alliance. It was completed by François Sicard in 1932 and donated by J F Archibald, one of the founders of the popular *Bulletin* literary magazine.

The *Emden* Gun, on the corner of College and Liverpool Streets, commemorates a World War I naval action. HMAS *Sydney* destroyed the German raider *Emden* off the Cocos Islands on 9 November 1914, and 180 crew members were taken prisoner.

❿ Australian Museum

See pp98–9.

⓫ Great Synagogue

187 Elizabeth St, entrance at 166 Castlereagh St. **Map** 1 B5. **Tel** (02) 9267 2477. 394, 396, 380, 382. **Open** for services and tours only. by arrangement. **Closed** public and Jewish hols. noon Tue & Thu. greatsynagogue.org.au

The longest established Jewish Orthodox congregation in Australia assembles in this synagogue (consecrated in 1878). Although Jews had arrived with the First Fleet, worship did not commence until the 1820s. With its carved porch columns and wrought-iron gates, the synagogue is perhaps the finest work of Thomas Rowe, architect of Sydney Hospital (see p117). The interior features a stunning panelled ceiling.

Candelabra in the Great Synagogue

⓬ Sydney Town Hall

483 George St. **Map** 4 E2. **Tel** (02) 9265 9189. George St routes. **Open** 8am–6pm Mon–Fri. **Closed** pub hols. sydneytownhall.com.au

The steps of Sydney Town Hall have been a favourite meeting place since it opened in 1869. Walled burial grounds originally covered the site. It is a fine example of High

Grand Organ in the 19th-century Centennial Hall

Victorian architecture. The original architect, J H Wilson, died during its construction, as did several of the architects who followed. The vestibule, an elegant salon with stained glass and a crystal chandelier, is the work of Albert Bond. The clock tower was completed by the Bradbridge brothers in 1884. From 1888–9, other architects designed Centennial Hall, with its imposing 19th-century Grand Organ with over 8,500 pipes.

Some people believe this became Sydney's finest building by accident, as each architect strove to outdo similar buildings in Manchester and Liverpool. Today, it makes a good venue for concerts.

⓭ St Andrew's Cathedral

Sydney Square, cnr George & Bathurst sts. **Map** 4 E3. **Tel** (02) 9265 1661. George St routes **Open** contact the cathedral for opening times and tours. sydneycathedral.com

While the foundation stone for the country's oldest cathedral was laid in 1819, the building was not consecrated until 1868. The Gothic Revival design, by Edmund Blacket, was inspired by York Minster in England. Inside are memorials to Sydney pioneers, a 1539 Bible and beads made from olive seeds collected in the Holy Land.

The southern wall includes stones from London's St Paul's Cathedral, Westminster Abbey and the House of Lords.

Game in progress on the giant chessboard in Hyde Park

⑩ Australian Museum

The Australian Museum, the nation's leading natural science museum, founded in 1827, was the first museum established and remains the premier showcase of Australian natural history. The main building, an impressive sandstone structure with a marble staircase, faces Hyde Park. Architect Mortimer Lewis was forced to resign his position when building costs began to far exceed the budget. Construction was completed in the 1860s by James Barnet. The collection provides a journey across Australia and the near Pacific, covering biology, and natural and cultural history. From Tuesday to Saturday, behind-the-scenes tours focus on some of the 18 million objects in the museum's collection and pioneering science work.

Original Museum Entrance
The façade features massive Corinthian square pillars or piers.

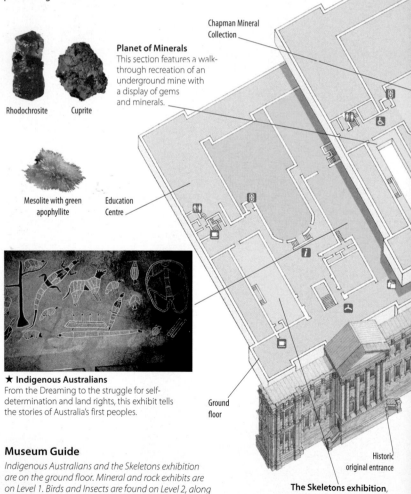

Planet of Minerals
This section features a walk-through recreation of an underground mine with a display of gems and minerals.

Rhodochrosite   Cuprite

Mesolite with green apophyllite

Education Centre

Chapman Mineral Collection

★ **Indigenous Australians**
From the Dreaming to the struggle for self-determination and land rights, this exhibit tells the stories of Australia's first peoples.

Ground floor

Historic original entrance

The Skeletons exhibition, on the ground floor, provides a different perspective on natural history.

Museum Guide

Indigenous Australians and the Skeletons exhibition are on the ground floor. Mineral and rock exhibits are on Level 1. Birds and Insects are found on Level 2, along with Kidspace, Surviving Australia and Dinosaurs.

★ **Search & Discover**
Sydneysiders bring bugs, rocks and bones here for identification. The public can also access electronic archives for research.

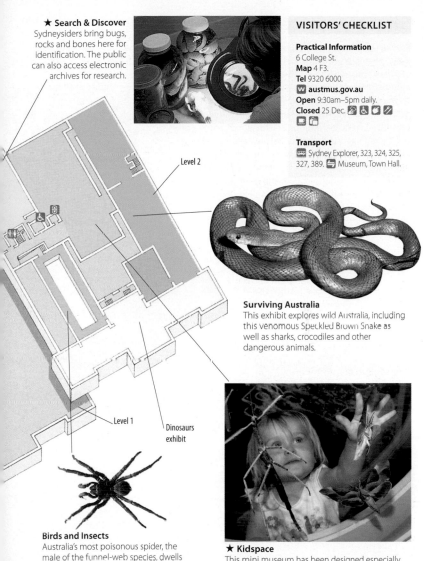

Level 2

Level 1

Dinosaurs exhibit

VISITORS' CHECKLIST

Practical Information
6 College St.
Map 4 F3.
Tel 9320 6000.
ⓦ austmus.gov.au
Open 9:30am–5pm daily.
Closed 25 Dec. 🅿 ♿ 🗎 ✏
🖥 📷

Transport
🚌 Sydney Explorer, 323, 324, 325, 327, 389. 🚇 Museum, Town Hall.

Surviving Australia
This exhibit explores wild Australia, including this venomous Speckled Brown Snake as well as sharks, crocodiles and other dangerous animals.

Birds and Insects
Australia's most poisonous spider, the male of the funnel-web species, dwells exclusively in the Greater Sydney region.

★ **Kidspace**
This mini museum has been designed especially for children aged five and under to investigate the natural world, with five "pods" – Bugs, Marine, Volcano, Observation and Imagination – to explore.

Key to Floorplan

- 🟦 Plants and minerals
- 🟦 Kidspace
- 🟦 Birds and insects exhibition
- 🟦 Indigenous Australians
- 🟦 The skeleton exhibition
- 🟦 Australian environments
- ⬜ Dinosaurs exhibition
- 🟦 Temporary exhibition space
- 🟦 Non-exhibition space
  Surviving Australia

"Welcome Stranger" Gold Nugget Cast

In 1869, the largest gold nugget ever found in Australia was discovered in Victoria. It weighed 71.06 kg (156 lb). The museum holds a cast of the original in a display examining the impact of the gold rush, when the Australian population doubled in ten years.

← 67.5 cm (26 1/2 in) wide →

Street-by-Street: Darling Harbour

Darling Harbour was New South Wales' bicentennial gift to itself. This imaginative urban redevelopment, close to the heart of Sydney, covers a 54-ha (133-acre) site that was once a busy industrial centre and international shipping terminal catering for the developing local wool, grain, timber and coal trades. In 1984 the Darling Harbour Authority was formed to examine the area's commercial options. The resulting complex opened in 1988, complete with the Australian National Maritime Museum and Sydney Aquarium, two of the city's tourist highlights. Free outdoor entertainment, appealing to children in particular, is a regular feature, and there are many shops, waterside cafés and restaurants, as well as several major hotels overlooking the bay (www.darlingharbour.com.au).

Harbourside Complex offers restaurants and cafés with superb views over the water to the city skyline. There is also a wide range of speciality shops, selling unusual gifts and other items.

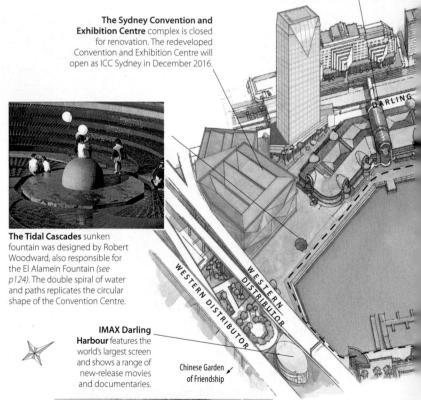

The Sydney Convention and Exhibition Centre complex is closed for renovation. The redeveloped Convention and Exhibition Centre will open as ICC Sydney in December 2016.

The Tidal Cascades sunken fountain was designed by Robert Woodward, also responsible for the El Alamein Fountain (see p124). The double spiral of water and paths replicates the circular shape of the Convention Centre.

IMAX Darling Harbour features the world's largest screen and shows a range of new-release movies and documentaries.

Chinese Garden of Friendship ↗

The Chinese Garden of Friendship is a haven of peace and tranquillity in the heart of Sydney. Its landscaping, with winding pathways, waterfalls, lakes and pavilions, offers an insight into the rich culture of China.

For hotels and restaurants in this area see pp482–3 and pp504–7

Pyrmont Bridge
opened in 1902 to service the busy harbour. It is the world's oldest swingspan bridge and opens for vessels up to 14 m (46 ft) tall. The monorail track above the walkway opens up for even taller boats.

Locator Map
See Central Sydney map pp66–7

Swingspan supports for Pyrmont Bridge are sunk 10 m (33 ft) below the harbour floor.

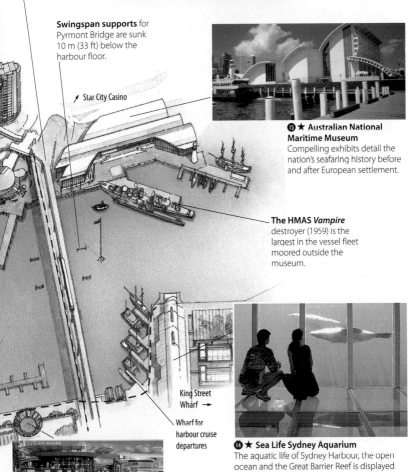

Star City Casino

⓯ ★ Australian National Maritime Museum
Compelling exhibits detail the nation's seafaring history before and after European settlement.

The HMAS *Vampire*
destroyer (1959) is the largest in the vessel fleet moored outside the museum.

King Street Wharf →

Wharf for harbour cruise departures

⓮ ★ Sea Life Sydney Aquarium
The aquatic life of Sydney Harbour, the open ocean and the Great Barrier Reef is displayed in massive tanks which can be seen from underwater walkways.

Cockle Bay Wharf is vibrant and colourful, and is an exciting food and entertainment precinct.

0 metres	100
0 yards	100

Key

— Suggested route

⑭ Sea Life Sydney Aquarium, Wild Life Sydney Zoo & Madame Tussaud's

Aquarium Pier, Darling Harbour. **Map** 4 D2. **Tel** 1800 614 069. George St routes, Sydney Explorer. Darling Harbour. Town Hall. Paddy's Markets. Aquarium: **Open** 9am–7pm daily. Zoo: **Open** Apr–Sep: 9:30am–5pm; Oct–Mar: 9:30am–7pm. Madame Tussaud's: **Open** 9:30am–8pm. Last adm: 1 hr before closing. sydneyaquarium.com.au sydneywildlifeworld.com.au madametussauds.com/sydney

These fascinating attractions are located adjacent to one another on Darling Harbour.

The aquarium contains more than 12,000 animals from approximately 650 species, held in a series of re-created marine environments. One of the highlights is the Shark Walk, 165 m (541 ft) of acrylic underwater tunnels passing through two floating oceanaria. These allow close observation of sharks, stingrays and schools of many types of fish. Other exhibits include a Great Barrier Reef display, a collection of sharks and a Discovery Rockpool, where visitors may touch marine invertebrates such

A tang fish in the Great Barrier Reef display

as sea urchins and tubeworms. Wild Life Sydney Zoo offers an authentic Australian wildlife experience, with more than 100 native species in nine different habitats. Highlights include the koala sanctuary and the kangaroo walkabout.

Madame Tussaud's is another fun destination, with life-size wax figures of the famous and powerful, including sporting heroes, historical figures, actors, musicians and celebrities from Australia and around the world.

⑮ Australian National Maritime Museum

See pp104–5.

⑯ King Street Wharf

Lime St, between King and Erskine sts. **Map** 4 D1. Paddy's Markets. George St routes. Darling Harbour. kingstreet wharf.com.au

Merchant bankers and city workers from nearby offices flock to this harbourside venue, which combines a modern glass-and-steel shrine to café society with a working wharf. Passengers arrive and depart in style on harbour cruises, ferries and water taxis, or on

Night lights at King Street Wharf, Darling Harbour

foot from the city. The complex is flush with bars and restaurants that vie for the best views. Midway along the wharf is the Pumphouse boutique brewery, with more than 50 beers. This is not just a party circuit, there are also low-rise residential apartments set back from the water.

⑰ Chinese Garden of Friendship

Darling Harbour. **Map** 4 D3. **Tel** (02) 9240 8888. George St routes, Sydney Explorer. Paddy's Markets. Darling Harbour. **Open** 9:30am–5pm daily. **Closed** Good Fri, 25 Dec. about 60 per cent. chinesegarden.com.au

The Chinese Garden was built in 1984. It is a tranquil refuge from the city streets. The garden's design was a gift to Sydney from its Chinese sister city of Guangdong. The Dragon Wall, in the lower section beside the lake, has glazed carvings of two

Structuralist design of the Aquarium Pier, the home of Sea Life Sydney Aquarium, Wild Life Sydney Zoo and Madame Tussaud's

For hotels and restaurants in this area see pp482–3 and pp504–7

Twin Pavilion in the Chinese Garden, decorated with carved flowers

dragons, one representing Guangdong province and the other the state of New South Wales. The lake is covered with lotus and water lilies for much of the year and a rock monster guards against evil. On the other side of the lake is the Twin Pavilion. Waratahs (New South Wales' floral symbol) and flowering apricots are carved into its woodwork in Chinese style, and are also planted at its base.

A tea house at the top of the stairs in the Tea House Courtyard serves Chinese and Western light refreshments.

⑱ Powerhouse Museum

See pp106 7.

⑲ Paddy's Markets

Cnr Thomas & Hay sts, Haymarket. **Map** 4 D4. **Tel** 1300 361 589. 🚌 George St routes, Sydney Explorer. 🚆 Town Hall. 🚇 Paddy's Markets. **Open** 9am–5pm Wed–Sun & public hols Mon. **Closed** 25 Apr, 25 Dec. ♿ *See also Shopping pp136–41.* 🌐 **paddysmarkets.com.au**

The Haymarket district, near Chinatown, is home to Paddy's Markets, Sydney's oldest and best-known market. It has been in this area, on a number of sites, since 1869 (with only one five-year absence). The origin of the name is uncertain, but is believed to have come from either the Chinese who originally supplied much of its produce, or the Irish who were among their main customers.

Once the shopping centre for the inner-city poor, Paddy's Markets is now an integral part of the Market City Shopping Centre, which includes cut-price fashion outlet stores, an Asian food court and a cinema complex. Yet despite this transformation, the familiar clamour, smells and chaotic bargain-hunting atmosphere of the original marketplace remain. Every weekend the market is filled with up to 800 stalls selling everything from fresh produce to electrical products, homewares, leather goods, and pets, including rabbits, puppies and chickens.

⑳ Chinatown

Dixon St Plaza, Sydney. **Map** 4 D4. 🚌 George St routes. 🚆 Town Hall. 🚇 Paddy's Markets.

Originally concentrated around Dixon and Hay streets, Chinatown is now expanding to fill Sydney's Haymarket area, stretching as far west as Harris Street, south to Broadway and east to Castlereagh Street. It is home to a pulsating mix of restaurants, noodle bars, hawker food stalls and quirky gift shops that stay open until late. It is the preferred destination of many of the city's top chefs in search of a late-night meal long after their own kitchens have closed.

For years, Chinatown was little more than a run-down district at the edge of the city's produce markets, where many Chinese immigrants worked at traditional businesses. Today, Dixon Street, its main thoroughfare, has been spruced up to equal many of the other popular Chinatowns around the world. There are authentic-looking street lanterns and archways, and a new wave of Southeast Asian and Chinese immigrants fills the now up-market restaurants.

Chinese food products in Chinatown

Chinatown is a distinctive area and is also home to vibrant Chinese New Year celebrations. There are many excellent greengrocers, traditional herbalists and butchers' shops with wind-dried ducks hanging in their windows. Asian jewellers, clothes shops and confectioners fill the lively arcades.

Traditional archway entrance to Chinatown in Dixon Street

⑮ Australian National Maritime Museum

Bounded as it is by the sea, Australia has a history inextricably linked to maritime traditions. The museum displays material in a broad range of permanent and temporary thematic exhibits, many with interactive elements. As well as artifacts relating to the enduring Aboriginal maritime cultures, the exhibits survey the history of European exploratory voyages in the Pacific, the arrival of convict ships, successive waves of migration, water sports and recreation, and naval life. Historic vessels on show at the wharf include a flimsy Vietnamese refugee boat, sailing, fishing and pearling boats, a navy patrol boat and a World War II commando raider.

Museum Façade
The billowing steel roof design by Philip Cox suggests both the surging sea and the sails of a ship.

Passengers
The model of the *Orcades* reflects the grace of 1950s liners. This display also charts harrowing sea voyages made by migrants and refugees.

Eora Indigenous Gallery – First People traces the seafaring traditions of Aboriginal peoples and Torres Strait Islanders.

The Tasman Light was used in a Tasmanian lighthouse.

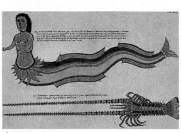

★ Navigators
This 1754 engraving of an East Indian sea creature is a European vision of the uncharted, exotic "great south".

The *Sirius* anchor is from a 1790 wreck off Norfolk Island.

Main entrance (sea level)

The Navy exhibit examines naval life in war and peace, as well as the history of colonial navies.

Museum Guide

The Watermarks, Navy and Linked by the Sea: USA Gallery exhibits are located on the main entrance level (sea level). The Eora – First People, Navigators, Passengers and Commerce sections are found on the first level.

Key to Floorplan

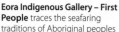

- Navigators and Eora – First People
- Passengers
- Commerce
- Watermarks
- Navy
- Linked by the Sea: USA Gallery
- Temporary exhibitions
- Non-exhibition space

Linked by the Sea honours enduring links between the US and Australia. American traders stopped off in Australia on their way to China.

Commerce
This 1903 Painters' and Dockers' Union banner was carried by waterfront workers in marches. It shows the *Niagara* entering the dry dock at Cockatoo Island.

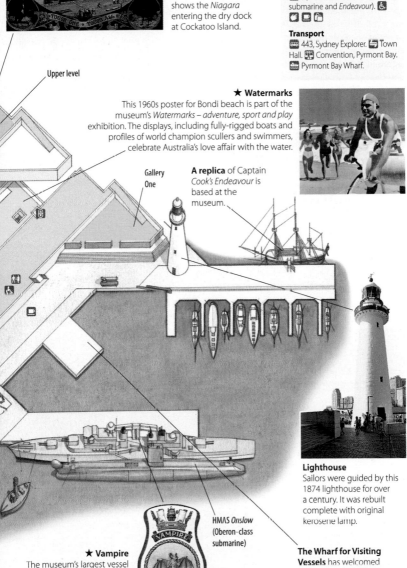

Upper level

★ **Watermarks**
This 1960s poster for Bondi beach is part of the museum's *Watermarks – adventure, sport and play* exhibition. The displays, including fully-rigged boats and profiles of world champion scullers and swimmers, celebrate Australia's love affair with the water.

Gallery One

A replica of Captain *Cook's Endeavour* is based at the museum.

Lighthouse
Sailors were guided by this 1874 lighthouse for over a century. It was rebuilt complete with original kerosene lamp.

HMAS *Onslow* (Oberon-class submarine)

★ **Vampire**
The museum's largest vessel is the 1959 Royal Australian Navy destroyer, whose insignia is shown here. Tours of "The Bat" are accompanied by simulated battle action sounds.

The Wharf for Visiting Vessels has welcomed many ships, including a replica of the 17th-century Dutch East India Company flagship *Batavia*.

⑱ Powerhouse Museum

This former power station, completed in 1902 to provide power for Sydney's tramway system, was redesigned to cater for the needs of an interactive, hands-on museum. Revamped, the Powerhouse opened in 1988. The early collection was held in the Garden Palace where the 1879 international exhibition of invention and industry from around the world was held. Few exhibits survived the devastating 1882 fire, and today's huge and ever-expanding collection was gathered after this disaster. The building's monumental scale provides an ideal context for the epic sweep of ideas encompassed within: everything from the realm of space and technology to the decorative and domestic arts. The museum emphasizes Australian innovations and achievements, celebrating both the extraordinary and the everyday.

What's It Like to Live in Space?
Find out how astronauts live and work in space and experience weightlessness in the zero gravity space lab.

★ Transport
See the vehicles that carry us from the cradle to the grave, including a pram, a hearse and everything inbetween: a penny farthing bicycle, boats and even flying machines.

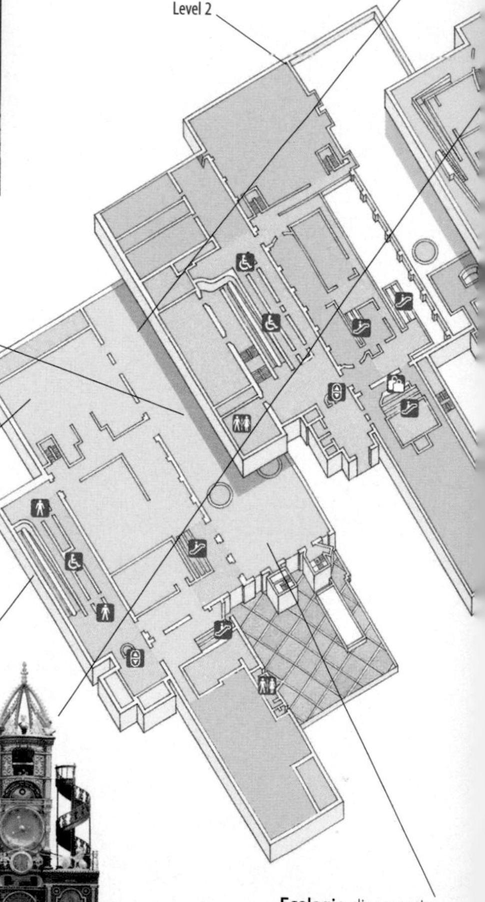

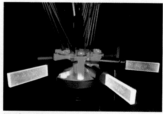

Nuclear Matters
Explore the complex world of nuclear science, medicine and power, and learn how many things in everyday life are slightly radioactive.

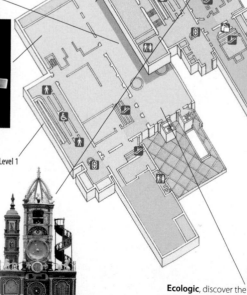

Level 2

Level 1

Strasburg Clock
This fascinating timepiece operates for six minutes every day, before the hour.

Ecologic, discover the science behind global warming and what can be done to prevent it.

Museum Guide

The museum houses more than 20 exhibitions on four levels, descending from Level 4. The shop, café, entrance, Boulton & Watt Engine, Robert Stephenson's Locomotive No. 1 and temporary exhibits are on Level 3. Level 2 has thematic exhibits. Level 1 has displays on space and transport, as well as interactive technology displays.

Level 4

Level 3

VISITORS' CHECKLIST

Practical Information
500 Harris St, Ultimo.
Map 4 D4.
Tel 9217 0111. **Open** 10am–5pm daily. **Closed** 25 Dec. 🅿 ♿ 🅟
🎞 📷 Ⓦ **maas.museum/ powerhouse-museum**

Transport
🚌 449, 501. 🚈 Darling Harbour.
🚉 Central. 🚊 Paddy's Markets.

★ Boulton & Watt Engine
The oldest surviving rotative steam engine in the world, it powered a London brewery for 102 years from 1875. It is regularly put into operation in the museum.

The Neville Wran Building, a 1980s addition, is based on the design of grand exhibition halls and railway stations of the 19th century.

Main entrance

Key to Floorplan

🔲 Temporary exhibitions
🔲 Social History & Design
🔲 Science & Technology
🔲 Non-exhibition space

★ Locomotive No. 1
Robert Stephenson built this locomotive in England in 1854. It hauled the first train in New South Wales in 1855. Using models and voices, the display re-creates a 19th-century day trip for a group of Sydneysiders.

BOTANIC GARDENS AND THE DOMAIN

This tranquil part of Sydney can seem a world away from the bustle of the city centre. It is rich in the remnants of Sydney's convict and colonial past: the site of the first farm and the boulevard-like Macquarie Street where the barracks, hospital, church and mint – bastions of civic power – are among the oldest surviving public buildings in Australia. This street continues to assert its dominance today as the location of the state government of New South Wales.

The Domain, an open, grassy space, was originally set aside by the colony's first governor for his private use. Today it is filled with joggers and touch footballers sidestepping picnickers and sunbathers. In January, during the Festival of Sydney, it hosts free outdoor concerts. The Royal Botanic Gardens has for almost 200 years collected, grown, researched and conserved plants from Australia and the rest of the world. The result is a parkland of great diversity and beauty.

Sights at a Glance

Historic Streets and Buildings
2 Conservatorium of Music
7 State Library of New South Wales
8 Parliament House
9 Sydney Hospital
10 The Mint
11 Hyde Park Barracks Museum

Museums and Galleries
5 Art Gallery of New South Wales
pp114–17

Churches
12 St James' Church

Islands
4 Fort Denison

Monuments
3 Mrs Macquaries Chair

Parks and Gardens
1 Royal Botanic Gardens *pp110–11*
6 The Domain

See also Street Finder, maps 1 and 4

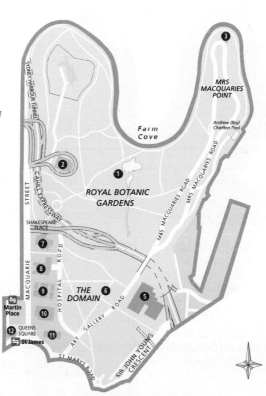

0 metres 250
0 yards 250

❶ Royal Botanic Gardens

The Royal Botanic Gardens, a 30-ha (75-acre) oasis in the heart of the city, occupies a superb position, wrapped around Farm Cove at the harbour's edge. Established in 1816 as a series of pathways through shrubbery, it is the oldest scientific institution in the country and houses an outstanding collection of plants from Australia and overseas. A living museum, the gardens are also the site of the first farm in the fledgling colony. Fountains, statues and monuments are today scattered throughout. The diversity is amazing: there are thousands of trees, stands of bamboo, a cactus garden, a rainforest walk, one of the world's finest collections of palms, a herb garden and a garden containing rare and threatened plant species.

Locator Map
See Central Sydney map pp66–7

★ **Palm Grove**
Begun in 1862, this cool summer haven is one of the world's finest outdoor collections of palms. There are about 180 species in the grove.

★ **Herb Garden**
Herbs from around the world used for a wide variety of purposes – culinary, medicinal and aromatic – are on display here. A sensory fountain and a sundial modelled on the celestial sphere are also features.

KEY

① **Conservatorium of Music**
(see p112).

② **Government House (1897)**

③ **The Fleet Steps** met those disembarking from ships in Farm Cove.

④ **Mrs Macquaries Chair,** where the governor's wife liked to watch the harbour, is marked by a rock ledge seat *(see p112).*

⑤ **Mrs Macquaries Road**

⑥ **Andrew (Boy) Charlton Pool** is a popular spot for inner-city swimming and sunbathing.

⑦ **Wollemi Pine**

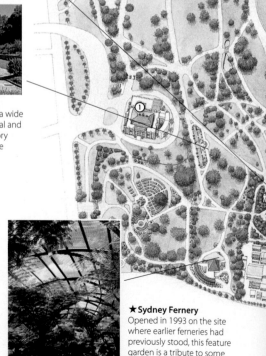

★ **Sydney Fernery**
Opened in 1993 on the site where earlier ferneries had previously stood, this feature garden is a tribute to some of the most ancient plants on earth.

Macquarie Wall
In 1810, work began on this 290-m- (950-ft-) long wall intended to separate the convict domain from the town's "respectable Class of Inhabitants". Only a small section remains standing today.

Choragic Monument *(1870)*
This sandstone replica of the marble monument by Lysicrates in Athens was sculpted by Walter McGill.

★ Australia's First Farm
Some oblong beds in the Middle Garden follow the direction of the first furrows ploughed in the colony.

National Herbarium of New South Wales
Over one million dried plant specimens document biological diversity. Discovery and study of new plants aims to slow down the extinction rate of entire species.

0 metres	200
0 yards	200

❷ Conservatorium of Music

Macquarie St. **Map** 1 C3. **Tel** (02) 9351 1222. 🚌 Sydney Explorer, Circular Quay routes. **Open** 9am–5pm Mon–Fri, 9am–4pm Sat, public areas only. Phone for details of concerts. ♿ **Closed** public holidays, Easter Sat, 24 Dec–2 Jan. 📷 phone 8256 2222 for details. 🔳 sydney.music.edu.au

When it was finished in 1821, this striking castellated Colonial Gothic building was meant to be the stables and servants' quarters for Government House, but construction of the latter was delayed for almost 25 years. That stables should be built in so grand a style, and at such great cost, brought forth cries of outrage and led to bitter arguments between the architect, Francis Greenway *(see p177)*, and Governor Macquarie – and a decree that all future building plans be submitted to London.

Between 1908 and 1915 "Greenway's folly" underwent a dramatic transformation. A concert hall, roofed in grey slate, was built on the central courtyard and the building in its entirety was converted for the use of the Sydney Conservatorium of Music.

The café holds lunchtime concerts during the school term and an upper level with great harbour views. "The Con" continues to be a training ground for future musicians and a great place to visit.

Resting on the carved stone seat of Mrs Macquaries Chair

❸ Mrs Macquaries Chair

Mrs Macquaries Rd. **Map** 2 E2. 🚌 Sydney Explorer, 111. ♿ 📷

The Scenic Mrs Macquaries Road winds alongside much of what is now the city's Royal Botanic Gardens, stretching from Farm Cove to Woolloomooloo Bay and back again. The road was built in 1816 at the instigation of Elizabeth Macquarie, wife of the Governor. In the same year, a stone bench, inscribed with details of the new road and its commissioner, was carved into the rock at the point where Mrs Macquarie would often stop to rest and admire the view on her daily stroll. Although today the outlook is much changed, it is just as arresting, taking in the broad sweep of the harbour with all its landmarks.

Rounding the cove to the west leads to Mrs Macquaries Point. These lawns are a popular picnic spot with Sydneysiders, particularly at sunset.

❹ Fort Denison

Sydney Harbour. **Map** 2 E1. **Tel** (02) 9247 5033. 🚌 Circular Quay. **Open** daily tours: for prices and times call 1300 072 757, or visit 🔳 national parks.nsw.gov.au. **Closed** 25 Dec. 📷 📷 📷 🔳 fortdenison.com.au

First named Rock Island, this prominent, rocky outcrop in Sydney Harbour was also dubbed "Pinchgut". This was probably because of the meagre rations given to convicts who were confined there as punishment. It had a grim history of incarceration in the early years of the colony.

In 1796, the convicted murderer Francis Morgan was hanged on the island in chains.

Fort Denison in 1907

His body was left to rot on the gallows for three years as a warning to the other convicts.

Between 1855 and 1857, the Martello tower (the only one in Australia), gun battery and barracks that now occupy the island were built as part of Sydney's defences. The site was renamed after the governor of the time. The gun, still fired at 1pm each day, helped mariners to set their ships' chronometers accurately.

Today the island is the perfect setting for watching the many harbour activities, such as the New Year fireworks displays *(see p45)*. Daily guided tours of Fort Denison are led by National Parks and Wildlife Service rangers.

❺ Art Gallery of New South Wales

See pp114–17.

Conservatorium of Music at the edge of the Royal Botanic Gardens

❻ The Domain

Art Gallery Rd. **Map** 1 C4. 🚌 Sydney Explorer, 111, 411. ♿

The tens of thousands of people who swarm to the January concerts and other Festival of Sydney events in The Domain are part of a long-standing tradition. They come equipped with picnic baskets and blankets to enjoy the ongoing entertainment.

Once the governor's private park, this extensive space is now public and has long been a rallying point for crowds of Sydneysiders whenever emotive issues of public importance have arisen. These have included the attempt in 1916 to introduce military conscription and the sudden dismissal of the elected federal government by the then governor-general in 1975.

From the 1890s, part of The Domain was also used as the Sydney version of "Speakers' Corner". Today, you are more likely to see joggers or office workers playing touch football in their lunch hours, or simply enjoying the shade.

View of Sydney Harbour from The Domain

❼ State Library of New South Wales

Macquarie St. **Map** 1 C4. **Tel** (02) 9273 1414. 🚌 Sydney Explorer, Elizabeth St routes. 🚉 Martin Place. **Open** 9am–8pm Mon–Thu, 9am–5pm Fri, 10am–5pm Sat & Sun. **Closed** most public hols, Mitchell Library closed Sun. ♿ 🚻 📷 ♿ 🖥 sl.nsw.gov.au

The state library is housed in two separate buildings connected by a passageway and a glass bridge. The older building, the Mitchell

Mosaic replica of the Tasman Map, State Library of New South Wales

Library wing (1910), is a majestic sandstone edifice facing the Royal Botanic Gardens *(see pp110–11)*. Huge stone columns supporting a vaulted ceiling frame the impressive vestibule. On the vestibule floor is a mosaic replica of an old map illustrating the two voyages made to Australia by Dutch navigator Abel Tasman in the 1640s *(see p53)*. The two ships of the first voyage are shown off the south coast, the two from the second voyage are seen to the northwest. The original Tasman Map is held in the Mitchell Library as part of its collection of historic Australian paintings, books, documents and pictorial records.

The Mitchell wing's vast reading room, with its huge skylight and oak panelling, is just beyond the main vestibule. There is also an attractive contemporary structure that faces Macquarie Street *(see pp118–19)*. This area houses the State Reference Library. Beyond the Mitchell wing is the Dixson Gallery, housing cultural and historical exhibitions which change regularly.

Outside the library, facing Macquarie Street, is a statue of the explorer Matthew Flinders, who first ventured into central Australia *(see pp56–7)*. On the windowsill behind him is a statue of his travelling companion, his cat, Trim.

❽ Parliament House

Macquarie St. **Map** 1 C4. **Tel** (02) 9230 2111. 🚌 Sydney Explorer, Elizabeth St routes. 🚉 Martin Place. **Open** 9am–5pm Mon–Fri. **Closed** public hols. ♿ 📷 (02) 9230 3444 to book. 🖥 parliament.nsw.gov.au

The central section of this building, which houses the State Parliament, is part of the original Sydney Hospital built from 1811–16 *(see p117)*. It has been a seat of government since 1829 when the newly appointed Legislative Council first held meetings here. The building was extended twice during the 19th century and again during the 1970s and 1980s. The current building contains the chambers for both houses of state parliament, as well as parliamentary offices.

Parliamentary memorabilia is on view in the Jubilee Room, as are displays showing Parliament House's development and the legislative history of the state.

The corrugated iron building with a cast iron façade tacked on at the southern end was a prefabricated kit from England. In 1856, this dismantled kit became the chamber for the new Legislative Council. Its packing cases were used to line the chamber; the rough timber can still be seen.

Malby's celestial globe, Parliament House

❺ Art Gallery of New South Wales

Established in 1871, the art gallery has occupied its present imposing building since 1897. Designed by the Colonial Architect W L Vernon, the gallery doubled in size following building extensions in 1988. Two equestrian bronzes – *The Offerings of Peace* and *The Offerings of War* – greet the visitor on entry. The gallery itself houses some of the finest works of art in Australia, with permanent collections of Australian, Aboriginal, European, Asian and Contemporary art. The Yiribana Gallery is among the largest in the world to exclusively exhibit Aboriginal and Torres Strait Islander art and culture. Free guided tours take place daily, covering Aboriginal art, highlights of the collection or major exhibitions.

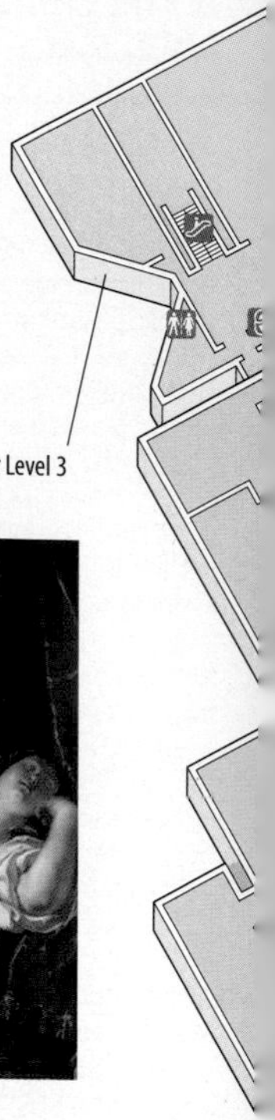

Lower Level 3

Mars and the Vestal Virgin (1638)
This oil on canvas by Parisian painter Jacques Blanchard (1600–38) depicts Mars' encounter with a Vestal Virgin, who subsequently gave birth to Romulus and Remus, founders of Rome.

★ **Pukumani Grave Posts** (1958)
Carved by the Tiwi people of Melville Island (north of Australia), these posts represent qualities of the deceased whose grave they solemnly surrounded.

Sofala (1947)
Russell Drysdale's visions of Australia show "ghost" towns laid waste by devastating natural forces such as drought.

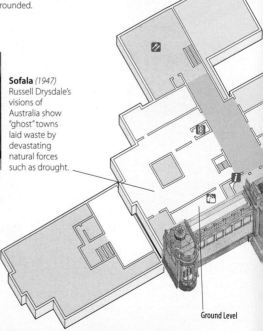

Gallery Guide

There are five levels. The Upper Level and Lower Level 1 host temporary exhibitions. The Ground Level has European and Australian works. On Lower Level 2 are the Contemporary galleries, which house the most extensive collection of modern art in the country. The Yiribana Aboriginal Gallery is on Lower Level 3.

Ground Level

For hotels and restaurants in this area see pp482–3 and pp504–7

VISITORS' CHECKLIST

Practical Information
Art Gallery Road, The Domain.
Map 2 D4. **Tel** 9225 1744.
W **artgallery.nsw.gov.au**
Open 10am–5pm daily (to 10pm Wed). **Closed** Good Fri, 25 Dec.

Transport
Sydney Explorer, 441.
Circular Quay. St James, Martin Place

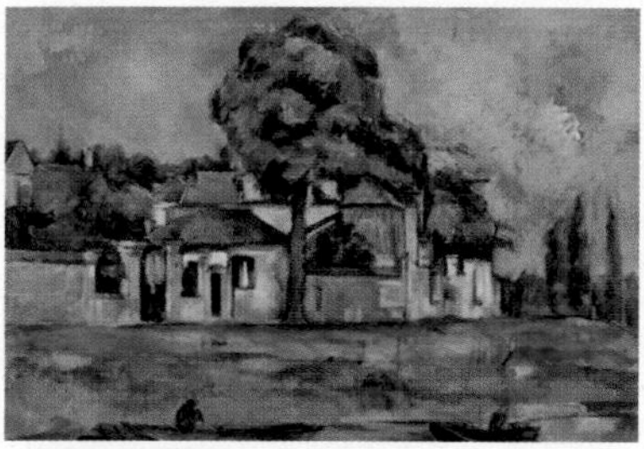

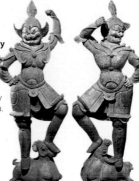

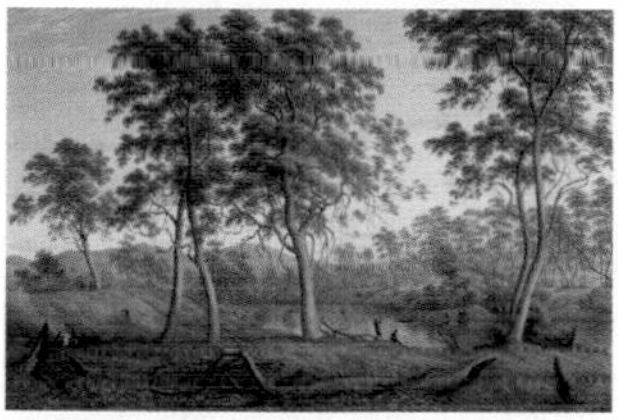

Lower Level 2
Lower Level 1
Mars and the Vestal Virgin

Banks of the Marne *(c. 1888)*
This landscape painting by the post-Impressionist artist Paul Cézanne is a highlight of the gallery's collection of modern art.

Guardians, Tang Dynasty
These 7th-century Chinese figures are part of a collection highlighting different traditions, periods and cultures from the many countries of Asia.

Natives on the Ouse River, Van Diemen's Land *(1838)*
English Australian artist John Glover was dubbed the father of Australian landscape painting for his bright depictions of the Van Dieman's Land bush (now Tasmania).

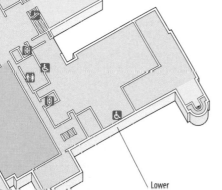

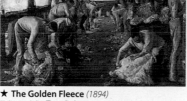

★ **The Golden Fleece** *(1894)*
This work by Tom Roberts portrays the vanished tradition of manual shearing, and captures the heroic quality of the men.

The sandstone entrance was added in 1909.

Key to Floorplan

- Australian Art
- European Art
- Asian Art
- Modern Gallery (20th-Century European Art)
- Contemporary Art
- Domain Theatre
- Yiribana Aboriginal Gallery
- Temporary exhibition space
- Non-exhibition space
- Photography Gallery

Exploring the Art Gallery's Collection

The gallery's early focus was on Australian and British art, and these areas continue to be well represented. Aboriginal art began to be added to the collection during the 1940s, with strong acquisition programmes in recent decades. The Contemporary galleries are an exciting addition, with both international and Australian pieces on display. The gallery stages major temporary exhibitions, and the annual Archibald, Wynne and Sulman prizes always entertain and usually stir controversy.

Grace Cossington Smith's *The Curve of the Bridge* (1928–9)

Australian Art

Among the most important colonial works is John Glover's *Natives on the Ouse River, Van Diemen's Land* (1838), an image of doomed Tasmanian Aborigines. The old wing holds paintings from the Heidelberg school of Australian Impressionism. *Departure of the Orient – Circular Quay* (1888) by Charles Conder and Tom Roberts's *The Golden Fleece* (1894) hang near the equally iconic *Fire's On* (1891) by Arthur Streeton.

Australia was slow to take up Modernism. *Implement Blue* (1927) by Margaret Preston is an

emphatic statement of its period. Some of Sidney Nolan's most powerful paintings exploiting myths and landscapes of Australia include *Hare in a Trap* (1946) and *Central Australia* (1950). There are also fine holdings of William Dobell, Russell Drysdale, Grace Cossington Smith and Brett Whiteley *(see p38).*

Yiribana Aboriginal Gallery

This gallery opened in 1994 and exhibits works by Aboriginal and Torres Strait Islanders. The name Yiribana implies a multiplicity of directions, reflecting the diversity of a collection representing artists from many different communities, including Emily Kam Ngwarray, John Mawurndjul and Pedro Wonaeamirri. Most of the works were produced after 1945 yet depict stories dating back thousands of years. The gallery received an important gift of 24 paintings on bark and works on paper from the Commonwealth Government's 1948 expedition to Arnhem Land. Between 1959 and 1962 more works and a set of Pukumani grave posts were also acquired.

Three Bathers, an Ernst Ludwig Kirchner painting from 1913

European Art

Among the Old Masters are some significant Italian works. Hogarth, Turner and Joshua Reynolds are represented, as are Neo-Classical works such as *The Visit of the Queen of Sheba to King Solomon* (1884–90) by Edward Poynter. *Chaucer at the Court of Edward III* (1845–51) by Ford Madox Brown is the most commanding Pre-Raphaelite painting.

Impressionists and Post-Impressionists are represented by Pissarro, Cézanne and Monet, as well as Bonnard, Kandinsky and Braque. *Old Woman in Ermine* (1946) by Max Beckmann and *Three Bathers* (1913) by Ernst Ludwig Kirchner are strong examples of German Expressionism. The gallery's first Picasso, *Nude in a Rocking Chair* (1956), was bought in 1981.

Photography

There are 4,500 photographs in the collection, celebrating the extraordinary diversity of the medium. The majority are Australian and half date from 1980 onwards. Major holdings of a wide variety of artists include Micky Allan, Mark Johnson, Max Pam, Lewis Morley, Tracey Moffatt and Bill Henson. Australian Pictorialism, as represented by Harold Cazneaux, is also a particular strength, as is the Modernism and postwar photodocumentary of artists such as Olive Cotton and Max Dupain.

Brett Whiteley's vivid *The balcony 2* from 1975

For hotels and restaurants in this area see pp482–3 and pp504–7

Asian Art

The Asian collections offer one of the largest pan-Asian displays of art in the southern hemisphere, including exquisite calligraphy, traditional and modern paintings, textiles, porcelain and an extraordinary legacy of Buddhist art. The galleries occupy two levels; the lower level displays the art of East Asia – China, Korea and Japan; the upper level displays the art of South and Southeast Asia and changing exhibitions. The upper gallery is housed within a white glass pavilion, inspired by floating lanterns typically found in Asia. The lower one includes a fully operational Japanese tearoom.

Amitabha Buddha, dating from between the late 8th and the mid-9th centuries

Contemporary Art

The Contemporary galleries were opened in 1974, initially showing only Australian artists, but later including international works. It now contains Australia's most comprehensive collection of contemporary artworks from the 1960s onwards, spanning abstract painting, expressionism, screen culture and pop art. Leading international and Australian artists represented include Sol LeWitt, Ugo Rondinone, Urs Fischer, Richard Long, Gilbert and George, Vanessa Beecroft, Christo and Jeanne-Claud, and Jeff Koons. International works focus on the influences of conceptual art, nouveau realism and minimalism.

Il Porcellino, the bronze boar in front of Sydney Hospital

❾ Sydney Hospital

Macquarie St. **Map** 1 C4. **Tel** (02) 9382 7111. 🚌 Sydney Explorer, Elizabeth St routes. 🚆 Martin Place. **Open** daily. 🎟 for tours. 🚻 📷 book in advance.

This imposing collection of Victorian sandstone buildings stands on the site of what was once the central section of the original convict-built Sydney Hospital. It was known locally as the Rum Hospital because the builders were paid by being allowed to import rum for resale. Both the north and south wings of the Rum Hospital survive as Parliament House (see p113) and the Sydney Mint. The central wing was demolished in 1879 and the new hospital, which is still operational, was completed in 1894.

The Classical Revival building boasts a Baroque staircase and elegant stained-glass windows in its central hall. Florence Nightingale approved the design of the 1867 nurses' wing. In the inner courtyard, there is a brightly coloured Art Deco fountain (1907), somewhat out of place among the surrounding heavy stonework.

At the front of the hospital sits a bronze boar called Il Porcellino. It is a replica of a 17th-century fountain in Florence's Mercato Nuovo. Donated in 1968 by an Italian woman whose relatives had worked at the hospital, the statue is an enduring symbol of

Stained glass at Sydney Hospital

the friendship between Italy and Australia. Like his Florentine counterpart, Il Porcellino is supposed to bring good luck to all those who rub his snout. Coins tossed in the pool at his feet for luck and fortune are collected for the hospital.

❿ The Mint

10 Macquarie St. **Map** 1 C5. **Tel** (02) 8239 2288. 🚌 Sydney Explorer, Elizabeth St routes. 🚆 St James, Martin Place. **Open** 9am–5pm Mon–Fri. **Closed** Good Fri, 25 Dec. 🚻 ground floor only. 🖥 🌐 sydneylivingmuseums.com.au/the-mint

The gold rushes of the mid-19th century transformed colonial Australia (see pp58–9). The Sydney Mint opened in 1854 in the south wing of the Rum Hospital in order to turn recently discovered gold into bullion and currency. This was the first branch of the Royal Mint to be established outside London, but it was closed in 1927 as it was no longer competitive with the mints in Melbourne (see p391) and Perth (see p309). The Georgian building then went into decline after it was converted into government offices. The Mint's artifacts are now in the Powerhouse Museum (see pp106–7). The head office of the Historic Houses Trust of NSW is now located here and you can look through the front part of the building.

⓫ Hyde Park Barracks Museum

Queens Square 10, Macquarie St.
Map 1 C5. **Tel** (02) 8239 2311.
🚌 Sydney Explorer, Elizabeth St
routes. 🚉 St James, Martin Place.
Open 10am–5pm daily. **Closed**
Good Fri, 25 Dec. 🎫 🚹 ground
floor only. 🎧 on request. 🛍
🌐 sydneylivingmuseums.com.au

Described by Governor
Macquarie as "spacious" and
"well-aired", the beautifully
proportioned barracks are the
work of Francis Greenway and
are considered his masterpiece
(see p177). They were completed
in 1819 by convict labour and
designed to house 600 convicts.
Until that time convicts had
been forced to find their own
lodgings after their day's work.

**Replica convict hammocks on the third
floor of Hyde Park Barracks**

Subsequently, the building then
housed, in turn, young Irish
orphans and single female
immigrants, before it later
became courts and legal offices.

Refurbished in 1990, the barracks
reopened as a museum on the
history of the site and its occupants. The displays include a
room reconstructed as convict
quarters of the 1820s, as well as
pictures, models and artifacts.
Many of the objects recovered
during archaeological digs at
the site and now on display
survived because they had
been dragged away by rats to
their nests; today the rodents
are acknowledged as valuable
agents of preservation.

The Greenway Gallery on the
first floor holds varied exhibitions
on history and culture. Elsewhere,
the Barracks Café, which incorporates the original cell area, offers
views of the courtyard, today
attractive but in the past the
scene of brutal convict floggings.

Macquarie Street

*Described in the 1860s as one of the gloomiest
streets in Sydney, this could now claim to be the
most elegant. Open to the harbour breezes and
the greenery of The Domain, a stroll down this
tree-lined street is a pleasant way to view the
architectural heritage of Sydney.*

This wing of the
library was built
in 1988 and
connected to
the old section
by a glass
walkway.

The Mitchell Library
wing's portico (1906) has
Ionic columns.

Parliament House was
once the convict-built Rum
Hospital's northern wing.

1. State Library of NSW *(1906–41)*

2. Parliament House *(1811–16)*

The roof of The Mint
has now been
completely restored to
replicate the original
wooden shingles in
casuarina (she-oak).

The Mint, like its twin,
Parliament House, has an
unusual double-colonnaded,
two-storeyed veranda.

**Hyde Park
Barracks Café**

4. The Mint *(1816)*

⑫ St James' Church

179 King St. **Map** 1 B5. **Tel** (02) 8227 1300. ☐ St James, Martin Place. **Open** 10am–4pm Mon–Fri, 9am–1pm Sat, 7:30am–5pm Sun. ♿ Concerts: 1:15pm Wed (free). 🅦 **sjks.org.au**

This fine Georgian building, constructed by convict labour, was originally designed as a courthouse in 1819. The architect, Francis Greenway, had to build a church instead when plans to construct a cathedral on George Street were abandoned. Greenway designed a simple yet elegant church. Consecrated in 1824, it is the city's oldest church. Many additions were carried out, including designs by John Verge in which the pulpit faced the high-rent pews, while convicts and the military sat directly behind the preacher where the service was inaudible. A Children's Chapel was created in 1929. Prominent members of early 19th-century society, many of whom died violently, are honoured with marble tablets. These tell the stories of luckless explorers, the governor's wife dashed to her death from her carriage, and shipwreck victims.

Detail from the Children's Chapel mural in the St James' Church crypt

The lamps hanging over the gateways of Parliament House are reproductions of the 19th-century gas lamps that used to stand here.

Corrugated iron and cast-iron façade

The entrance stairs of Pyrmont sandstone have set the tone for all renovations. The stone, quarried in colonial times, must be matched exactly.

Arcaded stone verandas with ornate balustrading

Arched sandstone bridges

Locator map

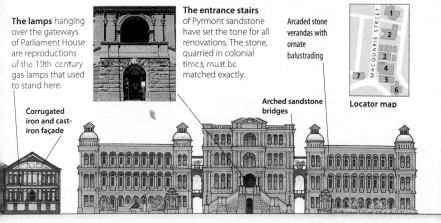

3. Sydney Hospital (1868–94)

Georgian sandstone façade

Statue of Prince Albert

The Land Titles Office, a W L Vernon building from 1908, has a Classical form with some fine Tudor Gothic detailing

The stained-glass windows in St James' Church are mostly 20th century. Those in the Chapel of the Holy Spirit represent air, earth, fire and water.

Copper spire

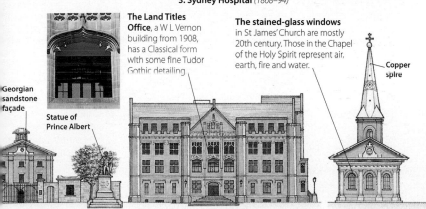

5. Hyde Park Barracks Museum (1817–19)

6. Land Titles Office (1908–13)

7. St James' (1820)

KINGS CROSS, DARLINGHURST AND PADDINGTON

Sydney's Kings Cross and Darlinghurst districts are still remembered for their 1920s gangland associations. However, both areas are now cosmopolitan and densely populated parts of the city. Kings Cross has a thriving café society, in spite of the nearby red-light district. Darlinghurst comes into its own every March, during the flamboyant

Gay and Lesbian Mardi Gras parade. The Victorian terraces of Paddington are still admired for their wrought-iron "lace" verandas. Paddington is also famed for its fine restaurants, galleries and antiques shops. On Saturdays, people flock to Paddington Markets, spilling out into the pubs and cafés of the surrounding area.

Sights at a Glance

Historic Streets and Buildings
- ❷ Victoria Street
- ❸ Elizabeth Bay House
- ❻ Old Gaol, Darlinghurst
- ❼ Darlinghurst Court House
- ❽ Five Ways
- ❾ Paddington Village
- ❿ Juniper Hall
- ⓫ Paddington Town Hall
- ⓬ Victoria Barracks
- ⓮ Paddington Street
- ⓰ The Entertainment Quarter

Parks and Gardens
- ❹ Beare Park
- ⓯ Centennial Park

Museums and Galleries
- ❺ Sydney Jewish Museum

Monuments
- ❶ El Alamein Fountain

Markets
- ⓭ Paddington Markets

See also Street Finder, maps 2, 5 and 6

0 metres 500
0 yards 500

◀ Colourful Victorian terrace houses in the Sydney suburb of Paddington

For keys to symbols see back flap

Street-by-Street: Potts Point

The substantial Victorian houses filling the streets of this old suburb are excellent examples of the 19th-century concern with architectural harmony. New building projects were designed to enhance rather than contradict the surrounding buildings and general streetscape. Monumental structures and fine details of moulded stuccoed parapets, cornices and friezes, even the spandrels in herringbone pattern, are all integral parts of a grand suburban plan. (This plan included an 1831 order that all houses cost at least £1,000.) Cool, dark verandas extend the street's green canopy of shade, leaving an impression of cold drinks enjoyed on summer days in fine Victorian style.

The McElhone Stairs were preceded by a wooden ladder that linked Woolloomooloo Hill, as Kings Cross was known, to the estate far below.

Horderns Stairs

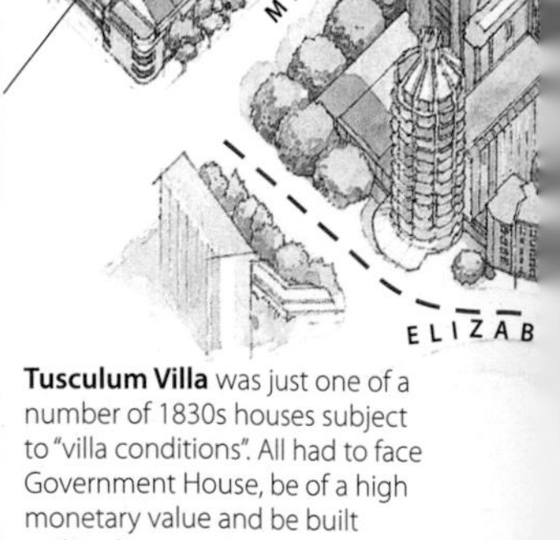

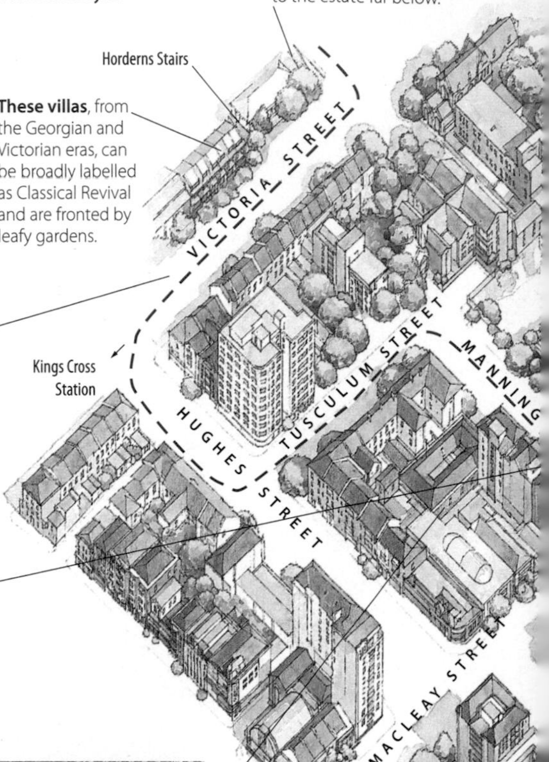

These villas, from the Georgian and Victorian eras, can be broadly labelled as Classical Revival and are fronted by leafy gardens.

Kings Cross Station

❷ ★ Victoria Street
From 1972–4, residents of this historic street fought a sometimes violent battle against developers wanting to build high-rise towers, motels and blocks of flats.

Werrington, a mostly serious and streamlined building, also has flamboyant Art Deco detailing which is now hidden under brown paint.

Tusculum Villa was just one of a number of 1830s houses subject to "villa conditions". All had to face Government House, be of a high monetary value and be built within three years.

VICTORIA STREET

TUSCULUM STREET

MANNING

HUGHES STREET

MACLEAY STREET

ELIZAB

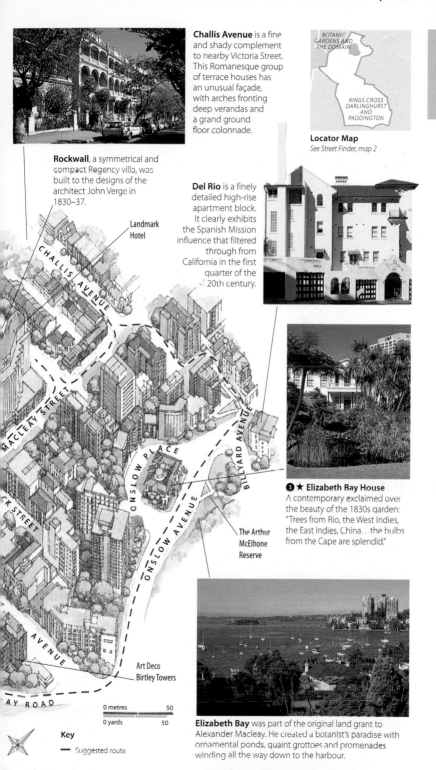

Challis Avenue is a fine and shady complement to nearby Victoria Street. This Romanesque group of terrace houses has an unusual façade, with arches fronting deep verandas and a grand ground floor colonnade.

Locator Map
See Street Finder, map 2

BOTANIC GARDENS AND THE DOMAIN

KINGS CROSS DARLINGHURST AND PADDINGTON

Rockwall, a symmetrical and compact Regency villa, was built to the designs of the architect John Verge in 1830–37.

Landmark Hotel

Del Rio is a finely detailed high-rise apartment block. It clearly exhibits the Spanish Mission influence that filtered through from California in the first quarter of the 20th century.

CHALLIS AVENUE

MACLEAY STREET

ONSLOW PLACE

ONSLOW AVENUE

BILLYARD AVENUE

CK STREET

The Arthur McElhone Reserve

AVENUE

AY ROAD

Art Deco Birtley Towers

❸ ★ Elizabeth Bay House
A contemporary exclaimed over the beauty of the 1830s garden: "Trees from Rio, the West Indies, the East Indies, China…the bulbs from the Cape are splendid."

0 metres   50
0 yards   50

Key

— Suggested route

Elizabeth Bay was part of the original land grant to Alexander Macleay. He created a botanist's paradise with ornamental ponds, quaint grottoes and promenades winding all the way down to the harbour.

El Alamein Fountain, commemorating the World War II battle

❶ El Alamein Fountain

Fitzroy Gardens, Macleay St, Potts Point. **Map** 2 E5. 🚌 222, 311.

This dandelion of a fountain in the heart of the Kings Cross district has a reputation for working so spasmodically that passers-by often murmur facetiously, "He loves me, he loves me not." Built in 1961, it commemorates the Australian army's role in the siege of Tobruk, Libya, and the battle of El Alamein in Egypt during World War II. At night, when it is brilliantly lit, the fountain looks surprisingly ethereal.

❷ Victoria Street

Potts Point. **Map** 5 B2. 🚌 311, 324, 325, 389.

At the Potts Point end, this street of 19th-century terrace houses, interspersed with a few incongruous-looking high-rise blocks, is, by inner-city standards, almost a boulevard. The gracious street you see today was once at the centre of a bitterly fought conservation struggle, one which almost certainly cost the life of a prominent heritage campaigner.

In the early 1970s, many residents, backed by the "green bans" put in place by the Builders' Labourers Federation of New South Wales, fought to prevent demolition of old buildings for high-rise development. Juanita Nielsen, heiress and publisher of a local newspaper, vigorously took up the conservation battle. On 4 July 1975, she disappeared without trace. An inquest into her disappearance returned an open verdict.

As a result of the actions of the union and residents, most of Victoria Street's superb old buildings still stand. Ironically, they are now occupied not by the low-income residents who fought to save them, but by the well-off professionals who eventually displaced them.

Juanita Nielsen

❸ Elizabeth Bay House

7 Onslow Ave, Elizabeth Bay. **Map** 2 F5. **Tel** (02) 9356 3022. 🚌 Sydney Explorer, 311. **Open** 11am–4pm Fri–Sun & Australia Day. **Closed** Good Fri, 25 Dec. 🔲 🔳 🔲 ground floor.
🔲 **sydneylivingmuseums.com.au**

Elizabeth Bay House contains the finest colonial interior on display in Australia. It is a potent expression of how the depression of the 1840s cut short the 1830s' prosperous optimism. Designed in Greek Revival style by John Verge, it was built for Colonial Secretary Alexander Macleay, from 1835–39. The oval saloon with its dome and cantilevered staircase is recognized as Verge's masterpiece. The exterior is less satisfactory, as the intended colonnade and portico were not finished owing to a crisis in Macleay's financial affairs. The present portico dates from 1893. The interior is furnished to reflect Macleay's occupancy from 1839–45, and is based on inventories drawn up in 1845 for the transfer of the house and contents to his son, William Sharp. He took the house in return for paying off his father's debts, leading to a rift that was never resolved.

Macleay's original 22-ha (55-acre) land grant was subdivided for flats and villas from the 1880s to 1927. In the 1940s, the house itself was divided into 15 flats. In 1942, the artist Donald Friend saw the ferry *Kuttabul* hit by a torpedo from a Japanese midget submarine from his flat's balcony.

The house was restored and opened as a museum in 1977. It is a property of the Historic Houses Trust of NSW.

The sweeping staircase under the oval dome, Elizabeth Bay House

❹ Beare Park

Ithaca Rd, Elizabeth Bay. **Map** 2 F5. 🚌 311, 350.

Originally a part of the Macleay Estate, Beare Park is now encircled by a jumble of apartment blocks.

A refuge from hectic Kings Cross, it is one of only a few parks serving a populated area. Shaped like a natural amphi-theatre, the park has glorious views of Elizabeth Bay.

The family home of J C Williamson, a famous theatrical entrepreneur who came to Australia from America in the 1870s, formerly stood at the eastern extremity of the park.

Star of David in the lobby of the Sydney Jewish Museum

❺ Sydney Jewish Museum

148 Darlinghurst Rd, Darlinghurst. **Map** 5 B2. **Tel** (02) 9360 7999. 🚌 Sydney, Bondi & Bay Explorer, 311, 389. **Open** 10am–4pm Sun–Thu, 10am– 2pm Fri. **Closed** Sat, Jewish hols. ♿ 🅿 📷
🌐 sydneyjewishmuseum.com.au

Sixteen Jewish convicts were on the First Fleet, and many more were to be transported before the end of the convict era. As with other convicts, most would endure and some would thrive, seizing all the opportunities the colony had to offer.

The Sydney Jewish Museum relates stories of Australian Jewry within the context of the Holocaust. The ground floor display explores present-day Jewish traditions and culture within Australia. Ascending the stairs to the mezzanine levels

1–6, the visitor passes through chronological and thematic exhibitions which unravel the tragic history of the Holocaust.

From Hitler's rise to power and *Kristallnacht*, through the evacuation of the ghettos and the Final Solution, to the ultimate liberation of the infamous death camps and Nuremberg Trials, the harrowing events are graphically documented. This horrific period is recalled using photographs and relics, some exhumed from mass graves, as well as audiovisual exhibits and oral testimonies.

Holocaust survivors act as guides and their presence, bearing witness to the recorded events, lends considerable power and moving authenticity to the exhibits in the museum.

❻ Old Gaol, Darlinghurst

Cnr Burton & Forbes sts, Darlinghurst. **Map** 5 A2. **Tel** (02) 9339 8744. 🚌 378, 380, 382, 389. **Open** 9am–5pm Mon– Fri. **Closed** public hols. ♿ 📷 11am, 1pm, 2pm & 3pm.

Originally known as the Woolloomooloo Stockade and later as Darlinghurst Gaol, this complex is now the National Art School. It was constructed over a 20-year period from 1822.

Surrounded by walls almost 7 m (23 ft) high, the cell blocks radiate from a central round-house. The jail is built of stone quarried on the site by convicts,

which was then chiselled by them into blocks.

No fewer than 67 people were executed here between 1841 and 1908. Perhaps the most notorious hangman was Alexander "The Strangler" Green, after whom Green Park, outside the jail, is thought to have been named. Green lived near the park until public hostility forced him to live in relative safety inside the jail.

Some of Australia's most noted artists, including Frank Hodgkinson, Jon Molvig and William Dobell, trained or taught at the art school which was established here in 1921.

The former Governor's house, Old Gaol, Darlinghurst

❼ Darlinghurst Court House

Forbes St, Darlinghurst. **Map** 5 A2. **Tel** 1300 679 272. 🚌 378, 380, 382. **Open** Feb–Dec: 10am–4pm Mon–Fri. **Closed** Jan, mid-Dec, public hols. ♿

Abutting the grim old gaol, to which it is connected by underground passages, and facing tawdry Taylor Square, this unlikely gem of Greek Revival architecture was begun in 1835 by colonial architect Mortimer Lewis. He was only responsible for the central block of the main building with its six-columned Doric portico with Greek embellishments. The side wings were not added until the 1880s.

The Court House is still used by the state's Supreme Court, mainly for criminal cases, and these are open to the public.

Beare Park, a quiet inner-city park with harbour views

Street-by-Street: Paddington

Paddington began to flourish in the 1840s, when the decision was made to build the Victoria Barracks. At the time much of it was "the most wild looking place… barren sandhills with patches of scrub, hills and hollows galore." The area began to fill rapidly, as owner builders bought into the area and built rows of terrace houses, many very narrow because of the lack of building regulations. After the Depression, most of the district was threatened with demolition, but was saved and restored by the large influx of postwar migrants.

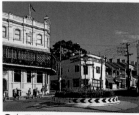

8 ★ Five Ways
This shopping hub was established in the late 19th century on the busy Glenmore roadway trodden out by bullocks.

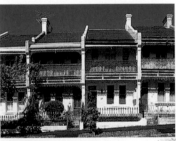

Duxford Street's terrace houses in toning pale shades constitute an ideal of town planning: the Victorians preferred houses in a row to have a pleasingly uniform aspect.

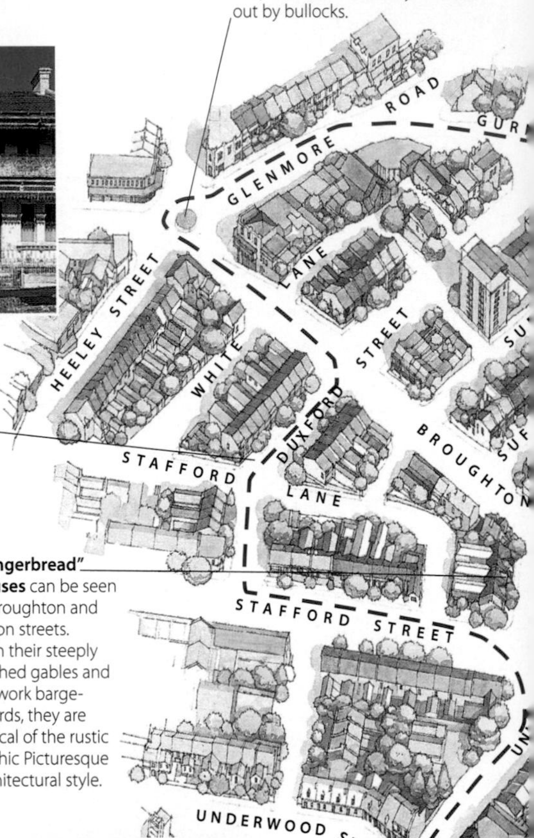

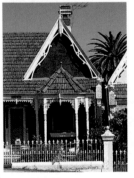

"Gingerbread" houses can be seen in Broughton and Union streets. With their steeply pitched gables and fretwork barge-boards, they are typical of the rustic Gothic Picturesque architectural style.

The London Tavern opened for business in 1875, making it the suburb's oldest pub. Like many of the pubs and delicatessens in this well-serviced suburb, it stands at the end of a row of terraces.

Key

— Suggested route

For hotels and restaurants in this area see pp482–3 and pp504–7

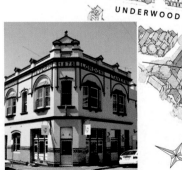

The Sherman Gallery was formerly housed in this strikingly modern building. It was designed to hold Australian and international contemporary sculpture and paintings. Suitable access gates and a special in-house crane enabled the movement of large-scale artworks, including textiles.

Locator Map
See Central Sydney map pp66–7

Paddington's streets are a treasure trove of galleries, bars and restaurants. A wander through the area should prove an enjoyable experience.

Warwick, built in the 1860s, is a minor castle lying at the end of a row of humble terraces. Its turrets, battlements and assorted decorations, in a style somewhat fancifully described as "King Arthur", even adorn the garages at the rear.

Windsor Street's terrace houses are, in some cases, a mere 4.5 m (15 ft) wide.

Street-making in Paddington's early days was often an expensive and complicated business. A cascade of water was dammed to build Cascade Street.

0 metres 50
0 yards 50

⑭ ★ Paddington Street
Under the established plane trees, some of Paddington's finest Victorian terraces exemplify the building boom of 1860–90. Over 30 years, 3,800 houses were built in the suburb.

Pretty cast-iron balcony, the typical architecture of Paddington

⑧ Five Ways

Cnr Glenmore Rd & Heeley St. **Map** 5 C3. 🚍 389.

At this picturesque intersection, where three streets cross on Glenmore Road, a shopping hub developed by the tramline that ran from the city to Bondi Beach (see p131). On the five corners stand 19th- and early 20th-century shops, one now a restaurant.

Much of the architecture in Paddington features decorative cast-iron "lacework" balconies, using mixed Victorian and Classical Revival styles. Streets lined with pretty houses make this one of Sydney's most desirable areas.

⑨ Paddington Village

Cnr Gipps & Shadforth sts. **Map** 5 C3. 🚍 378, 380, 382.

Paddington began its life as a working-class suburb of Sydney. The community mainly consisted of the carpenters, quarrymen and stonemasons who supervised the convict gangs that built the Victoria Barracks in the 1840s.

The 19th-century artisans and their families occupied a tight huddle of spartan houses crowded into the area's narrow streets. A few of these houses still remain. Like the barracks, these dwellings and surrounding shops and hotels were built of locally quarried stone.

The terraces of Paddington Village are now a popular address with young, up-and-coming Sydneysiders.

⑩ Juniper Hall

250 Oxford St. **Tel** (02) 9358 0123. **Map** 5 C3. 🚍 378, 380, 382. **Open** check website for exhibition dates. 🆆 juniperhall.com.au

The emancipist gin distiller Robert Cooper built this superb example of colonial Georgian architecture for his third wife, Sarah. He named it after the main ingredient of the gin that made his fortune.

Completed in 1824, the two-storey home is the oldest dwelling still standing in Paddington. It is probably also the largest and most extravagant house ever built in the suburb. It had to be: Cooper already had 14 children when he declared that Sarah would have the finest house in Sydney. Once resident in the new house, he subsequently fathered 14 more.

Juniper Hall was saved from demolition in the mid-1980s and has been restored. It is now home to the annual Moran Art Prize and holds exhibitions through the year.

⑪ Paddington Town Hall

Cnr Oxford St & Oatley Rd. **Map** 5 C3. 🚍 378, 380, 382. **Open** 10am–4pm Mon–Fri. **Closed** to the public except the cinema. 🆆 palacecinemas.com.au

Paddington Town Hall was completed in 1891. A design competition was won by local architect J E Kemp. The Classical Revival building still dominates the area. No longer a centre of local government, the building now houses a cinema, library and a large ballroom.

Paddington Town Hall

The archway at the Oxford Street entrance to Victoria Barracks

⑫ Victoria Barracks

Oxford St. **Map** 5 B4. **Tel** (02) 8335 5330. 🚍 378, 380, 382. Museum: **Open** 10am–1pm Thu (last adm noon), 10am–4pm first Sun of the month. 🚫 Sun. **Closed** Dec–Jan. ♿ 📷 Parade & tour: 10am Thu. 🆆 armymuseumnsw.com.au

Victoria Barracks is the largest and best-preserved group of late Georgian architecture in Australia, covering almost 12 ha (30 acres). They are widely considered to be one of the best examples of a military barracks in the world.

Designed by the colonial engineer Lieutenant Colonel George Barney, the barracks were built between 1841 and 1848 using local sandstone quarried by convict labour. Originally intended to house 800 men, they have been in continuous use ever since and still operate as a centre of military administration.

The main block is 225 m (740 ft) long and has symmetrical two-storey wings with cast-iron verandas flanking a central archway. The perimeter walls have foundations 10 m (40 ft) deep in places. A former gaol block now houses a military museum. The tour leaves sharp at 10am on Thursdays.

⑬ Paddington Markets

395 Oxford St. **Map** 6 D4. **Tel** (02) 9331 2923. 🚍 378, 380, 382. **Open** 10am–4pm Sat. **Closed** 25 Dec. ♿ See Shopping p137. 🆆 paddingtonmarkets.com.au

This market, which began in 1973 as Paddington Bazaar, takes place every Saturday, come rain or shine, in the grounds of Paddington Village Uniting Church. It is probably the most colourful in Sydney – a place to meet and be seen as much as to shop. Stallholders come from all over the world and young designers, hoping to launch their careers, display their wares. Other offerings are jewellery, pottery and other arts and crafts, as well as new and second-hand clothing. Whatever you are looking for you are more than likely to find it here.

Paddington Street terrace house

⑭ Paddington Street

Map 6 D3. 🚌 378, 380, 382.

With its huge plane trees shading the road and fine terrace houses on each side, Paddington Street is one of the oldest and loveliest of the suburb's streets.

Paddington grew rapidly as a commuter suburb in the late 19th century and most of the terraces were built for renting to Sydney's artisans. They were decorated with iron lace, Grecian-style friezes, worked parapets and cornices, pilasters and scrolls.

By the 1900s, the terraces became unfashionable and people moved out to newly emerging "garden suburbs". In the 1960s, however, their architectural appeal came to be appreciated again and the area was reborn.

Paddington Street now has a chic atmosphere where small art galleries operate out of quaint and grand shopfronts.

⑮ Centennial Park

Map 6 E5. **Tel** (02) 9339 6699.
🚌 Clovelly, Coogee, Maroubra, Bronte, Randwick, City, Bondi Beach & Bondi Junction routes, Bondi Explorer Bus.
Open permanently, but cars permitted only between sunrise and sunset. 🚻 ♿ 🅿 🚲 upon request.
🌐 centennialparklands.com.au

Entering this 220-ha (544-acre) park through one of its sandstone and wrought-iron gates, the visitor may wonder how such an extensive and idyllic place has survived so close to the centre of the city. Formerly a common, Centennial Park was dedicated "to the enjoyment of the people of New South Wales forever" in 1888 as part of the centenary of the foundation of the colony. On 1 January 1901, 100,000 people gathered here to witness the Commonwealth of Australia come into being, when the first Australian federal ministry was sworn in by the first governor-general (see p60).

The park boasts landscaped lawns, a rose garden, statues and a coordinated series of walks. Once the source of the city's water supply, the swamps are home to many species of waterbirds. Picnickers, painters, runners, cyclists, skaters and horse-riders all share this vast park. Equipment hire is available, as well as barbecues and a scenic café and restaurant. An adjacent golf course with a large driving range, and tennis courts offer even more sporting opportunities.

⑯ The Entertainment Quarter

Lang Rd, Moore Park. **Map** 5 C5.
Tel 8117 6700. 🚌 339, 355.
Open most retail shops: 10am–10pm; markets: early–3:30pm Wed & Sat.
🌐 eqmoorepark.com.au

There is a vibrant atmosphere in the Entertainment Quarter, which is located next door to the working studios that produced some very famous movies, such as *The Matrix* and *Moulin Rouge*.

There are 16 cinema screens where you can watch the latest movies, and at the La Premiere cinema you can enjoy your movie with wine and cheese, sitting on sofas. There are four live-entertainment venues which regularly feature the latest local and international acts. You can also enjoy bungy trampolining, bowling or seasonal ice-skating, and children love the play areas. There are many restaurants, cafés and bars offering a range of snacks, meals and drinks.

Every Wednesday you can savour fresh produce at the EQ Village Markets. More than 100 stalls feature regional products, with many offering free tastings. The weekend market features fresh produce on Saturday and the merchandise market, with its eclectic range of stalls, on Sunday. Shops are open until late every day, and there is a good selection of products. There is plenty of undercover parking and the Entertainment Quarter is a pleasant stroll from the Paddington end of Oxford Street.

The lush green expanse of Centennial Park

Further Afield

Beyond Sydney's inner city, around the harbour shores, are picturesque suburbs, secluded beaches and historic sights. Taronga Zoo, just a short ferry ride from the city, shelters 400 animal species. To the north is the beautiful landscape of Ku-ring-gai Chase National Park. Manly is the city's northern playground, while Bondi is its eastern counterpart. Further west at Parramatta are sites that recall and evoke the first days of European settlement.

Sights at a Glance

1. Ku-ring-gai Chase National Park
2. Manly
3. Taronga Zoo
4. Bondi Beach
5. Sydney Olympic Park
6. Parramatta

Key

▓ Central Sydney

═ Highway

═ Major road

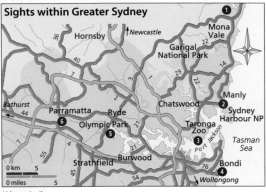

Sights within Greater Sydney

10 km = 6 miles

❶ Ku-ring-gai Chase National Park

McCarrs Creek Rd, Church Point.
ℹ Kalkari Discovery Centre (02) 9472 9300. **Open** 9am–5pm daily. **Closed** 25 Dec.

Ku-ring-gai Chase National Park lies on Sydney's northernmost outskirts, 30 km (19 miles) from the city, and covers 15,000 ha (37,000 acres). It is bounded to the north by Broken Bay, at the mouth of the Hawkesbury River, with its eroded valleys formed during the last Ice Age. Sparkling waterways and golden beaches are set against the backdrop of the national park. Picnicking, bushwalking, surfing, boating and windsurfing are popular with visitors.

The Hawkesbury River curls around an ancient sandstone landscape rich in Aboriginal rock art. The national park has literally hundreds of Aboriginal art sites, the most common being rock engravings thought to be 2,000 years old. They include whales up to 8 m (26 ft) long, sharks, wallabies and echidnas, as well as ancestral spirits.

❷ Manly

🚢 Manly. Manly Sea Life Sanctuary: West Esplanade. **Tel** 1800 199 742 or 1800 614 069. **Open** 9:30am–5pm daily. **Closed** 25 Dec. 🅿 🚻
Ⓦ **manlysealifesanctuary.com.au**

If asked to suggest a single excursion outside the city, most Sydneysiders would nominate the 11-km (7-mile) ferry ride from Circular Quay to Manly. This narrow stretch of land lying between the harbour and the ocean was named by Governor Phillip, even before the

Brass band playing on The Corso, Manly's esplanade

township of Sydney got its name, for the impressive bearing of the Aboriginal men.

To the right of Manly wharf are shops, restaurants and bars on the adjacent pier and, on the left, the tranquil harbour-side beach known as Manly Cove. **Manly Sea Life Sanctuary** is at the far end of Manly Cove, where visitors can see sharks, giant stingrays and other species in an underwater viewing tunnel. You can also dive with the sharks.

The Corso is a lively pedestrian thoroughfare that leads to Manly's ocean beach, popular with sunbathers, with its promenade lined by towering Norfolk pines.

❸ Taronga Zoo

Bradley's Head Rd, Mosman. **Tel** (02) 9969 2777. 🚢 from Circular Quay. 🚌 247 from Wynard. **Open** 9:30am–5pm daily (May–Aug: to 4:30pm). 🅿 🚻 ♿ 🚼 🛒 Ⓦ **taronga.org.au**

Taronga opened in 1916 in its idyllic harbourside location, with sweeping views across the water. It is home to 2,000 animals, and the protection and preservation of endangered creatures is at the heart of the zoo's prolific conservation programmes. Free daily presentations include a Free Flight Bird Show, while the Great Southern Ocean exhibit emulates the natural habitats of a superb range of marine life. Zoo volunteers allow visitors to view close-up and even touch some of the animals.

For hotels and restaurants in this area see pp482–3 and pp504–7

Crescent-shaped Bondi Beach, Sydney's most famous beach, looking towards North Bondi

❹ Bondi Beach

🚌 380, 382, 381.

This long crescent of golden sand has long drawn the sun and surf set (see pp148–9). The word *bondi* is Aboriginal for "water breaking over rocks". Surfers visit from far and wide in search of the perfect wave, and inline skaters hone their skills on the promenade.

People also seek out Bondi for its trendy seafront cafés and cosmopolitan milieu as much as for the world-famous beach. The pavilion, built in 1928 as changing rooms, is now a busy venue for festivals, plays, films and arts and crafts displays.

❺ Sydney Olympic Park

Sydney Olympic Park. **Tel** 9714 7888. 🚆 Olympic Park. Visitors' Centre: cnr Showground Rd & Herb Elliott Ave; **Open** 9am–5pm daily. **Closed** Good Fri, 25 Dec, 26 Dec, 1 Jan. 🚗 ♿ 🖥 ♿ 🆆 sydneyolympicpark.com.au

Once host to the 27th Summer Olympic Games and Paralympic Games, Sydney Olympic Park is situated at Homebush Bay. Visitors can buy a ticket for a guided tour of the park or the main Olympic Stadium. Bicycles can also be hired. There is a tour of the wetlands of Bicentennial Park as well as Breakfast with the Birds – breakfast after a morning

of birdwatching. All tickets for tours can be bought at the Visitors' Centre.

Other facilities include the Aquatic Centre with a waterpark, and a Tennis Centre. There is an arena that hosts concerts by major Australian and international acts.

❻ Parramatta

🚆 Parramatta. ⛴ Parramatta. 🛈 346a Church St (02) 8839 3311.

The fertile soil of this Sydney suburb resulted in its foundation as Australia's first rural settlement, celebrating its first wheat crop in 1789. **Elizabeth Farm**, dating from 1793, is the oldest surviving home in Australia. Once the home of John Macarthur, the farm played a major role in breeding merino sheep, so vital to the country's economy

(see p55). The house is now a museum, detailing the lives of its first inhabitants until 1850.

Old Government House in Parramatta Park is the oldest intact public building in Australia, built in 1799. The Doric porch, added in 1816, is attributed to Francis Greenway (see p177). A collection of early 19th-century furniture is housed inside.

St John's Cemetery on O'Connell Street is the final resting place of many of the First Fleet's settlers (see p54).

🏛 **Elizabeth Farm**
70 Alice St, Rosehill. **Tel** (02) 9635 9488. **Open** 10.30am–3.30pm Sat, Sun & school hols. **Closed** Good Fri, 25 Dec. ♿ 🏪 🗃 🖥

🏛 **Old Government House**
Parramatta Park (entry by Macquarie St). **Tel** (02) 9635 8149. **Open** daily. **Closed** Good Fri, 25 Dec. ♿ 🏪

Drawing room in Old Government House in Parramatta

GETTING AROUND SYDNEY

The best way to see the city's sights and attractions is on foot, coupled with public transport. Buses and trains serve the suburbs and outlying areas as well as the inner city. The Sydney Light Rail links the downtown area to the inner west. Passenger ferries provide a fast and scenic means of travel between the city and the many harbourside suburbs. It is wise to invest in a combined ticket that includes all modes of public transport. On Sundays, families with at least one adult and child enjoy unlimited travel on Sydney's public buses, trains, light rail and ferries for a flat fare of A$2.50 per person.

Driving in Sydney

Driving is not the ideal way to get around Sydney: the city road network is confusing, traffic is congested and parking can be expensive. If using a car, it is best to avoid the peak hours (about 7:30–9:30am and 4–7:30pm).

Overseas visitors can use their usual driving licences to drive in Sydney, but must have proof that they are simply visiting and keep the licence with them when driving.

Parking in Sydney is strictly regulated, with fines for any infringements. Vehicles can be towed away if parked illegally. Contact the **RMS's Transport Management Centre** if this happens. There are many car parks in and around the city. Also look for blue and white "P" signs or metered parking zones, many of which apply seven days a week, but it varies from council to council.

Taxis

Taxis are plentiful in the city: there are many taxi ranks and taxis are often found outside large hotels. Meters indicate the fare plus any extras, such as booking fees and waiting time. A 20 per cent tarif applies from 10pm. It is customary to round the fare up to the next dollar. A fleet of taxis caters for disabled passengers, including those in wheelchairs. Book these with any major taxi company.

Cycling in Centennial Park

Sydney by Bicycle

Cycling is permitted on all city and suburban roads, but stay in designated cycling tracks or areas with light motor traffic. Centennial Park is a popular cycling spot. Helmets are compulsory by law. Those who wish to take advantage of Sydney's undulating terrain can seek advice from **Bicycle New South Wales**. Bicycles are permitted on CityRail trains but you may have to pay an extra fare.

Walking

Take care when walking around the city. Vehicles are driven on the left. It is wise to use pedestrian crossings; there are two types. Push-button crossings are found at traffic lights. Zebra crossings are marked by yellow and black signs.

Composite Tickets

Sydney's transport is good value, particularly with one of the composite tickets available from **Sydney Buses Transit Shop**, information kiosks or railway stations.

The **Opal** card, an electronic smart-card, can be charged with as much credit as you wish and used on all forms of public transport. Paper-based Travel-Ten tickets, also available from newsagents and convenience stores, entitle you to make ten bus journeys. A MyMulti Day Pass allows one day's unlimited travel on Sydney's trains, buses, light rail and government ferries within stipulated zones, while MyMulti weekly passes allows seven days of unlimited travel. The Airport Link train requires a separate ticket.

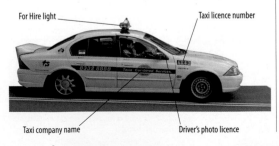
For Hire light

Taxi licence number

Taxi company name

Driver's photo licence

Travelling by Bus

Government-owned Sydney buses provide a punctual service that links up conveniently with the city's rail and ferry systems. As well as covering city and suburban areas, there are two excellent privately owned sightseeing buses – the Sydney Explorer and the Bondi Explorer. The **Transport Infoline** can advise you on routes, fares and journey times for all Sydney buses. Armed with the map printed on the inside back cover of this book and a composite ticket, you can enjoy travelling about the city without the difficulties and expense of city parking.

Using Sydney Buses

Route numbers and journey destinations are displayed on the front, back and left side of all Sydney buses. An "X" in front of the number means that it is an express bus. Buses also feature electronic displays that scroll to show the areas the bus travels through. When you see your bus approaching, raise your arm to signal to the driver that you want the bus to stop. Most buses now have stepless entries, which allow less mobile passengers and people with strollers to board with ease. Buses also have priority seating areas at the front for disabled, elderly or less mobile passengers.

Single-journey tickets can be purchased on board regular buses from the driver on routes outside the city centre. Try to have coins ready as drivers are not always able to change large notes. You will be given a ticket valid for that journey only. Buses with a "pre-pay" sign require you to buy a ticket or travel pass before you board. You must have pre-paid tickets to board buses in the city centre. These are available at main bus stops, convenience stores and news-agents. Insert pre-purchased tickets into the ticket reader when you board. If using a TravelTen ticket or TravelPass, it must also be inserted into the automatic stamping machine as you board. If sharing a TravelTen ticket, insert it into the machine once for each person travelling.

When you wish to alight, press one of the stop buttons well before the bus reaches your stop. The doors are electronic and can only be opened by the bus drivers.

Automatic stamping machine for validating composite tickets

Note that eating, drinking, smoking and playing music are prohibited on Sydney buses.

Bus stops

Bus stops are indicated by yellow and black signs displaying a profile of a bus. Below this symbol, the numbers of all buses along the route are clearly listed.

Timetables are usually found at main bus stops. They are also available from Sydney Buses Transit Shops, as well as some tourist information facilities.

Public holidays follow the Sunday timetable.

Sightseeing by Bus

Two Sydney bus services run by **Sydney Explorer**, the open-top double-decker Sydney Explorer and the Bondi Explorer, offer flexible sightseeing with commentaries. The Sydney Explorer covers a 32-km (20-mile) circuit and stops at 26 of the city's most popular attractions. The Bondi Explorer travels through a number of Sydney's eastern suburbs with eight additional stops, taking in much of the area's coastal scenery.

The red Sydney Explorer buses run daily every 15 to 20 minutes, the Bondi route every 30 to 45 minutes. The great advantage of these services is that you can explore at will, getting on and off the buses as often as you wish in the course of a day. Explorer bus stops are clearly marked. Tickets for both Explorer buses are valid for 24 or 48 hours and can be bought when boarding a bus. Tickets are also available from most hotels, information kiosks and some newsagents.

The 555 is a free shuttle bus operating in a loop between Circular Quay and Central Station along George and Elizabeth streets (9:30am–3:30pm daily; to 9pm Thu, to 6pm Sat & Sun).

Choose the sights you want to see and plan a basic itinerary; bus drivers can often advise you about the nearest stops for art galleries, museums and shops.

Sightseeing on the open-top Sydney Explorer

Travelling by Train

As well as being the key link between the city and suburbs, Sydney's railway network serves a large part of the central business district and reaches out to Newcastle to the north, Lithgow to the west, Nowra to the south and Goulburn to the southeast. Sydney Trains operates nine major suburban lines. The City Circle loop stops at Central, Town Hall, Wynyard, Circular Quay, St James and Museum stations. Most suburban lines pass through Central and Town Hall.

Pedestrian concourse outside Central
Railway Station

Finding Your Way Around Sydney Trains

The state government-owned Sydney Trains network is mainly used by commuters and covers the city and surburban Sydney. It is an efficient, economical and easy way to travel to and from the suburbs such as Parramatta. **Sydney Trains Information** has details of services and timetables.

Trains run from 4:15am until about midnight, when buses replace train services at railway stations. When using trains at night: use carriages near the train guard, marked by a blue light.

Using the Sydney Trains Route Map

Sydney Trains lines are colour-coded and route maps are displayed at all Sydney Trains stations and inside train carriages.

Note that the distances shown on the Sydney Trains map are not to the correct scale. Train stations are signposted with a white capital T in an orange circle.

Country and Inter-urban Trains

NSW Trains manages the inter-city and regional train network throughout the state. **NSW Trains Travel Centres** all over the city provide information about rail and coach services and take ticket bookings *(see their website)*.

Inter-urban trains run to a variety of areas, including the Blue Mountains *(see pp172–5)*, Wollongong *(see p190)* and Newcastle *(see p177)*.

Using the Sydney Light Rail

The **Sydney Light Rail** network provides convenient access to some of the most popular areas at the southern end of the city,

(see pp172–5), Wollongong *(see p190)* and Newcastle *(see p177)*.

including Paddy's Markets, Chinatown, Darling Harbour and the Sydney Fish Market.

Services are frequent – every 10–15 minutes during the day and every 30 minutes at night. A service linking Central Station and The Star casino operates 24 hours a day, every day. Services to stations beyond The Star run from 6am until 11pm daily, with extended hours on Fridays and Saturdays.

Tickets are available from the conductor on board. Return tickets for same-day travel are significantly cheaper than two single-journey tickets. Unlimited Light Rail travel is also included in the MyMulti pass *(see p132)*; however, note that this pass cannot be purchased on board.

DIRECTORY

Sydney Light Rail

Tel 131500.
W transportnsw.info

NSW Trains Travel Centre

Central Railway Station
Sydney Terminal. **Map** 4 E5.
Tel 131500. W transportnsw.info

Sydney Trains Information

Central Railway Station
Map 4 E5. **Tel** 131500.

Circular Quay Railway Station
Map 1 B3. **Tel** (02) 9224 3553.
W transportnsw.info

The Sydney Light Rail

The Sydney Light Rail is designed to link Central Railway Station with Glebe and the inner west, via Darling Harbour. These efficient and environmentally friendly trains offer a quicker and quieter means of travelling around parts of the city. Light Rail stations are indicated by a white capital L in a red circle.

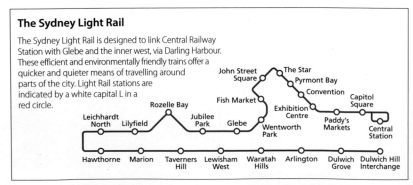

Travelling by Ferry and Water Taxi

For more than a century, Sydney ferries have been a picturesque, as well as a practical, feature of the Sydney scene. Today, they are as popular as ever. Travelling by ferry is both a pleasure and an efficient way to journey between Sydney's various harbour suburbs. Sightseeing cruises are operated by various private companies as well as by Sydney Ferries Corporation. Water taxis can be a convenient and fast alternative, although they are more expensive.

Sydney ferries coming and going at Circular Quay Ferry Terminal

A water taxi on Sydney Harbour

Water taxis

Small, fast taxi boats are available for hire to carry passengers around the harbour. You can flag them down like normal road cabs. Try King Street Wharf or Circular Quay, near the Overseas Passenger Terminal.

Water taxis will pick up and drop off passengers at any navigable pier. However, they are not cheap. Rates vary, depending on the distance. A short trip such as Darling Harbour to Circular Quay costs about $70 for four people, and $10 for each additional passenger.

Using Sydney's Ferries

There is a steady procession of Sydney Ferries traversing the harbour every day between 6am and midnight. They service most of Sydney Harbour, Manly and also several stops along the Parramatta River.

Ferry services are operated by Harbour City Ferries. For queries, information and timetables, call or visit the website of **Transport NSW**.

All ferry journeys start or end at the Circular Quay Ferry Terminal. Electronic destination boards at the entrance to each wharf indicate the wharf from which your ferry will leave. They also give departure times and list all the stops made en route. Tickets and TravelPasses can be bought from the ticket booths that are located on each wharf. On some ferries, tickets can be purchased on board.

Manly's ferry terminal is serviced both by regular ferries and a fast ferry service which operates during peak hours from Monday to Friday. Tickets and information can be obtained from the ticket windows in the centre of the terminal.

Sightseeing by Ferry

Sydney Ferries' extensive network offers an affordable alternative to commercial harbour cruises. Although there is no commentary, a ferry trip is a very cost-effective and pleasant way to experience Sydney Harbour. You can also travel between destinations for on-shore excursions to places such as Circular Quay, Darling Harbour, Taronga Zoo and Luna Park at Milson's Point.

The **itoursntix** provides bookings and information on all river and harbour cruises from Circular Quay and Darling Harbour.

DIRECTORY

Ferry Companies

itoursntix
Wharf 6, Circular Quay;
Harbourside Shopping Centre,
Darling Harbour.
Map 1 B3, 3 C2.
Tel (02) 9263 1100 or 1800 355 537. W itoursntix.com

Transport NSW
Tel 131500.
W transportnsw.info

Water Taxi Companies

Water Taxis Combined
Tel (02) 9555 8888.
W watertaxis.com.au

Yellow Water Taxis
Tel (02) 9299 0199.
W yellowwatertaxis.com.au

Electronic destination board for all ferries leaving Circular Quay

SHOPPING IN SYDNEY

For most travellers, shopping can be as much of a voyage of discovery as sightseeing. The variety of shops in Sydney is wide and the quality of goods is high. The city has two good quality department stores, many elegant arcades and shopping galleries, as well as several popular weekly and monthly markets. The range of merchandise available is vast and local talent is promoted. Nor does the most interesting shopping stop at the city centre; there are several "satellite" alternatives within close proximity.

A jumble of bric-a-brac in a typical Sydney junk shop

Shopping Hours

Most shops are open from 9am to 5:30pm every day, though some may close early on Saturdays and Sundays. High-end boutiques open from 10am to 6pm. On Thursdays, most shops stay open until 9pm. Most shops in Chinatown are open late every evening and on Sundays.

How to Pay

Major credit cards are accepted almost everywhere. You will need identification, such as a passport or driver's licence, when using traveller's cheques. Department stores will exchange goods or refund your money if you are not satisfied, provided you have kept your receipt. Other stores will only refund if an item is faulty or not as described. There is also a 10 per cent Goods and Services Tax (GST) which is included in the marked price and the amount indicated separately on the receipt.

Sales

Many shops conduct sales all year round. The big department stores of **David Jones** and **Myer** have two gigantic and chaotic clearance sales every year. The post-Christmas sales start on 26 December and last into January. The other major sale time starts in June in the lead up to the end of the financial year.

Tax-free Sales

Duty-free shops are found in the centre of the city as well as at Kingsford Smith Airport (see p554). You can save 10 per cent on goods such as perfume, jewellery and watches, and up to 30 per cent on alcohol at duty-free shops but you must show your passport and onward ticket. Some stores will also deliver your goods to the airport to be picked up on departure. Duty-free items must be kept in their sealed bags until you leave the city.

You can claim back the GST paid on most goods, purchased for (or in a single transaction of) A$300 or more, at the airport.

Chifley Tower, with the Chifley Plaza shopping arcade at its base

Arcades and Malls

Arcades and shopping malls in Sydney range from the ornately Victorian to modern marble and glass. The Queen Victoria Building (see p94) is Sydney's most palatial shopping space. Four levels contain more than 200 shops.

The elegant Strand Arcade (see p94) was originally built in 1892. Jewellery, lingerie, high fashion, antiques and fine cafés are its stock in trade.

Pitt Street Mall has several shopping centres including **MidCity** and **Westfield Sydney**, the city's largest mall, featuring department, up-market and speciality stores.

Next door to the Hilton, **The Galeries** houses the fantastic Kinokuniya bookstore, which sells Australian and American imprints, as well as Chinese and Japanese language books.

Both the **MLC Centre** and nearby **Chifley Plaza** cater to

Gleebooks, popular with students and Glebe locals (see pp138–9)

the prestige shopper. Gucci, Cartier and Tiffany & Co. are just some of the shops found in this area.

Harbourside Shopping Centre has dozens of shops selling articles of fine art, jewellery and Australiana, along with a range of waterfront restaurants.

Further afield, the **Westfield Bondi Junction** complex is only a 15-minute train ride from the centre of Sydney. It offers more than 440 stores, as well as bars, restaurants and an 11-screen cinema. The only problem is having the time and energy to make your way through this large centre, which can be filled with local shoppers on a wet weekend.

Best of the Department Stores

The spring floral displays and Christmas windows at **David Jones** are legendary, as is the luxurious perfumery and cosmetics hall on the ground floor. The store spreads out in two buildings, across the road from each other on Market and Elizabeth streets. The food hall is famous for its gourmet fare and fine wines. **Myer** has a ground floor packed with makeup and accessories, including a large MAC counter. Both stores sell women's clothing, lingerie, menswear, baby goods, children's clothes, toys, stationery, kitchenware, furniture, china, crystal and silver.

Part of the spring floral display in David Jones department store

Canopy over the harbourside Rocks Market

Markets

Scouring markets for the cheap, the cheerful and the unusual has become a popular pastime in Sydney.

Balmain Market, held each Saturday, includes a food hall selling Japanese, Thai and Indian dishes. The **Bondi Beach Market** on Sundays is known for its trendy second-hand clothing. The Saturday **Glebe Market** is a treasure-trove for the junk shop enthusiast and canny scavenger. The market is bright and popular with the inner-city grunge set.

The Rocks Market, held all weekend under a canopy, has around 140 stalls. Posters, lace, stained glass and leather are among the goods. You can watch a sculptor making art out of stone or have your portrait sketched in charcoal.

Sydney Fish Market is the place to go for fresh seafood. You can choose from more than 100 species, both live and prepared. Above the market, the Sydney Seafood School offers lessons in preparing and serving seafood. **The Sydney Morning Herald Growers' Market** sells everything you need for a gourmet feast, and is where you will find native Australian bushfoods, such as lemon myrtle linguini, dried bush tomatoes, nutty wattleseed and pepperberries.

The Growers Market is held on the first Saturday of the month (except January) and hosts additional events during October's Good Food Month.

Other good markets are Paddy's Markets (*see p103*), Fox Studio Markets and Paddington Markets (*see p128–9*).

(see p103), (see p128–9)

DIRECTORY

Arcades and Malls

Chifley Plaza
2 Chifley Square. **Map** 1 B4.
Tel (02) 9229 0165.
W chifleyplaza.com.au

The Galeries
2 Park St (cnr St George St).
Map 4 E2. **Tel** (02) 9265 6888.
W thegaleries.com

Harbourside Shopping Centre
Darling Harbour. **Map** 3 C2.
Tel (02) 8204 1888.
W harbourside.com.au

MidCity
Pitt St Mall. **Map** 4 E2.
Tel (02) 9210 4242.
W midcityshopping.com.au

MLC Centre
19–29 Martin Place. **Map** 1 B4.
Tel (02) 9224 8333.
W mlccentre.com.au

Westfield
500 Oxford St, Bondi Junction.
Tel (02) 9947 8000;
Cnr Pitt St & Market St, Sydney.
Tel (02) 8236 9200. **Map** 4 E2.

Department Stores

David Jones
Cnr Market & Castlereagh sts.
Map 1 B5. **Tel** (02) 9266 5544.
W davidjones.com.au

Myer
436 George St. **Map** 1 B5.
Tel (02) 9238 9111.
W myer.com.au

Markets

Balmain Market
Cnr Darling St & Curtis Rd, Balmain.

Bondi Beach Market
Bondi Beach Public School,
Campbell Parade, North Bondi.

Glebe Market
Glebe Public School, Glebe Point Rd, Glebe. **Map** 3 B5.

Paddy's Markets
Cnr Hay & Thomas Sts. **Map** 4 D4.
W paddysmarkets.com.au

Sydney Fish Market
Cnr Pyrmont Bridge Rd & Bank St,
Blackwattle Bay. **Map** 3 B2.

The Sydney Morning Herald Growers' Market
Pyrmont Bay Park. **Map** 3 C1.

The Rocks Market
George St, The Rocks. **Map** 1 B2.

Specialist Shopping in Sydney

Sydney offers an extensive range of gift and souvenir ideas, from unset opals and jewellery to Aboriginal art and hand-crafted souvenirs. Museum shops, such as at the Museum of Sydney (see p96) and the Art Gallery of NSW (see pp114–17), often have specially commissioned items that make great presents or reminders of your visit.

One-offs

Specialist shops abound in Sydney – some practical, some eccentric, others simply indulgent. **Wheels & Doll Baby** designs clothes that mix 1950s chic, rock'n'roll and Hollywood glamour. **The Hour Glass** stocks traditional watches, while **R.M. Williams** offers classic stockman's gear including boots, belts, clothes and accessories. Design concept store **Follow** has a selection of products created by Australian designers, including prints, jewellery, clothing, textiles and homewares

Napoleon Perdis Cosmetics sells a huge array of make-up and bears the name of Australia's leading "make-up artist to the stars".

For antiques and quirky artisan homewares, try **Elements I Love**.

Australiana

Australiana has become more than just a souvenir genre; it is now an art form in itself.

The **Ken Done Gallery** has distinctive prints by artist Ken Done on a selection of posters, prints, scarves and books at his small gallery story. **Australian Geographic** sells educational games and toys. Its Indigenous and Aussie Style ranges celebrate all that is Australian, from Aboriginal tools and art to books displaying the unique flora and fauna. The **Art Gallery of NSW** store stocks a wide range of Australian art books, prints, posters and giftware. The Queen Victoria Building (see p94) is dominated by shops selling Australiana: souvenirs, antiques, art and crafts.

The small shop at the Australian Museum (see pp98–9) sells slightly unusual gift items, such as native flower presses, bark paintings and Australian animal puppets, puzzles and games, as well as a collection of jewellery made from Australian minerals and products featuring Aboriginal designs.

Books

The large chain **Dymocks** has a good range of guide books and maps on Sydney. For more eclectic browsing, try **Abbey's Bookshop**, **Ariel** and **Gleebooks**, while **Berkelouw Books** has three floors of new, second-hand and rare books. **The Bookshop Darlinghurst** specializes in gay and lesbian fiction and non-fiction. The State Library of NSW (see p113) bookshop has a good choice of Australian books, particularly on history.

Music

Several specialist music shops of international repute can be found in Sydney. **Red Eye Records** is for the streetwise, with its collectables, rarities, alternative music and concert tickets. **Mojo Record Bar** sells vinyl records at the front and drinks out the back in its themed small bar space. **Birdland** has a good stock of blues, jazz, soul and avant-garde. **The Recordstore** specializes in vinyl records of many styles, including breakbeat, drum 'n' bass, dubstep and hip hop. **Waterfront** specializes in world and left-of-centre music, and **Utopia Records** in hard rock and heavy metal. Australia's largest classical and jazz music specialist, **Fish Fine Music**, is found in the QVB.

Aboriginal Art

Traditional paintings, fabric, jewellery, boomerangs, carvings and cards can be bought at the

Aboriginal and Pacific Art. You can find tribal artifacts from Aboriginal Australia at several shops in the Harbourside Shopping Centre, Darling Harbour. The **Coo-ee Aboriginal Art Gallery** boasts a large selection of limited edition prints, hand-printed fabrics, books and Aboriginal music.

The **Kate Owen Gallery** features three large floors of Aboriginal art, with friendly, knowledgeable staff who are happy to share their expertise. Works by urban indigenous artists can be found at the **Boomalli Aboriginal Artists' Cooperative**.

Opals

Sydney offers a variety of opals in myriad settings. **Flame Opals** is a family run store, selling stones from all the major Australian opal fields. At **Opal Fields** you can view a museum collection of opalized fossils, before buying from the wide range of gems. **Giulian's** has unset opals, including blacks from Lightning Ridge, whites from Coober Pedy and boulder opals from Quilpie.

Jewellery

Long-established Sydney jewellers with 24-carat reputations include **Fairfax & Roberts** and **Hardy Brothers**. World-class pearls are found in the waters off the northwestern coast of Australia. Rare and beautiful examples can be found at **Paspaley Pearls**.

The Family Jewels has been attracting jewellery buyers to its Paddington store since the 1980s. **Dinosaur Designs** made its name with colourful, chunky resin jewellery, while at **Love & Hatred**, jewelled wrist cuffs, rings and crosses recall lush medieval treasures.

Jan Logan is an iconic Australian jewellery designer, with stores in Melbourne, Hong Kong and London, as well as Sydney. Choose from beautiful and unusual contemporary pieces, otherwise the shop also carries antiques.

DIRECTORY

One-offs

Elements I Love
124 James St, Leichhardt.
Map 5 B3. **Tel** 9560 3867.

Follow
380 Cleveland St,
Surry Hills.
Map 5 A5.
Tel 8068 2813.

The Hour Glass
142 King St.
Map 1 B5.
Tel 9221 2288.

**Napoleon Perdis
Cosmetics**
74 Oxford St, Paddington.
Tel 9331 1702.
Map 5 A2.
W napoleoncosmetics.
com

R.M. Williams
Level 3, Westfield Sydney,
Pitt St. **Map** 4 E2.
Tel 8246 9136.

Wheels & Doll Baby
259 Crown St,
Darlinghurst.
Map 5 A2.
Tel 9361 3286.

Australiana

Art Gallery of NSW
Art Gallery Road,
The Domain.
Map 2 D4.
Tel 9225 1700.

**Australian
Geographic**
Shop 1001, Westfield
Bondi Junction.
Tel 9257 0060.

Ken Done Gallery
Level 2, 1 Hickson Rd.
Map 1 B2.
Tel 8274 4599.
W kendone.com.au

Books

Abbey's Bookshop
131 York St.
Map 1 A5.
Tel 9264 3111.

Ariel
42 Oxford St,
Paddington.
Map 5 B3.
Tel 9332 4581.

Berkelouw Books
19 Oxford St, Paddington.
Map 5 B3.
Tel 9360 3200.
Also at: 70 Norton St,
Leichhardt.
Tel 9560 3200.
W berkelouw.com.au

**The Bookshop
Darlinghurst**
207 Oxford St,
Darlinghurst.
Map 5 A2.
Tel 9331 1103.

Dymocks
424 George St.
Map 1 B5.
Tel 9235 0155.
One of many branches.

Gleebooks
49 Glebe Point Rd, Glebe.
Map 3 B5.
Tel 9660 2333.

Music

Birdland
Level 4, 428 George St.
Map 1 B4.
Tel 9231 1188.

Fish Fine Music
Level 2, Queen Victoria
Building.
Map 1 B5.
Tel 9264 6458.

Mojo Record Bar
Basement Level,
73 York St.
Map 1 A4.
Tel 9262 4999.

The Recordstore

255B Crown St,
Darlinghurst.
Map 5 A2.
Tel 9380 8223.

Red Eye Records
143 York St.
Map 1 A5.
Tel 9267 7440.

Utopia Records
Lower Ground Floor,
511 Kent St.
Map 1 A5.
Tel 9571 6662.

Waterfront
Online sales only.
Tel 9283 9301.
W waterfrontrecords.
com

Aboriginal Art

**Aboriginal and
Pacific Art**
2 Danks St,
Waterloo.
Tel 9699 2211.

**Boomalli Aboriginal
Artists' Cooperative**
55–59 Flood St,
Leichhardt.
Tel 9560 2541.

**Coo-ee Aboriginal
Art Gallery**
31 Lamrock Ave,
Bondi Beach.
Tel 9300 9233.

Kate Owen Gallery
680 Darling St,
Rozelle.
Tel 9555 5283.

Opals

Flame Opals
119 George Street,
The Rocks.
Map 1 B2.
Tel 9247 3446.

Giulian's
98 Harrington St.
Map 1 B3.
Tel 9247 5360.

Opal Fields

119 George St,
The Rocks.
Map 1 B3.
Tel 9247 6800.
One of two branches.

Jewellery

Dinosaur Designs
Level 1,
Strand Arcade.
Map 1 B5.
Tel 9223 2953.
One of two branches.

Fairfax & Roberts
44 Martin Place.
Map 1 B4.
Tel 9232 8511.

The Family Jewels
48 Oxford St,
Paddington.
Map 5 B3.
Tel 9331 6647.

Hardy Brothers
60 Castlereagh St.
Map 1 B5.
Tel 8262 3100.

Jan Logan
36 Cross St,
Double Bay.
Tel 9363 2529.

Love & Hatred
Strand Arcade.
Map 1 B5.
Tel 9233 3441.

Paspaley Pearls
2 Martin Place.
Map 1 B4.
Tel 9232 7633.

Clothes and Accessories

Australian style was once an oxymoron. Sydney now offers a plethora of chic shops as long as you know where to look. Top boutiques sell both men's and women's clothing, as well as accessories. The city's "smart casual" ethos, particularly in summer, means there are plenty of luxe but informal clothes available.

Australian Fashion

A number of Sydney's fashion designers have attained a global profile, including **Alex Perry** and **Akira Isogawa**. Perry's glamorous and breathtaking creations are often seen on the red carpet.

Young jeans labels such as **Sass & Bide** (women only) have also shot to fame, with celebrities wearing their denims. Nearby is **Scanlan & Theodore**, a stalwart of the Australian fashion scene.

Other shops are **Dragstar**, with its selection of retro women's and children's clothing, such as bright sundresses and minis. The quirky **Capital L** boutique houses the hottest names in Aussie fashion, while **Zimmermann** offers women's and girls' clothes and is famous for its swimwear. **Camilla** is the place to go for Camilla Frank's vibrant, playful and luxurious free-flowing designs. Head to **Farage Women** for tailored business wear.

High-street clothing can be found in and around Pitt Street Mall and Bondi Junction. Here you will find both international and homegrown fashion outlets. **Sportsgirl** sells funky clothes that appeal to both teens and adult women. The **Witchery** stores are a favourite among women for their stylish designs, as is **Country Road**, known for its classically tailored work and weekend wear. **Just Jeans** doesn't just sell jeans; it stocks the latest trends for men and women.

General Pants has funky street labels such as One Teaspoon and Just Ask Amanda. Surry Hills is the place for discount and vintage clothing; check out **Zoo Emporium**. New designers try out their wares in Bondi, Glebe and Paddington markets (see p137).

International Labels

Many Sydney stores sell designer imports. For the best ranges, visit **The Corner Shop**, an eclectic boutique that stocks a carefully chosen selection of clothing and accessories from emerging fashion names. In **Robby Ingham Stores** you will find women's and men's ranges including Chloé, Paul Smith and Comme des Garçons. **Cosmopolitan Shoes** stocks labels such as Dolce & Gabbana, Sonia Rykiel, Dior and Jimmy Choo. **Hype DC** also offers all the latest ranges. The designs of Vietnamese-born stylist **Alistair Trung** are inspired by architecture and urban zen. For stylish shoes, try **Varese** in Chifley Plaza.

Luxury Brands

Many visitors like to shop for international labels such as **Gucci** and **Prada**. You will find both in Westfield Sydney, with **Chanel** in nearby Castlereagh Street and **Versace** in Chifley Plaza. The Queen Victoria Building (see p94) is home to **Bally**, and Martin Place has resident designer A-listers such as **Armani**, while **Louis Vuitton** is just around the corner. **Girls with Gems** is further afield in Double Bay.

Surf Shops

For the latest surf gear, head to Bondi, where the streets are lined with shops selling clothing, swimwear as well as boards of all sizes to buy and hire. Surfers and novices should check out **Between the Flags** for boards, as well as **Bondi Surf Co**. Besides selling its own beachwear label, **Rip Curl** also sells Australian brands such as Tigerlily and Billabong. **Surfection** and **The Big Swim** are popular surf and swimwear shops packed with bikinis and the latest performance brands and accessories.

Clothes for Children

Department stores, **David Jones** and **Myer** (see p137), are one-stop shops for children's clothes, from newborn to teenage.

Size Chart

Women's clothes

Australian	6	8	10	12	14	16	18	20
American	4	6	8	10	12	14	16	18
British	6	8	10	12	14	16	18	20
Continental	38	40	42	44	46	48	50	52

Women's shoes

Australian	6–6$\frac{1}{2}$	7	7$\frac{1}{2}$–8	8$\frac{1}{2}$	9–9$\frac{1}{2}$	10	10$\frac{1}{2}$–11	
American	5	6	7	8	9	10	11	
British	3	4	5	6	7	8	9	
Continental	36	37	38	39	40	41	42	

Men's suits

Australian	44	46	48	50	52	54	56	58
American	34	36	38	40	42	44	46	48
British	34	36	38	40	42	44	46	48
Continental	44	46	48	50	52	54	56	58

Men's shirts

Australian	44	38	39	41	42	43	44	45
American	34	15	15$\frac{1}{2}$	16	16$\frac{1}{2}$	17	17$\frac{1}{2}$	18
British	34	15	15$\frac{1}{2}$	16	16$\frac{1}{2}$	17	17$\frac{1}{2}$	18
Continental	44	38	39	41	42	43	44	45

Men's shoes

Australian	7	7$\frac{1}{2}$	8	8$\frac{1}{2}$	9	10	11	12
American	7	7$\frac{1}{2}$	8	8$\frac{1}{2}$	9$\frac{1}{2}$	10$\frac{1}{2}$	11	11$\frac{1}{2}$
British	6	7	7$\frac{1}{2}$	8	9	10	11	12
Continental	39	40	41	42	43	44	45	46

Look out for good quality Australian labels such as Fred Bare and Gumboots. Mambo, Dragstar and Zimmermann also sell fun and unusual kidswear.

Accessories

The team behind **Dinosaur Designs** are some of Australia's most celebrated designers. They craft chunky bangles, necklaces and rings, and also bowls, plates and vases, from jewel-coloured resin. **Chilli Coral**, sells home decor and gifts including Australian-made Samantha Ronson bowls, Bison tableware, vintage bottles and handmade jewellery. At the **Art Gallery of NSW** (see p138) you can find brooches and bags featuring designs by Australian artists such as Brett Whiteley. In her plush store, **Jan Logan** sells exquisite jewellery, using all kinds of precious and semi-precious stones.

Australian hat designer **Helen Kaminski** uses fabrics, raffia, straw, felt and leather to make hats and bags. In a different style altogether, **Crumpler** use high-tech fabrics to make bags that will last a century. **Andrew McDonald**'s little studio shop in the beautiful Strand Arcade brings to life handcrafted shoes for men and women.

DIRECTORY

Australian Fashion

Akira Isogawa
12A Queen St, Woollahra.
Map 6 E4. **Tel** 9361 5221.

Alex Perry
Level 2, Strand Arcade.
Map 1 B5. **Tel** 9233 6555.

Camilla Boutique
132a Warners Ave, Bondi.
Tel 9130 1430.

Capital L
100 Oxford St,
Paddington. **Map** 5 B3.
Tel 9361 0111.

Country Road
Ground level, Queen
Victoria Building. **Map** 1 B5.
Tel 9261 2009.

Dragstar
535A King St, Newtown.
Map 1 B4. **Tel** 9550 1243.

Farage Women
Shops 54, Level 1 Strand
Arcade. **Map** 1 B5.
Tel 9233 1272.

General Pants
Ground level, Mid City
Shopping St, Pitt St Mall.
Map 4 E1. **Tel** 8275 5111.

Just Jeans
Ground Floor, Sydney
Westfield. **Map** 1 B5.
Tel 9231 2297.

Sass & Bide
132 Oxford St,
Paddington. **Map** 5 B3.
Tel 9360 3900.

Scanlan & Theodore
122 Oxford St,
Paddington. **Map** 5 B3.
Tel 9380 9388.

Sportsgirl
Street level, Westfield
Sydney, 188 Pitt St.
Map 1 B5. **Tel** 9223 8255.

Witchery
Shop 3, Met Centre, 273
George St. **Map** 1 B4.
Tel 9252 8450.

Zimmermann
2–16 Glenmore Rd,
Paddington. **Map** 5 B3.
Tel 9357 4700.

Zoo Emporium
180B Campbell St, Surry
Hills. **Tel** 9380 5990.

International Labels

Alistair Trung
128A Oxford St, Padding-
ton. **Map** 5 B3. **Tel** 9360
2288.

The Corner Shop
43 William St, Paddington.
Map 6 D3. **Tel** 9380 9828.

Cosmopolitan Shoes
Cosmopolitan Centre,
Knox St, Double Bay.
Tel 9362 0510.

Hype DC
Shop 50, Queen Victoria
Building. **Map** 1 B5.
Tel 9262 7444.

Robby Ingham Stores
424–426 Oxford St,
Paddington. **Map** 6 D4.
Tel 9332 2124.

Varese
Shop 19, Chifley Plaza,
Chifley Square. **Map** 1 B4.
Tel 9233 7477.

Luxury Brands

Armani
4 Martin Place. **Map** 1 B4.
Tel 8233 5888.

Bally
Ground floor, Queen
Victoria Building.
Map 1 B5. **Tel** 9267 3887.

Chanel
70 Castlereagh St.
Map 1 B5.
Tel 9233 4800.

Girls With Gems
Shop 15, 28–34 Cross St,
Double Bay. **Tel** 0413
488 823.

Gucci
Level 3, Westfield
Sydney. **Map** 1 B5.
Tel 8223 8222.

Louis Vuitton
365 George St. **Map** 1 B5.
Tel 1300 883 880.

Prada
Level 3, Westfield Sydney.
Map 1 B5. **Tel** 9231 3929.

Versace
Level 1, Queen Victoria
Building. **Map** 1 B5.
Tel 9267 6053.

Surf Shops

Between the Flags
1520158 Campbell
Parade, Bondi Beach.
Tel 9365 5611.

The Big Swim
74 Campbell Parade,
Bondi Beach.
Tel 9130 1511.

Bondi Surf Co.
80 Campbell Parade,
Bondi Beach.
Tel 9365 0870.

Rip Curl
82 Campbell Parade,
Bondi Beach.
Tel 9130 2660.

Surfection
31 Hall St, Bondi Beach.
Tel 9130 1051.

Clothes for Children

David Jones
Cnr Elizabeth & Market sts.
Map 1 B5.
Tel 9266 5544.

Myer
436 George St.
Map 1 B5.
Tel 9238 9111.

Accessories

Andrew McDonald
2nd Floor, Strand Arcade.
Map 1 B5.
Tel 8084 2595.

Art Gallery of NSW
Art Gallery Rd,
The Domain. **Map** 2 D4.
Tel 9225 1700.

Chilli Coral
401 Crown St, Surry Hills.
Map 5 A3. **Tel** 8021 7869.

Crumpler
Ground floor, Strand
Arcade. **Map** 1 B5.
Tel 9222 1300.

Dinosaur Designs
See pp138–9.

Helen Kaminski
Shop 3, Four Seasons
Hotel, 199 George St.
Map 1 B3.
Tel 9251 9850.

Jan Logan
36 Cross St, Double Bay.
Tel 9363 2529.

ENTERTAINMENT IN SYDNEY

Sydney has the standard of entertainment and nightlife you would expect from a cosmopolitan city. Everything from opera and ballet at Sydney Opera House to Shakespeare productions in the Royal Botanic Gardens is on offer. Venues such as the Capitol, the Lyric Theatre and the Theatre Royal play host to the latest musicals, while Sydney's many smaller theatres are home to interesting fringe theatre, modern dance and rock and pop concerts. Pub rock thrives in the inner city and beyond; and there are many nightspots for jazz, dance and alternative music. Movie buffs are well catered for with film festivals, art-house films and foreign titles, as well as the latest Hollywood blockbusters. One of the features of harbourside living is the free outdoor entertainment, which is very popular with children.

The Sydney Theatre on Hickson Road, Walsh Bay

Information

For details of events in the city, check the daily newspapers first. They carry cinema, and often arts and theatre, advertisements daily. The most comprehensive listings appear in the *Sydney Morning Herald's* entertainment guide every Friday. The *Daily Telegraph* has a daily gig guide, with opportunities to win free tickets to special events. The *Australian's* main arts pages appear on Fridays, and all the papers review new films in weekend editions.

Tourism NSW information kiosks have free guides and the quarterly *What's on in Darling Harbour*. Kiosks are found at Town Hall, Circular Quay and Martin Place. *Where Magazine* is available at the airport and the **Sydney Visitor Centre** at The Rocks. Hotels also offer free guides, or try whatson.cityofsydney.nsw. gov.au or timeout.com/sydney.

Music fans are well served by the free online guides including www.themusic.com.au, www. thebrag.com.au and www. inthemix.com.au found at video and music shops, pubs and clubs. Many venues have leaflets about forthcoming attractions, while the major venues have information telephone lines and websites.

Buying Tickets

Some of the most popular operas, shows, plays and ballets in Sydney are sold out months in advance. While it is better to book ahead, many theatres set aside tickets to be sold at the door on the night.

You can buy tickets from the box office, online or by telephone. Some orchestral performances do not admit children under seven, so check with the box office before buying. If you make a phone booking using a credit card, the tickets can be mailed to you. Online purchases can be sent as mobile tickets to a phone, or emailed to print yourself. Tickets can also be collected from the box office half an hour before the show. The major agencies will take overseas bookings.

Buying tickets from touts is not advisable, as you could be denied access to the event. If all else fails, hotel concierges have a reputation for being able to secure hard-to-get seats.

Choosing Seats

If booking online, you will be able to look at a seating plan and choose your seat. In Sydney, there is not as much difference in price between stalls and dress circle as in other cities. If booking by phone with one of the agencies, the computer will select the "best" tickets available at the time. You can't select your seat, but you can choose a price or seating category if there are different categories of tickets. This is important if an event has both general admission floor tickets (you will be standing) and reserved seating.

The annual Gay and Lesbian Mardi Gras Festival's dog show *(see p46)*

Booking Agencies

Sydney has two main ticket agencies: **Ticketek** and **Ticketmaster**. Between them, they represent all the major entertainment and sporting events. The quickest and easiest way to check ticket availability and book is via the agencies websites. Phone and in person bookings often involve waiting in long queues and give you less flexibility in comparing availability for different dates and choosing seats. Ticketek has more than 60 outlets throughout NSW and the ACT. Opening hours vary between agencies and call centres, so check with Ticketek to confirm. Phone bookings: 8.30am–10pm, Monday to Saturday, and 8:30am–5pm Sunday. For Internet bookings, visit their website.

Ticketmaster outlets are open 9am–5pm Monday to Friday. Phone bookings: 9am–9pm Monday to Saturday and 10am–5pm Sunday. Agencies accept cash, Visa, MasterCard and Amex. Some agencies do not accept Diners Club. Booking fees apply per ticket and a service and delivery fee applies per transaction (even if tickets are sent electronically). There are no refunds (unless a show is cancelled) or exchanges.

Discount Tickets and Free Entertainment

Tuesday is budget-price day at most cinemas. Some independent cinemas have special prices on other days. The Sydney Symphony Orchestra and Opera Australia *(see p144)* offer a special Student Rush price to full-time students under 28 but only if surplus tickets are available. These can be bought on the day of the performance, from the box office at the venue.

Outdoor events are especially popular in Sydney, and many are free *(see pp11–7)*. Sydney Harbour is a splendid setting for the New Year's Eve fireworks, with a display at 9pm for families as well as the midnight display. The Sydney Festival in January is a huge

The Spanish firedancers *Els Comediants* at the Sydney Festival

extravaganza of performance and visual art. Various outdoor venues in the Rocks, Darling Harbour and in front of the **Sydney Opera House** *(see pp88–9)* feature events to suit every taste, including musical productions, drama, dance, exhibitions and circuses. The most popular free events are the symphony and opera concerts held in the Domain. Also popular are the Darling Harbour Hoopla Circus and Street Theatre Festival at Easter, and the food and wine festival held in the first weekend of June at Manly.

A busker at Circular Quay

Disabled Visitors

Many older venues were not designed with the disabled visitor in mind, but this has been redressed in most newer buildings. It is best to phone the box office beforehand to request special seating and other needs

or call **Ideas Inc**, who have a list of Sydney's most wheelchair-friendly venues. The Sydney Opera House has disabled parking, wheelchair access and a loop system in the Concert Hall for the hearing impaired. The website of **Easy Access Australia**, is another source of information for seniors and people with disabilities.

DIRECTORY

Useful Numbers

Easy Access Australia
W easyaccessaustralia.com.au

Ideas Inc
Tel 1800 029 904.
W ideas.org.au

Sydney Opera House
Information Desk
Tel (02) 9250 7111.
Disabled Parking Information
Tel (02) 9250 7185.

Sydney Visitor Centre
Tel 8273 0000 or 9281 2244.
W sydney.com

Tourism NSW
W visitnsw.com

Ticket Agencies

Ticketek
Tel 13 28 49.
W ticketek.com.au

Ticketmaster
Tel 136 100.
W ticketmaster.com.au

Publicity shot of the Australian Chamber Orchestra *(see p144)*

Performing Arts and Cinema

Sydney has a wealth of orchestral, choral, chamber and contemporary music from which to choose, and of course every visitor should enjoy a performance of some kind at the Sydney Opera House. There is also a stimulating range of musicals, classic plays and Shakespeare by the Sea, as well as contemporary, fringe, experimental theatre and comedy. Prominent playwrights include David Williamson, Debra Oswald, Brendan Cowell, Stephen Sewell and Louis Nowra. Australian film-making has also earned an excellent international reputation. A rich variety of both local and foreign films are screened throughout the year.

Classical Music

Much of Sydney's orchestral music and recitals are the work of the famous **Sydney Symphony Orchestra (SSO)**. Numerous concerts are given, mostly in the Sydney Opera House Concert Hall *(see pp88–9)*, the **City Recital Hall** and the **Sydney Town Hall**.

The **Australian Chamber Orchestra** also performs at the Opera House and City Recital Hall, and has won high acclaim for its creativity. The **Australia Ensemble** is the resident chamber music group at the University of New South Wales.

Many choral groups and ensembles book St James' Church *(see p119)* for their performances because of its atmosphere and acoustics.

Formed in 1973, the respected **Sydney Youth Orchestra** stages performances in major concert venues. The **Australian Youth Choir** is booked for many private functions, but if you are lucky, you may catch one of their major annual performances.

Comprising the 120-strong Sydney Philharmonia Symphonic Choir and the 40-member Sydney Philharmonia Motet Choir, the **Sydney Philharmonia Choirs** are the city's finest.

One of Sydney's most impressive vocal groups is the **Café of the Gate of Salvation**, which has been described as an "Aussie blend of *a capella* and gospel".

Originally specializing in chamber music, **Musica Viva** now presents string quartets, jazz, piano groups, percussionists, soloists and international avant-garde artists as well.

Synergy is one of Australia's foremost percussion quartets. Its innovative performance style spans traditional and contemporary percussion from around the world.

Comedy

Sydney's most established comedy venue, the **Comedy Store** is known for its themed nights. Tuesday is open-mic night; Wednesday, new comics; Thursday, cutting edge; Friday and Saturday are reserved for the best of the best. Monday is comedy night at **The Old Manly Boatshed**, where both local and visiting comics perform. Tuesday is also comedy night at the **Harold Park Hotel**, where special events and entertainment is offered most nights of the week.

Dance

The **Australian Ballet** has two seven-week Sydney seasons at the Opera House: one in March/April, the other in November/December. **Sydney Dance Company** is the city's leading modern dance group. Productions are mostly staged at the Sydney Opera House.

Bangarra Dance Theatre uses traditional Aboriginal and Torres Strait Islander dance and music as its inspiration. The startling and original **Legs on the Wall** are a physical theatre group, brilliantly combining circus and aerial techniques with dance and narrative, often performed while suspended from skyscrapers.

Opera

In 1956, the Australian Opera (now called **Opera Australia**) was formed. It presented four Mozart productions in its first year. But it was the opening of the Sydney Opera House in 1973 that heralded new public interest. Opera Australia's summer season is held from early January to early March; the winter season from June to the end of October. Every year at the popular Opera in The Domain, members of Opera Australia perform excerpts from famous pieces.

Theatre

Sydney's larger, mainstream musicals are staged at the **Theatre Royal**, the opulent **State Theatre** *(see p94)* and the **Capitol Theatre**. **The Star** entertainment and casino complex boasts two theatres, the Showroom, and the first-rate Lyric Theatre for musical productions and stage shows.

Smaller venues also offer a range of interesting plays and performances. These include the **Seymour Theatre Centre**, the **Belvoir Theatre** and the **Ensemble Theatre**. The **Griffin Theatre** at The Stables specializes in works by new Australian playwrights, while the **Parade Theatre** at the National Institute of Dramatic Arts (NIDA) showcases work by NIDA's students. The well-respected **Sydney Theatre Company (STC)** has just introduced an ensemble of actors, employed full time, who will perform a minimum of two plays each season. Most STC productions are performed at **The Wharf**.

The **Bell Shakespeare Company** productions are ideal for the young or the more wary theatre-goers. **Shakespeare Australia** performs *The Wind in the Willows* in the Royal Botanic Gardens every year in January.

The **Sydney Festival** provides an enjoyable celebration of original, often quirky, Australian theatre, dance, music and visual arts.

Film

The city's main commercial cinema, the **Event Cinemas** complex, is on George Street. A similar Hoyts-run multiplex can be found in the Fox Studios Entertainment Quarter *(see p129)*. The **IMAX Theatre** in Darling Harbour has a giant, 8-storey screen – the world's largest – showing 2D and 3D films.

Cinephiles flock to **Palace Cinemas** on Norton Street and **Dendy Opera Quays** cinema at Circular Quay. **Cinema Paris** shows arthouse and indie films, as well as many Bollywood productions. The **Chauvel Cinema** in the Paddington Town Hall has long been the spiritual home of Australian film culture, screening the best of independent and world cinema.

Commercial cinema houses offer half-price tickets on Tuesday, while Palace does so on Monday. The Sydney Film Festival is one of the highlights of the city's calendar *(see p47)*. The main venue is the State Theatre. The **Flickerfest International Short Film Festival** is held at the Bondi Pavilion Amphitheatre at Bondi Beach in early January. It screens shorts and animated films. In December, **Tropfest** shows local short films.

Run by Queer Screen, the **Mardi Gras Film Festival** starts mid-February for 15 days.

DIRECTORY

Classical Music

Australia Ensemble
Tel 9385 4874.
W ae.unsw.edu.au

Australian Chamber Orchestra
Tel 1800 444 444 or 8274 3888. W aco.com.au

Australian Youth Choir
W niypaa.com.au

Café of the Gate of Salvation
W cafeofthegateof salvation.com.au

City Recital Hall
Angel Place. **Map** 1 B4.
Tel 8256 2222.
W cityrecitalhall.com

Musica Viva
Tel 8394 6666.
W mva.org.au

Sydney Philharmonia Choirs
Tel 9251 2024. W sydney philharmonia.com.au

Sydney Symphony Orchestra
Tel 8215 4600. W sydney symphony.com

Sydney Town Hall
483 George Street.
Map 4 E2. **Tel** 9265 9333.

Sydney Youth Orchestra
Tel 9251 2422.
W syo.com.au

Synergy
Tel 9663 5532. W synergy percussion.com

Comedy

Comedy Store
Entertainment Quarter, Driver Ave, Moore Park.
Map 5 C5. **Tel** 9357 1419.
W comedystore.com.au

Harold Park Hotel
78A Ross St, Glebe.
Tel 9660 4745.
W haroldparkhotel. com.au

The Old Manly Boatshed
40 The Corso, Manly.
Tel 9977 4443.
W oldmanlyboatshed. com.au

Dance

Australian Ballet
Tel 9252 5300.
W australianballet. com.au

Bangarra Dance Theatre
Tel 9251 5333.
W bangarra.com.au

Legs on the Wall
Tel 9560 9479.
W legsonthewall. com.au

Sydney Dance Company
Tel 9221 4811.
W sydneydance company.com

Opera

Opera Australia
Tel 9318 8200.
W opera.org.au

Theatre

Bell Shakespeare Company
Tel 8298 9000.
W bellshakespeare. com.au

Belvoir Theatre
25 Belvoir St, Surry Hills. **Tel** 9699 3444.
W belvoir.com.au

Capitol Theatre
13 Campbell St, Haymarket.
Map 4 E4. **Tel** 9320 5000.
W capitoltheatre. com.au

Ensemble Theatre
78 McDougall St, Kirribilli.
Box office: **Tel** 9929 0644.
W ensemble.com.au

Griffin Theatre
10 Nimrod St, Kings Cross.
Map 5 B1. **Tel** 9361 3817.
W griffintheatre.com.au

Parade Theatre
215 Anzac Parade, Kensington. **Map** 5 B4.
Tel 9697 7613.
W nida.edu.au

Seymour Theatre Centre
Cnr Cleveland St & City Rd, Chippendale.
Tel 9351 7940.
W seymourcentre.com

Shakespeare Australia
Tel 03 8676 7511 or 1300 122 344. W shakespeare australia.com.au

The Star
80 Pyrmont St, Pyrmont.
Map 3 B1. **Tel** 9777 9000.
W star.com.au

State Theatre
49 Market St. **Map** 1 B5.
Tel 9373 6852.
W statetheatre.com.au

Sydney Festival
Tel 8248 6500. W sydney festival.org.au

Sydney Theatre Co
Tel 9250 1999. W sydney theatre.com.au

Theatre Royal
MLC Centre, King St.
Map 1 B5. **Tel** 136 100 (Ticketmaster).
W theatreroyal.net.au

The Wharf
Pier 4, Hickson Rd, Walsh Bay. **Map** 1 A1.
Tel 9250 1777. W sydney theatre.com.au

Film

Chauvel Cinema
Paddington Town Hall, 249 Oxford St, Paddington.
Map 5 C3. **Tel** 9361 5398.
W palacecinemas. com.au

Cinema Paris
Entertainment Quarter, Driver Ave, Moore Park.
Map 5 C5. **Tel** 9332 1633.
W hoyts.com.au

Dendy Opera Quays
Shop 9/2, East Circular Quay. **Map** 1 C2. **Tel** 9247 3800. W dendy.com.au

Event Cinemas
505–525 George St.
Map 4 E3. **Tel** 9273 7300.
W eventcinemas.com.au

Flickerfest
Tel 9365 6888.
W flickerfest.com.au

IMAX Theatre
Southern Promenade, Darling Harbour.
Map 4 D3. **Tel** 9281 3300.
W imax.com.au

Mardi Gras Festival
Tel 9332 4938.
W queerscreen.org.au

Palace Cinemas
Palace Norton Street Cinema 99 Norton St, Leichhardt. **Tel** 9550 0122.
W palacecinemas. com.au

Tropfest
W tropfest.com

Music Venues and Nightclubs

Sydney attracts some of the biggest names in modern music all year round. Venues range from the cavernous Allphones Arena to small and noisy back rooms in pubs. Visiting international DJs frequently play sets at Sydney clubs. Some venues cater for a variety of music tastes – rock and pop one night, jazz, blues or folk the next. There are several free online gig guides available, including www.themusic.com.au, www.thebrag. com.au and www.inthemix.com.au which tell you what is on.

Getting In

Tickets for major shows are available through booking agencies such as Ticketek and Ticketmaster *(see p142)*. Prices vary considerably, depending on the shows that are going to take place. You may pay from A$30 to A$70 for a gig at the Metro, but over A$150 for seats for a concert by major International touring acts. **Moshtix** also sells tickets for smaller venues across Sydney and their website gives a good idea of the various venues and what is on. Buying online also prevents you from having to queue early for tickets from the door.

You can also pay at the door on the night at most places, unless the show is sold out. Nightclubs often have a cover charge, but some venues will admit you free before a certain time in the evening or on weeknights.

Most venues serve alcohol, so shows are restricted to those at least 18 years of age. This is the usual case unless a gig is specified "all ages". It is advisable that people under 30 years old carry photo identification, such as a passport or driver's licence, because entry to some establishments is very strict. You are also not allowed to carry any kind of bottle into most nightclubs or other venues. Similarly, any cameras and recording devices are usually prohibited.

Dress codes vary, but generally shorts (on men) and flip flops are not welcome. Wear thin layers, which you can remove when you get hot, instead of a coat, and avoid carrying a big bag, because many venues do not have a cloakroom.

Rock, Pop and Hip Hop

Pop's big names and famous rock groups perform at the **Enmore Theatre**, **Allphones Arena**, **Hordern Pavilion** and sports grounds such as the Allianz Stadium and ANZ Stadium at **Sydney Olympic Park** *(see p131)* in Homebush Bay. More intimate locations Include the **State Theatre** *(see p94)*, **Factory Theatre** and Sydney's best venue, **The Metro Theatre**. Hip hop acts usually play in rock venues rather than in nightclubs. You are almost as likely to find a crew rapping as a band strumming and drumming at the Metro Theatre, the **Gaelic Club** or the **Palace Hotel**. It is not unusual to catch a punk, garage or electro-folk band at **Spectrum** or the **Annandale Hotel** on Parramatta Road.

Pub rock is a constantly changing scene in Sydney. Weekly listings appear on Fridays in the entertainment section of the *Sydney Morning Herald* and in the street press *(see p142)*. Music stores are also full of flyers for gigs at the Metro Theatre and Gaelic Club, where international and Australian acts perform every week. These shows usually sell out very quickly.

Jazz, Folk and Blues

For many years, the first port of call for any jazz, funk, groove or folk enthusiast has been **The Basement**. Visiting luminaries play some nights, talented but struggling local musicians others, and the line-ups now also include increasingly popular world music and hip-hop bands. **505**, in Surry Hills, features live jazz, reggae, gypsy, latin, funk and folk styles Monday to Saturday. Experimental jazz is offered on Fridays and Saturdays at the **Seymour Centre** *(see p145)*. **The Vanguard**, a newer venue, also offers dinner and show deals, as well as show-only tickets, and has been drawing an excellent roster of jazz, blues and roots talent. Marrickville's **Camelot Lounge** presents jazz, folk, blues, cabaret and world music, while the **Cat & Fiddle Hotel** in Balmain is the place to go for acoustic music and folk.

House, Breakbeats and Techno

Sydney's long-time super club, **Home Sydney** in Cockle Bay, features three levels and a gargantuan sound system. Friday night is the time to go, as the DJs present a pulsating mix of house, trance, drum and bass and breakbeats. A mainstream crowd flocks to the nearby **Bungalow 8** on King Street Wharf. Once the sun has set, house DJs turn the place into a club. At **Pacha**, in the Ivy complex, you can experience hallucinatory burlesque with international artists every Saturday night. There are bands or DJs at the **World Bar** in Kings Cross every night.

For something a little more hip, try **Candy's Apartment** on Bayswater Road, or head a few doors down the street to **Hugo's Lounge**, three-time Nightclub of the Year winner. For the best of House, presented by Paul Strange, go to the **Arthouse Hotel** on Saturday nights. It is located in the 1836, heritage School of Arts Building next to the Hilton Hotel. Down the road, **Q Bar**, one of many bars in the Exchange Hotel on Oxford Street, Darlinghurst, has arcade games for when you need a breather from strutting your stuff. Or sample the low-ceilinged **Chinese Laundry** on Sussex Street, which you'll find tucked under the gentrified pub, Slip Inn.

Gay and Lesbian Pubs and Clubs

Sunday night is the big night for many of Sydney's gay community, although there is plenty of action throughout the week. A number of venues have a gay or lesbian night on one night of the week and attract a mainstream crowd on the other nights. Wednesday is lesbian night at the **Bank Hotel** in Newtown. **The Polo Lounge**, situated on the top floor of the Oxford Hotel, has great views of the city's skyline. Catch live music at the first-floor supper club.

ARQ on Flinders Street is the largest of the gay clubs, with pounding commercial house music. The main dance floor is overlooked by a mezzanine for watching the writhing mass of bodies below. **Midnight Shift** on Oxford Street is for men only, and **Stonewall** plays camp anthems and is patronized mostly by men and their straight female friends. The **Colombian** is the best of the Oxford Street bars, with a mock Central American jungle and large windows that open out to the street. The **Oxford Hotel** and its upper-level cocktail bar **Gingers** are popular too. There's always something on in the main bar and visiting acts often perform in its basement level underground bar. The **Imperial Hotel** has drag shows on most nights of the week. The **Oxford Art Factory** in Darlinghurst has live music as well as burlesque and cabaret evenings.

DIRECTORY

Rock, Pop and Hip Hop

Allphones Arena
Sydney Olympic Park, Homebush Bay. **Tel** 8765 4321. [W] allphones arena.com.au

Annandale Hotel
17–19 Parramatta Rd, Annandale. **Tel** 9550 1078. [W] annandalehotel.com

Enmore Theatre
130 Enmore Rd, Newtown. **Tel** 9550 3666/9519 9331. [W] enmore theatre. com.au

Factory Theatre
105 Victoria Rd, Marrickville. **Tel** 9550 2990. [W] factorytheatre. com.au

Gaelic Club
64 Devonshire St, Surry Hills. **Tel** 9211 1687. [W] thegaelic.com

Hordern Pavilion
Driver Ave, Moore Park. **Map** 5 C5. **Tel** 9921 5333. [W] playbillvenues.com

The Metro Theatre
624 George St. **Map** 4 E3. **Tel** 9550 3666. [W] metrotheatre.com.au

Moshtix
Tel 1300 438 849. [W] moshtix.com.au

Palace Hotel
730–742 George St, Haymarket. **Map** 4 E4. **Tel** 9212 2111. [W] palacehotel sydney.com.au

Spectrum
34 Oxford St, Darlinghurst. **Map** 4 F4. **Tel** 9360 1375. [W] spectrum.exchange sydney.com.au

State Theatre
49 Market St. **Map** 1 B5. **Tel** 9373 6852. [W] statetheatre.com.au

Sydney Olympic Park
Homebush Bay. **Tel** 9714 7888. [W] sydneyolympic park.com.au

Jazz, Folk and Blues

505
280 Cleveland St, Surry Hills. [W] venue505.com

The Basement
29 Reiby Place. **Map** 1 B3. **Tel** 9251 2797. [W] the basement.com.au

Camelot Lounge
Cnr 103 Railway Pde & 19 Marrickville Rd, Marrickville. **Tel** 9550 3777. [W] camelotlounge. wordpress.com

Cat & Fiddle Hotel
456 Darling St, Balmain. **Tel** 9810 7931. [W] thecatandfiddle.net

Seymour Centre
Cnr Cleveland St & City Rd, Chippendale. **Tel** 9351 7940. [W] seymourcentre.com

The Vanguard
42 King St, Newtown. **Tel** 9557 7992. [W] thevanguard.com.au

House, Breakbeats and Techno

Arthouse Hotel
275 Pitt St. **Map** 1 B5. **Tel** 9284 1200.

Bungalow 8
The Promenade, 3 Lime St, King St Wharf. **Tel** 9299 4660. [W] bungalow8 sydney.com

Candy's Apartment
22 Bayswater Rd, Kings Cross. **Map** 5 B1. **Tel** 9380 5600. [W] candys.com.au

Chinese Laundry
111 Sussex St (under Slip Inn). **Map** 1 A3. **Tel** 8295 9999. [W] chinese laundryclub.com.au

Home Sydney
101 Cockle Bay Wharf, Darling Harbour. **Map** 4 D2. **Tel** 9266 0600. [W] homesydney.com

Hugo's Lounge
Level 1, 33 Bayswater Rd, Kings Cross. **Map** 5 B1. **Tel** 9357 4411.

Pacha
Level 1, Ivy, 330 George St. **Map** 1 B4. **Tel** 9254 8100.

Q Bar at the Exchange Hotel
Level 2, 44 Oxford St, Darlinghurst. **Map** 4 F4. **Tel** 9360 1375. [W] qbar. exchangesydney.com.au

World Bar
24 Bayswater Rd, Kings Cross. **Map** 5 C1. **Tel** 9357 7700. [W] theworldbar.com

Gay and Lesbian Clubs and Pubs

ARQ
16 Flinders St, Taylor Square. **Map** 5 A2. **Tel** 9380 8700. [W] arqsydney.com.au

Bank Hotel
324 King St, Newtown. **Tel** 8568 1900. [W] bankhotel.com.au

Colombian
Cnr Oxford and Crown Sts, Surry Hills. **Map** 5 A2. **Tel** 9360 2151. [W] colombian.com.au

Gingers
Level 1, 134 Oxford St, Darlinghurst. **Map** 5 A2. **Tel** 9331 3467.

Imperial Hotel
35 Erskineville Rd, Erskineville. **Tel** 9519 9899.

Midnight Shift
85 Oxford St, Darlinghurst. **Map** 5 A2. **Tel** 9358 3848. [W] themidnightshift. com.au

Oxford Art Factory
38–46 Oxford St, Darlinghurst. **Map** 5 A2. **Tel** 9332 3711. [W] oxfordartfactory.com

Oxford Hotel
134 Oxford St, Darlinghurst. **Map** 5 A2. **Tel** 9331 3467. [W] theoxfordhotel. com.au

The Polo Lounge
Level 2, 134 Oxford St, Darlinghurst. **Map** 5 A2. **Tel** 9331 3467.

Stonewall
175 Oxford St, Darlinghurst. **Map** 5 A2. **Tel** 9360 1963. [W] stonewallhotel.com

Sydney's Beaches

Being a city built around the water, it is no wonder that many of Sydney's recreational activities involve the sand, sea and sun. There are many harbour and surf beaches in Sydney, most of them accessible by bus *(see p133)*. Even if you're not a swimmer, the beaches offer a chance to get away from it all for a day or weekend and enjoy the fresh air and relaxed way of life.

Scuba diving at Gordons Bay

Swimming

You can swim at either harbour or ocean beaches. Harbour beaches are generally smaller and sheltered. Popular ones are Camp Cove, Shark Bay and Balmoral Beach.

At the ocean beaches, surf lifesavers in their red and yellow or blue caps are on duty. Swimming rules are strongly enforced. Surf lifesaving carnivals are held throughout the summer. Call **Surf Life Saving NSW** for a calendar. Well-patrolled, safer surf beaches include Bondi, Manly and Coogee.

The beaches can become polluted, especially after heavy rain. The **Beach Watch and Harbour Watch Info Line** provides information.

Surfing

Surfing is more a way of life than a leisure activity for some Sydneysiders. If you're a beginner, try Bondi, Bronte, Palm Beach or Collaroy.

Two of the best surf beaches are Maroubra and Narrabeen. Bear in mind that local surfers know one another well and do not take kindly to "intruders"

who drop in on their waves. To hire a surfboard, try Bondi Surf Co on Campbell Parade, Bondi Beach, or Aloha Surf on Pittwater Road, Manly. If you would like to learn, there are two schools: **Manly Surf School** and **Lets Go Surfing** at Bondi Beach. They also hire out boards and wetsuits.

Windsurfing and Sailing

There are locations around Sydney suitable for every level of windsurfer. Boards can be hired from **Balmoral Sailing School**.

Good spots include Palm Beach, Narrabeen Lakes, La Perouse, Brighton-Le-Sands and Kurnell Point (for beginner and intermediate boarders) and Long Reef Beach, Palm Beach and Collaroy (for more experienced boarders).

One of the best ways to see the harbour is while sailing. A sailing boat, including a skipper, can be hired for the afternoon from the **East Sail** sailing club. The sailing club has two-day courses and also hires out sailing boats and motor cruisers to experienced sailors.

Scuba Diving

The great barrier reef it may not be, but there are some excellent dive spots around Sydney, especially in winter when the water is clear, if a little cold. Favoured spots are Shelly Beach, Gordons Bay and Camp Cove.

Pro Dive Coogee offers a complete range of courses, escorted dives, introductory dives for beginners, and hire equipment. **Dive Centre Manly** also runs courses, hires equipment and conducts boat dives seven days a week.

DIRECTORY

Balmoral Sailing School
Balmoral Park, The Esplanade, Mosman, Balmoral Beach. **Tel** 9960 5344. W **sailingschool.com.au**

Beach Watch/Harbour Watch
W **environment.nsw.gov. au/beach**

Dive Centre Manly
10 Belgrave St, Manly. **Tel** 9977 4355. W **divesydney.com.au** Also at Bondi and City.

East Sail
d'Albora Marinas, New Beach Rd, Rushcutters Bay. **Tel** 9327 1166. W **eastsail.com.au**

Lets Go Surfing
128 Ramsgate Ave, North Bondi. **Tel** 9365 1800. W **letsgosurfing.com.au**

Manly Surf School
North Steyne Rd, Manly. **Tel** 9977 6977. W **manlysurfschool. com.au**

Pro Dive Coogee
27 Alfreda St, Coogee. **Tel** 9665 6333. W **provdivesydney.com**

Surf Life Saving NSW
Tel 9471 8000. W **surflifesaving.com.au**

Rock baths and surf lifesaving club at Coogee Beach

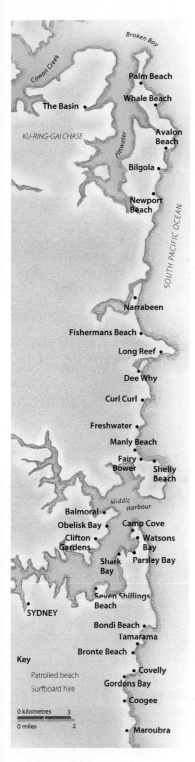

Top 30 beaches

These beaches have been selected for their safe swimming, water sports, facilities available or their picturesque setting.

	Swimming Pool	Surfing	Windsurfing	Fishing	Scuba Diving	Picnic/Barbecue	Restaurant/Café
Avalon	★	★	★	★		★	
Balmoral	★	★	★	★	★	★	
The Basin	★					★	
Bilgola							
Bondi Beach	★	★			★	★	★
Bronte	★	★		★	★	★	★
Camp Cove					★		
Clifton Gardens	★		★	★	★	★	
Clovelly				★	★	★	★
Coogee	★		★	★	★	★	★
Curl Curl	★	★		★			
Dee Why	★	★		★	★	★	★
Fairy Bower					★		
Fishermans Beach		★	★	★	★		
Freshwater	★	★		★	★	★	
Gordons Bay					★	★	
Long Reef		★	★	★	★		
Manly Beach	★	★			★	★	★
Maroubra		★	★	★	★	★	★
Narrabeen	★	★		★		★	
Newport Beach	★	★	★	★		★	
Obelisk Bay							
Palm Beach	★	★	★	★		★	★
Parsley Bay						★	
Seven Shillings Beach	★					★	
Shark Bay	★					★	★
Shelly Beach					★	★	★
Tamarama		★	★	★	★		★
Watsons Bay	★					★	★
Whale Beach	★	★	★	★		★	★

Fishing in Sydney

Surprisingly for a thriving city port, there is a wide variety of fish to be caught. From the rocks and headlands of the northern beaches, such as Palm Beach and Bilgola, tuna, whiting and blenny abound. The Narrabeen Lakes offer estuary fishing, with a population of flathead and bream. The sheltered Middle Harbour has many angling spots. A NSW Recreational Fishing Fee must be paid by everyone.

Triplefin blenny

SPORTING SYDNEY

Throughout Australia sport is a way of life, and Sydney is no exception. On any day you'll see locals on golf courses at dawn, running on the streets keeping fit, or having a quick set of tennis after work. At weekends, during summer and winter, there is no end to the variety of sports you can watch. Thousands gather at the Allianz Stadium and Sydney Cricket Ground (SCG) every weekend while, for those who are unable to make it, sport reigns supreme on weekend television.

Cricket

During the summer months Test cricket and one-day internationals are played at the Sydney Cricket Ground (SCG). Shorter Twenty Twenty international and domestic games played in the evening have a fun and exciting atmosphere. It is advisable to book well in advance (through **Ticketek**) for Test matches and for all the one-day international matches.

Australia versus the All Blacks

Rugby League and Rugby Union

The popularity of rugby league knows no bounds in Sydney. This is what people refer to as "the footy". There are three major competition levels: local, State of Origin – which matches Queensland against New South Wales – and Tests. The "local" competition fields teams from all over Sydney as well as Newcastle, Canberra, Brisbane, Melbourne, the Gold Coast, Far North Queensland and Auckland, New Zealand.

These matches are held all over Sydney, but the ANZ Stadium at Sydney Olympic Park is by far the biggest venue. Tickets for State of Origin and Test matches often sell out immediately. Call Ticketek to check availability.

Rugby union is the second most popular football code. Again, matches at Test level sell out very quickly. For some premium trans-Tasman rivalry, catch a Test match between Australia's "Wallabies" and the New Zealand "All Blacks". Phone Ticketek for details.

Golf and Tennis

Golf enthusiasts need not do without their round of golf. There are many courses throughout Sydney where visitors are welcome at all times. These include **Moore Park**,

St Michael's and Warringah golf courses. It is sensible to phone beforehand for a booking, especially at weekends.

Tennis is another favoured sport. Courts available for hire can be found all over Sydney. Many centres also have floodlit courts available for night time. Try **Cooper Park** or **Parkland Sports** Centre.

Playing golf at Moore Park, one of Sydney's public courses

Australian Rules Football

Although not as popular as in Melbourne, "Aussie Rules" has a strong following in Sydney. The local teams, Sydney Swans and Greater Western Sydney Giants, play their home games at the SCG and Spotless Stadium at Homebush. Check a local paper for details.

Rivalry between the Sydney supporters and their Melbourne counterparts is always strong. Fans from the south arrive to cheer on their teams. Tickets can be bought on the day of the game or through Ticketek and **Ticketmaster**.

Basketball

Basketball has grown in popularity as both a spectator and recreational sport in recent years. Sydney has male and female teams competing in the National Basketball League. The games, held at the Sydney Sports Centre at Homebush have

One-day cricket match between Australia and the West Indies, SCG

Aerial view of the Allianz Stadium at Moore Park

much of the pizzazz, colour and excitement of American basketball. Tickets can be purchased by phone or on the Internet from Ticketek.

Cycling and Inline Skating

Sydney boasts excellent, safe locations for the whole family to go cycling. One of the most frequented is Centennial Park (see p132). You can hire bicycles and safety helmets from **Centennial Park Cycles** and also from **Inner City Cycles** in Glebe, where you can hire out equipment by the day or by the week.

Another popular pastime in summer is inline skating. **Rollerbladingsydney.com.au** hires equipment and runs tours starting at Milsons Point to all parts of Sydney. They offer private and group lessons. Or keep both feet firmly on the ground and watch skateboarders and inline skaters practising their moves at the ramps at Bondi Beach (see p149).

Inline skaters enjoying a summer evening on the city's streets

Horse Riding

For a leisurely ride, head to Centennial Park or contact the **Centennial Parklands Equestrian Centre**. They will give you details of the four riding schools that operate in the park. **Shellby Equestrian Centre** conducts trail rides through Ku-ring-gai Chase National Park (see p130).

Further afield, you can enjoy the magnificent scenery of the Blue Mountains (see pp172–3) on horseback. The **Megalong Australian Heritage Centre** has trail rides from one hour to an overnight ride. All levels of experience are catered for.

Horse riding in one of the parks surrounding the city centre

Adventure Sports

Sydney offers a wide range of adventure sports for those seeking a more active and thrill-filled time. You can participate in guided bushwalking, mountain biking, canyoning, rock climbing and abseiling expeditions in the nearby Blue Mountains National Park. The **Blue Mountains Adventure Company** runs one-day or multi-day courses and trips for all standards of adventurer.

DIRECTORY

Blue Mountains Adventure Company
84a Bathurst Rd, Katoomba.
Tel 4782 1271.
W bmac.com.au

Centennial Park Cycles
50 Clovelly Rd, Randwick.
Tel 9398 5027.
W cyclehire.com.au

Centennial Parklands Equestrian Centre
Cnr Lang & Cook Rds,
Moore Park.
Tel 9332 2809.
W cpequestrian.com.au

Cooper Park Tennis Courts
1 Bunna Place, off Suttie Rd,
Double Bay.
Tel 9389 3100.

Inner City Cycles
151 Glebe Point Road, Glebe.
Map 3 B5.
Tel 9660 6605.

Megalong Australian Heritage Centre
Megalong Valley Rd, Megalong
Valley. **Tel** 4787 8188.
W megalongcc.com.au

Moore Park Golf Club
Cnr Cleveland St & Anzac Parade,
Moore Park. **Map** 5 B5.
Tel 9663 1064.
W mooreparkgolf.com.au

Parkland Sports
Lang Rd, Moore Park.
Tel 9662 7033.
W centennialparklands.com.au

Rollerbladingsydney.com.au
Tel 0411 872 022.
W rollerbladingsydney.com.au

St Michael's Golf Club
Jennifer St, Little Bay.
Tel 9311 0068.
W stmichaelsgolf.com.au

Shellby Equestrian Centre
90 Booralie Rd, Terrey Hills.
Tel 9450 1745.

Ticketek
Tel 13 28 49.
W ticketek.com.au

Ticketmaster
Tel 13 61 00.
W ticketmaster.com.au

Warringah Golf Club
397 Condamine St, North Manly.
Tel 9905 4028.

SYDNEY STREET FINDER

The page grid superimposed on the *Area by Area* map below shows which parts of Sydney are covered in this *Street Finder*. Map references given for all sights, shops and entertainment venues in Sydney described in this chapter refer to the maps in this section. All the major sights are clearly marked so they are easy to locate. The key, set out below, indicates the scale of the maps and shows what other features are marked on them, including railway stations, bus terminals, ferry boarding points, taxi ranks, emergency services, post offices and tourist information centres. Map references are also given for hotels *(see pp482–3)* and restaurants *(see pp504–7)*.

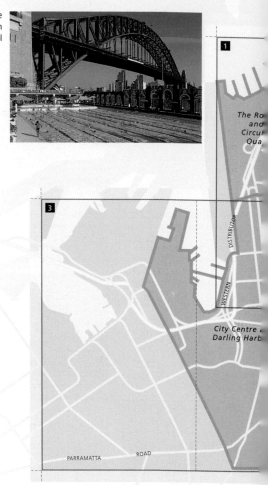

Sydney Harbour Bridge *(see pp84–5)* viewed from North Sydney Olympic Pool

Key

- Major sight
- Place of interest
- Other building
- Ferry boarding point
- Main railway station
- Bus station
- Sydney Trains station
- Light rail station
- Tourist information
- Hospital with casualty unit
- Police station
- Golf course
- Church
- Mosque
- Synagogue
- Highway
- Railway line
- Ferry route
- Pedestrianized street
- Tunnel

Scale of Map Pages

0 metres	250
0 yards	250

0 metres	500
0 yards	500

For additional map symbols *see back flap*

Statues on the Art Deco Anzac Memorial in
Hyde Park *(see p97)*

Enjoying coffee outside a café in
Darlinghurst

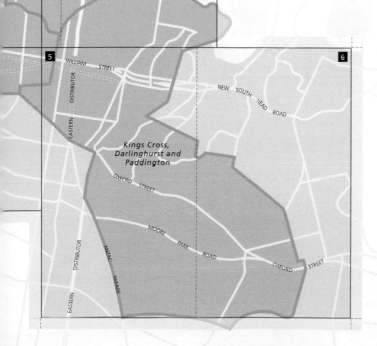

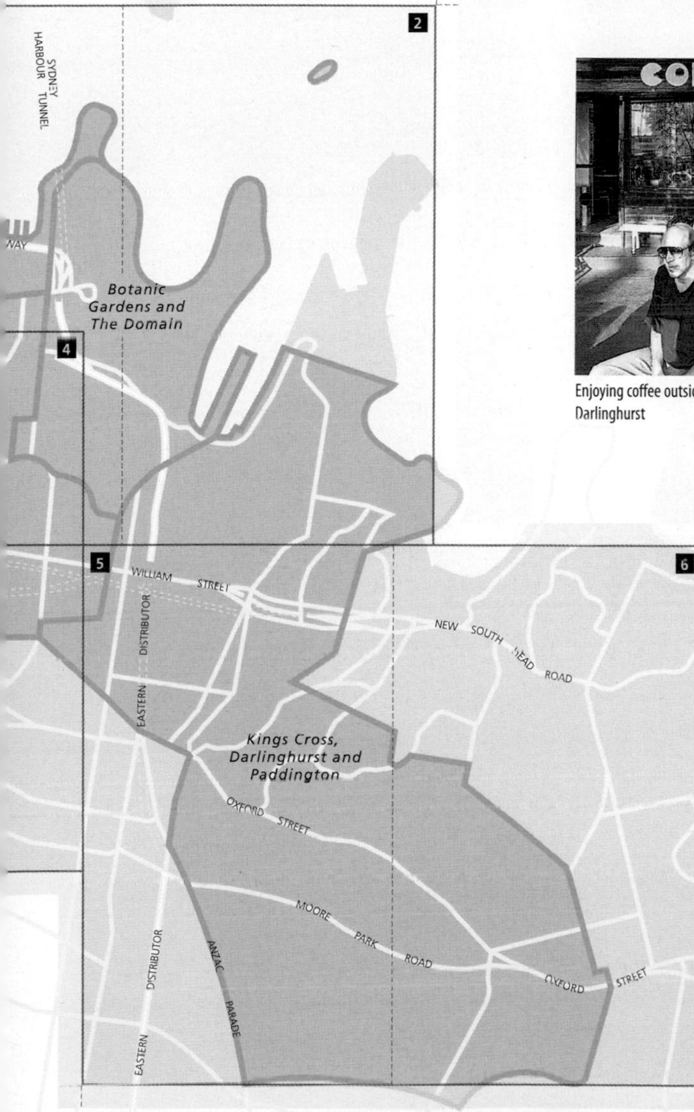

Sundial in the Royal Botanic Gardens *(see pp110–11)*

Botanic
Gardens and
The Domain

Kings Cross,
Darlinghurst and
Paddington

SYDNEY HARBOUR TUNNEL

WAY

WILLIAM STREET

EASTERN DISTRIBUTOR

NEW SOUTH HEAD ROAD

OXFORD STREET

MOORE PARK ROAD

ANZAC PARADE

EASTERN DISTRIBUTOR

OXFORD STREET

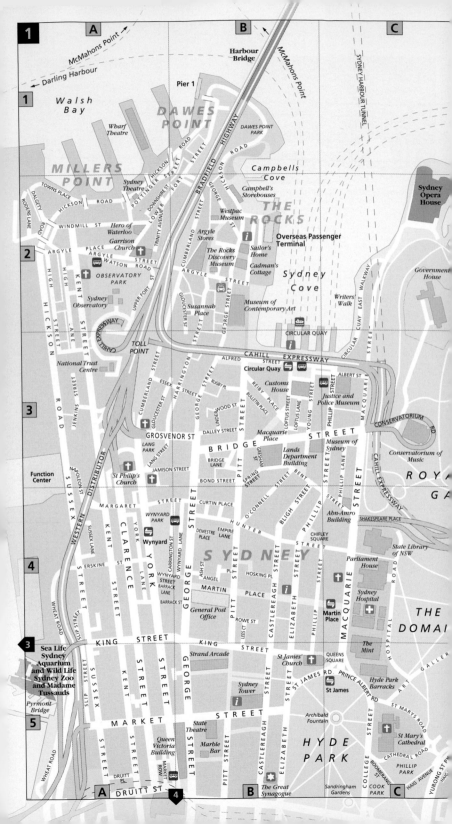

D   E   F   2

Neutral Bay

Mosman

Taronga Zoo

Manly

Rose Bay

1

Fort Denison
(Pinchgut)

Port

Jackson

GARDEN

ISLAND

2

Mrs Macquaries
Chair

MRS
MACQUARIES
POINT

Farm Cove

3

Andrew (Boy)
Charlton Pool

GARDEN ISLAND
NAVAL DOCKYARD

OTANIC
NS

CAPTAIN COOK
GRAVING DOCK

Woolloomooloo
Bay

Palm
ouse

Visitors
Centre

WHARF ROADWAY

WILDE STREET

4

Woolloomooloo
Finger Wharf

LINCOLN COURT

POTTS
POINT

GRANTHAM STREET

SAINT NEOT AVE

McDONALD ST

McDONALD LANE

CHALLIS AVENUE

Elizabeth
Bay

McELHONE
STAIRS

Gallery of
w South
Wales

TOLL
POINT

COWPER

BLAND STREET

NICHOLSON STREET

WILSON STREET

BOURKE STREET

PLUNKETT ST

GRIFFITHS ST

HARMER
ST

DOWLING STREET

McELHONE STREET

NESBITT ST

ROCKWALL
LANE

ROCKWALL
CREST

Elizabeth Bay
House

CROWELL
PLACE

ELIZABETH BAY AVENUE

ITHACA ROAD

Elizabeth
Point

BEARE
PARK

ESPLANADE

5

WOOLLOO MOOLOO

CHARLES

FORBES

STREET

YOUNG

PALMER

STREET

St ENE

CATHEDRAL

BOSSLEY
TERRACE

TURNER
LANE

CROSS
LANE

CATHEDRAL

STREET

RAE PL

HOURIGAN LANE

EARL STREET

BROUGHAM STREET

SPRINGFIELD AVE

VICTORIA STREET

HUGHES LANE

TUSCULUM LANE

TUSCULUM ST

HUGHES STREET

ORWELL STREET

ORWELL LANE

MANNING
ST

CRICK AVE

MACLEAY STREET

GREENKNOWE AVENUE

BICKLEY PL

BARONCA

ELIZABETH BAY ROAD

ROSLYN GDNS

30TH JULY LANE

ROSLYN LANE

ELIZABETH BAY RD

HOLDSWORTH
AVENUE

El Alamein
Fountain

D   E   5   F

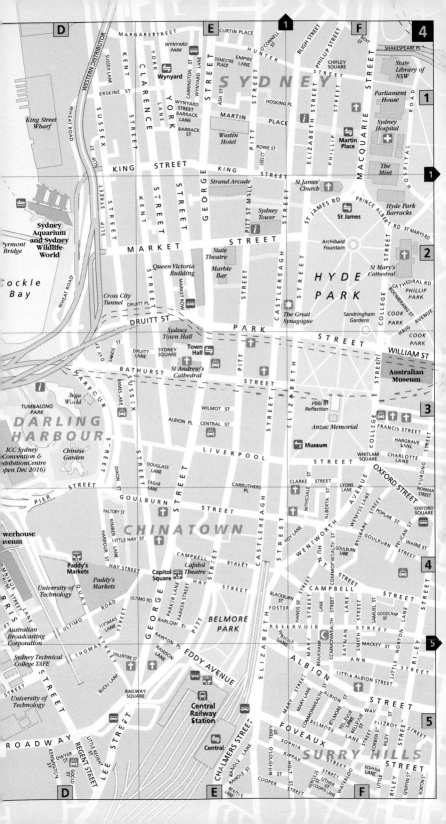

NEW SOUTH WALES AND ACT

New South Wales and ACT at a Glance

This southeastern corner of the continent, around Sydney Cove, was the site of the first European settlement in the 18th century and today it is the most densely populated and varied region in Australia, and home to its largest city, Sydney *(see pp64–159)*, as well as Canberra, the nation's capital. It also contains the country's highest mountain, Mount Kosciuszko. In the east there are farmlands and vineyards, the Blue Mountains and the ski resorts of the Snowy Mountains. To the west is a desert landscape. The coastline is tropically warm in the north, cooler in the south.

Locator Map

Broken Hill *(see p185)* is one of the few 19th-century mining towns in Australia that continues to survive on its mineral resources. It is also the location of the Royal Flying Doctor Service headquarters, and guided tours detailing the history of the service are popular with visitors.

Broken Hill

B•

The Blue Mountains and Beyond *(see pp168–85)*

Griffith

Wagga Wa•

0 kilometres 100

0 miles 100

Bourke's major attraction is its remote location. Irrigated by the Darling River, the town is also a successful agricultural centre *(see p185)*. A lift-up span bridge crosses the river.

◀ Aerial view of South Era Beach, part of the Royal National Park

Tamworth is the heart of Australian country music. The Big Golden Guitar Tourist Centre is fronted by the city's iconic large golden guitar (*see p181*).

Tenterfield's School of Arts building has a proud history as the site of Sir Henry Parkes' Federation speech in 1889, which was followed, 12 years later, by the founding of the Commonwealth of Australia (*see p60*). A museum in the town details the event.

Moree

Armidale

Tamworth

The Three Sisters rock formation is the most famous sight within the Blue Mountains National Park (*see pp172–3*). At night it is floodlit for a spectacular view.

Dubbo

Taree

Parkes

Maitland

Orange

Newcastle

Lithgow

Windsor

Gosford

Windsor is one of the best preserved 19th-century towns in the state (*see p176*). The Macquarie Arms Hotel is considered to be the oldest operational hotel in Australia.

Penrith

Sydney

nberra and ACT
(*see pp194–211*)

Camden

Goulburn

Wollongong

nberra

Nowra-Bomaderry

Canberra was designed as the new national capital in 1912 by architect Walter Burley Griffin. Anzac Parade offers fine views of New Parliament House, atop Capital Hill (*see pp198–9*).

The South Coast and
Snowy Mountains
(*see pp186–93*)

Mount Kosciuszko, in Kosciuszko National Park, is Australia's highest mountain. Panoramic views of the Snowy Mountains can be found at the Mount Kosciuszko Lookout, accessible via a walking trail or a chairlift (*see pp164–5*).

The Snowy Mountains

The Snowy Mountains stretch 500 km (310 miles) from Canberra to Victoria. Formed more than 250 million years ago, they include Australia's highest mountain, Mount Kosciuszko, and the country's only glacial lakes. In summer, wildflowers carpet the meadows; in winter, snow gums bend beneath the cold winds. The Snowy Mountains are preserved within the Kosciuszko National Park and are also home to two of Australia's largest ski resorts, Thredbo and Perisher. The Snowy Mountains Scheme dammed four rivers to supply power to much of inland eastern Australia *(see p187)*.

The Snowy Mountains are home to the Kosciuszko National Park which was declared a World Biosphere Reserve by UNESCO in 1997.

The Snowy River rises below Mount Kosciuszko and is now damned and diverted to provide hydroelectricity for Melbourne and Sydney as part of the Snowy Mountains Scheme.

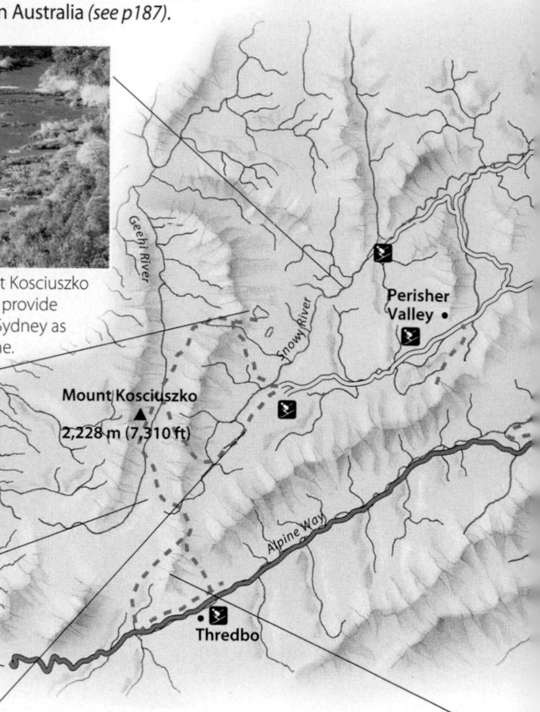

Blue Lake is a spectacular glacial lake, one of only a few in the country, which lies in an ice-carved basin 28 m (90 ft) deep.

Seaman's Hut, built in honour of a skier who perished here in 1928, has saved many lives during fierce blizzards.

The Alpine Way offers a spectacular drive through the mountains, best taken in spring or summer, via the Thredbo River Valley.

Geehi River

Snowy River

Perisher Valley •

Mount Kosciuszko
▲
2,228 m (7,310 ft)

Alpine Way

Thredbo

Prominent Peaks of the Snowy Mountains

Mount Kosciuszko is Australia's highest mountain, and may be approached by gentle walks across alpine meadows from Thredbo or from Charlottes Pass. Mount Townsend is only slightly lower but, with a more pronounced summit, is often mistaken for its higher and more famous neighbour.

Charlottes Pass marks the start of the summit walk to Mount Kosciuszko. It was named after Charlotte Adams, who, in 1881, was the first European woman to climb the peak.

Dead Horse Gap is a striking pass named after a group of "brumbies" (wild horses) that perished in a snowdrift here during the 19th century.

0 metres   5

0 yards   5

Key

▬▬ Major road

═══ Minor road

■ ■ Walking trail

Downhill and cross-country skiing and snow-boarding are popular in the Snowy Mountains between June and September.

Flora and Fauna

The Snowy Mountains are often harsh, windswept and barren, yet myriad flowers, trees and wildlife have evolved to survive all seasons. Almost all species here are unique to the alpine regions of Australia.

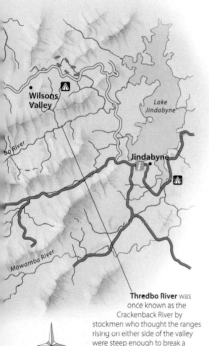

Silver snow daisies, with their white petals and yellow centres, are the most spectacular of all the alpine flowers en masse.

Mountain plum pine is a natural bonsai tree, which grows slowly and at an angle. The pygmy possum feeds on its berries.

Sphagnum moss surrounds the springs, bogs and creeks in the highest regions, and helps to protect primitive alpine plants.

Corroboree frogs live only in the fragile sphagnum moss bogs of the region.

Mountain pygmy possums live under the snow, high up in the mountains.

Thredbo River was once known as the Crackenback River by stockmen who thought the ranges rising on either side of the valley were steep enough to break a man's back.

The Yarrangobilly Caves, about 130 km (80 miles) north of Thredbo, are a system of 70 limestone caves formed 750,000 years ago. They contain magnificent white columns, cascading frozen waterfalls and delicate underground pools.

Brown and rainbow trout, both introduced species, thrive in the cool mountain streams.

Wines of New South Wales and ACT

New South Wales and ACT were the cradle of Australian wines. A small consignment of vines was on board the First Fleet when it landed at Sydney Cove in January 1788 (see pp54–5), and this early hope was fulfilled in the steady development of a successful wine industry. New South Wales is now the home of many fine wineries with an international reputation. The state is currently in the vanguard of wine industry expansion, planting new vineyards and developing established districts to meet steadily rising domestic and export demand.

Locator Map

New South Wales wine region

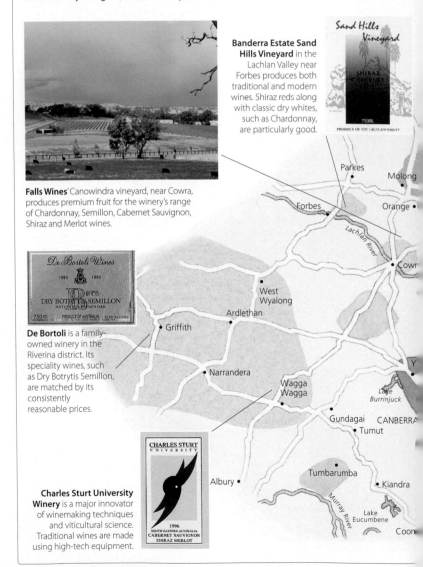

Banderra Estate Sand Hills Vineyard in the Lachlan Valley near Forbes produces both traditional and modern wines. Shiraz reds along with classic dry whites, such as Chardonnay, are particularly good.

Falls Wines' Canowindra vineyard, near Cowra, produces premium fruit for the winery's range of Chardonnay, Semillon, Cabernet Sauvignon, Shiraz and Merlot wines.

De Bortoli is a family-owned winery in the Riverina district. Its speciality wines, such as Dry Botrytis Semillon, are matched by its consistently reasonable prices.

Charles Sturt University Winery is a major innovator of winemaking techniques and viticultural science. Traditional wines are made using high-tech equipment.

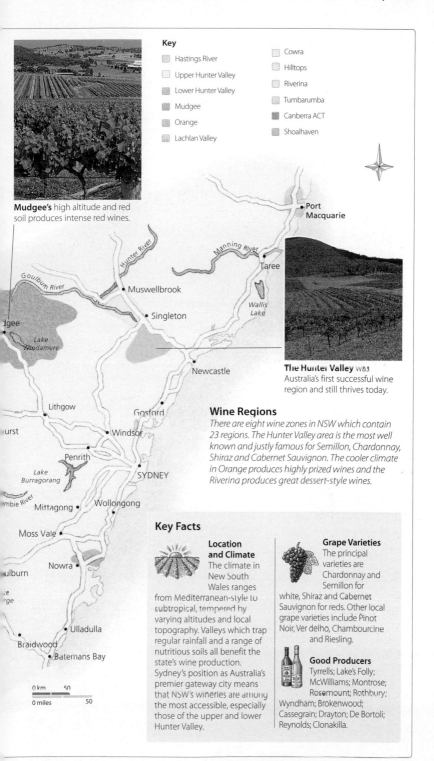

Key

- Hastings River
- Upper Hunter Valley
- Lower Hunter Valley
- Mudgee
- Orange
- Lachlan Valley
- Cowra
- Hilltops
- Riverina
- Tumbarumba
- Canberra ACT
- Shoalhaven

Mudgee's high altitude and red soil produces intense red wines.

The Hunter Valley was Australia's first successful wine region and still thrives today.

Wine Regions

There are eight wine zones in NSW which contain 23 regions. The Hunter Valley area is the most well known and justly famous for Semillon, Chardonnay, Shiraz and Cabernet Sauvignon. The cooler climate in Orange produces highly prized wines and the Riverina produces great dessert-style wines.

Key Facts

Location and Climate

The climate in New South Wales ranges from Mediterranean-style to subtropical, tempered by varying altitudes and local topography. Valleys which trap regular rainfall and a range of nutritious soils all benefit the state's wine production. Sydney's position as Australia's premier gateway city means that NSW's wineries are among the most accessible, especially those of the upper and lower Hunter Valley.

Grape Varieties

The principal varieties are Chardonnay and Semillon for white, Shiraz and Cabernet Sauvignon for reds. Other local grape varieties include Pinot Noir, Verdelho, Chambourcine and Riesling.

Good Producers

Tyrrells; Lake's Folly; McWilliams; Montrose; Rosemount; Rothbury; Wyndham; Brokenwood; Cassegrain; Drayton; De Bortoli; Reynolds; Clonakilla.

0 km   50
0 miles   50

THE BLUE MOUNTAINS AND BEYOND

Think of northern New South Wales and vibrant colours spring to mind. There are the dark blues of the Blue Mountains; the blue-green seas of the north coast; the verdant green of the rainforests near the Queensland border; and the gold of the wheat fields. Finally, there are the reds and yellows of the desert in the far west.

Ever since English explorer Captain James Cook claimed the eastern half of Australia as British territory in 1770 and named it New South Wales, Sydney and its surroundings have been at the forefront of Australian life.

On the outskirts of Sydney, at Windsor and Richmond, early convict settlements flourished into prosperous farming regions along the fertile Hawkesbury River. The barrier of the Blue Mountains was finally penetrated in 1812, marking the first spread of sheep and cattle squatters north, west and south onto the rich plains beyond. In the middle of the 19th century came the gold rush around Bathurst and Mudgee and up into the New England Tablelands, which led to the spread of roads and railways.

Following improved communications in the late 19th and early 20th centuries, northern New South Wales now contains more towns, a denser rural population and a more settled coastline than anywhere else in the country. Fortunately, all this development has not robbed the region of its natural beauty or assets. From the grand and daunting wilderness of the Blue Mountains to the blue waters and surf of Byron Bay, the easternmost point in Australia, the region remains easy to explore and a delight to the senses. It is most easily divided into three parts: the coastline and mild hinterland, including the famous Hunter Valley vineyards; the hills, plateaus and flats of the New England Tablelands and Western Plains with their rivers, national parks and thriving farming areas; and the remote, dusty Outback, west of the vast Great Dividing Range.

The combination of urban civilization, with all the amenities and attractions it offers, and the beautiful surrounding landscape, make this region a favourite holiday location with locals and tourists all year round.

Cape Byron lighthouse on Australia's most easterly point

◀ Hanging Rock, in the Blue Mountains National Park

Exploring the Blue Mountains and Beyond

Distances can be long in northern New South Wales, so the extent of any exploration will depend on the time available. Within easy reach of Sydney are historic gold rush towns such as Windsor and those between Bathurst and Mudgee, the cool retreats of the Blue Mountains, and the gentle, green hills of the Hunter Valley and its vineyards. The north coast and its hinterland are best explored as part of a touring holiday between Sydney and the Queensland capital, Brisbane, or as a short break to the beaches and fishing areas around Port Macquarie, Taree and Coffs Harbour.

Key

The Blue Mountains and Beyond

West of the Divide *pp184–5*

Impressive Three Sisters rocks in the Blue Mountains National Park

Sights at a Glance

❶ *Blue Mountains National Park pp172–5*
❷ Windsor
❸ Gosford
❹ Newcastle
❻ Barrington Tops WHA
❼ Armidale
❽ Gibraltar Range National Park
❾ Tenterfield
❿ Inverell
⓫ Tamworth
⓬ Mudgee

Tour

❺ Hunter Valley

West of the Divide

See pp184–5
⓭ Dubbo
⓮ Lightning Ridge
⓯ Bourke
⓰ Broken Hill
⓱ Willandra National Park
⓲ Wagga Wagga

For additional map symbols *see back flap*

Cape Byron, Byron Bay; mainland Australia's easternmost point

Getting Around

An extensive rail and bus network up the north coast and to major towns such as Coffs Harbour, Byron Bay and Armidale makes this region very accessible. However, a car is still the best way to see the natural highlights of the area. Highways are good, although rarely dual carriageway, with the exception of the coastal Princes Hwy and parts of the Hume Hwy. Other routes are the New England Hwy to the Northern Tablelands, the Newell Hwy to Moree and the Great Western Hwy through the Blue Mountains to Bathurst.

0 kilometres   50

0 miles   50

Key

■■■ Highway

— Major road

····· Minor road

— Scenic route

▬▬ Main railway

— Minor railway

— State border

Extensive green vineyards of the Hunter Valley

❶ Blue Mountains National Park

The landscape of the Blue Mountains was more than 250 million years in the making as sediments built up then were eroded, revealing sheer cliff faces and canyons. Home to Aboriginal communities for an estimated 14,000 years, the rugged terrain proved, at first, a formidable barrier to white settlers *(see p174)*, but since the 1870s it has been a popular holiday resort. The mountains get their name from the release of oil from the eucalyptus trees which causes a blue haze. Excellent drives and walking trails allow for easy exploration of the region.

Mount Wilson
A basalt cap, the result of a now extinct volcano, provides the rich soil for the gardens of this attractive summer retreat.

Flora and Fauna in the Blue Mountains

Possum

Many species of flora and fauna that are unique to Australia can be easily seen in the Blue Mountains. For example, the superb lyrebird is a fan-tailed bird found in the forests, distinguishable by its high-pitched cry. The sassafras (*Doryphora sassafras*) tree is one of the species of the warm temperate rainforest and produces tiny white flowers. The shy brushtail possum seeks shelter in the woodlands by day and forages at night.

MUDGEE

Lithgow

Bell

Hartley

Mount Victoria ③②

Blackheath

Hampton

Jenolan Caves
Nine spectacular limestone caves are open to the public; stalactites and stalagmites can be seen in beautiful and striking formations.

Key

▬▬ Major road
▭▭ Minor road
▬•▬ Railway

0 km		5
0 miles		5

For hotels and restaurants in this area see pp483–4 and pp507–9

VISITORS' CHECKLIST

Practical Information
Great Western Hwy. ℹ Blue
Mountains Visitor Information,
Great Western Hwy, Glenbrook
(1300 653 408). 🅿 ♿ 🎁 🛍

Transport
🚃 Katoomba.

Mount Tomah Botanic Garden
Cool-climate species from around the world
are grown here, including rhododendrons
from the Himalayas.

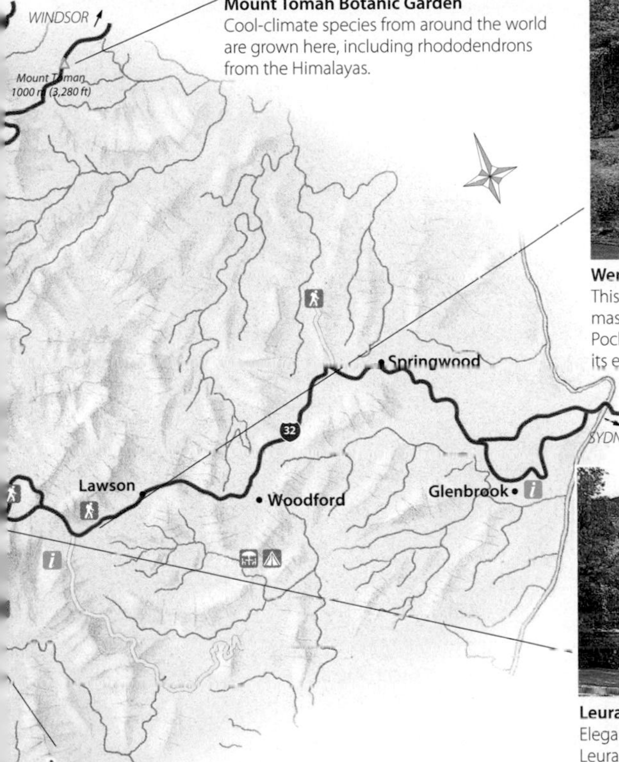

WINDSOR

*Mount Tomah,
1000 m (3,280 ft)*

Wentworth Falls
This waterfall is evidence of a
massive slip in the escarpment.
Pockets of rainforest thrive along
its edges.

Springwood

32

SYDNEY

Lawson • Woodford   Glenbrook • ℹ

Leura
Elegant old residences such as the
Leura Mansion are features of this
pretty village.

KEY

① **Katoomba** is the largest town in
the vicinity of the national park and
has a full range of accommodation
for tourists.

② **The Leuralla Toy and Railway
Museum** is home to the southern
hemisphere's largest collection of
toys, trains and related memorabilia.

③ **The Cathedral of Ferns** is an area
of green foliage set amid streams,
resembling tropical rainforest.

Three Sisters
Erosion formed this spectacular rock formation. Aboriginal legend
has it that it is in fact three sisters, imprisoned by their father to
protect them from a bunyip (a mythical swamp creature).

For additional map symbols *see back flap*

Exploring the Blue Mountains

The Blue Mountains, reaching 1,100 m (3,600 ft) above sea level at their highest point, at first made the early colonists virtual prisoners of the Sydney Cove area. Many settlers were convinced that plains suitable for grazing and crops would be found beyond the mountains, but attempts to reach the imagined pastures repeatedly failed. In 1813, however, three farmers, Gregory Blaxland, William Lawson and William Charles Wentworth, set out on a well-planned mission, following the ridge between the Grose and Cox rivers, and emerged successfully on the western side of the mountains. The construction of roads and a railway made the mountains an increasingly attractive destination, and resorts and country homes were soon established. In 1959, the Blue Mountains National Park was gazetted, ensuring the preservation of the large tracts of remaining wilderness.

🏛 Norman Lindsay Gallery and Museum

14 Norman Lindsay Crescent, Faulconbridge. **Tel** (02) 4751 1067. **Open** 10am–4pm daily. **Closed** 25 Dec. 🅿 ♿ 🆆 normanlindsay.com.au

Norman Lindsay, one of Australia's most recognized artists, inspired considerable controversy during his lifetime with his sumptuous nudes and risqué novels. Born in 1879, he bought his mountain retreat in 1913 and set about producing an enormous body of work, much of which reflects his rejection of the moral and sexual restraints of his era.

His beautifully preserved home is now a gallery for his many paintings, cartoons, mythological garden sculptures and children's books. There is a whole room devoted to *The Magic Pudding*, a perennial favourite. There is also a re-creation of the interior of his original studio, and a peaceful garden set amid the mountain bushland.

Leura

ℹ Echo Point, Katoomba. **Tel** 1300 653 408. 📅 first Sun of the month.

This small town on the Great Western Highway, with its European gardens and Art Deco architecture, recalls the elegance of life in the 1920s. Its secluded, tree-lined main street is a magnet for fine art galleries, cafés, shops, up-market restaurants and the Leuralla Toy and Railway Museum.

Six km (3.5 miles) from Leura, Everglades House is an Art Deco fantasy of curves, balconies and rose-pink walls. The Everglades gardens are considered classic examples of cool-climate design from the 1930s. They include a shaded alpine garden, a grotto pool, rhododendron stands and peacocks roaming around the grounds. Some other gardens in the area are opened to the public during the Leura Garden Festival each October (see p44).

Visitors can get an overview of the surrounding landscape by taking the Cliff Drive to Katoomba. The lookout at Sublime Point, at the end of Sublime Point Road, also provides startling views across the Jamison Valley.

Scenic Skyway ride over the Blue Mountains from Katoomba

Katoomba

ℹ Echo Point, Katoomba. **Tel** 1300 653 408. 🆆 visitbluemountains.com.au

Katoomba is the bustling tourism centre of the Blue Mountains and a good base from which to explore the mountains. However, it still manages to retain a veneer of its gracious former self, when it first attracted wealthy Sydneysiders in need of mountain air during the 1870s. The Paragon Café, with its dark-wood panelling and mirrored walls, is a reminder of these glory days, as are the imposing guesthouses with their fresh air and beautiful views across the Jamison Valley.

Within a few minutes' drive of the town are the region's most popular attractions. Echo Point is home to a large information centre and lookout, with views across to the imposing bulk of Mount Solitary and the most famous of icons, the Three Sisters (see pp172–3). A short walk leads down to this striking rock formation, while further on the Giant Staircase – steps hewn out

Picturesque tree-lined Main Street in Leura

For hotels and restaurants in this area see pp483–4 and pp507–9

of the rock face – curls around its eastern side. Beyond the Staircase is the Leura Forest, which is a warm temperate rainforest.

On the western side of town the world's first glass-floor Skyway, 270 m (885 ft) above the valley floor, departs regularly. The Scenic Skyway traverses 205 m (670 ft) above the mountains, while the Scenic Railway offers a nerve-wracking plummet down a mountain gorge. Reputed to be the steepest rail track in the world, it was originally built in the 1880s to transport miners down to the valley's rich coal deposits.

Blackheath

4,100. Govetts Leap Rd. **Tel** 1300 653 408.

Blackheath is a small village that offers a quieter prospect than many of the busy mountain towns further east. The excellent standard of restaurants and accommodation available in the town often induces visitors to stay one or two nights here, rather than make the return to Sydney the same day. But the real draw of this area is the chance to explore the mist enshrouded rifts and ravines of the beautiful Grose Valley.

The best place to start is the Heritage Centre, 3 km (2 miles) from Blackheath along Govetts Leap Road. Displays document the geological, Aboriginal and European histories of the region and local flora and fauna, while park officers are available to offer advice on the best walks in the area. Govetts Leap, with its heady views across Grose Valley, provides a point of orientation and is the starting place for a number of tracks. A clifftop track leads off in a southerly direction past Bridal Falls, the highest waterfalls in the Blue Mountains, and through stretches of exposed mountain heathland.

A steep and arduous 8-hour return trek into the valley leads to Blue Gum Forest Walk through the dense covered forest with towering blue-gum eucalyptus trees. The Grand Canyon is a destination only for the fit – this 5-hour walk, through deep gorges and

Eroded gorge in Grose Valley, near the town of Blackheath

sandstone canyons, sheds some light on the geological mysteries of the mountains.

Jenolan Caves

Jenolan Caves Rd. **Tel** (02) 6359 3311. **Open** 9am–5pm daily. to small section of Orient and Chifley caves. jenolancaves.org.au

The Jenolan Caves lie southwest of the mountain range. The Great Western Highway passes the grand old hotels of Mount Victoria before a south turn is taken at Hartley, the centre of the first grazing region established by Blaxland, Lawson and Wentworth from 1815 onwards. The southern stretch of the road, cutting across the escarpment of Kanimbla Valley, is one of the most scenic in the mountains. The Jenolan Caves

Limestone formations in the Jenolan Caves

were first discovered in 1838 and are remarkable for their complexity and accessibility. More than 300 subterranean chambers were formed in a limestone belt that was deposited more than 300 million years ago. The nine caves open to the public have a variety of delicate limestone formations, pools and rivers, including the ominously named Styx River.

Mount Tomah Botanic Gardens

Bells Line of Road. **Tel** (02) 4567 3000. **Open** Mar–Sep: 10am–4pm daily, Oct–Feb: 10am–5pm daily. **Closed** 25 Dec. bluemountainsbotanic garden.com.au

Mount Tomah lies along the Bells Line of Road, a quiet but increasingly popular route with tourists to the area.

Tomah takes its name from an indigenous word for "fern". The Botanic Gardens were set up as an annex to Sydney's Royal Botanic Gardens (see pp110–11) in order to house species that would not survive the coastal conditions. Of special interest are the southern hemisphere plants which developed in isolation once Australia broke away from Gondwanaland (see p27).

The overall layout of the gardens is a feat of engineering, and the views across Grose Valley are breathtaking.

❷ Windsor

🚗 1,850. 🚉 🚌 🚌 ℹ️ Hawkesbury Valley Way, Clarendon (02) 4560 4620.
🌐 hawkesburytourism.com.au

Windsor was named by Governor Macquarie and this well-preserved colonial settlement is one of the five "Macquarie towns". Established on the banks of the Hawkesbury River in 1794, the town provided farmers with both fertile land and the convenience of river transport.

In the centre of town, St Matthew's Church, designed by Francis Greenway, is a fine example of Georgian colonial architecture and is considered to be his most successful work. Other buildings of interest include the Macquarie Arms, which claims to be Australia's oldest hotel, and the **Hawkesbury Museum**, set in a Georgian residence. The museum chronicles Windsor's early colonial history.

🏛️ **Hawkesbury Museum**
8 Baker St, Windsor. **Tel** (02) 4560 4655. **Open** 10am–4pm Wed–Mon. **Closed** Good Fri, 25 Dec. 🅿️

Environs
One of the other five "Macquarie towns" is Richmond, which lies 6 km (3.5 miles) west of Windsor.

St Matthew's Church in Windsor, designed by Francis Greenway

This attractive settlement was established five years earlier, in 1789. The farmstead of Mountainview, built in 1804, is one of the oldest surviving homes in the country.

❸ Gosford

🚗 155,000. 🚉 🚌 🚌 🚢
ℹ️ 1300 130 708, (02) 4343 4444.
🌐 visitcentralcoast.com.au

Gosford is the principal town of the popular holiday region known as the Central Coast, and provides a good base for touring the surrounding area. The rural settlements that once dotted this

A kangaroo at the Forest of Tranquility

coastline have now evolved into one continuous beachside suburb, stretching as far south as Ku-ring-gai Chase National Park (see p130). Gosford itself sits on the calm northern shore of Brisbane Waters, an excellent spot for sailing and other recreational activities. The nearby coastal beaches are renowned for their great surf, clear lagoons and long stretches of sand. The beaches here are so numerous that it is still possible to find a deserted spot in any season except high summer. The **Forest of Tranquility – Australian Rainforest Sanctuary** is located in a valley of subtropical and temperate rainforest. There are undercover picnic areas, play areas, barbecue facilities, a kiosk and Function Centre, in addition to 5 km (3 miles) of beautiful rainforest walks.

The **Australian Reptile Park** is home to many types of reptiles, including crocodiles, massive goannas, snakes and other species. The park offers wildlife shows such as crocodile feeding, venomous snake and spider milking and a picnic area where you can hand-feed the friendly kangaroos that share the grassy space.

Memorial Park, located in the town of The Entrance, is a short drive north of Gosford. See dozens of pelicans vying for fish from the human feeders at the free pelican feeding show that takes place at 3:30pm daily on

Entrance to the Australian Reptile Park

For hotels and restaurants in this area see pp483–4 and pp507–9

the waterfront. The show also provides visitors with an entertaining and educational commentary about the area's pelicans, birds and marine life.

 Forest of Tranquility – Australian Rainforest Sanctuary
Ourimbah Creek Rd, Ourimbah.
Tel (02) 4362 1855. **Open** 10am–4pm daily. **Closed** 25 Dec. ⬛ ⬛ limited.
ⓦ forestoftranquility.com

Australian Reptile Park
Pacific Hwy, Somersby. **Tel** (02) 4340 1022. **Open** 9am–5pm daily.
Closed 25 Dec. ⬛ ⬛ ⓦ reptile park.com.au

Environs
There are several national parks within a short distance of Gosford. Bouddi National Park is one of the most diverse reserves in the state, with sandstone cliffs, secluded beaches and coastal heaths blanketed in wildflowers. Also worth a visit is the Bulgandry Aboriginal site in Brisbane Waters National Park, which has rock engravings of human and animal figures dating back thousands of years.

❹ Newcastle

🏙 140,000. ✈ 🚉 🚌 🚢
ⓦ visitnewcastle.com.au

One visitor to Newcastle, Australia's second-oldest city, remarked in the 1880s: "To my mind the whole town appeared to have woke up in fright at our arrival and to have no definite ideas of a rendezvous whereat to rally." The chaos to which he referred was largely the result of the city's reliance on coal mining and vast steel works. Building progressed with no planning as profits rose.

Today this chaos only adds to Newcastle's charm. The city curls loosely around a splendid harbour and its main streets rise randomly up the surrounding hills. Industry is still the mainstay, but this does not detract from the city's quaint beauty. The main thoroughfare of Hunter Street has many buildings of diverse architectural styles. The Courthouse follows a style known as Late Free

Italianate post office in Newcastle

Classical; the Court Chambers are High Victorian; the post office was modelled on Palladio's Basilica in Venice and the town's cathedral, Christ Church, is an elaborate and impressive example of Victorian Gothic.

The modern **Newcastle Region Art Gallery** houses works by some of the country's most prominent 19th- and 20th-century artists, including the Newcastle-born William Dobell, Arthur Boyd and Brett Whiteley *(see pp38–9)*.

Queens Wharf is the main attraction of the harbour foreshore. It was redeveloped during the 1980s as part of a bicentennial project. There are splendid views from its

promenade areas and outdoor cafés. On the southern side of the harbour, Nobbys Lighthouse sits at the end of a long causeway; the vista back over old Newcastle makes the brief walk worthwhile.

Further on lies **Fort Stratchley**, built originally to repel the coal-seeking Russians in the 1880s. Despite constant surveillance, the fort did not open fire until the 1940s, when the Japanese shelled Newcastle during World War II. Good surfing beaches lie on either side of the harbour's entrance.

🏛 **Newcastle Region Art Gallery**
Cnr Darby & Laman sts. **Tel** (02) 4974 5100. **Open** 10am–5pm Tue–Sun.
Closed 25 Dec, Good Fri. ⬛

🏰 **Fort Scratchley**
Nobbys Rd. **Tel** (02) 4974 2027.
Open 10am–4pm Wed–Mon (last tour departs at 2:30pm).
Closed Good Fri, 25 Dec. ⬛ ⬛
ⓦ fortscratchley.com.au

Environs
Four times the size of Sydney Harbour *(see pp78–107)*, Lake Macquarie lies 20 km (12 miles) south of Newcastle. The lake's vast size facilitates nearly every kind of watersport imaginable. On the western shore, at Wangi Wangi, is Dobell House, once home to the renowned local artist, William Dobell.

Francis Greenway, Convict Architect

Australian $10 notes once bore the portrait of the early colonial architect Francis Greenway. This was the only currency in the world to pay tribute to a convicted forger. Greenway was transported from England to Sydney in 1814 to serve a 14-year sentence for his crime. Under the patronage of Governor Lachlan Macquarie, who appointed him Civil Architect in 1816, Greenway designed more than 40 buildings, of which 11 still survive today. He received a full King's Pardon in 1819, but soon fell out of favour because he charged exorbitant fees for his architectural designs while still on a government salary. Greenway eventually died in poverty in 1837.

Francis Greenway (1777–1837)

❺ A Tour of the Hunter Valley

The first commercial vineyards in Australia were established on the fertile flats of the Hunter River in the 1830s. Originally a specialist area for fortified wines, Tyrrell's helped shift the focus towards new, high-quality modern wines. February and March are busy months with the Harvest Festival taking place from March to May and the Jazz in the Vines festival in October. With beautiful scenery and 74 wineries, mostly open daily, the Hunter Valley is one of the top tourist destinations in New South Wales.

③ **Lake's Folly** Max Lake started this vineyard in the 1960s, successfully growing Cabernet Sauvignon grapes in the Hunter Valley for the first time since the 1900s.

④ **Hope Estate** Cask Hall was the vision of the late wine writer Len Evans. The vineyard's wines are now world famous, as are its concerts.

⑤ **Tyrrells' Vineyards** The Tyrrell family has been making wine here since 1858. An outdoor tasting area gives views over the vineyards.

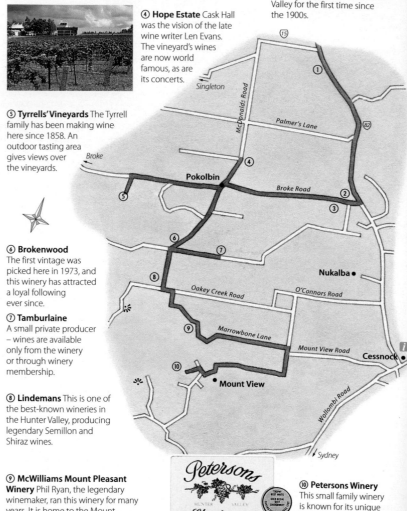

⑥ **Brokenwood**
The first vintage was picked here in 1973, and this winery has attracted a loyal following ever since.

⑦ **Tamburlaine**
A small private producer – wines are available only from the winery or through winery membership.

⑧ **Lindemans** This is one of the best-known wineries in the Hunter Valley, producing legendary Semillon and Shiraz wines.

⑨ **McWilliams Mount Pleasant Winery** Phil Ryan, the legendary winemaker, ran this winery for many years. It is home to the Mount Pleasant Elizabeth Semillon, one of Australia's best quality white wines.

⑩ **Petersons Winery** This small family winery is known for its unique experimentation with champagne-style wine production in the Hunter Valley.

① **Rothbury** An early morning champagne breakfast and hot-air balloon flight over the Hunter Valley from this town are a luxurious way to start a day touring the wineries.

② **The Hunter Valley Wine Society** This group organizes wine tastings from many local vineyards and offers excellent advice for the novice. Shiraz and Semillon are the two most recognizable Hunter Valley styles.

0 kilometres   5

0 miles   5

Key

▬▬ Tour route

══ Other road

Tips for Drivers

Tour length: 60 km (37 miles). While there are no limits on the numbers of wineries that can be visited, three or four in one day will give time to taste and discuss the wines leisurely. Don't forget Australia's strict drink-driving laws (see p561).

Starting point: Cessnock is the gateway to the Hunter Valley and is home to its major visitors' centre.

Stopping-off points: Apart from the picnic areas and restaurants at the wineries, Pokolbin has plenty of cafés, a general store and a bush picnic area. The Mount Bright lookout gives a panoramic view over the region.

Panoramic mountain view from Barrington Tops

❻ Barrington Tops World Heritage Area

🚉 Gloucester. 🛈 27 Denison St, Gloucester (02) 6558 1408. **Open** daily. 🌐 **gloucester.org.au**

Flanking the north of the Hunter Valley is the mountain range known as the Barringtons. One of the highest points in Australia, its high country, the "Barrington Tops", reaches 1,550 m (5,080 ft), and light snow is common in winter. The rugged mountains, cool-climate rainforest, gorges, cliffs and waterfalls make Barrington Tops a paradise for hikers, campers, birdwatchers and climbers. Its 280,000 ha (690,000 acres) of forest, with 1,000-year-old trees, are protected by the Barrington Tops National Park. The rainforest was declared a World Heritage Area in 1986 and a Wilderness Area in 1996 as part of the Gondwana Rainforests of Australia (formerly the Central Eastern Rainforest Reserves) (see pp30–31).

Barrington Tops is a favourite weekend escape for Sydney-siders. Tourist operators organize environmentally friendly 4WD trips into the heart of the wild forests, with camping along the Allyn River, hiking trails at Telegherry and Jerusalem Creek and swimming in the rock pool at Lady's Well.

Barrington Tops is best reached through Dungog or from Gloucester.

Spinning wheel from the Armidale Folk Museum

❼ Armidale

🏠 22,000. ✈ 🚉 🚌 🚌 🛈 82 Marsh St (02) 6770 3888. **Open** daily. 🌐 **armidaletourism.com.au**

Lying in the heart of the New England Tablelands, Armidale is a sophisticated university city surrounded by some of the state's most magnificent national parks, while concerts, plays, films and lectures fill its many theatres, pubs and university halls.

Some 35 buildings in Armidale are classified by the National Trust, testament to the land booms of the 19th century, including the town hall, courthouse and St Peter's Anglican Cathedral. The **New England Regional Art Museum** holds the A$20 million Howard Hinton and Chandler Coventry collections, with many works by Australian artists, including Tom Roberts and Norman Lindsay (see p38). To the east of Armidale is the 90-ha (220-acre) **Oxley Wild Rivers National Park**, containing the 220-m (720-ft) high Wollomombi Gorge, one of the highest waterfalls in Australia.

🏛 **New England Regional Art Museum**
106 Kentucky St. **Tel** (02) 6772 5255. **Open** 10am–5pm Tue–Fri, 10am–4pm Sat & Sun. **Closed** 1 Jan, Good Fri, 25 Dec. 💻 ♿ 🌐 neram.com.au

🌳 **Oxley Wild Rivers National Park**
145 Miller St, Armidale. **Tel** (02) 6738 9100. **Open** Mon–Fri. ♿ limited.

Wilderness stream in Gibraltar Range National Park

❽ Gibraltar Range National Park

Gwydir Hwy. **Tel** (02) 6739 0700.
Open daily. 🚫 only for camping
and facilities. ♿ Ⓦ **nationalparks.
nsw.gov.au**

Situated 70 km (43 miles) east
of Glen Innes, Gibraltar Range
National Park is known for its
giant rocky tors towering
1,200 m (4,000 ft) above sea
level, surrounded by heath and
swamp land. The area is at its
most beautiful in the summer,
when wildflowers such as
waratahs and Christmas bells
bloom. The park also has
good walking trails and
camping facilities.

Gibraltar Range National Park
is linked to Washpool National
Park by a 40-km (25-mile) World
Heritage walk. Washpool has
visitor facilities at Coombadjha
Creek but wilderness walking is
its main feature.

Glen Innes and its surrounding villages of Glencoe, Ben
Lomond and Shannon Vale are
known as Australia's "Celtic
Country". Settled by Scottish,
Welsh, Irish and Cornish
immigrants in 1852, the area's
heritage is celebrated by the

annual Australian Celtic Festival
(see p46). The town's Standing
Stones are a traditional
monument to all Celtic settlers.

Sapphire mining remains a
major industry. Public digging,
known as "fossicking", for
sapphires, topaz, garnet and
beryl is still possible near the
mining villages of Emmaville
and Torrington. Glen Innes
hosts a gem and mineral fair
in September each year.

❾ Tenterfield

🏙 3,500. ✈ 🚌 🚌 ℹ 157 Rouse St
(02) 6736 1082.

The rural town of Tenterfield,
to the north of the
New England Tablelands,
occupies a special
place in Australian
history. Often
described as the
"Birthplace of Our
Nation", it was at
the town's School
of Arts building
on 24 October
1889 that local
politician and towering figure of
19th-century Australian politics,
Sir Henry Parkes, made his

Plaque celebrating Henry
Parkes' speech

historic "One Nation" speech.
The address explained his
vision of all the colonies in
Australia uniting to form one
country. Parkes' Tenterfield
address led to a popular
movement of support, resulting
in Australian Federation on
1 January 1901 (see p60). The
School of Arts was the first
building to be acquired by
the New South Wales National
Trust because of its political
and historic importance.

Other historic buildings in
this small town include the
Victorian mansion Stannum
House, the bluestone saddlers'
shop (made famous in the
song "Tenterfield Saddler"),
and the restored courthouse
with its glass ceiling.

Also not to be
missed are Bald
Rock and Boonoo
Boonoo, which
are about 40 km
(25 miles) north
of Tenterfield.
Bald Rock is the
second biggest
monolith in
Australia after Uluru (see pp290–
93) and the largest exposed
granite rock, dating back to
the Lower Triassic period which
was over 200 million years ago.
It is 750 m (2,460 ft) long and
approximately 200 m (650 ft)
high. It offers magnificent
views of volcanic ranges to
the east, Girraween National
Park in Queensland to the
north and Mount McKenzie to
the south. Boonoo Boonoo
Falls cascade 210 m (690 ft)
into the gorge below, ideal for
swimming, and surrounded by
rainforest bathed in moisture
from the falls.

Tenterfield's School of Arts building

For hotels and restaurants in this area see pp483–4 and pp507–9

⑩ Inverell

🏙 11,000. 🚆 🚌 🚍 ℹ️ Water Towers Complex, Campbell St (02) 6728 8161. 🌐 **inverell.com.au**

Inverell is known as "Sapphire City" because so many of the world's sapphires are mined in the area. Many of the buildings in the main street were built during the 1880s mining boom and are well preserved. The **Inverell Pioneer Village** features buildings gathered from around the district and relocated to create this tourist theme town.

Just south of Inverell lies the mighty Copeton Dam. White-water rafting below the dam on the wild Gwydir River is an exhilarating experience.

🏛 **Inverell Pioneer Village** Tingha Rd, Inverell. **Tel** (02) 6722 1717. **Open** 10am–4pm Tue–Sun. **Closed** Good Fri, 25 Dec. 🐾 ♿ 🌐 **inverellpioneervillage.org.au**

⑪ Tamworth

🏙 36,000. 🚆 🏢 🚌 🚍 ℹ️ cnr Murray & Peel sts (02) 6767 5300. 🌐 **visittamworth.com**

Tamworth is a thriving rural city, located at the centre of fertile agricultural plains. Yet despite its history, fine old buildings and claim to fame as the first Australian city with electric street lighting, it remains best known as Australia's country music capital.

Every January, thousands of country music fans and performers flock here for the Country Music Festival, which includes country music, blue grass, busking, bush ballads, harmonica

Golden Guitar Tourist Centre, fronted by a huge golden guitar

playing and the Golden Guitar Awards *(see p45)*. Reflecting the city's main interest there is the Big Golden Guitar Tourist Centre, fronted by a large golden guitar, the Country Music Gallery of Stars, where Australia's country music greats are immortalized in wax, the Roll of Renown dedicated to musicians who have made a major contribution to the industry and the Country Music Hands of Fame cornerstone.

Tamworth's other source of fame is as the equestrian centre of Australia. The Quarter Horse Association and Appaloosa Association are based here, and rodeos and show-jumping events are held here.

⑫ Mudgee

🏙 8,500. 🚌 🚉 Lithgow. ℹ️ 84 Market St (02) 6372 1020. 🌐 **visitmudgeeregion.com.au**

Mudgee is a magnificent old rural town with gardens and grand buildings, many of which are protected by the National Trust.

Situated on the banks of the Cudgegong River, the town was first settled by William Lawson, who discovered its good grazing country in 1821. The settlement was surveyed and planned in 1824 by Robert Hoddle. The design was so successful that he copied Mudgee's grid layout 14 years later for the city of Melbourne *(see pp386–7)*. Historic buildings not to be missed include the Regent Theatre on Church Street, the many churches, banks and civic buildings on Market Street, the railway station and the restored West End Hotel that now

Sheep grazing under a tree in the Mudgee region

houses the excellent Colonial Inn Museum.

Mudgee is also famous for its surrounding wineries and the Mudgee Wine Festival held each September *(see p44)*. From the surrounding countryside come local gourmet foods such as yabbies (crayfish), trout, lamb, peaches and asparagus.

Environs

During the 1850s and 1860s, gold was discovered to the south of Mudgee, bringing thousands of hopeful prospectors to the region *(see pp58–9)*. The villages of Hill End, Hargraves, Windeyer and Sofala once had populations of more than 20,000 each, but became ghost towns once the boom was over. Hill End is the most famous of these and is now classed as a Living Historic Site with almost all of its buildings dating back to the 1870s. The creeks of Windeyer continued to yield alluvial gold until the 1930s. Panning for gold in the river is a popular tourist activity.

One of Australia's most famous writers, Henry Lawson, hailed from the region *(see p39)*, and Gulgong, a quaint gold rush village famous for being depicted on the original A$10 note, contains the **Henry Lawson Centre**.

🏛 **Henry Lawson Centre** 147 Mayne St, Gulgong. **Tel** (02) 6374 2049. **Open** 10am–3:30pm Mon–Sat, 10am–1pm Sun. **Closed** Good Fri, 25 Dec. 🐾 🌐 **henrylawson gulgong.org.au**

Northern New South Wales Coastline

The northern New South Wales coastline is known for its mix of natural beauty, mild climate and good resorts. Australia's most easterly mainland point, Byron Bay, is an attractive, up-market resort which is enhanced by its unspoiled landscape and outstanding beaches. Elsewhere, clean and isolated beaches directly abut rainforest, with some national parks and reserves holding World Heritage status *(see pp30–31)*. Sugar cane and bananas are commonly grown in the region.

④ Red Cliff Beach
Adjacent to the beautiful Yuraygir National Park, Red Cliff is one of several sandy, isolated beaches in the immediate vicinity.

⑤ Moonee Beach
A creek meandering through bush country to the ocean offers perfect opportunities for safe swimming, picnics and camping.

⑥ Urunga
Two rivers, the Bellingen and the Kalang, reach the ocean in this picturesque beach resort. Its safe waters make it a particularly popular holiday site for families.

Coffs Harbour is one of the most popular tourist destinations in New South Wales. Surrounded by excellent beaches, there is also an attractive man-made harbour and a range of top-quality tourist facilities.

⑨ Arakoon
This picturesque headland is part of a state recreation area. Nearby is Trial Bay Gaol, a progressive 19th-century prison that re-opened during World War I to house prisoners of war from various countries.

⑦ Third Headland Beach
Like its neighbour Hungry Head Beach, 5 km (3 miles) north, Third Headland is a popular surfing beach with strong waves hitting the headland cliffs.

Grafton is a quaint 19th-century rural town, with elegant streets and riverside walks. The town is best known for its abundance of jacaranda trees, whose striking purple blooms are celebrated in a festival each October *(see p45)*.

⑫ ★ Crowdy Bay
Part of a national park, Crowdy Bay's lagoons, forests and swamps are abundant with native wildlife. Coarse-fishing is a popular activity from the sea's edge.

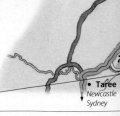

Dor▶

• Taree
Newcastle
Sydney

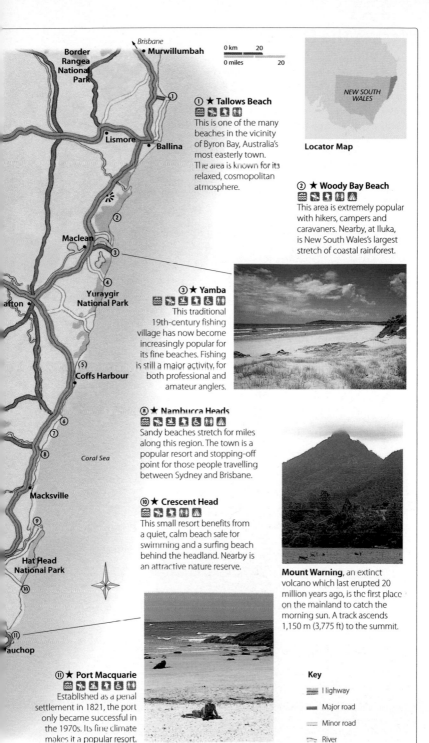

Brisbane
Murwillumbah

Border
Rangea
National
Park

Lismore

Ballina

①

Maclean
②

③

Yuraygir
National Park
④

atton

⑤
Coffs Harbour

⑥
⑦
⑧

Coral Sea

Macksville

⑨

Hat Head
National Park

⑩

⑪

auchop

0 km   20
0 miles   20

NEW SOUTH
WALES

Locator Map

① ★ Tallows Beach

This is one of the many beaches in the vicinity of Byron Bay, Australia's most easterly town. The area is known for its relaxed, cosmopolitan atmosphere.

② ★ Woody Bay Beach

This area is extremely popular with hikers, campers and caravaners. Nearby, at Iluka, is New South Wales's largest stretch of coastal rainforest.

③ ★ Yamba

This traditional 19th-century fishing village has now become increasingly popular for its fine beaches. Fishing is still a major activity, for both professional and amateur anglers.

⑧ ★ Nambucca Heads

Sandy beaches stretch for miles along this region. The town is a popular resort and stopping-off point for those people travelling between Sydney and Brisbane.

⑩ ★ Crescent Head

This small resort benefits from a quiet, calm beach safe for swimming and a surfing beach behind the headland. Nearby is an attractive nature reserve.

Mount Warning, an extinct volcano which last erupted 20 million years ago, is the first place on the mainland to catch the morning sun. A track ascends 1,150 m (3,775 ft) to the summit.

⑪ ★ Port Macquarie

Established as a penal settlement in 1821, the port only became successful in the 1970s. Its fine climate makes it a popular resort.

Key

━━ Highway

━━ Major road

┄┄ Minor road

〜 River

West of the Divide

In stark contrast to the lush green of the Blue Mountains and the blue waters of the New South Wales coastline, the western region of the state is archetypal of Australia's Outback. This dusty, dry landscape, parched by the sun, is an understandably remote area, dotted with a few mining towns and national parks. Dubbo and Wagga Wagga are the main frontier towns, but anything beyond is commonly referred to as "Back o' Bourke" and ventured into by only the most determined of tourists. Even the most adventurous should avoid the area in high summer.

Locator Map

▪ *West of the Divide*
▫ *The Blue Mountains pp168–83*

Sights at a Glance

⓭ Dubbo
⓮ Lightning Ridge
⓯ Bourke
⓰ Broken Hill
⓱ Willandra National Park
⓲ Wagga Wagga

Key

— Major road
═══ Minor road
– – Track
⌁ Main railway
— Regional border

0 kilometres 200
0 miles 200

⓭ Dubbo

🏠 39,500. ✈ 🚍 🚌 ℹ cnr Newell Hwy & Macquarie St (02) 6801 4450. 🅆 **dubbotourism.com.au**

Dubbo is located at the geographical heart of the state and is the regional capital of western New South Wales. The area was first noted for its rich agricultural potential in 1817 by explorer John Oxley, sited as it is on the banks of the Macquarie River. The city has since grown into a rural centre producing $45 million worth of food and agricultural goods annually.

Dubbo also has a strong colonial history and period architecture. Among the more interesting buildings are the 1876 Dubbo Museum, with its ornate ceilings and cedar staircase, the 1890 Italianate courthouse and the 1884 Macquarie Chambers, with their Tuscan columns and terracotta tiles.

At the **Old Dubbo Gaol**, visitors can hear the tragic story of Jacky Underwood, an Aborigine hung for his part in the Breelong massacre of 1900, when eleven white settlers were killed. Dubbo magistrate Rolf Boldrewood drew on the characters of the gaol's inmates to write the classic novel *Robbery Under Arms (see p38)*.

The most popular sight in Dubbo is the large **Western Plains Zoo**, 5 km (3 miles) from the town. The zoo's emphasis is

Rhinoceros in Western Plains Zoo

on breeding endangered species. Visitors can see over 1,000 animals.

🏛 **Old Dubbo Gaol**
Macquarie St. **Tel** (02) 6801 4460.
Open 9am–4:30pm daily.
Closed Good Fri, Dec 25. 🅆 **olddubbogaol.com.au**

🐾 **Western Plains Zoo**
Obley Rd. **Tel** (02) 6882 5888.
Open 9am–5pm daily. ♿ 🚻 🅿

⓮ Lightning Ridge

🏠 5,000. ✈ 🚌 ℹ Morilla St (02) 6829 1670.

Lightning Ridge is a small mining village and home of the treasured black opal – a rare dark opal shot with red, blue and green. Gem enthusiasts from around the world come to try their luck on the opal fields. The town is also famous for its hearty welcome to visitors, unusual within mining communities, and its mine tours, plethora of opal shops and hot bore spas.

⓯ Bourke

🏘 3,000. ✈ 🚌 🚃 ℹ 24 Anson St
(02) 6872 1321. 🆆 **visitbourke.com**

Situated on the Darling River, part
of Australia's longest river system,
Bourke is a colourful town that
was once the centre of the
world's wool industry. It still
produces 25,000 bales per year.

Bourke's heyday is evident in
the colonial buildings and the
old weir, wharf, lock and lift-up
span bridge which recall the
days of the paddlesteamer trade
to Victoria *(see p435)*. The town's
cemetery tells something of
Bourke's history: Afghan camel
drivers who brought the animal
to Australia from the Middle
East in the 19th century are
buried here.

⓰ Broken Hill

🏘 21,000. ✈ 🚉 🚌 🚃 ℹ cnr
Blende and Bromide sts (08) 8080
3560. 🆆 **visitbrokenhill.com.au**

The unofficial centre of Outback
New South Wales, Broken Hill
is a mining city perched on
the edge of the deserts of
Inland Australia. The town was
established in 1883, when vast
deposits of zinc, lead and silver
were discovered in a 7-km
(4-mile) long "Line of Lode" by
the then-fledgling company,
Broken Hill Pty Ltd. Broken Hill
has since grown into a major
town and BHP has become
Australia's biggest corporation.

Broken Hill's now declining
mining industry is still evident;
slag heaps are piled up, there are
more pubs per head than any
other city in the state and streets
are named after metals.

Mungo World Heritage Area

Lake Mungo is an area of great
archaeological significance.
For 40,000 years, it was a 10-m
(33-ft) deep lake, around
which Aborigines lived. The
lake then dried up, leaving its
eastern rim as a wind-blown
sand ridge known as the
Walls of China. Its age was
determined in the 1960s when
winds uncovered an Aboriginal
skeleton known as Mungo
Man. Lake Mungo has been
protected as part of the
Willandra Lakes World Heritage
Area since 1981 *(see pp30–31)*.

Walls of China sand ridges

Surprisingly, Broken Hill also
has more than 20 art galleries
featuring desert artists. The city
is also the base of the Royal
Flying Doctor Service *(see p261)*
and School of the Air.

To the northwest of Broken
Hill is **Silverton**, once a thriving
silver mining community and
now a ghost town. It is popular
as a location for films, such as
Mad Max and *Priscilla, Queen
of the Desert*.

⓱ Willandra National Park

ℹ 200 Yambil St, Griffith (02) 6966
8100. **Open** daily. **Closed** in wet
weather. 🐾 ♿ to homestead.
🆆 **nationalparks.nsw.gov.au**

Willandra National Park, on
the edge of a riverine plain
has significant wildlife and
historic values. The park covers
part of the once prosperous
Willandra Sheep Station and
contains the homestead and

shearing complexes of the
former station. The homestead
overlooks peaceful Willandra
Creek, where grasslands and
creek beds are home to
kangaroos, emus and ground-
nesting birds.

⓲ Wagga Wagga

🏘 57,000. ✈ 🚉 🚌
ℹ Tarcutta St, 1300 100 122.
🆆 **tourismwaggawagga.com.au**

Named by its original
inhabitants, the Widadjuri
people, as "a place of many
crows", Wagga Wagga has
grown into a large, modern
city serving the surrounding
farming community. It has won
many accolades for its wines
and the abundance of gardens
has earned it the title of "Garden
City of the South".

The large Botanic Gardens
and the Wagga Historical
Museum are well worth a visit.
The Widadjuri track is a popular
walk along the Murrumbidgee
River banks.

Environs

The gentle town of **Gundagai**,
nestling beneath Mount
Parnassus on the banks of the
Murrumbidgee River, has been
immortalized in the bush ballad
"Along the Road to Gundagai".
More tragic is Gundagai's place
in history as the site of
Australia's greatest natural
disaster when floods swept
away the town in 1852.

Historic pub in the ghost town of Silverton, near Broken Hill

THE SOUTH COAST AND SNOWY MOUNTAINS

Although the busiest highway in Australia runs through southern New South Wales, the area remains one of the most beautiful in the country. Its landscape includes the Snowy Mountains, the surf beaches of the far south, the historic Southern Highland villages and the farming towns of the Murray and Murrumbidgee plains.

Ever since European settlers crossed the Blue Mountains in 1812 *(see p174)*, the southern plains of New South Wales around Goulburn, Yass and Albury have been prime agricultural land. Yet the wilderness of the Snowy Mountains to the east and the steep escarpment which runs the length of the beautiful South and Sapphire coasts, from Wollongong to the Victoria border, has never been completely tamed. Today, the splendour of southern New South Wales is protected by a number of large national parks.

The great Snowy Mountains offer alpine scenery at its best. In summer, the wildflower-scattered meadows, deep gorges and cascading mountain creeks seem to stretch endlessly into the distance; in winter, the jagged snow-capped peaks and twisted snow gums turn this summer walking paradise into a playground for keen downhill and cross-country skiers.

The area also has a long and colourful cultural heritage: Aboriginal tribes, gold diggers and mountain cattlemen have all left their mark here. During the 1950s and 1960s, the region became the birthplace of multicultural Australia, as thousands of European immigrants came to work on the Snowy Mountains Scheme, an engineering feat which diverted the flow of several rivers to provide hydroelectricity and irrigation for southeastern Australia.

But southern New South Wales is more than just landscapes; civilization is never far away. There are excellent restaurants and hotels along the coast, Wollongong is an industrial city and the gracious towns of the Southern Highlands offer historic attractions.

Snowy Mountains landscape in autumn

◄ Bucolic landscape around the Thredbo River, in the Snowy Mountains

Exploring the South Coast and Snowy Mountains

The Great Dividing Range, which runs from the Blue Mountains (see pp172–5) down to the Snowy Mountains and into Victoria, divides the region into three areas. There is the coastal strip, a zone of beautiful beaches, which starts at Wollongong and runs south for 500 km (310 miles) to Eden, hemmed in by the rising mountain range to its west. On the range lie the Southern Highlands, Mount Kosciuszko and the Snowy Mountains. West of the range are the farming plains of the Murrumbidgee River.

Waterfall in the beautiful Morton National Park

Golden inlet at Ben Boyd National Park, on the southern tip of New South Wales

Getting Around

A car is essential to do full justice to this region, with the Hume Hwy providing excellent access to the Southern Highlands and the western farming towns. Wollongong and the southern beaches are linked from Sydney to the Victoria border by the coastal Princes Hwy. From Canberra, the Monaro Hwy is the best route to the Snowy Mountains. From Bega to the east or Gundagai and Tumut in the west, take the Snowy Mountains Hwy. A train service between Sydney and Canberra stops at the Southern Highlands and Hume Hwy towns, while the coastal resorts are serviced by buses from both Sydney and Melbourne.

0 kilometres 25

0 miles 25

Sydney

Campbelltown

Camden

1
ROYAL
NATIONAL
PARK

Picton

Mittagong

Berrima · Bowral

2 WOLLONGONG

Moss Vale

Port Kembla

3 SOUTHERN HIGHLANDS

Kiama

Fitzroy Falls

GOULBURN

Kangaroo Valley

Seven Mile Beach
National Park

MORTON NATIONAL PARK

Nowra-Bomaderry

5

Jervis
Bay

Jervis Bay

Wreck
Bay

Pigeon House Mountain 719m

Milton

Ulladulla

Budawang
National
Park

wood

52

Pebbly Beach

PRINCES HIGHWAY

Batemans Bay

Moruya

Deua
tional
Park

Bodalla

Montague
Island

Narooma

illiga
mal
rk

Tasman Sea

Bermagui

boka

Mimosa Rocks

Bega

Tathra

Merimbula

ests
al

PRINCES HIGHWAY

Eden

Ben Boyd
National
Park

Green Cape

Narrabarba

Bairnsdale

Key

═══	Highway
━━━	Major road
┄┄┄	Minor road
──	Scenic route
──	Main railway
──	Minor railway
──	State border
△	Summit

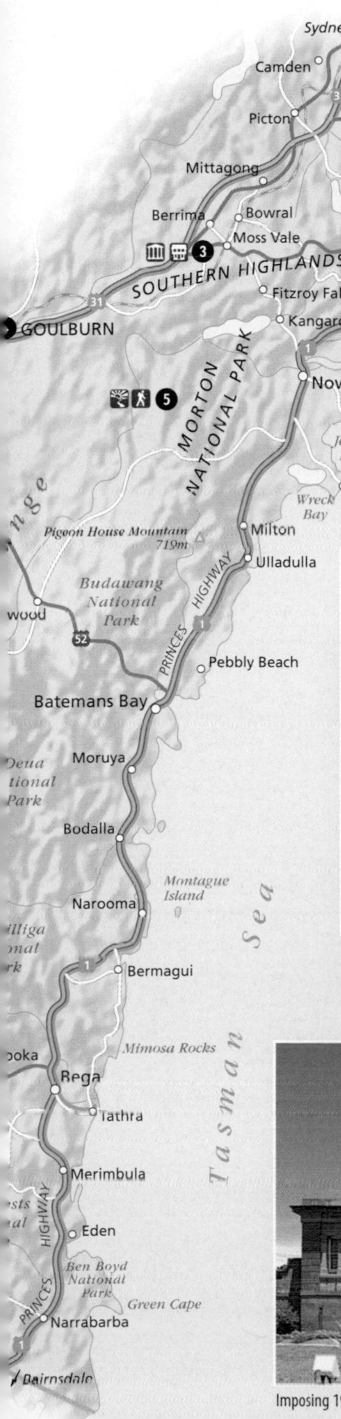

Snowy landscape near Thredbo Village

Imposing 19th-century architecture in Cooma

For additional map symbols *see back flap*

❶ Royal National Park

🚉 Loftus, then tram to Audley (Sun public hols only). 🚌 Bundeena from Cronulla. 🛈 Sir Bertram Stevens Drive, Audley (02) 9542 0648. 🅿️
Ⓦ nationalparks.nsw.gov.au

Designated a national park in 1879, the "Royal" is the oldest national park in Australia and the oldest in the world after Yellowstone in the USA. It covers 16,500 ha (37,000 acres) of spectacular landscape.

To the east, waves from the Pacific Ocean have undercut the sandstone and produced coastal cliffs, interspersed by creeks, waterfalls, lagoons and beaches. Sea eagles and terns nest in caves at the Curracurrang Rocks. Heath vegetation on the plateau merges with woodlands on the upper slopes and rainforest in the gorges. The park is ideal for bushwalking, swimming and bird-watching.

❷ Wollongong

🚹 280,000. 🚉 🚌 🚌
🛈 93 Crown St 1800 240 737.
Ⓦ visitwollongong.com.au

The third largest city in the state, Wollongong is situated on a coastline of beautiful surf beaches. Mount Kembla and Mount Keira provide a backdrop to the city. Originally a coal and steel industrial city – the BHP steel mill at Port Kembla is still a major employer – Wollongong is fast building a reputation as a leisure centre. Northbeach is the most famous of its 17 surf beaches. Flagstaff Point, with its lighthouse, boat harbour, beach views and seafood restaurants, is popular with visitors. Fresh seafood is also on offer at the fish market in Wollongong harbour. The city boasts Australia's largest regional art gallery, and the Nan Tien Temple, the largest Buddhist temple in the southern hemisphere, built for the region's Chinese community.

Figure in Nan Tien Temple

❸ The Southern Highlands

🚌 🚉 Bowral, Moss Vale, Mittagong, Bundanoon. 🛈 62–70 Main St, Mittagong 1300 657 559.
Ⓦ southern-highlands.com.au

Quaint villages, country guesthouses, homesteads and beautiful gardens are scattered across the lush landscape of the Southern Highlands. The region has been a summer retreat for Sydneysiders for almost 100 years. Villages such as Bowral, Moss Vale, Berrima and Bundanoon are also ideal places in the winter for pottering around antiques shops, dining on hearty soups, sitting by open fires and taking bushwalks and country drives. The region's gardens are renowned for their blaze of colours in the spring and autumn. The Corbett Gardens at Bowral are a showpiece during its Tulip Festival (see p44). Bowral is also home to the **Bradman Museum**, where a fascinating collection of photos and cricketing memorabilia commemorates the town's famous son, cricketer Sir Donald Bradman. Bradman is said to have first showed signs of greatness as a child, hitting a golf ball against a water tank stand with a stump-wide strip of wood.

Visiting the village of Berrima is like stepping back in time. The settlement, now home to an abundance of antiques and craft shops, is one of the most unspoilt examples of a small Australian town of the 1830s.

Popular walks in the area include Mount Gibraltar, Carrington Falls, the magnificent Fitzroy Falls at the northern tip of Morton National Park and the majestic Kangaroo Valley. The five Wombeyan Caves, west

Fishing boats moored along Wollongong Harbour

Impressive peak of Pigeon House in Morton National Park

of the town of Mittagong, form an imposing underground limestone cathedral.

🏛️ Bradman Museum

St Jude St, Bowral. **Tel** (02) 4862 1247. **Open** 10am–5pm daily. **Closed** 25 Dec. 🅿️ ♿ 📷 **W** bradman.com.au

Sandstone house in Goulburn

❹ Goulburn

🏔️ 24,500. 🚍 🚌 🚐 ℹ️ 201 Sloane St 1800 353 646. **W** igoulburn.com

Goulburn is at the heart of the Southern Tablelands, with its rich pastoral heritage. Proclaimed in 1863, the town's 19th-century buildings, such as the courthouse, post office and railway station, are testament to the continuing prosperity of the district.

The Big Merino, a giant, hollow concrete sheep, marks Goulburn as the "fine wool capital of the world".

Environs

The town of **Yass** is known for its fine wool and cool-climate wines. Worth a visit is the historic Cooma Cottage, now owned by the National Trust. It was once the home of Australian explorer Hamilton Hume, between 1839 and 1873.

❺ Morton National Park

📷 Bundanoon. 🚌 Fitzroy Falls. ℹ️ Fitzroy Falls (02) 4887 7270. **W** nationalparks.nsw.gov.au/morton

Morton National Park stretches along the rugged hinterland from north of the Shaolhaven Valley to the Ulladulla area. Fitzroy Falls are at the northern end of the park. At Bundanoon, magnificent sandstone country can be explored.

To the south, views of the coastline and Budawang wilderness can be found at Little Forest Plateau and the top of Pigeon House Mountain.

❻ Cooma and the Snowy Mountains

🏔️ 8,000. 🚂 🚌 🚐 ℹ️ 119 Sharp St (02) 6450 1742, 1800 636 525. **W** visitcooma.com.au

Colourful Cooma has a rich history as a cattle, engineering and ski town. During the construction of the Snowy Mountains Scheme (see p187), Cooma was also the weekend base for the thousands of immigrants working up in the mountains during the week. Stories surviving from this era include tales of frontier-like shootouts in the main street, interracial romances and bush mountain feats. However, Cooma is now a sleepy rural town that acts as the gateway to the Snowy Mountains and the southern ski slopes.

The modern resort town of Jindabyne on Lake Jindabyne is home to the Kosciuszko National Park information centre, a myriad of ski shops and lodges, and plenty of nightlife. The two major ski resorts are Thredbo Village along the Alpine Way and the twin resort of Perisher Blue, linked by the ski tube train to Lake Crackenback and the Blue Cow ski fields. Take the chairlift from Thredbo in summer to walk to the summit of Australia's highest mountain, Mount Kosciuszko (see p164), or simply to stroll among the wildflowers and snow gums in the alpine meadows. Another recommended walk is to Blue Lake and the Cascades from Dead Horse Gap. Lake Eucumbene and the Thredbo and Eucumbene rivers offer excellent fly-fishing.

Environs

The ghost settlement of **Kiandra** has a marked historic walking trail detailing the gold rush era in the town (see pp58–9). Nearby is the gentle ski resort of Mount Selwyn and the spectacular Yarrangobilly Caves with their underground walks set among limestone stalactites and stalagmites.

Resort town of Jindabyne in the Snowy Mountains

The South Coast

From Nowra to the border with Victoria, the south coast of New South Wales is a magical mix of white sand beaches, rocky coves and coastal bush covered with spotted gums and wattles, and alive with a variety of birds. The coastline is rich in Aboriginal sites, fishing villages and unspoilt beach settlements. The 400 km (250 miles) of coast are divided into three distinct areas – the Shoalhaven Coast to the north, the Eurobodalla ("Land of Many Waters") Coast in the centre and the Sapphire Coast in the far south.

Ulladulla is a small fishing village flanked by the dovecote-shaped peak of Pigeon House Mountain in the Morton-Budawang National Park. A bushwalk offers breathtaking coastal views.

Central Tilba is a delightful historic farming village, backed by the 800-m (2,600-ft) Mount Dromedary. The town itself is famous for its weatherboard cottages and shops, now housing some of the region's finest cafés and arts and crafts shops, and its cheese and wine. The cheese factory and wineries are all open to visitors.

⑦ ★ **Horseshoe Bay Beach, Bermagui**
🚌 ⛴ Writer Zane Grey brought fame to this tiny game fishing town with his tales of marlin fishing.

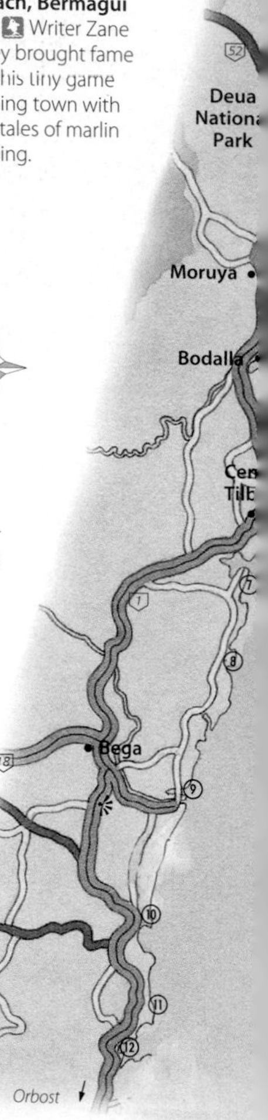

⑩ ★ **Merimbula Beach**
🚌 ⛴ The tourist centre of the Sapphire Coast is famous for its oysters, deep-sea fishing and surrounding white sandy beach.

⑪ ★ **Eden**
🚌 ⛴ ⛰ Set on the deep Twofold Bay, this was once a whaling station. It is now the centre of whale-watching on the south coast during spring. It is also a major tuna fishing town and centre for the local timber industry.

Nowra is the town centre of the beautiful Shoalhaven Coast, near the mouth of the Shoalhaven River. The name means "black cockatoo" in the local Aboriginal language. Nearby are the resorts of Culburra and Shoalhaven Heads, adjacent to Seven Mile Beach National Park.

0 kilometres   25

0 miles   25

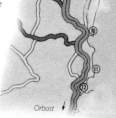

Deua National Park

Moruya

Bodalla

Central Tilba

Bega

Orbost

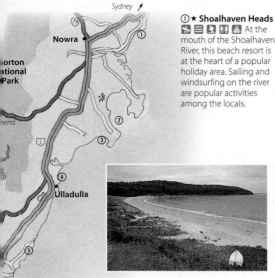

① ★ Shoalhaven Heads

At the mouth of the Shoalhaven River, this beach resort is at the heart of a popular holiday area. Sailing and windsurfing on the river are popular activities among the locals.

Locator Map

② ★ Jervis Bay

This is one of the most beautiful natural harbours in Australia, famous for its naval bases, national park, tiny settlements of Husskinson and Vincentia, and some of the whitest beaches and crystal clear waters in the world.

③ Wreck Bay

This area, within Jervis Bay National Park, abounds with Aboriginal history. The cultural centre offers walkabout tours of local bushlife and archaeology. Nearby Cave Beach is one of the region's most popular for its secluded location.

④ Lake Conjola

This lake, 10 km (6 miles) north of Ulladulla, is one of many lakes in the region popular with canoeists. Camp sites are also available.

⑥ Batemans Bay

The Clyde River enters the sea here, marking the start of the Eurobodalla coastline with its rivers, lakes and chain of heavenly quiet beaches popular with Canberrans.

⑧ Mimosa Rocks

This coastal park, just off the south coast road, offers exceptional bushwalking opportunities and idyllic beaches. Secluded camp sites, with minimum facilities, are popular with families and anglers.

⑨ Tathra Beach

This tiny fishing village and holiday haven includes a maritime museum, housed in a 150-year-old wharf building.

⑩ Ben Boyd National Park

Camping, bushwalks and fine beaches are all features of this park. Temperate rainforests begin to take over the landscape in the surrounding region. The ascent to Mount Imlay offers panoramic views of the coast.

⑤ ★ Pebbly Beach

Set within Murramarang National Park, this beach is famous for its tame kangaroos which sometimes venture into the water at dusk and dawn, and have been seen to "body surf".

Key

━━━ Highway

━━━ Major road

▭▭▭ Minor road

〰〰 River

CANBERRA AND AUSTRALIAN CAPITAL TERRITORY

Located within New South Wales, some 300 km (185 miles) southwest of Sydney, Canberra is Australia's capital and its political heartland. The city was planned in 1908 as the new seat of federal parliament to end rivalry between Sydney and Melbourne. The surrounding Australian Capital Territory (ACT) features bush and mountain terrain.

Canberra was once little more than a sheep station on the edge of the Molonglo River. American architect Walter Burley Griffin won an international competition to design the city. He envisaged a spacious, low-level, modern city, with its major buildings centred on the focal point of Lake Burley Griffin. Canberra (its name is based on an Aboriginal word meaning "meeting place") is a city of contradictions. It consists of more than just politics, diplomacy and monuments. Lacking the traffic and skyscrapers of Australia's other main cities, it has a serenity and country charm suited to strolling around the lake, bush driving and picnicking.

Canberra is the national capital and the centre of political and administrative power in Australia, yet it is also a rural city, ringed by gum trees, with the occasional kangaroo seen hopping down its suburban streets. The city holds the majority of the nation's political, literary and artistic treasures, and contains important national institutions such as the High Court of Australia, the Australian National University and the Australian War Memorial, but it has a population of fewer than 400,000. These contradictions are the essence of the city's attraction. Canberra's hidden delights include Manuka's elegant cafés, excellent wines and sophisticated restaurants. Special events include the annual spring flower festival, Floriade, which turns the north shore of the lake into a blaze of colour, and the spectacular hot-air ballooning festival in April.

Outside the city lie the region's natural attractions. Tidbinbilla Nature Reserve is home to wild kangaroos, wallabies, emus, koalas and platypuses. The Murrumbidgee River is excellent for canoeing, and the wild Namadgi National Park has bush camping, Aboriginal art sites, alpine snow gums and mountain creeks for trout fishing.

Hot-air ballooning festival over Lake Burley Griffin, near the National Library of Australia

◀ Entrance to Parliament House at Capital Hill, Canberra

Exploring Canberra and ACT

Central Canberra lies around Lake Burley Griffin, framed by
the city's four hills – Black Mountain and Mount Ainslie to
the north and Capital Hill and Red Hill to the south. Most of
Canberra's main sights are accessible from the lake. Scattered
throughout the northern suburbs are other places of interest
such as the Australian Institute of Sport. To the south lies the
wilderness and wildlife of Namadgi National Park.

The city of Canberra nestled around Lake Burley Griffin

Sights at a Glance

Historic Streets and Buildings
❷ Royal Australian Mint
❸ Government House
❺ Yarralumla
❼ Civic Square
❽ *Australian War Memorial pp204–5*
❿ Telstra Tower
⓮ Mugga-Mugga

Parks and Gardens
❶ Red Hill
❾ Australian National Botanic
   Gardens
⓲ *Namadgi National Park p211*

Modern Architecture
❹ *Parliament House pp202–3*

Museums and Galleries
❻ *National Gallery pp206–7*
⓬ Australian Institute of Sport
⓭ National Museum of Australia
⓰ Canberra Deep Space
   Communication Complex

Aquariums and Nature Reserves
⓫ National Zoo and Aquarium
⓱ Tidbinbilla Nature Reserve

Rivers
⓯ Murrumbidgee River

0 kilometres   1

0 miles   1

Getting Around

Many of the sights around Lake Burley Griffin are within walking distance of each other. The Canberra Day Tours Explorer Bus also travels between attractions. The city centre's layout can make driving difficult, but to explore the bush suburbs a car is essential as there is no suburban train system. Most of the sights in ACT are within half an hour's drive of the city.

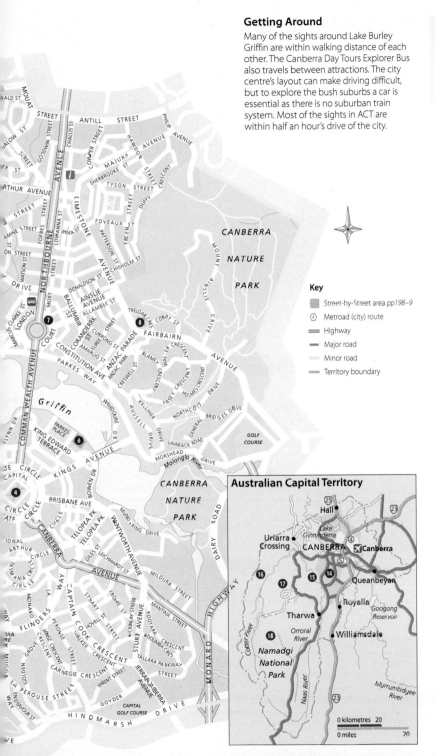

Key

- Street-by-Street area *pp198–9*
- ④ Metroad (city) route
- Highway
- Major road
- Minor road
- Territory boundary

Australian Capital Territory

For additional map symbols *see back flap*

The Parliamentary Triangle

Canberra's major monuments, national buildings and key attractions are all situated around Lake Burley Griffin within the Parliamentary Triangle. Designed to be the focal point of Canberra's national activities by the architect Walter Burley Griffin *(see p201)*, the Parliamentary Triangle has Capital Hill at its apex, topped by Parliament House. Commonwealth Avenue and Kings Avenue fan out from Capital Hill, cross the lake and end at Parkes Way. Running at a right angle from the base of the triangle is Anzac Parade, which leads to the Australian War Memorial *(see pp204–5)* and completes the basic symmetry of Burley Griffin's plan.

❹ ★ Parliament House
Completed in 1988, this is one of the world's most impressive parliamentary buildings.

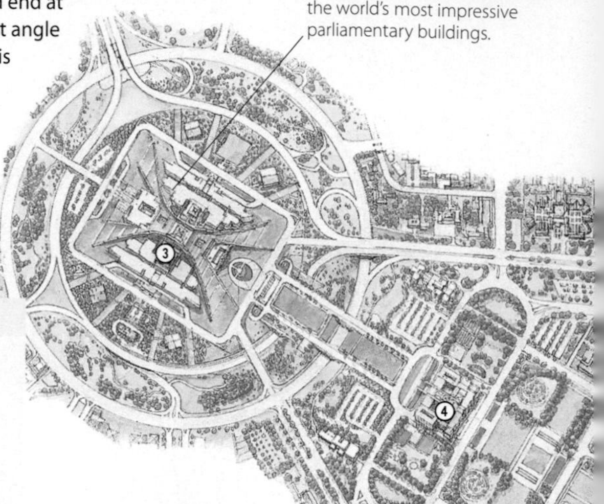

KEY

① **The High Court of Australia** is the highest court of justice in the country.

② **Kings Avenue**

③ **Capital Hill**

④ **Museum of Australian Democracy** was the first parliamentary building in Canberra. Built in 1927, it was the centre of Australian politics until 1988, when Parliament House became the home of federal government. It is open to the public.

⑤ **Questacon** is an action-packed science and technology centre with hundreds of hands-on displays.

⑥ **The National Library** is the country's largest and includes Captain Cook's original journals.

⑦ **Commonwealth Avenue**

⑧ **The Captain Cook Memorial Jet** in Lake Burley Griffin spurts water to a height of 147 m (480 ft).

⑨ **Commonwealth Park** is ablaze with colour during September and October when it is home to the city's annual spring flower festival, Floriade *(see p45)*.

⑩ **Parkes Way**

⑪ **St John the Baptist Church and Schoolhouse** were built in 1844 and are two of Canberra's oldest buildings.

⑫ **The Australian American Memorial** was given to Australia by the United States as a thank you for the Pacific alliance during World War II *(see pp61–2)*.

❻ ★ National Gallery of Australia
This impressive art gallery contains an excellent collection of Australian colonial and Aboriginal art, as well as many significant European works.

Blundell's Cottage
Built in 1858, this is a fine example of an early colonial cottage typical of remote farming life of the time.

Lake Burley Griffin
This artificial lake was created by damming the Molonglo River in 1963. The water feature was central to Walter Burley Griffin's elegant design for Canberra.

CANBERRA
Lake Burley Griffin

Locator Map

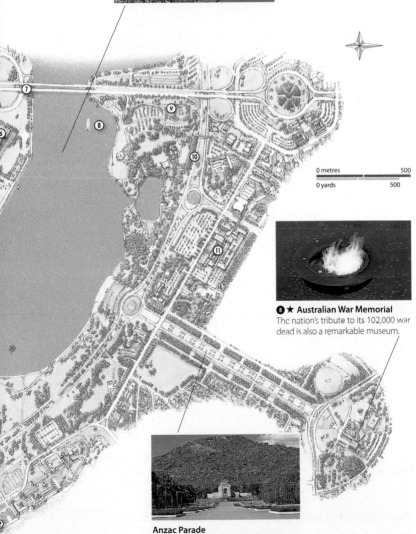

0 metres   500
0 yards   500

❽ ★ Australian War Memorial
The nation's tribute to its 102,000 war dead is also a remarkable museum.

Anzac Parade
Eleven memorials line the boulevard, commemorating Australia's war efforts in the 20th century.

Exploring the Parliamentary Triangle

Canberra, with its still lake and impressive national monuments and institutions, can at first glance appear cold and somewhat forbidding to visitors. But venture inside the various buildings dotted around Lake Burley Griffin within the Parliamentary Triangle, and a treasure trove of architecture, art, history and politics will be revealed. The lake itself, surrounded by gardens, cycle paths and outdoor sculptures and memorials, is a picturesque location for relaxing picnics and leisurely strolls. Exploring the entire Parliamentary Triangle can take one or two days. It is, however, more easily tackled by dividing it into two parts, taking in first the north and then the south of the lake.

🏛 Museum of Australian Democracy

King George Terrace, Parkes.
Tel (02) 6270 8222. Open 9am–5pm daily. Closed 25 Dec. 🅰🅱🅲🅳🅴
Ⓦ moadoph.gov.au

Built in 1927 as the first parliamentary building in the new national capital, Old Parliament House was the centre of Australian politics for more than 60 years. It was replaced by the new Parliament House in 1988 (see pp202–3).

This building has witnessed many historic moments: Australia's declaration of war in 1939; news of the bombing of Australia's northern shores by the Japanese in 1942; the disappearance and presumed drowning of Prime Minister Harold Holt in 1967 and the dismissal of the Whitlam government by Sir John Kerr in 1975 (see pp62–3).

Today the building is home to the Museum of Australian Democracy, which includes several historical exhibitions. Visitors can explore the Kings Hall, the old House of Representatives and Senate chambers, and see the peephole in the wall of the prime minister's office, discovered during renovations. The National Portrait Gallery's main collection is also held in the museum.

Blundell's Cottage

🏛 Blundell's Cottage

Wendouree Drive, Parkes.
Tel (02) 6272 2902. Open 10–11:30am, noon–4pm Thu & Sat. Closed 25 Dec.
🅰 Ⓦ nationalcapital.gov.au/nce

This small sandstone farmhouse was built in 1858 by the Campbell family, owners of a large farming property at Duntroon Station, for their head ploughman. It was later occupied by bullock driver George Blundell, his wife, Flora, and their eight children.

This excellent example of a colonial cottage conveys the remoteness of early farming life. The cottage once looked out over sheep paddocks, but these were flooded by Lake Burley Griffin (see pp198–9).

🏛 National Capital Exhibition

Commonwealth Park. Tel (02) 6272 2902. Open 9am–5pm Mon–Fri, 10am–4pm Sat & Sun. Closed 25 Dec and public hols (except Australia Day).
🅰🅱🅲
Ⓦ nationalcapital.gov.au/nce

The rotunda housing the National Capital Exhibition, north of Lake Burley Griffin at Regatta Point, is recommended as a starting point for any tour of Canberra. Inside are models, videos and old photographs showing the history and growth of Canberra as the federal capital of Australia. These provide a good orientation of the city.

From the windows of the rotunda is a clear view of Lake Burley Griffin, the Parliamentary Triangle and the Captain Cook Memorial Jet, National Carillion and Globe. The jet fountain and bronze, copper and enamel globe on the edge of the lake were part of the 1970 bicentennial commemoration of the claiming of the east coast of Australia by British navy officer Captain James Cook in 1770 (see p54). The elegant fountain lifts a column of water

Neo-Classical façade of the Museum of Australian Democracy and its impressive forecourt

147 m (480 ft) out of the lake from 11am until 2pm, provided the weather is not too windy. The National Carillion has 55 bronze bells and there are regular recitals.

National Library of Australia

Parkes Place, Parkes. **Tel** (02) 6262 1111. **Open** 10am–8pm Mon–Thu, 10am–5pm Fri & Sat, 1:30–5pm Sun. **Closed** Good Fri, 25 Dec. **nla.gov.au**

This five-storey library, an icon of 1960s architecture, is the repository of Australia's literary and documentary heritage. Containing more than 7 million books, as well as copies of most newspapers and magazines published in Australia, thousands of tapes, manuscripts, prints, maps and old photographs, it is the nation's largest library and leading research centre. There are also historic items in a rotating display such as Captain Cook's original journal from his *Endeavour* voyages.

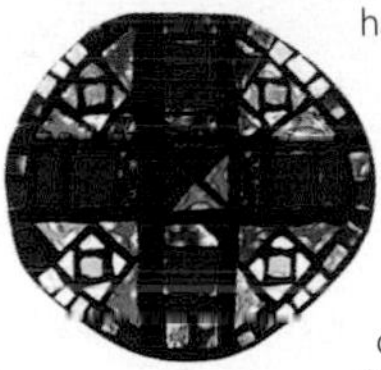
Leonard French stained glass

The building, designed by Sydney architect Walter Bunning (1912–1977) and completed in 1968, includes some notable works of art. Foremost are the modern stained-glass windows by Australian architect and artist Leonard French (1928–), made of Belgian chunk glass and depicting the planets. There are also the Australian life tapestries by French artist Mathieu Mategot.

Questacon – The National Science and Technology Centre

Cnr King Edward Terrace & Parkes Place, Parkes. **Tel** (02) 6270 2800. **Open** 9am–5pm daily. **Closed** 25 Dec. **questacon.edu.au**

With 200 hands-on exhibits in six different galleries arranged around the 27-m- (90-ft-) high cylindrical centre of the building, science need never be dull again. A must for anyone visiting Canberra, Questacon demonstrates that science can be fascinating, intriguing, fun and an everyday part of life.

Visitors can freeze their shadow to a wall, play a harp with no strings, experience an earthquake and feel bolts of lightning. You can also enjoy giant slides and a roller coaster simulator, and there are regular science demonstrations and special lectures.

High Court of Australia

Parkes Place, Parkes. **Tel** (02) 6270 6811. **Open** 9:45am–4:30pm Mon–Fri, noon–4pm Sun. **Closed** public hols. **hcourt.gov.au**

British and Australian legal traditions are embodied in this imposing lakeside structure, opened in 1980 by Queen Elizabeth II. The High Court is centred on a glass public hall, designed to instil respect for the justice system. Two murals by artist Jan Sensbergs look at the Australian constitution, the role of the Federation and the significance of the High Court. There are three courtrooms, and chambers for the Chief Justice and six High Court judges. Sittings are open to the public.

On one side of the ramp at the entrance is a sculpture of a waterfall made out of granite. It is intended to convey how the decisions of this legal institution trickle down to all Australian citizens.

Jan Sensbergs mural in the High Court

St John the Baptist Church and Schoolhouse Museum

Constitution Ave, Reid. **Tel** (02) 6248 8399. **Open** 10am–noon Wed, 2–4pm Sat, Sun. **Closed** Good Fri, 25 Dec. **stjohnscanberra.org**

Built in 1844 of local bluestone and sandstone, the Anglican church of St John the Baptist and its adjoining schoolhouse are Canberra's oldest surviving buildings. They served the pioneer farming families of the region. Memorials on the walls of the church commemorate many early settlers, including statesmen, scientists and scholars.

Within the schoolhouse is a museum containing various 19th-century memorabilia.

Walter Burley Griffin

Walter Burley Griffin

In 1911, the Australian government, then located in Melbourne, decided on Canberra as the best site for a new national capital. An international competition for a city plan was launched, and the first prize was awarded to a 35-year-old American landscape architect, Walter Burley Griffin. Influenced by the design of Versailles, his plan was for a garden city, with lakes, avenues and terraces rising to the focal point of Parliament House atop Capital Hill. On 12 March 1913, a foundation stone was laid by Prime Minister Andrew Fisher, but bureaucratic arguments and then World War I intervened. By 1921, little of Canberra had begun to be constructed, and Burley Griffin was dismissed from his design post. He stayed in Australia until 1935, when, reduced to municipal designs, he left for India. He died there in 1937, although his original vision lives on in the ever-expanding city of Canberra.

❶ Red Hill

Via Mugga Way, Red Hill.

One of the highlights of a visit to Canberra is a drive to the top of Red Hill, which offers excellent views over Lake Burley Griffin, Parliament House,

Panoramic view of Canberra from Red Hill

Manuka and the embassy suburb of Yarralumla *(see p204)*. Behind Red Hill stretch the southern suburbs of Canberra, with the beautiful green of the Brindabella Ranges to the west.

An alternative view of Canberra, offering a better understanding of Walter Burley Griffin's carefully planned city design, can be seen from the top of Mount Ainslie, on the north side of the lake behind the Australian War Memorial *(see pp204–5)*.

❷ Royal Australian Mint

Denison St, Deakin. **Tel** (02) 6202 6999 or 1 300 652 020. ▭ 30, 31. **Open** 8:30am–5pm Mon–Fri, 10am–4pm Sat–Sun, public hols. **Closed** Good Fri, 25 Dec. ▢ 10am & 2pm Mon–Fri. ⬧ ⬥ **ramint.gov.au**

The Royal Australian Mint is the sole producer of Australia's circulating coin currency. It has produced over 11 billion circulating coins and today has the capacity to mint over two million coins per day, or over 600 million per year. The Mint is dedicated to commemorating Australia's culture and history through its numismatic programme.

❹ Parliament House

Parliament House is the meeting place of Australia's Parliament and the centre of Australia's democracy. Opened in 1988, the building on Capital Hill is the third home of the Federal Parliament since 1901. The building is set on a 32-ha (80-acre) site and is the focal point of Canberra. Its architecture reflects Australia's commitment to open government.

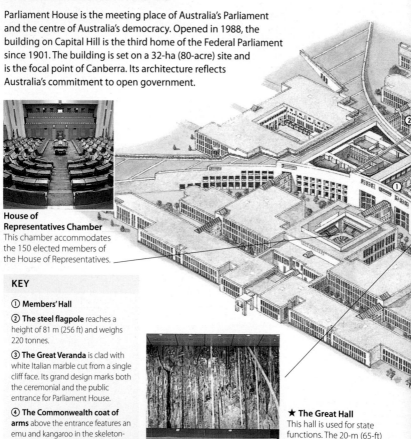

House of Representatives Chamber
This chamber accommodates the 150 elected members of the House of Representatives.

KEY

① **Members' Hall**

② **The steel flagpole** reaches a height of 81 m (256 ft) and weighs 220 tonnes.

③ **The Great Veranda** is clad with white Italian marble cut from a single cliff face. Its grand design marks both the ceremonial and the public entrance for Parliament House.

④ **The Commonwealth coat of arms** above the entrance features an emu and kangaroo in the skeleton-like style of Aboriginal rock paintings.

★ **The Great Hall**
This hall is used for state functions. The 20-m (65-ft) tapestry is based on an Arthur Boyd painting.

When touring the Mint you can see the history of Australian currency as well as how coins are made. You can even view the coins coming directly off the presses.

❸ Government House

Dunrossil Drive, Yarralumla.
Tel (02) 6283 3533. **Open** two days a year – phone ahead to check. 📷 🎥 obligatory.

Government House has been the official residence of the Governor General, the representative of the monarch in Australia, since 1927. The house was once part of a large sheep station called Yarralumla, which was settled in 1828, and is now where heads of state and the Royal Family stay when visiting Australia. The house is closed to the public, except on special open days; however, a lookout point on Lady Denman Drive offers good views of the residence and the large gardens.

Elegant façade and front grounds of Government House

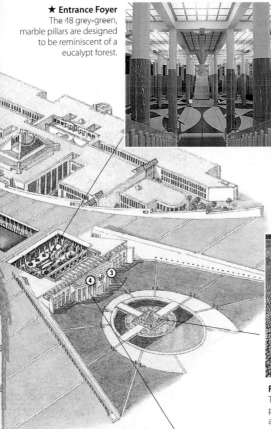

★ Entrance Foyer
The 48 grey-green, marble pillars are designed to be reminiscent of a eucalypt forest.

Entrance

Forecourt
The Aboriginal mosaic, red gravel and pool represent Australia's landscape and native inhabitants.

VISITORS' CHECKLIST

Practical Information
Capital Hill.
Tel (02) 6277 7111. 🌐 **aph.gov.au**
Open 9am–5pm daily (later on days parliament is sitting).
Closed 25 Dec. 🎥 10am, 1pm, 3pm daily. ♿ 📷

Transport
🚌 1, 31, 34, 39.

❺ Yarralumla

Yarralumla. **Tel** (02) 6205 0044
(Canberra Visitors' Centre). 🚌 901, 31.
🗓 for embassy open days. ♿
variable. 🅿

The suburb of Yarralumla, on
the edge of Capital Hill, is home
to more than 80 of Australia's
foreign embassies and
diplomatic residences. A drive
through the tree-lined streets
gives a fascinating view of the
architecture and cultures of
each country represented, as
embodied in their embassies and
grand ambassadorial residences.

The traditional style of the Chinese Embassy in Yarralumla

Distinctive buildings include
the vast Chinese Embassy at
No. 15 Coronation Drive, with
its red columns, dragon statues
and pagoda-shaped roofs.

On Moonah Place, the Indian
Embassy has pools, a shallow
moat and a white temple
building in the Mogul architectural style, with a gold spire on

❻ Australian War Memorial

The Australian War Memorial was built to
commemorate all Australians who have died
while serving their country. The Roll of Honour
and the symbolic Tomb of the Unknown
Australian Soldier serve as a reminder of the
horror and sadness of war. The Anzac Hall is the
stage for sound and light shows, one of which
recreates a bombing raid over Germany.

Façade of the Australian War Memorial

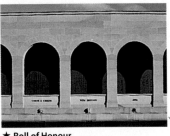

★ **Roll of Honour**
Names of all the 102,600 Australians killed
in action are written on bronze panels in
the cloisters.

KEY

① **Eternal flame**

② **The Pool of Reflection** is a
peaceful place where families can
mourn their loved ones. Rosemary
planted by the pool symbolizes
remembrance.

③ **Orientation Gallery**

④ **First World War Gallery**

⑤ **Aircraft Hall**

⑥ **Second World War Gallery**

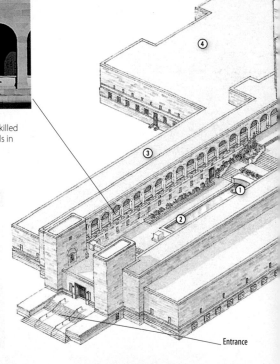

Entrance

top. The High Commission of Papua New Guinea on Forster Crescent is built as a Spirit House, with carved totem poles outside; the Mexican Embassy on Perth Avenue boasts a massive replica of the Aztec Sun Stone.

Just across Adelaide Avenue is The Lodge, the official residence of the Australian prime minister and his family.

❻ National Gallery of Australia

See pp206–7.

❼ Civic Square

Civic Centre. 🚌 many routes.

The commercial heart of Canberra is the Civic Centre, on the north side of Lake Burley Griffin close to the northwest corner of the Parliamentary Triangle *(see pp198–9)*. It is the centre of many administrative, legal and local government functions in Canberra, as well as having the highest concentration of offices and private sector businesses. It is also the

Ethos statue, Civic Square

city's main shopping area. The central Civic Square, as envisaged by Walter Burley Griffin in his original city plan, is a common meeting place and relaxing area. It is dominated by the graceful bronze statue of Ethos, by Australian sculptor Tom Bass, located at the entrance of the ACT Legislative Assembly. In the adjacent Petrie Plaza is a traditional carousel, a much-loved landmark among the citizens of Canberra.

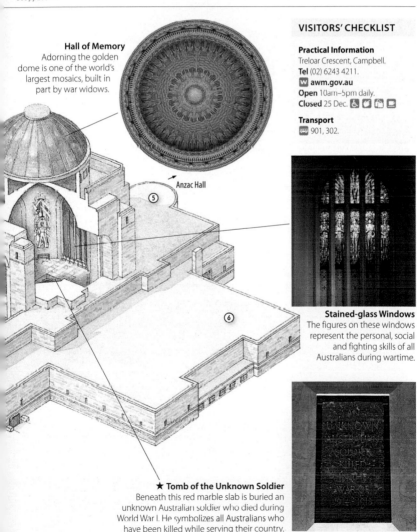

Hall of Memory
Adorning the golden dome is one of the world's largest mosaics, built in part by war widows.

Anzac Hall

⑤

⑥

VISITORS' CHECKLIST

Practical Information
Treloar Crescent, Campbell.
Tel (02) 6243 4211.
🆆 awm.gov.au
Open 10am–5pm daily.
Closed 25 Dec. 🦽 📷 🏠 💻

Transport
🚌 901, 302.

Stained-glass Windows
The figures on these windows represent the personal, social and fighting skills of all Australians during wartime.

★ Tomb of the Unknown Soldier
Beneath this red marble slab is buried an unknown Australian soldier who died during World War I. He symbolizes all Australians who have been killed while serving their country.

⊙ National Gallery of Australia

Australian society is diverse, multicultural and vibrant, and the 160,000 works of art owned by the National Gallery of Australia reflect the spirit of the country. The National Gallery opened in 1982, and the core of its collection consists of Australian art, from European settlement to present day, by some of its most famous artists, such as Tom Roberts, Arthur Boyd, Sidney Nolan and Margaret Preston *(see p38)*. The oldest art in Australia is that of its indigenous inhabitants *(see pp36–7)*, and the Aboriginal & Torres Strait Islander art collection offers fine examples of both ancient and contemporary works. The gallery's Asian and international collections are also growing. Modern sculptures are on display in the gardens.

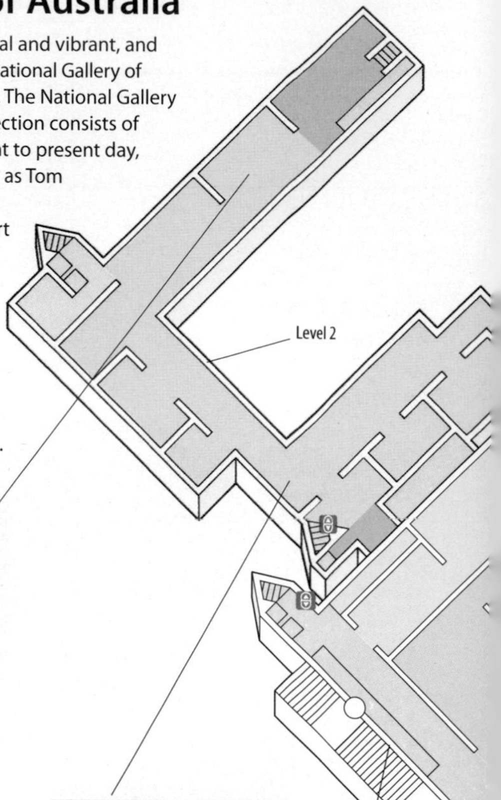

Level 2

★ In a Corner on the MacIntyre *(1895)*
Tom Roberts' depiction of this country's bushland is painted in the fractured light style of the Australian School of Impressionists.

Sandringham Beach *(c.1933)*
This dynamic painting by Clarice Beckett exudes a leisurely feel that captures Australia's passion for the beach as a place of relaxation and recreation.

Level 1
Entrance

Sculpture Garden

The National Gallery makes the most of its picturesque, lakeside gardens as the site for an impressive collection of sculptures, from classical, such as Aristide Maillol's *The Mountain*, to modern. Two of the best known and loved contemporary sculptures in the garden are *Cones* by Bert Flugelman and *The Pears* by George Baldessin.

The Mountain by Aristide Maillol

Gallery Guide

The National Gallery is easily visited within two hours, although an excellent one-hour tour of the highlights is offered twice daily. On the lower level is the largest Aboriginal art collection in the world and the Impressionism to Pop collections. Also highly recommended, on the upper level, is the extensive Australian art collection. Touring "blockbuster" art shows are hung in rooms in what is actually a later addition to the original building.

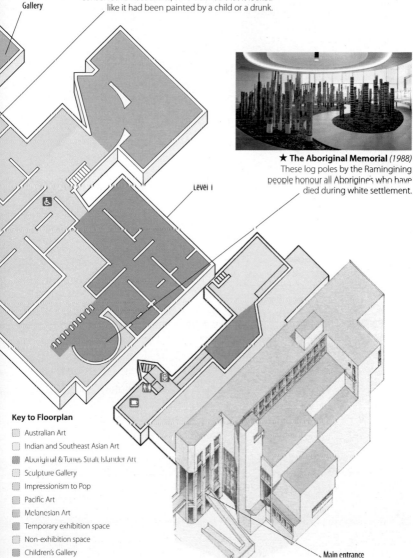

Blue Poles *(1952)*
When this work by US artist Jackson Pollock was bought for $1.2 million in 1973 it outraged conservative Australians, who claimed that it looked like it had been painted by a child or a drunk.

Orde Poyntan Gallery

★ The Aboriginal Memorial *(1988)*
These log poles by the Ramingining people honour all Aborigines who have died during white settlement.

Level 1

Key to Floorplan

- Australian Art
- Indian and Southeast Asian Art
- Aboriginal & Torres Strait Islander Art
- Sculpture Gallery
- Impressionism to Pop
- Pacific Art
- Melanesian Art
- Temporary exhibition space
- Non-exhibition space
- Children's Gallery
- East Asian Art

Main entrance

Rock Garden section of the Australian National Botanic Gardens

❾ Australian National Botanic Gardens

Clunies Ross St, Acton. **Tel** (02) 6250 9588. **Open** 8:30am–5pm daily (to 8pm in Jan). **Closed** 25 Dec. ♿ 📷 💻 **W** anbg.gov.au

On the slopes of Black Mountain, the Australian National Botanic Gardens hold the finest scientific collection of native plants in the country. Approximately 90,000 plants of more than 5,000 species are featured in its displays.

The Rainforest Gully, one of the most popular attractions, features plants from the rainforests of eastern Australia. One fifth of the nation's eucalypt species are found on the Eucalypt Lawn. The Aboriginal Trail is a self-guided walk that details how Aborigines have utilized plants over thousands of years.

❿ Telstra Tower

Black Mountain Drive, Acton. **Tel** 1800 806 718 or (02) 6219 6120. **Open** 9am–10pm daily. 🐾 ♿ 💻 **W** telstratower.com.au

Known affectionately by locals as "the giant syringe", Telstra soars 195 m (640 ft) above the summit of Black Mountain. The tower houses state-of-the-art communications equipment, such as television transmitters and cellular phone bases. The tower also features an exhibition on the history of telecommunications in Australia, from its first telegraph wire in Victoria in 1854 to the 21st century.

There are three viewing platforms at different levels offering spectacular 360° views of Canberra and the surrounding countryside. There is also a revolving restaurant. In 1989, Black Mountain Tower, as it was originally called, was made a member of the World Federation of Great Towers, which includes such buildings as the Empire State Building in New York.

⓫ National Zoo and Aquarium

Lady Denman Drive, Scrivener Dam. **Tel** (02) 6287 8400. **Open** 9:30am–5pm daily. **Closed** 25 Dec. 🐾 ♿ 📷 by arrangement. 💻 📷 **W** nationalzoo.com.au

A wonderful collection of Australia's fish, from native freshwater river fish to brilliantly coloured cold sea, tropical and coral species are on display in the National Zoo and Aquarium. This is Australia's only combined zoo and aquarium. There are about 20 aquariums on show, including a number of smaller tanks containing freshwater and marine animals. They have some eight different species of shark on display.

The 9-ha (22-acre) landscaped grounds of the adjacent **Zoo** have excellent displays of numerous native animals including koalas, wombats,

Turtle in the National Aquarium

dingoes, fairy penguins, Tasmanian devils, emus and kangaroos. As well as the native residents of the zoo there are many favourites from all over the world, including several big cats (the zoo has the largest collection of big cats in the country), primates, two giraffes and African antelopes.

The zoo also organizes "Meet a Cheetah" encounters. Under the supervision of a keeper, you will enter the cheetah enclosure and actually be able to touch and pat the animals. For even more close encounters, there is the two-hour ZooVenture tour, which would appeal to those animal lovers who want to enjoy a more hands-on behind-the-scenes kind of experience. Both this tour and "Meet a Cheetah" have age and height restrictions, and must be booked well ahead of your visit.

⓬ Australian Institute of Sport

Leverrier Crescent, Bruce. **Tel** (02) 6214 1010. 🚌 80. **Open** for tours only: 10am, 11:30am, 1pm, 2:30pm daily. **Closed** 25 Dec. 🐾 ♿ 📷 obligatory. **W** ais.org.au

Australian Olympic athletes are often on hand to show visitors around the world-class Australian Institute of Sport (AIS). This is the national centre of Australia's sports efforts. Here you can see where the athletes sleep, train and eat. You can see how your fitness levels compare and test your sporting skills. There is also an exhibition of interactive sports displays, the Sportex exhibition, which includes themes such as "Heroes and Legends" and "How do you measure up?" Athletes can take visitors on guided tours around the amazing facilities. A shop and a café are also open to visitors.

The *Harvest of Endurance* scroll, depicting the 1861 Lambing Flat Riots, in the National Museum of Australia

⓭ National Museum of Australia

Lawson Crescent, Acton Peninsula.
Tel (02) 6208 5000 or 1800 026 132.
🚌 34. **Open** 9am–5pm daily.
Closed 25 Dec. ♿ 🅿 by arrangement. 📷 (special exhibitions). 🖥 📷
🆆 nma.gov.au

Established by an Act of Parliament in 1980, the National Museum of Australia moved to its permanent home on the Acton Peninsula in early 2001. It shares its location with the Australian Institute of Aboriginal and Torres Strait Islander Studies. The innovative, purpose-built facility quickly became an architectural landmark. Its unique design was inspired by the idea of a jigsaw puzzle.

Before beginning a tour of the museum, visitors can experience an audiovisual introduction to the museum in the Circa, a novel rotating cinema. A huge, three-dimensional map of Australia is visible from three floors. Using digital animation and interactive media stations, it helps to place the displays in their geographical context.

The permanent exhibitions explore the people, events and issues that have shaped and influenced the country. The museum's aim is to be a focus for sharing stories and promoting debate, and interactive displays involve visitors by inviting their contributions.

The **First Australians** gallery is the largest permanent exhibition and relates the stories and experiences of Aboriginal and Torres Strait Islander people. It not only illuminates their history but also deals frankly with contemporary social issues. Displays include Central Australian desert art, stone tools and Aboriginal jewellery made from Tasmanian seashells and a Torres Island outrigger canoe.

In the **Landmarks** gallery, discover how Australia's cities, towns and communities have developed throughout history. The displays explore the ways people have engaged with landscapes, flora, fauna and technologies to build the Australia we recognise today.

The **Australian Journeys** exhibition reviews how immigration has shaped the country. Since 1788 more than 10 million people have arrived in Australia as immigrants, and this gallery uses individual stories, as well as objects from the museum's collection, to look at the remarkable diversity of the Australian experience.

One of the more moving exhibitions is **Eternity**, in which the personal stories of 50 Australians are brought to life. The intention of this unique display is to explore history through emotion. "Your Story", an interactive exhibit, allows visitors to record their own stories,

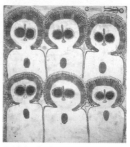

Untitled by Charlie Alyungurra, in the First Australians gallery

which then become part of the collection.

The museum also acknowledges the significance of the land in Australia's identity. In **Old New Land**, the relationship between people and the environment is examined.

The landscaping of the museum is also notable and includes the striking Garden of Australian Dreams, which incorporates many symbols of Australian culture. The Backyard Café spills out into the innovative garden.

In addition, the museum hosts a range of temporary exhibitions. There are also children's galleries and performance spaces, as well as a television broadcast studio.

The Mermaid Coffin by Gaynor Peaty, in Eternity

Further Afield in the ACT

More than 70 per cent of the Australian Capital Territory is bushland. A one-day tour along Tourist Drive 5 provides an opportunity to see native animals in the wild, swim in the majestic Murrumbidgee River, visit a deep-space tracking station, and relax in the lovely gardens of the historic Lanyon Homestead.

Interior of the small stone cottage at Mugga-Mugga

⓭ Mugga-Mugga

8 Narrabundah Lane, Symonston. **Tel** (02) 6239 5607. **Open** 1:30–4:30pm Sat–Sun. **Closed** 25 Dec. ♿

One of Canberra's earliest historic sites, Mugga-Mugga reflects the social and material history of a rural working class family who worked on Duntroon Estate. The site's main feature is a small stone cottage built for the estate's head shepherd in the 1830s. It has been adapted over time, but is still furnished with household items that belonged to the Curley family who moved to Mugga-Mugga in 1913. A galvanized iron garage near the cottage houses an exhibition on the issue of Federation (see p60).

⓮ Murrumbidgee River

ℹ️ ACT Parks and Conservation Service 13 2281.

The Murrumbidgee River meets the Cotter River at Casuarina Sands, a beautiful place to fish and canoe. Nearby is Cotter Dam, good for picnics, swimming and camping.

On the bank of the Murrumbidgee River south of Canberra is **Lanyon Homestead**, a restored 1850s home.

On the same property is the Sidney Nolan Gallery, which features the Ned Kelly series of paintings (see p38).

🏠 **Lanyon Homestead**
Tharwa Drive, Tharwa. **Tel** (02) 6235 5677. **Open** 10am–4pm Tue–Sun. **Closed** Good Fri, 24 & 25 Dec. ♿♿♿

⓰ Canberra Deep Space Communication Complex

Via Paddys River Rd (Tourist Drive 5). **Tel** (02) 6201 7880. **Open** 9am–5pm daily. **Closed** 25 Dec. ♿♿♿♿ by arrangement. 🌐 cdscc.nasa.gov

Canberra Deep Space Communication Complex is managed by the Commonwealth Scientific and Industrial Research Organization (CSIRO) and the American NASA organization. It is one of only three such deep-space tracking centres in the world linked to the NASA control centre in California. The complex has six satellite dishes, the largest of which measures 70 m (230 ft) in diameter and weighs a hefty 3,000 tonnes.

Visitors to the Space Centre can see a piece of moon rock 3.8 billion years old, examine an astronaut's space suit, learn about the role of the complex during the Apollo moon landings and see pictures sent back from Mars, Saturn and Jupiter.

Emu at Tidbinbilla Nature Reserve

⓱ Tidbinbilla Nature Reserve

Via Paddys River Rd (Tourist Drive 5). **Tel** 13 2281 or (02) 6215 1233. **Open** 9am–5pm daily (to 4:30pm in winter). **Closed** 25 Dec. ♿♿ limited. 📷

The tranquil Tidbinbilla Nature Reserve, with its 5,450 ha (13,450 acres) of forests, grasslands, streams and mountains, is a paradise for wildlife lovers. Kangaroos and their joeys bask in the sun, emus strut on the grassy flats, platypuses swim in the creeks, koalas thrive on the eucalypt branches and bower birds and superb lyrebirds can be seen in the tall forests.

The reserve is set at the end of a valley. Visitors hike up to Gibraltar Rock or take a night stroll with a ranger to see sugar gliders and possums. The Birrigai Time Trail is a 3-km (2-mile) walk through various periods of history. The visitors' centre features Aboriginal artifacts and pioneer relics.

Tracking dishes known as "antenna" at the Canberra Space Complex

⓲ Namadgi National Park

Namadgi National Park covers almost half of the Australian Capital Territory. It is a beautiful, harsh landscape of snow, mountains, river valleys and Aboriginal rock art. Only 35 km (22 miles) south of Canberra, Namadgi is remote and solitary. Many days could be spent exploring the park, but even a day's walking will reward you with breathtaking views of the country.

VISITORS' CHECKLIST

Practical Information

Namadgi Visitors' Centre, Naas Rd, 2 km (1 mile) sth of Tharwa 13 2281, (02) 6207 2900. **Open** 9am–4pm Mon–Fri (to 4:30pm Sat, Sun, public hols). **Closed** 25 Dec.

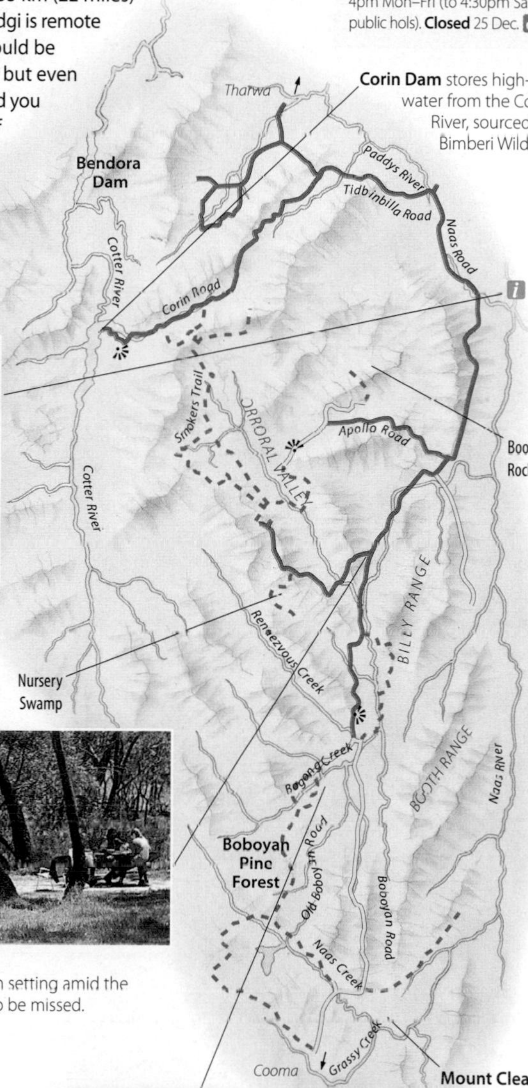

Corin Dam stores high-quality water from the Cotter River, sourced in the Bimberi Wilderness.

0 km 1

0 miles 1

Booromba Rocks

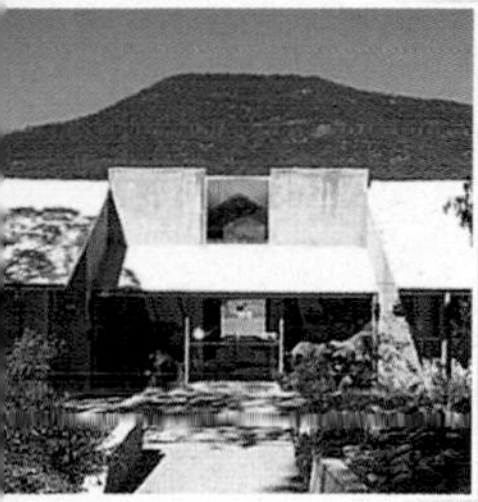

Visitors' Centre
Trail maps of the park and information on ranger-guided walks are available here.

Nursery Swamp

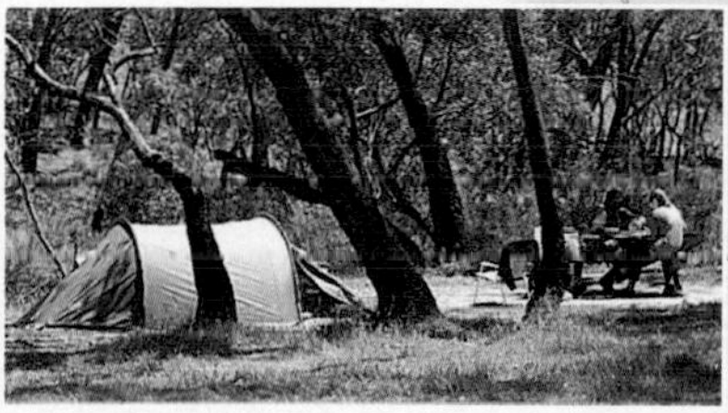

Orroral Bush Camp Site
Camping out in this wild, bush setting amid the wildlife is an experience not to be missed.

Key

- Major road
- Minor road
- Walking trail
- River

Mount Clear is one of three camping grounds in the park.

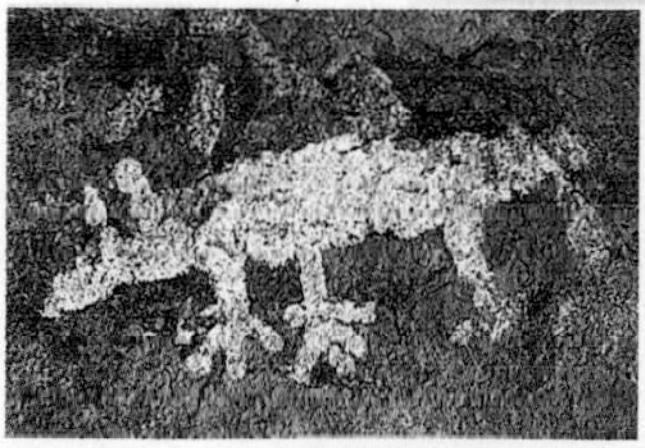

Yankee Hat
Ancient Aboriginal rock art thought to date back thousands of years has been discovered in this area.

For keys to symbols *see back flap*

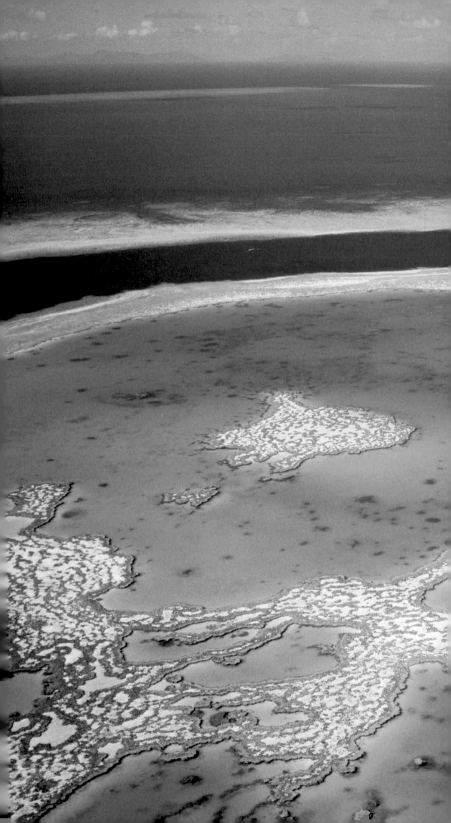

QUEENSLAND

Queensland at a Glance

Australia's second-largest state encompasses some 1,727,000 sq km (667,000 sq miles) and is the country's most popular tourist destination, after Sydney, due to its tropical climate. Brisbane, the state capital, is a modern city, with skyscrapers looking out over the Brisbane River. The southern coastline is a haven for surfers and is the region that most typifies the nation's beach culture. Further north is the Great Barrier Reef, one of the natural wonders of the world. Inland, cattle stations and copper mines generate Queensland's wealth. The Far North remains remote and unspoiled, with rainforests and savannah land abundant with native wildlife.

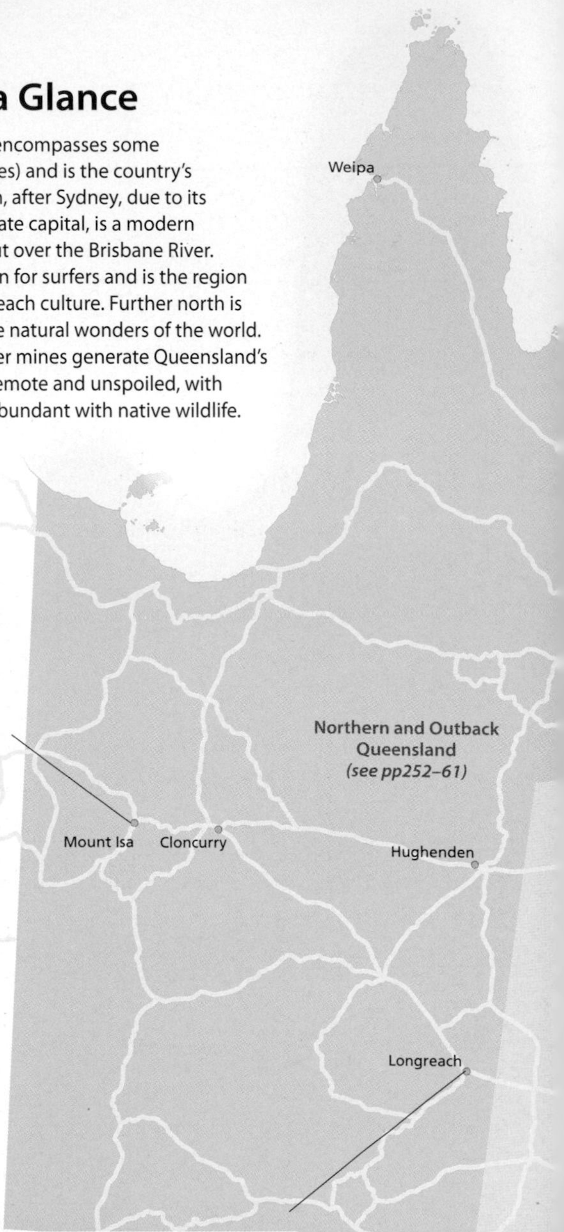

Weipa

Northern and Outback
Queensland
(see pp252–61)

Mount Isa   Cloncurry

Hughenden

Longreach

Charlevi

Cunnamulla

Mount Isa is one of Queensland's largest inland cities and revolves almost entirely around its copper, zinc and lead mining industries *(see p261)*.

0 km   100
0 miles   100

Longreach is in the heart of Queensland's Outback, and its most popular sight is the Stockman's Hall of Fame, documenting Australia's Outback history. Longreach is also the site of Qantas' original hangar *(see p261)*.

 The spectacular coral islands of the Great Barrier Reef

Locator Map

Cairns is Queensland's most northerly city and is a popular boarding point for touring the Great Barrier Reef. The city's hub is its esplanade, lined with cafés *(see p258)*.

The Great Barrier Reef is the largest coral reef in the world. Hundreds of islands scatter the coastline, but only a few are developed for tourists, who come here to dive among the coral and tropical fish *(see pp216–21)*.

Townsville

harters
owers   Bowen

Mackay

Emerald

Rockhampton

Gladstone

**South of
Townsville**
(see pp238–51)

Bundaberg

Maryborough

Gympie

Caloundra

Toowoomba

Brisbane

airns

Maryborough
has many typical
"Queenslander" houses, known
for their wide verandas
shading residents from the
tropical sun *(see p245)*.

Brisbane, the state capital, is a highly modern yet relaxing city *(see pp222–37)*. Skyscrapers blend with older edifices, such as the impressive City Hall.

Surfers Paradise is the vibrant centre of the Gold Coast and more than lives up to its name. Chic hotels, pulsating nightclubs, high fashion stores and beach poseurs can all be found here *(see p243)*.

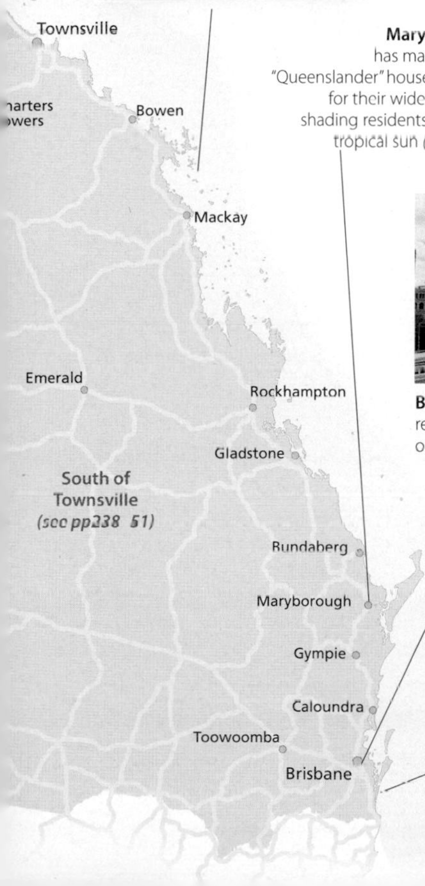

The Great Barrier Reef

Coral reefs are among the oldest and most primitive forms of life, dating back at least 500 million years. Today, the Great Barrier Reef is the largest reef system in the world, covering 2,000 km (1,250 miles) from Bundaberg to the tip of Cape York and an area of approximately 350,000 sq km (135,000 sq miles). Between the outer edges of the reef and the mainland, there are more than 2,000 islands and almost 3,000 separate reefs, of differing types. On islands with a fringing reef, coral can be viewed at close hand, although the best coral is on the outer reef, about 50 km (30 miles) from the mainland.

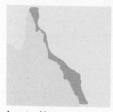

Locator Map

The channel of water between the inner reef and Queensland's mainland is often as deep as 60 m (200 ft) and can vary in width between 30 km (20 miles) and 60 km (40 miles).

Coral is formed by tiny marine animals called polyps. These organisms have an external "skeleton" of limestone. Polyps reproduce by dividing their cells and so becoming polyp colonies.

Fringing reefs surround islands or develop off the mainland coast as it slopes away into the sea.

Typical Section of the Reef

In this typical section of the Great Barrier Reef, a deep channel of water runs close to the mainland. In shallower water further out are a variety of reef features including coral cays, platform reefs and lagoons. Further out still, where the edge of the continental shelf drops off steeply, is a system of ribbon reefs.

Platform reefs form in shallow water, growing outwards in a circle or oval rather than upwards in a wall.

Platform reef

Coral cays are sand islands, formed when reef skeletons and other debris such as shells are exposed to the air and gradually ground down by wave movement into fine sand.

Queensland's tropical rainforest is moist and dense, thriving on the region's heavy, monsoon-like rains and rich soil.

Tidal flats consist of either dead or dying coral, since coral cannot survive exposure to air for an extended period of time.

Coral on the outer reef is built up in "walls" on ancient limestone bases. The coral survives down to a depth of about 30 m (100 ft), where enough sunlight penetrates the water and the temperature is above 17.5°C (65°F).

Ribbon reefs are narrow strips that occur only in the north along the edge of the continental shelf. Exactly why they form here remains a mystery to marine biologists.

How the Reef was Formed

The growth of coral reefs is dependent on sea level, as coral cannot grow above the water line or below 30 m (100 ft). As sea level rises, old coral turns to limestone, on top of which new coral can build, eventually forming barrier reefs. The Great Barrier Reef consists of thousands of separate reefs and is comparatively young, most of it having formed since the sea level rose after the end of the last Ice Age. An outer reef system corresponds with Queensland's continental shelf. Reef systems nearer the mainland correspond with submerged hills.

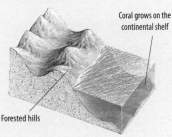

Coral grows on the continental shelf

Forested hills

1 Approximately 18,000 years ago, during the last Ice Age, waters were low, exposing a range of forested hills. Coral grew in the shallow waters of the continental shelf.

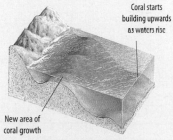

Coral starts building upwards as waters rise

New area of coral growth

2 Approximately 9,000 years ago, following the last Ice Age, the water level rose to submerge the hills. Coral began to grow in new places.

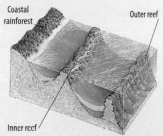

Coastal rainforest

Outer reef

Inner reef

3 Over succeeding millennia, coral formed "walls" on the continental shelf (the outer reef), while an array of fringing and platform reefs, coral cays and lagoons formed around the former hills (the inner reef).

Life on the Great Barrier Reef

More than 2,000 species of fish and innumerable species of hard and soft coral are found in the waters of the Great Barrier Reef. The diversity of life forms is extraordinary, such as echinoderms (including sea urchins), crustaceans and sponges. There is also an array of invertebrates, such as the graceful sea slug, some 12 species of sea grasses and 500 types of algae. The reef islands and coral cays support a wonderfully colourful variety of tropical birdlife. This environment is protected by the Great Barrier Reef Marine Park Authority, established by an Act of Parliament in 1975.

Diving amid the dazzling colours and formations of soft coral.

Hard coral *(see p217)* is formed from the outer skeleton of polyps. The most common species is staghorn coral.

Soft coral has no outer skeleton and resembles the fronds of a plant, rippling in the waves.

Wobbegongs are members of the shark family. They sleep during the day under rocks and caves, camouflaged by their skin tones.

Manta rays are huge fish, measuring up to 6 m (20 ft) across. Despite their size, they are gentle creatures that are happy to swim close to divers.

Potato cod are known for their friendly demeanour and are often happy to swim alongside divers.

Great white sharks are occasional visitors to the reef, although they usually live in the open ocean and swim in schools.

Giant clams, which are large bivalves, are sadly a gourmet delicacy. Australian clams are now protected by law to save them from extinction.

The sea bed of the Barrier Reef is 60 m (195 ft) deep at its lowest point.

Coral groupers inhabit the reef waters and grow up to 15 kg (33 lbs). They are recognizable by their deep red skin.

The Fragile Reef

Ecotourism is the only tourism that is encouraged on the Great Barrier Reef. The important thing to remember when on the reef is to look but not touch. Coral is easily broken; avoid standing on it and be aware that the taking of coral is strictly forbidden and carefully monitored. Camping on the reef's islands requires a permit from the Great Barrier Reef Marine Park Authority.

Beaked coralfish are abundant and some of the most attractive fish of the Barrier Reef. They often swim in pairs, in shallow waters and around coral heads.

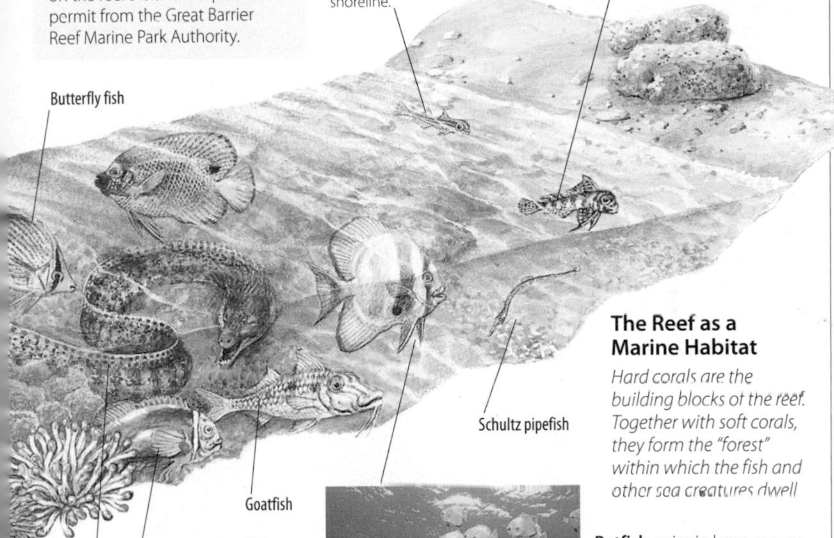

Gobies feed on sand, ingesting the organic matter. They are found near the shoreline.

Blenny

Butterfly fish

The Reef as a Marine Habitat

Hard corals are the building blocks of the reef. Together with soft corals, they form the "forest" within which the fish and other sea creatures dwell

Schultz pipefish

Goatfish

Clown anemonefish have an immunity to the stinging tentacles of sea anemones, among which they reside.

Moray eels grow to 2 m (6 ft) in length, but are gentle enough to be hand-fed by divers.

Batfish swim in large groups and colonize areas of the reef for long periods before moving on elsewhere. They mainly feed on algae and sea jellies.

The crown of thorns starfish feeds mainly on staghorn coral. In the 1960s, a sudden growth in the numbers of this starfish led to worries that it would soon destroy the whole reef. However, many now believe that such a population explosion is a natural and common phenomenon. It contributes to reef life by destroying old coral and allowing new coral to generate.

Birds of the Great Barrier Reef

Gulls, gannets, frigate birds, shearwaters and terns all make use of the rich environment of the islands of the Great Barrier Reef to breed and rear their young, largely safe from mainland predators such as cats and foxes. The number of sea birds nesting on some of the coral cays is astounding – for example, on the tiny area of Michaelmas Cay, 42 km (26 miles) northeast of Cairns, there are more than 30,000 birds, including herons and boobies.

Red-footed booby

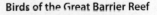

Activities on the Great Barrier Reef

Fewer than 20 of the Great Barrier Reef's 2,000 islands cater for tourists *(see map and table below)*. Accommodation on the islands ranges from luxury resorts to basic camp sites. To make the most of the coral, take a tourist boat trip to the outer reef; most operators provide glass-bottomed boats to view the coral. The best way of seeing the reef, however, is by diving or snorkelling. There are many day trips from the mainland to the reef and between the islands. Some resorts were devastated by a cyclone in 2011 and are still being rebuilt.

Reef walking involves walking over dead stretches of the reef at low tide. Wear strong shoes and be very careful to avoid standing on living coral under the water.

Snorkelling is one of the most popular activities in the Great Barrier Reef, offering the chance to see beautiful tropical fish at close range.

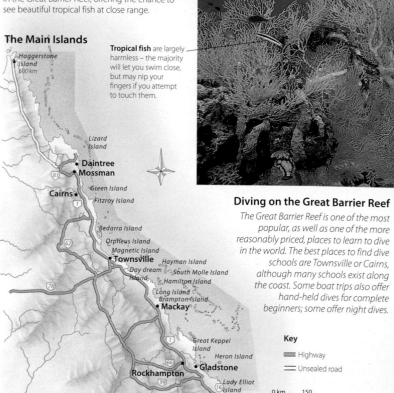

The Main Islands

Tropical fish are largely harmless – the majority will let you swim close, but may nip your fingers if you attempt to touch them.

Haggerstone
Island
600 km

Lizard
Island

● Daintree
● Mossman
(81)

Cairns ●

Green Island
Fitzroy Island

Bedarra Island

Orpheus Island
Magnetic Island
● Townsville
(62)

Hayman Island
Daydream
Island
South Molle Island
Hamilton Island
Long Island
Brampton Island
● Mackay
(78)

Great Keppel
Island
Heron Island

Rockhampton ●
(66)
Gladstone ●
(39)
Lady Elliot
Island
(15)
Bundaberg ●

Diving on the Great Barrier Reef

The Great Barrier Reef is one of the most popular, as well as one of the more reasonably priced, places to learn to dive in the world. The best places to find dive schools are Townsville or Cairns, although many schools exist along the coast. Some boat trips also offer hand-held dives for complete beginners; some offer night dives.

Key

▬▬ Highway
══ Unsealed road

0 km   150
0 miles   150

Heron Island is one of the few coral cay resorts and is known for its excellent diving. From October to March, turtle-spotting is a popular activity as they make their way up the beach to lay their eggs. Bird-watching is also popular as the island's pisonia trees are home to thousands of birds, including Noddy terns. Guided nature walks around the cay are available.

Gorgonian fan coral grows in thickets in the deep waters of the Barrier Reef and is recognizable by its orange-yellow colour.

Scuba is an acronym for Self-contained Underwater Breathing Apparatus.

Getting to the Tourist Islands

Bedarra Island: 🚢 from Dunk Island. Daydream Island: 🚢 from Port of Airlie, Airlie Beach. Fitzroy Island: 🚢 from Cairns. Great Keppel Island: ✈ from Rockhampton. Green Island: 🚢 from Cairns. Haggerstone Island: ✈ from Cairns. Hamilton Island: ✈ from state capitals & Cairns. 🚢 from Port of Airlie, Airlie Beach. Hayman Island: 🚢 from Port of Airlie, Airlie Beach. Heron Island: ✈ 🚢 from Gladstone. Lady Elliot Island: ✈ from Bundaberg, Hervey Bay. Lizard Island: ✈ from Cairns. Long Island: 🚢 from Port of Airlie, Airlie Beach. Magnetic Island: 🚢 from Townsville. Orpheus Island: ✈ from Cairns & Townsville. S. Molle Island: 🚢 from Port of Airlie, Airlie Beach.

Hamilton Island is a popular resort island featuring a wide range of activities, including parasailing, skydiving, golf, tennis and children's entertainments.

The Low Isles, 25 km (15 miles) offshore from Port Douglas, are a perfect example of the reef's day-trip opportunities. This glass-bottomed boat offers sunbathing areas, snorkelling, views of reef life and lunch, before returning to the mainland.

Activities on the Tourist Islands

These islands are easily accessible and offer a range of activities.

	DIVING	SNORKELLING	FISHING	DAY TRIPS	BUSH-WALKING	WATERSPORTS	FOR CHILDREN
Bedarra Island	●	●	●	●	●	●	
Daydream Island	●	●	●	●	●	●	●
Fitzroy Island	●	●	●	●	●	●	
Gt Keppel Island		●	●	●	●	●	●
Green Island *(see p257)*	●	●		●	●	●	
Haggerstone Island	●	●	●		●		●
Hamilton Island	●	●	●	●	●	●	●
Hayman Island	●	●	●	●	●	●	
Heron Island	●	●		●		●	
Lady Elliot Island	●	●		●			●
Lizard Island	●	●	●	●	●	●	
Long Island		●	●	●	●	●	●
Magnetic Island *(see p251)*	●	●	●	●	●	●	
Orpheus Island	●	●	●	●	●	●	
South Molle Island	●	●	●	●	●	●	

BRISBANE

Brisbane is the capital of Queensland and, with a population of over 2.2 million, ranks third in size in Australia after Sydney and Melbourne. Situated on the Brisbane River and surrounded by misty blue hills, the city is known for its scenic beauty, balmy climate and friendly atmosphere. Its tropical vegetation is a great attraction, particularly the bougainvillea, poinciana and fragrant frangipani.

In 1823, the Governor of New South Wales, Sir Thomas Brisbane, decided that some of the more intractable convicts in the Sydney penal settlement needed more secure incarceration. The explorer John Oxley was dispatched to investigate Moreton Bay, noted by Captain Cook on his journey up the east coast 50 years earlier. Oxley landed at Redcliffe and thought he had stumbled across a tropical paradise. He was soon disappointed and it was decided to move the colony inland up the Brisbane River. This was mainly due to Brisbane's more reliable water supply and the fact that the river had a bend in it, which made escape more difficult for the convicts.

Free settlers began arriving in 1837, although they were not permitted to move closer than 80 km (50 miles) to the famously harsh penal settlement. This set a pattern of decentralization which is still evident today: Brisbane consists of several distinct communities as well as the central area. The city's growth was rapid and, in 1859, when Queensland became a self-governing colony, Brisbane was duly named as the state capital.

As Queensland's natural resources, including coal, silver, lead and zinc, were developed, so its major city flourished. Brisbane's status as a truly modern city, however, is relatively recent, beginning with a mining boom in the 1960s. Hosting the Commonwealth Games in 1982 and the 1988 World Expo were also milestones, bringing thousands of visitors to the city. Today, Brisbane is a cosmopolitan place boasting some superb restaurants, streetside cafés and a lively arts scene. Yet amid all the high-rises and modernity, pockets of traditional wooden cottages with verandas can still be found. In January 2011, major floods severely damaged homes and businesses in the city.

The Streets Beach swimming lagoon on Brisbane's South Bank with the city's high-rise skyline as a backdrop

◄ Brisbane's River Street Pier area by night

Exploring Central Brisbane

Brisbane's city centre fits neatly in a U-shaped loop of the Brisbane River, so one of the best ways to get acquainted with the city is by ferry. The city centre can also be easily explored on foot. The streets follow a grid and are named after British royalty: queens and princesses run north–south, kings and princes run east–west. Brisbane's suburbs also have their own distinct feel: to the east is chic Kangaroo Point; just west of the centre is trendy Paddington; while to the northwest Fortitude Valley has a diverse and multicultural population.

Cenotaph in Anzac Square

Mount Coot-tha Botanic Gardens

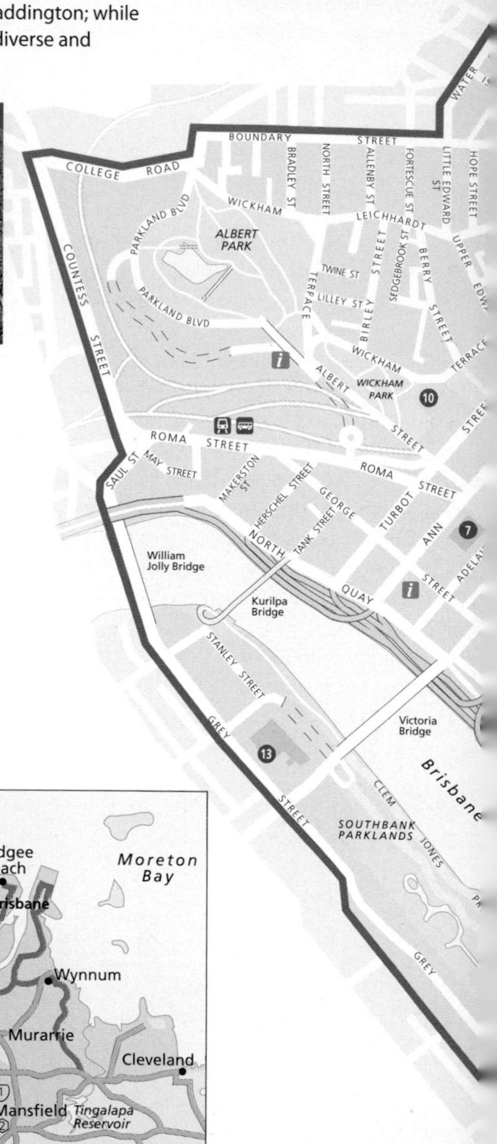

Key

— Highway
— Major road
= Minor road

| 0 metres | 500 |
| 0 yards | 500 |

Greater Brisbane

Brendale
Sandgate
Nudgee Beach
Moreton Bay
✈ Brisbane
Stafford
Pinkenba
Wynnum
The Gap
BRISBANE
Murarrie
Enoggera Reservoir
Cleveland
St Lucia
Mansfield *Tingalapa Reservoir*
Brisbane River

| 0 km | 5 |
| 0 miles | 5 |

For additional map symbols *see back flap*

Sights at a Glance

Historic Streets and Buildings
1 General Post Office
3 Commissariat Store Museum
4 Parliament House
6 Old Government House
7 City Hall
8 Customs House
9 Anzac Square
10 Old Windmill
12 Fortitude Valley and Chinatown
16 Story Bridge
17 Newstead House

Churches and Cathedrals
2 Cathedral of St Stephen
11 St John's Anglican Cathedral

Parks and Gardens
5 Brisbane City Botanic Gardens
14 South Bank Precinct
18 Lone Pine Koala Sanctuary
19 Brisbane Botanic Gardens
20 South D'Aguilar National Park

Museums and Galleries
13 Queensland Cultural Precinct pp232–3
15 Queensland Maritime Museum

Getting Around

Tours of the city centre are readily available and public transport is cheap and efficient. City centre bus stops are colour-coded for easy route identification and the Free Loop bus does a clockwise and anticlockwise loop around the main city area. The best place for boarding the city's ferries is Riverside Centre.

Street-by-Street: Central Brisbane

Central Brisbane is a blend of glass and steel
high-rises co-existing with graceful 19th-century
constructions. The latter fortunately managed to
survive the frenzy of demolishing old buildings
that took place throughout the country during
the 1970s. Queen Street, now a pedestrian mall,
is the hub of the city. Reflecting the city's
beginnings as a port, most of the historic
buildings are found near the river. Near the
city's first Botanical Gardens, which border
Alice Street, many old pubs have been
renovated to cater for a largely
business-lunch clientele.

Central Brisbane's modern skyline, looming over the
Brisbane River

② Cathedral of St Stephen
One of the landmarks of
Brisbane's city centre is this
Gothic-style cathedral. Particularly
notable are its white twin spires.

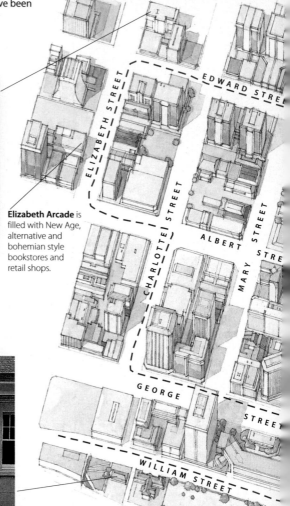

Elizabeth Arcade is
filled with New Age,
alternative and
bohemian style
bookstores and
retail shops.

③ ★ Commissariat Store Museum
The original façade of these former
19th-century granary stores has been
preserved, although the interior is now a
museum detailing Queensland's history.

The former Coal Board building was erected in the mid-1880s and is an example of the elaborate warehouses that once dominated the city.

Smellie & Co. was a 19th-century hardware merchant housed in this attractive building. Note the Baroque doorway on the eastern side.

Queensland Club
This charming old building has housed the private, men-only Queensland Club since 1884. Panelled wood walls and elegant columns were intended to emulate British gentlemen's clubs.

Locator Map

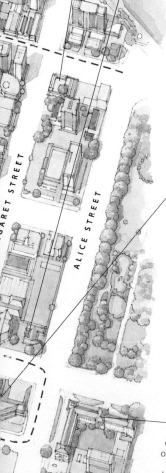

ARET STREET

ALICE STREET

The Mansions
The Mansions are a row of 1890s three-storey, red brick terrace houses. The arches of lighter coloured sandstone create a distinctive design. Stone cats sit atop the parapets at each end of the building.

Key

— Suggested route

0 metres   100

0 yards   100

❹ ★ **Parliament House**
This stained-glass window depicting Queen Victoria is one of the many beautiful features of this late 19th-century building. Unlike many early parliamentary buildings in Australia, it is still used for its original purpose.

The restored colonial Commissariat Store Museum

❶ General Post Office

261 Queen St. **Tel** 13 13 18.
🚇 Brisbane Central. 🚌 Free Loop.
⛴ Eagle St Pier. **Open** 7am–6pm
Mon–Fri. ♿

Built between 1871 and
1879, this attractive Neo-
Classical building was erected
to house the city's first official
postal service. It replaced the
barracks for female convicts
which had previously occupied
the site. The building continues
to operate as central Brisbane's
main post office.

Post Office Square, opposite
the General Post Office, is a
pleasant place to relax, while
looking out over the landscaped
greenery and fountains of
Anzac Square.

❷ Cathedral of St Stephen

249 Elizabeth St. **Tel** (07) 3324 3030.
🚇 Brisbane Central. 🚌 Free Loop.
⛴ Eagle St Pier. **Open** 8am–6pm
Mon–Fri, 7am–6pm Sat–Sun.
♿ 📷 10:30am Mon–Fri, by appt Sun.

Early settlers provided the funds
for this lovely English Gothic-
style Catholic cathedral,
designed by noted colonial
architect Benjamin Backhouse
and completed in 1874. The
main façade features restored
twin spires on each side of the
elaborate stained-glass windows.

Next door is St Stephen's
Chapel, the original cathedral.
It was designed by A W Pugin,
an English architect who also
worked on London's Houses
of Parliament.

❸ Commissariat Store Museum

115 William St. **Tel** (07) 3221 4198.
🚇 South Brisbane. 🚌 Free Loop.
⛴ North Quay. **Open** 10am–4pm
Tue–Fri. **Closed** Good Fri, Easter Sun,
25 Dec, 26 Dec. 📷 ♿

The Commissariat Stores,
constructed by convict labour
in 1829, is the only surviving
building from Brisbane's penal
colony days open to the public.
Having been restored in 2000,
it is now open to visitors and
houses the Royal Historical
Society of Queensland.

❹ Parliament House

Cnr George and Alice sts. **Tel** (07)
3406 7111. 🚇 Brisbane Central.
🚌 1a, 1b, 5, 5b, 5c, 7, 7a, Free Loop.
⛴ Gardens Point. **Open** 9am–
4:15pm Mon–Fri (on sitting days).
Closed public hols. ♿

Queensland's Parliament House
was designed in French
Renaissance style by architect
Charles Tiffin, who won an
architectural competition.

Begun in 1865, it was
completed in 1868. Tiffin added
features more suited to
Queensland's tropical climate,
such as shady colonnades,
shutters and an arched roof
which is made from Mount
Isa copper *(see p261)*. Other
notable features are the cedar
staircases and the intricate
gold leaf detailing on the
Council Chamber ceilings.

The building is still used for its
original purpose and the public
is permitted into the chambers
when parliament is not in
progress. Unlike other state
parliaments, consisting of an
Upper and Lower House,
Queensland has only one
parliamentary body.

Parliament House is also
notable as being the first
legislative building in the British
Empire to be lit by electricity.

Interior of the Assembly Chamber in
Parliament House

❺ Brisbane City Botanic Gardens

Alice St. **Tel** (07) 3403 8888. 🚇 Brisbane
Central. 🚌 Free Loop. ⛴ Edward St.
Open 24 hours. ♿ 📷 Guided walks:
11am & 1pm Mon–Sat (free).

Brisbane's first Botanic Gardens
on the Brisbane River are the
second oldest botanic gardens
in Australia. Their peaceful location is a welcome haven from

Mangrove boardwalk in the Botanic Gardens

Arcade and arches of the north façade of Old Government House

the city's high-rise buildings. In its earliest incarnation, the area was used as a vegetable garden by convicts. It was laid out in its present form in 1855 by the colonial botanist Walter Hill, who was also the first director of the gardens. An avenue of bunya pines dates back to the 1850s, while an avenue of weeping figs was planted in the 1870s.

Hundreds of water birds, such as herons and plovers, are attracted to the lakes dotted throughout the gardens' 18 ha (44 acres). Brisbane River's renowned mangroves are now a protected species and can be admired from a specially built boardwalk.

6 Old Government House

Queensland University of Technology Campus, Gardens Point, 2 George St. **Tel** (07) 3138 8005. 🚇 Brisbane Central. 🚌 Free Loop. 🚢 Gardens Point. **Open** 10am–4pm Sun–Fri. 🛗 🖥 📷 10:30am Tue–Thu. **W** ogh.qut.edu.au

Home to the National Trust of Queensland since 1973, the state's first Government House was designed by colonial architect Charles Tiffin and completed in 1862. The graceful sandstone building served not only as the state governor's residence, but also as the administrative base and social centre of the state of Queensland until 1910. It was then occupied by the fledgling University of Queensland. Old Government House reopened

in 2009 after renovation. It now has an art gallery dedicated to the works of William Robinson, one of Australia's greatest living landscape artists.

7 City Hall

King George Sq, Adelaide and Ann sts. **Tel** (07) 3403 8888; Museum: (07) 330 0800. 🚇 Brisbane Central. 🚌 Free Loop. 🚢 Eagle St Pier. **Open** 8am–5pm daily (from 9am Sat & Sun). 🛗 📷 Clocktower. **Open** 10am–5pm daily. **Closed** public hols. Museum of Brisbane: **Open** 10am–5pm daily. **W** brisbane.qld.gov.au; **W** museumofbrisbane.com.au

Completed in 1930, the Neo-Classical City Hall is home to Brisbane City Council, the largest council in Australia, and the Museum of Brisbane.

Brisbane's early settlement is depicted by a beautiful sculpted tympanum above the main entrance. In the King George Square foyer, some fine examples of traditional craftsmanship are evident in the

floor mosaics, ornate ceilings and woodwork carved from Queensland timbers. City Hall's 92-m (300-ft) Italian Renaissance-style tower gives a panoramic view of the city from a platform at its top. A display of contemporary art and Aboriginal art and ceramics is housed in the Museum of Brisbane. The Shingle Inn, an iconic 1936 walnut-panelled café/bakery in City Hall, has been restored to its former glory and serves meals and snacks.

The attractive King George Square, facing City Hall, continues to resist the encroachment of high-rise office blocks and has several interesting statues, including *Form del Mito* by Arnaldo Pomodoro. The work's geometric forms and polished surfaces, for which this Italian sculptor is noted, reflect the changing face of the city from morning through to night. The bronze *Petrie Tableau*, by Tasmanian sculptor Stephen Walker, was designed for Australia's bicentenary.

City Hall, with its Italian Renaissance clocktower

❽ Customs House

399 Queen St. **Tel** (07) 3365 8999.
🚇 Brisbane Central. 🚌 Free Loop.
⛴ Riverside. **Open** from 9am daily.
Closed public hols. ♿ 📷 Sun. 🚫
🌐 customshouse.com.au

Restored by the University of
Queensland in 1994, Customs
House, with its landmark copper
dome and stately Corinthian
columns, is now open to the
public. Commissioned in 1886,
this is one of Brisbane's oldest
buildings, predating both City
Hall *(see p229)* and the Treasury.
Early renovations removed the
hall and staircase, but these have
now been carefully reconstructed
from the original plans. Today,
the building is used for
numerous civic functions and
there is also a restaurant; call
ahead for opening times.

❾ Anzac Square

Ann & Adelaide sts. 🚇 Brisbane
Central. 🚌 Free Loop. ⛴ Waterfront
Place, Eagle St Pier.

All Australian cities commemorate those who have
given their life for their
country. Brisbane's war
memorial is centred on Anzac
Square, an attractive park
planted with, among other flora,
rare boab (baobab) trees. The
Eternal Flame burns in a Greek
Revival cenotaph at the Ann
Street entrance to the park.
Beneath the cenotaph is the
Shrine of Memories, containing
various tributes and wall
plaques to those who gave
their lives in war.

The distinctive Old Windmill

❿ Old Windmill

Wickham Terrace. 🚇 Brisbane Central.
🚌 City Sights. **Closed** to public.

Built in 1828, the Old Windmill
is one of two buildings still
standing in Brisbane from convict
days, the old Commissariat
Stores being the other survivor
(see p228). Originally the
colony's first industrial building,
it proved unworkable without
the availability of trained
operators, so it was equipped
with treadmills to punish
recalcitrant convicts. It later
served as a time signal, with a
gun fired and a ball dropped
each day at exactly 1pm.
    The picturesque mill was
also chosen as the first television image in Australia in the
1920s. The windmill is not open
to the public, but it makes a
striking photograph.

⓫ St John's Anglican Cathedral

373 Ann St. **Tel** (07) 3835 2231.
🚇 Brisbane Central. 🚌 Free Loop.
⛴ Riverside Centre. **Open** daily (call
for worship or tour times). ♿ 📷

Designed along French Gothic
lines in 1888, with the foundation
stone laid in 1901, St John's
Anglican Cathedral is regarded
as one of the most splendid
churches in the southern
hemisphere. The interior is of
Helidon sandstone. On display
are numerous examples of local
needlework, wood, glass and
stone craft. Over 400 cushions
depicting Queensland's flora and
fauna attract a lot of interest.
    It was at the adjacent Deanery
in 1859 that Queensland was
made a separate colony (it
had been part of NSW). The
Deanery was the temporary
residence of Queensland's
first governor.

Nave and altar of St John's
Anglican Cathedral

⓬ Fortitude Valley and Chinatown

Ann and Wickham sts, Fortitude Valley.
🚇 Brunswick St. 🚌 City Sights.

The ship *Fortitude* sailed from
England and up the Brisbane
River in 1859 with 250 settlers
on board, and the name stuck
to the valley where they
disembarked. For a time the
area was the trading centre of
the city and some impressive
buildings were erected during
the 1880s and 1890s. It then

Greek cenotaph in Anzac Square

Entrance to the Pedestrian Hall in Chinatown, Fortitude Valley

degenerated into one of Brisbane's seedier areas.

In the 1980s, the city council began to revive the district. It is now the bohemian centre of Brisbane, with some of the city's best restaurants (see pp512–14). McWhirter's Emporium, an Art Deco landmark, was originally a department store. Shops now occupy the lower levels with apartments above. On weekends, there is also a busy outdoor market in Brunswick Street.

Also within the valley is Brisbane's Chinatown, a bustling area of Asian restaurants, supermarkets, cinemas and martial arts centres. The lions at the entrance to the area were turned around when a feng shui expert considered their original position to be bad for business.

⑬ Queensland Cultural Precinct

See pp232–3.

⑭ South Bank Precinct

Brisbane River foreshore, South Bank. 🚆 South Bank. 🚍 12, Adelaide St & George St routes. 🚢 South Bank 1, 2, 3. ♿ Visitors' Centre: **Tel** (07) 3156 6366. **Open** 9am–5pm daily. 🌐 visitsouthbank.com.au

The South Bank of the Brisbane River was the site of Expo '88 and is now a 17 ha (42 acres) centre of culture, entertainment and recreation. The area known as the parklands includes the Queensland Performing Arts Centre, the State Library, the Queensland Museum & Science Centre, and Queensland Art Gallery and Gallery of Modern Art (see pp232–3), the Conservatorium, Opera Queensland, two colleges and an exhibition centre.

The South Bank area abounds with restaurants, cafés, weekend market stalls and street entertainers. Classical music and pop concerts are also regularly held here. There is even a man-made lagoon with

Butterfly at South Bank Parklands

a "real" sandy beach, complete with suntanned lifesavers. South Bank Cinema screens the latest-release movies.

South Bank also features the Wheel of Brisbane, offering breathtaking views of the city, and Goodwill Bridge, a 450-m (1,500-ft) pedestrian and cycle bridge, linking the area with the Botanic Gardens.

⑮ Queensland Maritime Museum

End of Goodwill Bridge, South Bank. **Tel** (07) 3844 5361. 🚆 South Bank. 🚍 174, 175, 203, 204. 🚢 River Plaza, South Bank 3. **Open** 9:30am–4:30pm daily. **Closed** Good Fri, 25 Apr (am), 24–26 Dec. 🌐 maritimemuseum.com.au

Queensland Maritime Museum lists among its exhibits shipbuilders' models, reconstructed cabins from early coastal steamers and relics from early shipwrecks in the area. In the dry dock, as part of the National Estate, sits HMAS Diamantina, a frigate that served during World War II.

A coal-fired tug, Forceful, is maintained in running order and cruises with passengers to Moreton Bay two seasons a year. Also on display is the pearling lugger Penguin and the bow of a Japanese pleasure boat, a yakatabume, donated to Brisbane by Japan after Expo '88.

HMAS Diamantina at the Queensland Maritime Museum

⑬ Queensland Cultural Precinct

The Queensland Cultural Precinct is the hub of Brisbane's arts scene, with a spectacular setting on the South Bank. It incorporates the Queensland Art Gallery (QAG), the Gallery of Modern Art (GOMA), the Queensland Museum & Science Centre, the State Library of Queensland and the Queensland Performing Arts Centre.

First established in 1895, QAG has a fine collection of Australian art, including works by Sidney Nolan and Margaret Preston, together with Indigenous Australian art. The international collection includes 15th-century European art and Asian art from the 12th century. QAG and GOMA together create QAGOMA, Australia's second-largest public art museum, offering distinct yet complementary experiences.

Bathers *(1906)*
One of Australia's most highly regarded artists, Rupert Bunny gained international fame with paintings of Victorian life.

Bushfire *(1944)*
Russell Drysdale is known for his depiction of harsh Outback life, such as this farm house destroyed by a fire. It is an abstract piece with slightly discordant colours.

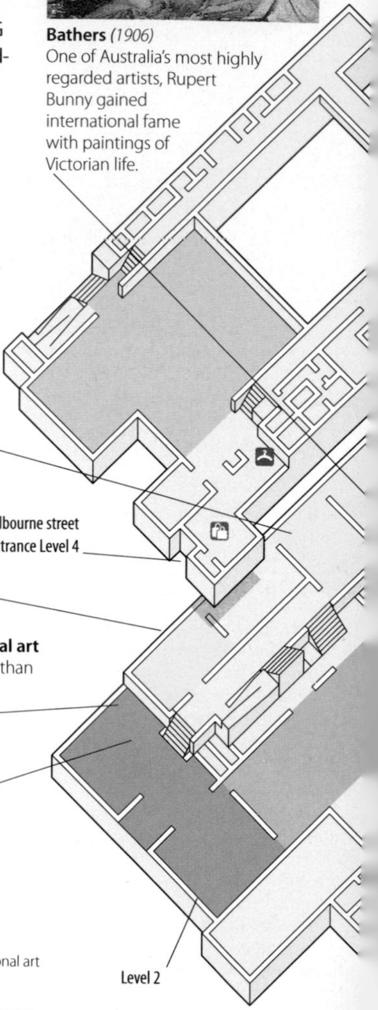

Melbourne street entrance Level 4

Level 3

Asian and international art
is represented by more than 3,000 European and American works.

★ **La Belle Hollandaise** *(1905)*
One of Picasso's transitional works between his blue and rose periods, this was painted during a visit to the Netherlands. The gallery paid a then world record price of £55,000 in 1959 for the work of a living artist.

Level 2

Key

- ▧ Asian and international art
- ☐ Australian art
- ▨ Indigenous Australian art
- ■ Watermall
- ▦ Sculpture courtyard
- ▨ Temporary/Feature exhibition
- ☐ Non-exhibition space
- ▩ Queensland artists

For hotels and restaurants in this area see p486 and pp512–14

Queensland Art Gallery Guide

The collection is housed over three levels. Fine collections of Asian and International art from the 12th century are on Level 2. Indigenous Australian art begins on Level 2 and moves up to Level 4. Level 3 contains Australian art after 1970. The work in this gallery is complemented by the contemporary art housed in GOMA. QAGOMA's Children's Art Centre presents engaging exhibitions and events for all ages. Also of interest is the Watermall's indoor water feature.

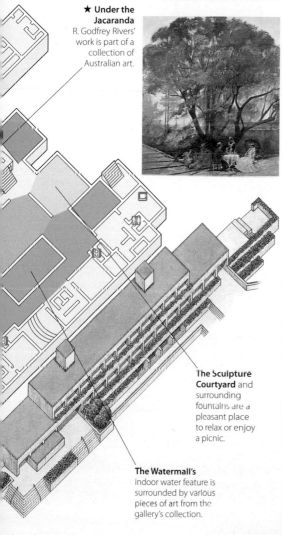

★ **Under the Jacaranda**
R. Godfrey Rivers' work is part of a collection of Australian art.

The Sculpture Courtyard and surrounding fountains are a pleasant place to relax or enjoy a picnic.

The Watermall's indoor water feature is surrounded by various pieces of art from the gallery's collection.

Gallery of Modern Art (GOMA)

Australia's largest gallery of modern and contemporary art focuses on 20th- and 21st-century works from Australia, Asia and the Pacific. The cinemas here feature films by influential and popular directors and artists.

Queensland Museum & Sciencentre

Tel (07) 3840 7555. **Open** 9:30am–5pm daily. **Closed** Good Fri, 25 Apr (open 1:30pm), 25 Dec. (Science Centre only).

This natural history museum is filled with full-scale models, both prehistoric and current. A large-scale model of Queensland's unique dinosaur, the *Mutta-burrasaurus*, stands in the foyer. The Sciencentre offers hands-on, interactive exhibitions.

State Library of Queensland

Tel (07) 3840 7666. **Open** 10am–8pm Mon–Thu, 10am–5pm Fri–Sun daily. **Closed** Good Fri, 25–26 Dec.

The State Library houses collections from around the world. Its extensive resources cover all interests and most of its services are free. There are innovative exhibitions, an Indigenous Knowledge Centre and The Edge, a digital culture space.

Performers of the acclaimed Queensland Ballet company

Queensland Performing Arts Centre (QPAC)

Tel (07) 3840 7444. **Open** performances only. advise when booking.
The Queensland Performing Arts Centre comprises a main concert hall and three theatres where internationally acclaimed opera, classical music and theatrical productions are staged.

River view from Brisbane's
Story Bridge

⑯ Story Bridge

Level 1, 170 Main St, Kangaroo Point.
Tel 1300 254 627 or (07) 3514 6900.
Open daily. 🔲 💿 🌐 **sbac.net.au**

Brisbane's iconic Story Bridge
was constructed during the
Great Depression, taking five
years to build and opening in
July 1940. With a bridge already
across the Brisbane River, this
new bridge was more a means
of creating jobs and boosting
the city's morale.

The Story Bridge Adventure
Climb is a spectacular way to
discover Brisbane. Climbs take
place several times a day as well
as at night. Throughout the
two-and-a-half hour experience,
the climb leader reveals the
history of the bridge and talks
about the city's transition from
a 19th-century penal settlement
to a 21st-century metropolis.
At the summit, climbers enjoy
views of Brisbane, its river and
the surrounding mountains.

⑰ Newstead House

Newstead Park, Breakfast Creek Rd,
Newstead. **Tel** (07) 3216 1846.
🔲 Bowen Hills. 🚌 300, 306, 322.
🚢 Newstead Point. **Open** 10am–4pm
Mon–Fri, 2–5pm Sun. **Closed** Sat,
Good Fri, 25 Apr, 25–26 Dec. 🔲 💿
by arrangement. 🌐 **newsteadhouse.
com.au**

Built in 1846 for Patrick Leslie,
one of the first European settlers
in the Darling Downs region,
Newstead House is the oldest
surviving home in Brisbane.
This charming building was sold

in 1847 to government resident
and magistrate, Captain
John Wickham.

The centre of the new colony's
social life, Newstead House
was the scene of lavish parties.
A huge fig tree, under which
elegant carriages once waited,
still graces the drive. In 1939,
it became the first Australian
house to be preserved by its
very own act of parliament.
Restored by the Newstead House
Trust from 1976, the house is
furnished with Victorian antiques.

Decorated Victorian music box in
Newstead House

⑱ Lone Pine Koala Sanctuary

Jesmond Rd, Fig Tree Pocket. **Tel** (07)
3378 1366. 🚌 430, 445. 🚢 North
Quay. **Open** 8:30am–5pm daily;
8:30am–4pm on 25 Dec. **Closed** until
1:30pm 25 April. 🔲 💿 💿 🔲
🌐 **koala.net**

The oldest Koala Sanctuary in
Australia, opened in 1927, is now
one of Brisbane's most popular
tourist attractions. Lone Pine has
more than 100 koalas, as well as

kangaroos, emus, possums,
dingoes, wombats, reptiles and
many Australian birds, including
various species of parrot. Lone
Pine insists that it is more than
just a zoo, a claim that is
supported by its nationally
respected koala breeding
programme. For a small fee,
visitors can have their photograph taken holding a koala.

A pleasant and scenic way to
get to Lone Pine Sanctuary is by
ferry. There are daily departures
at 10am from Victoria Bridge.

⑲ Brisbane Botanic Gardens

Mt Coot-tha Rd, Toowong. **Tel** (07) 3403
2535. 🚌 333. **Open** Apr–Aug: 8am–
5pm; Sep–Mar: 8am–5:30pm. 🚻

Brisbane Botanic Gardens, in
the foothills of Mount Coot-tha
Forest Park 8 km (5 miles) from
the city centre, were founded
in 1976 and feature more than
20,000 specimens, representing
5,000 species, of exotic herbs,
shrubs and trees laid out in
themed beds. Highlights
include eucalypt groves, a
Japanese Garden, a Tropical
Display Dome, which includes
lotus lilies and vanilla orchids,
a Lagoon and Bamboo Grove,
Fern House, National Freedom
Wall (celebrating 50 years of
peace) and a large collection
of Australian native plants.
Many arid and tropical plants,
usually seen in greenhouses,
thrive in the outdoor setting.
Also in the Gardens complex,
the Sir Thomas Brisbane
Planetarium is the largest of

Koala at Lone Pine Koala Sanctuary

Lush landscape of the Brisbane Botanic Gardens

Australia's planetariums. Mount Coot-tha Forest Park offers both spectacular views and attractive picnic areas. The Aboriginal name means "place of wild honey", a reference to the tiny bees found in the area. On a clear day, from the summit lookout you can admire a spectacular panorama that encompasses the skyscrapers of central Brisbane, encircled by the winding river, Moreton and Stradbroke islands, the Glasshouse Mountains and the Lamington Plateau backing onto the Gold Coast (see pp242–3). The park also offers easygoing walking trails through the woodland, including Aboriginal trails which detail traditional uses of native plants.

㉑ South D'Aguilar National Park

385. ℹ️ The Gap (07) 3512 2300 or 13 74 68. Visitor Centre: **Open** 9am–4:30pm daily. **Closed** 1–2 Jan, 25–26 & 31 Dec.

South D'Aguilar National Park, within the D'Aguilar Mountain Range, stretches for more than 50 km (30 miles) northwest of Brisbane city centre. Covering more than 28,500 ha (70,250 acres) of natural bushland and eucalypt forests, the park offers driving routes with breathtaking views over the surrounding countryside. The most scenic driving route is along Mount Nebo Road, which winds its way through

the lush mountains. Another scenic drive extends from Samford up to the charming mountain village of Mount Glorious and down the other side. It is worth stopping from time to time to hear the distinctive calls of bellbirds and whipbirds.

Six km (4 miles) past Mount Glorious is the Wivenhoe Outlook, with spectacular views down to Lake Wivenhoe, an artificial lake created to prevent the Brisbane River from flooding the city. One km (half a mile) north of Mount Glorious is the entrance to Maiala Recreation Area, where there are picnic areas, some wheelchair accessible, and several walking trails of varying lengths, from short walks to longer, 8-km

(5-mile) treks. These pass through the rainforest, which abounds with animal life. Other excellent walks are at Manorina and at Jolly's Lookout, the oldest formal lookout in the park, which has a good picnic area. Also in the park is the Westridge Outlook, a boardwalk with sweeping views.

The engrossing **South East Queensland Wildlife Centre at Walkabout Creek** park's headquarters is a re-created large freshwater environment. Water dragons, pythons, water rats, catfish and tiny rainbow fish flourish within these natural surroundings. Visitors also have the chance to see the extraordinary lungfish, a unique species which is equipped with both gills and lungs. The on-site restaurant looks out over the beautiful bush landscape.

About 4 km (2 miles) from the park headquarters is Bellbird Grove, which includes an outdoor Aboriginal collection of bark huts. It has a picnic area and also grassed picnic areas at Ironbark Gully and Lomandra.

🏞️ **South East Queensland Wildlife Centre at Walkabout Creek** 60 Mt Nebo Rd, The Gap. **Tel** (07) 3300 2558. **Open** 9am–4:30pm daily. **Closed** Good Fri, 25 Dec & 25 Apr (until 1:30pm). 🔲 limited. 🌐 **nprsr.qld.gov.au/parks/daguilar/walkabout-creek.html**

Spectacular waterfall in South D'Aguilar National Park

BRISBANE PRACTICAL INFORMATION

Brisbane, built around a serpentine river, takes full advantage of its idyllic subtropical weather. Trendy riverside cafés, heritage trails, miles of boardwalk and a floating walkway, ferries and fast catamaran-style CityCats make Brisbane a relaxed holiday destination. The city offers centrally located five-star hotels, budget inns and historic guesthouses *(see pp486)*. There are dining choices in all price ranges, such as silver service at luxury hotels, riverfront cafés, ethnic cuisine and alfresco restaurants, most offering menus based on superb local produce and fresh seafood *(see pp512–14)*. Public transport is reasonably priced and easily accessed. Taxi stands are well signposted, and tourist information centres, identified by the international "I" symbol, are situated throughout the city.

Shopping

Brisbane is a shopping heaven, with its hidden arcades, small boutiques, quaint tea shops, pedestrian malls and multi-storied shopping centres. Finding what you are looking for is not difficult as the city is divided into small precincts, each offering a unique shopping experience. The pedestrianized **Queen Street Mall** has more than 1,000 speciality stores, including six shopping centres. **Brisbane Arcade**, one of Brisbane's most elegant shopping areas, runs off the Mall. With classic marbled interior and polished wood balustrades, it was opened in 1923 and offers quality jewellers and stylish fashion. Using the river to move from one precinct to another is a convenient option.

The South Bank, dominated by the Wheel of Brisbane

Restored interior of the 19th-century Brisbane Arcade

The **Fireworks Gallery** exhibits aboriginal art and local artists, and is just another river stop away at Stratton Street, in Newstead. The **James Street Precinct** in Fortitude Valley has developed around an urban inner-city lifestyle. It is a great place for coffee, small delicatessens, trendy fashion shops, designer boutiques and galleries. Brisbane's weather encourages outdoor markets. The **Riverside Markets** with over 250 stalls are open every Sunday, displaying a huge variety of local arts, crafts, clothes and jewellery. The **Collective Markets at South Bank** feature unique and eclectic artisan goods and are held every Friday night and on weekends. Its parklands, man-made beach, cafés and restaurants make the South Bank a great place for a shopping experience.

Entertainment

The **Queensland Performing Arts Centre** has an exciting calendar of events, including opera, classical and contemporary dance, and live stage shows. The **La Boite Theatre** in Spring Hill is a 200-seat theatre in the round, and home to one of the oldest production companies in Australia. Brisbane hosts a myriad of music festivals, including the Brisbane River Festival. For live music there are nightclubs in the Fortitude Valley and Caxton Street areas. **Treasury Casino** is open 24 hours. Entertainment listings can be found online at www. visitbrisbane.com.au and in free magazines such as *Time Off*, which offers a great gig guide. Tickets for most events can be obtained from **Ticketek**.

CityCat ferry service on the Brisbane River

Getting Around

Brisbane is a compact city which can be explored on foot. Maps are available from most hotels and information centres. There are excellent self-guided heritage trails and riverside pathways on both sides of the river.

Public transport in Brisbane includes buses, commuter trains and ferries. **The TransLink** system allows for use of one ticket for all forms of transport. The river has become one of the main ways of moving about the city. **CityCat** ferries service some of the most popular locations including South Bank, Eagle Street, Riverside, Dockside, New Farm and Kangaroo Point. The two main points of departure are in Eagle Street.

The most economical way to travel on all Brisbane's public transport is with a SEEQ card, which provides three or five days' unlimited travel on TransLink public buses, trains and ferries. Single-journey paper tickets and electronic "go cards" that cover all public transport services are

CityCat ferry sign

also available. Another flexible and economical way to see the city is on a **Brisbane Explorer Bus Tour**. Buy a 24/48 hour ticket and you can get on and off at any of the Explorer bus stops along two routes, which take in major sights and landmarks.

Brisbane's Free Loop service travels around the centre of the city, with a bus every ten minutes. The Cityxpress buses service the suburbs with limited stops. All buses stop at the Queen Street Bus Station.

Commercially operated bus companies also offer tours of the city's highlights, as well as to the surrounding areas, including Stradbroke Island, Moreton Bay and Surfers Paradise *(see pp242–3)* and the mountainous hinterland *(see pp244–5).*

All types of public transport run until midnight, and taxis are plentiful in the city centre at night. Driving is increasingly difficult but there are numerous, well-maintained bike tracks around the city.

A Translink public bus – a popular form of transport in Brisbane

---

DIRECTORY

Shopping

Brisbane Arcade
160 Queen St Mall.
Tel (07) 3231 9777.

The Collective Markets at South Bank
Stanley St, South Bank.
Tel (07) 3844 2440.

Fireworks Gallery
52a Doggett St, Newstead.
Tel (07) 3216 1250.

James Street Precinct
James Street, Fortitude Valley.
Tel (07) 3850 0111.
W jamesst.com.au

Queen Street Mall
Queen Street.
Tel (07) 3006 6290.

Riverside Markets
Markets Cnr Eagle & Charlotte sts.
Tel (07) 3870 2807.

Entertainment

Treasury Casino & Hotel
21 Queen St. **Tel** (07) 3306 8888.
W treasurybrisbane.com.au

La Boite Theatre
21 Queen St. **Tel** (07) 3007 8600.
W laboite.com.au

Queensland Performing Arts Centre
Cnr Grey & Melbourne sts, South Bank. **Tel** (07) 3840 7444.
W qpac.com.au

Ticketek
Tel 13 28 49. W ticketek.com.au

Public Transport

Administration Centre
George Street. **Tel** phone TransLink (see below).

Brisbane Explorer Bus Tour
Tel (02) 9567 8400.
W theaustralianexplorer.com.au

TransLink
(for public transport information)
Tel 13 12 30 or (07) 3851 8700.
W translink.com.au

Tourist Information Centres

Brisbane Visitor Information
Tel (07) 3006 6290.
W visitbrisbane.com.au

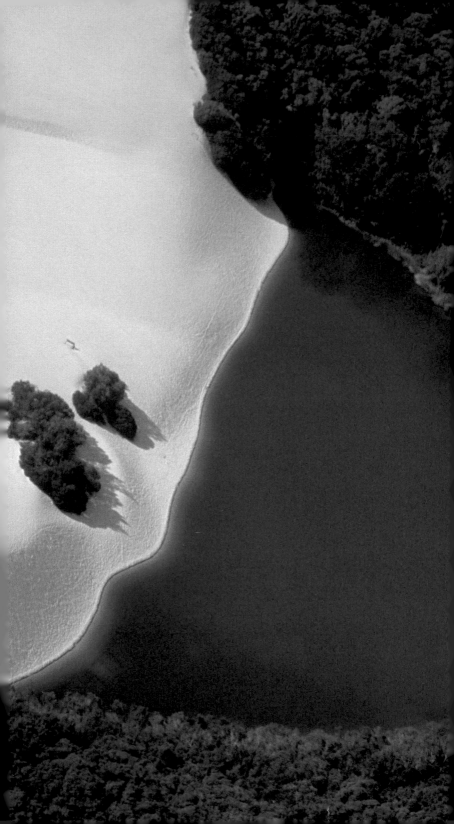

SOUTH OF TOWNSVILLE

Southern Queensland is renowned for two distinct features: its fine coastal surfing beaches and, inland, some of the richest farming land in Australia. The area is the centre of the country's beef and sugar industries, and the Burdekin River Delta supports a fertile "salad basin" yielding tomatoes, beans and other small crops. Ports such as Mackay and Gladstone service some rich inland mines.

Recognizing the land's potential, pastoralists followed hard on the heels of the explorers who opened up this region in the 1840s. Sugar production had begun by 1869 in the Bundaberg area and by the 1880s it was a flourishing industry, leading to a shameful period in the country's history. As Europeans were considered inherently unsuited to work in the tropics, growers seized on South Sea Islanders for cheap labour. Called Kanakas, the labourers were paid a pittance, housed in substandard accommodation and given the most physically demanding jobs. Some Kanakas were kidnapped from their homeland (a practice called "black-birding"), but this was outlawed in 1868 and government inspectors were placed on all Kanakas ships to check that their emigration was voluntary. It was not until Federation in 1901 that the use of island labour stopped but by then some 60,000 Kanakas had been brought to Queensland.

In tandem with this agricultural boom, southern Queensland thrived in the latter half of the 19th century when gold was found in the region. Towns such as Charters Towers have preserved much of their 19th-century architecture as reminders of the glory days of the gold rush. Although much of the gold has been extracted, the region is still rich in coal and has the world's largest sapphire fields. Amid this mineral landscape, there are also some beautiful national parks.

Today, the area is perhaps best known for its coastal features. Surfers from all over the world flock to the aptly named resort of Surfers Paradise, and the white sand beaches of the Gold Coast are crowded throughout the summer months. The region is also the gateway to the southern tip of the Great Barrier Reef and the Whitsunday Islands, and is popular with both locals and visitors.

Surfers trying to catch the best wave in Surfers Paradise

◀ Lake Wabby, the deepest lake on the largest sand island in the world

Exploring South of Townsville

With easy access from Brisbane *(see pp222–37)*, the southern coastline of Queensland is one of the most popular holiday locations in Australia, with its sunny climate, sandy beaches and good surf. Fraser Island is one of the region's undisputed highlights with its vast beaches, cool blue lakes and interior rainforests. Behind the fertile coastal plains are many of the 1850s gold rush "boom towns", while the Capricorn Hinterland, inland from Rockhampton, has the fascinating sapphire gem fields near Emerald and the dramatic sandstone escarpments of the Carnarvon and Blackdown Tableland national parks. To the north of the region is the busy city of Townsville, a major gateway to the Whitsundays and the islands of the Great Barrier Reef *(see pp216–21)*.

Irrigating sugar cane fields in Mackay, near Eungella National Park

Sights at a Glance

1. Lamington National Park
2. Darling Downs
3. Sunshine Coast Hinterland
4. Maryborough
5. Hervey Bay
6. *Fraser Island p246*
7. Mon Repos Conservation Park
8. Gladstone
9. Rockhampton
10. Blackdown Tableland National Park
11. *Carnarvon National Park p249*
12. Eungella National Park
13. Whitsunday Islands
14. Ayr
15. Charters Towers
16. Townsville and Magnetic Island

Key

━━ Highway
━━ Major road
┄┄┄ Minor road
– – Track
━━ Scenic route
━━ Main railway
━━ Minor railway
━━ State border
△ Summit

0 kilometres   100

0 miles   100

For additional map symbols *see back flap*

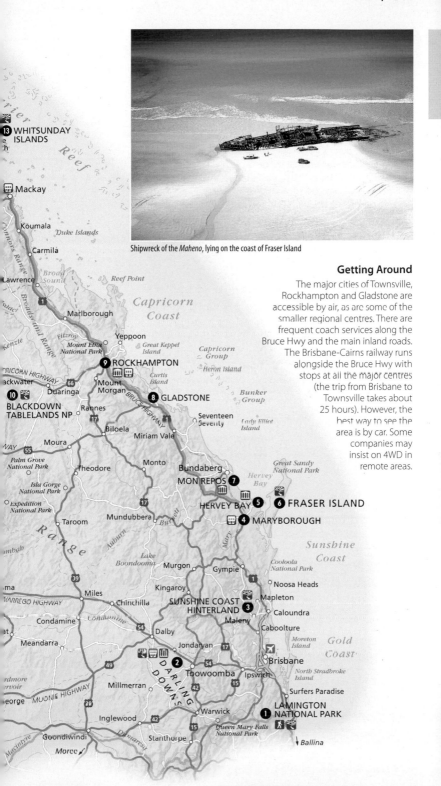

Shipwreck of the *Maheno*, lying on the coast of Fraser Island

Getting Around

The major cities of Townsville, Rockhampton and Gladstone are accessible by air, as are some of the smaller regional centres. There are frequent coach services along the Bruce Hwy and the main inland roads. The Brisbane-Cairns railway runs alongside the Bruce Hwy with stops at all the major centres (the trip from Brisbane to Townsville takes about 25 hours). However, the best way to see the area is by car. Some companies may insist on 4WD in remote areas.

13 WHITSUNDAY ISLANDS

Mackay

Koumala
Duke Islands
Carmila

Lawrence
Broad Sound
Reef Point

Capricorn Coast

Marlborough

Yeppoon
Great Keppel Island
Capricorn Group
Mount Etna National Park
Heron Island

CAPRICORN HIGHWAY 66
9 ROCKHAMPTON
ackwater
Duaringa
Mount Morgan
Curtis Island

10 BLACKDOWN TABLELANDS NP
Rannes
17
8 GLADSTONE
Bunker Group

Moura
Biloela
Miriam Vale
Seventeen Seventy
Lady Elliot Island

Palm Grove National Park
Theodore
Monto
Bundaberg
MON REPOS 7
Great Sandy National Park
Hervey Bay

Isla Gorge National Park
Expedition National Park
Mundubbera
17
HERVEY BAY 5
6 FRASER ISLAND

Taroom
4 MARYBOROUGH

Range
Lake Boondooma
Murgon
Gympie
Cooloola National Park
Sunshine Coast

39
Miles
Kingaroy
Noosa Heads

ma
Chinchilla
SUNSHINE COAST HINTERLAND 3
Mapleton
Caloundra

WARREGO HIGHWAY
Condamine
54
Dalby
Maleny
Caboolture
Moreton Island
Gold Coast

Meandarra
Jondaryan
17
Brisbane
North Stradbroke Island

49
Millmerran
2 Toowoomba
Ipswich
Surfers Paradise

rdmore
ervoir
MOONIE HIGHWAY 29
Warwick
42
15
1 LAMINGTON NATIONAL PARK

eorge
Inglewood
42
Goondiwindi
Stanthorpe
15
Queen Mary Falls National Park
Ballina

Moree

Southern Queensland Coastline

An hour's drive either north or south of Brisbane, the southern Queensland coast is Australia's most popular beach playground. The famous Gold Coast extends 75 km (45 miles) south of Brisbane and is a flashy strip of holiday apartments, luxury hotels, shopping malls, nightclubs, a casino and, above all, 42 km (25 miles) of golden sandy beaches. To the north, the Sunshine Coast is more restrained and elegant. Inland, the Great Dividing Range provides a cool alternative to the hot coastal climate, with flourishing arts and crafts communities, superb bushwalking and wonderful panoramas.

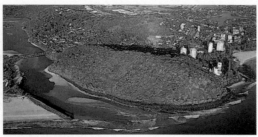

Burleigh Heads National Park is a tiny park that preserves the dense eucalypt forests that once covered the entire region. The nutritious volcanic soil stemming from Mount Warning, 30 km (20 miles) southwest of the park, allows the rainforest to thrive.

The Gold Coast has three theme parks. Sea World has dolphin, sea lion and penguin displays; Warner Bros. Movie World features stunts and tours of replica film sets; Dreamworld fairground park has wildlife such as Bengal tigers. There are also two water parks: Wet 'n' Wild® and Whitewater World.

Australia Zoo began life as a small, four-acre park known as Beerwah Reptile Park. Its founder, the late Steve "the Croc Hunter" Irwin, became a household name and today the zoo is a 70-acre entertainment mecca with more than 1,000 animals.

② **Tewantin** 🚻
This well-known town is in the heart of the Sunshine Coast area, with spectacular sunsets and beautiful beaches. It is also the ferry access point to Cooloola National Park.

Maryborou

⑤ **Maroochydore Beach**
🏃 🏖 🧗 🚻 ♿ 🚹
An ocean beach and the Maroochy riverfront make the main commercial centre of the Sunshine Coast a popular holiday destination, with good hotels and restaurants.

⑥ **Mooloolaba Wharf**
🏃 🏖 🧗 🚻 ♿
The wharf at Mooloolaba is a popular tourist development. Underwater World, said to be the largest oceanarium in the southern hemisphere, contains crocodiles and barramundi.

⑦ **Bulcock Beach, Caloundra** 🏖 🧗 🚻 ♿ 🚹
The central location of sandy Bulcock Beach means it is often crowded with tourists and families. Nearby Golden Beach and Shelly Beach are also beautiful, but quieter.

⑧ **Moreton Bay**
🏖 🧗 🚻 ♿ 🚹
This is the access point to some 370 offshore islands, the most popular being Moreton, Bribie and South Stradbroke. Fishing, birdwatching and boating are the main activities.

⑫ **Coolangatta**
🏃 🏖 🧗 🚻 ♿ 🚹
On the Queensland–New South Wales border, Coolangatta has some of the best surfing waters in the area, but relatively uncrowded beaches. Surfing tuition and boards for hire are available here.

For additional map symbols see back flap

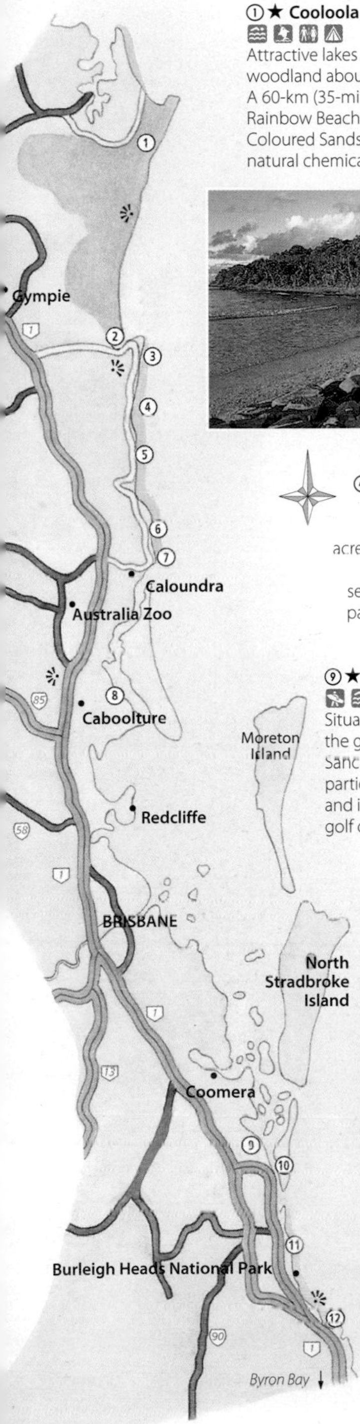

Locator Map

① ★ Cooloola National Park

Attractive lakes and sclerophyll woodland abound in this area. A 60-km (35-mile) 4WD to Rainbow Beach passes the Teewah Coloured Sands, produced by natural chemicals.

③ ★ Noosa Heads, Main Beach

Extraordinary natural beauty, a north-facing beach and an extensive river system have combined to make Noosa a fashionable holiday resort.

④ ★ Noosa National Park

Consisting of 380 ha (940 acres) of headland surrounded by coastline containing secluded coves, this national park is inhabited with koalas.

⑨ ★ Sanctuary Cove

Situated on Hope Island, the glamorous resort of Sanctuary Cove is aimed particularly at golfers and includes two luxury golf courses.

⑩ ★ South Stradbroke Island Beach

This unspoiled sand island offers peaceful but relatively basic accommodation. Catching crabs and bird-watching are popular activities.

⑪ ★ Surfers Paradise Beach

This is the focal point of the Gold Coast with block after block of high-rise developments and a range of entertainment options for visitors.

0 km   20
0 miles   20

Key

- Highway
- Major road
- Minor road
- River
- Viewpoint

Gympie

Caloundra

Australia Zoo

Caboolture

Moreton Island

Redcliffe

BRISBANE

North Stradbroke Island

Coomera

Burleigh Heads National Park

Byron Bay ↓

QUEENSLAND

❶ Lamington National Park

🚌 Canungra. ℹ️ Park Ranger Office (07) 5544 0634 or 13 74 68. **Open** daily. 🌐 **nprsr.qld.gov.au/ parks/lamington**

Lamington National Park, set within the McPherson Mountain Range, is one of Queensland's most popular parks. Declared in 1915, it contains 200 sq km (78 sq miles) of thick wooded country, with more than 160 km (100 miles) of walking tracks through subtropical rainforests of hoop pine, black booyongs and strangler figs. The highest ridges in the park reach more than 1,000 m (3,280 ft) and are lined with Antarctic beech trees – the most northerly in Australia. Some 150 species of birds, such as the Albert's lyrebird, make bird-watching a popular pastime. The global importance of the area was recognized in 1994, when Lamington was declared a World Heritage Area.

Nearby Macrozamia National Park has macrozamia palms (cycads) – one of the oldest forms of vegetation still growing in the world.

Stunning king parrot

❷ Darling Downs

🚌 Toowoomba. ℹ️ Toowoomba (07) 4639 3797 or 1800 331 155.

Only 90 minutes' drive from Brisbane, stretching west of the Great Dividing Range, is the fertile country of the Darling Downs. The first area to be settled after Brisbane, the region encompasses some of the most productive agricultural land in Australia, as well as one of the most historic areas in Queensland.

Toowoomba is the main centre of the Downs and is also one of Queensland's biggest cities. Early settlers transformed this one-time swamp into the present "Garden City", famous for its jacarandas and Carnival of Flowers (see p44).

About 45 km (28 miles) north-west of Toowoomba along the

Warrego Hwy is **The Woolshed at Jondaryan**. Built in 1859 to handle 200,000 sheep in one season, it has now been restored as a working memorial to the early pioneers of the district.

South of Toowoomba is Warwick, the oldest town in Queensland after Brisbane and known for its roses and its 19th-century sandstone buildings. It also claims one of the oldest rodeos in Australia, dating from 1857 when £50 (a year's pay) was wagered on the outcome of the riding contest. Today the rodeo follows the Rose and Rodeo Festival in October and offers prize money of more than A$70,000 (see p45).

About 60 km (40 miles) south of Warwick and 915 m (3,000 ft) above sea level, Stanthorpe actively celebrates its freezing winter temperatures with the

Brass Monkey Season (see p47). The town is at the heart of the Granite Belt, one of Queensland's few wine regions (see p41).

Near Warwick, Queen Mary Falls National Park is a 78-ha (193-acre) rainforest park with picnic areas and a 40-m (130-ft) waterfall.

🏛️ **The Woolshed at Jondaryan** Evanslea Rd, Jondaryan. **Tel** (07) 4692 2229. **Open** 9am–4:30pm daily. **Closed** 25 & 26 Dec. 🅿️ ♿ 🌐 **jondaryanwoolshed.com**

❸ Sunshine Coast Hinterland

🚌 Glasshouse Country Coaches (07) 5496 9249. ℹ️ Cnr 6th Ave & Melrose Pde, Maroochydore (07) 5458 8842. 🌐 **glasshousecoaches.com.au**

To the west of the Sunshine Coast is the Blackall Range. The area has become a centre for artists and artisans, with numerous guesthouses and some fine

Waterfall in Queen Mary Falls National Park, Darling Downs

The Glasshouse Mountains, a Queensland landmark on the hinterland of the Sunshine Coast

restaurants. The most attractive centres are Montville and Maleny. The drive from Maleny to Mapleton is one of the most scenic in the region, with views across to Moreton Island, encompassing pineapple and sugar cane fields.

Consisting of ten volcanic cones, the Glasshouse Mountains were formed 20 million years ago. The craggy volcanic peaks were named by Captain Cook in 1770 because they reminded him of the glass furnaces in his native Yorkshire.

❹ Maryborough

🏙 21,300. ✈ 🚗 🚌 🚆 City Hall, Kent St (07) 4190 5742 or 1800 811 728. 🌐 visitmaryborough.info

Situated on the banks of the Mary River, Maryborough has a strong link with Australia's early history. Founded in 1843, the town provided housing for Kanakas' labour *(see p239)* and was the only port apart from Sydney where free settlers could enter. This resulted in a thriving town – the buildings reflecting the wealth of its citizens.

Many of these buildings survive, earning Maryborough the title of "Heritage City". A great many of the town's private residences also date from the 19th century, ranging from simple workers' cottages to beautiful old "Queenslanders". These houses are distinctive to the state, set high off the ground to catch the cool air currents and with graceful verandas on all sides.

❺ Hervey Bay

🏙 41,000. ✈ 🚌 🚆 🛈 227 Maryborough-Hervey Bay Rd, Torquay, Hervey Bay (07) 4197 4730 or 1800 811 728. 🌐 visitherveybay.info

As recently as the 1970s Hervey Bay was just a string of five fishing villages. However, the safe beaches and mild climate have quickly turned it into a metropolis of over 40,000 people and one of the fastest-growing holiday centres in Australia.

Hervey Bay is also the best place for whale-watching. Humpback whales migrate more than 11,000 km (7,000 miles) every year from the Antarctic to northern Australian waters to mate and calve. On their return, between August and October, they rest at Hervey Bay to give the calves time to develop a protective layer of blubber before they

Bundaberg rum

begin their final run to Antarctica. Since whaling was stopped in the 1960s, numbers have quadrupled from 300 to approximately 5,000.

Environs
The sugar city of central Queensland, Bundaberg is 62 km (38 miles) north of Hervey Bay. It is the home of Bundaberg ("Bundy") rum, the biggest-selling spirit label in Australia. Bundaberg is an attractive town with many 19th-century buildings. The city's favourite son, Bert Hinkler (1892–1933), was the first man to fly solo from England to Australia in 1928. His original "Ibis" aircraft is displayed in the **Hinkler Hall of Aviation.**

🏛 **Hinkler Hall of Aviation**
Young St, Botanic Gardens. **Tel** (07) 4130 4400. **Open** 9am–4pm daily. **Closed** Good Fri, 25 Apr, 25 Dec. ♿ 📷 🌐 hinklerhallofaviation.com

Classic Queenslander-style house in Maryborough

⑥ Fraser Island

Situated off the Queensland coast near Maryborough *(see p245)*, Fraser Island World Heritage area is the largest sand island in the world. Measuring 123 km (76 miles) in length and 25 km (16 miles) across, the island is a mix of hills and valleys, rainforest and clear lakes. Ferries to the island operate from Urangan, River Heads and Inskip Point. There is a range of resorts and numerous camp sites on the island. Vehicle (4WD only) and camping permits are required.

VISITORS' CHECKLIST

Practical Information
ℹ️ Hervey Bay Visitor Information Centre 1800 811 728.

Transport
🚌 from Urangan, River Heads & Inskip Point.

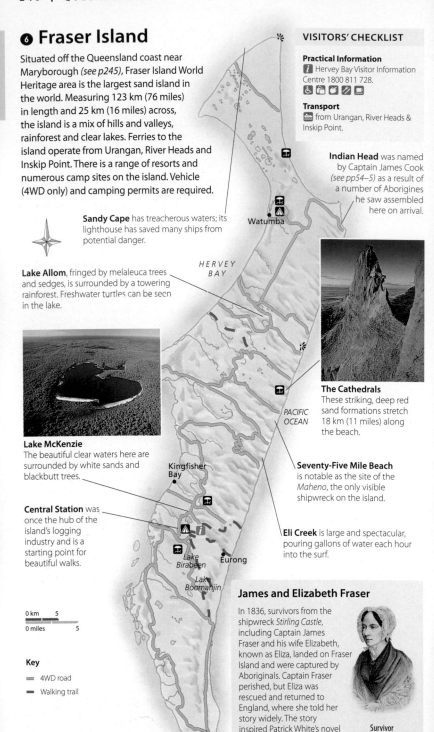

Sandy Cape has treacherous waters; its lighthouse has saved many ships from potential danger.

HERVEY BAY

Lake Allom, fringed by melaleuca trees and sedges, is surrounded by a towering rainforest. Freshwater turtles can be seen in the lake.

Lake McKenzie
The beautiful clear waters here are surrounded by white sands and blackbutt trees.

Central Station was once the hub of the island's logging industry and is a starting point for beautiful walks.

Kingfisher Bay

Lake Birabeen

Eurong

Lake Boomanjin

Watumba

Indian Head was named by Captain James Cook *(see pp54–5)* as a result of a number of Aborigines he saw assembled here on arrival.

The Cathedrals
These striking, deep red sand formations stretch 18 km (11 miles) along the beach.

PACIFIC OCEAN

Seventy-Five Mile Beach is notable as the site of the *Maheno*, the only visible shipwreck on the island.

Eli Creek is large and spectacular, pouring gallons of water each hour into the surf.

James and Elizabeth Fraser

In 1836, survivors from the shipwreck *Stirling Castle*, including Captain James Fraser and his wife Elizabeth, known as Eliza, landed on Fraser Island and were captured by Aboriginals. Captain Fraser perished, but Eliza was rescued and returned to England, where she told her story widely. The story inspired Patrick White's novel *A Fringe of Leaves (see p39)*.

Survivor **Elizabeth Fraser**

Hook Point

0 km 5
0 miles 5

Key

═══ 4WD road

▬ Walking trail

Loggerhead turtle laying eggs on Mon Repos Beach

❼ Mon Repos Conservation Park

Tel (07) 4159 1652, tour bookings (07) 4153 8888. **Open** daily. 🐢 Turtle tours. 🚻 🎫 obligatory Nov–Mar. 🆆 nprsr.qld.gov.au/parks/mon-repos

Mon Repos Beach, 15 km (9 miles) from Bundaberg *(see p245)*, is one of the most significant and accessible turtle rookeries on the Australian mainland. Egg-laying of loggerhead and other turtles takes place from November to February. By January, the first young turtles begin to hatch and make their way down the sandy beach to the ocean.

An information centre within the environmental park has videos and other information about these fascinating reptiles. Supervised public viewing ensures that the turtles are not unduly disturbed.

Just behind Mon Repos Beach is an old stone wall built by Kanakas and now preserved as a memorial to these South Sea Island inhabitants *(see p239)*.

❽ Gladstone

🏘 29,000. ✈ 🚉 🚌 🚐
ℹ Gladstone Marina, Bryan Jordan Drive (07) 4972 9000.
🆆 gladstoneregion.info

Gladstone is a town dominated by industry. However, industry is in harmony with tourism and the environment. Tours of the area are popular with visitors. The world's largest alumina refinery is located here, processing bauxite mined in Weipa on the west coast of Cape York Peninsula. Five per cent of the nation's wealth and 20 per cent of Queensland's wealth is generated by Gladstone's industries. Gladstone's port, handling more than 35 million tonnes of cargo a year, is one of the busiest in Australia.

There are, however, more attractive sights in and around the town. The town's main street has an eclectic variety of buildings, including the Grand Hotel, rebuilt to its 1897 form after fire destroyed the original in 1993. Gladstone's Botanic Gardens were first opened in 1988 as a bicentennial project and consist entirely of native Australian plants. South of Gladstone are the tiny coastal villages of Agnes Waters and the quaintly named "1770" in honour of Captain Cook's brief landing here during his journey up the coast *(see p54)*. About 20 km (12 miles) out of town lies the popular holiday location of Boyne Island.

Gladstone is also the access point for Heron Island, considered by many to be one of the most desirable of all the Great Barrier Reef islands, with its wonderful coral and diving opportunities. Other islands in the southern half of the reef can also be accessed from Gladstone by boat or helicopter *(see pp220–21)*.

Pretty coastal village of Agnes Waters, near Gladstone

⑨ Rockhampton

🏔 61,000. 🚉 🚌 🚌 ℹ Capricorn Info. Centre, Gladstone Rd (07) 4927 2055.

Rockhampton is situated 40 km (25 miles) inland, on the banks of the Fitzroy River. Often referred to as the "beef capital" of Australia, the town is also the administrative and commercial heart of central Queensland. A spire marks the fact that, geographically, the Tropic of Capricorn runs through the town.

Rockhampton was founded in 1854 and contains many restored 19th-century buildings. Quay Street flanks the tree-lined river and has been classified in its entirety by the National Trust. Particularly outstanding is the sandstone Customs House. The beautiful **Botanic Gardens** were established in 1869, and have a fine collection of tropical plants. There is also on-site accommodation.

Built on an ancient tribal meeting ground, the **Aboriginal Dreamtime Cultural Centre** is owned and operated by local Aboriginals. Imaginative displays give an insight into their life and culture.

🌿 **Botanic Gardens**
Spencer St. **Tel** (07) 4922 1654.
Open 6am–6pm daily. ♿

🏛 **Aboriginal Dreamtime Cultural Centre**
Bruce Hwy. **Tel** (07) 4936 1655.
Open 9am–3:30pm Mon–Fri.
Closed public hols. 🍴 📷
ⓦ dreamtimecentre.com.au

Sandstone cliff looking out over Blackdown Tableland National Park

Environs

The heritage township of Mount Morgan is 38 km (25 miles) southwest of Rockhampton. A 2 sq km (0.5 sq mile) open-cut mine of first gold, then copper, operated here for 100 years and was an important part of the state's economy until the minerals ran out in 1981.

Plaque at base of the Tropic of Capricorn spire

Some 25 km (15 miles) north of Rockhampton is Mount Etna National Park, containing spectacular limestone caves, discovered in the 1880s. These are open to the public via Olsen's Capricorn Caverns and Camoo Caves. A major feature of the caves is "cave coral" – stone-encrusted tree roots that have forced their way through the rock. The endangered ghost bat, Australia's only carnivorous bat, nests in these caves.

The stunning sandy beaches of Yeppoon and Emu Park are only 40 km (25 miles) northeast of the city. Rockhampton is also the access point for Great Keppel Island (*see pp220–21*).

⑩ Blackdown Tableland National Park

Off Capricorn Hwy, via Dingo. Park Ranger **Tel** (07) 4986 1964. ♿

Between Rockhampton and Emerald, along a 20-km (12-mile) untarmacked detour off the Capricorn Highway, is Blackdown Tableland National Park. A dramatic sandstone plateau which rises 600 m (2,000 ft) above the flat surrounding countryside, the Tableland offers spectacular views, escarpments, open forest and tumbling waterfalls. Wildlife includes gliders, brushtail possums, rock wallabies and the occasional dingo.

Emerald is a coal mining centre and the hub of the central highland region, 75 km (45 miles) west of the park; the town provides a railhead for the surrounding agricultural areas. Its ornate 1900 railway station is one of the few survivors of a series of fires that occurred between 1936 and 1969, which destroyed much of the town's heritage. About 60 km (37 miles) southwest of Emerald is Cullin-la-ringo, where there are headstones marking the mass grave of 19 European settlers killed in 1861 by local Aboriginals. At Comet is a tree carved with the initials of explorer Ludwig Leichhardt during his 1844 expedition to Port Essington (*see p253*).

More in tune with its name, Emerald is also the access point for the largest sapphire fields in the world. The lifestyle of the gem diggers is fascinating, making it a popular tourist area.

Façade of Customs House on Quay Street, Rockhampton

For hotels and restaurants in this area see pp486–8 and pp514–15

⓫ Carnarvon National Park

The main access to Carnarvon National Park lies 250 km (155 miles) south of Emerald, while the park itself covers some 298,000 ha (730,000 acres). There are several sections of the park, but the stunning Carnarvon Gorge is the most accessible area to visitors. A 32-km (20-mile) canyon carved by the waters of Carnarvon Creek, the gorge consists of white cliffs, crags and pillars of stone harbouring plants and animals which have survived through centuries of evolution. The area is also rich in Aboriginal culture, and three cultural sites are open to the public. Comfortable cabin accommodation is available or there are various camp sites, provided you have an advance booking and a camping permit *(see p481)*.

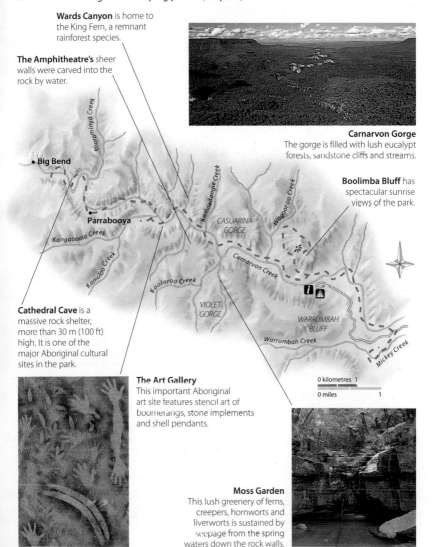

Wards Canyon is home to the King Fern, a remnant rainforest species.

The Amphitheatre's sheer walls were carved into the rock by water.

Carnarvon Gorge
The gorge is filled with lush eucalypt forests, sandstone cliffs and streams.

Boolimba Bluff has spectacular sunrise views of the park.

Cathedral Cave is a massive rock shelter, more than 30 m (100 ft) high. It is one of the major Aboriginal cultural sites in the park.

The Art Gallery
This important Aboriginal art site features stencil art of boomerangs, stone implements and shell pendants.

0 kilometres 1
0 miles 1

Moss Garden
This lush greenery of ferns, creepers, hornworts and liverworts is sustained by seepage from the spring waters down the rock walls.

For keys to symbols *see back flap*

Stunning estuary at Whitehaven Beach, the highlight of the Whitsundays

⑫ Eungella National Park

🚌 Mackay. 🚍 Mackay. 🛈 Mackay (07) 4944 5888.

Eungella National Park is the main wilderness area on the central Queensland coast and encompasses some 50,000 ha (125,000 acres) of the rugged Clarke Ranges. Volcanic rock covered with rainforest and subtropical flora is cut by steep gorges, crystal clear pools and impressive waterfalls tumbling down the mountainside.

Finch Hatton Gorge is the main destination for tourists, where indigenous wildlife includes gliders, ring-tailed possums, bandicoots and pademelons (a kind of wallaby). Broken River is one of the few places in Australia where platypuses can be spotted at dusk and dawn.

The main access point for Eungella is the prosperous sugar town of **Mackay**. Somewhat low-key from a tourist point of view, Mackay boasts a balmy climate by way of the surrounding mountains trapping the warm coastal air even in winter. Thirty beautiful white sand beaches are lined with casuarinas. All around the town sugar cane can be seen blowing in the wind in the many sugar cane fields.

The town centre of Mackay has a number of historic buildings worth visiting, including the Commonwealth Bank and Customs House, both classified by the National Trust.

The second-largest coal-loader in the world is at Hay Point, where trains more than 2 km (1 mile) long haul coal from the western mines for shipping overseas.

⑬ Whitsunday Islands

🚍 Proserpine. 🚌 Airlie Beach. ✈ Hamilton Island; Proserpine. ⛴ Port of Airlie, Airlie Beach. 🛈 (07) 4945 3967. 🌐 tourismwhitsundays.com.au

The Whitsunday Islands are an archipelago of 74 islands, situated within the Great Barrier Reef Marine Park, approximately 1,140 km (700 miles) north of Brisbane and 640 km (400 miles) south of Cairns. These beautiful islands and sandy atolls are among the most stunning holiday destinations in Australia. Whitehaven Beach on Whitsunday Island is recognized as one of the world's best beaches, with 9 km (6 miles) of pure white silica sand and turquoise sea.

Only a few of the islands offer accommodation, including Hamilton, Daydream, Hayman, South Molle and Long, while some 66 islands remain uninhabited. A wide range of accommodation is available including luxury hotels, hostels, guesthouses and self-catering apartments.

There are many activities on offer including scuba diving, whale watching, seaplane flights and charter sailing.

Many companies at Airlie Beach on the mainland offer sailing packages, which include diving or snorkelling and a night or two moored on the Great Barrier Reef.

⑭ Ayr

🏙 8,000. 🚍 🚌 🛈 Plantation Park, Bruce Hwy (07) 4783 5988.

The busy town of Ayr, at the heart of the Burdekin River Delta, is the major sugar cane-growing area in Australia.

Within the town itself is the modern Burdekin Cultural Complex, which includes a 530-seat theatre, a library and an art gallery. Among its art collection are the renowned "Living Lagoon" sculptures by the contemporary Australian sculptor Stephen Walker. The Ayr Nature Display consists of an impressive rock wall made from 2,600 pieces of North Queensland rock, intricate pictures made from preserved insects and a display of Australian reptiles, shells, fossils and Aboriginal artifacts. In Plantation Park is the Juru walking trail and Gubulla Munda, a giant snake sculpture 15 m (50 ft) long.

Environs

Approximately 55 km (35 miles) north of Ayr is Alligator Creek, which is the access point for Bowling Green Bay National Park. Here you will find geckos and chirping cicadas living alongside each other in this lush landscape. Within the park are rock pools, perfect for swimming, and plunging waterfalls.

"Living Lagoon" sculpture at the Burdekin Complex, Ayr

Ornate 19th-century façade of City Hall in Charters Towers

⓯ Charters Towers

🏙 8,000. 🚗 🚌 🚋 ℹ️ 74 Mosman St (07) 4761 5533.

Charters Towers was once the second-largest town in Queensland with a population of 27,000, following the 1871 discovery of gold in the area by a 10-year-old Aboriginal boy. Gold is still mined in the area, as well as copper, lead and zinc.

The old Charters Towers Stock Exchange is a historic gem set amid a group of other splendid 19th-century buildings in the city centre. This international centre of finance was the only such exchange in Australia outside a capital city and was built during the gold-mining days. Charters Towers fell into decline when the gold ran out in the 1920s. Its economy now depends on the beef industry and its status as the educational centre for Queensland's Outback and Papua New Guinea – school students make up one-fifth of the population.

⓰ Townsville and Magnetic Island

🏙 129,000. ✈️ 🚗 🚌 🚋 🛳 ℹ️ Flinders Square (07) 4721 3660.

Townsville is the second-largest city in Queensland and a major port for the beef, sugar and mining industries. Boasting, on average, 300 sunny days a year, the beachfront is a source of local pride. The city was founded in the 1860s by Robert Towns, who began the practice of "blackbirding" – kidnapping Kanakas from their homeland and bringing them to Australia as cheap labour (see p239).

Among the city's tourist attractions is **Reef HQ**, a "living coral reef aquarium" and the **Museum of Tropical Queensland**, which displays artifacts from the shipwreck *Pandora*. Townsville is also an access point for the Barrier Reef and a major diving centre, largely because of the nearby wreck of the steamship *Yongala*, which sank in 1911.

Situated 8 km (5 miles) off-shore and officially a suburb of Townsville, Magnetic Island has 2,500 inhabitants and is the only reef island with a significant permanent population. It was named by Captain Cook, who erroneously believed that magnetic fields generated by the huge granite boulders he could see were causing problems with his compass. Today, almost half of the island is a national park.

🏖 **Reef HQ**
Flinders St East. **Tel** (07) 4750 0800. **Open** 9:30am–5pm daily. **Closed** 25 Dec. 🅿️ 🛗 ♿ 🏠 🌐 reefhq.com.au

🏛 **Museum of Tropical Qld**
Flinders St East. **Tel** (07) 4726 0600. **Open** 9:30am–5pm daily. **Closed** Good Fri, 25 Apr (am), 25 Dec. ♿

Idyllic blue waters of Rocky Bay on Magnetic Island

NORTHERN AND OUTBACK QUEENSLAND

European explorers who made epic journeys into the previously impenetrable area of Northern and Outback Queensland in the 1800s found a land rich in minerals and agricultural potential. They also discovered places of extreme natural beauty, such as the Great Barrier Reef and other unique regions now preserved as national parks.

Northern Queensland was first visited by Europeans when Captain Cook was forced to berth his damaged ship, the *Endeavour*, on the coast. The area remained a mystery for almost another 100 years, however, until other intrepid Europeans ventured north. These expeditions were perilous and explorers were faced with harsh conditions and hostile Aboriginal tribes. In 1844, Ludwig Leichhardt and his group set out from Brisbane to Port Essington, but most of the men were wounded or killed by Aboriginals. In 1848, Edmund Kennedy led an expedition from Cairns to the top of Cape York. All but two of this party perished, including Kennedy, who was killed by Aboriginals.

In the late 19th century, Northern Queensland found sudden prosperity when gold was discovered in the region. The population rose and towns grew up to service the mines, but by the beginning of the 20th century much of the gold had dried up. These once thriving "cities" are now little more than one-street towns, lined with 19th-century architecture as a reminder of their glory days. Today, much of the area's wealth stems from its booming tourist trade. Luxury resorts line the stunning coastline, and tourists flock to experience the spectacular natural wonders of the Great Barrier Reef.

Queensland's Outback region has a strong link with Australia's national heritage. The Tree of Knowledge at Barcaldine marks the meeting place of the first Australian Labor Party during the great shearer's strike of 1891. The town of Winton is where "Banjo" Paterson *(see p39)* wrote Australia's national song "Waltzing Matilda" in 1895. Today, the vast Outback area is known for agriculture and a wide range of mining operations.

A rodeo rider and clown perform in Laura near Lakefield National Park in Northern Queensland

◀ A shoal of bigeye trevally swimming in a spiral pattern at the Great Barrier Reef

Exploring Northern Queensland

The area north of Townsville leading up to Cairns is Australia's sugar-producing country, the cane fields backed by the Great Dividing Range. Northern Queensland is sparsely populated: Cairns is the only city, while Port Douglas and Mossman are small towns. The only other villages of note in the region are Daintree and Cooktown. Cape York Peninsula is one of the last untouched wildernesses in the world, covering 200,000 sq km (77,220 sq miles) – roughly the same size as Great Britain. The landscape varies according to the time of year: in the green season (November–March) the rivers are swollen and the country is green; during the dry winter the riverbeds are waterless and the countryside is bare and arid.

Lush rainforest in Daintree National Park, near Cairns

Getting Around

Cairns is well served by public transport, with regular air, train and coach connections from southern Queensland and the other states. It also benefits from an international airport. The tropical terrain north of Cape Tribulation to Cooktown and the Outback requires approved 4WD hire cars unless you take an organized tour. Many car rental companies will insist on a 4WD all the way along the 326-km (202-mile) coast road from Cairns to Cooktown. During the wet season, Cape York is generally impassable.

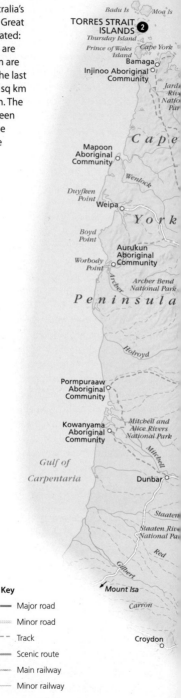

The Pier shopping centre and Marlin Marina in Cairns

Key

— Major road

⋯⋯ Minor road

-- Track

— Scenic route

—•— Main railway

— Minor railway

For additional map symbols *see back flap*

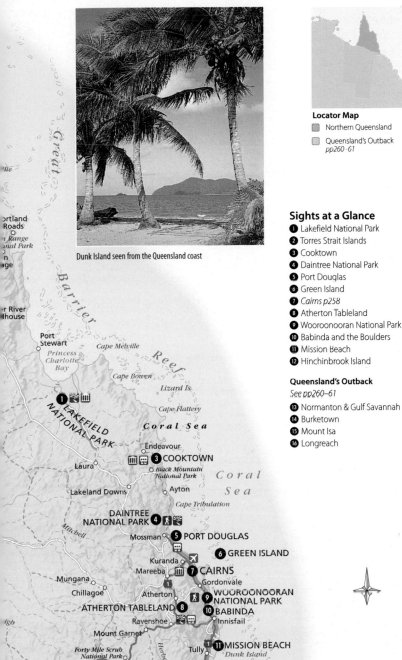

Dunk Island seen from the Queensland coast

Locator Map
▨ Northern Queensland
▨ Queensland's Outback
pp260–61

Sights at a Glance

1 Lakefield National Park
2 Torres Strait Islands
3 Cooktown
4 Daintree National Park
5 Port Douglas
6 Green Island
7 *Cairns p258*
8 Atherton Tableland
9 Wooroonooran National Park
10 Babinda and the Boulders
11 Mission Beach
12 Hinchinbrook Island

Queensland's Outback
See pp260–61

13 Normanton & Gulf Savannah
14 Burketown
15 Mount Isa
16 Longreach

0 kilometres 100
0 miles 100

❶ Lakefield National Park

🚌 Cooktown. ℹ️ Cooktown (07) 4069 6004. Park Office (07) 4060 3271. Campsite bookings 13 74 68. **Open** Jun–Nov: Mon–Fri. 🆆 **nprsr.qld.gov.au/parks/ rinyirru-lakefield**

Covering approximately 540,000 ha (1,300,000 acres), Lakefield National Park is the second-largest national park in Queensland. It encompasses a wide variety of landscapes, including river forests, plains and coastal flats. The centre of the park abounds with birds. Camping is the only accommodation option and a permit must be obtained at the self-registration stations throughout the park. The park is largely inaccessible during the wet season between December and April when the rivers flood the plains.

The nearby town of **Laura**, at the base of the Cape York Peninsula, is a typical Australian Outback town, with a sealed road flanked by a pub, a general store and a few houses. In the late 19th century, Laura was the rail terminus for the Palmer River gold fields and some 20,000 people passed through each year. Today, it is almost forgotten, but the discovery in 1959 of Aboriginal art sites of great antiquity is reviving interest in the area. One of its most notable sites is the "giant horse gallery", which contains huge horse paintings thought to record the first sightings of European explorers.

River forest landscape in Lakefield National Park

Thursday Island, in the Torres Strait island group

❷ Torres Strait Islands

✈️ from Cairns. 🚢 from Cairns. ℹ️ Cairns (07) 4051 3588.

The Torres Strait divides the northern coastline of Australia from Papua New Guinea and is dotted with numerous islands. Approximately 19 of these islands are inhabited and have been governed by Queensland since 1879.

Thursday Island is the "capital" island and was once the centre of the local pearling industry. Many Japanese pearlers who lost their lives in this occupation are buried in the island's cemetery. In 1891, Green Hill Fort was built to prevent invasion by the Russians. Murray Island was the birthplace of Eddie Mabo, who, in 1992, won his claim to traditional land in the Australian High Court and changed Aboriginal-European relations (*see p62*).

❸ Cooktown

🗺️ 1,300. ✈️ 🚌 🚌 🚢 ℹ️ Charlotte St (07) 4069 6004.

When the *Endeavour* was damaged by a coral reef in 1770, Captain Cook and his crew spent six weeks in this area while repairs to the ship were made (*see pp54–5*). Cooktown's proud boast, therefore, is that it was the site of the first white settlement in Australia. Like most towns in the area, Cooktown originally serviced the gold fields and its present-day population of less than 2,000 is half the 4,000 inhabitants who once sustained its 50 pubs. However, many of its historic buildings survive, including the Westpac Bank, originally the Old National Bank, with its stone columns supporting an iron-lace veranda. The **James Cook Museum**, which houses the old anchor from the *Endeavour*, started life in the 1880s as a convent. In the cemetery of the town, a memorial and numerous gravestones are testimony to the difficulties faced by the many Chinese who came to the gold fields in the 1870s (*see p59*).

Chinese gravestone in Cooktown

Between Cooktown and Bloomfield, Black Mountain National Park is named after the geological formation of huge black granite boulders. The boulders were formed around 260 million years ago below the earth's surface and were gradually exposed as surrounding land surfaces eroded away.

🏛️ **James Cook Museum**
Cnr Helen & Furneaux sts. **Tel** (07) 4069 5386. **Open** Nov–Jan & Mar: 9:30am–4pm daily; Feb: 10am–1pm Tue–Sat; Apr–Oct: 9am–4pm daily. 🅿️ ♿ limited.

❹ Daintree National Park

🚌 from Port Douglas. ℹ️ Port Douglas (07) 4099 5599 or 13 74 68. 🌐 **nprsr.qld.gov.au/parks/daintree**

Daintree National Park, north of Port Douglas, covers more than 76,000 ha (188,000 acres). The Cape Tribulation section of the park is a place of great beauty, and one of the few places where the rainforest meets the sea. Captain Cook named Cape Tribulation in rueful acknowledgment of the difficulties he was experiencing navigating the Great Barrier Reef. Today, it is a popular spot with backpackers.

The largest section of the park lies inland from Cape Tribulation. It is a mostly inaccessible, mountainous area, but 5 km (3 miles) from Mossman lies the Mossman Gorge, known for its easy and accessible 2.7-km (1-mile) track through the rainforest.

❺ Port Douglas

🏙️ 3,500. 🚌 🚌 ℹ️ 23 Macrossan St (07) 4099 5599.

Situated 75 km (47 miles) from Cairns, Port Douglas was once a tiny fishing village. Today it is a tourist centre, but it has managed to preserve some of its village atmosphere.

At the end of Macrossan Street is the beautiful Four-Mile Beach, which is a very

Tropical Myall Beach in Daintree National Park

popular walking spot. Many 19th-century buildings still line the street, such as the Courthouse Hotel, and the modern shopping centres have been designed to blend with the town's original architecture.

The original port was set up during the gold rush of the 1850s, but it was superseded by Cairns as the main port of the area. A disastrous cyclone in 1911 also forced people to move elsewhere, leaving the population at less than 500. The construction of the luxurious Sheraton Mirage Resort in the early 1980s heralded the beginning of a new boom, and now a range of accommodation and restaurants is on offer *(see p488 and p516)*.

Port Douglas is an alternative departure point to Cairns for Great Barrier Reef tours.

❻ Green Island

🚌 from Cairns. ℹ️ (07) 4031 3300. ♿ 🌐 **nprsr.qld.gov.au/parks/green-island** or 🌐 **greenislandresort.com.au**

Green Island is one of the few inhabited coral cays of the Great Barrier Reef *(see pp220–21)*. Despite its small size (a walk around the entire island takes about 15 minutes), it is home to a small scale eco-resort.

Green Island's proximity to the mainland means its coral is not as colourful as the outer reef, but it offers snorkelling from shore and visitors can spot sea turtles feeding on sea grass from the long jetty. Its accessibility by a ferry trip from Cairns makes it popular with day trippers.

The Islands Marineland Melanesia complex has daily crocodile feeding shows and is home to Cassius, the world's largest crocodile in captivity.

Green Island, a coral cay at the heart of the Great Barrier Reef

❼ Cairns

Cairns is the main centre of Northern Queensland. Despite its beachfront esplanade, it has a city atmosphere and instead of sandy beaches there are mudflats, abundant with native birdlife. Its main attraction is as a base for exploring the Great Barrier Reef *(see pp216–21)*, the Daintree Rainforest *(p257)* and the Atherton Tableland *(p259)*. However, Cairns itself does have several places of interest to visit.

⊠ Flecker Botanic Gardens

Collins Ave, Edge Hill. **Tel** (07) 4044 3398. **Open** daily. ♿ ▣
Dating from 1886, the Flecker Botanic Gardens are known for their collection of more than 100 species of palm trees. They also house many other tropical plants. The gardens include an area of Queensland rainforest with native birdlife. The Centenary Lakes were created in 1976 to commemorate the city's first 100 years.

⑪ Cairns Historical Society Museum

City Place, cnr Lake & Shield sts.
Tel (07) 4051 5582. **Open** 10am–4pm Mon–Sat. **Closed** Good Fri, 25 Apr, 25 Dec. ▨ Ⓦ cairnsmuseum.org.au
Housed in the 1907 School of Arts building, this museum

Tropical orchid in the Flecker Botanic Gardens

is a fine example of the city's early architecture. Among the exhibits are the contents of an old Chinese joss house.

▦ Reef Fleet Terminal

Pier Point Rd.
This is the departure point for most cruises to the Great Barrier Reef. Some 19th-century

façades nearby offer a glimpse of the city's early life.
Cairns is the game-fishing centre of Australia and, from August to December, tourists crowd Marlin Jetty to see the anglers return with their catch.
Adjacent Pier Marketplace has boutiques, restaurants, markets and accommodation.

Environs

On the eastern edge of the Atherton Tablelands is the tiny village of **Kuranda**. A hippie hang-out in the 1960s, it has since developed into an arts and crafts centre with markets held here daily. Nearby, at Smithfield, is the Tjapukai Cultural Centre, home to the renowned Aboriginal Tjapukai Dance Theatre.

Cairns City Centre

① Flecker Botanic Gardens
② Cairns Historical Society Museum
③ Reef Fleet Terminal

Mount Hypipamee Crater's green lake, Atherton Tableland

❽ Atherton Tableland

ℹ️ Cnr Silo & Main St, Atherton 1300 363 242 or (07) 4091 4222. **Open** 9am–5pm daily. **Closed** 1 Jan, Good Fri, Easter Sun, 25 Dec, 26 Dec. 🅆 ltablelands.com.au

Rising sharply from the coastal plains of Cairns, the northern landscape levels out into the lush Atherton Tableland. At their highest point, the tablelands are 900 m (3,000 ft) above sea level. The cool temperature, heavy rainfall and rich volcanic soil make this one of the richest farming areas in Queensland. For many decades, tobacco was the main crop, but, with the worldwide decline in smoking, farmers have diversified into peanuts, macadamia nuts, sugar cane, bananas and avocados.

The town of **Yungaburra**, with its many historic buildings, is listed by the National Trust. Nearby is the famed "curtain fig tree". Strangler figs attach themselves to a host tree and eventually kill the original tree. In this case, the aerial roots, growing down from the tree tops, form a 15-m (50-ft) screen. Southwest of Yungaburra is the eerie, green crater lake at Mt Hypipamee. Stretching 60 m (200 ft) in diameter.

Millaa Millaa contains the most spectacular waterfalls of the region. A 15-km (9-mile) sealed circuit drive takes in the Zillie and Ellinjaa falls, while not far away are the picturesque Mungalli Falls. **Atherton** is the main town of the region, named after its first European settlers, John and Kate Atherton, who established a cattle station here in the mid-19th century. The wealthy agricultural centre of Mareeba now stands on the site of this former ranch.

❾ Wooroonooran National Park

🚉 Innisfail. 🚌 Innisfail. ℹ️ 1 Edith St, Innisfail 13 74 68. 🅆 nprsr.qld.gov. au/parks/wooroonooran

Wooroonooran National Park contains the state's two highest mountains. Bartle Frere, reaching 1,611 m (5,285 ft) and Bellenden Ker, rising to 1,591 m (5,220 ft), are often swathed in cloud. Cassowaries (large flightless birds, under threat of extinction) can be spotted on the mountains.

Much of the park is wilderness, although tracks do exist. A popular area to visit is Josephine Falls to the south of the park, about 8 km (5 miles) from the Bruce Highway.

❿ Babinda and the Boulders

🗺️ 1,300. ℹ️ Cnr Munro St & Bruce Hwy, Babinda (07) 4067 1008.

The rural town of Babinda is a quaint survivor of old-world Queensland, lined with veranda-fronted houses and a wooden pub.

The Babinda Boulders, 7 km (4 miles) inland, are water-worn rock shapes and a popular photographic subject.

⓫ Mission Beach

🚉 Tully. 🚌 Mission Beach. 🚌 Mission Beach. ℹ️ Mission Beach (07) 4068 7099. 🅆 missionbeachtourism.com

Located halfway between Cairns and Townsville, Mission Beach comprises four beach villages linked by 14 km (9 miles) of golden sand in an unspoilt, natural environment. Its boutiques, galleries and restaurants are set against a rainforest backdrop and views across to nearby Dunk Island, just 4 km (2.5 miles) off the coast. Dunk Island's rugged terrain is covered with a variety of vegetation. Day trips from Mission Beach are popular, offering snorkelling, diving and windsurfing.

⓬ Hinchinbrook Island

🚉 Ingham. 🚌 Cardwell. 🚢 Lucinda, Cardwell. ℹ️ Ingham (07) 4776 4792.

Hinchinbrook is the largest island national park in Australia, covering 635 sq km (245 sq miles). Dense rainforest, much of which remains unexplored, makes the island popular with bushwalkers. Hinchinbrook's highest point, Mount Bowen, rises 1,121 m (3,678 ft) above sea level and is often capped with cloud. The native wildlife includes wallabies, dugongs and the magnificent blue Ulysses butterfly. The island is separated from the mainland town of Cardwell by a narrow, mangrove-fringed channel.

Water-worn boulders near the town of Babinda

Queensland's Outback

In stark contrast to the lush green of the eastern rainforests, the northwest of Queensland is made up of dry plains, mining areas and Aboriginal settlements. The vast distances and high temperatures often dissuade tourists from venturing into this harsh landscape; yet those willing to make the effort will be rewarded with unique wildlife and an insight into Australia's harsh Outback life.

Locator Map

■ Queensland's Outback

□ Northern Queensland
pp252–59

Sights at a Glance

⑬ Normanton and Gulf Savannah
⑭ Burketown
⑮ Mount Isa
⑯ Longreach

Key

— Major road
⋯⋯ Minor road
‒ ‒ Track
— Minor railway
— State border

---

⑬ Normanton and Gulf Savannah

Normanton. 🚌 29–33 Haig St, Normanton (07) 4747 8422.

Normanton, situated 70 km (45 miles) inland on the Norman River, is the largest town in the region. It began life as a port, handling copper from Cloncurry and then gold from Croydon. The famous Gulflander train still commutes once a week between Normanton and Croydon.

En route from Normanton to the Gulf of Carpentaria, savannah grasses give way to glistening salt pans, barren of all vegetation. Once the rains come in November, however, this area becomes a wetland and a breeding ground for millions of birds, including jabirus, brolgas, herons and cranes, as well as crocodiles, prawns and

barramundi. Karumba, at the mouth of the Norman River, is the access point for the Gulf of Carpentaria and the head-quarters of a multi-million-dollar prawn and fishing industry. It remains something of an untamed frontier town, especially when the prawn trawlers are in.

Covering approximately 350,000 sq km (135,000 sq miles), the most northwesterly region of Queensland is the Gulf Savannah. Largely flat and

covered in savannah grasses, abundant with bird and animal life, this is the remotest landscape in Australia. The economic base of the area is fishing and cattle. Prawn trawlers go out to the Gulf of Carpentaria for months at a time and cattle stations cover areas of more than 1,000 sq km (400 sq miles). Given the distances, local pastoralists are more likely to travel via light aircraft than on horseback.

Gum trees and termite mounds on the grassland of Gulf Savannah

For additional map symbols *see back flap*

Mount Isa, dominated by Australia's largest mine

⓮ Burketown

🏚 1/0. ✈ ℹ 19 Musgrave St
(07) 4745 5111, City Council, 65
Musgrave St (07) 4745 5111.

In the late 1950s, Burketown
found fleeting fame as the
setting for Neville Shute's
famous novel about life in a
small Outback town, *A Town
Like Alice*. Situated 30 km
(18 miles) from the Gulf of
Carpentaria, on the Albert River,
Burketown was once a major
port servicing the hinterland.
The spectacular propagating
roll cloud known as a Morning
Glory appears here in the early
mornings from September to
November. Burketown is rich
in history and Aboriginal
culture. It is also famous for
the World Barramundi Fishing
Championship.

About 150 km (90 miles)
west of Burketown is Hell's
Gate, an area so named at the
beginning of the 20th century
because it was the last outpost
where the state's police
guaranteed protection.

⓯ Mount Isa

🏚 19,000. ✈ 🚌 🚍
ℹ 19 Marian St (07) 4749 1555.

Mount Isa is the only major
city in far western Queensland.
Its existence is entirely based
around the world's largest
silver and lead mine, which
dominates the town's industry
and landscape. Ore was first
discovered at Mount Isa in
1923 by a prospector called
John Campbell Miles and the

first mine was set up in the
1930s. In those early days, "the
Isa" was a shanty town, and Tent
House, now owned by the
National Trust, is an example
of the half-house-half-tents
that were home to most early
settlers. Also in town is **Outback
at Isa**, which incorporates mine
tours, the Riversleigh Fossil
Centre and Isa Experience
Gallery *(see pp30–31)*.

One of the most popular
events in town is the Mount
Isa Rodeo in August *(see p47)*.
With prize money totalling
more than A$100,000, riders
come from all over the world
to perform spectacular
displays of horsemanship.

🏛 **Outback at Isa**
19 Marian St. **Tel** (07) 4749 1555.
Open daily. **Closed** Good Fri, 25 Dec.
🦽 ♿ 🅦 outbackatisa.com.au

The Royal Flying Doctor Service

The Royal Flying Doctor Service
was founded by John Flynn, a
Presbyterian pastor who was
sent as a missionary to the
Australian Outback in 1912.
The young cleric was disturbed to
see that many of his flock died
due to the lack of basic medical
care and he founded the
Australian Inland Mission together
with Hudson Fysh (the founder of
Qantas), self-made millionaire Hugh Victor McKay, Alfred Traeger
(the inventor of the pedal wireless) and Dr Kenyon St Vincent Welch.
Today, the Royal Flying Doctor Service deals with some 130,000
patients a year, and most Outback properties have an airstrip on
which the Flying Doctor can land. Emergency medical help is
rarely more than two hours away and advice is available over a
special radio channel.

A Royal Flying Doctor plane flying over
Australia's Outback

Environs

Cloncurry, 120 km (75 miles) east
of Mount Isa, was the departure
point for the Queensland and
Northern Territory Aerial Service's
(QANTAS) first flight in 1921.
Now Australia's national airline,
Qantas is also the oldest airline
in the English-speaking world.

⓰ Longreach

🏚 3,000. ✈ 🚌 🚍 ℹ Qantas
Park, Eagle St (07) 4658 4150.
🅦 longreachtourism.com.au

Situated in the centre of
Queensland, Longreach is the
main town of the central west
of the state.

From 1922 to 1934, Longreach
was the operating base of
Qantas and there is a Founders
Museum at Longreach Airport.
The **Australian Stockman's Hall
of Fame** is a fascinating tribute
to Outback men and women.
Aboriginal artifacts, as well as
documented tales of the early
European explorers are included
in the impressive displays.

There are daily flights or a
17-hour coach ride from Brisbane
to Longreach. Other access points
are Rockhampton and Townsville.

🏛 **Australian Stockman's
Hall of Fame**
Landsborough Hwy.
Tel (07) 4658 2166. **Open** daily.
Closed 25 Dec. 🦽 ♿ 💻 📷
🅦 outbackheritage.com.au

THE NORTHERN TERRITORY

The Northern Territory at a Glance

That most famous of Australian icons, the red monolith of Uluṟu (Ayers Rock) lies within the Northern Territory, but it is just one of the area's stunning natural features, which also include the tropical splendour of Kakadu National Park. The main centres are Darwin in the lush north and Alice Springs in the arid Red Centre. Much of the Outback land is Aboriginal-owned. The Northern Territory has yet to achieve full statehood owing to its low population and relatively small economy, but it has been self-governing since 1978.

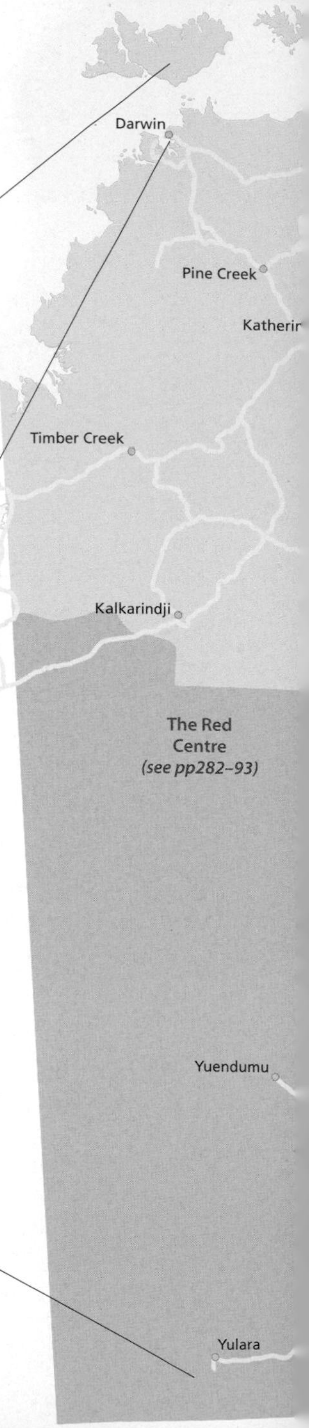

Darwin

Pine Creek

Katherir

Timber Creek

Kalkarindji

The Red
Centre
(see pp282–93)

Yuendumu

Yulara

Tiwi Islands *(see p278)* lie 80 km (50 miles) off the north coast. The islands are inhabited by Tiwi Aboriginals, who have preserved a culture distinct from the mainland which includes unique characteristics such as these burial poles.

0 kilometres 150
0 miles 150

Darwin *(see pp274–7)* is the Northern Territory's capital city with an immigrant population of more than 50 nationalities *(see pp268–9)*. The colonial Government House is one of the few 19th-century survivors in what is now a very modern city.

Uluṟu-Kata Tjuṯa National Park *(see pp290–93)* is dominated by the huge sandstone rock rising up out of the flat, arid desert and the nearby Olgas, a series of 36 mysterious rock domes.

◀ A "beware of kangaroos" road sign next to Uluṟu (Ayers Rock)

Kakadu National Park *(see pp280–81)* is an ancient landscape of tropical rainforest and majestic rock formations. Covering 1.7 million ha (4.3 million acres), it is the largest national park in Australia. The Jim Jim Falls are the most impressive in the park, and the Aboriginal rock art sites are among the most important in the country.

Locator Map

Roper Bar

Darwin and the Top End
(see pp270–81)

Borroloola

Daly Waters

Dunmarra

Elsey Homestead Replica, 110 km (70 miles) southeast of Katherine *(see pp278–9)*, was the setting for Jeannie Gunn's novel *We of the Never Never*, depicting 19th-century Outback life.

Karlu Karlu/Devil's Marbles *(see p289)* are a remarkable collection of granite boulders in the heart of the flat, sandy desert. Caused by millions of years of erosion, they are traditionally believed to be the eggs of the Rainbow Serpent.

Cape Crawford Roadhouse

ree Ways oadhouse

Tennant Creek

Alice Springs *(see pp286–7)* lies at the heart of Australia. Its Old Telegraph Station Historical Reserve was the site of the area's first settlement in 1871.

Ti Tree   Utopia

Aileron

Harts Range

Alice Springs

Chambers Pillar Historical Reserve *(see p288)* is a strange, 50-m (165-ft) sandstone column which served as a landmark for explorers of the area in the 19th century.

Idunda

Aboriginal Lands

Aboriginal people are thought to have lived in the Northern Territory for between 20,000 and 50,000 years. The comparatively short 200 years of European settlement have damaged their ancient culture immensely, but in the Northern Territory more traditional Aboriginal communities have survived intact than in other states – mainly due to their relatively greater numbers and determination to preserve their identity. Nearly one-third of the Northern Territory's people are Aboriginal and they own almost 50 per cent of the land through native title legislated enacted by the federal government (see p63). For Aboriginals, the concept of land ownership is tied to a belief system that instructs them to care for their ancestral land.

This X-ray image (see p37) of the dreaming spirit Namarrgon at Nourlangie Rock is centuries old, but was continually repainted until the 1900s.

Nourlangie Rock in Kakadu National Park is significant to Aborigines as home of the Lightning Dreaming (see pp280–81).

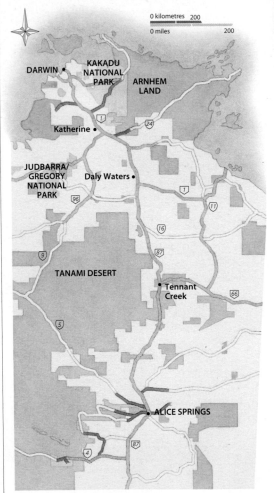

Key

- Aboriginal land
- National park
- Highway
- Major road
- Unsurfaced road

Access and Permits

Northern Land Council
Tel (08) 8920 5100.
For access to all Aboriginal land in the Top End, including Arnhem Land. W nlc.org.au

Parks and Wildlife Commission of the Northern Territory
Tel (08) 8999 4555.
For permits to Garig Gunak Barlu National Park.
W nt.gov.au/nreta/parks

Tiwi Land Council
Tel (08) 8970 9373.
For access to Melville and Bathurst (Tiwi) islands.
W tiwilandcouncil.com

Central Land Council
Tel (08) 8951 6211. For access to all Central Australian Aboriginal lands. W clc.org.au

Aboriginal Tourism

Most visitors who come to the Northern Territory are keen to learn more about the region's unique Aboriginal culture. There are now many Aboriginal organizations which take tourists into Aboriginal areas that would otherwise be inaccessible, and explain the Aboriginal view of the land. Excursions available include boat trips in Kakadu National Park *(see pp280–81)* with a Guluyambi guide; bush camping with the Manyallaluk community near Katherine; or a safari camp in Arnhem Land with Umorrduk Safaris. Also well worth visiting are the information and cultural centres, such as those in Kakadu and Uluṟu-Kata Tjuṯa national parks, where native owners share their creation stories and culture, adding another layer to visitors' appreciation of these special places.

Ubirr in Kakadu National Park is one of the finest Aboriginal rock art sites in the Northern Territory. Many paintings in Ubirr's gallery depict the area's wildlife in an X-ray style *(see p37)*, such as this barramundi. They date from 20,000 years ago to the present day.

Visitors climbing to the lookout at Ubirr

Uluṟu *(see pp290–93)* has many sites sacred to the Anangu people around its base. Most are closed to the public, but it is possible to walk around the area, including a route around the entire perimeter of Uluṟu, and learn the associated stories.

Bush Tucker Dreaming, painted in 1991 by Gladys Napanangka of the Papunya community of the Central Western Desert, records the Dreaming or creation stories passed down to the artist through hundreds of generations *(see pp34–5)*.

Aboriginal Culture and Law

Every Aboriginal clan lives according to a set of laws linking the people with their land and their ancestors. These laws have been handed down through generations and are embedded in Aboriginal creation stories. The stories, which tell how the first spirits and ancestors shaped and named the land, also form a belief system which directs all aspects of Aboriginal life. All Aboriginals are born into two groups: their family clan and a "Dreaming" totem group such as the crocodile – determined by place and time of birth. These decide their links with the land and place in the community and the creation stories they inherit.

Aboriginals in body make-up for a traditional tribal dance

Multicultural Northern Territory

The Northern Territory, with its proximity to Indonesia and the Pacific Islands, has long served as Australia's "front door" to immigrants. Around 500 years ago, Portuguese and Dutch ships charted the waters of the northern coast and from the 1700s traders from the Indonesian archipelago visited the northern shores. From 1874, when Chinese gold prospectors arrived in Darwin, the tropical north has appealed to Southeast Asians and, being closer to Indonesia than to Sydney or Melbourne, the city markets itself as Australia's gateway to Asia. There are now more than 50 ethnic groups living in Darwin, including Greeks and Italians who arrived in the early 20th century, and East Timorese, Indonesians, Thais and Filipinos, together with the town's original mix of Aboriginals and those of Anglo-Celtic stock.

Harry Chan, elected in 1966, was the first Mayor of Darwin of Chinese descent.

Mindil Markets are among several Asian-style food markets in the Darwin area. More than 60 food stalls serve Thai, Indonesian, Indian, Chinese, Sri Lankan, Malaysian and Greek cuisine (*see p276*).

The Indonesian language Bahasa is taught in many of Darwin's schools due to Indonesia's proximity to the city.

The Chinese in the Top End

In 1879, a small carved figure dating from the Ming dynasty (1368–1644) was found in the roots of a tree on a Darwin beach, causing much speculation that a Chinese fleet may have visited this coast in the 15th century. If so, it was the start of an association between China and the Top End which endures today. Chinese came here in search of gold in the 1870s. By 1885, there were 3,500 Chinese in the Top End, and 40 years later Darwin had become a Chinese-run shanty town with Chinese families managing its market gardens and

Chinese man using buffalo to haul wood in early 19th-century Darwin

general stores. Today, many of the area's leading families are of Chinese origin; Darwin has had two Lord Mayors of Chinese descent, and fifth-generation Chinese are spread throughout the city's businesses.

Aboriginal people are believed to have arrived in the Northern Territory 20,000 to 50,000 years ago, overland from Asia when the sea level was much lower. Here, young male initiates from an Arnhem Land tribe are carried to a ceremony to be "made men".

With a quarter of its present population born overseas and another quarter Aboriginal, Darwin's racial mix is best seen in the faces of its children.

The Children of Darwin

The faces of Darwin's children show an incredible ethnic diversity, something many believe will be typical of all of Australia in 50 years' time. The Northern Territory, and especially Darwin, is renowned for a multicultural society, with significant Indigenous and Asian communities.

Darwin's children, whatever their ethnic origin, are united by their casual Australian clothes and relaxed attitude.

The Filipino community in Darwin preserves its traditions, as seen by these two girls in national costume at the Festival of Darwin.

Paspaley Pearls is Darwin's wealthiest local company. Founded by Greek settlers, it owns pearl farms across northern Australia.

The East Timorese community of Darwin performs traditional dancing at a city arts festival. Most of the East Timorese have arrived in the city since 1975, in the wake of Indonesia's invasion of East Timor.

DARWIN AND THE TOP END

The tropical tip of the Northern Territory is a lush, ancient landscape. For thousands of years it has been home to large numbers of Aboriginals and contains one of the oldest collections of rock art in the world. Its capital, Darwin, is small and colourful. The World Heritage-listed Kakadu National Park has a raw beauty combined with the fascinating creation stories of its Aboriginal tribes.

The Port of Darwin was first named in 1839, when British captain John Lort Stokes, commander of HMS *Beagle*, sailed into an azure harbour of sandy beaches and mangroves, and named it after his friend Charles Darwin. Although the biologist would not publish his theory of evolution in the *Origin of the Species* for another 20 years, it proved to be a wonderfully apt name for this tropical region, teeming with unique and ancient species of birds, plants, reptiles and mammals. The Aboriginal tribes that have lived for many thousands of years in the northern area known as the Top End are recognized by anthropologists as one of the world's oldest races.

Darwin itself is a city that has fought hard to survive. From 1869, when the first settlement was established at Port Darwin, it has endured isolation, bombing attacks by the Japanese in World War II *(see p274)* and devastation by the force of Cyclone Tracy on Christmas Eve in 1974 *(see p276)*. Despite having been twice rebuilt, it has grown into a multicultural modern city, with a relaxed atmosphere, great beauty and a distinctly Asian feel.

Beyond Darwin is a region of Aboriginal communities and ancient art sites, wide rivers and crocodiles, lotus-lily wetlands and deep gorges. For visitors, Kakadu National Park superbly blends sights of great scenic beauty with a cultural and spiritual insight into the complex Aboriginal culture. Also to be enjoyed are the plunging waterfalls and giant termite mounds of Litchfield National Park, the deep red-rock gorge of Nitmiluk (Katherine Gorge) National Park, and expeditions into the closed Aboriginal communities of Arnhem Land and Melville and Bathurst Islands.

An Aboriginal child gathering water lilies in the lush and tropical Top End

◄ Jim Jim Falls, in Kakadu National Park, at the end of the wet season

Exploring Darwin and the Top End

The Top End is a seductive, tropical region on the remote tip of the Northern Territory. On the turquoise coast there are palm trees; inland are winding rivers, grassy wetlands, gorge pools and sandstone escarpments. The Territory's capital, Darwin, has many attractions and is a good base for day trips to areas such as Berry Springs and Melville and Bathurst Islands. The climate is hot, but the dry season has low humidity, making it the best time to visit. The wet season, however, compensates for its humidity and tropical downpours with the spectacle of thundering rivers and waterfalls, and lush vegetation. Some seasonal businesses, including restaurants, remain closed during the wet season.

Pearl lugger-turned-cruise boat in Darwin Harbour

Getting Around

The Top End's reputation as an isolated region is long gone. Darwin is linked by the Stuart Highway to Alice Springs, Adelaide and Melbourne in the south, and along interstate highways to Mount Isa, Cairns and Brisbane in the east. The centre of Darwin can be explored on foot or using the open trolley Tour Tub which stops at all the main attractions in an hourly circuit. The Top End's major attractions, such as Kakadu National Park and Katherine Gorge, can be visited without driving on a dirt road. Bus connections to the main towns are regular, but a car is vital to make the most of the scenery. Distances are not great for Australia; Kakadu is 210 km (130 miles) from Darwin and Katherine 300 km (186 miles) away on the Stuart Hwy.

Spectacular Jim Jim Falls in Kakadu National Park

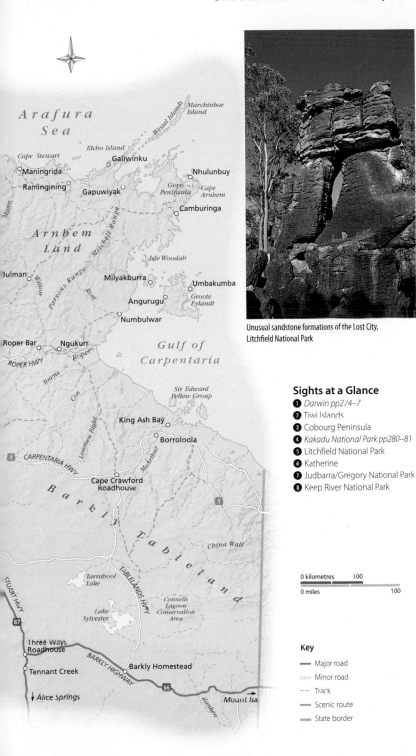

Arafura Sea

Cape Stewart

Maningrida

Ramingining

Arnhem Land

Bulman

Roper Bar

Ngukurr

ROPER HWY

CARPENTARIA HWY

Elcho Island

Galiwinku

Gapuwiyak

Mann

Mitchell Range

Parsons Range

Wilton

Roee

Towns

Cox

Wessel Islands

Marchinbar Island

Nhulunbuy

Gove Peninsula

Cape Arnhem

Camburinga

Isle Woodah

Milyakburra

Angurugu

Numbulwar

Umbakumba

Groote Eylandt

Limmen Bight

McArthur

King Ash Bay

Borroloola

Cape Crawford Roadhouse

Gulf of Carpentaria

Sir Edward Pellew Group

Barkly Tableland

China Wall

Tarrabool Lake

Lake Sylvester

Connells Lagoon Conservation Area

STUART HWY

Three Ways Roadhouse

Tennant Creek

Alice Springs

TABLELANDS HWY

BARKLY HIGHWAY

Barkly Homestead

Ranken

Mount Isa

87

66

1

1

Unusual sandstone formations of the Lost City, Litchfield National Park

Sights at a Glance

1 *Darwin pp274–7*
2 Tiwi Islands
3 Cobourg Peninsula
4 *Kakadu National Park pp280–81*
5 Litchfield National Park
6 Katherine
7 Judbarra/Gregory National Park
8 Keep River National Park

0 kilometres   100

0 miles   100

Key

— Major road

···· Minor road

– – Track

— Scenic route

— State border

For additional map symbols *see back flap*

❶ Darwin

Following European settlement in 1864, for the first century of its life Darwin was an outpost of the British Empire, with vast cattle farms established around it. In its short, colourful history it has experienced the gold rush of the 1890s, life as an Allied frontline during World War II and almost total destruction in 1974 by the fearful winds of Cyclone Tracy (see p276). Darwin has now emerged as a modern but relaxed town where more than 50 ethnic groups mingle, including Asian-born Australians, Aboriginals, Europeans, particularly Greeks, and Chinese.

Shady palm trees in Bicentennial Park, seen from The Esplanade

🌳 Bicentennial Park
The Esplanade. 🚻

This lush, green park, with its pleasant shady walks and panoramic lookouts, is home to many World War II memorials. One commemorates the attack by Japanese bombers which flew over Darwin Harbour on 19 February 1942, sinking 21 of the 46 US and Australian naval vessels in port and killing 243 people. It was the closest Australia came to war on its own soil.

🏛 Old Admiralty House
Cnr Knuckey St & The Esplanade.

Across the road from Lyons Cottage is Old Admiralty House, once the headquarters of the Australian navy and one of the oldest surviving buildings in Darwin. It was built in the 1930s by the territory's principal architect, Beni Carr Glynn Burnett, in an elevated tropical style using louvres, open eaves and three-quarter-high walls to aid ventilation.

🏛 Smith Street Mall
Bennett & Knuckey sts. 🚻

The heart of Darwin's shopping area is Smith Street Mall, with its glass air-conditioned plazas shaded by tall tropical trees. Always full of buskers, tour operators offering trips, locals and visitors, the mall is a favourite meeting place. Noteworthy buildings include the 1890 Victoria Hotel, one of the few old structures in town to survive Cyclone Tracy. During the dry season, many outdoor events are held at Raintree Park, at the northern end of the mall.

🏛 Parliament House
Mitchell St, State Square. Tel (08) 8946 1512. Open 8am–4:30pm daily. 📷 May–Aug. 🚻

Dominating the edge of Darwin's sea cliffs is the new Parliament House. With architecture that appears to borrow from both Middle Eastern and Russian styles, this imposing building is home to the Territory's 25 parliamentarians, who administer just 200,000 people. It has a granite and timber interior which is filled with Aboriginal art. Visitors may also get a glimpse of the parliamentarian chambers and use the library – the largest in the territory.

🏛 Old Town Hall
Smith St. 🚻

The limestone ruin of the Old Town Hall lies at the bottom of Smith Street. The original council chambers, built in 1883, became a naval workshop and store in World War II. Later it was a bank and then a museum, before being destroyed by Cyclone Tracy in 1974. Curved brick paving built against the remaining wall symbolizes the fury of the cyclone's winds.

🏛 Brown's Mart
12 Smith St. Tel (08) 8981 5522. 🚻

Opposite the town hall ruins is Brown's Mart, built during the gold boom in 1885. A former mining exchange, it now houses an intimate theatre. On Friday afternoons local musicians perform in its courtyard.

Front entrance of Parliament House

🏛 Old Police Station and Courthouse
Cnr Smith St & The Esplanade. Tel (08) 8999 7103. 🚻

The 1884 limestone Old Police Station and Courthouse have both been restored after being damaged by Cyclone Tracy and are now used as the Office of the Administrator.

Across the road, overlooking the harbour, is Survivors' Lookout, where photographs and written accounts tell of Darwin's wartime role as an Allied frontline. Thousands of US and Australian troops were based in the Top End, which endured 63 bombing raids by Japanese forces (see p61).

Darwin's Old Police Station and Courthouse

🏛 Government House

The Esplanade. **Tel** (08) 8999 7103. ♿

On a natural plateau above the harbour, Government House, also known as the House of Seven Gables, is Darwin's oldest surviving building, dating back to 1871. It has withstood bomb raids, cyclones, earthquakes and infestations of white ants. This gracious sandstone building with stunning tropical gardens is the residence of the Administrator of the Northern Territory.

🏛 Stokes Hill Wharf

McMinn St. ♿ 💻

The long, wooden Stokes Hill Wharf, stretching out into Darwin Harbour, was once the

town's main port area. Now a centre for tourist and local life, it has restaurants and shops. Boats leave on tours from the wharf.

At the wharf entrance is the excellent Indo-Pacific Marine exhibit, which has re-created local coral reef ecosystems, with bright tropical fish in its tanks. In the same building, the Australian Pearling Exhibition describes the history and science of local pearl farming.

Restaurant at the end of Stokes Hill Wharf overlooking the harbour

Darwin City Centre

① Bicentennial Park
② Old Admiralty House
③ Smith Street Mall
④ Parliament House
⑤ Old Town Hall
⑥ Brown's Mart
⑦ Old Police Station and Courthouse
⑧ Government House
⑨ Stokes Hill Wharf

0 metres 250
0 yards 250

For keys to symbols *see back flap*

Greater Darwin

Many of Darwin's best attractions are not in the city centre but located a short drive away. The Tour Tub, an open-sided trolley bus that picks up from major hotels, does an hourly circuit of tourist attractions, allowing visitors to hop on and off at will for a daily charge. Outside Darwin, alongside the mango farms and cattle stations, there are some fine bush and wetland areas which provide excellent opportunities for swimming, fishing and exploring.

Feeding the friendly fish at Aquascene in Doctor's Gully

🦈 Aquascene
28 Doctor's Gully Rd, cnr of Daly St & The Esplanade. **Tel** (08) 8981 7837. **Open** daily, with the tide. **Closed** 25 Dec. ♿

Ever since the 1950s, the fish of Darwin Harbour have been coming in on the tides for a feed of stale bread in Doctor's Gully. At Aquascene, visitors can feed and play with hundreds of catfish, mullet and milkfish. Feeding times vary from day to day.

Delicious offerings at a Thai food stall at Mindil Beach Sunset Market

🏮 Mindil Beach Sunset Market
Mindil Beach. **Tel** (08) 8981 3454. **Open** May–Oct: 5–10pm Thu, 4–9pm Sun. ♿

Thursday and Sunday nights during the dry season are when Darwinians flock to Mindil Beach at dusk to enjoy some 60 outdoor food stalls, street theatre, live music and over 200 craft stalls.

🌺 George Brown Darwin Botanic Gardens
Gardens Rd, Stuart Park. **Tel** (08) 8981 1958. **Open** daily. ♿ limited.

Just north of town, the 42-ha (100-acre) Botanic Gardens, established in the 1870s, boast over 1,500 tropical species, including 400 palm varieties and wetland mangroves.

🎖 East Point Military Museum and Fannie Bay Gaol
Alec Fong Lim Drive, East Point. **Tel** (08) 8981 9702. **Open** 9:30am–5pm daily. ♿♿

An attraction for all the family, this pleasant harbourside reserve contains an artificial lake that is ideal for swimming and the fascinating East Point

Military Museum. Nearby Fannie Bay Gaol now houses an interesting museum.

🏛 Australian Aviation Heritage Centre
557 Stuart Hwy, Winnellie. **Tel** (08) 8947 2145. ♿ 5, 8. **Open** 9am–5pm daily. **Closed** Good Fri, 25 Dec. ♿♿

Along the Stuart Highway at Winnellie, 6 km (4 miles) from the city centre, Darwin's Aviation Centre displays a variety of historic and wartime aircraft. Its exhibits are dominated by a B-52 bomber, one of only two in the world on display outside the US.

🦘 Territory Wildlife Park
Cox Peninsula Rd, Berry Springs. **Tel** (08) 8988 7200. **Open** 8:30am–6pm daily. **Closed** 25 Dec. ♿♿🍴Ⓦ territorywildlife park.com.au

Only 60 km (37 miles) from Darwin is the town of Berry Springs and the Territory Wildlife Park with its hundreds of unique indigenous species, in natural surroundings. Nearby, Berry Springs Nature Reserve has a series of deep pools, fringed with vegetation, that make for great swimming.

🌴 Howard Springs Nature Park
Howard Springs Rd. **Tel** (08) 8983 1001. **Open** daily. ♿ limited.

This nature park, 35 km (22 miles) south of Darwin, has clear, freshwater spring-fed pools, filled with barramundi and turtles. It's an ideal place to have a barbecue or a picnic in the shade after a hot day of exploring.

Cyclone Tracy

Late Christmas Eve, 1974, a weather warning was issued that Cyclone Tracy, gathering force off the coast, had turned landward and was heading for Darwin. Torrential rain pelted down and winds reached a record 280 km/h (175 mph) before the measuring machine broke. On Christmas morning, 66 people were dead,

Cyclone Tracy's devastation

thousands injured and 95 per cent of the buildings flattened. More than 30,000 residents were airlifted south in the biggest evacuation in Australia's history. The city ruins were bulldozed and Darwin has been rebuilt, stronger and safer than before.

For hotels and restaurants in this area see p489 and pp517–18

Museum and Art Gallery of the Northern Territory

The Museum and Art Gallery of the Northern Territory has exhibitions on regional Aboriginal art and culture, maritime history, visual arts and natural history.

The museum's collection of Aboriginal art is considered to be the best in the world and has some particularly fine carvings and bark paintings, along with explanations of Aboriginal culture. Other displays include a chilling exhibition on Cyclone Tracy and displays that explain the evolution of some of the Top End's unique and curious wildlife, including the popular stuffed crocodile named "Sweetheart".

VISITORS' CHECKLIST

Practical Information
Conacher St.
Tel (08) 8999 8264.
🅦 magnt.nt.net.au
Open 9am–5pm Mon–Fri,
10am–5pm Sat & Sun.
Closed some public hols.
🈳 🅱 🈴 🈺 ▢

Transport
🚌 4, 5.

Key

- ▢ Indigenous Art Gallery
- ▢ Natural Sciences Gallery
- ▢ Cyclone Tracy Gallery
- ▢ Visual Art Gallery
- ▢ Amphitheatre
- ▢ Maritime Galleries
- ▢ Temporary exhibitions
- ▢ Non-exhibition space
- ▢ Monsoon Forest Pathway
- ▢ Fish Pond

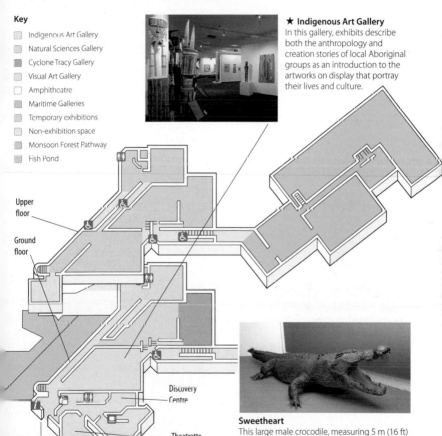

★ **Indigenous Art Gallery**
In this gallery, exhibits describe both the anthropology and creation stories of local Aboriginal groups as an introduction to the artworks on display that portray their lives and culture.

Upper floor

Ground floor

Discovery Centre

Theatrette

Entrance

Sweetheart
This large male crocodile, measuring 5 m (16 ft) in length, is called Sweetheart. It was caught in 1979 in the Finnis River, which is between Darwin and Kakadu. He drowned while being captured, after becoming entangled with a log.

Façade of the Museum and Art Gallery
Located 4 km (2 miles) north of Darwin's centre, the museum's stylish low-level building is in a tropical beachside setting overlooking Fannie Bay.

Tiwi islander making handicrafts from local fibres, Bathurst Island

❷ Tiwi Islands

🚗 ℹ️ Tiwi Tours, Mitchell St, Darwin (08) 8923 6523.

Just 80 km (50 miles) north of Darwin lie the Tiwi Islands, the collective name given to the small island of Bathurst and its larger neighbour, Melville. The latter is the second-largest island off the Australian coast after Tasmania and is rich in history and Aboriginal culture. The islands' inhabitants, the Tiwi people, had little contact with mainland Aboriginals until the 20th century.

With beautiful waters, sandy beaches and lush forest, the islands are a tropical paradise, but only Bathurst can be visited on tours from Darwin. Day trips (May–Oct) offer a glimpse of the unique blend of Aboriginal, Indonesian and Tiwi traditions. Tourists can visit Aboriginal art centres, Tiwi printworks for screen-printed fabrics and a *pukumani* burial site.

❸ Cobourg Peninsula

ℹ️ Venture North Australia, Darwin (08) 8927 5500. 🌐 venturenorth.com.au

The Cobourg Peninsula is one of the most remote parts of Australia. It is only accessible by vehicle during the dry season and with an access permit *(see p266)*, travelling through the closed Aboriginal Arnhem Land to the wild coastal beaches of

Garig Gunak Barlu National Park. The number of vehicles allowed to enter the region each week is restricted and there are permit fees, too, so going on a tour is sometimes a convenient option.

Garig is a large park, with sandy beaches and the calm waters of Port Essington. Two attempts by the British to settle this area in the early 1800s were abandoned, due to the inhospitable environment and malaria epidemics. The ruins of Victoria Settlement can be reached by boat from Smith Point. Luxury accommodation is available at Seven Spirit Bay Wilderness Lodge, reached by plane from Darwin; the Venture North company, which tours the region, has a safari-style camp overlooking Port Essington.

❹ Kakadu National Park

See pp280–81.

❺ Litchfield National Park

ℹ️ Parks and Wildlife Commission of the Northern Territory (08) 8999 4555. 🌐 nt.gov.au/nreta/parks

The spectacular Litchfield National Park, only 129 km (80 miles) south of Darwin, is very popular with Darwinians. There are waterfalls, gorges and deep, crocodile-free pools for swimming at Florence Falls, Wangi, in the wet season, and

Giant magnetic termite mound in Litchfield National Park

Buley Rockhole. The park has some amazing giant magnetic termite mounds. They are so-called because they point north in an effort by the termites to control temperature by having only the mound's thinnest part exposed to the sun. Also popular are the sandstone block formations further south, known as the "Lost City" due to their resemblance to ruins.

❻ Katherine

🏔️ 11,000. 🚗 🚌 🚌 ℹ️ Cnr Stuart Hwy & Lindsay St (08) 8972 2650. 🌐 visitkatherine.com.au

The town of Katherine, situated on the banks of the Katherine River, 320 km (200 miles) south of Darwin, is both a thriving regional centre and a major Top End tourist destination. Home for thousands of years to the Jawoyn people, Katherine River has long been a rich source of food for the Aboriginal people. The river was first crossed by white explorers in 1844, and the area was not settled by Europeans until 1872, with the completion of the Overland Telegraph Line. Springvale Homestead was built on the Katherine River in 1879. It is now the oldest homestead in the Territory and is open to the public. Tours are offered at 3pm daily during dry season.

Only 30 km (20 miles) from town lies the famous **Nitmiluk (Katherine Gorge) National Park**. Its string of 13 separate gorges along 50 km (30 miles) of the Katherine River has been carved out by torrential seasonal rains cutting through cliffs of red sandstone which are 1,650 million years old. The result is a place of deep pools, silence and grandeur.

The best way to explore the park is by boat or canoe. Canoe trips are guided or self-guided, with nine navigable gorges and overnight camping possible. There are also cruise trips operated by the Jawoyn people, who own the park and run it in conjunction with the Parks and Wildlife Commission of the Northern Territory. There are also around 100 km (60 miles) of

Upper waterfall and pools of Edith Falls, Nitmiluk (Katherine Gorge) National Park near Katherine

marked trails in the park, ranging from the spectacular lookout walk to the five-day 72-km (45-mile) Jatbula Trail to Edith Falls, which can also be reached by car from the Stuart Highway.

Environs

Just 27 km (17 miles) south of Katherine are the Cutta Cutta caves, limestone rock formations 15 m (50 ft) under the earth's surface and formed five million years ago. They are home to both the rare orange horseshoe bat and the brown tree snake.

Further southeast, 110 km (70 miles) from Katherine, lies the small town of Mataranka. This is "Never Never" country, celebrated by female pioneer Jeannie Gunn in her 1908 novel, *We of the Never Never*, about life at nearby Elsey Station at the turn of the century. The area is called Never Never country because those who live here find they never, never want to leave it. About 8 km (5 miles)

east of Mataranka is Elsey National Park. Visitors can swim in the hot waters of the Mataranka Thermal Pool which flow from Rainbow Springs to this idyllic spot. Built in 1916 **Mataranka Homestead** is now backpacker accommodation and part of the Mataranka Homestead resort, which includes a motel, cabins and camping.

Mataranka Homestead
Tel (08) 8975 4544. **Open** daily.

❼ Judbarra/Gregory National Park

Timber Creek (08) 8975 0888, Bullita (08) 8975 0833. **Open** 7am–4pm Mon–Fri. **W** nt.gov.au/nreta/parks

This massive national park is 280 km (174 miles) by road southwest of Katherine. Broken into two sections, its eastern part contains a 50-km (31-mile) section of the Victoria River gorge accessible by a 2WD boat ramp for much of the year. In the north of the larger western section of the park are some crocodile-infested areas of the Victoria River. Here boat trips combine close-up views of the crocodiles.

A "no swimming" policy covers the entire park. In the west of the park, the stunning Limestone Gorge has dolomite blocks, huge cliffs and good fishing opportunities.

Walking trail by a sandstone escarpment, Keep River National Park

❽ Keep River National Park

Victoria Hwy (08) 9167 8827. **Open** Apr–Sep: daily; Oct–Mar: Mon–Fri. Closed when inaccessible.

Located only 3 km (2 miles) from the Western Australian border, Keep River National Park includes the dramatic Keep River gorge and some of Australia's most ancient rock art sites. The park, once the location of an ancient Aboriginal settlement, today has some superb walking trails for all levels of trekkers.

Limestone Gorge, Judbarra/Gregory National Park

❹ Kakadu National Park

The vast 19,757 sq km (7,628 sq miles) of Kakadu
National Park, with its stunning diversity of stony
plateaux, red escarpment cliffs, waterfalls, billabongs,
long twisting rivers, flood plains and coastal flats,
is one of Australia's most extraordinary places.
A UNESCO World Heritage Area *(see pp30–31)*, Kakadu
encompasses both scenic wonders and huge galleries
of Aboriginal rock art. The park is Aboriginal land
leased back to the government *(see p63)* and is
managed jointly. The entire catchment area of
the South Alligator River lies within the park,
and is home to thousands of plant and
animal species. Some areas in Kakadu are
not accessible during the wet season.

Yellow Water
A cruise on the wetlands of Yellow Water shows
Kakadu in all its glory. Lotus lilies, crocodiles,
kookaburras, magpie geese, jabirus and other
bird species can be seen.

Flora and Fauna in Kakadu National Park

More than one-third of all bird species
recorded in Australia live in Kakadu National
Park; as do more than 60 mammal species,
117 reptile species, 1,700 plant species
and at least 10,000 insect species.
Approximately 10 per cent of the
birds are estimated to be unique
to Kakadu. Magpie geese are
especially abundant; at times there
are three million in the park, which is
60 per cent of the world's population.

The stately jabiru, seen near shallow
water in the dry season

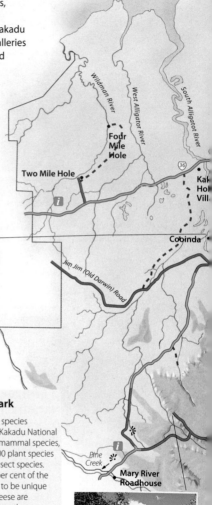

Gunlom Waterhole
The southern and drier end of Kakadu is less visited,
but holds some magical places such as the Gunlom
plunge pool and waterfall, home to the Rainbow
Serpent, Borlung, in Aboriginal legend.

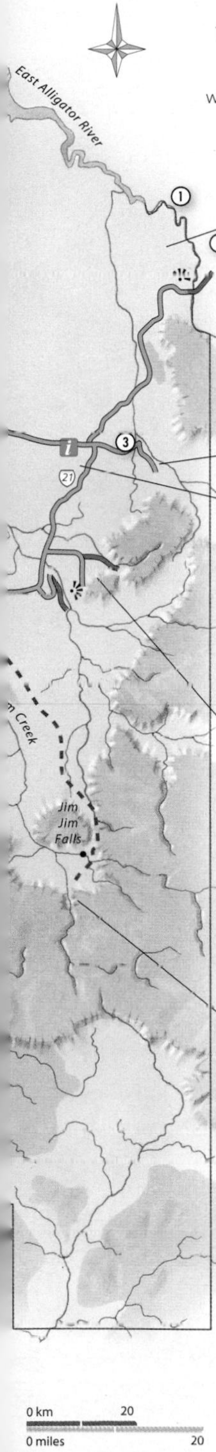

Ubirr

This rock has many Aboriginal rock art galleries, some with paintings more than 20,000 years old *(see p37)*.

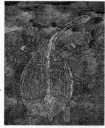

Ranger Uranium Mine

This mine is rigorously monitored to ensure that the natural and cultural values of the park are not endangered.

Bowali Visitors' Centre

This award-winning centre features excellent displays describing the animals, Aboriginal culture and geology of Kakadu.

Nourlangie Rock

Another fine Aboriginal rock art site, this includes paintings of Namarrgon, the Lightning Man *(see p266)*.

Key

▬ Highway

▬ Major road

= = 4WD only

— National park boundary

Twin Falls

This waterfall (accessible by 4WD and boat transfer) is most dramatic in the wet season, when it thunders over a high plateau into rock pools. Scenic flights go over the top of these falls.

0 km   20

0 miles   20

East Alligator River

m Creek

Jim Jim Falls

For additional map symbols *see back flap*

THE RED CENTRE

The Red Centre stretches roughly from Tennant Creek to the South Australian border, and is made up almost entirely of huge desert areas. The region occupies the centre of the Australian continent, with its main town, Alice Springs, at the country's geographical heart. Its signature colour is red: red sand, soil, rocks and mountains are all pitched against a typically blue sky.

The Red Centre contains some of the finest natural scenery in the world, much of it dating back about 800 million years. At that time, central Australia was covered by an inland sea; here sediments were laid down which form the basis of some of the region's best-known topographical features today. These include the huge monolith Uluṟu (formerly Ayers Rock), the domes of Kata Tjuṯa (also known as the Olgas), the giant boulders of Karlu Karlu/Devil's Marbles and the majestic MacDonnell Ranges. Between these sights are vast open spaces where remnants of tropical plant species grow beside desert-hardy stock. Verdant plants fed by occasional rains flourish next to animal skeletons.

Aboriginal people have lived in the region for more than 30,000 years, and their ancient tradition of rock painting is one of many tribal rituals still practised. By comparison, the history of white settlement here is recent. Explorers first arrived in the area during the 1860s. Alice Springs, founded in 1888, was a tiny settlement until improved communications after World War II led to the town's growth. It is now a modern, bustling town with much to offer. Tennant Creek, the only other sizeable settlement in the area, lies on the main Stuart Highway that bisects the Red Centre.

Much of the Territory has now been returned to its Aboriginal owners (see pp266–7), and today many Aborigines are actively involved in tourism. Access to Aboriginal lands is restricted but visiting them is a rewarding encounter to add to the unforgettable experience of the Red Centre.

Trekking through the desert landscape on a camel safari near Alice Springs

◀ The red monolith Uluṟu (Ayers Rock), sacred to the Aborigines

Exploring the Red Centre

The Red Centre's biggest draw is its stunning array of natural features. Alice Springs is the main city, with other towns at Yulara (Ayers Rock Resort) and Tennant Creek. The best time to travel is from April to October, thus avoiding the intense summer heat. The MacDonnell Ranges run like a huge spine on either side of Alice Springs; elsewhere the land is largely flat, formed by millions of years of erosion, and covered by spinifex grasslands. The region's gorges have been carved out by rivers, many of which flow only once or twice a year, soaking the surrounding desert plains.

The striking Olga Gorge in Uluṟu-Kata Tjuṯa National Park

Getting Around

There is a wide range of transport options available in central Australia. Domestic airports serve Alice Springs and Yulara. Overland, coaches connect the region with all the state capital cities, and the famous Ghan railway (see p287) operates between Darwin, Alice Springs and Adelaide. The most popular way to explore the region, however, is by car, and there are many car rental companies in the area. Standard vehicles are adequate for most journeys, but 4WD is advisable for off-road travel. Alternatively, many guided tours are also available. The Stuart Hwy is the main road running through the area, linking Port Augusta in South Australia with Darwin in the north. Alice Springs itself has taxis, bike hire and a town bus service, but the relatively short distances within the city also make walking popular.

Katherine

Kalkarindji   96   Cattle

BUCHANAN HWY

Halls Creek

Lajamanu

Winnecke

T a n a m i

D e s e r t

Rabbit Flat

Lake Surprise

The Granites

Lake White

Mount Theo △ 583m

Yuendumu   5

Lake Mackay

Central Mount Wedge 1094m △   Tilmou W

Papunya Aboriginal Community

Mount Liebig △ 1274m   *Ormiston Gorg*

Lake Macdonald   MACDONNE

Lake Neale   KING'S CANYON 7   *Finke Go National Pa*

Watarrka National Park

Kaltukatjara Community o (Docker River)

Yulara   LASSETER HWY   Im

Kata Tjuta (The Olgas) o

ULURU-KATA TJUTA NATIONAL PARK 8   △ *Uluru (Ayers Rock)* 867m

Sights at a Glance

1. *Alice Springs pp286–7*
2. Chambers Pillar Historical Reserve
3. Henbury Meteorites Conservation Reserve
4. MacDonnell Ranges
5. Karlu Karlu/Devil's Marbles Conservation Reserve
6. Tennant Creek
7. Kings Canyon
8. *Uluṟu-Kata Tjuṯa National Park pp290–93*

A mural painted on a shopping centre in Alice Springs

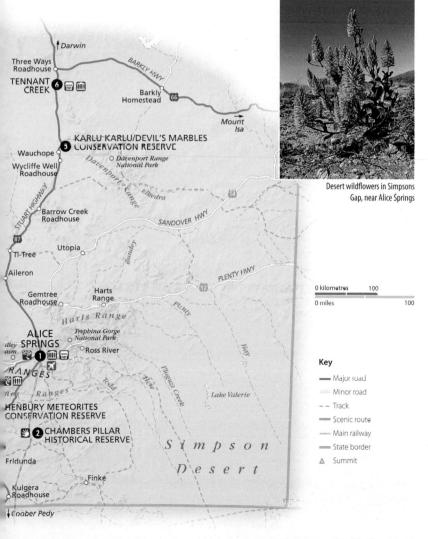

Desert wildflowers in Simpsons Gap, near Alice Springs

Key

— Major road
····· Minor road
– – Track
— Scenic route
····· Main railway
— State border
△ Summit

For additional map symbols *see back flap*

❶ Alice Springs

Alice Springs is named after the Alice Spring permanent waterhole, near which a staging post for the overland telegraph line was built in the 1870s. The waterhole was named after Alice Todd, wife of the line's construction manager. The town developed nearby in the 1880s, but, with no rail link until 1929 and no surfaced road link until the 1940s, it grew slowly. The huge increase in tourism since the 1970s, however, has brought rapid growth and Alice Springs is now a lively city with around 400,000 visitors a year, many of whom use it as a base from which to tour the surrounding spectacular natural sights.

Exploring Alice Springs

Although many of its sights are spread around the city, Alice Springs is small enough to tour on foot. Its compact centre, just five streets across running from Wills Terrace in the north to Stuart Terrace in the south, contains many of the town's hotels and restaurants and the pedestrianized Todd Mall. The city's eastern side is bordered by Todd River, dry and sandy most of the time and scene of the celebrated Henley-on-Todd Regatta (see p47).

Meteorite fragment in the Museum of Central Australia

🏵 Anzac Hill

Anzac Hill Rd. 🚹

At the northern end of Alice Springs, Anzac Hill overlooks the city and affords fine views of the MacDonnell Ranges (see p288). Named after the 1934 Anzac memorial at the site, the hill is a perfect vantage point for visitors to familiarize themselves with the city's layout, as well as for viewing the area at sunrise or sunset.

🏛 Museum of Central Australia

Alice Springs Cultural Precinct, Memorial Ave. **Tel** (08) 8951 1121. **Open** daily. **Closed** Good Fri, two weeks over Christmas. 🅿️ 🚹

This museum, situated in the Cultural Precinct, focuses on local natural history with displays of fossils, flora and fauna, meteorite pieces and minerals. It also houses fine pieces of Aboriginal art and artifacts.

🏯 Adelaide House Museum

Todd Mall. **Tel** (08) 8952 1856. **Open** 10am–2pm Mon–Fri. **Closed** Good Fri. 🅿️ 🚹

Adelaide House Musuem, Alice Springs' first hospital, opened in 1926. It was designed by John Flynn, founder of the Royal Flying Doctor Service (see p261), and is preserved as a museum dedicated to his memory.

🏯 Old Courthouse

Cnr Parsons & Hartley sts. **Tel** (08) 8953 6073. **Open** on request. 🅿️ 🚹

Built in 1928 by Emil Martin, who was also responsible for

The Residency, the Old Courthouse was in use until 1980, when new law courts were opened nearby.

Old Stuart Town Gaol

🏯 Old Stuart Town Gaol

8 Parsons St. **Tel** (08) 8953 6073. **Open** Wed, Thu & Sat. **Closed** mid-Dec–1 Feb, public hols. 🅿️ 🚹

The oldest building in central Alice Springs is the Old Stuart Town Gaol, which operated as a jail between 1909 and 1938, when a new prison was built on Stuart Terrace. The gaol is now open to the public, but call ahead to be granted access.

🏯 The Residency

Cnr Parsons & Hartley sts. **Tel** (08) 8953 6073. **Open** 11am–3pm Mon–Fri. **Closed** Dec–Mar, public hols. 🅿️ Donation.

The Residency, built in 1927 for the regional administrator of Central Australia, was the home of Alice Springs' senior public servant until 1973. After restoration, it was opened to the public in 1996 and now houses a local history display.

🏛 National Pioneer Women's Hall of Fame

Old Alice Springs Gaol, 2 Stuart Tce. **Tel** (08) 8952 9006. **Open** 10am–5pm daily. **Closed** late Dec–early Feb. 🅿️ 🚹 🌐 pioneerwomen.com.au

The displays in this museum document the achievements of Australia's pioneering women.

🏯 Alice Springs Telegraph Station Historical Reserve

Off Stuart Hwy. **Tel** (08) 8952 3993. **Open** 9am–5pm daily. **Closed** 25 Dec. 🅿️ 🚹

This, the site of the first settlement in Alice Springs, features

View over central Alice Springs from the top of Anzac Hill

Plane used for the Royal Flying Doctor Service

🏛 **Royal Flying Doctor
Service Visitor Centre**
8–10 Stuart Terrace. **Tel** (08) 8958
8411. **Open** 9am–5pm Mon–Sat,
1–5pm Sun & public hols. **Closed** 25
Dec, 1 Jan. 🎟 🎫 obligatory. 🖼 🎫
♿ 🌐 flyingdoctor.org.au

The centre can only be visited
accompanied by a guide, and
visitors are taken on a 45-minute
tour of the base that includes the
Radio Communications centre,
where staff recount the history of
the Service and explain the day-
to-day operations. There is also a
museum, containing old medical
equipment, model aircraft and
an original Traeger Pedal Radio.
The Visitor Centre opened in
the late 1970s but has been
extended to include a café
and a souvenir shop.

the original buildings and
equipment of the telegraph
station built in 1871. A small
museum describes the
amazing task of setting up
the station and operating
the overland telegraph.

🏞 **Alice Springs Desert Park**
Off Larapinta Drive. **Tel** (08) 8951 8788.
Open 7:30am–6pm daily (last entry
4:30pm). **Closed** 25 Dec. 🎟 ♿
🌐 alicespringsdesertpark.com.au

An excellent introduction to
Central Australia, this park lies
on the western edge of the
town and features three habitat
types: desert river, sand country
and woodlands. Visitors may

see many of the birds and
animals of Central Australia
here at close range.

🏛 **National Road
Transport Hall of Fame**
1 Norris Bell Ave. **Tel** (08) 8953
8940. **Open** 9am–5pm daily.
🌐 roadtransporthall.com

This museum pays homage to
all the great trucks, buses and
other vehicles that have crossed
the Australian continent. The
Ghan, the first train to run from
Adelaide to Alice Springs in
1929, is commemorated with
a fascinating collection of
vintage memorabilia.

Alice Springs Town Centre

① Royal Flying Doctor Service
   Visitor Centre
② Anzac Hill
③ Old Stuart Town Gaol
④ The Residency
⑤ Old Courthouse
⑥ Museum of Central Australia
⑦ Adelaide House Museum
⑧ National Pioneer Women's Hall
   of Fame

❷ Chambers Pillar Historical Reserve

Tel (08) 8951 8250. 🚗 Alice Springs. 🚌 Alice Springs. 🚗 W **nt.gov.au/ nreta/parks**

Chambers Pillar, a 50-m (165-ft) high sandstone obelisk, was used by explorers as an important navigational landmark during early colonial exploration. The pillar is made of mixed red and yellow sandstone deposited more than 350 million years ago. Many of the explorers, such as John Ross who visited the area in 1870, carved their names and inscriptions into the rock.

Located 160 km (110 miles) south of Alice Springs, with the final section of the journey accessible only by 4WD vehicles, the pillar is also a sacred Aboriginal site.

❸ Henbury Meteorites Conservation Reserve

Tel (08) 8951 8250. 🚗 Alice Springs. 🚌 Alice Springs. 🚗

This cluster of 12 craters, located 145 km (89 miles) southwest of Alice Springs, was formed by a meteorite which crashed to earth several thousand years ago. It is believed that local Aborigines witnessed the event, as one of the Aboriginal names for the area suggests a fiery rock falling to earth. The largest crater in the group is 180 m (590 ft) across and is 15 m (50 ft) deep. Signs on a trail mark significant features.

Lush Palm Valley in Finke Gorge National Park, MacDonnell Ranges

❹ MacDonnell Ranges

🚗 Alice Springs. 🚌 Alice Springs. 🛈 Alice Springs (08) 8951 8250. Simpsons Gap: **Open** daily. 🚻 Standley Chasm: **Open** daily. 🚻 🚻 W **nt.gov.au/nreta/parks**

The MacDonnell Ranges are the eroded remnants of an ancient mountain chain which was once as monumental as the Himalayas. Still impressive and filled with striking scenery, the East and West MacDonnells contain gorges, waterholes and walking tracks. Running east and west of Alice Springs and easily accessible, they are popular with day-trippers. Visitors will notice the layers of rock thrust up in the ranges, evidence of geological movements more than 300 million years ago. Culturally, they contain many areas sacred to the Aranda people.

In the West MacDonnells, 7 km (4 miles) from Alice Springs, is John Flynn's Memorial Grave, which honours Presbyterian minister, Rev John Flynn, who founded the Royal Flying Doctor Service (see p261).

A further 10 km (6 miles) from town, **Simpsons Gap** is the first of a series of attractive gorges in the MacDonnells. A pretty spot, it is home to some rare local plant species. Nearby is **Standley Chasm**, a narrow, deep gorge whose sheer rock-faces glow a glorious red, particularly under the midday sun.

The large 18-m (60-ft) deep permanent waterhole within Ellery Gorge at Ellery Creek Big Hole is a good swimming spot. Serpentine Gorge, 20 km (12 miles) further west, is another narrow gorge created by an ancient river. A walking track leading to a lookout gives a fine view of its winding path.

Pushed up out of Ormiston Creek, the 300-m (985-ft) high walls of Ormiston Gorge are an awesome sight. The gorge consists of two layers of quartzite, literally doubled over each other, thus making it twice the height of others in the region.

Along Larapinta Drive is the small Aboriginal settlement of Hermannsburg, site of an 1870s Lutheran Mission which pre-dates Alice Springs. Famous as the home of the popular Aboriginal painter Albert Namatjira (1902–59), most of the town is contained within the **Hermannsburg Historic Precinct**, which includes a museum devoted to the mission and an art gallery. Twenty km (12 miles) south of here lies

Sacred site of Corroboree Rock in the East MacDonnell Ranges near Alice Springs

the popular **Finke Gorge National Park**, home to Palm Valley, an unusual tropical oasis in the dry heart of the country with rare, ancient palm species.

On the other side of Alice Springs, the East MacDonnell Ranges boast some beautiful sites accessible via the Ross Highway. Close to town is Emily Gap, one of the most significant Aranda sites in Australia. Further east, Corroboree Rock, a strangely shaped outcrop, has a crevice once used to store sacred Aranda objects. Trephina Gorge is the most spectacular of the East MacDonnell sights, with quartzite cliffs and red river gums.

🏛 **Hermannsburg Historic Precinct**
Larapinta Drive. **Tel** (08) 8956 7402. **Open** daily. **Closed** 25 Dec. 🅿 🔥
🌐 hermannsburg.com.au

🏕 **Finke Gorge National Park**
Tel (08) 8951 8250.
🚌 🚍 Alice Springs.

Spherical boulders of the Devil's Marbles

🟡 Karlu Karlu/ Devil's Marbles Conservation Reserve

Tel (08) 8951 8250, Tennant Creek Office (08) 8962 4599. 🚍 from Tennant Creek Tourist Information. 🔥 📷

Approximately 104 km (65 miles) south of Tennant Creek, this reserve features a series of huge, spherical, red-granite boulders, scattered across a shallow valley in the Davenport Ranges. The result of geological activity from 1,700 million years ago, the boulders were created when molten lava was compressed to create huge domes just below the earth's surface. Subsequent erosion of the overlying rock exposed the marbles.

Mining building at Battery Hill, Tennant Creek

🟡 Tennant Creek

🏕 3,500. ✈ 🚍 ℹ Battery Hill Mining Complex, Peko Rd (08) 8962 1281.

Tennant Creek was chosen as the site of a telegraph station on the Overland Telegraph Line in 1872. The town grew after gold was discovered in the area in 1932. The **Battery Hill Mining Centre** has two museums and an underground mine. The complex also houses the Tennant Creek Visitor Information Centre.

Tennant Creek today is the second-largest town in the Red Centre. Nearly 500 km (310 miles) north of Alice Springs, it is also a major stopover along the Stuart Highway, between Darwin and South Australia. Other local attractions include the recreational Lake Mary Ann, 5 km (3 miles) out of town and ideal for sailing and swimming. The remote **Tennant Creek Telegraph Station**, 12 km (8 miles) north of the town, built in 1874, is now a museum.

🏛 **Battery Hill Mining Centre**
Battery Hill, Peko Rd. **Tel** (08) 8962 1281. **Open** daily. **Closed** Good Fri; 7, 8 & 25 Dec. 🅿 🔥 📷

🏛 **Tennant Creek Telegraph Station**
Stuart Highway. **Tel** (08) 8962 4599.

🟡 Kings Canyon

🚌 Alice Springs. 🚍 Alice Springs, Yulara. ℹ Alice Springs (08) 8951 8250. 🌐 nt.gov.au/nreta/parks

The spectacular sandstone gorge of Kings Canyon, set within Watarrka National Park, has walls more than 100 m (330 ft) high that have been formed by millions of years of erosion. They contain the fossilized tracks of ancient marine creatures, and even ripplemarks of an ancient sea are visible. Several walking tracks take visitors around the rim of the gorge where there are some stunning views of the valley below. Watarrka National Park has many waterholes and areas of lush vegetation that contain more than 600 plant species. The park also provides a habitat for more than 100 bird species and 60 species of reptiles.

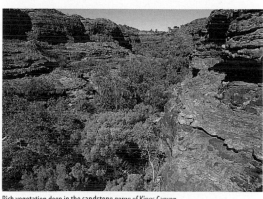
Rich vegetation deep in the sandstone gorge of Kings Canyon

❽ Uluṟu-Kata Tju̱ta National Park

The most instantly recognizable of all Australian symbols is the huge, red monolith of Uluṟu (Ayers Rock). Rising high above the flat desert landscape, Uluṟu is one of the world's natural wonders, along with the 36 rock domes of Kata Tju̱ta (The Olgas) and their deep valleys and gorges. Both sights are in Uluṟu-Kata Tju̱ta National Park, 463 km (288 miles) southwest of Alice Springs, which was established in 1958 and was named as a World Heritage site in 1987 *(see pp30–31)*. The whole area is sacred to Aboriginal people and, in 1985, the park was handed back to its indigenous owners and its sights reassumed their traditional names. As Aboriginal land, it is leased back to the Australian government and jointly managed with the local Anangu people. Within the park is an excellent cultural centre which details the Aboriginal lives and traditions of the area. Yulara, 12 km (7 miles) from Uluṟu, is the park's growing tourist resort *(see p293)*.

The Maruku Gallery
This Aboriginal-owned gallery sells traditional and modern Aboriginal crafts.

Kata Tju̱ta (The Olgas)
This magnificent view of Kata Tju̱ta's domes is from the sunset viewing area. The site has drinking water and interpretive panels giving information on local flora and fauna.

KEY

① **Kata Tju̱ta's** domes rise in the distance behind Uluṟu.

② **Uluṟu** is famous for its colour changes, which range from deep red at sunrise and sunset to shiny black after rain.

③ **Vegetation** is sparse on this desert plain except for a few areas of greenery found in sheltered spots where rainwater collects.

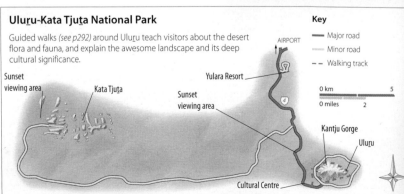

Uluṟu-Kata Tju̱ta National Park

Guided walks *(see p292)* around Uluṟu teach visitors about the desert flora and fauna, and explain the awesome landscape and its deep cultural significance.

AIRPORT

Sunset viewing area

Kata Tju̱ta

Yulara Resort

Sunset viewing area

Kantju Gorge

Uluṟu

Cultural Centre

Key

— Major road

— Minor road

-- Walking track

0 km 5
0 miles 2

Olga Gorge

This scenic gorge runs between two of Kata Tjuta's huge domes. A walking track leads to a cliff face at the end where there is a rock pool and a trickling stream.

Hare Wallaby

This mammal is significant to the Anangu people, who call it *Mala*. According to tradition, Mala people lived at Uluru and created many of the rock formations that are seen today.

Dehydration in the Desert

Uluru-Kata Tjuta National Park is in the heart of Australia's vast desert region. It can experience summer daytime temperatures of more than 45°C (113°F). To avoid dehydration and heat exhaustion all visitors are advised to wear hats, long-sleeved shirts with collars and sunscreen, and to avoid any strenuous activity between 10am and 4pm. Most importantly, each person should drink one litre of water per hour while walking in hot weather.

Mala Walk

This free, ranger-guided walk leads visitors to places created and used by the ancestral Mala people. It ends at Kantju Gorge, sacred to the Anangu, which contains a waterhole beneath a waterfall.

Exploring Uluṟu-Kata Tjuṯa National Park

It is impossible to arrive at Uluṟu-Kata Tjuṯa National Park and not be filled with awe. The sheer size of the world's largest monolith, Uluṟu, rising from the flat desert plain, is a moving and impressive sight. Just as magical are the rounded humps of Kata Tjuṯa not far distant. All the rocks change colour from oranges and reds to purple during the day. Getting around the park, understanding some of its deep Aboriginal significance and learning about its geology, flora and fauna should not be rushed. There is much more to this fascinating area than can be seen or experienced in one day, and a two- or three-day stay is recommended.

Tourists enjoying the Mala walk around part of the base of Uluṟu

Blue-tongued lizard basking in the sun

🦎 Uluṟu (Ayers Rock)

Uluṟu, 3.6 km (2.25 miles) long and 2.4 km (1.5 miles) wide, stands 348 m (1,142 ft) above the plains. It is a single piece of sandstone extending 5 km (3 miles) beneath the desert surface. Besides its immense Aboriginal cultural significance, Uluṟu is an outstanding natural phenomenon, best observed by watching its changing colours at dusk and taking a guided walk at the rock's base.

There are a number of walking trails around Uluṟu. The three-hour, 9.5-km (6-mile) tour around the base gives the greatest sense of its size and majesty. Sacred sights en route are fenced off, and entering is an offence. The Mala (hare wallaby) walk takes in several caves, some with rock art. The Liru (snake) walk starts at the cultural centre, with Aboriginal tour guides explaining how they use bush materials in their daily lives. The Kuniya (python) walk visits the Mutijulu waterhole on the southern side of Uluṟu where local Anangu people tell creation stories and display art describing various legends. Details of all walks can be found at the Uluṟu-Kata Tjuṯa Cultural Centre.

🦎 Kata Tjuṯa (The Olgas)

Kata Tjuṯa, meaning "many heads", is a collection of massive rounded rock domes, 42 km (25 miles) to the west of Uluṟu. Beyond lies a vast, remote desert; permits from the Central Land Council (see p266), 4WDs and full travel survival kits are needed in this inhospitable land.

Kata Tjuṯa is not one large rock; it is a system of gorges and valleys that you can walk around, making it a haunting, quiet and spiritual place. To the Anangu people, it is of equal significance to Uluṟu, but fewer stories about it can be told as they are restricted to initiated tribal men. The tallest rock, Mount Olga, is 546 m (1,790 ft) high, nearly 200 m (660 ft) higher than Uluṟu. There are two recommended walking trails. The Valley of the Winds walk takes about three hours and wanders through several deep gorges. This walk is partially closed when the temperature exceeds 36°C (97°F).

Climbing Uluṟu

The climbing of Uluṟu by the chain-rope path that has been in place since the 1960s is a contentious issue. Physically, it is a steep, 1.6-km (1-mile) climb in harsh conditions, and several tourists die each year from heart attacks or falls. Culturally, the route to the top follows the sacred path taken by the ancestral Mala (hare wallaby) men for important ceremonies. The Anangu ask that visitors respect their wishes and do not climb the rock; a push to ban all climbing on Uluṟu is now gathering pace.

If you do decide to climb, the ascent takes about two hours. Climbing the rock is banned for the remainder of the day if the temperature reaches 36°C (97°F) at any point of the climb. A dawn climb is most popular.

Sign warning tourists of the dangers of climbing Uluṟu

The Anangu of Uluru

Archaeological evidence suggests that Aboriginal people have lived at Uluru for at least 22,000 years and that both Uluru and Kata Tjuta have long been places of enormous ceremonial and cultural significance to a number of Aboriginal tribes.

The traditional owners of Uluru and Kata Tjuta are the Anangu people. They believe that both sites were formed during the creation period by ancestral spirits who also gave them the laws and rules of society that they live by today. The Anangu believe they are direct descendants of these ancestral beings and that, as such, they are responsible for the protection and management of these lands.

The Anangu Aborigines performing a traditional dance

The Olga Gorge (Walpa Gorge) walk leads up the pretty Olga Gorge to its dead-end cliff face and a rock pool. Walkers here may spot the small brown spinifex bird or the thorny devil spiked lizard.

🏛 Uluru-Kata Tjuta Cultural Centre

Tel (08) 8956 1128. **Open** 7am–6pm (last entry 5:30pm) daily. Information desk: 8am–5pm. 🅿 🅰

Near to the base of Uluru is an award-winning cultural centre, with multilingual displays, videos and exhibitions. It is an excellent introduction to the park and well worth visiting before exploring the rock and its surrounding area. The Nintiringkupai display focuses on the history and management of Uluru-Kata Tjuta National Park and includes up-to-date brochures and information on walking trails, sights and tours. The Tjukurpa display, with its art, sounds and videos, is a good introduction to the complex system of Anangu beliefs and laws. Attached to the cultural centre is the Aboriginal-owned Maruku Arts and Craft shop,

where artists are at work and dancers and musicians give performances for tourists. The traditional art, on bark and canvas, tells the story of Uluru Tjukurpa legends.

Ayers Rock Resort

Yulara Drive. ☎ 1300 134 044.
🌐 ayersrockresort.com.au

Yulara is an environmentally friendly, modern tourist village well equipped to cater for the 500,000 annual visitors. Nestling between the desert dunes 20 km (12 miles) north of Uluru and just outside the national park boundary, it serves as a comfortable, green and relaxing base for exploring Uluru and Kata Tjuta. The resort offers all standards of accommodation, from five-star luxury to backpacker accommodation and camping grounds, and is the only option for those who want to stay in the immediate vicinity *(see pp489–90)*.

The visitors' centre at Yulara has information about the park and its geology, flora and fauna. It also sells souvenirs and helps to arrange tours with the licensed operators in the park. Every day at 7:30am there is a free guided walk through the wonderful native garden of the Sails in the Desert Hotel (174 Yulara Drive; Tel: 08 8957 7417). Each evening at the Amphitheatre there is an hour-long concert of Aboriginal music featuring a variety of indigenous instruments, including the didgeridoo. A Night Sky Show is also available, and this describes both the Anangu and ancient Greek stories of the stars.

Yulara also has a shopping centre, which includes a post office, bank and supermarket, and many different restaurants and outdoor eating options *(see pp518–19)*. Other facilities include a childcare centre for children up to the age of eight.

Aerial view of Yulara Resort, with Uluru in the distance

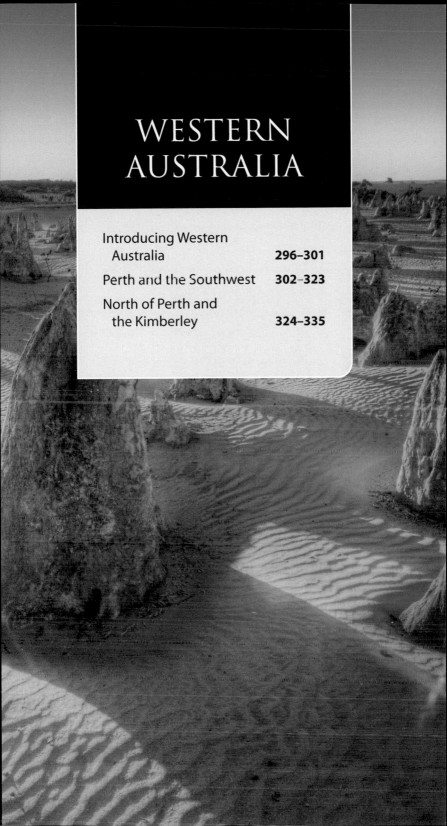

WESTERN AUSTRALIA

Western Australia at a Glance

The huge state of Western Australia encompasses a land mass of more than 2,500,000 sq km (1,000,000 sq miles). In recent years, the state's popularity as a tourist destination has increased, with large numbers of visitors drawn to its many areas of extreme natural beauty. The landscape ranges from giant karri forests, imposing mountains and meadows of wildflowers to vast expanses of untamed wilderness with ancient gorges and rock formations. The coastline has an abundance of beaches, ideal for surfing, and some stunning offshore reefs. In the east, great deserts stretch to the state border. The capital, Perth, is home to 80 per cent of the state's population, but there are many historic towns scattered around the southwest, such as the gold field settlements of Kalgoorlie and Coolgardie.

Locator Map

Karijini National Park is in the Pilbara region and is a spectacular landscape of gorges, pools and waterfalls. The area is particularly popular with experienced hikers; guided tours are also available for more novice bushwalkers (see p333).

Shark Bay World Heritage and Marine Park is Australia's westernmost point. Visitors flock to this protected area to watch the dolphins swim in the waters close to the shore (see pp330–31).

Perth is Australia's most isolated yet most modern state capital. Gleaming skyscrapers, an easy-going atmosphere and its coastal setting make it a popular destination (see pp306–11).

Fremantle's heyday as a major port was at the end of the 19th century. Many of its historic buildings remain. Today the town is renowned for its crafts markets (see pp314–15).

Port Hedland

Exmouth

Coral Bay

Carnarvon

Meekatha

Mount Magne

Kalbarri

Geraldton

Perth

Frema

Mandurah

Bunbury

Busselton

◀ Dawn at the Pinnacles, in Nambung National Park

Purnululu (Bungle Bungle) National Park is one of Australia's most famous natural sights, with its multi-coloured rock domes. Access is limited, but helicopter flights offer views of the area *(see p335)*.

Derby

Broome

Fitzroy Crossing

North of Perth and the Kimberley *(see pp324–35)*

vman

Wiluna

Kalgoorlie made its name in the 1890s when gold was discovered in the region. Much of its 19th-century architecture has been preserved *(see p322–3)*.

Menzies

Perth and the Southwest *(see pp302–23)*

Kalgoorlie-Boulder

Coolgardie

Cocklebiddy

Norseman

Esperance

Wave Rock is 15 m (50 ft) high, 110 m (360 ft) long and is so named because its formation resembles a breaking wave. The illusion is further enhanced by years' worth of water stains running down its face *(see p322)*.

Albany

0 kilometres 200

0 miles 200

Wildflowers of Western Australia

Western Australia is truly the nation's wildflower state. In the spring, from June to November, more than 12,000 species of flowers burst into brilliantly coloured blooms, carpeting deserts, plains, farmland and forests with blazing reds, yellows, pinks and blues.

A staggering 60 per cent of these flowers are unique to the state, giving it one of the world's richest floras. It is home to such remarkable plants as the kangaroo paw, the cowslip orchid and the carnivorous Albany pitcher plant, as well as giant jarrah and karri forests.

The elegant kangaroo paw looks exactly like its name suggests. The state's floral emblem, it has many different species and mostly grows in coastal heath and dry woodland areas.

When and Where to see the Wildflowers

Bushwalking or driving among the flower carpets of Western Australia is an experience not to be missed. Most of the wildflowers bloom in spring, but exactly when depends on their location in this vast state. The wildflower season begins in the northern Pilbara in July and culminates in the magnificent flowering around the Stirling Ranges and the south coast in late October and November.

The Albany pitcher plant grows near coastal estuaries around Albany in the southwest. One of the world's largest carnivorous plants, it traps and devours insects in its sticky hairs.

The magnificent royale hakea is one of many hakea species in Western Australia. It is found on the coast near Esperance and in Fitzgerald River National Park.

Much of Western Australia is arid, dusty outback country where the only vegetation is dry bush shrubs and, after rainfall, wildflowers.

Many wild flowers possess an incredible ability to withstand even the driest, hottest ground.

Red flowering gum trees in the Stirling Ranges burst into bright red flowers every November, attracting honey bees.

The cowslip orchid is a bright yellow orchid with red streaks and five main petals. It can usually be found in October, in the dramatic Stirling Ranges region.

Leschenaultia biloba is a brilliant blue, bell-shaped flower found in jarrah forests near Collie, or in drier bush and plain country where it flowers in carpets of blue.

The boab tree is a specimen related to the African baobab. Growing in the rocky plains of Kimberley (see pp300–301), it holds a great deal of water in its swollen trunk and can grow many metres in circumference.

The bright daisy flowers of the everlastings come in a host of creams, pinks, yellows, oranges and reds.

Giants of the Western Australian Forest

It is not only the native flowers that are special to Western Australia. So, too, are the trees – especially the towering jarrah and karri eucalypts of the southern forests. A major hardwood timber industry, harvesting the jarrah and karri, remains in the state's southwest near Manjimup and Pemberton. Today, however, thousands of trees are preserved in national parks such as Shannon and Walpole-Nornalup, which has a walkway high in the trees for visitors.

Giant karri trees grow to a height of 85 m. They live for up to 300 years, reaching their maximum height after 100 years.

Everlasting Flowers

Native to Australia, everlastings carpet vast areas in many parts of Western Australia. Especially prolific in the southeast, they can also be seen from the roadside in the north, stretching as far as the eye can see.

Everlastings are so called because the petals stay attached to the flower even after it has died.

The scarlet banksia, is one of 41 banksia species found in Western Australia. It is named after Sir Joseph Banks, the botanist who first noted this unusual tree and its flower in 1770.

Sturt's desert pea is actually South Australia's floral emblem, but is also prolific in the dry inland areas of Western Australia. Its bright flowers spring up after rain in the deserts, sometimes after lying dormant for years.

The Kimberley

One of the last truly remote regions in Australia, the Kimberley in northwestern Australia covers 423,000 sq km (164,000 sq miles), yet has a population of less than 35,000. Geologically it is one of the oldest regions on earth. Its rocks formed up to 2,000 million years ago, with little landscape disturbance since. Aboriginal people have lived here for thousands of years, but this unique land has been a tourist attraction only since the 1980s.

Key

═══ Highway

▬▬▬ Major road

═══ Unsealed road

▬▬ National park boundary

The Bungle Bungles

The tiger-striped beehive mountains that comprise the Bungle Bungle range were only discovered by tourists in the 1980s. These great geological and scenic wonders are now protected in Purnululu National Park *(see p335)*. The large, weathered sandstone domes are most easily viewed by air from Kununurra or Halls Creek, but visitors who make the effort to explore this 4WD-only park will also encounter some stunning narrow gorges and clear pools.

The black and orange moulded domes of the Bungle Bungles

Windjana Gorge National Park is one of the three stunning Devonian Reef national parks.

The Great Northern Highway is a sealed road that runs from the Northern Territory border to Broome and Perth beyond.

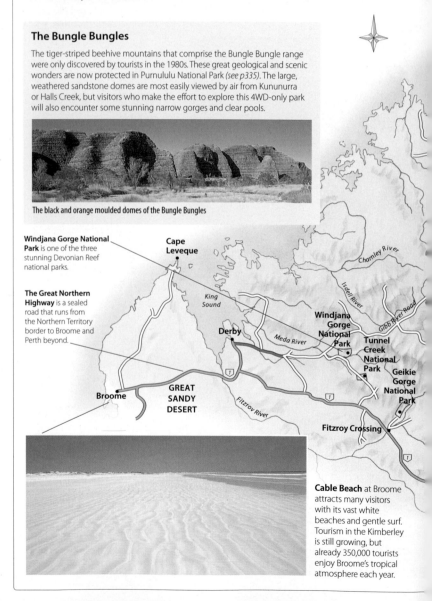

Cape Leveque

Charnley River

Isdell River

King Sound

Windjana Gorge National Park

Gibb River Road

Derby

Meda River

Tunnel Creek National Park

Geikie Gorge National Park

Broome

GREAT SANDY DESERT

Fitzroy River

Fitzroy Crossing

Cable Beach at Broome attracts many visitors with its vast white beaches and gentle surf. Tourism in the Kimberley is still growing, but already 350,000 tourists enjoy Broome's tropical atmosphere each year.

The Cockburn Ranges have deep, inaccessible caves and sandstone cliffs separating the summit from the surrounding plains. The ranges tower above the crocodile-infested Pentecost River on the Gibb River Road. As with many sites in the region, they hold great Aboriginal significance.

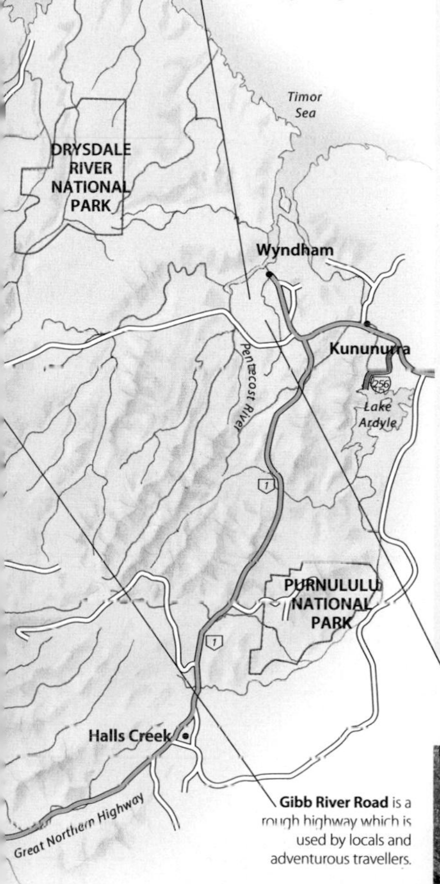

The Aborigines of the Kimberley

Legend suggests that the first Aborigines arrived on the continent, near Broome, 200,000 years ago *(see p51)*. While this view has yet to be validated by scientific evidence, the fact that many of the "songlines" *(see p35)* marked by landmarks and ceremonial sites all end or start around the Kimberley certainly suggests that the area has seen a very long period of human habitation.

Two thirds of the region's population remains Aboriginal, and Aboriginal culture here is one of the most traditional in Australia. Local Aboriginal communities equip their children with a strong identity to help them cope with the demands of living in a mixed-race society.

Aboriginal art in the Kimberley differs from most other parts of Australia. Instead of dot art, there are the outstanding Wandjina figures of the central Kimberley and the object paintings of the Purnululu community based near the Bungle Bungles.

The mysterious Wandjina figures can be seen throughout the Kimberley region.

Aboriginal rock art in the Kimberley has now been dated back 125,000 years, 80,000 years earlier than previously thought.

Timor Sea

DRYSDALE RIVER NATIONAL PARK

Wyndham

Kununurra

Lake Argyle

PURNULULU NATIONAL PARK

Halls Creek

Great Northern Highway

Gibb River Road is a rough highway which is used by locals and adventurous travellers.

| 0 km | 100 |
| 0 miles | 100 |

Emma Gorge is one of hundreds of deep, cool waterholes hidden across the Kimberley. Located near El Questro Station, it was made by waterfalls cascading off the red sandstone plateau into gorges and valleys below.

PERTH AND THE SOUTHWEST

Western Australia's pretty capital, Perth, is the most isolated city in the world, closer to Southeast Asia than it is to any other Australian city. The state's stunning southern region takes in magnificent forests and diverse coastal scenery. To the east, the vast Nullarbor Plain covers more than 250,000 sq km (100,000 sq miles), and rolling wheat fields lead to the arid interior and the gold fields.

Aborigines have lived in the southern region of Western Australia for at least 30,000 years. However, within 20 years of the settlement of the state's first European colony, in 1829, most Aboriginal groups had been either forcibly ejected from the region, imprisoned or stricken by European diseases.

Europeans visited the southern part of the state as early as 1696, but it was not until 1826 that British colonist Captain James Stirling arrived in the Swan River area, declaring the Swan River Colony, later Perth, in 1829. Convicts arrived in 1850 and helped to build public buildings and the colony's infrastructure, until transportation to Western Australia ceased in 1868.

In the 1890s, gold strikes in Coolgardie and Kalgoorlie led to a wave of prosperity in the region. Many ornate late Victorian-style buildings were erected, several of which are still standing.

The beginning of the 20th century saw huge changes: a telegraph cable was laid connecting Perth with South Africa and London, and, in 1917, the railway arrived to join Kalgoorlie with the eastern states. In the 1920s, immigrants and returning World War I servicemen were drafted to the area to clear and develop land under the Group Settlement Scheme. Much of the land, however, was intractable and many people abandoned it.

Today, Perth and the Southwest are fast becoming popular international tourist destinations. Blessed with superb beaches and a glorious climate, the region has everything to offer visitors from climbing the tallest fire-lookout tree in the country to whale-watching along the coast. World-class wineries abound in the Margaret River region and, in springtime, vast tracts of the south are covered with wildflowers.

Dramatic beauty of the Stirling Ranges rising from the plains in the southwest of the state

◄ Architectural contrast of Victorian and modern buildings in Perth

Exploring Perth and the Southwest

The city of Perth lies on the Swan River, just 20 km (12 miles) from where it flows into the Indian Ocean. The coastal plain on which it stands is bordered to the north and west by the Darling Range, beyond which lie the region's wheat fields. To the south is a diverse landscape: forests with some of the tallest trees on earth, mountains that dramatically change colour during the course of each day and a spectacular coastline. Inland are the gold fields that kept the colony alive in the 1890s; beyond lies the Nullarbor Plain, bordering the raging Southern Ocean.

Beach and raging surf in Leeuwin Naturaliste National Park, near the mouth of the Margaret River

Getting Around

Perth's public transport is fast and reliable, and travel by bus within the city centre is free. TransWa, Greyhound and Skywest (a state-based airline) offer rail, coach and air services to many of the region's towns. Distances are not overwhelming, so travelling by car allows visits to the many national parks in the area. The arterial routes are fast roads often used by gigantic road trains. However, there are many tourist routes which lead to places of interest and great natural beauty. Some national parks have unsealed roads, and a few are accessible only by 4WD.

Sights at a Glance

Koorda

Wongan Hills

Mukinbudin

Trayning

Walgoolan

Merredin   *Kalgoorlie*

94

NORTHAM   Cunderdin   Kellerberrin

Muntadgin

13 YORK

Beverley

Narembeen

GREAT SOUTHERN HIGHWAY

Corrigin

40   Brookton   Kondinin   Hyden

40

Kulin

120   Wickepin

Pingaring

Narrogin

Williams   Lake Grace

107

Wagin   Dumbleyung   *Chinocup Nature Reserve*

Arthur River   *Dumbleyung Lake*   Nyabing

ALBANY HIGHWAY   Pingrup

Katanning

Kojonup   Jerramungup   *Esperance*

120   Gnowangerup   Ongerup

Tambellup

Cranbrook   **12**

102   MUIRS HIGHWAY   STIRLING RANGE NATIONAL PARK   Bremer Bay

Cape Knob

innon tional Park   Mount Barker   1

DENMARK   Cheyne Beach

alpole   **10**   *Cape Vancouver*

Nornalup   **11**   ALBANY

Locator Map
- Perth and the Southwest
- The Goldfields and Nullarbor Plain pp322–3

London Court, a Tudor-style shopping arcade in Perth

Key
— Major road
━ Highway
--- Track
— Scenic route
— Main railway

0 kilometres   50

0 miles   50

❶ Street-by-Street: Perth

The history of Perth has been one of building and rebuilding. The makeshift houses of the first settlers were soon replaced with more permanent buildings, many erected by convicts in the latter half of the 19th century. The gold rush of the 1890s and the mining boom of the 1960s and 70s brought waves of prosperity, and the citizens replaced their older buildings with more prestigious symbols of the state's wealth. As a result, much of the early city has gone, but a few traces remain, hidden between skyscrapers or in the city's public parks.

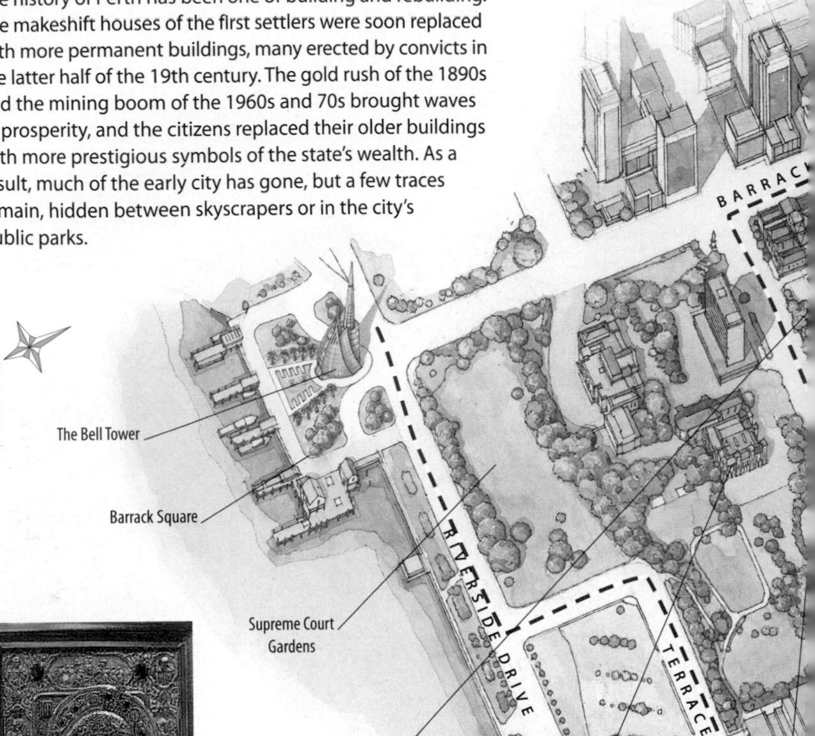

BARRACK

The Bell Tower

Barrack Square

Supreme Court Gardens

RIVERSIDE DRIVE

TERRACE ROAD

★ St George's Anglican Cathedral
This Victorian Gothic Revival-style cathedral, built in the late 19th century, has a fine rose window *(see p308)*.

Government House
Hidden behind walls and trees, the original residence of the state governor was built by convicts between 1859 and 1864. The building's patterned brickwork is typical of the period.

Key

— Suggested route

The Deanery
Built in 1859, the Deanery was originally the residence of the Dean of St George's. It now houses the Cathedral administration.

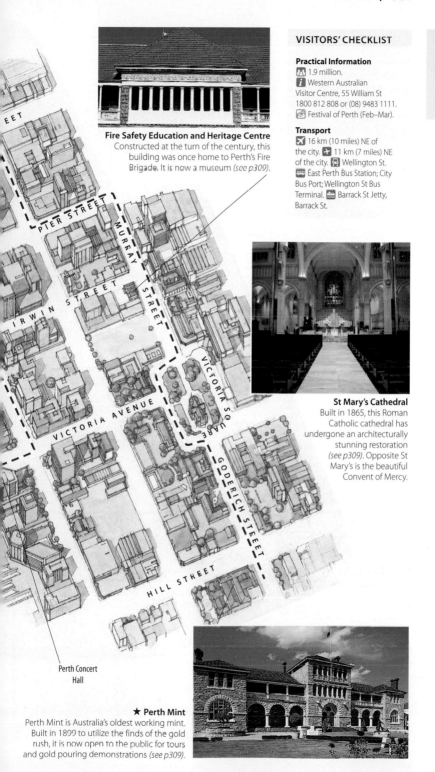

Fire Safety Education and Heritage Centre
Constructed at the turn of the century, this building was once home to Perth's Fire Brigade. It is now a museum *(see p309)*.

VISITORS' CHECKLIST

Practical Information

🗺 1.9 million.
ℹ️ Western Australian Visitor Centre, 55 William St 1800 812 808 or (08) 9483 1111.
🎭 Festival of Perth (Feb–Mar).

Transport

✈️ 16 km (10 miles) NE of the city. 🛫 11 km (7 miles) NE of the city. 🚉 Wellington St. 🚌 East Perth Bus Station; City Bus Port; Wellington St Bus Terminal. ⛴ Barrack St Jetty, Barrack St.

St Mary's Cathedral
Built in 1865, this Roman Catholic cathedral has undergone an architecturally stunning restoration *(see p309)*. Opposite St Mary's is the beautiful Convent of Mercy.

Perth Concert Hall

★ **Perth Mint**
Perth Mint is Australia's oldest working mint. Built in 1899 to utilize the finds of the gold rush, it is now open to the public for tours and gold pouring demonstrations *(see p309)*.

Central Perth

Perth is a relatively small and quiet city compared with those on the east coast. Its main commercial and shopping areas can be easily explored on foot. The city's atmosphere is brisk but not hurried. Redevelopment projects in the 1970s brought skyscrapers and more roads, but they also made space for city parks and courtyards lined with cafés and shady trees. The city centre is bordered to the south and east by a wide stretch of the Swan River known as Perth Water, and to the north lies Northbridge, Perth's restaurant and entertainment centre.

The elaborately decorated Brass Monkey Hotel on William Street

Exploring Central Perth

St Georges Terrace is Perth's main commercial street. At its western end stands Parliament House, and in front of this is Barracks Archway. Further east, the Cloisters, built in 1850 as a school, boast some fine decorative brickwork. Nearby is the Old Perth Boys' School, a tiny one-storey building that was Perth's first school for boys.

Perth's shopping centre lies between William and Barrack streets. It is a maze of arcades, plazas and elevated walkways. The main areas are Hay Street Mall and Murray Street Mall. On the corner of William Street and St Georges Terrace lies the Town Hall (1870), close to the site where Perth was founded.

Beyond the railway tracks is Northbridge, the focus of much of Perth's nightlife. James Street is lined with many restaurants, cafés and food halls offering a variety of ethnic cuisines. The ornate façade of the former Brass Monkey Hotel (now a pub), is a perfect example of colonial gold rush architecture.

🏛 Barracks Archway

Cnr St Georges Terrace & Elder St. Barracks Archway is all that remains of the 1863 barracks that once housed the soldiers who were brought in to police the convict population.

🏛 Perth Cultural Centre

James St. Art Gallery of Western Australia: **Tel** (08) 9492 6622. **Open** 10am–5pm Wed–Mon. **Closed** Good Fri, 25 Apr, 25 Dec. Donations. 🚻 🚾 **mra. wa.gov.au/projects-and-places**

The Perth Cultural Centre is a pedestrianized complex on several levels. The centre is home to the Art Gallery of Western Australia, which has a collection of modern Aboriginal and Australian art, and some international pieces. The Perth Institute of Contemporary Art (PICA), State Library and State Theatre are also here.

🏛 Western Australian Museum – Perth

Perth Cultural Centre, James St. **Tel** (08) 9212 3700. **Open** 9:30am–5pm daily; 25 Apr: 1–5pm. **Closed** 1 Jan, Good Fri, 25–26 Dec. 🚻 limited. 🚾 **museum.wa.gov.au**

Within the Perth Cultural Centre stands the Western Australian Museum complex. Among its buildings are the Old Perth Gaol (1856), with exhibitions on life in the original Swan River colony. The exhibition "Western Australia Land and People" tells the story of Western Australia from dinosaurs to indigenous beginnings and the environmental issues now facing the state. International and temporary exhibitions enhance the permanent displays.

🏛 St George's Anglican Cathedral

38 St Georges Terrace. **Tel** (08) 9325 5766. **Open** daily. 🚻

St George's Cathedral, consecrated in 1888, was only the second permanent Anglican place of worship in Perth. The city's first Anglican church was built between 1841 and 1845 in Classical Revival style close to the site of the existing cathedral. In 1875 a more prestigious place of worship was required, and the old church was demolished. Some artifacts from the original church remain, however, such as some of the jarrah pews and the carved eagle lectern. This Gothic Revival building has some notable features including the intricate English alabaster *reredos* at the base of the east window, the modernistic medallions cast for the Stations of the Cross and some original 19th-century Russian icons.

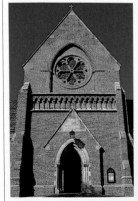

Western façade of St George's Cathedral showing rose window

For hotels and restaurants in this area see p490 and pp519–21

🖩 Perth Mint

310 Hay St. **Tel** (08) 9421 7222.
Open 9am–5pm daily. **Closed** 1 Jan,
Good Fri, 25 Apr, 25–26 Dec. 🅿 &
W perthmint.com.au

Perth Mint was
opened in 1899,
under British control,
to refine gold from
Western Australia's
gold fields to make
British sovereigns
and half-sovereigns.

**Perth Fire Station's
original fire bell**

Although it no
longer produces coins for
circulation, the mint produces
proof coins and specialist pure
precious-metal coins, making
it Australia's oldest operating
mint. The mint has an
interesting exhibition with
coins, precious metal exhibits
and displays on gold mining
and refining. In addition, every
hour a "Gold Pour" takes place
in the Melting House that
has been in operation for
over a century.

🏛 DFES Education and Heritage Centre

25 Murray St. **Tel** (08) 9395 9860.
Open 10am–4pm Tue–Thu. **Closed**
1 Jan, Good Fri, 25 Apr, 25–26 Dec. &
W dfes.wa.gov.au

Perth City Fire Brigade
moved from this, its
original home, to a much
larger site in 1979. The
old fire station became
a fascinating museum
charting the history of
the fire service in Perth
and Western Australia, and a fire
safety centre. Exhibits here
include some well-preserved
old fire appliances and
reconstructions of rooms.

🏠 St Mary's Cathedral

Victoria Sq. **Tel** (08) 9224 1350.
Open 7am–6pm daily. &

Following an extensive
restoration project, St Mary's
Cathedral is an architectural
delight. The cathedral has retained
its splendid stained-glass
windows and rich heritage,
while also providing a
modern space, seating 1,400
people. St Mary's is renowned
for its superb choir.

🖩 The Bell Tower: Home of the Swan Bells

Barrack Sq. **Tel** (08) 6210 0444. **Open**
10am–4pm daily. **Closed** Good Fri, 25
Dec. 🅿 & **W** thebelltower.com.au

One of Perth's main attractions,
the Bell Tower contains 12 bells
from St Martin-in-the-Fields in
London, England. There are
displays and exhibitions inside
the tower, including the oldest
bell in Australia – the Upon
Grey Bell – cast in 1550, a
restored late Victorian turret
clock which is wound daily for
visitors, and an observation
deck. Expert bell ringers give
a brief history of bell ringing,
and the bells ring daily, except
Wednesday and Friday, when
there is a bell handling
demonstration instead.

Perth City Centre

① Barracks Archway
② Perth Cultural Centre
③ Western Australian Museum – Perth
④ DFES Education and Heritage Centre
⑤ St Mary's Cathedral
⑥ Perth Mint
⑦ St George's Anglican Cathedral
⑧ The Bell Tower

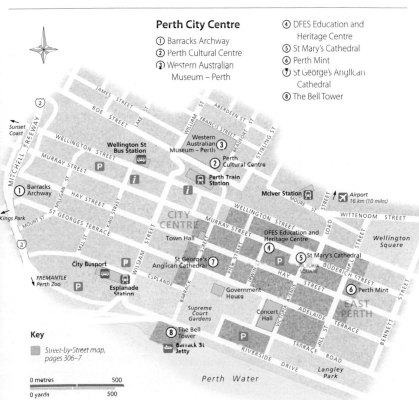

Key

▭ Street-by-Street map, pages 306–7

0 metres — 500
0 yards — 500

For **additional map symbols** *see back flap*

Exploring Greater Perth

Beyond the city centre, Greater Perth covers the Darling Range in the northeast to the Indian Ocean in the west. It has several large parks, including Kings Park, overlooking the river. On the coast, beaches stretch from Hillarys Boat Harbour in the north to Fremantle in the south *(see pp314–15)*. Perth's suburbs are accessible by train, local bus or car.

Sights at a Glance

❶ Kings Park
❷ Sunset Coast
❸ Hills Forest
❹ Whiteman Park
❺ Perth Zoo
❻ AQWA
❼ Swan Valley

Key

▨ Central Perth
▬ Highway
▬ Major road
= Minor road

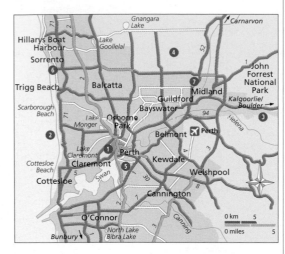

Snorkellers and qualified divers can explore the reef at AQWA

🐟 AQWA, Aquarium of Western Australia

Hillarys Boat Harbour, 91 Southside Drive, Hillarys. **Tel** (08) 9447 7500. **Open** 10am–5pm daily. **Closed** 25 Dec. 🅿 ♿ 🆆 aqwa.com.au

At Hillarys Boat Harbour, to the north of Perth's Sunset Coast, is this magnificent aquarium complex. A transparent submerged tunnel allows visitors to observe native sea creatures, including sharks and stingrays. There is a Touch Pool, where rays and sharks can be stroked. The denizens of the outside seal pool never fail to delight.

🍇 Swan Valley

Swan Valley Visitor Centre, Guildford Courthouse, cnr Meadow & Swan Sts, Guildford. **Tel** (08) 9207 8899. **Open** 9am–4pm daily. **Closed** 25 Dec. 🆆 swanvalley.com.au

Western Australia's oldest wine-growing region is only a 25-minute drive from Perth. The historic suburb of Guildford is the gateway to a mix of award-winning wineries, breweries and gourmet offerings. Contact the Visitor Centre for details of wine tours and tastings.

🍇 Sunset Coast

Via West Coast Hwy.

Perth's Sunset Coast is lined with 30 km (20 miles) of white sandy beaches, many of them virtually deserted during the week. There are beaches to suit all tastes. Cottesloe Beach, at the southern end, is fringed with grassland and trees, and offers safe swimming and good services, making it popular with families, as is Sorrento Beach in the north. Scarborough Beach is

🏞 Kings Park

Fraser Ave, Kings Park. **Tel** (08) 9480 3600. **Open** daily. ♿ 🆆 bgpa.wa.gov.au

Established at the end of the 19th century, Kings Park is 400 ha (1,000 acres) of both wild and cultivated parkland. Situated on Mount Eliza, it offers views of the city and the Swan River. Most of the park is bushland, which can be seen from the DNA Tower.

A landscaped parkland area on the eastern side includes the 17 ha (42 acres) Western Australian Botanic Garden. Treetops Walkway, a 629-m- (689-yd-) long elevated walkway, gives another perspective of the garden. The State War Memorial on Anzac Bluff is dedicated to the Western Australians who died in the two world wars. The Minmara

Gun Gun and Pioneer Women's Memorial are monuments to the women who helped build the Swan River Colony and, later, the state.

Bronze statue of a mother and child in Kings Park Western Australian Botanic Garden

very popular with surfers, but it is for experienced swimmers only as strong currents can make it dangerous on windy days. Trigg Beach just above Scarborough is also a good surfing spot. Just north of Cottesloe, Swanbourne Beach is a naturist beach.

Many of the city's beaches have no shade whatsoever and Perth residents are constantly reminded that the sun's rays, unshielded due to the hole in the ozone layer, can burn within minutes. Beachgoers are strongly advised to take sunscreen, a hat, t-shirt and sun umbrella (see p549).

Students admiring a magnificent tiger in Perth Zoo

Surfing on Scarborough Beach

◧ Perth Zoo
20 Labouchere Rd. **Tel** (08) 9474 0444. **Open** 9am–5pm daily. 🅦 perthzoo.wa.gov.au

In South Perth, a ferry-ride away from the city centre, lies Perth Zoo. Dedicated to conservation, it has all the features of an international-standard zoo. Attractions include a Nocturnal House, a wildlife park, an African savannah exhibit, an Australian walkabout and an Asian rainforest zone.

◧ Hills Forest
Via Great Eastern Hwy.

Only 30 minutes' drive from Central Perth, Hills Forest lies in the Darling Range and offers a wide range of bush-related activities. Conserved since 1919 as the catchment area for the Mundaring Reservoir, which provided water for the southern gold fields in the 19th century (see p59), Hills Forest is now managed as a conservation and recreation area. It is well served with barbecue and picnic areas and camp sites. At Mundaring Weir landscaped gardens are a lovely backdrop for picnics. On the northern edge of the forest is John Forrest National Park, Western Australia's first national park. It consists of woodland and heathland with trails leading to beautiful pools and waterfalls, including Hovea Falls.

◧ Whiteman Park
Lot 99 Lord St, Whiteman. **Tel** (08) 9209 6000. **Open** 8:30am–6pm daily. 🖳 🕭

Northeast of the city centre lies popular Whiteman Park. Visitors can tour the park on a 1920s tram or by train. A craft village displays local craftsmanship and there is also a motor museum with a collection of vehicles from the last 100 years. Within Whiteman Park, Caversham Wildlife Park is home to 200 species of native Australian animals from koalas to Tasmanian devils.

A Chrysler Newport on display by the entrance to the motor museum in Whiteman Park

❷ Rottnest Island

Less than 20 km (12 miles) west of Fremantle lies the idyllic island of Rottnest. Settled by Europeans in 1831, it was used as an Aboriginal prison between 1838 and 1902. In 1917, in recognition of its scenic beauty and rich bird life, the island became a protected area and today it is a popular tourist destination. Rottnest's oldest settlement, Thomson Bay, dates from the 1840s. The island's other settlements, all built in the 20th century, are found at Longreach Bay, Geordie Bay and Kingstown. Rottnest's rugged coastline comprises beaches, coves and reefs – ideal for many water-based activities – salt lakes and several visible shipwrecks. Private cars are not allowed on the island, so the only way to get around is by bicycle or bus, or on foot.

Aerial View of Rottnest
Rottnest is 11 km (7 miles) long, 4.5 km (3 miles) wide, and is governed by strict conservation regulations.

Wadjemup Lighthouse
The lighthouse on Wadjemup Hill was built in 1895. "Wadjemup" is the Aboriginal name for the island.

Rocky Bay
Overlooked by the sandy Lady Edeline beach, this popular, picturesque bay also contains the wreck of the barque *Mira Flores*, which sank in 1886.

Cape Vlamingh Lookout
Named after Dutch explorer Willem de Vlamingh, Rottnest's most famous early European visitor, this lookout stands at the furthest tip of the island, 10.5 km (6.5 miles) from Thomson Bay. The view is spectacular.

KEY

① **Strickland Bay** was named after Sir Gerald Strickland, governor of Rottnest from 1909 to 1912, and is a prime surfing spot.

② **City of York Bay** was named after Rottnest's most tragic shipwreck. In 1899, the captain of the *City of York* mistook a lighthouse flare for a pilot's signal and headed towards the rocks.

③ **Parakeet Bay** is popular with snorkellers. It is also an excellent spot to see the rock parrots after which it is named.

④ **The Basin** is the most popular beach on Rottnest

Island, particularly with families with children, as it is easily accessible on foot from Thomson Bay.

⑤ **The Rottnest Museum** is housed in the old granary, which dates from 1857. Exhibits cover the island's geology, its many shipwrecks, flora and fauna, and memorabilia of the early settlers and convicts.

⑥ **Henrietta Rocks** are a hazardous place for shipping. No less than three ships have been wrecked in the waters off this point.

⑦ **Mabel Cove**

For hotels and restaurants in this area see p490 and pp519–21

Hotel Rottnest
With its turrets and crenellations, this was built in 1864 as the state governor's summer residence. Formerly the Quokka Arms, it is now a hotel (see p490).

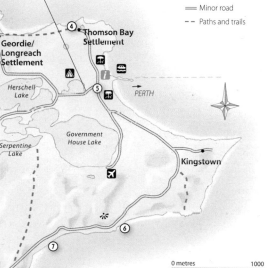

Key
━━━ Minor road
– – – Paths and trails

Thomson Bay Settlement
Geordie/ Longreach Settlement
Lake Baghdad
Herschell Lake
PERTH
Government House Lake
Serpentine Lake
Kingstown

0 metres 1000
0 yards 1000

The Quokka

When de Vlamingh first visited Rottnest in 1696, he noted animals somewhat bigger than a cat, with dark fur. Thinking they were a species of rat, he called the island the "rats' nest". In fact the animals were a type of wallaby, called quokkas by the Aborigines. Although there is a small mainland population in Western Australia, this is the best place to see these timid creatures in areas of undergrowth. On Rottnest such habitat is scarce, and they are often visible at dusk. Quokkas are wild and should not be fed.

Oliver Hill
At this lookout stand two 9.2-inch (23.5-cm) guns, brought here for coastal defence purposes in 1937, but obsolete since the end of World War II. A railway to the hill has been renovated by volunteers.

For additional map symbols see back flap

❸ Fremantle

Fremantle is one of Western Australia's most historic cities. A wealth of 19th-century buildings remains, including superb examples from the gold rush period. Founded on the Indian Ocean in 1829, at the mouth of the Swan River, Fremantle was intended to be a port for the new colony, but was only used as such when an artificial harbour was dredged at the end of the 19th century. The town still has thriving harbours and, in 1987, it hosted the America's Cup. Many sites were renovated for the event, and street cafés and restaurants sprang up.

Busy fruit and vegetable stall in the Fremantle Markets

Twelve-sided Round House

🕼 The Round House

Below High St. **Tel** (08) 9336 6897. **Open** 10:30am–3:30pm daily. Donation. 🚻 limited.

Built in 1830, the Round House is Fremantle's oldest building. It was the town's first gaol and, in 1844, site of the colony's first hanging. Beneath is a tunnel, dug in 1837 to allow whalers to transfer cargo from the jetty to the High Street. To the left of the site are clear views across Bathers Bay to Rottnest Island (see pp312–13).

🏛 Western Australian Museum – Shipwreck Galleries

Cliff St. **Tel** (08) 9431 8469. **Open** 9:30am–5pm daily (25 Apr: 1–5pm). **Closed** 1 Jan, Good Fri, 25–26 Dec. Donation. 🚻
W **museum.wa.gov.au**

Housed in the Commissariat building, an 1850s convict-built government storehouse, the Shipwreck Galleries is a renowned centre for maritime archaeology and exploration. The museum's prize possession is a reconstruction of part of the hull of the Dutch East Indiaman *Batavia* from timbers discovered at the wreck off the Abrolhos Islands in 1629 (see p328). The exhibit tells the story of the shipwreck and mutiny of the vessel and gives an insight into life on board.

🛒 Fremantle Markets

Cnr South Terrace & Henderson St. **Tel** (08) 9335 2515. **Open** 9am–8pm Fri–Sun (to 6pm public hols). **Closed** 25 Dec. 🚻

In 1897, a competition was announced to design a suitable building to act as Fremantle's market hall. The winning design still stands today, having been renovated in 1975. There are more than 170 stalls offering everything from vegetables to opals. The market is open until 8pm on Fridays.

🏛 St John the Evangelist Anglican Church

Cnr Adelaide & Queen sts. **Tel** (08) 9335 2213. **Open** 9am–5pm daily. 🚻

This charming church, completed in 1882, replaced a smaller church on the same site. Its Pioneer Window tells the story of a pioneer family across seven generations, from its departure from England in the 18th century, to a new life in Western Australia. The window next to it is from the old church. The ceiling and altars are of local jarrah wood.

🏛 Western Australian Museum – Maritime

Victoria Quay. **Tel** (08) 9431 8444. **Open** 9:30am–5pm daily (25 Apr: 1–5pm). **Closed** 1 Jan, Good Fri, 25–26 Dec. 🚻 🚻
W **museum.wa.gov.au**

This museum houses the *Australia II*, the racing yacht with the winged keel that won the America's Cup in 1983. Also popular is the submarine HMAS *Ovens*, which can be toured. Visitors can find out what life is like aboard a submarine and immerse themselves in Fremantle's wartime history.

The America's Cup Bonanza

The America's Cup yachting race has been run every four years since 1851. Not until 1983, however, did a country other than the United States win this coveted trophy. This was the year that *Australia II* carried it home. In 1987, the Americans were the challengers, and the races were run in *Australia II*'s home waters, off Fremantle. Investment poured into the town, refurbishing the docks, cafés, bars and hotels for the occasion.

The Americans regained the trophy, but Fremantle remains forever changed by being, for once, under the world's gaze.

The 1983 winner, *Australia II*

🏛 Fremantle Arts Centre

Cnr Ord & Finnerty Vale sts. **Tel** (08) 9432 9555. **Open** 10am–5pm daily. **Closed** Good Fri, 25–26 Dec & 1 Jan. 🦽 limited. 🅆 fac.org.au

This beautiful Gothic Revival mansion with its shady gardens was first conceived as an insane asylum. The main wing was built between 1861 and 1865, and an extension was added between 1880 and 1902.

The building, which after its use as an asylum became the wartime headquarters for US forces, was slated for demolition in 1967. But, principally through the efforts of Fremantle's mayor, it was rescued and renovated to become the Fremantle Arts Centre.

The centre is one of Western Australia's most dynamic multi-arts organisations, offering a rich cultural program of exhibitions, residences, art courses, music and events. It also showcases local contemporary artists, with many of the works for sale.

During the summer months (October to March), the centre's Sunday Music series takes place from 2–4pm. The outdoor event is free and features an extensive line up of established local acts, touring artists and young up-and-coming musicians.

🏛 Fremantle Prison

1 The Terrace. **Tel** (08) 9336 9200. **Open** 9am–5pm daily. **Closed** Good Fri, 25 Dec. 🚫 📷 🦽 limited. 🅆 fremantleprison.com.au

In the 1850s, when the first group of convicts arrived in the Swan River Colony, the need arose for a large-scale prison. Fremantle Prison, an imposing building with a sturdy gatehouse and cold, forbidding limestone cell blocks, was built by those first convicts in 1855. It was used as a maximum-security prison until 1991. Today, visitors tour the complex, visiting cells, punishment cells, the chapel and the chilling gallows

room, last used in 1964. The torchlight tours and tunnel tours are highly recommended.

Fremantle Prison's striking façade

Fremantle City Centre

① The Round House
② WA Museum – Shipwreck Galleries
③ Fremantle Markets
④ St John the Evangelist Anglican Church
⑤ WA Museum – Maritime
⑥ Fremantle Arts Centre
⑦ Fremantle Prison

The Southern Coastline

Western Australia's southwest corner has diverse coastal scenery. Two oceans meet here, the Indian and the Southern, resulting in discernible climate changes: the southern coastline is often windy and cooler than the western coast, and the oceans are much less gentle. Lined by national parks, the coast incorporates limestone, reefs, granite formations, beautiful sand dunes and crags topped by low vegetation. There are also world-class surfing spots in the region.

⑤ ★ Flinders Bay, Augusta

Augusta was founded in 1830 and is the third oldest settlement in the state. Only 5 km (3 miles) from Cape Leeuwin, the southwestern tip of the continent, today it is a popular holiday resort. The beautiful Flinders Bay is particularly favoured by windsurfers.

0 km   20
0 miles   20

④ ★ Hamelin Bay

This busy beach in the centre of Cape Leeuwin is particularly attractive to families, with its calm waters and fine swimming and fishing opportunities.

① Bunker Bay, Dunsborough

This excellent beach in the tourist resort of Dunsborough benefits from dolphin- and whale-watching in season and fine views of Cape Naturaliste.

② Smiths Beach, Yallingup

This popular honeymoon spot is also a haven for surfers. Nearby is the spectacular Yallingup Cave. Yallingup is the indigenous word for "palace of lovers".

③ Boodjidup Beach, Margaret River

The coastline in this holiday town consists of long beaches, sheltered bays and cliff faces looking out on to the surf.

⑦ Peaceful Bay

Keen anglers and sailors can often be spotted within this aptly named inlet, which is also a popular picnic spot. Nearby Walpole is the gateway to Walpole-Nornalup National Park, with its impressive karri and eucalypt trees.

⑩ Middleton Beach, Albany

The waters of Middleton Beach are regularly filled with windsurfers and bodyboarders. A short drive around the point is Torndirrup National Park, with a multitude of natural coastal formations, including offshore islands and some excellent locations for whale-watching in season.

For additional map symbols see back flap

Lake Cave, near Margaret River, is just one of an estimated 200 underground caves along the Leeuwin-Naturaliste Ridge that runs from Busselton to Augusta. It is one of the few caves open to the public and is a fairyland of limestone formations, reflected in dark underground waters.

Locator Map

D'Entrecasteaux National Park, 40 km (25 miles) southwest of Pemberton, is a wild and rugged park with spectacular coastal cliffs, pristine beaches and excellent coastal fishing. Much of the park, including some isolated beach camp sites, is only accessible by 4WD. Inland, heathland is home to a range of animal and plant habitats.

Leeuwin-Naturaliste National Park is a 15,500-ha (40,000-acre) protected area of scenic coastline, caves, heathlands and woodlands. Its rugged limestone coast with long beaches and sheltered bays faces the Indian Ocean. It has long been popular as a holiday destination and has excellent opportunities for swimming, surfing and fishing.

⑧ ★ Ocean Beach, Denmark

Denmark is a popular haunt for surfers from many countries. Ocean Beach, in particular, is the setting for international surfing competitions.

⑨ ★ Wilson Inlet

From Denmark's main street it is a relatively short walk through well-kept woodland to Wilson Inlet where there are some spectacular and varied coastal views.

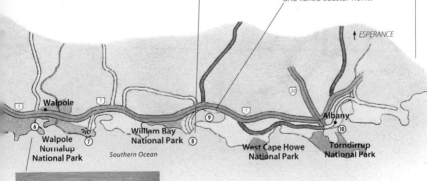

⑥ ★ Conspicuous Beach

Impressive cliffs face on to the beautiful white sands of Conspicuous Beach. It is also the access point for the Valley of the Giants, with its massive red tingle trees.

Key

═══ Highway

─── Major road

▭▭▭ Minor road

〰 River

Wide first-floor veranda and ornate ironwork of the Rose Hotel, Bunbury

❹ Bunbury

🏙 50,000. 🚉 🚌 🚕 🚢 ℹ️ Old Railway Station, Carmody Place (08) 9792 7205. 🌐 visitbunbury.com.au

The city of Bunbury lies about 180 km (110 miles) south of Perth at the southern end of the Leschenhault Inlet. The state's second-largest city, it is the capital of the southwest region. Since the 19th century it has grown into a thriving port and a centre for local industry. It is also a popular holiday destination, with many water sports available.

Historic buildings in Bunbury include the Rose Hotel, built in 1865, with its first-floor veranda and intricate ironwork detail. The Anglican St Boniface Cathedral contains some pretty stained glass. Nearby are the Bunbury Art Galleries, housed in the former Sisters of Mercy convent built in the 1880s. Today they are the centre for community arts events.

On the beachfront stands the **Dolphin Discovery Centre**, which has fascinating audio-visual exhibits and a shallow pool where visitors can interact with dolphins. Wild dolphins regularly appear off the beach in front of the centre, and visitors come to see them and swim with them. The centre also runs cruises and swim-with-dolphin tours.

The **King Cottage Museum**, is run by the Bunbury Historical Society. It exhibits local artifacts dating from the 1880s to the 1920s and a wealth of photographs.

🐬 Dolphin Discovery Centre
Lot 830 Koombana Drive. **Tel** (08) 9791 3088. **Open** Jun–Sep: 9am–2pm; Oct–May: 8am–4pm. **Closed** 25 Dec. 🅿️ ♿

🏛 King Cottage Museum
77 Forrest Ave. **Tel** (08) 9721 7546. **Open** 2–4pm daily. **Closed** 1 Jan, Good Fri, 25 Apr, 25–26 Dec. 🅿️ ♿ limited.

❺ Busselton

🏙 29,000. ✈️ 🚌
ℹ️ 38 Peel Terrace (08) 9752 5800.
🌐 geographebay.com

Standing on the shores of Geographe Bay, Busselton offers more than 30 km (19 miles) of beaches and an array of water-based activities, including fishing, whale-watching and scuba-diving. Busselton Jetty, 2 km (1 mile) long and once the longest in Australia, is a reminder of the town's origins as a timber port.

Some of Busselton's oldest surviving buildings are located at the Old Courthouse site, now

Entrance to Busselton's original courthouse building

used as an arts complex. Here, the jail cells, police offices, courthouse and bond store all date from 1856. Local crafts are sold in the old jail cells, and other outbuildings act as studio space for artists.

The 1871 *Ballarat*, the first steam locomotive used in the state, stands in Victoria Park.

Environs
About 10 km (6 miles) north of Busselton is **Wonnerup House,** a lovingly restored house built by pioneer George Layman in 1859 and now owned by the National Trust. Three other buildings share the site, the earliest being the first house Layman erected in the 1830s. Both buildings stand in pretty grounds within farmland and are furnished with Layman family memorabilia and artifacts. In 1874, Layman's son built a school and in, 1885, a teacher's house close by.

About 20 km (12 miles) north of Busselton is the beautiful Ludlow Tuart Forest National Park, probably the largest area of tuart trees left in the world.

🏠 Wonnerup House
935 Layman Rd. **Tel** (08) 9752 2039. **Open** 10am–4pm Thu–Mon. **Closed** Good Fri, 25 Dec. 🅿️ ♿

❻ Margaret River

🏙 100,000. ✈️ 🚌 🚕
ℹ️ 100 Bussell Hwy (08) 9780 5911.
🌐 margaretriver.com

The attractive town of Margaret River, close to the Indian Ocean, was first settled by Europeans in the 1850s. The town became the centre of an agricultural and timber region, but in the past few decades has gained fame for its wineries *(see pp40–41)*, and for its splendid surfing beaches.

Within the town are many galleries, studios and gourmet food and beverage specialists. The **Margaret River Gallery** showcases works by Western Australian artists. Featuring painting, sculpture, jewellery and furniture, the gallery also hosts exhibition openings. Set in 12 ha (30 acres) of bush on the outskirts of town, the **Eagles**

Heritage Raptor Wildlife Centre has a collection of birds of prey and gives eagle-flying displays.

☐ Margaret River Gallery
Shop 4 no. 1 Charles West Ave. **Tel** (08) 9757 2729. **Open** 10am–5pm Mon–Sat, 11am–3pm Sun. **Closed** 1 Jan, Good Fri, 25 Dec. ♿

☒ Eagles Heritage Raptor Wildlife Centre
341 Boodjidup Rd. **Tel** (08) 9757 2960. **Open** 10am–4:15pm (last adm). **Closed** Fri (except WA school hols), Good Fri, 25 Dec. ♿

Environs
Eight km (5 miles) north of Margaret River stands the region's first homestead, Ellensbrook, built by pioneer Alfred Bussell in the 1850s. The stone cottage is close to a forest trail which leads to the pretty Meekadarribee Falls.

Margaret River's outlying wineries are very popular. Many, from Vasse-Felix, the oldest, to the large Leeuwin Estates Winery, offer tastings.

Ellensbrook Pioneer Homestead, near the town of Margaret River

❼ Bridgetown
🏠 4,000. 🚍 🏋 154 Hampton St (08) 9761 1740. 🔲 **bridgetown.com.au**

Nestled amid rolling hills on the banks of Blackwood River, Bridgetown began as a single one-room homestead in the 1850s. It was built by settler John Blechynden and can still be seen standing next to the second home he built, Bridgedale House. Both are National Trust properties.

The town's visitors' centre is home to its municipal history museum and the unusual Brierly

Hilltop view of picturesque Bridgetown

Jigsaw Gallery, which has hundreds of puzzles.

Sutton's Lookout, off Philips Street, offers panoramic views of the town and surrounding countryside. The Blackwood River and local jarrah and marri forests afford opportunities for walks and drives, and several river-based activities, including canoeing and marron fishing.

❽ Manjimup
🏠 5,000. 🚍 🏋 Giblett St (08) 9771 1831. 🔲 **manjimupwa.com**

If you are travelling south from Perth, Manjimup acts as the gateway to the great karri forests for which the southwest is so famous. The town was settled in the late 1850s, and has been associated with the timber industry ever since. **Manjimup Timber Park** has a Timber Museum, Historical Hamlet and Bunnings Age of Steam Museum. A sculpture of a woodsman at the entrance commemorates the region's timber industry pioneers.

☐ Manjimup Timber & Heritage Park
Cnr Rose & Edwards sts. **Tel** (08) 9771 7777. **Open** 9am–5pm daily. **Closed** 25 Dec. ♿

Environs
About 25 km (16 miles) west of Manjimup on Graphite Road lies Glenoran Pool, a pretty swimming

hole on the Donnelly River. The adjacent One-Tree Bridge is the site where early settlers felled a huge karri and used it to carry a bridge across the river. Nearby are the Four Aces, four giant karri trees in a straight line, thought to be up to 300 years old.

❾ Pemberton
🏠 1,400. 🚍 🏋 Brockman St (08) 9776 1133. 🔲 **pembertonvisitor.com.au**

At the heart of karri country, Pemberton has the look and feel of an old timber town. The Pemberton Tramway, originally built to bring the trees to mills in town, now takes visitors through the forests. The **Pemberton Pioneer Museum** is a fascinating tribute to the pioneers of the area.

☐ Pemberton Pioneer Museum
Brockman St. **Tel** (08) 9776 1133. **Open** daily. **Closed** Good Fri, 25 & 26 Dec. Donations. ♿

Environs
Southeast of the town lies Gloucester National Park, home to the famous giant karri, the Gloucester Tree. At 61 m (200 ft), it is one of the highest fire look-out trees in the world. Southwest of Pemberton is Warren National Park with its cascades, swimming holes and fishing spots. Attractive Beedelup National Park is northwest of Pemberton.

Sculpture of a woodsman at Manjimup Timber Park

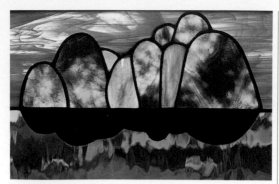
Example of local artist Andy Ducker's stained glass in Denmark

⑩ Denmark

🏠 5,000. 🚌 ℹ️ 73 Southcoast Hwy (08) 9848 2055. 🆆 denmark.com.au

Lying on Western Australia's southern coastline, Denmark was founded as a timber company settlement in 1895, but by the 1920s it was a fully fledged town. The town now attracts a host of visitors, many of whom come seeking the good surf of the Southern Ocean. There is also a large population of artists and artisans, and the atmosphere is distinctly bohemian.

Denmark's oldest building is St Leonard's Anglican Church, built by volunteers in 1899. Its Scandinavian-style pitched roof and interior detail are reminders of the Norwegian timber workers in the town at that time.

Nearby are the Old Butter Factory Galleries and the Wildwood Gallery, just two of Denmark's galleries where visitors can admire and buy paintings and craftwork from the region.

Berridge Park is often the scene for open-air, riverfront concerts.

Environs

A popular surfing spot is Ocean Beach; more sheltered locations for swimmers include Cosy Corner and Peaceful Bay. The coastline and Wilsons Inlet are popular with boaters and anglers.

⑪ Albany

🏠 31,000. ✈️ 🚌 🚌 ℹ️ Old Railway Station, Proudlove Parade (08) 9841 9290. 🆆 albanytourist.com.au

Albany was first visited by Captain Vancouver in 1791, but it was not until 1826 that the British settled here. Until Fremantle harbour was constructed (see pp314–15), Albany acted as the colony's main port and the harbour is still the commercial heart of the city. Whale migrations bring them close to the city's shores, which made it a base for whalers in the last century.

The **National Anzac Centre** in Albany was opened in 2014 to celebrate the 100-year anniversary of the Anzac landing at Gallipoli. Artifacts, interactive multimedia and images tell the stories of those who fought in the war. Albany includes many old buildings. **St John the Evangelist Anglican Church**, built in 1848, was the first Anglican church consecrated in Western Australia and is the epitome of an English country church.

Ship's wheel in Discovery Bay

The Residency Museum, originally part of the convict hiring depot built in the 1850s, details the history of the town and its surrounding area. The convict hiring depot itself and the Old Gaol now house the collection of the Albany Historical Society. In Duke Street is Patrick Taylor Cottage, built before 1836 of wattle and daub,

and the oldest building in Albany. On Albany's foreshore is a fully-fitted replica of the brig *Amity*, which brought the first settlers here from Sydney in 1826.

🏛️ **National Anzac Centre**
1347 Forts Rd. **Tel** (08) 9841 9369. **Open** 9am–5pm daily. **Closed** 25 Dec. 🈂️ ♿ 🆆 nationalanzaccentre.com.au

⛪ **St John the Evangelist Anglican Church**
York St. **Tel** (08) 9841 5015. **Open** daily. ♿ 🆆 anglicanchurchalbany.org.au

Environs

The world's largest whaling museum is **Discovery Bay**. Tour guides take visitors around the remains of the Cheyne Beach whaling station and explain the process of extracting whale oil. From July to October, breaching displays of migrating whales can sometimes be seen offshore.

🏛️ **Discovery Bay**
81 Whaling Station Rd, Frenchman Bay. **Tel** (08) 9844 4021. **Open** 9am–5pm daily. **Closed** 25 Dec. 🈂️ 🖥️ 📷 ♿

Replica of the brig *Amity*

⑫ Stirling Range National Park

🚌 Albany. ℹ️ Albany (08) 9841 9290. Park Ranger & information: **Tel** (08) 9827 9230.

Overlooking the rolling farm-land to the north of Albany is the Stirling Range National Park. The mountain peaks, noted for their colour changes from purple to red to blue, rise to more than 1,000 m (3,300 ft) above sea level and stretch for more than 65 km (40 miles). The highest peak is Bluff Knoll, which reaches 1,073 m (3,520 ft). Because of its sudden rise from the surrounding plains,

Stirling Range National Park as seen from Chester Pass Road

the park has an unpredictable climate which encourages a wide range of unique flora and fauna, including ten species of mountain bell. No less than 60 species of flowering plants are endemic to the park. They are best seen from September to November, when they are likely to be in flower. The park offers visitors a number of graded and signposted walks in the mountains (all are steep) and there are several picturesque barbecue and picnic areas.

⓭ York

🏔 3,200. 🚌 ℹ 81 Avon Terrace (08) 9641 1301. 🎷 York Jazz Festival (Nov). 🌐 yorkwa.org

The town of York was founded in 1831, in the new colony's drive to establish its self-sufficiency via agriculture. Now registered as a historic town, it retains many mid–19th-century buildings, the majority of which are on Avon Terrace, the main street. The cells of York's Old Gaol, in use from 1865 until 1981, provide a chilling insight into the treatment of 19th-century offenders. Other historic buildings include Settler's House (1860s), now a hotel and restaurant (see p490), and Castle Hotel, built in stages between 1850 and 1932, with its unusual timber verandas. Nearby stands the **York Motor Museum**, with

one of the largest collections of veteran cars and vehicles in Australia. These include the 1886 Benz (the world's first car), the very rare 1946 Holden Sedan Prototype and the extraordinary Bisiluro II Italcorsa racing car.

Also of note is the York Residency Museum, housed in the former home of York magistrate Walkinshaw Cowan, father-in-law to Edith Cowan, the state's first female Member of Parliament (see p60). This extensive collection of artifacts and photographs is justly said to be the finest small museum in the state.

York's 1892 flour mill has now been converted into the Jah-Roc Mill Gallery, which exhibits and sells furniture made from jarrah wood.

🏛 York Motor Museum
116 Avon Terrace. **Tel** (08) 9641 1288. **Open** daily. **Closed** Good Fri, 25 Dec. 🎫 ♿

⓮ Northam

🏔 7,000. 🚉 🚌 ℹ 2 Grey St (08) 9622 2100.
🌐 visitnorthamwa.com.au

At the heart of the Avon Valley and the state's wheat belt, Northam is Western Australia's largest inland town. Settled as an agricultural centre early in the colony's history, the town became a gateway to the gold fields of Kalgoorlie Boulder for prospectors in the 1890s (see p322). It retains a number of historic buildings, including the Old Girls' School (1877), now the town's Art Centre, and the beautiful St John's Church (1890). The town's jewel is Morby Cottage, built in 1836 and a fine example of the architectural style adopted by the early colonists.

Spanning the Avon River is the longest pedestrian suspension bridge in the country, offering views of the river.

The Northam Suspension Bridge stretching across the Avon River

The Gold Fields and Nullarbor Plain

Western Australia's southeast is a sparsely populated, flat region of extreme aridity and little fresh water. Vast stretches of its red, dusty landscape are inhabited by small Aboriginal communities and mining companies. The gold rush around Kalgoorlie in the 1890s ensured the state's success, but many places waned and ghost towns now litter the plains. Traversing the Nullarbor Plain, the Eyre Highway runs from Norseman to South Australia, 730 km (455 miles) away, and beyond. To the south is the windswept coast of the Great Australian Bight.

Locator Map

☐ The Gold Fields and Nullarbor Plain

☐ Perth and the Southwest pp302–21

Sights at a Glance

⑮ Wave Rock
⑯ Kalgoorlie-Boulder
⑰ Norseman
⑱ Esperance
⑲ Nullarbor Plain

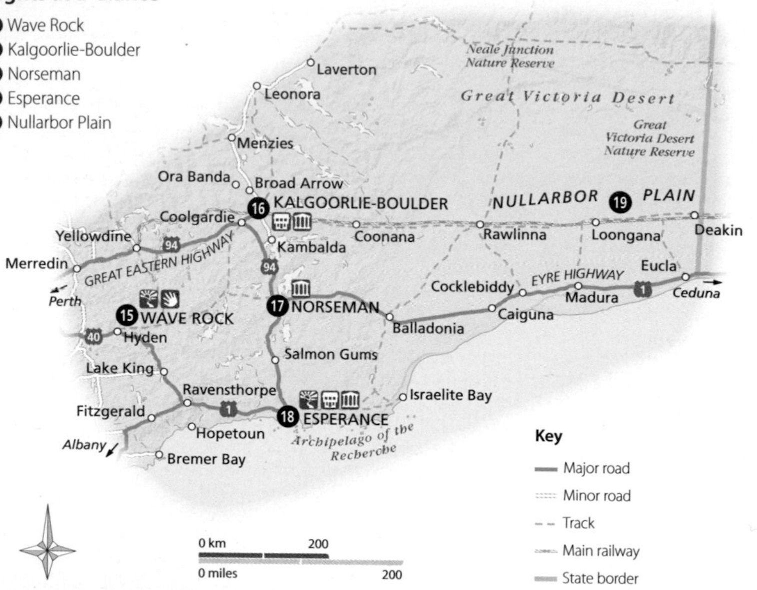

Neale Junction Nature Reserve
Laverton
Leonora
Great Victoria Desert
Menzies
Great Victoria Desert Nature Reserve
Ora Banda
Broad Arrow
KALGOORLIE-BOULDER ⑯
NULLARBOR ⑲ PLAIN
Coolgardie
Yellowdine
Coonana
Rawlinna
Loongana
Deakin
Merredin
Kambalda
GREAT EASTERN HIGHWAY
Perth
Cocklebiddy
EYRE HIGHWAY
Eucla
WAVE ROCK ⑮
⑰ NORSEMAN
Madura
Ceduna
Hyden
Caiguna
Lake King
Balladonia
Salmon Gums
Ravensthorpe
Israelite Bay
Fitzgerald
⑱ ESPERANCE
Albany
Hopetoun
Archipelago of the Recherche
Bremer Bay

Key

— Major road
⋯⋯ Minor road
– – Track
⋯⋯ Main railway
— State border

0 km   200
0 miles   200

Wave Rock, in the shape of a perfect wave about to break

⑮ Wave Rock

🏠 Hyden. Wave Rock Visitors' Centre: **Tel** (08) 9880 5022. **Open** 9am–5pm daily. 🅿️ ♿ 🛍️ by arrangement.

In Western Australia's wheat belt, 5 minutes' drive east of the small settlement of Hyden, stands one of the state's most surprising rock formations. A great granite wave has been created from a huge outcrop by thousands of years of chemical erosion, and reaction with rainwater has given it red and grey stripes. Other rock formations nearby include the Breakers and Hippo's Yawn. Facing Wave Rock, Lace Place is the unusual location for the largest collection of lacework in the southern hemisphere.

About 18 km (11 miles) northeast of Hyden lies Mulka's Cave, where several Aboriginal rock paintings can be seen.

⑯ Kalgoorlie-Boulder

🏔️ 35,000. ✈️ 🚉 🚌 🚐 ℹ️ 316 Hannan St (08) 9021 1966. 🌐 **kalgoorlietourism.com**

Kalgoorlie and the nearby town of Boulder, with which it was amalgamated in 1989, constantly remind visitors of their gold-fever past. Gold was first discovered here by Irishman Paddy Hannan in 1893, and, within weeks, the area was besieged with prospectors. Gold fields in other areas soon dwindled, but this field has yielded rich pickings to this day, bolstered by nickel finds in the 1960s. Today, gold is mined in the world's largest open-cut mine and more than 150,000 visitors a year come to see historic Kalgoorlie.

A variety of heritage trails and tours are available, and details are at the tourist office. The **WA Museum Kalgoorlie– Boulder** has an impressive collection of gold nuggets and jewellery, as well as natural history displays and a history of the gold rush. Visitors can ride in a glass lift for magnificent views of the gold fields, or step back in time at a 1930s miner's cottage.

The ornate buildings hastily erected during the boom years are best seen on Hannan Street, in the York and Exchange hotels, classic examples of gold rush architecture, and Kalgoorlie Town Hall.

Around Kalgoorlie-Boulder are ghost towns, such as Ora Banda and Broad Arrow, deserted by prospectors in search of new mines.

Bronze statue of Paddy Hannan

🏛 WA Museum Kalgoorlie–Boulder
17 Hannan St. **Tel** (08) 9021 8533. **Open** 10am–4:30pm daily (25 Apr. till 1pm). **Closed** 1 Jan, Good Fri, 25–26 Dec. Donation. ♿

Baxters Cliff, east of Esperance, on the shores of the Southern Ocean

⑰ Norseman

🏘 16,000. 🚌 ℹ 68 Roberts St (08) 9039 1071.

At the start of the Eyre Highway, Norseman is the gateway to the Nullarbor Plain and the eastern states beyond. Like Kalgoorlie-Boulder, the town stands on a gold field, discovered when a horse pawed the ground, uncovering gold deposits. In gratitude, miners named the town after the horse, and its statue was erected in the main street. Many visitors try fossicking, or learn more about the history of gold mining in the area at the **The Norseman Historical Museum** housed in the old School of Mines. Nearby, Beacon Hill offers a panoramic view of the town and surrounding countryside.

🏛 The Norseman Historical Museum
Battery Rd. **Tel** (08) 9039 0367. **Open** 10am–1pm Mon–Sat. **Closed** Good Fri, Easter Mon, 25 Apr, 25 Dec. 📷

⑱ Esperance

🏘 10,000. ✈ 🚌 ℹ Historic Museum Village, Dempster St (08) 9083 1555. 🌐 **visitesperance.com**

Although this area was visited by Europeans as far back as 1627, it was not until 1863 that British colonists established a settlement here. Fronting the Southern Ocean, this part of the coast is said to have some of the most beautiful beaches in Australia. Offshore is the Recherche Archipelago, with its 110 islands, one of which, Woody Island, is a wildlife sanctuary and can be visited.

In Esperance itself, Historic Museum Village includes the town's art gallery, and Esperance Municipal Museum contains local artifacts.

⑲ Nullarbor Plain

🚉 Kalgoorlie. 🚌 Norseman. ℹ Norseman (08) 9039 1071.

The Nullarbor Plain stretches across the southeast of the state and into South Australia (see p371). "Nullarbor" derives from the Latin meaning "no trees", and this is indeed a vast treeless plain. Only one road, the Eyre Highway, leads across the plain – one of the great Australian road journeys.

A few tiny settlements consisting only of roadhouses lie along the Eyre Hwy. Cocklebiddy, lying 438 km (270 miles) east of Norseman, has one of the world's longest caves and, at Eucla, 10 km (6 miles) from the state border, a telegraph station's remains can be seen. Nearby Eucla National Park has some fine views of the coastal cliffs.

The gold rush architecture of the York Hotel in Hannan Street, Kalgoorlie

NORTH OF PERTH AND THE KIMBERLEY

Western Australia covers one-third of Australia, and visitors to the area north of Perth start to get a feel for just how big the state really is. The region has many treasures: Ningaloo Reef and the Pinnacles rock formations; the Kimberley gorges; and a host of national parks, including the amazing Bungle Bungles.

The first people to set foot on the Australian land mass, the Aborigines, did so some 60,000 years ago in the north of Western Australia. This area is rich in Aboriginal petroglyphs, and some are thought to be more than 20,000 years old. The north of Western Australia was also the site of the first European landing in 1616 (*see p53*). In 1688, English explorer William Dampier charted the area around the Dampier Peninsula and, on a later voyage, discovered Shark Bay and the area around Broome.

In the 1840s, the Benedictines set up a mission in New Norcia and, by the 1860s, settlements had sprung up along the coast, most significantly at Cossack, where a pearling industry attracted immigrants from Japan, China and Indonesia. In the 1880s, pastoralists set up cattle and sheep stations in a swathe from Derby to Wyndham. Gold was struck in 1885 at Halls Creek, and the northern part of the state was finally on the map. In the 1960s, mining came to prominence again with the discovery of such minerals as iron ore, nickel and oil, particularly in the Pilbara region.

Today, the region is fast becoming a popular tourist destination, particularly with those visitors interested in ecotourism (*see p540*). Its climate varies from Mediterranean-style just north of Perth to the tropical wet and dry pattern of the far north. Wildlife includes endangered species such as the dugongs of Shark Bay. Even isolated spots, such as the Kimberley and the resorts of Coral Bay and Broome, are receiving more visitors every year.

The daily ritual of feeding wild dolphins at Monkey Mia beach

◀ Stromatolites in Hamelin Pool, part of Shark Bay Marine Park

Exploring North of Perth

The north of Western Australia is a vast area of diverse landscapes and stunning scenery. North of Perth lies Nambung National Park, home to the bizarre Pinnacles Desert. Kalbarri National Park is a region of scenic gorges on the Murchison River. The Indian Ocean coastline offers uninhabited islands, coral reefs, breathtaking cliffs and sandy beaches, none more spectacular than in Shark Bay World Heritage and Marine Park. At the tip of the region is the Pilbara, the state's mining area and home to the fascinating national parks of Karijini and Millstream-Chichester.

St Francis Xavier Cathedral, Geraldton

The Pinnacles in Nambung National Park at dusk

Sights at a Glance

1. New Norcia
2. Nambung National Park
3. Geraldton
4. Houtman Abrolhos
5. Kalbarri National Park
6. *Shark Bay World Heritage and Marine Park pp330–31*
7. Carnarvon
8. Ningaloo Reef Marine Park
9. Exmouth
10. Dampier
11. Roebourne
12. Cossack Historical Town
13. Point Samson
14. Karijini National Park

The Kimberley and the Deserts
See pp334–5

15. Broome
16. Derby
17. Halls Creek
18. Purnululu (Bungle Bungle) National Park
19. Wyndham

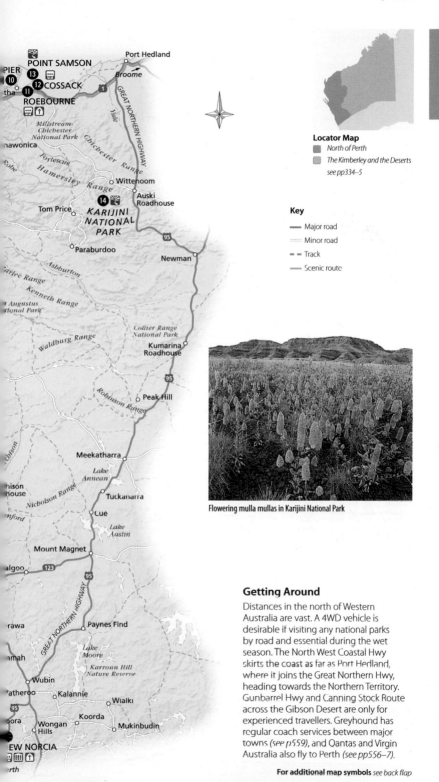

POINT SAMSON
COSSACK
PIER
ROEBOURNE

Port Hedland
Broome

Millstream-
Chichester
National Park

nawonica

Wittenoom

Auski
Roadhouse

Tom Price

KARIJINI
NATIONAL
PARK

Paraburdoo

Newman

Charlee Range

Kennedy Range

Augustus
tional Park

Waldburg Range

Collier Range
National Park

Kumarina
Roadhouse

Robinson Range

Peak Hill

Meekatharra

Lake
Annean

hison
house

Nicholson Range

Tuckanarra

Cue

Lake
Austin

Mount Magnet

algoo

rawa

Paynes Find

Lake
Moore

Karroun Hill
Nature Reserve

Wubin

atheroo

Kalannie

Wialki

oora

Wongan
Hills

Koorda

Mukinbudin

EW NORCIA

rth

Locator Map

North of Perth

The Kimberley and the Deserts
see pp334–5

Key

— Major road

⋯⋯ Minor road

– – Track

— Scenic route

Flowering mulla mullas in Karijini National Park

Getting Around

Distances in the north of Western
Australia are vast. A 4WD vehicle is
desirable if visiting any national parks
by road and essential during the wet
season. The North West Coastal Hwy
skirts the coast as far as Port Hedland,
where it joins the Great Northern Hwy,
heading towards the Northern Territory.
Gunbarrel Hwy and Canning Stock Route
across the Gibson Desert are only for
experienced travellers. Greyhound has
regular coach services between major
towns (see p559), and Qantas and Virgin
Australia also fly to Perth (see pp556–7).

For additional map symbols see back flap

❶ New Norcia

🗺 70. 🚌 ⓘ New Norcia Museum and Art Gallery, Great Northern Highway (08) 9654 8056.

One of Western Australia's most important heritage sites is New Norcia, 130 km (80 miles) northeast of Perth. A mission was established here by Spanish Benedictine monks in 1846, and it is still home to a small monastic community who own and run the historic buildings. There are daily tours of the monastery and visitors can stay at a guesthouse.

The town, known for its Spanish colonial architecture, has a pretty cathedral, built in 1860, at its centre. Also of note are two elegant colleges built early in the 20th century: St Gertrude's Residence for Girls and St Ildephonsus' Residence for Boys. The **New Norcia Museum and Art Gallery** has some fine art treasures and artifacts tracing the town's history.

🏛 **New Norcia Museum and Art Gallery**
Great Northern Hwy. **Tel** (08) 9654 8056. **Open** daily. **Closed** 25 & 26 Dec.
🚫 ♿ ground floor only.

Minarets adorning St Ildephonsus' Residence for Boys, New Norcia

❷ Nambung National Park

ⓘ Pinnacles Visitors' Centre, Cadiz St (inside Post Office) (08) 9652 7700.
Open 9am–5:30pm Mon–Sat (to 5pm Sun). 🌐 **visitpinnaclescountry. com.au**

This national park is composed of beach and sand dunes, with the dunes extending inland from the coast. It is best seen in spring when wildflowers bloom and the heat is not oppressive. The park is famous for the

The extraordinary Pinnacles, Nambung National Park

Pinnacles, a region of curious limestone pillars, the tallest of which stand 4 m (13 ft) high. Visitors can take a 3-km (2-mile) driving trail or a shorter walking trail which leads to lookouts with stunning views of the Pinnacles and the coastline. Most of the park animals are nocturnal, but some, including kangaroos, emus and many reptiles, may be seen in the cool of dawn or dusk.

❸ Geraldton

🗺 37,000. ✈ 🚌 🚌 ⓘ cnr Chapman Rd & Bayly St (08) 9956 6670. 🌐 **visitgeraldton.com.au**

The city of Geraldton lies on Champion Bay, about 425 km (265 miles) north of Perth. It is known as "Sun City" because of its average eight hours of sunshine per day. The pleasant climate brings hordes of sun-seekers from all over Australia who take advantage of fine swimming and surfing beaches. It can also be very windy at times, a further enticement to windsurfers, for whom Geraldton (particularly Mahomets Beach) is a world centre.

The history of European settlement in the area extends back to the mutiny of the Dutch ship *Batavia*, after it was wrecked on the nearby Houtman Abrolhos in 1629. Two crew members were marooned here as a punishment. In 1721, the Dutch ship *Zuytdorp* was wrecked, and it is thought that survivors settled here for a brief period. Champion Bay was first mapped in 1849 and a lead mine was established shortly afterwards. Geraldton grew up as a lead shipping point, and today is a port city with a large rock-lobster fleet.

The city retains many of its early historic buildings. The **WA Museum – Geraldton** includes the Shipwrecks Gallery, which contains relics of the area's early shipwrecks. The Old Railway Building has exhibits on local history, wildlife and geology. Geraldton has two cathedrals: the modern Cathedral of the Holy Cross, with its beautiful stained glass, and St Francis Xavier Cathedral, built from 1916 to 1938, in Byzantine style. Point Moore Lighthouse, with its distinctive red and white stripes, was shipped here from Britain and has been in continuous operation since 1878. The 1876 **Lighthouse Keeper's Cottage**, the town's first lighthouse, now houses Geraldton's Historical Society. Also in town, the **Geraldton Regional Art Gallery** is one of the best galleries in the state, exhibiting the work of local artists and pieces from private and public collections.

A number of lookouts such as Separation Point Lookout and Mount Tarcoola Lookout give panoramic views of the city and ocean.

Geraldton's Point Moore Lighthouse

For hotels and restaurants in this area see pp490–91 and pp521–2

🏛 WA Museum – Geraldton
1 Museum Place, Batavia Coast Marina. **Tel** (08) 9921 5080. **Open** 9:30am–4pm daily. **Closed** 1 Jan, Anzac Day (opens noon), Good Fri, 25 & 26 Dec. Donation. ♿

🏠 Lighthouse Keeper's Cottage
355 Chapman Rd. **Tel** (08) 9923 1837. **Open** 10am–3: 30pm Tue, Thu, Fri. **Closed** Good Fri, 25 Dec. 📷

🏛 Geraldton Regional Art Gallery
24 Chapman Rd. **Tel** (08) 9964 7170. **Open** 10am–4pm Mon–Sat, 1–4pm public hols. **Closed** Sun, Good Fri, 25 & 26 Dec & 1 Jan. ♿

❹ Houtman Abrolhos

🚌 Geraldton. ⛴ from Geraldton. 🛈 Geraldton (08) 9956 6670.

About 60 km (37 miles) off Geraldton lie more than 100 coral islands called the Houtman Abrolhos – the world's southernmost coral island formation. While it is not possible to stay on the islands, tours enable visitors to fly over them or to dive among the coral.

❺ Kalbarri National Park

🚌 Kalbarri. 🛈 Kalbarri (08) 9937 1140. **Open** sunrise–sunset daily. 📷 🌐 kalbarri.org.au

The magnificent landscape of Kalbarri National Park includes stunning coastal scenery and beautiful inland gorges lining the Murchison River. The park has a number of coastal and river walking trails which lead to breathtaking views and fascinating rock formations. The trails vary in length, from brief two-hour strolls to four-day hikes. Highlights of the park include Hawks Head, a picnic area with views of the gorge; Nature's Window, where a rock formation frames a view of the river; and Ross Graham Lookout, where visitors can bathe in the river pools. By the ocean, Pot Alley provides awesome views of the rugged coastal cliffs and Rainbow Valley is made up of layers of multi-coloured rocks.

The access town for the park, Kalbarri, is situated on the coast and provides good tourist facilities. The park's roads are accessible to most vehicles, but are unsuitable for caravans or trailers. The best time to visit is from July to October, when the weather is dry and the temperatures are not prohibitive. In summer, they can soar to 40°C (104°F).

❻ Shark Bay World Heritage and Marine Park

See pp330–31.

A bridge across the Gascoyne River in Carnarvon

❼ Carnarvon

🏕 7,000. ✈ 🚌 🚌 🛈 21 Robinson St, (08) 9941 1146. 🌐 carnarvon.org.au

The town of Carnarvon, standing at the mouth of the Gascoyne River, acts as the commercial and administrative centre for the surrounding Gascoyne region, the gateway to Western Australia's north. Tropical fruit plantations line the river here, some offering tours and selling produce.

In Carnarvon itself, One Mile Jetty on Babbage Island is a popular place for fishing, and Jubilee Hall, built in 1887, houses a fine arts and crafts centre. Carnarvon is also home to a busy prawn and scallop processing industry.

Environs
About 70 km (43 miles) north of Carnarvon lie the Blowholes, a spectacular coastal rock formation where air and spray is forced through holes in the rocks in violent spurts up to 20 m (66 ft) high.

Stunning gorge views from Hawks Head Lookout, Kalbarri National Park

❻ Shark Bay World Heritage and Marine Park

Shark Bay Marine Park was designated a World Heritage Area in 1991 *(see pp30–31)*. The park is home to many endangered species of plants and animals, and various unusual natural processes have, over the millennia, given rise to some astounding natural features and spectacular coastal scenery. Because this is a World Heritage Area, visitors are asked to abide by conservation rules, particularly when fishing. The only way to travel around the park is by car, and large areas are only accessible by 4WD.

François Peron National Park
At the tip of Peron Peninsula, this national park, now accessible by 4WD, was a vast sheep station until 1990.

Bernier Island

Dorre Island

Dirk Hartog Island

④

Denham Sound

François Peron National Park

Useless Loop

Useless Loop Road

Peron Homestead
Originally the centre of the Peron sheep station, the homestead offers an insight into pastoral life. The station also has two artesian bores that carry hot water (44°C, 111°F) to tubs at the surface in which visitors may bathe.

KEY

① **The Zuytdorp Cliffs** are named after the Dutch ship *Zuytdorp*, wrecked in these waters in 1721.

② **Steep Point** faces the Indian Ocean and is the westernmost point of mainland Australia. From here it is possible to see the Zuytdorp Cliffs.

③ **Denham** was originally settled as a pearling community, but is now mainly a fishing and tourist centre.

④ **Cape Inscription** is the place where Dutchman Dirk Hartog became the first known European to set foot in Australia in 1616 *(see p53)*.

⑤ **Northwest Coastal Highway**

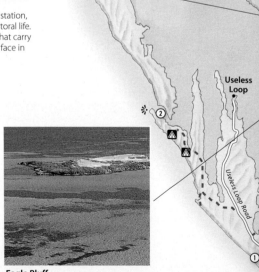

Eagle Bluff
The top of this bluff offers fine panoramic views across Freycinet Reach, with a chance of seeing the eagles that nest on the offshore islands and marine creatures in the clear ocean waters.

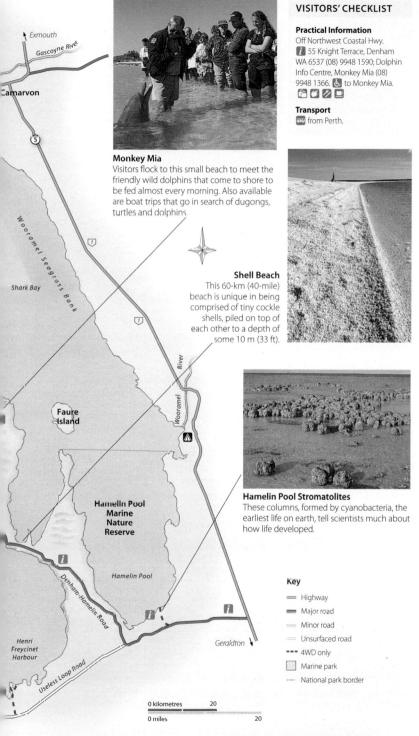

VISITORS' CHECKLIST

Practical Information
Off Northwest Coastal Hwy.
🛈 55 Knight Terrace, Denham
WA 6537 (08) 9948 1590; Dolphin
Info Centre, Monkey Mia (08)
9948 1366. 🛆 to Monkey Mia.
🏨 📷 🖊 🖵

Transport
🚌 from Perth.

Monkey Mia
Visitors flock to this small beach to meet the
friendly wild dolphins that come to shore to
be fed almost every morning. Also available
are boat trips that go in search of dugongs,
turtles and dolphins.

Shell Beach
This 60-km (40-mile)
beach is unique in being
comprised of tiny cockle
shells, piled on top of
each other to a depth of
some 10 m (33 ft).

Hamelin Pool Stromatolites
These columns, formed by cyanobacteria, the
earliest life on earth, tell scientists much about
how life developed.

Key

━━ Highway

▬▬ Major road

┈┈ Minor road

┈┈ Unsurfaced road

╍╍ 4WD only

▢ Marine park

— National park border

Exmouth

Gascoyne River

Carnarvon

Wooramel Seagrass Bank

Shark Bay

River

Wooramel

Faure Island

Hamelin Pool Marine Nature Reserve

Hamelin Pool

Henri Freycinet Harbour

Denham-Hamelin Road

Useless Loop Road

Geraldton

0 kilometres   20

0 miles   20

❽ Ningaloo Reef Marine Park

🚌 Exmouth. ℹ️ Milyering Discovery Centre, Yardie Creek Rd, Cape Range National Park (08) 9949 2808. **Open** daily. **Closed** 25 Dec.

This marine park runs for 260 km (162 miles) along the west coast of Exmouth Peninsula and around the tip into Exmouth Gulf. The Ningaloo Reef is the largest fringing barrier reef in the state and offers many of the attractions of the east coast's Great Barrier Reef *(see pp216–21)*. In many places, it lies very close to the shore, and its turquoise waters are popular with snorkellers. Apart from numerous types of coral and brightly coloured fish, the marine park also protects a number of species. Several beaches at the northern end of the park are used by sea turtles as mating and breeding areas. Further offshore, it is possible to see the gentle whale shark from late March to May. Capable of growing to up to 18 m (60 ft), this is the largest fish in the world.

The best areas for snorkelling are Turquoise Bay or the still waters of Coral Bay. A number of companies offer organized scuba diving outings. Visitors can camp on the park's coastline at several sites mana-ged by the Department of Environment and Conservation (DEC). Fishing is another popular pursuit here, but catches are very strictly controlled.

Yardie Creek Gorge in Cape Range National Park, near Exmouth

❾ Exmouth

🏙️ 3,100. ✈️ 🚌 ℹ️ Murat Rd (08) 9949 1176. 🌐 **visitningaloo.com.au**

Situated on the eastern side of the Exmouth Peninsula, this small town was originally built in 1967 to service the local airforce base. A military presence is still very much in evidence, but today the town is more important as a tourist destination, used as a base for exploring the Ningaloo Reef Marine Park and the Cape Range National Park. Giant turtles and whale sharks can frequently be seen from the nearby coastline.

Slightly outside of town, at Vlaming Head, lies the wreck of the SS *Mildura*, a cattle transporter which sank in 1907 and is still visible from the shore. Nearby stands the Vlaming

Lighthouse, on a high bluff offering striking, panoramic views across the entire peninsula.

Environs

Cape Range National Park contains a low mountain range with spectacular gorges and rocky outcrops. This area was originally under water and it is possible to discern the fossils of ancient coral in the limestone. Local wildlife includes kangaroos, emus and large lizards. There are two main wilderness walks, but visitors should not attempt these in summer as temperatures can reach as high as 50°C (120°F).

Yardie Creek is on the western side of the park, only 1 km (0.5 miles) from the ocean. A short walk along gorge cliffs leads to the spectacular canyon, where you may catch sight of rock wallabies on the far canyon wall. A cruise through the gorges is also available.

❿ Dampier

🏙️ 1,400. ✈️ 🚌 ℹ️ Dampier Seafarers Centre, The Esplanade, Dampier WA 6713 (08) 9183 1424.

Dampier stands on King Bay on the Burrup Peninsula, facing the 40 or so islands of the Dampier Archipelago. It was established and still acts as a service centre and port for mining areas inland; natural gas from the nearby Northwest Shelf Project is processed here for domestic and export markets. The town also has the largest desalination plant in Australia. This can be viewed from the Dampier Solar Evaporated Salt Mine Lookout. Dampier is also a popular base for offshore and beach anglers. Every August, game-fishing enthusiasts converge on the town for the Dampier Classic and Game Fishing Classic.

The Burrup Peninsula is one of the most renowned ancient Aboriginal art sites in Australia, created by the Yapurrara Aborigines.

Environs

The Dampier Archipelago, within 45 km (28 miles) of the town, offers a range of activities

White sands of Turquoise Bay in Ningaloo Reef Marine Park

Honeymoon Cove, one of the most popular beaches in Point Samson

from game fishing to whale-watching. Sport fishing here is particularly good, with reef and game species such as tuna, trevally and queenfish on offer.

Almost half of the islands are nature reserves and are home to rare species, including the Pilbara olive python and the king brown snake. Access to the islands is by boat only.

Simple façade of the Holy Trinity Church in Roebourne

⓫ Roebourne

🏠 2,600. 🚏 ℹ Queen St (08) 9182 1060.

About 14 km (9 miles) inland, Roebourne, established in 1866, is the oldest town in the Pilbara. The town retains several late 19th-century stone buildings, including the Old Gaol which now houses the tourist office and a craft gallery and the Holy Trinity Church (1894). Roebourne also marks the start of the 52 km (32-mile) Emma Withnell Heritage Trail, which takes a scenic route from here to Cossack and Point Samson. Trail guides are available at the tourist office.

Environs
Some 150 km (93 miles) inland lies the 200,000-ha (500,000-acre) Millstream-Chichester National Park with its lush freshwater pools.

⓬ Cossack Historical Town

🚌 ℹ Queen St, Roebourne (08) 9182 1060. 🆆 roebourne.org.au

In 1863, the town of Tien Tsin Harbour was established and quickly became the home of a burgeoning pearling industry that attracted people from as far away as Japan and China. The settlement was renamed Cossack in 1872 after a visit by Governor Weld aboard HMS *Cossack*. However, the town's moment soon passed. The pearling industry moved on to Broome (see p334) and by 1910 Cossack's harbour had silted up. In the late 1970s, restoration work of this ghost town began and today, under the management of the Shire of Roebourne, it has become a curiosity that continues to fascinate many visitors.

Old courthouse in Cossack Historical Town

⓭ Point Samson

🏠 200. ℹ Queen St, Roebourne (08) 9182 1060.

This small settlement was founded in 1910 to take on the port duties formerly performed by Cossack. Today, there is a modest fishing industry and two harbours. The town's best beaches are found at Honeymoon Cove and Samson Reef, where visitors can snorkel among the coral or search for rock oysters at low tide.

⓮ Karijini National Park

ℹ Central Rd, Tom Price (08) 9188 5488. **Open** daily (weather permitting). 🆆 tomprice.org.au

Set in the Hamersley Range, in the heart of the Pilbara region, Karijini National Park covers some 600,000 ha (1,500,000 acres). It is the second-largest national park in the state after Purnululu National Park (see p335).

The park has three types of landscape: rolling hills and ridges covered in eucalypt forests; arid, low-lying shrubland; and, in the north, spectacular gorges. The best times to visit the park are in winter, when the days are temperate, and in spring, when carpets of wildflowers are in spectacular bloom.

The Kimberley and the Deserts

Australia's last frontier, the Kimberley is a vast, remote upland region of dry, red landscape. Deep rivers cut through mountain ranges, and parts of the coastline have the highest tidal range in the southern hemisphere. Seasonal climatic extremes add to the area's sense of isolation as the harsh heat of the dry season and the torrential rains of the wet hamper access to the hostile terrain. April to September is the best time to visit, offering views of the country's best natural sights such as the Wolfe Creek Meteorite Crater and the Bungle Bungles. To the south lie the huge, inhospitable Great Sandy and Gibson deserts.

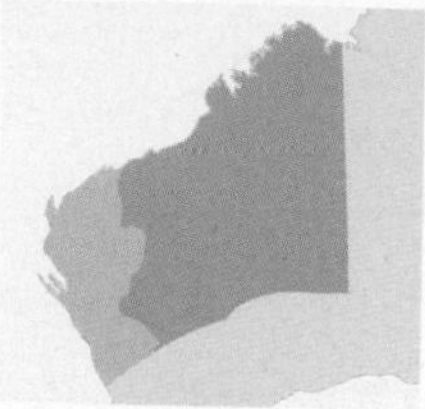

LOCATOR MAP

⬛ *The Kimberley and the Deserts*
⬜ *North of Perth pp326–33*

⓯ Broome

🏔 14,500. ✈ 🚌 🚐
ℹ 1 Hamersley St (08) 9195 2200.
ⓦ visitbroome.com.au

Broome, first settled by Europeans in the 1860s, soon became Western Australia's most profitable pearling region. Pearl divers from Asia swelled the town in the 1880s and helped give it the multicultural flavour that remains today. The tourist industry has now superseded pearling, but the town's past can still be seen in several original stores, as well as the Chinese and Japanese cemeteries that contain the graves of hundreds of pearl divers.

Just outside town is the popular Cable Beach. Nearby, the **Malcolm Douglas Crocodile Park** offers daily tours to see these animals (feeding tour is at 3pm).

🏞 **Malcolm Douglas Crocodile Park**
Broome Hwy. **Tel** (08) 9193 6580.
Open 2–5pm daily. **Closed** 25 Dec. 🖼

Camel trekking along the famous Cable Beach near Broome

Sights at a Glance

⓯ Broome
⓰ Derby
⓱ Halls Creek
⓲ Purnululu (Bungle Bungle)
   National Park
⓳ Wyndham

Key

— Major road
═ Minor road
-- Track
▬ State border

For additional map symbols *see back flap*

A freshwater crocodile basking in the sun, Windjana Gorge, near Derby

⑯ Derby

🏠 5,000. ✈ 🚌 𝒊 30 Loch St (08) 9191 1426, 1800 621 426.

Derby is the gateway to a region of stunning gorges. Points of interest in the town include the 1920s Wharfingers House, Old Derby Gaol, and the Botanical Gardens.

South of town is the 1,000-year old Prison Boab (baobab) tree, 14 m (45 ft) in circumference. At the end of the 19th century, it was used to house prisoners overnight before their final journey to Derby Gaol.

Environs
Derby stands at the western end of the Gibb River Road, which leads towards the three national parks collectively known as the **Devonian Reef National Parks**. The parks of Windjana Gorge, Tunnel Creek and Geikie Gorge contain spectacular gorge scenery.

🌳 **Devonian Reef National Parks** 🚌 to Derby. 𝒊 Derby (08) 9191 1426. **Open** Apr–Nov: daily. **Closed** Dec–Mar.

⑰ Halls Creek

🏠 1,400. 🚏 𝒊 Great Northern Hwy (08) 9168 6262.

Halls Creek was the site of Western Australia's first gold rush in 1885, and today is a centre for mineral mining. Close to the original town site is a vertical wall of quartz rock, known as China Wall. About 130 km (80 miles) to the south

is the world's second-largest meteorite crater, in **Wolfe Creek Crater National Park**.

🌳 **Wolfe Creek Crater National Park** 🚌 Halls Creek. 𝒊 Halls Creek (08) 9168 6262. **Open** Apr–Sep: daily. **Closed** wet weather (roads impassable).

⑱ Purnululu (Bungle Bungle) National Park

🚌 Halls Creek. 𝒊 Purnululu National Park (08) 9168 7300. **Open** Apr–Nov: daily. 🐾 📷

Covering some 320,000 ha (790,000 acres) of the most isolated landscape in Western Australia, Purnululu National Park was declared in 1987. It is home to the local Kija and Jaru

The intriguing domes of the Bungle Bungles, Purnululu National Park

people, who co-operate with national park authorities to develop cultural tourism.

The most famous part of the park is the Bungle Bungle Range, consisting of unique beehive-shaped domes of rock encased in a skin of silica and cyanobacterium.

⑲ Wyndham

🏠 900. ✈ 🚌 𝒊 Kimberley Motors, 6 Great Northern Hwy (08) 9161 1281.

The port of Wyndham lies at the northern tip of the Great Northern Highway, on Cambridge Gulf. The town was established in 1888, partly to service the Halls Creek gold rush and partly as a centre for the local pastoral industry. It also provided supplies, which were carried by Afghan camel-trains, for cattle stations in the northern Kimberley. The town's Afghan cemetery is a reminder of those traders who were essential to the survival of pioneer home-steads in the interior.

The part of the town known as Old Wyndham Port was the original town site and still con-tains a number of 19th-century buildings, including the old post office, the old courthouse and Anthon's Landing, where the first jetty was erected. The Port Museum displays a vivid photo-graphic history of the port.

The area around Wyndham has a large crocodile population. Freshwater and saltwater crocodiles can be seen occasionally in the wild at Blood Drain Crocodile Lookout and Crocodile Hole. To complete the picture, a 4-m (13-ft) high concrete saltwater crocodile greets visitors at the entrance to the town. Saltwater crocodiles have a taste for people, so exercise caution.

About 25 km (15 miles) from Wyndham, Aboriginal petro-glyphs can be seen at the picnic spot of Moochalabra Dam. Also worth mentioning is the Five Rivers Lookout located at the highest point from which to view the landscape. It provides a spectacular view of the five rivers which enter the Cambridge Gulf and surrounding mangroves.

SOUTH AUSTRALIA

South Australia at a Glance

South Australia contains a wide range of landscapes. A striking coastline of sandy beaches and steep cliffs gives way to lush valleys, mountains and rolling plains of wheat and barley. Further inland, the terrain changes starkly as the climate becomes hotter and drier. The South Australian Outback encompasses huge areas and includes the Flinders Ranges and Coober Pedy, the opal-mining town with "dugout" homes. Most of the population lives in the capital, Adelaide, and the wine-making regions of Clare Valley and the Barossa.

Locator Map

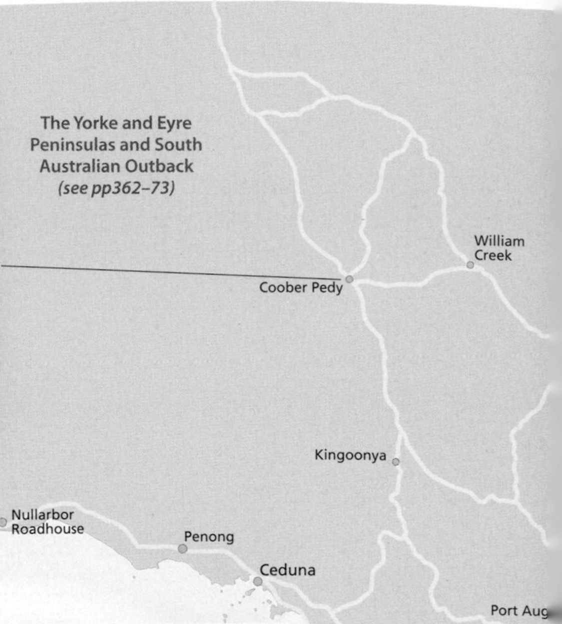

The Yorke and Eyre
Peninsulas and South
Australian Outback
(see pp362–73)

William
Creek

Coober Pedy

Kingoonya

Nullarbor
Roadhouse

Penong

Ceduna

Port Aug

Kyancutta

Whya

Port Lincoln

Coober Pedy's golf course is one of the few features above ground in this strange Outback mining town. Many of the town's houses are built underground to escape the area's harsh, dusty climate *(see p372)*.

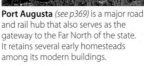

Port Augusta *(see p369)* is a major road and rail hub that also serves as the gateway to the Far North of the state. It retains several early homesteads among its modern buildings.

Kangaroo Island *(see p358)* is an unspoilt haven for abundant native wildlife. At Kirkpatrick Point in the southwest lie the Remarkable Rocks, sculpted by the wind, rain and sea.

0 km		100
0 miles		100

◀ Coastline around Pearson Island, in the Eyre Peninsula

Quorn *(see p373)* was an important railway town at the end of the 19th century and has many reminders of its pioneerng days. Today it marks the start of the Pichi Richi Railway, a restored track running vintage trains and locomotives for tourists.

The Flinders Ranges *(see p373)* stretch from north of St Vincent's Gulf far into the Outback. They include some of South Australia's most rugged scenery and offer fine bushwalking.

Moomba

rree

The Barossa wine region encompasses the Barossa Valley and Eden Valley. Both are lush areas of rolling hills and home to dozens of famous wineries dating from the 19th century *(see pp360–61)*.

Pirie

Adelaide *(see pp348–63)* is an elegant state capital with many well-preserved colonial buildings. Its cosmopolitan atmosphere is enhanced by a lively restaurant, arts and entertainment scene.

delaide

Adelaide and
the Southeast
(see pp344–61)

Mount Gambier

Mount Gambier *(see p358)* lies on the slopes of an extinct volcano of the same name. One of the volcano's crater lakes, Blue Lake, shows its intense hue in the summer months.

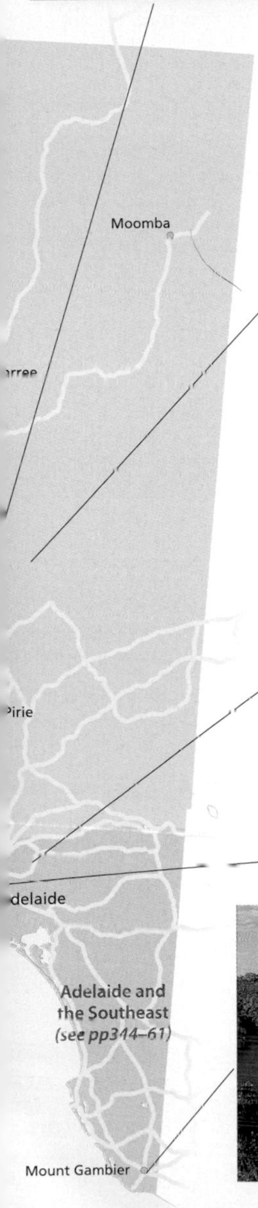

Birds of South Australia

The vast, varied habitats of South Australia are home to some 380 bird species. Gulls, sea eagles and penguins live along the coast, while waders, ducks and cormorants are found in the internal wetlands. Parrots are common in Adelaide's parkland. The mallee scrub, which once covered much of the state, is home to the mallee fowl and an array of honeyeaters. The Flinders Ranges and the South Australian Outback are the domain of birds of prey such as the peregrine falcon and the wedge-tailed eagle. Although much land has been cleared for farming, many habitats are protected in the national parks.

Fairy penguins are the smallest penguins found in Australia. The only species to breed on the mainland, they feed on fish and squid skilfully caught underwater.

The Flinders Ranges and Outback Habitat

The rugged mountains and deep gorges of the Flinders Ranges support a wide variety of bird species. Most spectacular are the birds of prey. Wedge-tailed eagles' nests can be found in large gum trees or on rock ledges, and the eagles are commonly seen feeding on dead animals in the arid Outback regions.

Mallee Scrub Habitat

Much of this low-level scrubland has been cleared for agriculture. Remaining areas such as Billiat National Park near Loxton provide an important habitat for several elusive species. Golden whistlers, red and brush wattlebirds and white-eared honeyeaters can be seen here by patient bird-watchers. The best seasons to visit are late winter, spring and early summer.

Wedge-tailed eagles, with their huge wingspan of up to 2.3 m (7 ft 6 in), typically perch on dead trees and telephone poles.

Mallee fowls, a wary species, stand 60 cm (24 in) tall. They spend most of the year building mounds, made of soil, leaves and twigs in which to lay their eggs.

Peregrine falcons do not build nests, but lay their eggs on bare ledges or in tree hollows. Magnificent in flight, they descend on their prey at great speed with wings half or fully closed.

Southern scrub robins hop along the ground to forage for food around mallee trees and shrubs. The female lays a single green-grey egg, the colour providing camouflage within the scrub.

The Emu

Emus are huge flightless birds unique to Australia. Second only to the ostrich in height, they stand 1.5–1.9 m (5–6 ft 3 in) tall. They have long powerful legs and can run at speeds of up to 50 km/h (30 mph) over short distances. The females have a distinctive voice like a thudding drum. They lay their eggs on the ground on a thin layer of grass and leaves. The male incubates them for seven weeks, then broods and accompanies the young for up to 18 months. Common all over Australia, emus are found mainly in open, pastoral areas. Moving alone or in flocks, they are highly mobile and have a large home range.

Alert gaze of the Australian emu

Soft, grey-black plumage of an emu

Wetland Habitat

Wetlands such as Coorong National Park (see p355) are vital feeding and breeding grounds for a wide range of water birds. They provide essential refuge in times of drought for many endangered birds. Migratory birds, such as sharp-tailed sandpipers from Siberia, use these areas to feed and rest before continuing on their annual journeys.

Brolgas stand up to 1.3 m (4 ft 3 in) tall, with a wingspan of up to 2.3 m (7 ft 6 in). They are renowned for their impressive dancing displays, leaping, bowing and flapping.

Freckled ducks are similar to primitive waterfowl, with swan-like characteristics. Dark, with no obvious markings, they are hard to spot. This is one of the world's rarest ducks.

Woodland Habitat

Habitats in woodland areas such as the Belair National Park near Adelaide support many species such as honeyeaters, rosellas and kookaburras. There is usually an abundance of food in such places and good opportunities to nest and roost. Despite increased human settlement in these areas, the birdlife is still rich. Dawn and dusk are the best times for seeing birds.

Adelaide rosellas are commonly found in the Mount Lofty Ranges and the parklands of Adelaide. Their plumage is in brilliant shades of red, orange and blue.

Laughing kookaburras are the world's largest kingfishers. They are renowned for their loud, manic laughing call, often begun by one bird and quickly taken up by others.

Wines of South Australia

South Australia produces almost half of Australia's wines, including many of its finest. From its numerous vineyards comes a dazzling diversity of wines – several are made from some of the oldest vines in the world. The state has a long history of wine-making and is home to some very famous producers, such as Hardys, Penfolds, Jacob's Creek and Banrock Station. Virtually all wineries welcome tourists for tastings.

Sevenhill Cellars is in the heart of the Clare Valley, one of South Australia's prime wine-producing regions.

Knappstein Winery, owned by Lion Nathan, is located in the Enterprise Brewery in Clare Valley and produces Riesling that is European in style.

Bridgewater Mill winery is renowned in the area for its excellent restaurant. Daily tastings of its own labels and Petaluma wines are offered at the cellar door.

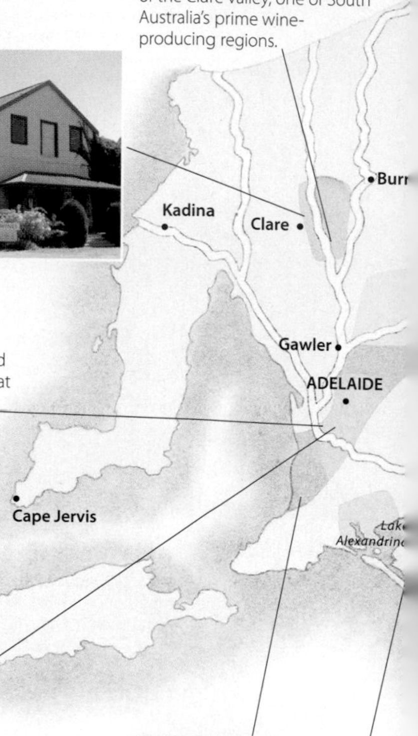

Wine Regions

South Australia has eight designated wine zones and within these zones are many well-known regions. These include the Barossa (see pp360–61), which has been producing wine for 150 years; the Clare Valley, which is noted for its Riesling, Cabernet Sauvignon and Shiraz; and Coonawarra, which is Australia's best red wine region, due to its soil. McLaren Vale, the Murray Valley, the Adelaide Plains, the Riverland, the Limestone Coast, and the Adelaide Hills are the other major districts.

Kadina •   Clare •   • Burr

Gawler •

ADELAIDE

• Cape Jervis

Lake Alexandrine

Cabernet Sauvignon grapes are very successful in the state, with a ripe, fruity flavour.

The Adelaide Hills are known for their excellent Pinot Noir, Chardonnay and Riesling grapes.

Key

- Clare Valley
- Barossa Valley
- Eden Valley
- Adelaide Hills
- McLaren Vale
- Riverland
- Langhorne Creek
- Padthaway
- Wrattonbully
- Coonawarra

Wolf Blass' Barossa Black Label has a rich, oaky flavour, and is just one of this world-renowned vintner's individual wines. Blass has earned more than 2,000 international medals for his wine.

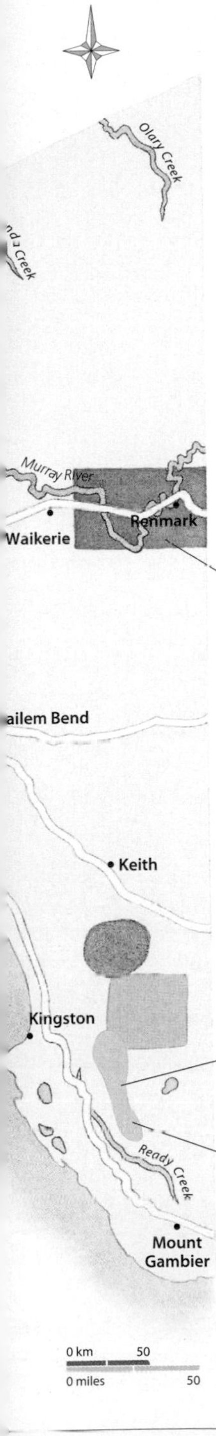

Key Facts

Location and Climate
The climate of Australia's central state ranges from Mediterranean-style in the Murray Valley to the cool Adelaide Hills and districts in the southeast. Vintage begins in high summer, when grapes are often picked and crushed at night to preserve maximum flavour.

Grape Varieties
The diverse climate ensures that a wide range of grape varieties is planted. These include the whites of Riesling, Semillon, Sauvignon Blanc, Chardonnay; and the reds of Shiraz, Grenache, Pinot Noir, Cabernet Sauvignon, Merlot.

Good Producers

Penfolds, Bethany, Grant Burge, St Hallett, Henschke, Seppelt, Charles Melton, Turkey Flat, Mountadam, Hardys, Orlando, Wolf Blass, Yalumba, Rockford, Willows, Petaluma, Grosset, Wendoree, Pauletts, Pikes, Wynns, Bowen, Chapel Hill, d'Arenberg, Peter Lehmann, Noons, Bridgewater Mill, Hollicks.

Olary Creek

nd a Creek

Murray River

Waikerie

Renmark

ailem Bend

Keith

Kingston

Ready Creek

Mount Gambier

0 km   50

0 miles   50

Barrel maturation at the Berri Renmano winery in the Murray Valley is one of the traditional techniques still used in the production of top-quality table wines.

Wynns Winery at Coonawarra is known for fine Cabernet Sauvignon and other reds. The winery itself is equally distinctive – an image of its triple-gable architecture appears on the wine labels.

Yalumba 'Menzies' Vineyard, founded in 1849, is one of the oldest in the Coonawarra region. The grapes are grown here, but the wine is made at the winery in the Barossa Valley (see p360–61). The climate in the Coonawarra area is similar to that of Bordeaux in France.

ADELAIDE AND THE SOUTHEAST

The Southeast is a region rich with pine forests, wineries and a spectacular coastline. The state capital, Adelaide, is a vibrant city, whose surrounding hills abound with vineyards from the Barossa to McLaren Vale. To the east, the great Murray River meanders from the Victoria border down to the Southern Ocean. Just off the Fleurieu Peninsula lies Kangaroo Island, a haven for wildlife.

Home to Aborigines for more than 50,000 years, this region was settled by Europeans in 1836 when Governor John Hindmarsh proclaimed the area a British colony. William Light, the Surveyor General, chose the site of the city of Adelaide.

The settlement was based on a theory of free colonization funded solely by land sales, and no convicts were transported here. Elegant Adelaide was carefully planned by Colonel Light: its ordered grid pattern, centred on pretty squares and gardens, is surrounded by parkland. Wealth from agriculture and mining paid for many of Adelaide's fine Victorian buildings. In the mid-20th century, the city established a significant manufacturing industry, in particular

of motor vehicles and household appliances. Adelaide still has a focus on high technology.

South Australia has always had a tradition of tolerance. Many of the first settlers were non-conformists from Great Britain seeking a more open society. Other early migrants included Lutherans escaping persecution in Germany. They settled in Hahndorf and the Barossa, where they established a wine industry.

With high rainfall and irrigated by the Murray River, the region is the most fertile in the state. The coastline includes the Fleurieu Peninsula and the beautiful Coorong National Park. Offshore, Kangaroo Island has stunning scenery and bountiful native wildlife.

Port and sherry casks at a winery in the Barossa

◀ Evening falls on the vineyards of the Barossa

Exploring Adelaide and the Southeast

Adelaide and the Southeast area encompass the most bountiful and productive regions of South Australia. Adelaide, the state's capital city and the most obvious base for exploring the region, lies on a flat plain between the Mount Lofty Ranges and the popular white sandy beaches of Gulf St Vincent, to the east of Cape Jervis. The city itself is green and elegant, with many historic sites to explore. To the northeast, beyond the Adelaide Hills, are quaint 19th-century villages and the many wineries of the Barossa. To the east and south lies Australia's largest river, the Murray River, and the rolling hills of the Fleurieu Peninsula. Further to the southeast the beauty of the coastal Coorong National Park and the Southern Ocean coastline contrasts with the flat, agricultural area inland. Offshore lies the natural splendour of Kangaroo Island, with its abundance of native wildlife and striking rock formations.

Sights at a Glance

1. Adelaide pp348–53
2. Belair National Park
3. Gorge Wildlife Park
4. Hahndorf
5. Strathalbyn
6. Mount Lofty
7. Birdwood
8. Kangaroo Island
9. Mount Gambier
10. Penola
11. Naracoorte Caves National Park
12. Murray River

Tour

13. The Barossa

St Peter's Anglican Cathedral, seen across Adelaide's parkland

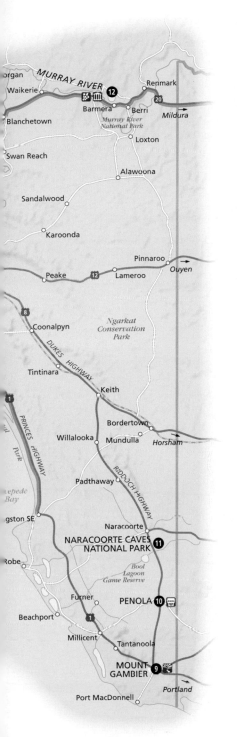

Murray River winding between Swan Reach and Walker Flat

Getting Around

The inner city of Adelaide is best explored on foot; it is compact, well laid out and flat. There is a public transport system of mostly buses, and some trains, throughout the metropolitan area, although services are often restricted at weekends. However, for those with a car, the city's roads are good and the traffic generally light. Outside Adelaide, public transport is very limited, although coach tours are available to most areas. A car provides the most efficient means of exploring the region, with a network of high-standard roads and highways. In addition, a domestic air service operates between Adelaide and Mount Gambier. Kangaroo Island is serviced by air from Adelaide and also by ferry from Cape Jervis. The predominantly flat landscape also makes this a popular area for cyclists and walkers.

Key

- ▬ Highway
- ▬ Major road
- ▭▭ Minor road
- ▬ Scenic route
- ▬▬ Main railway
- ▬▬ Minor railway
- ▬ State border

0 kilometres — 50

0 miles — 50

For additional map symbols see back flap

❶ Street-by-Street: Adelaide

Adelaide's cultural centre lies between the grand, tree-lined North Terrace and the River Torrens. Along North Terrace is a succession of imposing 19th-century public buildings, including the state library, museum and art gallery and two university campuses. To the west, on the bank of the river, is the Festival Centre. This multipurpose complex of theatres, including an outdoor amphitheatre, is home to the renowned annual Adelaide Festival *(see p45)*. To the east, also by the river, lie the botanic and zoological gardens and the National Wine Centre of Australia.

River Torrens
Visitors can hire paddleboats to travel along this gentle river and see Adelaide from water level.

Festival Centre
Completed in 1977, this arts complex enjoys a picturesque riverside setting and is a popular place for a picnic.

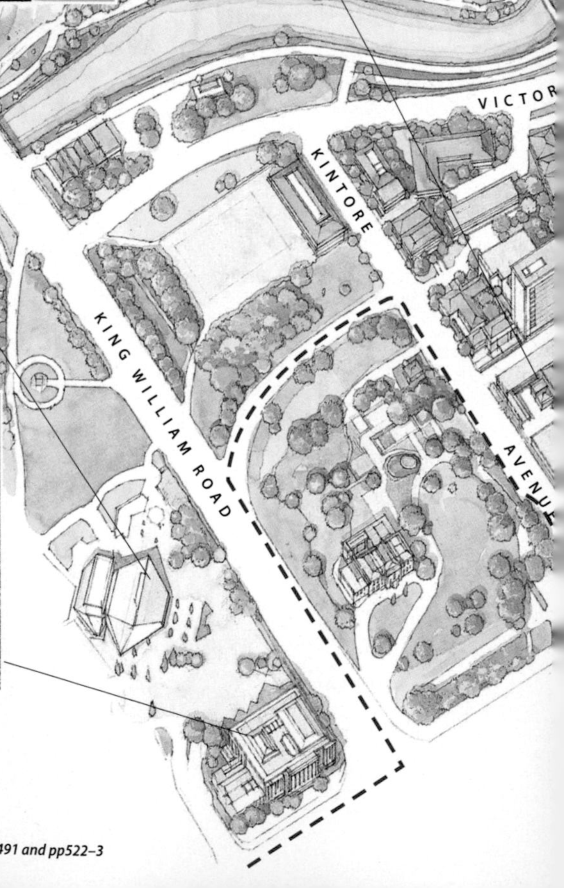

The Migration Museum tells the stories of the thousands of people from more than 100 nations who left everything behind to start a new life in South Australia.

VICTOR

KINTORE

KING WILLIAM ROAD

AVENUE

Parliament House
Ten marble Corinthian columns grace the façade of Parliament House, which was completed in 1939, more than 50 years after construction first began.

For hotels and restaurants in this area see p491 and pp522–3

★ **Adelaide Botanic Garden**
Begun in 1855, these peaceful gardens cover an area of 20 ha (50 acres). They include artificial lakes and the beautiful Bicentennial Conservatory, in which a tropical rainforest environment has been re-created.

VISITORS' CHECKLIST

Practical Information
🏛 1.2 million.
ℹ️ 108 North Terrace
1300 655 276. 🎭 Adelaide
Fringe; Adelaide Festival;
WOMADelaide (all in Feb/Mar).

Transport
✈️ West Beach, 10 km
(6 miles) W of the city.
🚉 North Terrace (suburban);
Richmond Rd, Keswick
(interstate). 🚌 Central Bus
Station, Franklin St.

Art Gallery of South Australia
Contemporary works, such as Christopher Healey's *Drinking Fountains*, feature here alongside period painting and sculpture.

Key
— Suggested route

```
0 metres        100
0 yards         100
```

The State Library of South Australia houses an extensive collection of reference material and various exhibitions, such as *South Australiana*, a permanent exhibition that explores South Australia's history and culture.

★ **South Australian Museum**
Chiefly a natural history museum, the South Australian Museum has an excellent reputation for its fine Aboriginal collection, including this painting on bark, *Assembling the Totem*, by a Melville Island artist *(see p278)*.

Exploring Adelaide

Adelaide, a city of great charm with an unhurried way of life, is easily explored on foot. Well planned on a grid pattern, it is bordered by wide terraces and parkland. Within the city are a number of garden squares and gracious stone buildings. However, while Adelaide values its past, it is very much a modern city. The balmy climate and excellent local food and wine have given rise to an abundance of streetside restaurants and cafés. With its acclaimed Adelaide Festival (see p45), the city prides itself on being an important bastion of traditional arts and culture.

Detail of the ornate front parapet of Edmund Wright House

🏛 Victoria Square
Flinders & Angas sts.

Victoria Square lies at the geographic heart of the city. At the southern end of the square stands a fountain designed by sculptor John Dowie in 1968. Its theme is the three rivers from which Adelaide draws its water: the Torrens, the Murray and the Onkaparinga. Government buildings were erected around much of the square during colonial days and many of these buildings still stand as reminders of a bygone age.

On the north side of Victoria Square stands the General Post Office, an impressive building with an ornate main hall and a clock tower. Opened in 1872, it was hailed by English novelist Anthony Trollope as the "grandest edifice in the town".

On the corner of Wakefield Street, to the east of Victoria Square, stands St Francis Xavier Catholic Cathedral. The original cathedral, dedicated in 1858, was a simpler building and plans for expansion were hampered by the lack of rich Catholics in the state. The cathedral was

only completed in 1996, when the spire was finally added.

To the south of the square is Adelaide's legal centre and the Magistrates Court. The Supreme Court, built in the 1860s, has a Palladian façade.

🏛 Adelaide Town Hall
128 King William St. **Tel** (08) 8203 7590. **Open** Mon–Fri. **Closed** public hols. 🚻 W adelaidetownhall.com.au

When Adelaide Town Hall, designed in Italianate style by Edmund Wright, was built in 1866, it became the most significant structure on King William Street. It was not long before it took over as the city's premier venue for concerts and civic receptions and is still used as such today. Notable features include its grand staircase and decorative ceiling.

🏛 Edmund Wright House
59 King William St. 🚻

Edmund Wright House, originally built for the Bank of South Australia in 1878, was set to be demolished in 1971. However, a general outcry led to its public purchase and

restoration. The building was renamed after its main architect, Edmund Wright. The skill and workmanship displayed in the finely proportioned and detailed façade is also evident in the beautiful interior. Today the building is the Migrant Resource Centre with limited access to the public.

Further along King William Street, at the corner of North Terrace, stands one of Adelaide's finest statues, the South African War Memorial. It shows a "spirited horse and his stalwart rider" and stands in memory of those who lost their lives in the Boer War.

Apples on display in Adelaide Central Market

🏛 Central Market
Gouger St. **Tel** (08) 8203 7494. **Open** Tue–Sat (limited stalls on Wed). **Closed** public hols. 🚻

Just west of Victoria Square, between Gouger and Grote streets, Adelaide Central Market has provided a profusion of tastes and aromas in the city for more than 125 years. The changing ethnic pattern of Adelaide society is reflected in the diversity of produce available today. Asian shops now sit beside older European-style butchers and delicatessens, and part of the area has become Adelaide's own little Chinatown. Around the market are dozens of restaurants and cafés.

Victoria Square in the centre of Adelaide

For hotels and restaurants in this area see p491 and pp522–3

🏛 Tandanya

253 Grenfell St. **Tel** (08) 8224 3200.
Open 10am–5pm daily. **Closed** Good
Fri, 25 Dec, 1 Jan. 🅿 📷 ♿
W tandanya.com.au

Tandanya, the Kaurna Aboriginal people's name for the Adelaide area (it means "place of the red kangaroo"), is an excellent cultural institute celebrating the Aboriginal and Torres Strait Islander art and cultures. It was established in 1989 and is the first Aboriginal-owned and run arts centre in Australia. The institute features indigenous art galleries, educational workshops and performance areas. It is also possible for visitors to meet indigenous people. A great gift shop sells authentic artifacts, arts and crafts.

🏛 Migration Museum

82 Kintore Ave. **Tel** (08) 8207 7580.
Open 10am–5pm Mon–Fri, 1–5pm
Sat & Sun. **Closed** Good Fri, 25 Dec.
♿ **W** history.sa.gov.au

The Migration Museum is located behind the State Library in what was once Adelaide's Destitute Asylum. It reflects the cultural diversity of South Australian society by telling the stories of people from many parts of the world who came here to start a new life. Exhibits, including re-creations of early settlers' houses, explain the immigrants' reasons for leaving their homeland and their hopes for a new life. The Memorial Wall acknowledges that many people were forced to leave their homelands.

🏛 South Australian Museum

North Terrace. **Tel** (08) 8207 7500.
Open 10am–5pm daily.
Closed Good Fri, 25 Dec. ♿
W samusuem.sa.gov.au

This museum, whose entrance is framed by huge whale skeletons, has a number of interesting collections including an Egyptian room and natural history exhibits. Its most important collection is its internationally acclaimed collection of Aboriginal artifacts which boasts more than 37,000 individual items and 50,000 photographs, as well as many sound and video recordings.

A street performer in Rundle Mall, Adelaide's main shopping precinct

🚻 Rundle Mall

Rundle Mall. **Tel** (08) 8203 7200.
Open daily. **Closed** Good Fri, 25 Dec,
public hols. **W** rundlemall.com

Adelaide's main shopping area is centred on Rundle Mall, with its mixture of small shops, boutiques and department stores. Several arcades run off the mall, including Adelaide Arcade. Built in the 1880s, it has Italianate elevations at both ends and a central dome. The interior was modernized in the 1960s, but has since been fully restored to its former glory.

Adelaide City Centre

1. Central Market
2. Victoria Square
3. Adelaide Town Hall
4. Edmund Wright House
5. Migration Museum
6. South Australian Museum
7. Rundle Mall
8. Ayers House
   (see pp352–3)
9. Tandanya

0 metres 500
0 yards 500

For keys to symbols *see back flap*

Ayers House

Ayers House is one of the best examples of colonial Regency architecture in Australia. It was the home of Sir Henry Ayers, a former Premier of South Australia and an influential businessman, from 1855 until his death in 1897. The original house was quite simple but was expanded over the years with the growing status and wealth of its owner. The final form of this elegant mansion is due largely to the noted colonial architect Sir George Strickland Kingston. The restored house is now run by the National Trust and also incorporates a function centre. The oldest section is open to the public and houses a fine collection of Victorian furniture, furnishings, memorabilia and art.

Front of the house viewed from North Terrace

★ **Bedroom**
The main bedroom has been carefully restored to its late-Victorian style. Its authentic furnishings reflect the prosperity brought by South Australia's rich mining discoveries in the 1870s.

KEY

① **The Library**, furnished with a long dining table, can be hired for functions.

② **Slate roof**

③ **The Conservatory** is based around the original stables and coachhouse. Now a function centre, the whole area has been flooded with light by the addition of a glass roof.

④ **Local bluestone** was used in constructing the house, as with many 19th-century Adelaide houses. The north façade faces onto North Terrace, one of the city's main streets (see pp348–9).

⑤ **Veranda's original chequered tile flooring**

⑥ **The family drawing room** along with the adjacent family dining room, had test strips removed from its walls and ceiling to uncover some stunning original decoration. These rooms have now been fully restored.

Ballroom
This intricately decorated cornice dates from the 1870s. It is likely that it was painted by Charles Gow, an employee of the Scottish firm of Lyon and Cottier, who is believed to have undertaken extensive work at the house.

★ **State Dining Room**
Sir Henry loved to entertain, and lavish dinners were often held here. It boasts a hand-painted ceiling, grained woodwork and the original gas-lamp chandeliers.

VISITORS' CHECKLIST

Practical Information
288 North Terrace, Adelaide.
Tel (08) 8223 1234.
Open 10am–4pm Tue–Fri;
1–4pm Sat, Sun & public hols.
Closed Mon, Good Fri, 25 Dec.
🖼 📷 ♿ ♿ ground floor only.

Transport
🚌 99c.

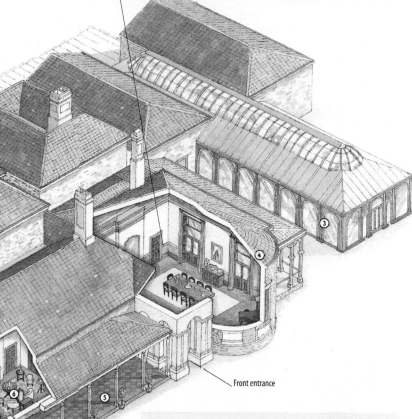

Front entrance

The story of Sir Henry Ayers

Sir Henry Ayers (1821–97) was born in Hampshire, England, the son of a dock worker. He married in 1840 and, a month later, emigrated with his bride to South Australia. After working briefly as a clerk, Ayers made his fortune in the state's new copper mines. Entering politics in 1857, he was appointed South Australia's Premier seven times between 1863 and 1873, and was President of the Legislative Council, 1881–93. Among many causes, he supported exploration of the interior (Ayers Rock, now Uluru, was named after him), but is chiefly remembered for his prominent role in the development of South Australia.

Statesman and businessman,
Sir Henry Ayers

Fleurieu Peninsula and Limestone Coast

The coastline south of Adelaide is rich and varied with beautiful beaches, magnificent coastal scenery and abundant birdlife. The southern coastline of the Fleurieu Peninsula is largely exposed to the mighty Southern Ocean. Here there are surfing beaches, long expanses of sand, sheltered bays and harbours and stark, weathered cliffs. The western side of the peninsula is more sheltered. There are very few commercial developments on the southeast's coastline and it is easy to find quiet, secluded beaches for swimming, surfing, fishing or walking. Just off South Australia's mainland, Kangaroo Island boasts both pristine swimming beaches and ruggedly beautiful windswept cliffs.

② ★ Cape Jervis
Visitors to the tiny hamlet of Cape Jervis can catch the ferry to Kangaroo Island across Backstairs Passage. The cape has good boating and fishing and is a hang-gliding centre.

Normanville

Fleurieu Peninsula

McLaren Vale

①

②

④

⑤

③

Flinders Chase National Park

Kangaroo Island

③ ★ Kingscote, Kangaroo Island
Kingscote, the island's largest town, has a small sandy beach with a tidal pool. There is rich birdlife in swampland south of the town.

① Port Noarlunga
Port Noarlunga boasts a fantastic beach and a protected reef with marine ecosystems that can be explored by snorkellers and scuba divers on a fully marked 800-m (2,600-ft) underwater trail.

④ Waitpinga Beach
Waitpinga Beach, on the southern coast of the Fleurieu Peninsula and part of Newland Head Conservation Park, is a spectacular surfing beach with waves rolling in off the Southern Ocean. Strong, unpredictable currents make the beach unsafe for swimming and suitable for experienced surfers only. The long stretch of clean white sand is a favourite for beach walkers.

⑤ Victor Harbor
During the early 19th century, Victor Harbor gained notoriety as a whaling station. Today, the southern right whales frolicking offshore from June to October are a popular tourist attraction.

⑥ Port Elliot
Port Elliot, together with nearby Victor Harbor, has long been a favourite place to escape the summer heat of Adelaide. Established in 1854 as a port for the Murray River trade, the town has a safe swimming beach and a fine cliff-top walk.

⑦ Hindmarsh Island
The quiet escapist destination of Hindmarsh Island can be reached by bridge from the town of Goolwa. On the island there are several good vantage points from which visitors can see the mouth of the Murray River.

Seal Bay, a windswept beach on the south coast, is a major Kangaroo Island tourist attraction, with visitors taking guided tours to see the endangered sea lions.

For keys to symbols see back flap

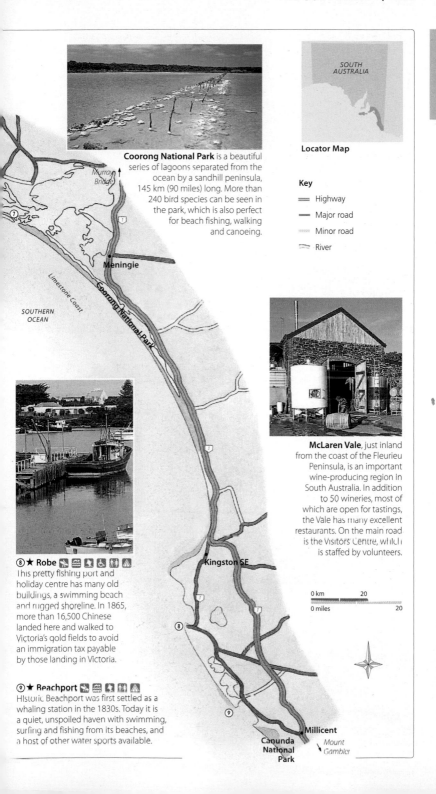

Coorong National Park is a beautiful series of lagoons separated from the ocean by a sandhill peninsula, 145 km (90 miles) long. More than 240 bird species can be seen in the park, which is also perfect for beach fishing, walking and canoeing.

Locator Map

Key

━━━ Highway

━━━ Major road

┄┄┄ Minor road

∿∿ River

McLaren Vale, just inland from the coast of the Fleurieu Peninsula, is an important wine-producing region in South Australia. In addition to 50 wineries, most of which are open for tastings, the Vale has many excellent restaurants. On the main road is the Visitors Centre, which is staffed by volunteers.

⑧ ★ **Robe**
This pretty fishing port and holiday centre has many old buildings, a swimming beach and rugged shoreline. In 1865, more than 16,500 Chinese landed here and walked to Victoria's gold fields to avoid an immigration tax payable by those landing in Victoria.

⑨ ★ **Beachport**
Historic Beachport was first settled as a whaling station in the 1830s. Today it is a quiet, unspoiled haven with swimming, surfing and fishing from its beaches, and a host of other water sports available.

Old Government House in Belair National Park

❷ Belair National Park

Tel (08) 8278 5477. 🚆 from Adelaide. **Open** 8am–sunset daily. **Closed** 25 Dec. 🅿 for cars only. ♿ limited. 🌐 **environment.sa.gov.au**

Established in 1891, Belair is the eighth-oldest national park in the world. Only 9 km (5 miles) from Adelaide, it is one of the most popular parks in South Australia. Tennis courts and pavilions are available for hire and there are picnic facilities throughout the park. Visitors can meander through the tall eucalypt forests and cool valleys, and see kangaroos, emus, echidnas and other native wildlife.

In spring, many native plants bloom. The park is closed occasionally in summer on days of extreme fire danger. Within the park lies **Old Government House**. Built in 1859 as the governor's summer residence, it offers a glimpse of the lifestyle enjoyed by the colonial gentry.

🏛 **Old Government House**
Belair National Park. **Tel** (08) 8278 5477. **Open** 1–4pm Sun & public hols. **Closed** Good Fri, 25 Dec. 🅿

❸ Gorge Wildlife Park

Redden Drive, Cudlee Creek. **Tel** (08) 8389 2206. 🚌 Adelaide. **Open** 9am–5pm daily. **Closed** 25 Dec. 🅿 🏕 🌐 **gorgewildlifepark.com.au**

Situated on 5.5 ha (14 acres) of land, Gorge Wildlife Park is home to an abundance of native Australian species, including kangaroos, dingos, wombats, wallabies and fruit bats. There are also birds – from ostriches to fairy wrens – and a colony of free-flying rainbow lorikeets. For those who prefer their animals crawling or swimming, there is a reptile house. The most popular residents of the park, however, are the koalas. Cuddling sessions with these friendly marsupials are held three times daily (11:30am, 1:30pm and 3:30pm, subject to weather conditions). The park also offers a kiosk, a souvenir shop, picnic areas and free gas BBQs.

A koala at Gorge Widlife Park

❹ Hahndorf

🏘 1,800. 🚌 from Adelaide. 🛈 68 Mount Barker Rd (08) 8388 1185. 🌐 **hahndorfsa.org.au**

Hahndorf is the oldest surviving German settlement in Australia. The first settlers arrived in 1838 aboard the *Zebra* under the command of Captain Dirk Hahn. Escaping religious persecution in their homeland, they settled in the Adelaide Hills and established Hahndorf (Hahn's Village), a German-style town.

The tree-lined main street has many examples of classic German architecture, such as houses with *fachwerk* timber framing filled in with wattle and daub, or brick. Visitors can take a stroll around the town and enjoy its historic atmosphere.

Wallabies roaming through Gorge Wildlife Park

For hotels and restaurants in this area see pp491–2 and pp522–5

Nineteenth century mill in the historic town of Hahndorf

Just outside Hahndorf is **The Cedars**, the former home of South Australia's best-known landscape artist, the late Sir Hans Heysen *(see p38)*. Both his home and his studio are open to the public. South of the town is Nixon's Mill, a stone mill built in 1842.

⚏ The Cedars
Heysen Rd. **Tel** (08) 8388 7277. **Open** 10am–4:30pm Tue–Sun & public hols. **Closed** Good Fri, 25 & 26 Dec. 🎨 🚻
w hansheysen.com.au

❺ Strathalbyn

🏠 6,000. 🚌 **ℹ** Railway Station, South Terrace 1300 007 842.

The designated heritage town of Strathalbyn was originally settled by Scottish immigrants in 1839. Links with its Scottish ancestry can still be seen today in much of the town's architecture, which is reminiscent of small highland towns in Scotland.

Situated on the banks of the Angas River, Strathalbyn is dominated by St Andrew's Church with its sturdy tower. A number of original buildings have been preserved. The police station, built in 1858, and the 1865 courthouse together house the National Trust Museum. The prominent two-storey London House, built as a general store in 1867, has, like a number of buildings in or near the High Street, found a new use as an antiques store. As in many country towns in Australia, the hotels and banks are also architectural reminders of the past. About 16 km (10 miles) southeast of Strathalbyn, on the banks of the Bremer River, is Langhorne Creek,

renowned as one of the earliest wine-growing regions in Australia; wine has been produced here since the 1850s.

St Andrew's Church, Strathalbyn

❻ Mount Lofty

🚌 Mount Lofty Summit Rd. **ℹ** Mount Lofty Summit Information Centre (08) 8370 1054. 🅿 🚻 The Summit **Open** 9am–5pm Mon–Fri, 8:30am–5pm Sat & Sun. 🖥 **w** mtloftysummit.com

The hills of the Mount Lofty Ranges form the backdrop to Adelaide. The highest point, Mount Lofty, reaches 727 m (2,385 ft) and offers a fine view

of the city from the modern lookout at the summit, where there is also an interpretive centre. The hills are dotted with grand summer houses to which Adelaide citizens retreat during the summer heat.

Just below the summit is the **Cleland Wildlife Park** where visitors can stroll among the kangaroos and emus, have a photograph taken with a koala or walk through the aviary to observe native birds at close quarters.

About 1.5 km (1 mile) south of here, Mount Lofty Botanic Gardens feature temperate-climate plants such as rhodo-dendrons and magnolias.

⚏ Cleland Wildlife Park
365 Mount Lofty Summit Rd, Crafters. **Tel** (08) 8339 2444. **Open** 9:30am–5pm daily. **Closed** 25 Dec. 🎨 🚻 🅿
🖥 **w** environment.sa.gov.au

❼ Birdwood

🏠 1,300. **ℹ** FJ Café, Shannon St (08) 8568 5577.

Nestled in the Adelaide Hills is the quiet little town of Birdwood. In the 1850s, wheat was milled in the town and the old wheat mill now houses Birdwood's most famous asset: the country's largest collection of vintage, veteran and classic motor cars, trucks and motorbikes. The **National Motor Museum** has more than 300 on display and is considered to be one of the best collections of its kind in the world.

⛬ National Motor Museum
Shannon St. **Tel** (08) 8568 4000. **Open** 10am–5pm daily. **Closed** 25 Dec. 🎨 🚻 **w** motor.history.sa.gov.au

Hand-feeding kangaroos at Cleland Wildlife Park, Mount Lofty

❽ Kangaroo Island

🚢 Sea Link ferry connection from Cape Jervis. ➡️ ℹ️ Kangaroo Island Gateway Visitor Information Centre, Howard Drive, Penneshaw (08) 8553 1185. ♿ 📧 🌐 **tourkangarooisland.com.au**

Kangaroo Island, Australia's third-largest island, is 155 km (96 miles) long and 55 km (34 miles) wide. Located 16 km (10 miles) off the Fleurieu Peninsula, the island was the site of South Australia's first official free settlement, established at Reeves Point in 1836. The settlement was short-lived, and within just four years had been virtually abandoned. The island was then settled by degrees during the remainder of the 19th century as communications improved with the new mainland settlements.

There is no public transport on the island and visitors must travel on a tour or by car (available for hire at Kingscote Airport). It is also possible to bike or hike. Though the roads to the main sights are good, many roads are unsealed and extra care should

Remarkable Rocks at Kirkpatrick Point, Kangaroo Island

be taken. Sparsely populated and geographically isolated, the island has few introduced predators and is a haven for a wide variety of animals and birds, many protected in its 19 conservation and national parks.

At Kingscote and Penneshaw fairy penguins can often be seen in the evenings, and the south coast windswept beach of Seal Bay is home to a large colony of Australian sea lions.

In Flinders Chase National Park, kangaroos will sometimes approach visitors, but feeding them is discouraged.

The interior is dry, but does support tracts of mallee scrub, and eucalypts. The coastline, however, is varied. The north coast has sheltered beaches ideal for swimming. The south coast, battered by the Southern Ocean, has more than 40 shipwrecks. At Kirkpatrick Point to the southwest stands a group of large rocks. Aptly named Remarkable Rocks, they have been eroded into weird formations by the winds and sea.

❾ Mount Gambier

👥 26,000. ➡️ 🚌 🚌 ℹ️ The Lady Nelson Visitor Centre, 35 Jubilee Hwy East (08) 8724 9750. 🌐 **mount gambiertourism.com.au**

Mount Gambier, a major regional city midway between Adelaide and Melbourne, is located on the slopes of an extinct volcano. Established in 1854, it is now surrounded by farming country and large pine plantations. The volcano has four crater lakes which are attractive recreation spots, with walking trails, picnic facilities and a wildlife park. The Blue Lake, up to 85 m (280 ft) deep, is a major draw between November and March when its water mysteriously turns an intense blue. From April to October, it remains a dull grey.

There are also a number of caves to explore within the city. Engelbrecht Cave is popular with cave divers.

Strange and vividly coloured water of Mount Gambier's Blue Lake

For hotels and restaurants in this area see pp491–2 and pp522–5

Sharam's Cottage, the first house built in Penola

❿ Penola

🗺 1,500. 🚌 ℹ Penola Coonawarra Visitor Information Centre, 27 Arthur St (08) 8737 2855. 🆆 **penola.org**

One of the oldest towns in the Southeast, Penola is the commercial centre of the Coonawarra wine region (see pp342–3). The region's first winery was built in 1893. There are now some 20 wineries, most of which are open for sales and tastings.

Penola itself is a quiet town which takes great pride in its history. A heritage walk takes visitors past most of its early buildings, including the restored Sharam's Cottage, which was built in 1850 as the first dwelling in Penola.

Environs
Situated 40 km (25 miles) north of Penola, Bool Lagoon Game Reserve (designated a wetland of international significance by UNESCO), is an important refuge for an assortment of native wildlife including more than 150 species of birds. The park provides an opportunity to observe at close quarters many of these local and migratory birds (see p341).

⓫ Naracoorte Caves National Park

Tel (08) 8762 2340. 🚌 from Adelaide. **Open** 9am–5pm daily (last tour 3:30pm). **Closed** 25 Dec. 🅿 📷 🖼 🆆 naracoortecaves.sa.gov.au

Located 19 km (12 miles) south of Naracoorte is the Naracoorte Caves National Park. Within this 600-ha (1,500-acre) park, there are 26 known caves (only four are open to the public), most notably Victoria Cave, which has been placed on the World Heritage

List as a result of the fossil deposits discovered here in 1969 (see pp30–31). Guided tours of this and two other caves are available. From November to February thousands of bent-wing bats come to breed in the Bat Cave. They can be seen leaving the cave en masse at dusk to feed in summer. Entrance to this cave is forbidden, but visitors can view the inside via infra-red cameras in the park.

Ancient stalactites inside one of the Naracoorte caves

⓬ Murray River

🚌 from Adelaide. ℹ Renmark (08) 8586 6704. 🆆 **murrayriver.com.au**

Australia's largest river is a vital source of water in this, the driest state in Australia. As well as supplying water for Adelaide it supports a vigorous local agricultural industry that produces 40 per cent of all Australian

wine (see pp342–3). It is also a popular destination for houseboating, water-skiing and fishing.

The town of Renmark, close to the Victoria border, lies at the heart of the Murray River irrigation area and is home to the Riverlands' first winery. At the town's wharf is the restored paddlesteamer Industry, now a floating museum and a reminder of days gone by.

Just south of Renmark, Berri is the area's commercial centre and site of the largest combined distillery and winery in the southern hemisphere. The Murray River meanders through Berri and on to the small town of Loxton before winding up towards the citrus centre of Waikerie. Surrounded by more than 5,000 ha (12,000 acres) of orchards, Waikerie is a favourite gliding centre and has hosted world gliding championships.

Another 40 km (25 miles) downstream, the Murray River reaches the town of Morgan, its northernmost point in South Australia, before it turns south towards the ocean. The **Morgan Museum**, located in the old landseer warehouse, aims to recapture the river-trading days, telling the story of what was once the second-busiest port in the state. Local crafts are for sale in the original railway ticket office.

🏛 **Morgan Museum**
Lanosa Rd, near Morgan Railway Station. **Tel** (08) 8540 2136 or 8540 2641, **Open** 10am–4pm daily. **Closed** 25 Dec. 📷

An old paddlesteamer cruising along the Murray River

⑬ Barossa Tour

The Barossa, which is comprised of the Barossa and Eden valleys, is one of Australia's most famous wine regions and has an international reputation. First settled in 1842 by German Lutheran immigrants, villages were established at Bethany, Langmeil (now Tanunda), Lyndoch and Light's Pass. Signs of German traditions can be seen in the 19th-century buildings, churches and in the region's food, music and festivals. The Barossa Vintage Festival takes place every April.

⑤ Seppeltsfield
Between Tanunda and Greenock, this winery was established in 1851 by the pioneering German family Seppelt. A historic complex of splendid stone buildings, it is reached via an avenue of palm trees planted in the 1920s.

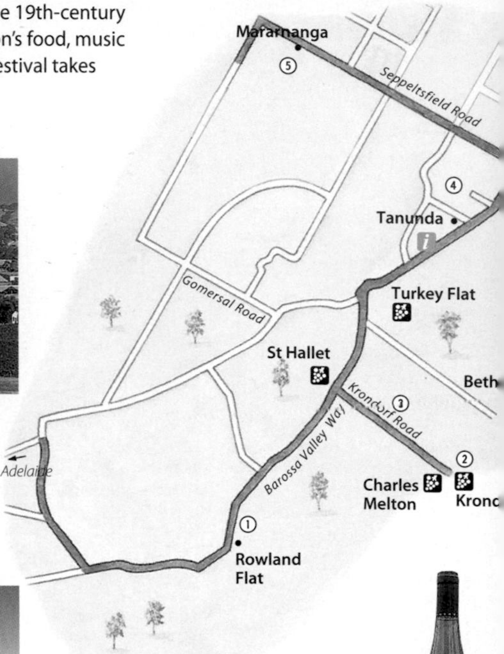

① Jacob's Creek Visitor Centre
Established in 1847 by Bavarian-born Johann Gramp, Jacob's Creek winery is famous for its vast range of wines and its restaurant, and has won numerous awards for tourism.

② Grant Burge
Grant and Helen Burge founded this historic winery in 1988. Visitors have the option of stopping at Krondorf to enjoy the pretty views, sip on excellent wine and have a light meal. The Meshach Shiraz is one of the region's finest wines.

④ Peter Lehmann
A significant producer of quality Barossa wines, this winery was established by the late Peter Lehmann, a well-known character in the valley. The winery was awarded International Winemaker of the Year in 2003 & 2006.

③ Rockford
This winery uses 100-year-old equipment to make its famous traditional hand-crafted wines. In the summer months visitors can see the old equipment working. The winery itself is also more than a century old.

Key

▬▬	Tour route
▬▬	Other road
🏵	Vineyard

0 km   4

0 miles   4

Map labels: Marananga, Seppeltsfield Road, Tanunda, Turkey Flat, Gomersal Road, St Hallet, Beth, Krondorf Road, Adelaide, Barossa Valley Way, Charles Melton, Kronc, Rowland Flat

⑥ Penfolds

Established in 1844, Penfolds moved to this site on the outskirts of Nuriootpa in 1974. This major winery (home of the famous Grange) matures its range of red and white table wines and ports in American oak barrels. Many wines are available for tasting and buying at the cellar door.

⑦ Wolf Blass

One of the younger wineries in the Barossa, established in 1973, Wolf Blass boasts elaborate tasting rooms and a wine-heritage museum. It specializes in premium red and white table wines, and sparkling and fortified wines.

⑧ Saltram

Established in 1859, this historic winery is set in beautiful gardens on a Barossa hillside outside Angaston. Popular with red- and fortified-wine enthusiasts, Saltram also has a restaurant, which is open for lunch daily (10am–3pm) and late on Friday nights from September to April.

SALTRAM

⑨ Collingrove Homestead, Angaston

Now owned by the National Trust, Collingrove was built in 1856 as a home for a member of the influential pioneering Angas family. It has original furnishings and is set in an English-style garden. Accommodation is available.

⑩ Henschke

This winery is one of the world's greatest producers. Their wines are made from single vineyards. After visiting the cellar be sure to walk through the vineyards – the vines, some up to 100 years old, are among the oldest in the world.

Tips for Drivers

Although a tour of the Barossa can be made in a day from Adelaide, the region is best seen and enjoyed by taking advantage of the excellent local accommodation and restaurants. The roads are generally good, although drivers should take special care on those that are unsealed. Visitors planning to visit a number of wineries and sample the produce may prefer to take one of the many tours or hire a chauffeur-driven vehicle.

THE YORKE AND EYRE PENINSULAS AND SOUTH AUSTRALIAN OUTBACK

From the lush Clare Valley and the dunes of the Simpson Desert, to the saltbush of the Nullarbor Plain, the land to the north and west of Adelaide is an area of vast distances and dramatic changes of scenery. With activities ranging from surfing on the coast to bushwalking in the Flinders Ranges, one is never far from awesome natural beauty.

South Australia was first settled by Europeans in 1836, but suffered early financial problems partly due to economic mismanagement. These were largely remedied by the discovery of copper at Kapunda, north of Adelaide, in 1842, and at Burra, near Clare, in 1845. As these resources were depleted fresh discoveries were made in the north of the Yorke Peninsula, in the area known as Little Cornwall, at the town of Wallaroo and Kadina in 1859 and at Moonta in 1861. By the 1870s, South Australia was the British Empire's leading copper producer, and copper, silver and uranium mining still boosts the state's economy today.

The Yorke and Eyre peninsulas are major arable areas, producing more than 10 per cent of Australia's wheat and much of its barley. They also have several important fishing ports, most notably Port Lincoln, the tuna-fishing capital of the country. Both peninsulas have stunning coastal scenery. The Yorke Peninsula, only two hours' drive from Adelaide, is a popular holiday

destination with excellent fishing, reef diving and surfing opportunities. The much larger Eyre Peninsula is also renowned for fishing and has many superb beaches. Despite extensive arable use, it still retains about half of its land area as parks, reserves and native bushland.

To the west, the vast Nullarbor Plain stretches far into Western Australia *(see p323)*, with the Great Victoria Desert extending above it. Much of this region is protected Aboriginal land and the RAAF Woomera Test Range.

North of the Yorke Peninsula lies the rugged majesty of the Flinders Ranges. Rich with sights of deep Aboriginal spiritual and cultural significance, the ranges are also home to abundant flora and fauna, and make for superb bushwalking. Further north, the immense, inhospitable but starkly beautiful desert regions of the South Australian Outback provide a challenging but rewarding destination for adventurous travellers.

Oyster beds in Coffin Bay at the southern tip of the Eyre Peninsula

◀ Red-sand dune in the Simpson Desert, in the South Australian Outback

Exploring the Yorke and Eyre Peninsulas

Just north of Adelaide *(see pp348–53)* lie the green hills of
the Clare Valley; then, further inland, as the rainfall diminishes,
the countryside changes dramatically. First comes the
grandeur of the Flinders Ranges with rugged mountains
and tranquil gorges. West of Adelaide are two peninsulas,
at the head of which is the industrial triangle of Port Pirie,
Port Augusta and Whyalla. The Yorke Peninsula is Australia's
richest barley growing district. Eyre Peninsula is also a
wheat- and barley-producing area. From here the Nullarbor
Plain runs beyond the Western Australian border.

Fishing boats moored in the harbour
of Port Lincoln

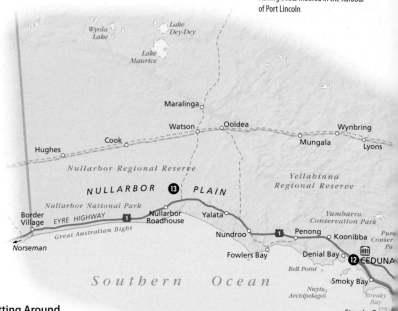

Getting Around

Despite the sparse population,
there is an extensive road network throughout the region.
The Stuart Hwy runs up
from Adelaide to Coober Pedy
and beyond into the Northern
Territory, and the Eyre Hwy
wends its way from Adelaide
along the tops of the Yorke and
Eyre peninsulas, across the
Nullarbor Plain and into Western
Australia. There is no state railway,
but interstate trains running from
Sydney to Perth, and Adelaide to
Alice Springs and Melbourne,
stop at major towns in the region.
Scheduled buses serve most
towns, and there are air services
from Adelaide to regional airports
in Port Lincoln, Ceduna, Coober
Pedy, Whyalla, and Port Augusta.

Raging waters of the Great Australian Bight

Sights at a Glance

1. Yorketown
2. Minlaton
3. Port Victoria
4. Maitland
5. Little Cornwall
6. Clare Valley
7. Port Pirie
8. Port Augusta
9. Whyalla
10. Port Lincoln
11. Coffin Bay National Park
12. Ceduna
13. Nullarbor Plain

South Australian Outback
See pp372–3

14. Coober Pedy
15. Witjira National Park
16. Simpson Desert Conservation Park
17. Lake Eyre National Park
18. Flinders Ranges

Locator Map

The Yorke and Eyre
Peninsulas

South Australian Outback
pp372–3

Saltbush landscape of the Eyre Peninsula

Key

— Major road

⋯⋯ Minor road

– – Track

— Scenic route

⊢⊢ Main railway

– – Minor railway

— State border

△ Summit

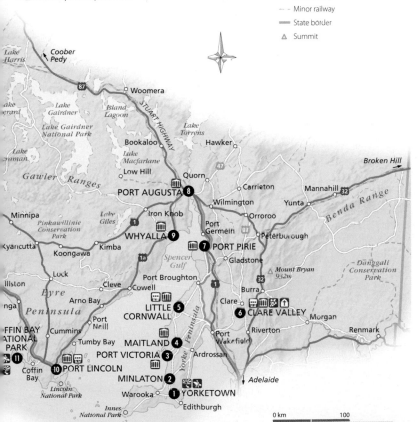

For additional map symbols *see back flap*

❶ Yorketown

🏠 685. 🚌 ❼ 29 Main St, Minlaton
(08) 8853 2600 or 1800 202 445.

Yorketown is the commercial centre of the earliest settled area on the southern Yorke Peninsula. It lies at the heart of a region scattered with nearly 200 salt lakes, many of which mysteriously turn pink at various times of the year, depending on climatic conditions. From the late 1890s until the 1930s, salt harvesting was a major industry in this part of South Australia.

Approximately 70 km (40 miles) southwest of Yorketown, at the tip of the Yorke Peninsula, is the spectacular Innes National Park. The park's geography changes from salt lakes and low mallee scrub inland to sandy beaches and steep, rugged cliffs along the coast. Kangaroos and emus have become accustomed to the presence of humans and are commonly seen, but other native inhabitants, such as the large mallee fowl, are more difficult to spot.

There is good surfing, reef diving and fishing in the park, especially at Browns Beach, the wild Pondalowie Bay, Chinamans Creek and Salmon Hole. Other beaches are considered unsafe for swimming. Also in the park are the rusting remains of the shipwrecked barque *Ethel*, which ran aground in 1904 and now lies with part of its hull protruding through the sand below the limestone cliffs of Ethel Beach.

"Red Devil" fighter plane in Minlaton

❷ Minlaton

🏠 770. 🚌 🚌 ❼ Yorke Pennisula Visitors Information Centre, 29 Main St (08) 8853 2600 or 1800 202 445.

Centrally located, Minlaton is a service town to the surrounding farming community. Minlaton's claim to fame, however, is as the destination of the very first air mail flight across water in the southern hemisphere. Pilot Captain Harry Butler, a World War I fighter ace, set off on this record-breaking mission in August 1919 from Adelaide. Minlaton's Butler Memorial houses his 1916 Bristol fighter plane, "Red Devil", believed to be the only one left in the world, as well as displays detailing Butler's life.

❸ Port Victoria

🏠 345. ❼ 29 Main St, Minlaton (08) 8853 2600 or 1800 202 445.

Lying on the west coast of the Yorke Peninsula, Port Victoria is today a sleepy holiday destination, popular with anglers, swimmers and divers. In the early part of the 20th century, however, it was a busy sea port with large clippers and windjammers loading grain bound for the northern hemisphere. The last time a square rigger used the port was in 1949. The story of these ships and their epic voyages is told in the **Maritime Museum**, located adjacent to the jetty.

About 10 km (6 miles) off the coast lies Wardang Island, around which are eight known shipwrecks dating from 1871. Divers can follow the Wardang Island Maritime Heritage Trail to view the wrecks, each of which has an underwater plaque. Boats to the island can be chartered, but permission to land must be obtained from the Community Council in Point Pearce, the nearby Aboriginal settlement which administers the island.

🏛 **Maritime Museum**
Main St, Foreshore. **Tel** (08) 8834 2268. **Open** 2–4pm Sat, Sun, pub hols. 🅿 ♿

❹ Maitland

🏠 1,050. 🚌 🚌 ❼ CHATT Centre, 3 Robert St, Maitland (08) 8832 2174. 🅦 **maitlandsa.com**

Surrounded by some of the most productive farmland in Australia, Maitland lies in the centre of the Yorke Peninsula, on a ridge overlooking the Yorke Valley and Spencer Gulf.

Vast expanse of the salt lakes in the Yorketown region

For hotels and restaurants in this area see pp491–2 and pp522–5

Originally proclaimed in 1872, it is now the service centre for the surrounding community.

The pretty town, laid out on a classic grid pattern, retains many fine examples of colonial architecture, including the Maitland Hotel, built in 1874, and the 1875 St Bartholomew's Catholic Church.

The **CYP National Trust Museum** has an agricultural and folk collection housed in four buildings and focuses on the region's history and development.

🏛 **CYP National Trust Museum**
Cnr Gardiner & Kilkerran terraces. **Tel** (08) 8832 2220. **Open** 2–4pm Sun, public & school hols. **Closed** Good Fri, 25 Dec. 🚗 &

Miners' cottages at Moonta Mines, Little Cornwall

❺ Little Cornwall

🚌 Kadina. 🚌 Kadina. 🛈 50 Moonta Rd, Kadina (08) 8821 2333.

The three towns of Moonta, Kadina and Wallaroo were established after copper discoveries on Yorke Peninsula in 1859 and 1861. Collectively the towns are known as "The Copper Coast", and Moonta as "Australia's Little Cornwall". Many miners from Cornwall, England, came here in the 19th century seeking their fortunes. The biennial festival "Kernewek Lowender" (see p46) celebrates this Cornish heritage. The wealth created by the mines has left the towns with fine architecture.

Wallaroo, the site of the first copper ore smelting works, was also a shipping port for ore

Former timber shed now home to the CYP National Trust Museum, Port Victoria

When mining finished, the port was important for agricultural exports. The **Wallaroo Heritage and Nautical Museum** is in the old post office.

Moonta, once home to Australia's richest copper mine, contains a group of sites and buildings in the **Moonta Mines State Heritage Area**. The 1870 Miner's Cottage is a restored wattle and daub cottage. The history museum is in the old Moonta Mines Model School. Also of interest is the Moonta Mines Railway, a restored light-gauge locomotive.

Kadina, where copper was originally found, is the Yorke Peninsula's largest town.

The **Farm Shed Museum and Tourism Centre** has interesting displays on mining and folk history of the area.

🏛 **Wallaroo Heritage and Nautical Museum**
Jetty Rd. **Tel** (08) 8823 3015. **Open** 10am–4pm daily. **Closed** 25 Dec. 🚗 &

🚌 **Moonta Tourist Office**
Verran Terrace. **Tel** (08) 8825 1891. **Open** 9am–5pm daily. **Closed** 25 Dec. 🚗 &

🏛 **Farm Shed Museum and Tourism Centre**
50 Moonta Rd. **Tel** (08) 8821 2333. **Open** 9am–5pm Mon–Fri, 10am–4pm Sat & Sun. **Closed** Good Fri, 25 Dec. 🚗 &

Fishing and Diving on the Yorke Peninsula

There are fantastic opportunities for on- and offshore fishing and diving in the waters off the Yorke Peninsula. Many of the coastal towns have jetties used by keen amateur fishermen, and around Edithburgh anglers may catch tommy ruff, garfish and snook. Divers can enjoy the southern coast's stunning underwater scenery with brightly coloured corals and fish.

Offshore, the wreck of the *Clan Ranald* near Edithburgh is a popular dive and, off Wardang Island, eight wrecks can be explored on a unique diving trail. Angling from boats can be equally fruitful and local charter boats are available for hire.

A large blue grouper close to a diver in waters off the Yorke Peninsula

Restored 19th-century buildings at Burra Mine near the Clare Valley

❻ Clare Valley

🚌 Clare. 🅵 The Clare Valley Discovery Centre, 33 Old North Rd, Clare. 1800 242 131. 🆆 clarevalley.com.au

Framed by the rolling hills of the northern Mount Lofty Ranges, Clare Valley is a picturesque and premium wine-producing region. At the head of the valley lies the town of Clare. This regional centre has many historic buildings, including the Old Police Station Museum, housed in the old Police Station, and Wolta Wolta, an early pastoralist's home, built in 1846, which has a fine collection of antiques. Visitors have the option of staying here.

Sevenhill Cellars, 7 km (4 miles) south of Clare, is the oldest vineyard in the valley. It was established by Austrian Jesuits in 1851, originally to produce altar wine for the colonies. The adjacent St Aloysius Church was completed in 1875. The winery is still owned by Jesuits and now produces both altar and table wines.

East of Sevenhill lies the heritage town of Mintaro, with many buildings making extensive use of the slate quarried in the area for more than 150 years. Also worth visiting is **Martindale Hall**, an elegant 1879 mansion situated just southeast of town.

Twelve km (7 miles) north of Clare lies **Bungaree Station**. This self-contained Merino sheep-farming complex was established in 1841 and is now maintained as a working 19th-century model. The historic exhibits here reveal the life and work at the station.

About 35 km (22 miles) north-east of Clare is the charming town of Burra. Five years after copper was discovered here in 1845, Burra was home to the largest mine in Australia. As such it was the economic saviour of the fledgling state, rescuing it from impending bankruptcy. Burra is now a State Heritage Area.

The **Burra Mine Site**, with its ruins and restored buildings around the huge open cut, is one of Australia's most exciting industrial archaeological sites. Morphett's Engine House Museum (open every morning) is a renovated three-storey Cornish engine house. An interpretive centre at the Bon Accord Mining Museum allows visitors access to the original mine shafts. The miners' dugouts, still seen on the banks of Burra Creek, were once home to more than 1,500 mainly Cornish miners. Paxton Square Cottages, built between 1849 and 1852, are unique in Australian mining history as the first decent accommodation provided for miners and their families. Many old buildings, including the police lockup and stables, the Redruth Gaol and the Unicorn Brewery Cellars, have been restored, as have a number of the 19th-century shops and houses. A museum chronicling the history is located in Burra market square.

🍷 Sevenhill Cellars
College Rd, Sevenhill 5453. **Tel** (08) 8843 4222. **Open** 10am–5pm daily. **Closed** 1 Jan, Good Fri, Easter Sun, 25 & 26 Dec. ♿

🏛 Martindale Hall
Manoora Rd, Mintaro 5415. **Tel** (08) 8843 9088. **Open** daily. 🅿

🏛 Bungaree Station
431 Bungaree Rd, Clare. **Tel** (08) 8842 2677. **Open** accommodation available, check website. 🅿 ♿
🆆 bungareestation.com.au

🏛 Burra Visitor Information Centre
2 Market St, Burra. **Tel** (08) 8892 2154. **Open** 9am–5pm daily. **Closed** 25 Dec. 🅿 ♿ limited.

❼ Port Pirie

🗺 17,333. 🚃 🚌 🚌 🅵 3 Mary Elie St 1800 000 424.

Port Pirie was the state's first provincial city. An industrial hub, it is the site of the largest lead smelter in the southern hemisphere.

In the town centre, the National Trust Museum comprises three well-preserved buildings: the pavilion-style railway station built in 1902, the former customs house and the old police building. The Regional Tourism and Arts Centre, located in the former 1967 railway station, features artworks on lead, zinc and copper panels interpreting the city's historic wealth.

Port Pirie also boasts a miniature railway. Visitors can enjoy a ride on the 1st or 3rd Sunday of every month.

🏛 National Trust Museum
73–77 Ellen St. **Tel** (08) 8632 3435. **Open** daily. **Closed** 25 Dec. ♿ limited.

Victorian grandeur of Port Pirie's old railway station

Harbour view of Port Augusta, backed by its power stations

❽ Port Augusta

🏚 13,000. ✈ 🚌 🚊 🚍
ℹ 41 Flinders Terrace 1800 633 060.

Situated at the head of Spencer Gulf, Port Augusta is at the crossroads of Australia; here lies the intersection of the Sydney–Perth and Adelaide–Alice Springs railway lines, as well as the major Sydney–Perth and Adelaide–Darwin highways. Once an important port, its power stations now produce 40 per cent of the state's electricity. The coal-fired Northern Power Station, which dominates the city's skyline, offers free conducted tours.

Port Augusta is also the beginning of South Australia's Outback region. The School of the Air and the Royal Flying Doctor Service offices, both of which provide essential services to inhabitants of remote stations, are open to the public *(see p261)*. The **Wadlata Outback Centre** imaginatively tells the story of the Far North from 15 million years ago when rainforests covered the area, through Aboriginal and European history, up to the present day and into the future.

Australia's first **Arid Lands Botanic Garden** was opened nearby in 1996. This 200-ha (500-acre) site is an important research and education facility, as well as a recreational area.

It also commands panoramic views of the Flinders Ranges to the east *(see p373)*.

🏛 Wadlata Outback Centre
41 Flinders Terrace. **Tel** (08) 8641 9193. **Open** 9am–5.30pm Mon–Fri, 10am–4pm Sat & Sun. **Closed** 25 Dec. 🌐 ♿

🌿 Arid Lands Botanic Garden
144 Stuart Hwy. **Tel** (08) 8641 9116. **Open** 7:30am–sunset daily. 🖥

❾ Whyalla

🏚 21,000. ✈ 🚍 ℹ Port Augusta Rd, Lincoln Hwy, 1800 088 589.

At the gateway to the Eyre Peninsula, Whyalla is the state's largest provincial city. Originally a shipping port for iron ore mined at nearby Iron Knob, the city was transformed in 1939 when a blast furnace was established, a harbour created and a shipyard constructed. The shipyard closed in 1978; however, the first ship built there, the HMAS *Whyalla* (1941), is now a major display of the **Whyalla Maritime Museum**.

Although an industrial centre, Whyalla has a number of fine beaches and good fishing. In recent years, Whyalla's foreshore has been extensively redeveloped. Today, it is home to a bustling marina, lush gardens and cafés.

🏛 Whyalla Maritime Museum
Lincoln Hwy. **Tel** (08) 8645 8900. **Open** 10am–3pm daily. **Closed** Good Fri, 25 Dec. 🌐 🎬 HMAS *Whyalla* can be accessed on guided tours only. ♿ museum only 🖥 **whyalla maritimemuseum.com.au**

HMAS *Whyalla*, docked beside the Whyalla Maritime Museum

Stunning coastline of Whalers Way at the southern end of the Eyre Peninsula near Port Lincoln

⑩ Port Lincoln

🏠 14,000. ✈ 🚌 𝒊 3 Adelaide Pl 1300 788 378 or (08) 8683 3544.

At the southern end of the Eyre Peninsula, Port Lincoln sits on the shore of Boston Bay, one of the world's largest natural harbours. A fishing and seafood processing centre, it is home to Australia's largest tuna fleet.

Locals celebrate the start of the tuna season every January with the Tunarama Festival *(see p45)*. This raucous event includes processions, concerts and a tuna-tossing competition.

Fishing and sailing are popular activities. Visitors can take a boat trip to Dangerous Reef, 31 km (20 miles) offshore, to view great white sharks from the relative safety of the boat or submerged cage. In the middle of the bay lies Boston Island, a working sheep station.

The Port Lincoln area has several buildings of note. South of Port Lincoln, **Mikkira Station**, established in 1842, is one of the country's oldest sheep stations. Today it is ideal for picnics or camping, with a restored pioneer cottage and a koala colony.

The **Koppio Smithy Museum**, located in the Koppio Hills 40 km (25 miles) north of Port Lincoln, is an agricultural museum with a furnished 1890 log cottage and a 1903 smithy that gives a glimpse into the lives of the pioneers.

Just 20 km (12 km) south of Port Lincoln is Lincoln National Park with its rocky hills, sheltered coves, sandy beaches and high cliffs. The park is also rich in birdlife. Emus and parrots are common and ospreys and sea eagles frequent the coast. Just west of the park, Whalers Way has some of Australia's most dramatic coastal scenery.

This land is private and entry is via a permit available from the visitors' centre.

🏠 **Mikkira Station**
621 Mikkira Lane. **Tel** (08) 8685 6020.
Closed when temperature exceeds 30°C (86°F). 🦘

🏛 **Koppio Smithy Museum**
Koppio Rd. **Tel** (08) 8684 4243.
Open 10am–5pm Tue–Sun.
Closed 25 Dec. 🦘 ♿

The prime surfing spot of Almonta Beach in Coffin Bay National Park

⑪ Coffin Bay National Park

🚌 Port Lincoln. 𝒊 (08) 8688 3111.
Open daily. **Closed** 25 Dec. 🚗 per vehicle. ♿ limited. 🌐 environment. sa.gov.au

To the west of the southern tip of the Eyre Peninsula is Coffin Bay Peninsula, which is part of the Coffin Bay National Park. This unspoilt area of coastal

Wildlife of the Eyre Peninsula

An enormous variety of wildlife inhabits the Eyre Peninsula. Emus and kangaroos are common, and the hairy-nosed wombat is found in large numbers on the west coast. Wedge-tailed eagles soar over the Gawler Ranges, while sea eagles, ospreys, albatrosses and petrels are all seen over the coast. In the water, dolphins, sea lions and occasional great white sharks feast on an abundance of marine life. The most spectacular sight, however, are the southern right whales which breed at the head of the Great Australian Bight every June to October. They can be seen from the cliffs at Head of the Bight, just east of the Nullarbor National Park.

Wedge-tailed eagle

For hotels and restaurants in this area see pp491–2 and pp522–5

wilderness has exposed cliffs, sheltered sandy beaches, rich birdlife and fantastic fishing. Wildflowers in the park can be quite spectacular from early spring to early summer.

There are several scenic drives through the park, but some roads are accessible to 4WD vehicles only. A favourite route for conventional vehicles is the Yangie Trail from the small town of Coffin Bay to Yangie and Avoid bays. To the east of Point Avoid is one of Australia's best surfing beaches, Almonta Beach.

Coffin Bay town has long been a popular centre for windsurfing, swimming, sailing and fishing. It now also produces oysters. The Oyster Walk is a pleasant walking trail along the foreshore through native bushland.

⑫ Ceduna

🏠 2,300. ✈ 🚌 ℹ 58 Poynton St (08) 8625 3343. 📷 Oysterfest (Oct).
🌐 **ceduna.net**

At the top of the west side of the Eyre Peninsula, sitting on the shores of Murat Bay, Ceduna is the most westerly significant town in South Australia before the start of the Nullarbor Plain. The town's name comes from the Aboriginal word *cheedoona*, meaning "a place to rest".

Today, Ceduna is the commercial centre of the far west. Within the town is the **Old Schoolhouse National Trust Museum** with its collections of restored farm equipment from

An Indian-Pacific train crossing the vast Nullarbor Plain

early pioneer days. It also has a display on the British atomic weapons tests held at nearby Maralinga in the 1950s, and a selection of Aboriginal artifacts.

In the 1850s, there was a whaling station on St Peter Island, just off the coast of Ceduna, but now the town is a base for whale-watchers. Southern right whales can be seen close to the shore from June to October from the head of the Bight, 300 km (185 miles) from Ceduna.

The oyster-farming industry has established itself west and east of Ceduna at Denial and Smoky bays. Between Ceduna and Penong, a tiny hamlet 73 km (45 miles) to the west, there are detours to surfing beaches including the legendary Cactus Beach. Keen surfers are found here all year round trying to catch some of the best waves in Australia, rolling in from the great Southern Ocean.

🏛 Old Schoolhouse National Trust Museum
Park Terrace. **Tel** (08) 8625 2210. **Open** Mon–Sat. **Closed** 25 Dec. 📷 🚻

⑬ Nullarbor Plain

🚌 Port Augusta. 🚌 Ceduna. ℹ Ceduna (08) 8625 3343. **Open** 9am–5:30pm Mon–Fri, 10am–4pm Sat–Sun. **Closed** Good Fri, 25 Dec.

The huge expanse of the Nullarbor Plain stretches from Nundroo, about 150 km (95 miles) west of Ceduna, towards the distant Western Australia border 330 km (200 miles) away, and beyond into Western Australia (*see p323*).

This dry, dusty plain can be crossed by rail on the Trans-Australian Railway or by road on the Eyre Highway. The train travels further inland than the road, its route giving little relief from the flat landscape. The highway lies nearer the coast, passing a few isolated sights of interest on its way west. Visitors should plan ahead if they intend to drive as petrol stations are few and far between here.

Just south of the small town of Nundroo lies Fowlers Bay. Good for fishing, it is popular with anglers seeking solitude. West of here, the road passes through the Yalata Aboriginal Lands. Bordering Yalata to the west is Nullarbor National Park. This runs from the Nullarbor Roadhouse hamlet, 130 km (80 miles) west of Nundroo, to the border with Western Australia 200 km (125 miles) away. The Eyre Highway passes through the park, close to the coastal cliffs. This stretch of the plain has some spectacular views over the Great Australian Bight.

The world's longest cave system runs beneath the plain, and the border area has many underground caves and caverns. These should only be explored by experienced cavers, however, as many are flooded and dangerous.

Watching southern right whales from Head of the Bight, near Ceduna

South Australian Outback

South Australia's outback is an enormous area of harsh but often breathtaking scenery. Much of the region is untamed desert, broken in places by steep, ancient mountain ranges, huge salt lakes, gorges and occasional hot springs. Although very hot and dry for most of the year, many places burst into life after heavy winter rains and hundreds of species of wildflowers, animals and birds can be seen. The area's recent history is one of fabled stock routes, now Outback tracks for adventurous travellers. Isolated former mining and railway towns now cater for Outback tourists. Vast areas in the west form extensive Aboriginal lands, accessible by permit only.

Locator Map

- *South Australian Outback*
- *The Yorke and Eyre Peninsulas see pp362–71*

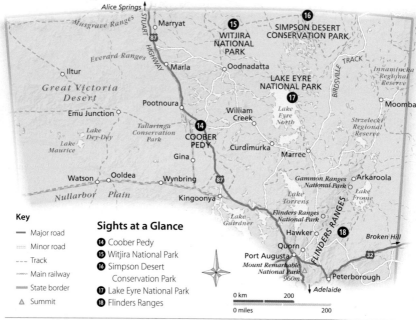

Key

— Major road
··· Minor road
--- Track
▪▪▪ Main railway
— State border
△ Summit

Sights at a Glance

⓮ Coober Pedy
⓯ Witjira National Park
⓰ Simpson Desert Conservation Park
⓱ Lake Eyre National Park
⓲ Flinders Ranges

0 km   200
0 miles   200

⓮ Coober Pedy

🗺 1,400. ✈ 🚌 ℹ 773 Hutchison St, 1800 637 076 or (08) 8672 5298.
🌐 opalcapitaloftheworld.com.au

One of Australia's most famous Outback towns, Coober Pedy, 850 km (530 miles) northwest of Adelaide, is an unusual settlement in the heart of an extremely hostile landscape. Frequent duststorms and a colourless desert landscape littered with abandoned mines contribute to the town's desolate appearance, yet the small population has a cultural mix of over 42 nationalities.

Opal was discovered here in 1915, and today Coober Pedy produces 70 per cent of the world's supply. Mining claims, limited to one per person, can measure no more than 100 m by 50 m (320 ft by 160 ft). For this reason opal mining is the preserve of individuals, not large companies, and this adds to the town's "frontier" quality. Coober Pedy's name comes

Underground "dugout" home in Coober Pedy

from the Aboriginal *kupa piti*, meaning "white man in a hole", and it is apt indeed. Not only the mines, but also houses, hotels and churches are built underground. This way, the residents escape the extreme temperatures of up to 50°C (122°F) during the day and 0°C (32°F) at night. Several such homes are open to the public.

The **Underground Art Gallery** displays Aboriginal art. It also has displays relating to opal mining, and visitors can dig for their own opals.

🏛 **Underground Art Gallery**
Main St. **Tel** (08) 8672 5985.
Open daily. **Closed** 25 Dec. 🅿 ♿

⓯ Witjira National Park

ℹ️ Pink Roadhouse, Oodnadatta (08) 8670 7822. **Open** daily. Park Office: 1800 816 078. **Open** 24 hours. Desert Parks pass required. 🖼️

About 200 km (125 miles) north of Coober Pedy lies the small town of Oodnadatta, where drivers can check the road and weather conditions before heading further north to Witjira National Park.

Witjira has dunes, saltpans, boulder plains and coolibah woodlands, but it is most famous for its hot artesian springs. Dalhousie Springs has more than 60 active springs with warm water rising from the Great Artesian Basin. These springs supply essential water for Aborigines, pastoralists and wildlife, including water snails, unique to the area.

⓰ Simpson Desert Conservation Park

ℹ️ Pink Roadhouse, Oodnadatta (08) 8670 7822. **Open** daily. Desert Parks pass required. Park Office: 1800 816 078. **Open** 24 hours. 🖼️

The Simpson Desert Conservation Park is at the very top of South Australia, adjoining both Queensland and the Northern Territory. It is an almost endless series of sand dunes, lakes, spinifex grassland and yidgee woodland.

The landscape is home to some 180 bird, 92 reptile and 44 native mammal species, some of which have developed nocturnal habits as a response to the aridity of the region.

Dunes stretching to the horizon in Simpson Desert Conservation Park

⓱ Lake Eyre National Park

ℹ️ Coober Pedy, (08) 8672 5298. **Open** Mon–Fri. **Closed** public hols. Park Office: 1800 816 078. **Open** 24 hours. 🖼️

Lake Eyre National Park encompasses all of Lake Eyre North and extends eastwards into the Tirari Desert. Lake Eyre is Australia's largest salt lake, 15 m (49 ft) below sea level at its lowest point, with a salt crust said to weigh 400 million tonnes. Vegetation is low, comprising mostly blue bush, samphire and saltbush. On the rare occasions when the lake floods, it alters dramatically: flowers bloom and birds such as pelicans and gulls appear, turning the lake into a breeding ground.

⓲ Flinders Ranges

🚍 Hawker, Wilpena. ℹ️ Wilpena (08) 8648 0048. **Open** daily. Park office: (08) 8648 0049. 🖼️

The Flinders Ranges extend for 400 km (250 miles) from Crystal Brook, just north of the Clare Valley, far into South Australia's Outback. A favourite with bushwalkers, the ranges encompass a great diversity of stunning scenery and wildlife, much of it protected in several national parks.

In the southern part of the Flinders Ranges is Mount Remarkable National Park, renowned for its fine landscape, abundant wildflowers and excellent walking trails.

About 50 km (30 miles) north of here is the town of Quorn, start of the restored Pichi Richi Railway. North of Quorn lie the dramatic Warren, Yarrah Vale and Buckaring gorges.

Much of the central Flinders Ranges are contained within the Flinders Ranges National Park. This beautiful park's best-known feature is Wilpena Pound, an elevated natural basin covering some 90 sq km (35 sq miles) with sheer outer walls 500 m (1,600 ft) high.

To the north is Gammon Ranges National Park, with mountain bushwalking for the experienced only. Just outside the park is **Arkaroola**, a tourist village with a wildlife sanctuary and a state-of-the-art observatory.

🏨 **Arkaroola**
Via Wilpena or Leigh Creek. **Tel** (08) 8648 4848. **Open** daily. 🖼️ for tours.

Shimmering expanse of Lake Eyre, the largest salt lake in Australia

VICTORIA

Victoria at a Glance

The state of Victoria can be easily divided into two distinct geographical halves, east and west. Western Victoria is known for its unusual landforms, including the Grampians and the Twelve Apostles. It was also the site of Australia's wealthiest gold rush during the 19th century, the legacy of which can be seen in the ornate buildings in the many surviving gold rush towns (see pp58–9). Eastern Victoria's cooler climate benefits the vineyards that produce world-class wines, while the Alps are Victoria's winter playground. The rugged coastline is known for its lakes, forests and wildlife. Melbourne, the state's capital, is the second most populous city in Australia.

Mildura

Western Victoria
(see pp426–41)

Horsham

Ballarat

Portland   Warrnambool   Geel

Halls Gap is the main entrance to the Grampians National Park *(see p431)*. This beautiful area is filled with dramatic rock formations, spectacular ridges and wildflowers unique to the region.

Ballarat's Arch of Victory on the Avenue of Honour commemorates the soldiers of World War I. It is also the western entrance to this provincial city, which grew up during the 1850s gold rush *(see pp438–9)*.

The Twelve Apostles is the evocative name given to these eroded limestone rock formations in Port Campbell National Park, seen from the Great Ocean Road *(see pp432–33)*. Sunset is the best time to fully appreciate the view.

◄ Skiers at Mount Hotham, in the Victorian Alps

Tahbilk Wines is one of the best known of all the northeastern Victorian vineyards, not only for its excellent wines but also for the pagoda-style architecture of its winery. Eastern Victoria's cool climate has led to a range of successful wineries *(see pp454–5)*.

Locator Map

The Victorian Alps come into their own during the winter months as a ski area *(see p452–3)*.

Shepparton

Wangaratta

ndigo

Eastern Victoria
(see pp442–55)

| 0 kilometres | 100 |
| 0 miles | 100 |

Sunbury

chus Marsh

Melbourne

ribee

Dandenong

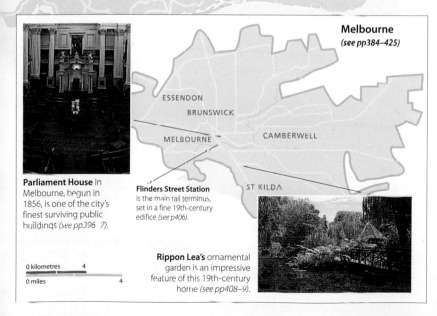

Melbourne
(see pp384–425)

ESSENDON

BRUNSWICK

MELBOURNE

CAMBERWELL

ST KILDA

Parliament House in Melbourne, begun in 1856, is one of the city's finest surviving public buildings *(see pp396–7)*.

Flinders Street Station is the main rail terminus, set in a fine 19th-century edifice *(see p406)*.

Rippon Lea's ornamental garden is an impressive feature of this 19th-century home *(see pp408–9)*.

| 0 kilometres | 4 |
| 0 miles | 4 |

Melbourne's Best: Parks and Gardens

Visitors to Melbourne should not miss the city's magnificent public and private gardens. A large proportion of the city's parks and gardens were created in the 19th century and have a gracious quality which has earned Victoria the nickname of Australia's "Garden State". Central Melbourne is ringed by public gardens, including the outstanding Royal Botanic Gardens, visited by more than 1.6 million people each year. Melbourne also has a network of public parks which offer a mix of native flora and fauna with recreational activities. The annual Open Garden Scheme *(see p44)* allows visitors into some of the best private gardens in Victoria and Australia.

Statue of Queen Victoria in her eponymous gardens

Landscape Gardens

Melbourne abounds with carefully planned and formal 19th-century gardens, designed by prominent landscape gardeners.

A variety of trees from all over the world lines the formal avenues of **Carlton Gardens**, designed in 1857 by Edward La Trobe Bateman. The aim of the design was for every path and flowerbed to focus attention on the Exhibition Building, constructed in 1880 *(see p399)*. The main entrance path leads from Victoria Street to the Hochgurtel Fountain, in front of the Exhibition Building, decorated on its upper tier with stone birds and flowers which are indigenous to the state of Victoria.

Statue of Simpson and his donkey in Kings Domain

The attractive **Fitzroy Gardens** in the heart of the city were also first designed by Bateman in 1856. His original plans were later revised by a Scotsman, James Sinclair, to make them more sympathetic to the area's uneven landscape. The avenues of elms that lead in to the centre of the gardens from the surrounding streets create the shape of the Union Jack flag and are one of the most distinctive features of the gardens *(see pp396–7)*. Fitzroy Gardens' Conservatory is renowned for its five popular annual plant shows. The **Queen Victoria Gardens** are considered one of the city's most attractive

gardens. They were created as a setting for a new statue of the queen, four years after her death, in 1905. Roses now surround the statue. A floral clock near St Kilda Road was given to Melbourne by Swiss watchmakers in 1966. It is embedded with some 7,000 flowering plants.

Kings Domain *(see p402)*, established in 1854, was the dream of a German botanist, Baron von Mueller, who designed this impressive garden. The garden is dominated by elegant statues, including one of Simpson, a stretcher bearer during World War I, with his faithful donkey. The Shrine of Remembrance and Government House are located here.

Botanic Gardens

Begun in 1846, the **Royal Botanic Gardens** now cover 36 ha (90 acres). Botanist Baron von Mueller became the director of the gardens in 1857 and began to plant both indigenous and exotic shrubs on the site, intending the gardens to be a scientific aid to fellow biologists. Von Mueller's successor, William Guilfoyle, made his own mark on the design, by adding wide paths across the gardens and an ornamental lake.

Conservatory of flowers in Fitzroy Gardens

Ornamental lake in the Royal Botanic Gardens

Where to Find the Parks and Gardens

Alexandra Gardens **Map** 3 A2.
Carlton Gardens **Map** 2 D1.
Fawkner Park **Map** 3 C5.
Fitzroy Gardens **Map** 2 E2.
Flagstaff Gardens **Map** 1 A2.
Kings Domain *pp402–3*.
Princes Park, Royal Parade, Carlton.
Queen Victoria Gardens **Map** 2 D4.
Royal Botanic Gardens *pp402–3*.
Treasury Gardens **Map** 2 E3.
Yarra Park **Map** 2 F3.

Today, the gardens are home to more than 10,000 plant species *(see pp402–3)*.

Recreational Gardens and Parks

Melburnians are avid sports participants as well as spectators, and many of the city's gardens offer a range of sporting facilities in attractive surroundings.

Flagstaff Gardens take their name from the site's role as a signalling station from 1840, warning of ships arriving in the Port of Melbourne. In the 1880s, with advances in communication, this role was no longer required and gardens were laid out on the land instead. Today the gardens are used for their recreational facilities, which include tennis courts, a children's playground and a barbecue area.

The **Alexandra Gardens** were designed in 1904 as a riverside walk along the Yarra River. Today, as well as the major thoroughfare of Alexandra Avenue, there is an equestrian path, a cycle path, boat sheds and barbecue facilities. The **Treasury Gardens** were designed in 1867 and are lined along its avenues with Moreton Bay Figs, which

offer very welcome shade in the summer heat. The location in the centre of the city makes these gardens very popular with office workers during their lunch breaks. The gardens also host regular evening concerts and other entertainment gatherings.

Established in 1856, **Yarra Park** is today home to the city's most well-known sports ground, the impressive Melbourne Cricket Ground *(see p401)*. The wood and bark of the indigenous river red gums in the park were once used for canoes and shields by local Aborigines and many still bear the scars.

Fawkner Park, named after Melbourne's co-founder, John Pascoe Fawkner, was laid out in 1862 and became a large sports ground in the 1890s. Despite a temporary role as a camp site for the Armed Services during World War II, the 40 ha (100 acres) of the park are still used for cricket, football, hockey and softball games.

Another popular sporting area with Melburnians is **Princes Park**. Two sports pavilions were constructed in 1938, as were two playing fields. The park now contains a football oval and a large timber adventure playground, as well as a jogging track lined with exercise equipment at stages along its 3-km (1.8-mile) route. A gravel running track was also added in 1991.

Cricket match in progress in Fawkner Park

Melbourne's Best: Architecture

In 1835, Melbourne was a village of tents and impermanent dwellings. Fed by the wealth of the 1850s' gold rush and the economic boom of the 1880s, it rapidly acquired many graceful buildings. Today, the city's architecture is very eclectic, with a strong. Victorian element. The range of architectural styles is impressive, from beautiful restorations to outstanding contemporary novelties. The city's tallest building is the Eureka Tower, which is 300 m (985 ft) high.

Early colonial Cook's Cottage

Early Colonial

In colonial days, it was quite common for small edifices, such as La Trobe's Cottage, to be shipped from England as skilled builders were in short supply. Other imported structures included timber cottages and corrugated iron dwellings.

Wood structure · Wooden shutters · Chimney

La Trobe's Cottage is a prefabricated wooden cottage of 1839.

High Victorian

During the 19th century, Melbourne erected several grand state buildings equal to those in the USA and Europe. State Parliament House, begun in 1856, included a central dome in its original design which was omitted due to lack of funds *(see p397)*. South of the city is the 1934 Shrine of Remembrance, which demonstrates the 20th century's yearning for classical roots *(see p402)*.

Detail of Parliament House

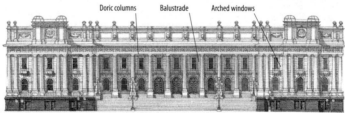
Doric columns · Balustrade · Arched windows

State Parliament House has an impressive entrance with its grand Doric columns.

Cast-iron lacework at Tasma Terrace

Terrace Housing

Terrace houses with cast-iron lace balconies were popular during the Victorian era. Tasma Terrace (1878) was designed by Charles Webb and is unusual for its three-storey houses, double-storey being more typical.

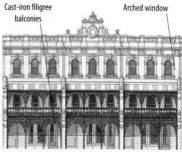
Cast-iron filigree balconies · Arched window

Tasma Terrace is now home to the National Trust.

Modernism and Post-modernism

The latter half of the 20th century has seen a range of post-modern buildings erected in Melbourne. The National Gallery of Victoria (see p407) was designed by Sir Roy Grounds and completed in 1968 (further modified in 2003 by Mario Bellini). It was the first time bluestone, widely used in the 19th century, was used in a modern structure. The stained-glass ceiling of the Great Hall was designed by Leonard French.

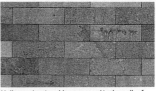

Melbourne's unique bluestone used in the walls of the National Gallery of Victoria

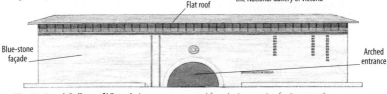

Flat roof

Blue-stone façade

Arched entrance

The National Gallery of Victoria has a monumental façade, impressive for its smooth simplicity and lack of ornamental details.

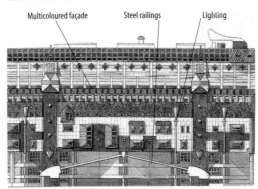

Multicoloured façade Steel railings Lighting

Royal Melbourne Institute of Technology's Building 8 façade is a complex blend of bright colours and diverse shapes.

Contemporary

Melbourne is known for its vibrant, experimental architecture scene. Some of the most radical Australian buildings of the 1990s can be found here. The Royal Melbourne Institute of Technology's Building 8 was designed by Peter Corrigan and completed in 1993. The building's interior and façade is both gaudy and Gaudían, with its bold use of primary colours. Whatever your view, it cannot help but attract the attention of every visitor to the northern end of the city.

Sports Architecture

Melbourne's modern architecture clearly reflects the importance of sport to its citizens. Rod Laver Arena at Melbourne Park, opened in 1988, has a retractable roof, a world first, and seats more than 15,000 people.

Aerial view of Melbourne Park, with Rod Laver Arena on the left

Where to Find the Buildings

La Trobe's Cottage p403.
National Gallery of Victoria p407.
Rod Laver Arena at Melbourne Park **Map** 2 F4.
Royal Melbourne Institute of Technology's Building 8, Swanston St **Map** 1 C2.
Shrine of Remembrance p402.
State Parliament House p397.
Tasma Terrace, Parliament Place **Map** 2 E2.

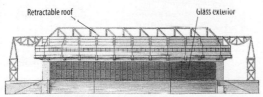

Retractable roof Glass exterior

Rod Laver Arena was designed by Philip Cox and now hosts the annual Australian Open tennis championships.

Wines of Victoria

Victoria has approximately 850 wineries located in 21 distinct wine regions, some easily reached in less than an hour by car from the state capital, Melbourne. The northeast is famous for its unique fortified Muscats and Tokays (often described as liquid toffee), while from the cooler south come silky Chardonnays and subtle Pinot Noirs. There is no better way to enjoy Victorian wine than in one of the many restaurants and bistros in cosmopolitan Melbourne *(see pp526–9)*.

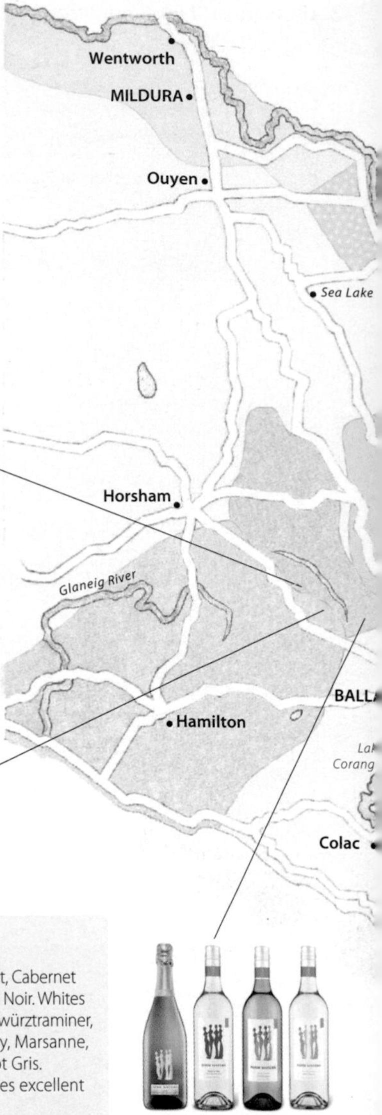

Best's is one of the oldest family-owned wineries in Australia. This producer makes excellent Shiraz, Merlot, Dolcetto and Riesling wines. Self-guided tours of its 150-year-old wooden cellar are free and available every day.

Wentworth
MILDURA
Ouyen
Sea Lake
Horsham
Glaneig River
BALL...
Hamilton
La...
Corang...
Colac

Cellar stacked with wine at Seppelt Great Western

Key facts

Location and Climate
Warm in the north, cool in the south, Victoria's climate spectrum yields a diversity of wines. Many small, high-quality producers have been in the vanguard of the Australian wine revolution, which began in the 1970s.

Grape Varieties

Victoria's varied climate and soil means it is possible to grow a full range of grape varieties. Reds include Shiraz, Merlot, Cabernet Sauvignon and Pinot Noir. Whites include Semillon, Gewürztraminer, Riesling, Chardonnay, Marsanne, Frontignac and Pinot Gris. Victoria also produces excellent sparkling wine.

Good Producers
Morris, Campbells, Brown Bros, de Bortoli, Trentham Estate, Seppelt, Best's, Mount Langi Ghiran, Jasper Hill, Yarra Yering, Coldstream Hills, Tahbilk Wines, Mitchelton.

Four Sisters has established itself as a pioneer by winemaker Trevor Mast.

How Victoria's famous Muscats and Tokays are made

Brown Muscat and Muscadelle grapes are picked late, when they are at their sweetest, to produce fine Muscats and Tokays respectively. Once the grapes have been crushed, the resulting juice is often fermented in traditional open concrete tanks which have been in use for generations. The wine is then fortified with top-quality grape spirit, which will give it an ultimate alcohol strength of around 18.5 per cent. The solera system, in which young vintages are blended with older ones, gives more depth to the wines and also ensures that they retain a consistent quality. Some wineries, such as Morris, use a base wine combined with vintages going back more than a century. The flavour of wine in the oldest barrel is so intense that one teaspoon can add a new dimension to 200 l (45 gal) of base wine.

Mick Morris sampling his famous Muscat from barrels

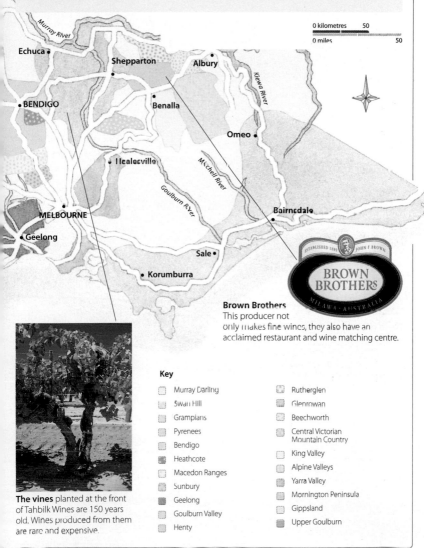

0 kilometres 50

0 miles 50

Murray River

Echuca

Shepparton

Albury

Kiewa River

BENDIGO

Benalla

Omeo

Healesville

Mitchell River

Goulburn River

MELBOURNE

Bairnsdale

Geelong

Sale

Korumburra

Brown Brothers
This producer not only makes fine wines, they also have an acclaimed restaurant and wine matching centre.

BROWN BROTHERS
ESTABLISHED 1889 · JOHN F BROWN
MILAWA · AUSTRALIA

The vines planted at the front of Tahbilk Wines are 150 years old. Wines produced from them are rare and expensive.

Key

- Murray Darling
- Swan Hill
- Grampians
- Pyrenees
- Bendigo
- Heathcote
- Macedon Ranges
- Sunbury
- Geelong
- Goulburn Valley
- Henty
- Rutherglen
- Glenrowan
- Beechworth
- Central Victorian Mountain Country
- King Valley
- Alpine Valleys
- Yarra Valley
- Mornington Peninsula
- Gippsland
- Upper Goulburn

MELBOURNE

John Batman, the son of a Sydney convict, arrived in what is now known as the Port Phillip district in 1835 and met with Aboriginal tribes of the Kulin, from whom he "purchased" the land. In just over two decades Melbourne grew from a small tent encampment to a sprawling metropolis. Today it is thriving as the second-largest city in Australia.

Melbourne's rapid growth was precipitated in the 1850s by the huge influx of immigrants seeking their fortunes on the rich gold fields of Victoria. This caused a population explosion of unprecedented proportions as prospectors decided to stay in the city. The enormous wealth generated by the gold rush led to the construction of grand public buildings. This development continued throughout the land boom of the 1880s, earning the city the nickname "Marvellous Melbourne". By the end of the 19th century, the city was the industrial and financial capital of Australia. It was also the home of the national parliament until 1927, when it was moved to purpose-built Canberra (see p195).

Fortunate enough to escape much damage in World War II, Melbourne hosted the summer Olympics in 1956. Dubbed the "Friendly Games", the event generated great changes in the city's consciousness. The postwar period also witnessed a new wave of immigrants who sought better lives here. Driven by the will to succeed, they introduced Melburnians to a range of cultures, transforming the British traditions of the city. This transformation continues today with the arrival of immigrants from all parts of Asia.

Melbourne holds many surprises: it has the most elaborate Victorian architecture of all Australian cities, it has a celebrated range of restaurant cuisines and its calendar revolves around hugely popular spectator sports and arts events (see pp44–5). While the climate is renowned for its unpredictability, Melburnians still enjoy an outdoor lifestyle, and the city possesses a unique charm that quietly bewitches many visitors.

The beautiful city of Melbourne across the Yarra River

◄ The Neo-Gothic interior of St Paul's Cathedral

Exploring Melbourne

Melbourne is organized informally into precincts.
Collins Street is a business centre and the site of the city's
smartest stores. To the east is the parliamentary precinct.
Swanston Street contains some fine Victorian architecture.
The south bank of the river is arts-orientated and includes
the Arts Centre Melbourne. The city also devotes much land
to parks and gardens.

Eureka Tower and Melbourne skyline

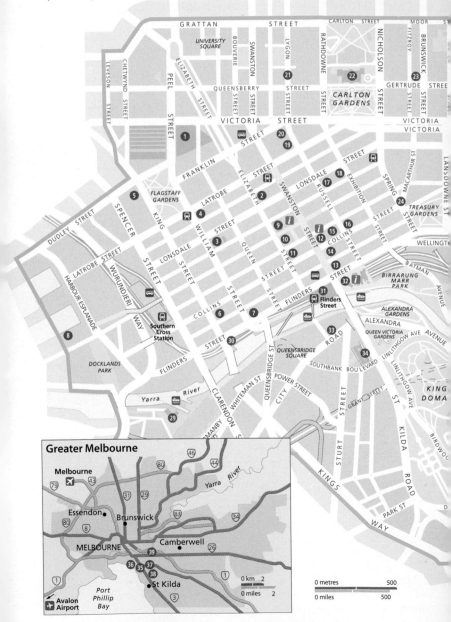

Getting Around

Despite the comprehensive Metro transport system of trams, trains and buses, many Melburnians use cars for commuting *(see pp416–17)*. This has resulted in a network of major roads and highways that lead in all directions from Melbourne's central grid through inner and outer suburbs. CityLink is a tollway linking several of the major access routes; drivers must purchase a pass prior to travelling on or within three days of using CityLink roads. The city's flat landscape is also well suited to bicycles.

Sights at a Glance

Historic Streets and Buildings

- ❸ Supreme Court
- ❹ Melbourne Mint
- ❽ Docklands
- ❾ General Post Office
- ⑫ Melbourne Town Hall
- ⑭ Regent Theatre
- ⑯ No. 120 Collins Street
- ⑰ Chinatown
- ⑲ Old Magistrate's Court
- ⑳ Old Melbourne Gaol
- ㉑ Lygon Street
- ㉓ Brunswick Street & Fitzroy
- ㉛ Flinders Street Station
- ㉜ Federation Square
- ㉟ Fitzroy & Acland streets
- ㊲ Chapel Street
- ㊳ *Rippon Lea pp408–9*
- ㊴ Como Historic House and Garden

Shops and Markets

- ❶ Queen Victoria Market
- ⑩ Royal Arcade
- ⑪ Block Arcade

Churches and Cathedrals

- ❷ St Francis' Church
- ❺ St James' Old Cathedral
- ⑬ St Paul's Cathedral
- ⑮ Scots' Church

Museums and Galleries

- ❼ Immigration Museum
- ⑱ Museum of Chinese Australian History
- ㉒ Melbourne Museum
- ㉔ Old Treasury Building
- ㉕ National Sports Museum
- ㉙ Polly Woodside
- ㉚ Melbourne Aquarium
- ㉞ National Gallery of Victoria

Parks and Gardens

- ㉘ *Royal Botanic Gardens and Kings Domain pp402–3*

Modern Architecture

- ❻ Rialto Towers
- ㉝ Eureka Tower

Sports Grounds

- ㉖ Melbourne Cricket Ground
- ㉗ Melbourne Park
- ㊱ Albert Park

Key

▧ Place of interest

Gothic turrets of the Old Magistrate's Court

For keys to symbols *see back flap*

Swanston Street Precinct

Swanston Street, home to Melbourne's town hall and other major civic buildings, has always been a hub of the city. It is an eclectic illustration of the city's Victorian and 20th-century public architecture and exemplary of one of the most interesting relics of Melbourne: an ordered grid of broad, evenly measured and rectilinear streets, lanes and arcades. This major thoroughfare was named after Captain Charles Swanston, a banker, politician and member of the Port Phillip Association.

Classically inspired Storey Hall, neighbour of the RMIT Building

The City Baths are set in a beautiful Edwardian building with twin cupolas as a distinctive feature. They have been carefully restored to their original 1903 condition.

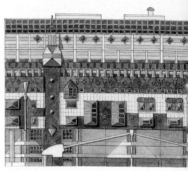

① City Baths

② RMIT Building 8

⑬ St Paul's Cathedral
Architect William Butterfield designed St Paul's in a Gothic Revival style in the 1880s.

⑫ Melbourne Town Hall
The city's town hall was built in 1867, funded by proceeds of the gold rush (see pp58–9).

Sandstone façade

Neo-Classical columns

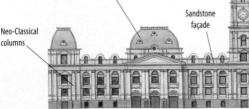

④ Melbourne Town Hall

⑤ St Paul's Cathedral

For hotels and restaurants in this area see pp493–4 and pp526–9

Building 8, RMIT (Royal Melbourne Institute of Technology), is a gaudy, contemporary blend of bold, primary colours utilized within horizontal and vertical lines. It was met with very mixed reviews by Melburnians when it was completed.

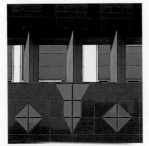

Locator Map
See Melbourne Street Finder, map 1

The State Library was the first design by noted architect Joseph Reed in 1854. Inside is an attractive octagonal reading room, covered by the central dome which was added in 1913.

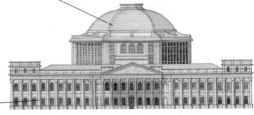

Neo-Classical Corinthian columns line the façade.

③ State Library of Victoria

③ Flinders Street Station
Melbourne's busiest rail terminus is one of the most recognizable sights in the city.

Station clock

Young and Jackson's, a 19th-century hotel known for its nude portrait *Chloe*, is protected by the National Trust.

The Atrium in Federation Square is a remarkable building made of glass, steel and zinc. The Square itself has become the cultural centre of the city, with its restaurants, various attractions and outdoor events.

⑥ Flinders Street Station

⑦ Young and Jackson's

⑧ Federation Square

Fruit stall in Queen Victoria Market

❶ Queen Victoria Market

Elizabeth, Therry, Peel & Victoria sts.
Map 1 B2. **Tel** (03) 9320 5822.
🚇 Flagstaff & Melbourne Central
(Elizabeth St exit). 🚊 Elizabeth St
routes. **Open** 6am–2pm Tue & Thu;
6am–5pm Fri; 6am–3pm Sat; 9am–4pm
Sun. **Closed** public hols. ♿ 📷
🖳 **qvm.com.au**

Melbourne's main fresh produce
and general goods market has
a strange history, occupying the
site of the original Melbourne
General Cemetery, which was
first used in 1837. In 1877, the
idea of converting part of the
original cemetery into a marketplace for fruit and vegetables
was considered a practical one.
At the time, it involved the
relocation of only three graves.
However, the choice created
controversy which did not
settle down for some time, as
the market's popularity made
it necessary to acquire further
portions of the cemetery.
In 1917, an act of Parliament
granted the removal of the
remains. However, only 900
were taken away. The rest still lie
there, mainly under the car park.
   The market began with the
construction of the Wholesale
Meat Market. In 1884, the Meat
Market and Elizabeth Street
shop façades were built. Further
extensions continued to
be built until 1936. Today
the complex, occupying 7 ha
(17 acres), attracts 130,000 visitors
per week. Its decorative high-
vaulted ceilings and open sides
add to its ornate atmosphere.
About 1,000 stalls sell fresh fruit

and vegetables, fish, meat,
cheese, organic food and
souvenirs and clothing. Every
Wednesday from November
to February there is a Night
Market (5:30–10pm).

❷ St Francis' Church

326 Lonsdale St. **Map** 1 C2. **Tel** (03)
9663 2495. 🚇 Melbourne Central.
🚊 Elizabeth St routes. **Open** 7am–
6:30pm daily. ♿ 📷 by arrangement.
🖳 **stfrancismelbourne.org.au**

St Francis' Church today is
Australia's busiest Roman
Catholic church, with 10,000
visitors each week. Built
between 1841 and 1845 on
the site of an earlier church,
it is also Victoria's oldest.
   Renowned for its beauty,
the church began as a simple
Neo-Gothic building and has
undergone many alterations.
It was the target of a $2.8 million
restoration appeal, and major
renovations were completed

in the early 1990s. During the
ceiling restoration, treasures
from the 1860s, such as a
painting of angels, stars and a
coat of arms, were discovered
and beautifully restored.
Vandalized statues have since
been replaced by faithful copies.
   The church holds regular
services, and has one of Australia's
most celebrated resident choirs.

Roof detail of St Francis' Church

❸ Supreme Court

210 William St. **Map** 1 B3. **Tel** (03) 9603
6111. 🚇 Flagstaff. 🚊 City Circle &
Bourke St routes. **Open** 9:30am–4pm
Mon–Fri (5pm Fri); courts sit
10am–4:15pm. ♿ 📷

When the Port Phillip district
was still part of the New South
Wales colony, criminal and
important civil cases were
heard in Sydney. To ease the
inconvenience, Melbourne's
first resident judge arrived in
1841 to set up a Supreme Court
in the city. Following the

Domed library in the Supreme Court

For hotels and restaurants in this area see pp493–4 and pp526–9

Separation Act of 1851, which established the Colony of Victoria, the city set up its own Supreme Court in 1852. The court moved to the present building, with a design inspired by the Four Courts of Dublin in Ireland, in 1884.

The Supreme Court is an imposing building, with street façades on Lonsdale, William and Little Bourke streets. Its style is Classical, with a projecting portico and a double arcade with Doric and Ionic columns. Internally, a labyrinthine plan is centred on a beautiful domed library. The large bronze figure of Justice, defying tradition, is not blindfolded: rumour has it that an early Melbourne judge persuaded the authorities that Justice should be "wide-eyed if not innocently credulous". The Supreme Court Library is now classified by the National Trust.

❹ Melbourne Mint

280 William St. **Map** 1 D3. **Tel** (03) 8602 5188. ⓕ Flagstaff. ⓣ 24, 30. ⓢ Lonsdale & Queen sts routes. **Closed** to the public. ⓦ **melbournemint.com.au**

This former Mint, built between 1871 and 1872, contains two courts which were formerly used to cope with the overflow from the Supreme Court.

The building replaced Melbourne's first Exhibition Building, erected in 1854 and subsequently destroyed by fire. When the mint opened in 1872 it processed finds from the Victoria gold fields and was a branch of the Royal Mint of London. The actual coining processes took place in an area now occupied by the car park. After the Commonwealth of Australia was founded in 1901 (see p60), new silver coinage was designed, which the mint produced from 1916 to the mid-1960s. The Melbourne site ceased production in 1967

when the Mint was relocated to Canberra. Although the Melbourne Mint building is now closed to the general public, visitors can still take in its imposing structure from the outside.

St James' Old Cathedral tower

❺ St James' Old Cathedral

Cnr King & Batman sts. **Map** 1 A2. **Tel** (03) 9329 0903. ⓕ Flagstaff. ⓣ 24, 30, 48, 75. ⓢ 220, 232. **Open** 10am–4pm Mon–Fri; 10am service Sun. **Closed** public hols. ⓖ ⓒ by appointment.

St James' was the first Anglican cathedral in the city, used until St Paul's opened in 1891 (see p393). It was first built near the corner of Little Collins and William streets to replace a wooden hut, known as the "Pioneers' Church". It was relocated to its present site between 1913 and 1914. The stones were numbered to ensure that the original design was replicated. However, a few changes were made, such as a lower ceiling, a shortening of the sanctuary and a reshaping of the bell tower.

St James' was designed in a colonial Georgian style. The foundations are made of bluestone and the main walls were constructed with local sandstone. The cathedral was opened for worship on 2 October 1842, but was not consecrated until 1853.

Melbourne Mint crest

Charles Perry, the city's first bishop, was enthroned here in 1848. The cathedral is still used for regular services. A small museum contains photographs, historic documents and cathedral mementos.

❻ Rialto Towers

525 Collins St (between King and William sts) **Map** 1 B4. ⓕ Southern Cross Station. ⓣ Collins St routes. **Open** 10am–10pm daily. ⓐ ⓖ ⓦ **rialto.com.au**

Rialto Towers is a member of the World Federation of Great Towers. It has 58 floors above street level and 8 below. From street level up, it measures 253 m (830 ft).

The structure was built in 1986 by Australian developer Bruno Grollo, who was also responsible for the Eureka Tower (see p407). The former observation deck, on the 55th floor, is now the setting for the Vue de Monde restaurant including the sophisticated Lui Bar. This fine establishment is one of the city's most spectacular places to dine, with panoramic views over Melbourne. The bar area is also open to non-diners.

The lift travels from the ground floor to the 55th floor in 38 seconds and is one of the fastest in the world.

The mighty Rialto Towers

❼ Immigration Museum

400 Flinders St. **Map** 1 B4.
Tel 13 11 02. 🚇 Southern Cross
Station. 🚊 Collins St routes. **Open**
10am–5pm daily. **Closed** Good Fri,
25 Dec. 🅿 ♿ 🌐 **museumvictoria.**
com.au/immigrationmuseum

The Immigration Museum
explores the stories – some sad,
some funny, but all engaging –
of real people from all over the
world who have migrated to
Victoria. Located in the Old
Customs House, it uses moving
images, personal and community
memories, and memorabilia to
recreate the journey and arrival
of immigrants and to explore
the impact of immigration on
indigenous people.

❽ Docklands

Map 1 A4. **Tel** 1300 66 3008.
🚇 Southern Cross Station.
🚊 City Circle 31, 48, 86.
🚌 236. ⛴ Yarra River Shuttle.
🌐 **docklands.com**

The spectacular redevelopment of Melbourne Docklands
makes it worth visiting for the
modern architecture alone.
The total redevelopment area
is 200 ha (490 acres),
with 3 km (2 miles) of Yarra
River frontage. The final stage
of the project is to be completed in 2020. Docklands is
also home to the Melbourne
Star ferris wheel.
    The area has a beautiful
harbour and marina, magnificent public spaces, such as
Harbour Esplanade, Grand Plaza
and Docklands Park, historic
wharves, urban art (by
Australian artists such as Bruce

General Post Office's magnificent and architecturally eclectic interior

Armstrong), shops and
restaurants. It hosts events
such as the Summer Boat
Show and is home to Etihad
Stadium where sports
events are held.

❾ General Post Office

Cnr Little Bourke St Mall & Elizabeth St.
Map 1 C3. **Tel** (03) 9290 0200.
🚇 Flinders St & Melbourne Central.
🚊 Bourke & Elizabeth sts routes.
Open 10am–6pm Mon–Thu & Sat,
10am–8pm Fri, 11am–5pm Sun.
Closed Good Fri, 25 Dec, 1 Jan.
♿ via Little Bourke St.

Melbourne's postal service
moved to this site in 1841.
The present structure was
begun in 1859 and completed
in 1907. The first and second
floors were built between
1859 and 1867, with the third
floor and clocktower added
between 1885 and 1890. This
has resulted in an unusual
combination of styles, with
Doric columns on the ground
floor, Ionic on the second and
Corinthian on the top level.
    The building had a post-
World War I redesign under

the direction of architect
Walter Burley Griffin (see p201).
It closed as a post office in 1993
and is now an H&M megastore
containing some of the biggest
names in international and
Australian fashion.

Royal Arcade entrance

❿ Royal Arcade

Elizabeth, Bourke & Little Collins sts.
Map 1 C3. **Tel** (03) 9670 7777.
🚇 Flinders St. 🚊 Bourke, Elizabeth &
Collins sts routes. **Open** 9am–6pm
Mon–Thu, 9am–9pm Fri, 9am–5:30pm
Sat, 10am–5pm Sun.

Royal Arcade is Melbourne's
oldest surviving arcade. It is
part of a network of lanes and
arcades which sprang up to
divide the big blocks of the
city grid into smaller segments.
The network was designed
in 1837 by the government
surveyor, Robert Hoddle.
    The original arcade, built in
1869 and designed by Charles
Webb, runs between Bourke
Street Mall and Little Collins
Street. An annexe, with an
entrance on Elizabeth Street,
was added in 1902. A statue

Docklands with the Etihad Stadium and the city's CBD in the background

For hotels and restaurants in this area see pp493–4 and pp526–9

of Father Time, originally on the Bourke Street façade, is now located inside the arcade at the northern end.

The arcade's most famous inhabitants are statues of Gog and Magog, mythical representations of the conflict between the ancient Britons and the Trojans. They are modelled on identical figures in the Guildhall in the City of London. Between them is Gaunt's Clock, crafted by an original tenant of the arcade, Thomas Gaunt.

Chapel of Ascension in St Paul's Cathedral

⓫ Block Arcade

282 Collins St. **Map** 1 C3. **Tel** (03) 9654 5244. 🚇 Flinders St. v Swanston & Collins sts routes. **Open** 10am–6pm daily (to 9pm Thu & Fri, to 5pm Sat & Sun). **Closed** Good Fri, 25 Dec. 🚻 🖾 Thu only, booking essential.

Built between 1891 and 1893, with period details including a mosaic floor and a central dome, Melbourne's most opulent arcade was named after the promenade taken by fashionable society in the 1890s. Known as "doing the block", the walk involved strolling down Collins Street between Elizabeth and Swanston streets.

The arcade was restored in 1988. It still includes the Hopetoun Tea-rooms, which have been in place since the structure was opened. Guided tours of the arcade are available.

Block Arcade façade

⓬ Melbourne Town Hall

Swanston St. **Map** 1 C3. **Tel** (03) 9658 9658. 🚇 Flinders St. 🚋 Swanston & Collins sts routes. **Open** 9am–6pm Mon–Fri, 9am–5pm Sat–Sun (ground level foyer only). **Closed** public hols. 🚻 🖾 11am & 1pm daily, obligatory for areas other than ground level foyer.

Melbourne Town Hall was completed in 1870, designed by Joseph Reed's company, Reed & Barnes. The portico was added in 1887. From here there are views of Swanston Street (see pp388–9) and the Shrine of Remembrance in the Botanic Gardens (see p402).

An adjacent administration block and the council's second chamber were added in 1908. This chamber combines a Renaissance-style interior with uniquely Australian motifs, such as a ceiling plasterwork of gum nuts.

A fire in 1925 destroyed much of the building's interior, including the main hall which had to be rebuilt. The entrance to the building shows four motifs on the young city's coat of arms: a whale, a ship, a bull and a sheep, signifying the main colonial industries. In 1942, the College of Arms ordered an inversion of the motifs according to heraldic convention. This explains the discrepancy between earlier and later coats of arms.

Stained glass in Melbourne Town Hall

⓭ St Paul's Cathedral

Cnr Swanston & Flinders sts. **Map** 2 D3. **Tel** (03) 9653 4333. 🚇 Flinders St. 🚋 Swanston, Flinders & Collins sts routes. **Open** 8am–6pm Sun–Fri, 9am–4pm Sat. 🚻 🖾

St Paul's Cathedral was built in 1866 to replace a far smaller church of the same name on the site.

Construction, however, was plagued by difficulties, with dissension between the English architect, William Butterfield, and the Cathedral Erection Board. Building began in 1880, but Butterfield tendered his resignation in 1884. The final stages of construction were supervised by the architect Joseph Reed, who also designed many of the fittings. The cathedral was eventually consecrated in 1891.

There are many outstanding internal features, including the reredos (altar screen) made in Italy from marble and alabaster inset with glass mosaics. The organ, made by T C Lewis & Co. of London, is the best surviving work of this great organ-builder. The cathedral also has a peal of 13 bells – a rarity outside the British Isles.

The cathedral underwent a five-year restoration, completed in 2009, which included the cleaning and upgrading of the spectacular stained-glass windows.

⓮ Regent Theatre

191 Collins St. **Map** 2 D3. **Tel** (03) 9299 9500. 🚉 Flinders St. 🚃 Swanston & Collins sts routes. ♿ 🎫 outside performance times & by appt. 🎭

When the Regent Theatre's auditorium was destroyed by fire in April 1945, the Lord Mayor of Melbourne promised the public that it would be rebuilt, despite the scarcity of building materials due to World War II, such was the popularity and local importance of the theatre.

Known as "Melbourne's Palace of Dreams", it was first constructed and opened in 1929 and later sold to the Hoyts Theatre Company. Its lavish interiors emulated both the glamour of Hollywood and New York's impressive Capitol Theater.

The building had two main venues. The auditorium upstairs, for live stage and musical entertainment, was known as the Regent Theatre. Downstairs, the Plaza Theatre was originally a ballroom but, following the success of the "talkies", it was converted into a cinema.

Fortunately, the magnificent decor of the Plaza Theatre was not damaged in the fire of 1945 and the renovated auditorium re-opened in 1947.

Assembly hall adjacent to Scots' Church

The advent of television soon resulted in dwindling cinema audiences, and the Regent Theatre closed for almost three decades. The complex was restored in 1996 and is now listed by the National Trust.

⓯ Scots' Church

99 Russell St (cnr Collins St). **Map** 2 D3. **Tel** (03) 9650 9903. 🚉 Flinders St & Parliament. 🚃 Swanston & Collins sts routes. **Open** 11am–2:30pm Mon–Fri. 🕐 1pm, Wed; 11am & 7pm, Sun. ♿ 📷 on request.

Scots' Church, completed in 1874, was intended at the time to be "the most beautiful building in Australia". It was designed by Joseph Reed in a

"decorated Gothic" style, with bluestone used in the foundations and local Barrabool stone making up the superstructure.

The site also includes an assembly hall which was completed in 1913.

⓰ No. 120 Collins Street

120 Collins St. **Map** 2 D3. 🚉 Flinders St & Parliament. 🚃 Collins St routes. **Open** 7am–7pm Mon–Fri. ♿

Built in 1991, No. 120 Collins Street was designed by Daryl Jackson and Hassell Architects and houses the offices of many blue-chip corporations. In the heart of Melbourne's central business district, the office

Grandiose foyer of the Regent Theatre, restored to its original glory

For hotels and restaurants in this area see pp493–4 and pp526–9

block is now a city landmark. Its communications tower was for many years the highest point in the city, at 265 m (869 ft). Original 1908 Federation-style professional chambers, built on the grounds of the 1867 St Michael's Uniting Church, are incorporated into the building.

Chambers at No. 120 Collins Street

⑰ Chinatown

Little Bourke St. **Map** 2 D2.
🚇 Parliament. 🚋 Swanston & Bourke sts routes.

When Chinese immigrants began arriving in Melbourne to seek gold during the 1850s, many European residents were decidedly hostile. Only recent arrivals in the area themselves, they were still insecure about how strongly their own society had been established. This led to racial tension and violence.

The very first Chinese immigrants landed in Australia as early as 1818, but it was during the late 1840s that larger contingents arrived. These newcomers replaced the pool of cheap labour which had dried up with the winding down of convict settlements in the new colonies. This wave of immigration was harmonious until the vast influx of Chinese visitors who came not for labour, but to seek their fortune in the Victorian gold fields in the 1850s. The large numbers of immigrants and a decline in gold finds made the Chinese targets of vicious and organized riots.

This attitude was sanctioned by government policy. The Chinese were charged a poll tax in most states of £10 each – a huge sum, particularly as many were peasants. Even harsher was a restriction on the number of passengers that boat-owners could carry. This acted as a disincentive for them to bring Chinese immigrants to Australia. What resulted were "Chinese marathons", as new arrivals dodged the tax by landing in "free" South Australia and walking to the gold fields, covering distances of up to 800 km (500 miles) (see pp58–9).

As an immigrant society in Melbourne, the Chinese were highly organized and self-sufficient. A city base was established during the 1850s, utilizing the cheap rental district of the city centre. As with other Chinatowns around the world, traders could live and work in the same premises and act as a support network for other Chinese immigrants. The community largely avoided prejudice by starting up traditional Asian businesses which included market gardening, laundering, green grocers and furniture-making (but work had to be stamped "Made by Chinese labour").

Traditional gateway in Little Bourke Street, Chinatown

Today, Chinatown is known for its restaurants and Chinese produce shops, with the community's calendar culminating in its New Year celebrations in January or February (see p45). Ironically, in view of the early prejudices, this community is now one of Australia's oldest and most successful.

⑱ Museum of Chinese Australian History

22 Cohen Place (off Little Bourke St).
Map 2 D2. **Tel** (03) 9662 2888.
🚇 Parliament. 🚋 Swanston & Bourke sts routes. **Open** 10am–5pm daily.
Closed 1 Jan, Good Fri, 25 Dec. ♿
♿ 🅿 🅦 chinesemuseum.com.au

Opened in 1985 to preserve the heritage of Australians of Chinese descent, this museum is in the heart of Chinatown. The subjects of its displays range from the influx of Chinese gold-seekers in the 1850s to exhibitions of contemporary Chinese art, thus offering a comprehensive history of the Chinese in Victoria and their cultural background. The second floor holds regular touring exhibitions from China and displays of Chinese art. On the third floor is a permanent exhibition covering many aspects of Chinese-Australian history, including elaborate costumes, furniture and temple regalia.

Stone lion in the Museum of Chinese Australian History

In the basement, another permanent exhibition traces the experiences of Chinese gold miners – visitors step into a booth which creaks and moves like a transport ship, then view dioramas of gold field life, a Chinese temple and a tent theatre used by Chinese performers to entertain miners. A guided heritage walk through Chinatown is also available.

The museum also houses the beautiful Melbourne Chinese dragon, the head of which is the largest of its kind anywhere in the world.

Street-by-Street: Parliament Area

The Parliament precinct on Eastern Hill is a gracious area of great historic interest. Early founders of the city noted the favourable aspect of the hill and set it aside for Melbourne's official and ecclesiastical buildings. The streets still retain the elegance of the Victorian era; the buildings, constructed with revenue from the gold rush *(see pp58–9)*, are among the most impressive in the city. The Fitzroy Gardens, on the lower slopes of the hill, date back to the 1850s *(see pp378–9)* and provide a peaceful retreat complete with woodlands, glades, seasonal plantings and magnificent elm tree avenues.

The Hotel Windsor, with its long and ornate façade, was built in 1883 and is the grandest surviving hotel of its era in Australia *(see p493)*.

Stanford Fountain
The beautiful centrepiece of the elegant Gordon Reserve was sculpted by the prisoner William Stanford while he was serving his sentence.

★ **Old Treasury Building**
This Renaissance Revival-style building was designed by draughtsman John James Clark in 1857. Built as government offices, with vaults to house the treasury's gold, it now holds permanent and temporary exhibitions.

Cook's Cottage
This cottage was the English home of the parents of Captain James Cook *(see p54)*. It was shipped to Australia in 1934 piece by piece and now houses displays about Cook and 18th-century life.

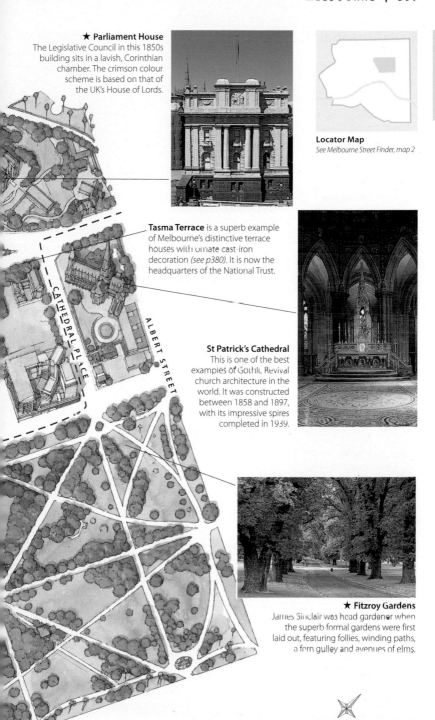

★ **Parliament House**
The Legislative Council in this 1850s building sits in a lavish, Corinthian chamber. The crimson colour scheme is based on that of the UK's House of Lords.

Locator Map
See Melbourne Street Finder, map 2

Tasma Terrace is a superb example of Melbourne's distinctive terrace houses with ornate cast-iron decoration *(see p380)*. It is now the headquarters of the National Trust.

St Patrick's Cathedral
This is one of the best examples of Gothic Revival church architecture in the world. It was constructed between 1858 and 1897, with its impressive spires completed in 1939.

CATHEDRAL PLACE

ALBERT STREET

★ **Fitzroy Gardens**
James Sinclair was head gardener when the superb formal gardens were first laid out, featuring follies, winding paths, a fern gulley and avenues of elms.

0 metres   100
0 yards   100

Key
— Suggested route

⑲ Old Magistrate's Court

Cnr La Trobe & Russell sts. **Map** 1 C2. **Tel** (03) 8663 7228. 🚇 Melbourne Central. 🚋 La Trobe & Swanston sts routes. **Open** during school hols and peak periods. 🅿 📷

The Melbourne Magistrate's Court, also called City Court, occupied this building until 1995. The area was formerly known as the police precinct – this is because the court lies opposite the former police headquarters, a very striking Art Deco skyscraper completed in the early 1940s, and next door to the Old Melbourne Gaol.

Built in 1911, the court's façades are made of native Moorabool sandstone. The building's intricate, Romanesque design features gables, turrets and arches. It originally contained three courtrooms. Court One is open to the public during school holidays and peak periods as part of the Old Melbourne Gaol Crime and Justice Experience.

Ornate Romanesque tower of the Old Magistrate's Court

⑳ Old Melbourne Gaol

Russell St. **Map** 1 C2. **Tel** (03) 8663 7228. 🚇 Melbourne Central. 🚋 La Trobe & Swanston sts routes. **Open** 9:30am–5pm daily; also for night tours Mon, Wed, Fri & Sat. **Closed** Good Fri, 25 Dec. 🅿 📷 ♿ limited.
🌐 **oldmelbournegaol.com.au**

Visiting the Old Melbourne Gaol, Victoria's first extensive gaol complex, is a chilling

Corridor of cells in Old Melbourne Gaol

experience, especially on a night tour. Between 1845 and 1929, it was the site of 133 executions. While much of the original complex has been demolished, the imposing Second Cell Block still stands and is home to a fascinating museum.

Ghosts are often reported at the gaol, which is hardly surprising given the tragic and grisly accounts of prisoners' lives and deaths. Conditions, based on London's Pentonville Model Prison, were grim, regulated and silent. When first incarcerated, prisoners were held in solitary confinement and were not permitted to mix with other prisoners until a later date, set according to their sentence. Exhibits showing these conditions include prisoners' chains and a frame used for flogging. But perhaps the most

compelling exhibits are the many accounts of prisoners who were condemned to die at the gaol, accompanied by their death masks. Ned Kelly's death mask is the most famous of those on display. Visitors can also see the original gallows where executions took place.

Included with a ticket to the Old Melbourne Gaol, visitors can now tour the former city Watch House, which served as a central "lock up" for police from 1908 to 1994. With a Charge Sergeant as a guide, visitors are "arrested" and processed through the lock up, experiencing first hand an environment that has not changed since the police and inmates left it. The Watch House has a long and fascinating history, with characters such as the 1920s gangster Squizzy

Ned Kelly

The most well-known execution at the Melbourne Gaol was that of Ned Kelly, Australia's most famous bushranger, on 11 November 1880. Edward "Ned" Kelly was the son of Ellen and ex-convict "Red" Kelly. At the time of Ned's final imprisonment and execution, Ellen was serving a sentence in the gaol's Female Ward after hitting a policeman over the head at her house when he came to arrest her son, Dan.

Ned Kelly's death mask

She was therefore able to visit Ned, who had been captured at Glenrowan on 28 June 1880 *(see p455)*. A crowd of 5,000 waited outside the gaol when Kelly was executed, most of them to lend their support to a man perceived to be rightfully rebelling against the English-based law and police authorities. In one instance, the Kelly Gang burned a bank's records of outstanding loans so they no longer had to be repaid. The controversy over whether Kelly was hero or villain continues to this day.

Taylor, last man hanged Ronald Ryan and infamous Chopper Read all having been locked up here. The experience is enhanced by informative multimedia displays that illustrate the stories of former inmates.

Italian restaurant in Lygon Street

㉑ Lygon Street

Lygon St, Carlton. **Map** 1 C1. 🚋 1, 8. 🚌 200, 201, 207.

This Italian-influenced street is one of the main café, restaurant and delicatessen areas in central Melbourne *(see pp526)*.

The strong Italian tradition of Lygon Street began at the time of mass post-World War II immigration. With a general exodus to the suburbs in the 1940s, Carlton became unfashionable and new immigrants were able to buy its 19th-century houses and shops cheaply. More importantly, the immigrants were central in protecting these Victorian and Edwardian houses, which were built with post-gold rush wealth, from government plans to fill the area with low-income Housing Commission homes.

A distinctive architectural trait of Lygon Street's two-storey shops is their street verandas, built to protect both customers and merchandise from the sun. In the mid-1960s, the area became fashionable with university students, many of whom moved in to take advantage of its cheap accommodation, then stayed on after graduating to become the base of the suburb's contemporary middle-class and professional community. The street is only one

block from the main University of Melbourne campus and can be reached from the city centre by foot, bus or tram. Its wide street resembles a French boulevard and is well suited to the Carlton Italian Festa held here every year *(see p44)*.

㉒ Melbourne Museum

Carlton Gardens, Melbourne. **Map** 2 D1. **Tel** (03) 8341 7777. 🚌 86, 96. **Open** 10am–5pm daily. **Closed** Good Fri, 25 Dec. 🏪 🖥 📷 ♿ **W** melbourne.museum.vic.gov.au

Housed in an ultra-modern facility in verdant Carlton Gardens, it has exhibits over six levels, half of which are below ground level. Diverse displays offer insights into science, technology, the environment, the human mind and body, Australian society and indigenous cultures.

One of the highlights is Bunjilaka, the Aboriginal Centre. It combines exhibition galleries with a performance space and meeting rooms. *Wurreka*, the 50-m- (150-ft-) long zinc wall etching at the entrance is by Aboriginal artist Judy Watson. The Two Laws gallery deals with the Indigenous Australians' systems of knowledge, law and property.

The Forest Gallery is a living, breathing exhibit, featuring 8,000 plants from 120 different species. It is also home to

Coffee grinder in a Lygon Street coffee house

around 20 different vertebrate species, including snakes, birds, fish and hundreds of insects. This gallery explores the complex ecosystem of Australia's temperate forests, using plants and animals, art and multimedia installations, soundscapes and other activities.

A dedicated children's museum is in a gallery that resembles a tilted, blue cube. The Blue Box houses multi-sensory displays exploring the theme of growth. There are also Children's Pathways throughout the rest of the museum, providing activities for children in other galleries.

One of the most popular exhibits is in the Australia Gallery. This treats the life of Phar Lap, the champion Australian racehorse of the early 1930s. Exhibits include race memorabilia of the period. Phar Lap himself is seen in an Art-Deco inspired showcase. Other curiosities on show in the museum include the skeleton of a blue whale, a car from Melbourne's first tram, a windmill and the Hertel, the first car to be imported.

Adjacent to the Melbourne Museum is the **Royal Exhibition Building**, offering an interesting 19th-century counterpoint to the Museum's modern architecture. The Exhibition Building was built for the 1880 International Exhibition and is one of the few remaining structures from the 19th-century world fairs. It was designed by Joseph Reed, whose work can be found throughout Melbourne.

Elegant Royal Exhibition Building, near the Melbourne Museum

Cyclists passing a clothing store on Brunswick Street

㉓ Brunswick Street and Fitzroy

Brunswick St. **Map** 2 E1.
🚋 112.

Next to the university suburb of Carlton, Fitzroy was the natural choice for a post-1960s populace of students and other bohemian characters, who took advantage of the area's cheap postwar Housing Commission properties, unwanted by wealthier Melburnians. Despite becoming gentrified, Fitzroy's main strip, Brunswick Street, maintains an alternative air and a cosmopolitan street life.

Today, Brunswick Street is a vibrant mix of cafés, restaurants and trendy shops, especially popular are the numerous vintage stores where anyone can hunt for an undiscovered treasure. Vegie Bar (p528), a vegetarian restaurant on the Brunswick street strip, is famous in Melbourne and a must-visit. From September to October, this street comes to life during the Melbourne Fringe Festival, featuring comedy acts, dance, cabaret, music and more. A little to the south is Gertrude Street, which has an eclectic mix of record stores, bars and galleries.

Nearby Johnston Street is home to Melbourne's Spanish quarter and in November, The Fiesta, an outdoor festival celebrating Hispanic-Latin American culture. All the streets in this area are most lively on Saturday nights and easily accessible on a tram.

㉔ Old Treasury Building

Old Treasury Building, Spring Street (top of Collins Street). **Map** 2 E2.
Tel (03) 9651 2233. 🚋 109, 112.
Open 10am–4pm Sun–Fri (other times group bookings only).
Closed Good Fri, 25 & 26 Dec. 🎨
🎫 group tours by request. ♿ 📷
W oldtreasurybuilding.org.au

Melbourne's beautiful, 19th-century Old Treasury Building (see p396) was designed in 1857 by John James Clark, a nineteen-year-old architectural prodigy. It provided secure storage for gold that flooded into Melbourne from the wealthy Victorian gold fields. It also served as office accommodation for the Governor of Victoria (a role it still fulfils to this day).

As well as an opportunity to see the building itself, a visit to the museum includes a look at the gold vaults that lie beneath the building. The vaults contain a dynamic multi-media exhibition Built on Gold, which tells the story of how Melbourne developed into a city of enormous wealth in a remarkably short period of ten years. In this time it went from a small colonial outpost to a vibrant city with magnificent buildings and grand boulevards, a dynamic theatre culture, a passion for sport and political activism.

㉕ National Sports Museum

Melbourne Cricket Ground, Yarra Park, Jolimont. **Map** 2 F3.
Tel (03) 9657 8879. 🚉 Richmond.
🚋 48, 70, 75. **Open** 10am–5pm daily.
Closed Good Fri, 25 Dec.
🎨 ♿ 📷

Following the redevelopment of the Melbourne Cricket Ground (MCG) for the 2006 Commonwealth Games, the MCG has become the home of the National Sports Museum. The museum honours all things sporting, including Aussie Rules football, cricket and the Olympic Games among others.

Located across two levels of the refurbished Olympic Stand, visitors can view some of the finest sports-related memorabilia using state-of-the-art technology. The Olympic Museum has displays of the history of all summer Olympic meets.

The Australian Cricket Hall of Fame, which opened with ten Australian players as initial members, includes Sir Donald Bradman. Each player is presented through a comprehensive historical display.

After you have wandered through the museum, you can take a tour which includes the Arena, the Great Southern Stand, the Ponsford Stand, the football and cricket changing rooms, heritage artworks and the corporate suites. Tours leave from Gate No.3 every half hour between 10am and 3pm, but only on non-event days. Booking is not essential.

Olympic Cauldron on display in the Olympic Museum

World-famous Melbourne Cricket Ground backed by the city skyline

ⓩ Melbourne Cricket Ground

Yarra Park, Jolimont. **Map** 2 F3. **Tel** (03) 9657 88/9. 🚆 Jolimont. 🚊 48, 70, 75 (special trams run on sports event days). **Open** for tours (10am–3pm daily, except event days) or sports events. 🚶 ♿ 📷 obligatory. **W** mcg.org.au

Melbourne Cricket Ground (MCG) is Australia's premier sports stadium and a cultural icon. The land was granted in 1853 to the Melbourne Cricket Club (MCC), itself conceived in 1838.

The MCG predominantly hosts cricket and Australian Rules football, being the site for test matches and the first one-day international match and for the Australian Football League Grand Final, held on the last Saturday of September (see p44). Non-sporting events, such as pop concerts, are also held here.

There have been numerous stands and pavilions over the years, each superseded at different times by reconstructions of the ground. An 1876 stand, now demolished, was reversible, with spectators able to watch cricket on the ground and football in the park in winter. Following massive redevelopment of the ground ahead of the 2006 Commonwealth Games, the MCG can now seat crowds of more than 100,000. Guided tours usually take visitors to the members' pavilion, which includes the Melbourne Cricket Club (MCC) Museum. It traces the history of the MCG with an exhibition of information and artifacts. The Mythical Ashes is a fascinating display of Ashes mementoes.

ⓩ Melbourne Park

Batman Ave. **Map** 2 E4. **Tel** (03) 9286 1600. 🚆 Flinders St & Richmond. 🚊 70. **Open** for events. Tours of Rod Laver Arena at 11:30am, 1pm, 2:30pm Mon–Fri, 11:30am, 1pm Sat & Sun (call 1300 836 647 to book). **W** mopt.com.au

Melbourne Park (formerly the National Tennis Centre) on the northern bank of the Yarra River, is Melbourne's sports and large-scale concerts venue. Events include the Australian Open (see p45), one of the four Grand Slam competitions of tennis, played under Rod Laver Arena's unique retractable roof (see p381). There are also 22 outdoor and seven indoor tennis courts for public use.

Next to Melbourne Park is the Hisense Arena, which is home to Melbourne Vixens netball team. It also hosts a stadium for cycling, dance performances, family shows, concerts and other entertainment. Opposite the park is the Westpac Centre, which was originally built for the 1956 Olympics but has been redeveloped.

Nearby Olympic Park, formerly the location for international and national athletics, is the training ground for Collingwood Football Club. The AAMI Park is also a venue for soccer events. Construction of the park began in 2007 and was completed in 2010.

Australian Open tennis match on one of the outdoor courts at Melbourne Park

⑳ Royal Botanic Gardens and Kings Domain

These adjoining gardens, established in 1852, form the green heart of Melbourne on what was originally a swamp on the edge of the city. The Botanic Gardens house one of the finest collections of botanic species in the world, as well as being highly regarded for their landscape design. William Guilfoyle, curator of the Gardens between 1873 and 1909, used his knowledge of English garden design to create a horticultural paradise. Kings Domain, once an inner-city wilderness, became instead a gracious parkland. Its civic function grew over the years, with the establishment of its monuments, statues, cultural venues and the hilltop residence of the Governor of Victoria.

Pioneer Women's Garden
This sunken, formal garden was built in 1934 to honour the memory of Victoria's founding women. A still, central pool is adorned by a bronze, female statue.

KEY

① **Observatory Gate Precinct**

② **Sidney Myer Music Bowl** is an architecturally acclaimed music "shell" which can accommodate up to 15,000 people for open-air concerts and ballets.

③ **The Temple of the Winds**

④ **The Perennial Border**, based on designer Gertrude Jekyll's traditional colour scheme, is planted with pastels, contrasting with grey and silver foliage.

⑤ **The Ian Potter Foundation Children's Garden**

⑥ **La Trobe's Cottage** was shipped from England in 1839 and was home to Victoria's first governor, Charles La Trobe. The building is now preserved by the National Trust.

★ **Shrine of Remembrance**
Based on the description of the Mausoleum of Halicarnassus in Asia Minor, now Turkey, this imposing monument honours Australian soldiers who gave their lives in war.

For hotels and restaurants in this area see pp493–4 and pp526–9

★ **Government House**
This elaborate Italianate building is a landmark of the gardens. Tours of the state rooms are held each week.

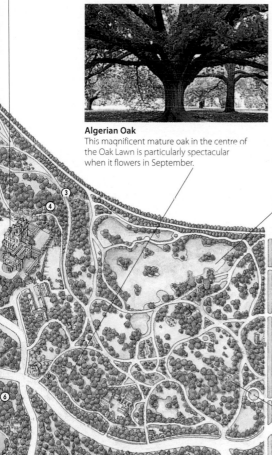

Algerian Oak
This magnificent mature oak in the centre of the Oak Lawn is particularly spectacular when it flowers in September.

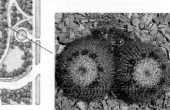

★ **Ornamental Lake**
William Guilfoyle's lake forms the centrepiece of the Gardens. It reflects his adherence to 18th-century English garden design, which used water as a feature.

Arid Garden
Desert region plants from Australia and around the world thrive in this special garden, watered by a small stream which acts as a natural oasis.

0 metres   200
0 yards   200

The Yarra River

The Yarra River winds for 240 km (150 miles) from its source in Baw Baw National Park to the coast, emptying in Port Phillip Bay. The river has always been vital to the city, not just as its major natural feature, but also in early settlement days as its gateway to the rest of the world. Today, the Yarra is a symbol of the boundary between north and south Melbourne and many citizens live their whole lives on one side or the other. Since the 1980s, the rejuvenation of the central section of the river has given the south bank an important focus. The river is also used for sport: rowers in training are a daily sight and cycle trails run along much of the river.

Locator Map
See Melbourne Street Finder, maps 1, 2

Arts Centre Melbourne holds performances by the Australian Ballet and the Melbourne Theatre Company. Its 162-m (531-ft) spire is a local landmark. There is also a spiegeltent (Feb–Apr, Jul & Aug).

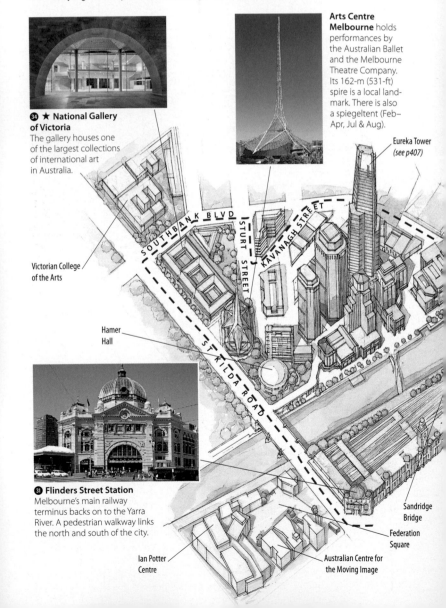

㉞ ★ National Gallery of Victoria
The gallery houses one of the largest collections of international art in Australia.

Eureka Tower *(see p407)*

Victorian College of the Arts

SOUTHBANK BLVD

STURT STREET

KAVANAGH STREET

Hamer Hall

ST KILDA ROAD

㉛ Flinders Street Station
Melbourne's main railway terminus backs on to the Yarra River. A pedestrian walkway links the north and south of the city.

Ian Potter Centre

Australian Centre for the Moving Image

Sandridge Bridge

Federation Square

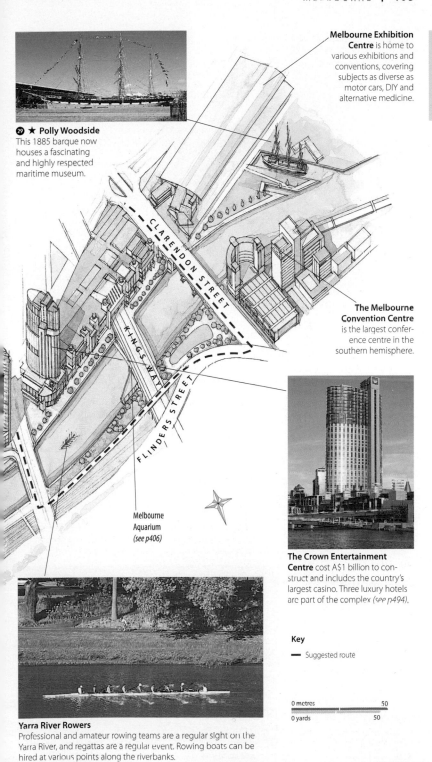

Melbourne Exhibition Centre is home to various exhibitions and conventions, covering subjects as diverse as motor cars, DIY and alternative medicine.

㉙ ★ Polly Woodside
This 1885 barque now houses a fascinating and highly respected maritime museum.

The Melbourne Convention Centre is the largest conference centre in the southern hemisphere.

Melbourne Aquarium (see p406)

The Crown Entertainment Centre cost A$1 billion to construct and includes the country's largest casino. Three luxury hotels are part of the complex (see p494).

Key

— Suggested route

0 metres   50
0 yards   50

Yarra River Rowers
Professional and amateur rowing teams are a regular sight on the Yarra River, and regattas are a regular event. Rowing boats can be hired at various points along the riverbanks.

Polly Woodside barque moored on the Yarra River

㉙ Polly Woodside

Lorimer St East, Southbank. **Map** 1 A5. **Tel** (03) 9656 9800. ☷ Southern Cross. ☷ 96, 109, 112. ☷ Grimes Street Bridge. **Open** 10am–4pm daily. **Closed** Good Fri, 25 Dec. ☷ ☷ except for ship. ☷ book in advance. ☷ pollywoodside.com.au

The *Polly Woodside* is an 1885 barque built in Belfast. When she was retired from service in the 1960s, she was the only deep-water commercial ship still afloat in Australia. Even in 1885, she was rare, as only one in four ships were then built with sails. Most of the last 40 years of her working life were spent as a coal hulk. Donated to the National Trust in 1968, she has since been restored. Interactive displays explore life at sea and working on Melbourne's docks.

Polly Woodside exhibit

㉚ Melbourne Aquarium

Cnr Flinders & King sts. **Map** 1 B4. **Tel** (03) 9923 5925. ☷ Southern Cross, Flinders St. ☷ 70. **Open** 9:30am–6pm daily (to 9pm in Jan). ☷ ☷ ☷ ☷ ☷ melbourneaquarium.com.au

Featuring species from the Australian, southern and tropical oceans, the Melbourne Aquarium puts humans close to some of the exotic inhabitants of the deep. Among the exhibits is the Oceanarium, approached through a viewing cylinder and housing sharks and rays as well as vibrantly coloured fish. Melbourne Aquarium is the only place in Victoria where you can see King and Gentoo penguins.

㉛ Flinders Street Station

Cnr Flinders & Swanston sts. **Map** 1 C4. **Tel** 13 16 38. ☷ Swanston St and Flinders St routes. ☷

Flinders Street Station is the central metropolitan train terminus of Melbourne and one of the city's favourite meeting places. Generations of Melburnians have met each other on the corner steps of the station "under the Clocks". Although the original clocks are now operated by computer rather than by hand, they remain in working order. The Flinders Street site has been part of the public transport network since the city's early days. The first steam train in Australia left Flinders Street Station, then a small wooden building at the end of Elizabeth Street, in 1854. The present station building, completed in 1910, was designed by Fawcett & Ashworth. The bronze domed building with its bright yellow brickwork was fully restored and refurbished in 1984.

㉜ Federation Square

Cnr Flinders & Swanston sts. **Map** 2 D3/4. **Tel** (03) 9655 1900. ☷ Swanston St and Flinders St routes. ☷ ☷ fedsquare.com.au The Ian Potter Centre – NGV: **Tel** (03) 8662 1555. ACMI: **Tel** (03) 8663 2200.

One of Melbourne's newest public spaces, Federation Square opened in October 2002 to commemorate the centenary of the federation of the Australian states.

The square hosts up to 2,000 events each year. Its architectural highlight is the geometric design of the Atrium building, a covered public space that is a hotspot for exhibitions, festivals, book markets, wine showcases and public art installations. There are many outstanding attractions. **The Ian Potter Centre – NGV:** Australia, an offshoot of the National Gallery of Victoria *(see p407)*, is the world's first major gallery dedicated exclusively to the display of Australian art, and well worth a visit. Nearby, the **Australian Centre for the Moving Image (ACMI)** celebrates images on multimedia and film. Across four floors of the Alfred Deakin Building, the ACMI has two multi-format cinemas and the world's largest screen gallery. The square has two information points: the Melbourne Visitor Centre *(see p415)* and the Melbourne Mobility Centre at the bottom of the Federation Square car park.

Modern architecture of the Atrium building at Federation Square

View of Albert Park Lake and its wetlands

③ Eureka Tower

7 Riverside Quay. **Map** 1 C4.
Tel (03) 9693 8888. **Open** 10am–
10pm daily. 🚇 for Skydeck 🛗
🌐 eurekaskydeck.com.au

This 300-m (985-ft) tower
was named after the Eureka
Stockade, a rebellion that took
place during the Victoria gold
rush *(see p438)*. The skyscraper's
gold crown and gold-plated
windows refer back to this era.
The Skydeck on the 88th floor
has numerous viewfinders and
a glass cube called "The Edge",
which slides out 3 m (10 ft)
from the side of the building
with visitors inside.

④ National Gallery of Victoria

180 St Kilda Rd and Federation Square.
Map 2 D4. **Tel** (03) 8620 2222.
Open 10am–5pm daily **Closed** Good
Fri, 25 Apr, 25 Dec. NGV Australia: Mon;
NGV International: Tue. 🛗 🎥 📷
🌐 ngv.vic.gov.au

The first public art gallery in
Australia, the National Gallery
of Victoria opened in 1861
and housed the original State
Museum. The gallery moved to
St Kilda Rd in 1968 and contains
the largest and widest-ranging
art collection in the country.
Its most significant bequest
was from Melbourne
entrepreneur Alfred Felton
in 1904. Its collections of Old
Masters and contemporary
Australian art are outstanding.
    The international collection is
at 180 St Kilda Road *(see p404)*;
the Australian collection is
at the Ian Potter Centre in
Federation Square *(see p406)*.

⑤ Fitzroy and Acland Streets

St Kilda. **Map** 5 B5. 🚋 16, 96, 112.
🚌 246, 600, 623, 606. ⛴ St Kilda Pier.

Situated 6 km (4 miles) south
of the city centre, St Kilda
has long been the most
popular seaside suburb of
Melbourne. During the
boom-time era of the 1850s
(see pp58–9), the suburb was
inhabited by many wealthy
families. Other well-off
Victorians would holiday in
St Kilda during the summer.
St Kilda Pier, still a magnet for
visitors, was erected in 1859.
    Today St Kilda is densely
populated, with many Art
Deco apartment blocks. The
neighbourhood's main streets
are Fitzroy and Acland. The
latter, renowned as a district
of Jewish delicatessens and
cake shops, is packed with
visitors on Sundays. Fitzroy
Street is filled with upmarket
restaurants and shops.
Rejuvenated in the 1980s, the
beachside esplanade attracts
crowds to its busy arts and
crafts market each Sunday.

Melbourne tram running along the St Kilda
Beach route No. 16

③⑥ Albert Park

Canterbury Rd, Albert St & Lakeside
Drive. **Map** 5 B3. 🚋 1, 96, 112.

Encompassing the remains of
a former natural swampland,
Albert Park Lake is the attractive
centrepiece of a 225-ha (555-
acre) parkland which includes
sporting fields, a public golf
course and many other
recreational facilities. However,
it is now predominantly known
as the site of the annual
Australian Formula One Grand
Prix, which covers a 5,260-m
(5,754-yd) circuit around the
lake *(see p46)*. Apart from the
Grand Prix, the park is used for a
variety of purposes. The popular
Melbourne Sports and Aquatic
Centre is located here. Wetlands
have also been developed to
promote a diverse wildlife.
Sailing here is another popular
activity, whether by small yacht,
rowing boat or model boat.
    A large, ancient river red
gum tree standing in the centre
of the park is also reputed to
have been the site of many
Aboriginal *corroborees* (festive
night dances).

③⑦ Chapel Street

South Yarra, Prahran and Windsor.
Map 6 E3. 🚉 South Yarra, Prahan.
🚋 6, 8, 72.

Chapel Street, Melbourne's
most fashionable street, with
price-tags to match, is lined
with shops selling local and
international fashion designs.
A youthful clientele swarms
the street at weekends.
Up-market restaurants and
cafés abound and the nearby
Prahran Market sells the best
in fresh, delicatessen produce.
    Crossing Chapel Street is
Toorak Road, whose "village"
is patronized by Melbourne's
wealthiest community. More
akin to the bohemian area of
Brunswick Street *(see p400)* is
Greville Street to the west,
with its cafés, bars and chic
second-hand shops.
    A food and fashion festival
is sometimes held on the last
Sunday before the Melbourne
Cup *(see p45)*.

③ Rippon Lea

Rippon Lea Mansion, designed by Joseph Reed and built in 1868, is now part of the National Trust's portfolio. The house is a much loved fixture of the city's heritage. The first family of Rippon Lea were the Sargoods, who held many balls and parties during the 1880s and 1890s. The next owner, Premier Sir Thomas Bent, sold off parts of the estate in the early 1900s. The Nathans bought Rippon Lea in 1910 and restored its reputation as a family home. Benjamin Nathan's daughter Louisa added a ballroom and swimming pool to the house, which were the venue for parties in the 1930s and 1940s. The formal gardens are a highlight.

Façade of the elegant mansion, Rippon Lea

Victorian Bathroom
The decor of the bathroom remains in its original Victorian style as installed by the Sargoods. The earth closets were ingeniously processed into liquid manure and recycled for use in the garden.

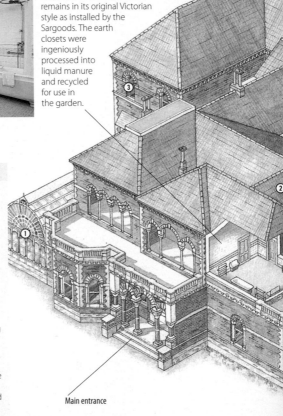

Main entrance

KEY

① **The conservatory** housed ferns and orchids, beloved flowers of both Frederick Sargood and Benjamin Nathan. Horticultural experts were regularly invited to Rippon Lea.

② **The main staircase** is oak and mahogany like much of the rest of the house. Mirrors, another recurring theme in the house, are fitted into an archway at the foot of the stairs, courtesy of Louisa Jones.

③ **Arched windows** are a recurring decorative theme throughout the house, bordered by polychrome bricks.

④ **The Tower** was an unusual feature in the design of a domestic house. In this case, it may have been inspired by Sargood, who wanted his home to have the ornateness of a church.

⑤ **The brickwork** was inspired by a trip by Joseph Reed to Lombardy in Italy, where he came across this polychrome design.

★ **Dining Room**
American walnut blends with an Italian Renaissance style for the dining furniture of Louisa Jones.

Como House and its driveway

⓷⓪ Como Historic House and Garden

Cnr Williams Rd & Lechlade Ave, South Yarra. **Map** 4 F4. **Tel** (03) 9827 2500. 🚉 South Yarra. 🚋 8. **Open** only for group tours of 15 or more, arranged in advance. **Closed** Good Fri, 25 Dec. 🖼 ♿ ground floor and grounds only. 🎥 obligatory. W comohouse.com.au

Begun in 1847 by Edward Eyre Williams, Como House was occupied by the Armytage family for almost a century (1865–1959).

One of Como's highlights is its vast collection of original furnishings. These include pieces collected by the Armytage matriarch, Caroline, while on a Grand Tour of Europe during the 1870s, and include marble and bronze statues. The tour was undertaken as an educational experience for her nine children after the death of her husband, Charles Henry. It was important to this prominent Melbourne family to be seen as well educated. On their return, they held a series of sophisticated parties here.

Set in the picturesque remnants of its once extensive gardens, the house overlooks Como Park and the Yarra River. The original facets of the magnificent grounds, designed by William Sangster (who also had an input at Rippon Lea), remain: the fountain terrace, croquet lawn and hard standing area at the front of the house.

Como was managed by the Armytage women from 1876 until it was purchased by the National Trust in 1959. The house has undergone major restoration work over the years since then.

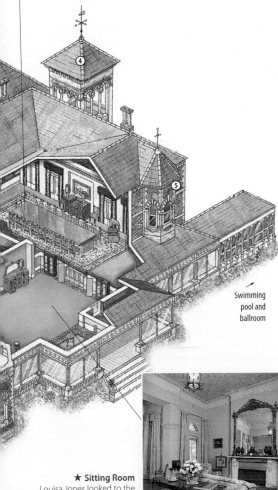

Swimming pool and ballroom

★ **Sitting Room**
Louisa Jones looked to the grand mansions of Hollywood film stars in the 1930s for much of her interior design, including the plush sitting room.

SHOPPING IN MELBOURNE

The Central Business District (CBD) is a magnet for the city's shoppers. Major department stores are supplemented by a network of boutiques and specialist shops, many of which are tucked away in arcades and lanes. There is also a network of inner-city and suburban shopping streets: fashionable clothing and retail stores abound in urban areas, while large one-stop shopping towns are a feature of Greater Melbourne.

There are areas known for particular products, such as High Street, which runs through Armadale and Malvern, with its antiques stores. The city's multicultural society is also reflected in its shopping districts: Victoria Street, Richmond, has a stretch of Vietnamese stores; Sydney Road, Brunswick, is renowned for its shops selling Middle Eastern goods; and Carlisle Street, St Kilda, has many Jewish delicatessens.

Ornate and elegant Royal Arcade, which was built in 1869

Shopping Hours

In Victoria, most traders are open every day. Some small businesses close on Sundays but, increasingly, many stay open, competing with the long hours of chain stores and supermarkets (some of which are open 24 hours a day). Standard hours are 9am to 5:30pm (10am to 6pm in the CBD), although some retailers have extended hours on Thursdays or Fridays. Hours can vary at weekends. Most shops close on Christmas Day and Good Friday.

Department Stores

There are two major department stores in central Melbourne: **Myer** and **David Jones**, both are open for business seven days a week.

Australia's largest department store, Myer, encompasses a full two blocks of the city centre, with seven floors in Lonsdale Street and six in Bourke Street. Its main entrance is in Bourke

Street Mall. Myer have nine other stores throughout Melbourne. David Jones, known to locals as DJs, has more up-market stock and high-quality service. The store has three sites within the city, with a main entrance adjacent to Myer in Bourke Street Mall; opposite is its menswear department. A third section is accessed in Little Bourke Street, again adjacent to Myer.

Two other popular stores are **Target** and K-mart. Both offer discounted prices on a range of goods. There are many branches of K-mart but they are located outside the CBD.

Arcades, Malls and Shopping Centres

Melbourne's best arcades and malls are located in the heart of the CBD. Chief among these are Bourke Street Mall, with shopfronts for the Myer and David Jones department stores. Occupied mostly by speciality stores and boutiques, other

arcades and malls include the Galleria Shopping Plaza, with an emphasis on Australiana and Australian-owned stores. The ABC Shop sells merchandise associated with the national television and radio network, such as books, videos and DVDs. Australian Geographic is an excellent shop for information on Australian landscape and geology.

Located on Collins Street, renowned for its up-market shops, clothing and shoes, are Australia on Collins, Block Arcade *(see p393)* and 234 Collins Street. Australia on Collins comprises 60 shops on five levels, with fashion, homeware and other retail stores. The Sportsgirl Centre, at 234 Collins Street, is known for its designer fashion shops, which are located on three levels. Both complexes have food halls. Block Arcade, itself of historic interest, sells more classic clothing amid a beautifully restored 1890s interior; there is an entrance

Up-market window display in Melbourne Central shopping centre

Locally grown fruit on sale at Queen Victoria Market

on Elizabeth Street. Also on Elizabeth Street is the GPO *(see p392)*, which is now a popular H&M megastore.

Further up on Collins Street, past Russell Street, there are stores located in Collins Place, and in the Royal Arcade *(see p392)* nearby, which is also of historic and architectural interest. Running between Bourke Street Mall and Little Collins Street, further east, you will find **The Walk Arcade**, containing a small selection of smart and exclusive boutiques.

Little Bourke Street, above Elizabeth Street, and the intersecting Hardware Lane, are well known for a range of stores specializing in travel and adventure products.

Melbourne Central and **QV** are two outstanding shopping centres located on Lonsdale and Swanston streets. Between them, there are literally hundreds of shops to visit. Adjoining Melbourne Central is the more recently opened **Emporium Melbourne**, which is architecturally stunning and contains a mix of food icons, designer brands and flagship stores. Away from the city centre, the **Southgate Complex**, with its 40 shops on three levels, should not be missed by the avid shopper.

Markets

Melbourne has a number of fresh food markets. The most notable is the Queen Victoria Market *(see p390)*.

Other kinds of market are also popular. There is a huge range of second-hand goods for sale each Sunday at the **Camberwell Market**. For arts and crafts, **The Esplanade Market** is held on Sundays on Upper Esplanade. Other Sunday markets include the food market in **Prahran** and the arts and crafts market at the Arts Centre *(see p415)*. One of the oldest markets is the **South Melbourne Market**, which has has been in continuous operation since 1867. It is open every Friday to Sunday, and also Wednesdays.

Brunswick Street has vintage clothing stores and retro boutiques

Shopping Strips

Village-style shopping centres abound in the many suburbs of Melbourne. Popular spots include High Street in Armadale; Sydney Road in Brunswick; Brunswick and Gertrude streets in Fitzroy; Bridge Road in Richmond; Chapel Street in South Yarra; and Maling Road in Canterbury

Another major shopping centre in South Yarra is the **Como Centre**, which has stores selling furniture, homewares and fashion.

DIRECTORY

Department Stores

David Jones
310 Bourke St Mall. **Map** 1 C3.
Tel (03) 9643 2222.
W davidjones.com.au

Myer
314 Bourke St Mall. **Map** 1 C3.
Tel (03) 9661 1111.
W myer.com.au

Target
236 Bourke St. **Map** 1 C3. **Tel** (03) 9653 4000. W target.com.au

Arcades, Malls and Shopping Centres

Australia on Collins
260 Collins St. **Map** 1 C3.
Tel (03) 9650 4355.
W AustraliaonCollins.com.au

Como Centre
650 Chapel St, South Yarra.
Map 4 E5. **Tel** (03) 9370 5411.
W como.centre.com.au

Emporium Melbourne
287 Lonsdale St, Melbourne.
Map 1 C2. **Tel** (03) 8609 8221.

Galleria Shopping Plaza
Cnr Bourke & Elizabeth sts.
Map 1 C3. **Tel** (03) 9604 5800.

Melbourne Central
300 Lonsdale St. **Map** 1 C2.
Tel (03) 9922 1100.
W melbournecentral.com.au

QV
Cnr Swanston and Lonsdale sts.
Map 1 C2. **Tel** (03) 9658 0100.
W qv.com.au

Southgate Complex
3 Southgate Ave, Southbank.
Map 2 C4. **Tel** (03) 9686 1000.

The Walk Arcade
309-325 Bourke St Mall. **Map** 1 C3.
Tel (03) 9654 6744.

Markets

Camberwell Market
Station St, Camberwell
W sundaymarket.com.au

The Esplanade Market
Upper Esplanade, St Kilda.
Tel (03) 9209 6764.

Prahran Market
Commercial Rd (near Chapel St).
Map 6 D1. **Tel** (03) 8290 8220.
W prahranmarket.com.au

South Melbourne Market
Cnr Cecil and Coventry sts.
Tel (03) 9209 6295. W south melbournemarket.com.au

Specialist Shops and Souvenirs

Melbourne is Australia's most fashion-conscious capital and hosts major fashion weeks. The Melbourne Fashion Festival in March sees young designers launch their autumn/winter collections, while established labels showcase their spring/summer collections during Spring Fashion Week in September. New boutiques have opened in the Flinders Lane and Little Collins Streets precincts, either side of Swanston Street, and in the Central Business District's (CBD) revitalized arcades and laneways. This area rivals Fitzroy's Brunswick Street for funky shopping. Melbourne is also a great place to buy outdoor gear, with several retailers located around Hardware Lane and Little Bourke Street. The city has a reputation for excellent bookshops and record stores, most of which are found in the city centre and inner suburbs of Carlton, Fitzroy, St Kilda and South Yarra.

Men's Clothing

The **Marcs** range is characterized by lightweight and colourful sweaters, shirts, t-shirts and trousers. Myer department store *(see pp410–11)* stocks a limited range of Marcs items, often on sale. For sharp designer suits, head for **Calibre**, who also stock imported designer accessories. Little Collins Street east of Swanston Street has a selection of menswear stores, including **Déclic**, which specialises in business shirts and designer ties with names such as Duchamp, Vivienne Westwood and Zegna. Down the hill, **H&M** has a good range of smart casual gear. **Out of the Closet**, opposite Flinders Street Station, stocks groovy vintage wear. They also have a store in Brunswick Street, Fitzroy. Nearby is **Dangerfield**, a Melbourne label, which promotes edgy Rock and Roll style. Everything from the 50's, 60's and 70's fashion to the latest trends are available here. Brunswick Street is a good place to browse for vintage clothing, and Chapel Street, South Yarra is great for jeanswear.

Women's Clothing

The CBD is the centre for haute couture in Melbourne. **Alannah Hill**'s and **Bettina Liano**'s fashions are feminine and sophisticated, the latter with a glam edge. **Scanlon & Theodore** have made a name for themselves with elegant outfits, earthy tones and breezy designs. **Issey Miyake** is one of several international design houses represented in Melbourne. The appointment-only **Le Louvre**, in South Yarra, has been Melbourne society's couturier for decades. Young design outfit **Fat** has shops in Fitzroy and Prahran. **Kinki Gerlinki** stocks a appealing range of retro clothing. H&M and Marcs stock a good range of casual gear for women. **Peter Alexander** has several branches throughout the city centre and is well regarded for a range of sleepwear, while **Smitten Kitten** offers imported lingerie, jewellery and exotic accessories.

Bridge Road, Richmond has numerous discount fashion outlets. Another favourite label for fashion accessories – from handbags to jewellery and shoes – is **Mimco**.

Children's Clothing

Brunswick Street, Fitzroy is a good starting point for hunting down kids' clothes. Check out **Pumpkin Patch** for a comprehensive range of quality kidswear. **World Wide Wear**, which started life in Fitzroy, has relocated to an outer-suburban shopping centre, but it is worth the trip to lay your hands on groovy kids' t-shirts, jackets, jeans and outdoor gear.

Jewellery

Kozminsky's on Bourke Street has been a Melbourne institution for decades. It specialises in fine art and antique jewellery.

Collins Street has a profusion of jewellery stores and international fashion labels, including **Bulgari**. **Maker's Mark** showcases exquisite designer jewellery and glassware. Their flagship store is opposite the Rialto Building on Collins Street.

Dinosaur Designs fashion distinctive and contemporary jewellery, and homewares from lustrous resins. They have several stores, including one in Chapel Street. **Studio Ingot** sells contemporary pieces made by over 60 artisans.

Shoes and Bags

The Westin hotel building in Collins Street is home to **Miss Louise**, a favourite with Melbourne's well-heeled women. Melbourne's **Catherine Manuell** designs colourful handbags, daypacks, kids' bags and travel gear.

Crumpler bags are the brainchild of a former bicycle courier who saw a market for comfortable, durable and funky shoulder bags. They come in a variety of styles and types to suit everything from laptops, to videos to homework: a Melbourne design icon.

Outdoor Gear

To stock up on ski equipment and apparel, rock-climbing gear, tents, sleeping bags, maps and designer outdoor clothing, head for the Hardware Lane and Little Bourke Street precinct. There are numerous shops with good quality gear. Both **Paddy Pallin**, an established name in outdoor equipment, and **Snowgum**, which has shops across Melbourne, are recommended outlets. Smith Street, Collingwood has several factory shops for outdoor retailers selling discount clothing.

Books and Music

Collins Booksellers, an Australian chain, has several outlets including the **Hill of Content Bookshop**, which has an interesting range of local and overseas books. **Readings** is another homegrown favourite, which regularly hosts literary events. Its flagship store is in Carlton and it has a branch in Acland Street, St Kilda. The **Brunswick Street Bookstore** is a quiet and relaxed venue for browsing quality books and magazines. **Discurio**, in a quiet corner of the CBD, is the place for Bach, Coltrane and alternative grooves. **Blue Moon Records** stocks a range of world music.

DIRECTORY

Men's Clothing

Calibre
483 Chapel St, Sth Yarra 3141. **Map** 6 E1.
Tel (03) 9826 4394
W calibre.com.au

Dangerfield
224 Flinders St, Melbourne 3000. **Map** 1 C3.
W shop.dangerfield.com.au

Déclic
186 Little Collins St, Melbourne 3000.
Map 1 C3.
Tel (03) 9650 2202.
W declic.com.au

H&M
323 Little Bourke St, Melbourne.
W hm.com/au

Marcs
576-584 Chapel St, Sth Yarra 3141. **Map** 6 E1.
Tel (03) 9826 4906.
W marcs.com.au

Out of the Closet
238B Flinders St, Melbourne 3000. **Map** 1 C3. **Tel** (03) 9639 0980.

Women's Clothing

Alannah Hill
533 Chapel St, Sth Yarra 3141. **Map** 4 E5.
Tel (03) 9826 2755.
W alannahhill.com.au

Bettina Liano
269 Little Collins St, Melbourne 3000. **Map** 1 C3. **Tel** (03) 9654 1912.
W bettinaliano.com.au

Fat
272 Chapel St, Sth Yarra 3141. **Map** 6 F2. **Tel** (03) 9510 2311. W fat4.com

Issey Miyake
Shop 2, 177 Toorak Rd, Sth Yarra 3141. **Map** 4 E5.
Tel (03) 9826 4900.
W isseymiyake.com

Kinki Gerlinki
22 Centre Place, Melbourne 3000. **Map** 1 C3. **Tel** (03) 9650 0465.

Le Louvre
2 Daly St, Sth Yarra 3141.
Map 4 E5.
Tel (03) 9823 5300.
W lelouvre.com.au

Mimco
4/567 Chapel St, Sth Yarra 3141. **Map** 4 E5.
Tel (03) 9827 0259.
W mimco.com.au

Peter Alexander
Level 2, Shop 228 Melbourne Central, 300 Lonsdale St, Melbourne 3000. **Map** 1 C2.
Tel (03) 9639 1299
W peteralexander.com.au

Scanlon & Theodore
566 Chapel St, Sth Yarra 3141. **Map** 4 E5. **Tel** (03) 9824 1800. W scanlonandtheodore.com.au

Smitten Kitten
Shop 6, Degraves St, Melbourne 3000. **Map** 1 C3. **Tel** (03) 9654 2073.
W smittenkitten.com.au

Children's Clothing

Pumpkin Patch
Centrepoint Mall, 283–297 Bounce St Mall. **Map** 1 C3.
Tel (03) 9650 1503.

World Wide Wear
Shop B10-B11, Chadstone Shopping Centre, 1341 Dandenong Rd, 3148.
Tel (03) 9530 9864.

Jewellery

Bulgari
119 Collins St, Melbourne 3000.
Map 2 D3.
Tel (03) 9663 8100.
W bvlgari.com.au

Dinosaur Designs
562 Chapel St, Sth Yarra 3141. **Map** 4 E5.
Tel (03) 9827 2600.
W dinosaurdesigns.com.au

Kozminsky
421 Bourke St, Melbourne 3000.
Map 1 C3.
Tel (03) 9670 1277.
W kozminsky.com.au

Maker's Mark
464 Collins St, Melbourne 3000.
Map 1 B4.
Tel (03) 9621 2488.
W makersmark.com.au

Studio Ingot
Shop 2, 234 Brunswick St, Fitzroy 3065.
Tel (03) 9415 6000.
W studioingot.com.au

Shoes and Bags

Catherine Manuell
273 Little Lonsdale St, Melbourne 3000.
Map 1 C2.
Tel (03) 9499 9844.
W catherinemanuelldesign.com

Crumpler
355 Little Bourke St, Melbourne 3000.
Map 1 C3.
Tel (03) 9600 3799.
W crumpler.com.au

Miss Louise
The Westin, 205 Collins St, Melbourne 3000. **Map** 2 D3. **Tel** (03) 9654 7730

Outdoor Gear

Paddy Pallin
360 Little Bourke St, Melbourne 3000.
Map 1 C3.
Tel (03) 9670 4845.
W paddypallin.com.au

Snowgum
370 Little Bourke St, Melbourne 3000.
Map 1 C3
Tel (03) 9642 4340.
W snowgum.com.au

Books and Music

Blue Moon Records
54 Johnston St, Fitzroy 3065.
Tel (03) 9415 1157.

Brunswick Street Bookstore
305 Brunswick Street, Fitzroy 3065.
Tel (03) 9416 1030.
W brunswickstreetbookstore.com

Discurio
113 Hardware St, Melbourne 3000.
Map 1 B3.
Tel (03) 9600 1488.
W discurio.com.au

Hill of Content Bookshop
86 Bourke St, Melbourne 3000.
Map 2 D2.
Tel (03) 9662 9472.

Readings
309 Lygon St, Carlton 3053.
Tel (03) 9347 6633.
112 Acland St, St Kilda, 3182.
Tel (03) 9525 3852.
W readings.com.au

ENTERTAINMENT IN MELBOURNE

Melbourne could be defined as Australia's city of the arts. All year round there is a wealth of cultural events and entertainment on offer. The city's major festivals include the Melbourne Food and Wine Festival and Moomba *(see pp45–8)*. There are also fringe festivals and many other independent events. Arts Centre Melbourne, which includes

Hamer Hall *(see p404)*, stages productions by the state's theatrical companies and hosts both national and international groups. Large concerts are held at Rod Laver Arena in Melbourne Park Entertainment Centre or the Melbourne Cricket Ground *(see p401)*. Cinema chains are supplemented by smaller, arthouse cinemas.

Evening concert at the Sidney Myer Music Bowl *(see p402)*

Information

The best guide to the range of events in Melbourne is the entertainment guide in the *Age*, published each Friday. This has comprehensive listings, along with more information on all the up-coming highlights. The tabloid newspaper *Herald Sun* and both newspapers' Saturday editions are also good sources of information and reviews. There is an array of free publications covering arts, entertainment and the nightclub scene. Visitors can obtain these from retailers and cafés in main inner-city precincts such as Fitzroy *(see p407)* and St Kilda. The **Melbourne Visitor Information Centre** has

a range of publications listing events.

There are also a number of websites that provide good events coverage, as well as other information helpful to visitors: www.theurbanlist.com/melbourne, www.visitvictoria.com and www.thatsmelbourne.com.au are worth a look. **Arts Centre Melbourne** *(see p404)* has a bi-monthly diary which it mails out free of charge worldwide, covering all up-to-date events at the complex. Most ticket agencies and some venues also provide information on events taking place in the city.

Ticket Booking Agencies

Buying tickets in Melbourne is reasonably straightforward. There are two major ticket booking agencies in Victoria, **Ticketmaster** (with more than 50 outlets) and **Ticketek** (with more than 30 outlets). Both agencies offer ticketing for all major sporting events, concerts, theatre performances and festivals, as well as for theme parks and other attractions. There are some

Grand 1930s foyer of the Regent Theatre *(see p394)*

venues which handle their own bookings independently, but these are rare and tickets for most major events are more easily purchased at these agencies.

Bookings can either be made in person at the various outlets, or with a credit card by phone, fax or post. Alternatively, bookings can be made online. The agencies also accept bookings from overseas. If not bought directly over the counter, tickets can be mailed out to customers for a small handling fee. If the event is impending, tickets can usually be picked up at the venue half-an-hour before the booked performance starts.

The hours for outlets vary according to their location, but almost all are open Monday through to Saturday, and some are open on Sundays. Neither Ticketmaster nor Ticketek offer refunds or exchanges, unless a show is cancelled. Remember that a nominal booking fee will be added to all ticket prices bought via a ticket agency.

Façade of the Princess Theatre, opposite the Parliamentary Precinct *(see p396)*

Street entertainers, a regular sight throughout Melbourne

Ticket Deals

Some major companies, especially those playing at the Arts Centre Melbourne, offer special "rush hour" ticket deals. These are available for tickets purchased in person after 6pm. The **Half Tix** booth at the Melbourne Town Hall on Swanston Street offers half-price deals for many events or try www.lasttix.com. au. Tickets must be bought in person and paid for in cash. They are also generally available only on the day of performance. Shows with tickets available are displayed at the booth.

Half Tix ticket booth sign on Swanston Street

Securing the Best Seats

If booking in person or online, you can usually consult a floor-plan showing the location of available seats. Over the telephone, both Ticketmaster and Ticketek have a "best available" system, with remaining seats arranged in a best-to-last order by individual venues. It is also possible to request particular seats and the booking agency will check their availability. Some seats are retained for sale at the venue itself and this can be a way of getting good seats at the last minute.

Disabled Visitors

The vast majority of venues have access and facilities for disabled visitors. Booking agencies will take this into account. You should also enquire at individual venues and the Mobility Centre, Federation Square (www.melbourne.vic.gov.au).

Outdoor and Street Entertainment

Melbourne has a strong tradition of outdoor and street entertainment. Every summer there is a broad programme of theatre and music for adults and children in most major parks and gardens. During February, the Melbourne Symphony Orchestra (MSO) presents a series of free concerts at the Sidney Myer music bowl.

Street buskers, many travelling on an international circuit, also frequent a number of areas, the most popular being Fitzroy (see p407) and St Kilda, and appear at festivals. The main spot for regular street performances is the Bourke Street Mall, outside Myer and David Jones department stores and at the Southgate Complex (see p411). The Arts Centre Melbourne also has regular programmes featuring free weekend street entertainment.

(see p407)
(see p411)

DIRECTORY

Information Centre

Melbourne Visitor Information Centre
Federation Square, cnr Swanston & Flinders sts. **Map** 2 D3. **Tel** (03) 9658 9658. W visitvictoria.com

Major Venues

Arts Centre Melbourne
100 St Kilda Rd. **Map** 2 D4.
Tel 1300 182 183.
W artscentremelbourne.com.au

Athenaeum Theatre
188 Collins St. **Map** 2 D3.
Tel (03) 9650 1500.
W athenaeumtheatre.com.au

Comedy Theatre
240 Exhibition St. **Map** 2 D2.
Tel (03) 9299 4950.

CUB Malthouse
113 Sturt St. **Map** 2 D4
Tel (03) 9685 5111.
W malthousetheatre.com.au

Forum Theatre
154 Flinders St. **Map** 2 D3.
Tel (03) 9299 9700.
W forummelbourne.com.au

Her Majesty's
219 Exhibition St. **Map** 2 D2.
Tel (03) 8643 3300.
W hmt.com.au

Melbourne Town Hall
Cnr Swanston & Collins sts.
Map 1 C3. **Tel** (03) 9658 9658.
W melbournetownhall.com.au

Palais Theatre
3182 Lower Esplanade, St Kilda.
Map 5 B5. **Tel** (03) 9525 3240.
W palaistheatre.net.au

Princess Theatre
163 Spring St. **Map** 2 D2.
Tel (03) 9299 9800.

Regent Theatre
191 Collins St. **Map** 2 D3.
Tel (03) 9299 9500.

Ticket Agencies

Half Tix
Melbourne Town Hall, cnr Swanston and Collins sts.
Map 1 C3. **Tel** (03) 9650 9420.
W halftixmelbourne.com

Ticketek
Tel 132 849. W ticketek.com

Ticketmaster
Tel 136 100.
W ticketmaster.com.au

MELBOURNE PRACTICAL INFORMATION

Melbourne is well served by public transport and is easy to negotiate, given the grid structure of the city centre and the flat layout of its suburbs. Many of the public facilities have been upgraded, with the aim of attracting both business and tourists.

Driving in the city is also easy and taxis are plentiful. Bureaux de change and automatic cash dispensers are located throughout the city. Melbourne is safe compared with many major cities, but common sense will also keep you out of trouble.

Driving and Cycling

Driving in Melbourne is easy. However, at particular intersections in the CBD marked by "Safety Zone" signs, a "hook turn" is required; cars must queue on the left to turn right in order to give way to trams. Cars left in No Standing zones will be towed away. The city has a tollway system known as **CityLink**, which uses electronic tolling: drivers must purchase a pass before travelling. Melbourne's flat landscape is well suited to cyclists and there are many cycle tracks. Helmets are compulsory. Information on bicycle hire and good cycle routes can be found at **Bicycle Victoria**. The **Melbourne Bike Share** scheme is also popular.

Travelling by Public Transport

Melbourne has a comprehensive system of trains, buses and trams, known as Metro or Yarra Trams. This system also provides access to country and interstate travel, operated by the **V/Line** network.

The main railway station for suburban services is Flinders Street Station (see p406). Southern Cross Station is the main terminus for country and interstate trains.

The City Circle Tram circuits the city every 15 minutes, while the City Explorer hop-on hop-off tourist bus departs at half-hour intervals. Details are available from the **Melbourne Visitor Information Centre**. Another way to get around the city is via water taxis and cruises along the Yarra River.

Tram Routes

Melbourne's famous electric tram network covers 240 km (150 miles), reaching many of the city's attractions. Stops are located on central islands within the CBD area, and by the roadside in suburban areas. Tickets can be purchased from coin-only ticket machines on board the tram, but weekly tickets must be bought at the railway station or selected retail outlets. Most routes operate at regular intervals (10 to 20 minutes) from 5am until midnight daily.

Flinders Street Station, the city's main suburban rail terminus

Tickets

Melbourne Visitor Information Centre sells **Smartvisit** cards which allow entry to over 50 attractions and include use of public transport. The **Myki** system operates with a card that can be purchased from all 7Eleven stores ($6) then topped up online, at 7Eleven stores, train stations, and some tram stops. Tap the card before boarding trams, buses and trains. Fines apply for fare evading.

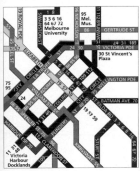
Central Melbourne area

Key

- ■ Swanston Street
- ▢ Elizabeth Street
- ■ William Street
- ■ Latrobe Street
- ■ Bourke Street
- ■ Collins Street
- ■ Flinders Street
- ■ Batman Avenue
- ● City Circle
- ■ Suburban trams

Tourist Information

The main Tourist Information stop is the Melbourne Visitor Information Centre, which has free maps and guides to all attractions and activities. They also provide information on accommodation and arrange bookings.

There is a range of free travel publications available from information centres, covering attractions in Melbourne and Victoria.

Disabled Travellers

The useful "CBD Mobility Map" is available from the Melbourne Visitor Information Centre and shows the smoothest path of travel along the city's streets. The majority of public facilities in the city have disabled access and toilets. Parking zones are allocated in the city and suburbs for disabled drivers; disabled driver permits are available from Melbourne Town Hall (see p393).

River cruise boats providing a leisurely way to see the city

DIRECTORY

Driving and Cycling

Bicycle Victoria
Tel (03) 8636 8888.
W bv.com.au

CityLink
Tel 13 26 29.
W citylink.com.au

Melbourne Bike Share
W melbournebikeshare.com.au

Royal Automobile Club of Victoria
Tel 13 11 11.
W racv.com.au

Transport Information Line
Tel 13 16 38.

Public Transport

Myki
W ptv.vic.gov.au

Public Transport Victoria
Tel 1800 800 007.
W ptv.vic.gov.au

Skybus Information Service
Tel (03) 9600 1711.
W skybus.com.au

Southern Cross Coach Terminal
Spencer St. Tel 13 61 96.
W vline.com.au

V/Line
Spencer Street Station.
Tel 13 61 96. W vline.com.au

River Cruises

Melbourne Water Taxis
No 4 Southgate (outside Langham Hotel). Tel 0416 068 655.
W melbournewatertaxis.com.au

Williamstown Ferries: Bay and River Cruises
Gem Pier Williamstown/No. 1 Southgate/Vault 12 Federation Square City. Tel (03) 9517 9444 (info), (03) 9682 9555 (booking).
W williamstownferries.com.au

Tourist Information

Melbourne Visitor Information Centre
Federation Sq, Cnr Swanston & Flinders sts. Tel 13 28 42.

Smartvisit Card
Tel 1300 661 711.
W onlymelbourne.com.au

Victorian Tourism Information Service
Tel 13 28 42. W visitvictoria.com

MELBOURNE STREET FINDER

The key map below shows the areas of Melbourne covered in the *Street Finder*. All places of interest in these areas are marked on the maps in addition to useful information, such as railway stations, bus termini and emergency services. The map references given for sights described in the Melbourne chapter refer to the maps on the following pages. Map references are also given for the city's shops and markets *(see pp410–13)*, entertainment venues *(see pp414–15)*, as well as hotels *(see pp493–4)* and restaurants *(see pp526–9)*. The different symbols used for sights and other major features on the *Street Finder* maps are listed in the key below.

Key

- ■ Major sight
- ■ Place of interest
- □ Other building
- 🚢 Ferry boarding point
- 🚉 Railway station
- 🚌 Bus station
- ℹ️ Tourist information
- ➕ Hospital with casualty unit
- 👮 Police station
- ⛳ Golf course
- ✝️ Church
- ☪️ Mosque
- ✡️ Synagogue
- ═ Highway
- ⟋ Railway line
- ▬ Pedestrian street

Scale of Map Pages

0 metres	250
0 yards	250

0 km	1
0 mile	1

Deborah Halpern sculpture at the city's Southgate Plaza *(see pp404–5)*

Red brick façade of the City Baths on Swanston Street *(see pp388–9)*

Ornamental lake at Rippon Lea *(see pp408–9)*

The Collins Street area as seen from Princes Bridge on the Yarra River

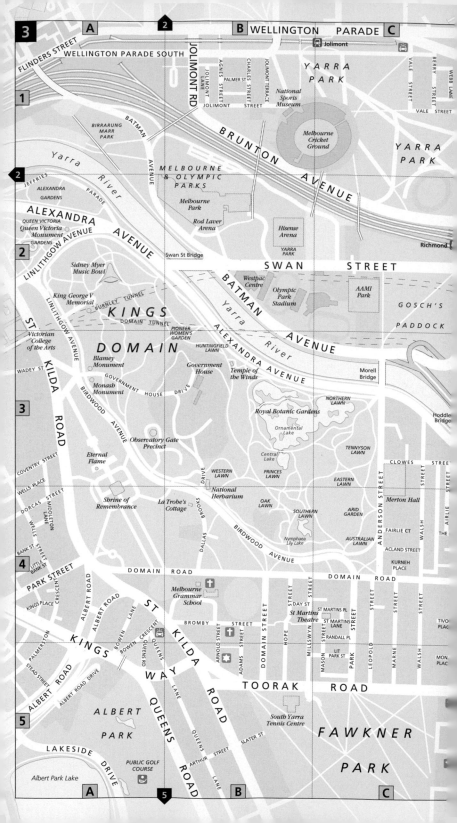

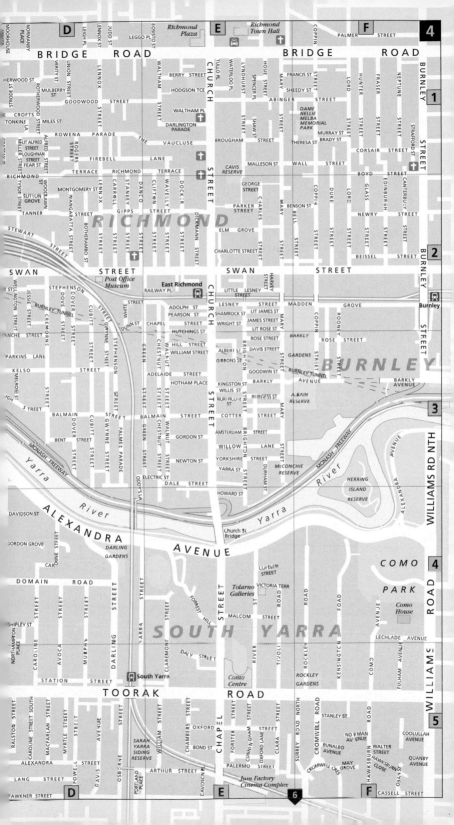

WESTERN VICTORIA

The theme of Western Victoria is diversity. For nature lovers, there is the bare beauty of the mallee deserts of the north or the forested hills and coastal scenery of the south. For a sense of the region's history, 19th-century gold-mining towns lie in the centre, surrounded by beautiful spa towns which have attracted visitors for more than a century. The area's sights are all within easy reach of one another.

Just as the Aboriginal tribes of Western Victoria had their lives and culture shaped by the region's diverse landscape, so the lives of the early European settlers were inevitably determined by the region's geographical features and immense natural resources.

The discovery of gold was the single most important event in Victoria's economic history, drawing prospectors from all over the world and providing the state with unprecedented wealth. Part of the legacy of this period is seen in the grand 19th-century buildings still standing in a number of central western towns. Also of interest are the spa towns clustered nearby, which draw their therapeutic waters from the same mineral-rich earth.

To the northwest, Victoria's major agricultural region, the Murray River, supports several large townships. The area is blessed with a Mediterranean-type climate, resulting in wineries and fruit-growing areas.

In the south, the spectacular Grampian mountain ranges have long been of significance to the Aborigines. Fortunately, the steep cliffs and heavily forested slopes offered little prospect for development by early settlers and this beautiful area is today preserved as a wilderness. Wheat and sheep farmers have settled in parts of the Mallee region in the north of Western Victoria but, as in the Grampians, other settlers have been discouraged by its semi-arid conditions, and large areas of this stunning desert vegetation and its native wildlife have been left intact.

The southwestern coast was the site of the first settlement in Victoria. Its towns were developed as ports for the rich farmland beyond and as whaling stations for the now outlawed industry. Besides its history, this coastline is known for its extraordinary natural scenery of sandstone monoliths, sweeping beaches, forests and rugged cliffs.

Pioneer Settlement Museum, a re-created 19th-century port town on the Murray River at Swan Hill

◀ The jagged edge of the Great Ocean Road coastline, with some of the Twelve Apostles

Exploring Western Victoria

Western Victoria abounds with holiday possibilities. The spa towns close to Melbourne make perfect weekend retreats, with excellent facilities set amid gentle rural scenery. By contrast, the large number of historic sites and architectural splendours of the Goldfields region requires an investigative spirit and sightseeing stamina. The Grampians National Park contains trekking opportunities and rugged views, while the Mallee region offers wide open spaces and undulating sandhills. The Murray River towns have their fair share of historic sites, as well as many recreational facilities, restaurants and accommodation. The Great Ocean Road is a popular touring destination – set aside several days to explore the historic towns and scenic beauty of the coastline.

Rupertswood mansion in the Macedon Ranges

Getting Around

The roads in Western Victoria are well signed and offer good roadside facilities. The Western Hwy is the route to Ballarat, the Grampians and the Mallee region. The Calder Hwy leads to the spa country and beyond to Bendigo, where it connects with highways to Mildura, Swan Hill and Echuca. Take the Princes Hwy to reach Geelong and the Great Ocean Road. All these places can also be reached by rail or a combination of rail and connecting coaches. However, in remoter areas, public transport may be a problem. A good solution is to take one of the tours from Melbourne offered by Metlink or V/Line (see p417).

Sandstone arch at Loch Ard Gorge along the Great Ocean Road

Sights at a Glance

1 Werribee Park
2 Bellarine Peninsula
3 Geelong
4 Grampians National Park
5 Big Desert Wilderness
6 Hattah-Kulkyne National Park
7 Mildura
8 Swan Hill

9 Echuca
10 Bendigo
11 Maldon
12 Castlemaine
13 *Ballarat pp438–9*
14 Sovereign Hill

Tour

15 Daylesford and the Macedon Ranges

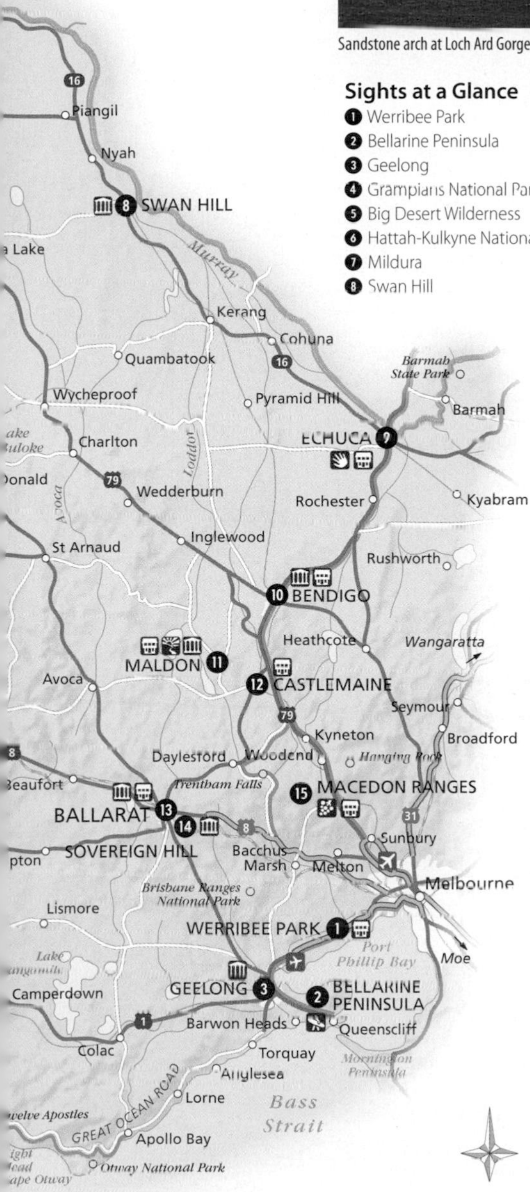

Striking rock formations of Grampians National Park

Key

— Highway
— Major road
····· Minor road
-- Track
— Scenic route
— Major railway
— Minor railway
— State border

For additional map symbols *see back flap*

Flamboyant Italianate façade of Werribee Park Mansion

❶ Werribee Park

K Rd, Werribee. **Tel** (03) 8734 5100.
🚃 Werribee. **Open** daily. 🅿 ♿ 🅲
💻 ✎ 🆆 **parkweb.vic.edu.au**

From 1860 until 1890, the wool
boom made millionaires of
Australia's sheep farmers, with
the Chirnside family of Werribee
Park and later of Victoria's
Western District among the
richest and most powerful.
Their former mansion is a
striking Italianate house,
built between 1873 and 1878.
It has now been restored to
reflect the lifestyle of wealthy
pastoral families. Visitors can
stroll through the sandstone
mansion and see the room
where renowned opera singer
Dame Nellie Melba once slept.
A wing added in the 1930s
has been converted into a
luxury hotel.

Next to Werribee Park
Mansion and its formal gardens
with popular picnic areas is the
Victoria State Rose Garden,
laid out in a symbolic Tudor
Rose-shaped design. It contains
more than 5,000 beautiful rose
bushes of different varieties
and colours
that are in
flower from
November
to April. Also
attached to
Werribee Park is
Werribee Open Range Zoo,
containing a range of exotic
animals, including giraffes and
hippopotami. The National
Equestrian Centre is also part
of the estate. This is home to
some of Australia's premier

Chaise longue in Werribee Park

show-jumping and polo events.
For bird-watchers, the nearby
Werribee sewage farm and
Point Cook Coastal Park provide
magnificent views of some
rare species from specially
designated hides. Migratory
birds such as the eastern curlew
and tiny red-necked stint spend
the whole summer in these
protected wetlands before flying
north to Japan and Siberia.

🦓 **Werribee Open Range Zoo**
Werribee Park Mansion.
Tel 1300 966 784. **Open** 9am–5pm
daily. 🅿 ♿ 🅲 🆆 **zoo.org.au**

❷ Bellarine Peninsula

🚌 Geelong. 🛈 1251–1269 Bellarine
Highway, Wallington 1800 755 611.
🆆 **visitgeelongbellarine.com.au**

The Bellarine Peninsula, at the
western entrance to Port Phillip
Bay, is one of Melbourne's many
summer resorts. The white sand
beaches of Barwon Heads, Point
Lonsdale and Ocean Grove
mark the
start of the
Great Ocean
Road and its
famous surf
beaches (see
pp432–3).
The little
village of **Point
Lonsdale** lies at the entrance to
the treacherous Heads – the
most dangerous entry to any
bay in the world due to its
churning seas and whirlpools.
It is only 3 km (2 miles) from
Point Lonsdale, across the

swirling water (known as the
Rip) with its hidden rocks, to
Point Nepean on the Morn-
ington Peninsula in Eastern
Victoria (see p446).

The graceful old town of
Queenscliff faces Port Phillip
Bay so its beaches are calm.
Its fort was the largest British
defence post in the southern
hemisphere during the 1880s,
when a Russian invasion was
feared. At the time Queenscliff
was also a fashionable resort
for Melburnians – its elegant
hotels, such as the Vue Grand,
are reminders of that opulent
era. St Leonards and
Portarlington are also popular
holiday villages.

The peninsula has around
20 wineries, most offering
cellar door sales and tastings.

Graceful wrought-iron detail on a
Queenscliff façade

❸ Geelong

🏠 180,000. ✈ 🚊 🚌 🚢 🛈 26–32
Moorabool St (03) 5222 2900.
🆆 **visitgeelongbellarine.com.au**

Geelong is the second largest
city in the state and has a rural
and industrial past. Positioned
on the north-facing and
sheltered Corio Bay, the city has
started to look once again on its
port as a recreational front door,
so popular in the first years of the
20th century. The wooden 1930s
bathing complex at Eastern
Beach, with its lawns, sandy
beach and shady trees, was
restored to its former Art Deco
glory in 1994. Steampacket Place
and Pier were part of an extensive
redevelopment project that saw
the gradual renovation of the
old warehouses into a thriving
waterfront quarter filled with
excellent seafood restaurants,

cafés, shops and hotels. Opposite Steampacket Place are the historic wool stores. Wool was auctioned, sold and stored here prior to its being shipped around the globe from the 1880s until the 1970s. This generated Geelong's wealth. These buildings have been transformed; the largest houses the award-winning **National Wool Museum**, tracing Australia's wool heritage from the shearing shed to the fashion catwalks.

A short drive from Geelong is the Brisbane Ranges National Park, near Anakie, with lovely walks and native wildflowers, such as grevilleas, wattles and wild orchids, in bloom between August and November. Nearby is Steiglitz, a ghost town from the 1850s gold rush. Few buildings remain of this once thriving town, among them the elegant 1870s courthouse, which is closed to the public.

🏛 **National Wool Museum**
26–32 Moorabool St. **Tel** (03) 5227 4701. **Open** daily. **Closed** Good Fri, 25 Dec. 🅿 ♿ 📷 🌐 **geelong australia.com.au/nwm**

❹ Grampians National Park

🚆 Stawell. 🚌 Halls Gap. 🛈 Stawell (03) 5358 2314; Brambuk National Park and Cultural Centre (03) 5361 4000. **Open** daily. 🌐 **parkweb.vic.gov. au/explore/parks/grampians-national-park**

The mountains, cliffs and sheer rock faces of the Grampians

Flora and Fauna of the Grampians

The Grampians are a haven for a wide range of birds, animals, native wildflowers and plants. The park is home to almost one-third of all Victorian plant species, with many, such as the Grampians guinea flower and boronia, found only within its rocky walls. Koalas grunt at night around Halls Gap and the kangaroos at Zumsteins are unusually tame and friendly. The air, trees and scrub teem with beautiful blue wrens, rainbow lorikeets, gang gang cockatoos, scarlet robins and emus. In spring, various wildflowers, orchids and pink heath burst from every valley, and the creeks and rivers are full of rare brown-tree frogs. Just south of the Grampians in the town of Hamilton, a few surviving eastern barred bandicoots, once thought to be extinct, were discovered on the town rubbish tip. They were quickly rescued and have now become part of an active breeding and protection programme.

Rainbow lorikeet

rise like a series of waves above the flat western plains. Within this awesome national park, the third largest in Victoria, is a diversity of natural features and wildlife.

There are craggy slopes, cascading waterfalls and sandstone mountain tops, all formed 400 million years ago by an upthrust of the earth's crust. It has been known as *gariwerd* for thousands of years to local Aboriginal tribes, for whom it is a sacred place, and 80 per cent of Victoria's indigenous rock art is here. The Brambuk National Park and Cultural Centre is partly run by local Aboriginal communities who conduct

tours to the many sites. The Grampians offer many different experiences for tourists. Day trips take in the spectacular MacKenzie Falls and the Balconies rock formation. Longer stays offer bush camping, wildflower studies, exploration of the Victoria Valley over the mountains from Halls Gap and overnight hiking trips in the south of the park. Experienced rock climbers come from around the world to tackle the challenging rock forms in the park and also at the nearby Mount Arapiles.

Excellent maps of the area and guides to the best walks are all available from the park's visitors' centre.

Panoramic view from the rugged crags of the Grampians

The Great Ocean Road Coastline

The Great Ocean Road is one of the world's great scenic drives. Close to Melbourne, pretty holiday towns are linked by curving roads with striking views at every turn. Inland, the road cuts through the Otways, a forested landscape, ecologically rich and visually splendid. Between Port Campbell and Port Fairy is a landscape of rugged cliffs and swirling seas. The giant eroded monoliths, the Twelve Apostles, in Port Campbell National Park, are an awesome spectacle. To the far west, old whaling ports provide an insight into one of Australia's early industries; at Warrnambool, Southern Right Whales can still be seen.

Portland, a deep-water port at the end of the Princes Highway, was the site of the first European settlement in Victoria in 1834. Stunning scenery of craggy cliffs, blowholes and rough waters can be found near the town at Cape Bridgewater.

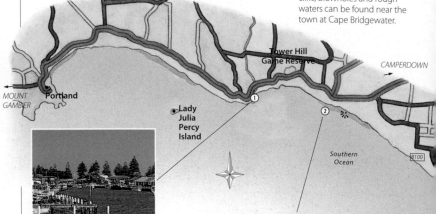

MOUNT GAMBIER — Portland — Tower Hill Game Reserve — CAMPERDOWN

Lady Julia Percy Island

Southern Ocean

B100

① ★ Port Fairy

The tiny cottages of Port Fairy are reminders of the days when the town thrived as a centre for whaling in the 1830s and 1840s. Although the whaling industry has come to an end, the town is now a popular tourist destination.

② ★ Warrnambool

This coastal town is best known for the Southern Right Whales that can often be spotted off Logans Beach between May and October. The town itself has many fine art galleries, museums and old churches.

| 0 kilometres | 25 |
| 0 miles | 25 |

Key

= Highway
— Major road
= Minor road
≈ River

Tower Hill Game Reserve, 13 km (8 miles) west of Warrnambool, is set in an extinct volcano crater. Dusk is the best time to visit and spot emus, koalas and kangaroos roaming the forests.

Locator Map

Otway National Park provides an introduction to some of the species of the southern temperate rainforest, including a famed 400-year-old myrtle beech tree.

⑤ ★ **Loch Ard Gorge** 🦽
This treacherous area claimed the clipper *Loch Ard* in 1878. Local walks focus on the shipwreck, geology and Aboriginal history of the site.

⑨ ★ **Lorne** 🏄🏖🏊🚣♿🚶🏕
Very popular in summer, this charming seaside village boasts excellent cafés, restaurants and accommodation. Nearby forests provide a paradise for walkers.

⑦ ★ **Johanna Beach** 🏄🏖🚣🚶🏕
Another of Victoria's renowned surf beaches is backed by rolling green hills. The area is quite remote, but popular with campers in summer.

GEELONG

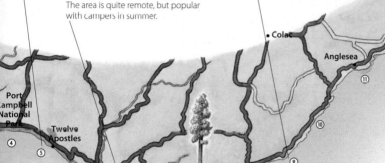

• Colac

Anglesea

⑫

⑪

Port Campbell National Park

④

⑤

Twelve Apostles

⑥ ⑦

⑩

⑨

Otway National Park

⑧

⑧ ★ **Apollo Bay** 🏄🏖🏊🚣♿🚶🏕
Fishing is the main activity here, and fishing trips can be taken from the town's wharf. The town itself has a relaxed village atmosphere and excellent restaurants.

③ **Peterborough** 🏄🏖🚣🚶🏕
Victoria's dairy industry is based on this stretch of coastline. A popular rock pool beneath the cliff is known as the Grotto.

④ **Port Campbell** 🏄🏖🏊🚣♿🚶🏕
Port Campbell beach is a sandy bay, safe for swimming. The town, set on a hill, has great views of the ocean.

⑥ **Moonlight Head** 🚶
Massive cliffs give way to rock platforms here in the heart of Otway National Park. Embedded anchors are reminders of the many ships lost along this perilous coastline.

⑩ **Aireys Inlet** 🏄🏖🏊🚣♿🚶🏕
The red and white lighthouse is a landmark of this tiny coastal town with its beautiful ocean views.

⑪ **Point Addis** 🏄🚶
The Great Ocean Road leads right to the headland with spectacular views from the car park of waves beating the rocks. There are also steps leading down the cliff for a more exhilarating experience of the rolling surf.

⑫ **Bells Beach** 🏄🚶🚶
A natural underwater rock platform contributes to the excellent surfing conditions at Bells. An international surfing competition is held here at Easter, bringing thousands of tourists to the area *(see p46)*.

Murrayville track in the Big Desert Wilderness Park

❺ Big Desert Wilderness

🚌 Hopetoun. 🚌 Hopetoun. ℹ️ 75 Lascelles St, Hopetoun (03) 5083 3001; Parks Victoria Information Line 131963. 🌐 **parkweb.vic.gov.au**

Victoria is so often seen as the state of mountains, green hills, river valleys and beaches that many visitors don't realize that a large part of the west of the state consists of arid desert and mallee scrubland.

These are areas of beauty and solitude, with sand hills, dwarf she-oaks, lizards, snakes and dry creek systems. Big Desert Wilderness Park and Murray-Sunset National Park are true deserts, with hot days and freezing nights. Murray-Sunset National Park is also home to Australia's rarest bird, the black-eared miner.

To the south, Wyperfeld and Little Desert national parks are not true deserts, as they contain lake systems that support diverse flora and fauna, including a wide range of reptiles.

❻ Hattah-Kulkyne National Park

🚌 Mildura. 🚌 Mildura. ℹ️ Mildura (03) 5018 8380; Parks Victoria Information Line 13 19 63. 🌐 **parkweb.vic.gov.au**

Unlike its drier Mallee region counterparts, Hattah-Kulkyne National Park is a haven of creeks and lakes that are linked to the mighty Murray River through a complex billabong (natural waterhole) overflow system.

Its perimeters are typical dry Mallee country of low scrub, mallee trees and native pine woodland, but the large lakes, including Lake Hattah, Mournpoul and Lockie, are alive with bird and animal life. Ringed by massive red gums, the surrounding habitat is home to an abundance of emus, goanna lizards and kangaroos. The freshwater lakes teem with fish, while pelicans, ibis, black swans and other water birds flock on the surface.

The lakes are ideal for canoeing, and the twisting wetlands and billabongs along the Murray River and in the Murray-

Kulkyne section of the park make for fine fishing, picnics, camping and bird-watching. Murray-Sunset National Park is also home to Victoria's largest flower, the Murray lily.

❼ Mildura

🏘️ 50,000. ✈️ 🚌 🚌 ℹ️ 180–190 Deakin Ave (03) 5018 8380. 🌐 **visitmildura.com.au**

In 1887, Mildura was little more than a village on the banks of the Murray River, situated in the middle of a red sandy desert. That year, two Canadian brothers, William and George Chaffey, came to town direct from their successful irrigation project in California and began Australia's first large-scale irrigation scheme. Since then, the red soil, fed by the Murray and Darling rivers, has become a vast plain of farms stretching for nearly 100 km (60 miles).

Today, Mildura is a modern city with a thriving tourist trade. The former home of William Chaffey, the **Rio Vista** is worth a visit. Built in 1890, it has been restored with its original furnishings and is now an Arts Centre. Grapes, olives, avocados and citrus fruit are grown successfully in the region and the area is rapidly expanding its vineyards

The Murray River Paddlesteamers

Old paddlesteamer on the Murray River

Between the 1860s and 1880s, Australia's economy "rode on the sheep's back" – from the Western District of Victoria to the Diamantina Plains in central Queensland, wool was king. But the only way to transport it from the remote sheep stations to coastal ports and then on to its thriving English market was by river. There were no roads other than a few dirt tracks, so the paddlesteamers that plied the Murray, Murrumbidgee and Darling river systems were the long-distance lorries of the day. Towing barges loaded with wool, they reached the Port of Echuca after sailing for days from inland Australia. Then, stocked up with supplies for the sheep stations and distant river settlements, they returned upriver. However, by the 1890s railway lines had crept into the interior and the era of the paddlesteamer was gone. Now the Port of Echuca is once again home to beautifully restored, working paddlesteamers, such as the PS *Adelaide* and PS *Success* (www.portofechuca.org.au).

Rio Vista, the elaborate home of irrigation expert William Chaffey, in Mildura

and wineries *(see pp382–3)*. The stark desert of Mungo National Park is only 100 km (60 miles) to the northeast of town.

🏛 Rio Vista
199 Cureton Ave. **Tel** (03) 5018 8330. **Open** 10am–5pm daily. **Closed** Good Fri, 25 Dec. 🔲 🔲

❽ Swan Hill

🔲 10,000. 🔲 🔲 🔲 🔟 306 Campbell St (03) 5032 3033.

Black Swans are noisy birds, as the early explorer Major Thomas Mitchell discovered in 1836 when his sleep was disturbed by their early morning calls on the banks of the Murray River. That's how the vibrant river town of Swan Hill got its name, and the black swans are still a prominent feature.

One of the most popular attractions of Swan Hill is the **Pioneer Settlement Museum**, a 3-ha (7-acre) living and working re-creation of a river town in the Murray-Mallee area during the period from 1830 to 1930. The settlement buzzes with the sound of printing presses, the blacksmith's hammer, the smell of the bakery and general daily life. "Residents" dress in period clothes and produce old-fashioned goods to sell to tourists. Some of the log buildings are made of

Murray pine, a hardwood tree impenetrable to termites. The sound and light show at night (bookings essential) is particularly evocative, providing a 45-minute journey through the town with accompanying sound effects, such as pounding hooves and a thundering steam locomotive.

🏛 Pioneer Settlement Museum
Monash Drive, Swan Hill. **Tel** (03) 5036 2410. **Open** 9:30am–4pm daily. **Closed** 25–26 Dec. 🔲 🔲 🔲
W pioneersettlement.com.au

❾ Echuca

🔲 14,000. 🔲 🔲 🔲
🔟 2 Heygarth St (03) 5480 7555.
W echucamoama.com

Ex-convict and entrepreneur Henry Hopwood travelled to the Murray River region in 1853, at the end of his prison sentence. He seized upon the need for a river punt at the Echuca crossing by setting up a ferry service, as well as the Bridge Hotel. However, Echuca really came into its own in 1864 when the railway from Melbourne reached the port. Suddenly the town, with its paddlesteamers on the Murray River, became the largest inland port in Australia. Today the port area features horse-drawn

carriages, working steam engines and old-fashioned timber mills. Tours of the area are available, along with regular river trips on a paddlesteamer. Visit the Star Hotel and discover the secret tunnel that let patrons leave after hours. There is also a paddlesteamer display opposite the hotel.

Approximately 30 km (19 miles) upstream from Echuca is Barmah Forest, the largest red gum forest in the world. A drive in the forest, with its 300-year-old river red gums and important Aboriginal sites, is highly recommended, as is the wetlands ecocruise that operates out of Barmah.

Gum trees on the road to Barmah Forest, outside Echuca

⑩ Bendigo

85,000. 🚉 🚌 ⛴ ✈
ℹ 51–67 Pall Mall (03) 5434 6060.
Open daily. **Closed** 25 Dec.
w bendigotourism.com

Bendigo celebrated the gold rush like no other city, and with good reason – the finds here were legendary. In 1851, the first year of gold mining, 23 kg (50 lbs) of gold were extracted from only one bucketful of dirt. When the surface gold began to disappear, the discovery of a gold-rich quartz reef in the 1870s reignited the boom.

Reflecting the city's wealth, Bendigo's buildings are vast and extravagant, often combining several architectural styles within one construction. Government architect G W Watson completed two buildings, the Law Courts and Post Office, in the French and Italian Renaissance styles. The tree-lined boulevard Pall Mall is reminiscent of a French provincial city. The elegant Hotel Shamrock opened to great fanfare in 1897 and is still in operation *(see p494)*. The European-style building is given a distinctly Australian feel with its front veranda. Self-guided heritage walk brochures are available from Bendigo's information centre, and the Vintage Talking Tram provides an excellent commentary on the town's history.

A major part of Bendigo's gold rush history was made by its Chinese population. The **Joss House**, dating from the 1860s, is a restored Chinese temple. The

Entrance to the Chinese Joss House in Bendigo

Typical 19th-century building in Maldon

Golden Dragon Museum also has displays that chart the history of the Chinese in the city. A ceremonial archway links the museum with the **Garden of Joy**, built in 1996. Based on a traditional Asian design, the garden resembles the Chinese landscape in miniature, with mountains, trees and streams.

The **Bendigo Art Gallery** has a splendid collection of Australian painting, including works depicting life on the gold fields. Nearby are shops selling pieces from Australia's oldest working pottery, Bendigo Pottery, established in 1858.

Bendigo's
local pottery

The **Central Deborah Goldmine** offers visitors tours 86 m (260 ft) down to the last deep reef mine in town.

🏛 **Joss House**
Emu Point, Finn St, North Bendigo.
Tel (03) 5442 1685. **Open** 11am–4pm daily. **Closed** 25 Dec. ♿
w bendigojosshouse.com

🏛 **Golden Dragon Museum and Garden of Joy**
1–11 Bridge St. **Tel** (03) 5441 5044.
Open 9:30am–5pm daily.
Closed 25 Dec. ♿ ♿ ♿
w goldendragonmuseum.org

🏛 **Bendigo Art Gallery**
42 View St. **Tel** (03) 5434 6088. **Open** 10am–5pm Tue–Sun. **Closed** 25 Dec. ♿ ♿ by arrangement.
w bendigoartgallery.com.au

🏛 **Central Deborah Goldmine**
76 Violet St. **Tel** (03) 5443 8322.
Open 9am–5pm daily.
Closed 25 Dec. ♿ ♿

⑪ Maldon

1,200. 🚌 ⛴ ℹ 93 High St (03) 5475 2569.

The perfectly preserved town of Maldon offers an outstanding experience of an early gold-mining settlement. This tiny town is set within one of the loveliest landscapes of the region. The hills, forests and exotic trees are an attractive setting for the narrow streets and 19th-century buildings. Maldon was declared Australia's "First Notable Town" by the National Trust in 1966. Cafés, galleries and museums cater to the town's stream of tourists.

Other attractions include Carmen's Tunnel, an old gold mine, and a 70-minute round-trip ride aboard a steam train to Muckleford. Visit at Easter to see the glorious golden leaves of the plane, oak and elm trees. There is also an Easter Fair, including an Easter parade and a street carnival *(see p46)*.

⑫ Castlemaine

7,000. 🚌 ⛴ ✈ ℹ Market Building, 44 Mostyn St (03) 5471 1795.

Castlemaine's elegance reflects the fact that gold finds here were brief but extremely prosperous. The finest attraction is the Market Hall, built in 1862. Architect William Benyon Downe designed this building in the Palladian style, with a portico and a large arched entrance leading into the building's restrained interior. The building is now the Visitors' Information Centre. **Buda Historic Home and Garden** was occupied from 1863 to 1981 by two generations of Hungarian silversmith, Ernest Leviny and his family. The house displays an extensive collection of arts and crafts works. The property is also noted for its largely intact 19th-century garden, a unique survivor of its period.

Castlemaine is also home to many writers and artists from Melbourne and has a lively collection of museums, cafés and restaurants.

🏠 **Buda Historic Home and Garden**
42 Hunter St. **Tel** (03) 5472 1032. **Open** noon–5pm Wed–Sat, 10am–5pm Sun & public hols. **Closed** Good Fri, 25 Dec. 🚻 🅿 teahouse and upper garden area. 🌐 budacastlemaine.org.au

⑬ Ballarat

See pp438–9.

⑭ Sovereign Hill

Bradshaw St, Ballarat. **Tel** (03) 5337 1100. **Open** 10am–5pm daily. **Closed** 25 Dec. 🚻 🅿 🅿 🌐 sovereignhill.com.au

Sovereign Hill is the gold fields' living museum. Located on the outskirts of Ballarat (see pp438–9), it offers visitors the chance to

The Chinese on the Gold Fields

The first Chinese gold-seekers landed in Melbourne in 1853. Their numbers peaked at around 40,000 in 1859. They worked hard in large groups to recover the tiniest particles of gold, but the Europeans became hostile, claiming that the new arrivals were draining the colony's wealth. In 1857, several Chinese were murdered. The state government tried to quell hostility by introducing an entry tax on Chinese who arrived by boat – the Chinese then landed in neighbouring states and walked overland to Victoria. At the end of the gold rush many stayed on to work as gardeners, cooks and factory hands. There is still a large Chinese community in the state.

Chinese workers on the gold fields

explore a unique period of Australia's history. Blacksmiths, hoteliers, bakers and grocers in full period dress ply their trades on the main streets, amid the diggers' huts, tents, old meeting places and the Chinese Village. Among the most absorbing displays are those that reproduce gold-mining methods. The town's fields produced an estimated 640,000 kg (630 tonnes) of gold before being exhausted in the 1920s.

The nearby Gold Museum is part of the Sovereign Hill complex. Its changing exhibits focus on the uses of gold throughout history.

Sovereign Hill opens in the evenings for an impressive sound and light show, which re-enacts the events of the Eureka Stockade (see p438).

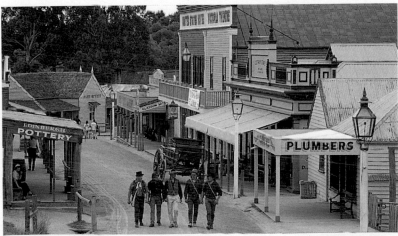

Actors in period costume walking along the main street in Sovereign Hill

⑬ Ballarat

In 1851, the cry of "Gold!" shattered the tranquillity of this pleasant, pastoral district. Within months, tent cities covered the hills and thousands of people were pouring in from around the world, eager to make their fortune. While there were spectacular finds, the sustainable prosperity was accrued to traders, farmers and other modest industries, and Ballarat grew in proportion to their growing wealth. The gold rush petered out in the late 1870s. However, the two decades of wealth can still be seen in the lavish buildings, broad streets, ornate statuary and grand gardens. Today, Ballarat is Victoria's largest inland city.

Ornate façade of Her Majesty's Theatre on Lydiard Street

⊞ Lydiard Street

The wealth of the gold fields attracted a range of people, among them the educated and well travelled. Lydiard Street reflects their influence as a well-proportioned streetscape, boasting buildings of exemplary quality and design.

At the northern end lies the railway station. Built in 1862, it features an arched train entrance and Tuscan pilasters. A neat row of four banks was designed by prominent architect Leonard Terry, whose concern for a balanced streetscape is clearly expressed in their elegant façades. Her Majesty's Theatre is an elaborate 19th-century structure and Australia's oldest surviving purpose-built theatre.

Opposite the theatre is Craig's Royal Hotel, begun in 1852. The hotel was extensively renovated in 1867 for a visit by Prince Alfred, Duke of Edinburgh, including the construction of a special Prince's Room. In 1881,

royal lanterns were constructed outside to honour a visit by the Duke of Clarence and the Duke of York (later King George V). This historic hotel is still in operation.

🏛 Art Gallery of Ballarat

40 Lydiard St North. **Tel** (03) 5320 5858. **Open** 10am–5pm daily. **Closed** Good Fri, 25 Dec. 🅿 ♿ 🅦 artgalleryof ballarat.com.au

Ballarat has always enjoyed the spirit of benefaction. Huge fortunes were made overnight and much of these found their way into the town's institutions. The Art Gallery of Ballarat has been a major recipient of such goodwill, enabling it to establish an impressive reputation as Australia's largest and arguably best provincial art institution.

More than 6,000 works chart the course of Australian art from colonial to contemporary times. Gold field artists include Eugene von Guerard, whose work *Old Ballarat as it was in the summer of 1853–54* is an extraordinary evocation of the town's early tent cities. The gallery's star exhibit is the original Eureka Flag, which has since come to symbolize the basic democratic ideals which are so much a part of modern Australian society.

🏛 Museum of Australian Democracy at Eureka (M.A.D.E)

Cnr Stawell Sth and Eureka streets. **Tel** 1800 287 113. **Open** 10am–5pm daily. 🅿 ♿ 🅦 made.org

The Museum of Australian Democracy at Eureka is located in East Ballarat, at what was the site of the Eureka Stockade. The

The Eureka Stockade

An insurrection at Eureka in 1854, which arose as a result of gold diggers' dissatisfaction with high licensing fees on the gold fields, heralded the move towards egalitarianism in Australia. When hotel-owner Peter Bentley was acquitted of murdering a young digger, James Scobie, after a row about his entry into the Eureka Hotel, it incited anger among the miners. Led by the charismatic Peter Lalor, the diggers built a stockade, burned their licences and raised the blue flag of the Southern Cross, which became known as the Eureka Flag. On Sunday, 3 December 1854, 282 soldiers and police made a surprise attack on the stockade, killing around 30 diggers. After a public outcry over the brutality, however, the diggers were acquitted of treason and the licence system was abolished.

Rebel leader Peter Lalor

Lily pond in Ballarat's beautiful Ballarat Botanical Gardens

centre celebrates the concept of democracy (from the Greek *demos* and *kratos*, meaning "people" and "power") through a series of interactive displays. The main gallery is surrounded by a cyclorama timeline that highlights the main events in the history of democracy, from its origins in Athens until the present day. The centre also hosts film screenings, photographic exhibitions and workshops, all focused on the struggle for democracy.

Ballarat Botanical Gardens

Wendouree Drive. **Tel** (03) 5320 5135. **Open** daily. **Closed** 25 Dec.

These gardens, in the northwest of the city, are a telling symbol of Ballarat's desire for Victorian gentility. The rough and ready atmosphere of the gold fields could be easily overlooked here among the statues, lush green lawns and exotic plants. The focus of the gardens has always been aesthetic rather than botanical, although four different displays are exhibited each year in the Robert Clark Conservatory. The most famous of these is the lovely begonia display, part of the Begonia Festival held here each March (*see p46*).

There is a Statuary Pavilion featuring female biblical figures in provocative poses, as well as a splendid centrepiece, *Flight from Pompeii*. The Avenue of Prime Ministers is a double row of staggered busts of every Australian prime minister to date, stretching off into the distance. The gardens run along the shores of the expansive Lake Wendouree.

Ballarat Town Centre

① Ballarat Botanical Gardens
② Lydiard Street
③ Art Gallery of Ballarat
④ Museum of Australian Democracy at Eureka (M.A.D.E)

⑮ Tour of Daylesford and the Macedon Ranges

Daylesford and the Macedon Ranges lie to the northwest of Melbourne. The landscape is dotted with vineyards, small townships, craft markets and bed-and-breakfasts. The tour follows the Calder Highway, once taken by gold prospectors to the alluvial fields of Castlemaine and Bendigo (see pp436–7) before heading west into the spa country around Daylesford. The region's wealthy past is reflected in the 19th-century bluestone buildings, including wool stores and stately homes.

⑧ **Malmsbury**
During the gold rush, this peaceful hamlet was a busy stop for prospectors on their way to the gold fields.

⑨ **Hepburn Springs**
The Mineral Springs Reserve is a large area of native bushland. It is an idyllic place for walkers and those who want to "take the waters" from the old-fashioned pumps.

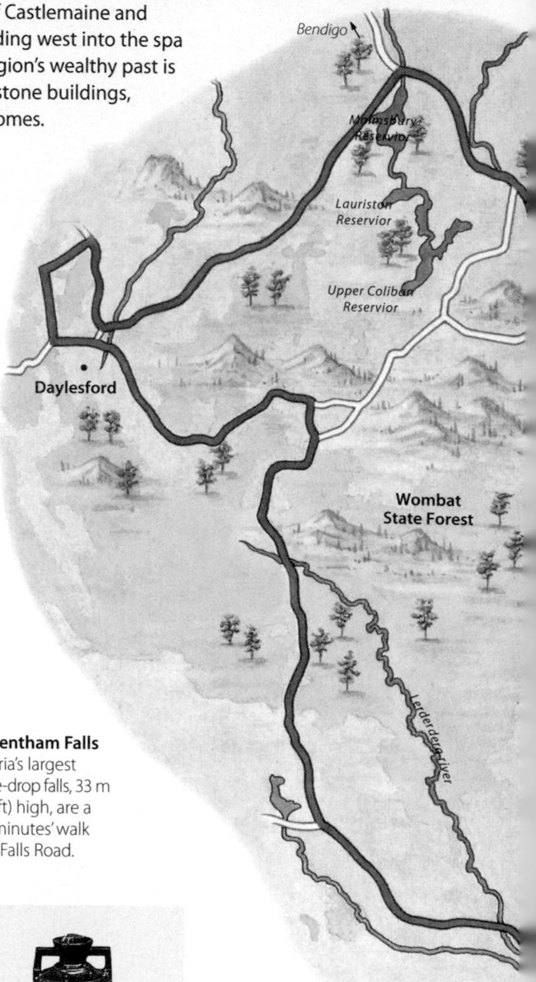

⑩ **Trentham Falls**
Victoria's largest single-drop falls, 33 m (108 ft) high, are a few minutes' walk from Falls Road.

Rupertswood and the Ashes

During the Christmas of 1882, eight members of the touring English cricket team were house guests of Sir William John Clarke at Rupertswood. The English won a social game between them and their hosts. Lady Clarke burnt a bail, placed the ashes in an urn and presented them to the English captain, Ivo Bligh. The urn was later presented to Marylebone Cricket Club by Bligh's widow, and thus the cricketing tradition of contesting for The Ashes began.

The original 1882 Ashes urn

0 kilometres 5

0 miles 5

Key

▬▬ Tour route
═══ Other roads

⑦ Kyneton
Historic Kyneton was once a supply town for diggers during the gold rush. It still has part of its 19th-century streetscape intact. The town has some good cafés and antique shops.

⑥ Woodend
Named for its location at the edge of the Black Forest, Woodend has long been a haven for travellers. It has many restaurants, hotels and speciality shops.

⑤ Hanging Rock
This rock was formed 6 million years ago when lava rose up from the earth's surface and solidified. Erosion has caused the fissures through which you can now walk. Scene of the film *Picnic at Hanging Rock*, the area is steeped in Aboriginal history.

④ Mount Macedon
A short walk from the summit car park leads to the memorial cross reserve and spectacular views over the Keilor Plains to Melbourne, Port Phillip Bay, the You Yangs and the Dandenong Ranges *(see p447)*.

③ Rupertswood
This Italianate mansion was built in 1874. The estate includes the cricket field on which The Ashes were created. The once magnificent grounds are now used by a boys' school.

② Goona Warra
The original vineyards of this 1863 bluestone winery were replanted during the 1980s. They now produce highly respected wines, available for tasting and sales daily from the cellar door.

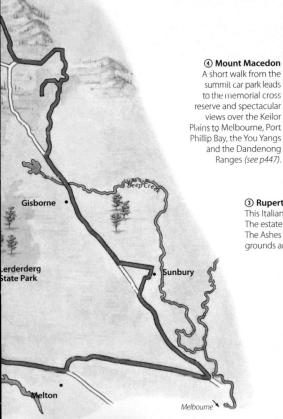

Melbourne

① Organ Pipes
These 20-m (65-ft) basalt columns were formed by lava flows a million years ago. The Pipes can be seen from a viewing area near the car park or via a trail down to the creek bed.

Tips for Drivers

Tour length: 215 km (133 miles).
Stopping off points: There are numerous places to stay and eat along the route, particularly at Woodend and Daylesford. Daylesford is also ideal for a romantic dinner or weekend lunch *(see p530)*.

EASTERN VICTORIA

Eastern Victoria is a region of immense natural beauty with snow-topped mountains, eucalyptus forests, fertile inland valleys, wild national parks and long sandy beaches. Some of the state's finest wine-growing areas are here, set around historic towns of golden sandstone. Fast rivers popular with rafters flow through the region and ski resorts resembling Swiss villages are found in the Victoria Alps.

Eastern Victoria has a range of attractions for the visitor. The fertile plains of the northeast, crossed by the Goulburn, Ovens, King and Murray rivers, offer a feast for the tastebuds: Rutherglen red wines; Milawa mustards; local cheeses; and luscious peaches, pears and apricots from Shepparton. Historic 19th-century towns such as Beechworth and Chiltern are beautifully preserved from their gold-mining days. Glenrowan is the site where Australia's most famous bushranger, Ned Kelly, was captured. An old-fashioned paddlesteamer rides regularly on the broad Murray River near Wodonga.

But towards the Victorian Alps and the towns of Bright and Mansfield another landscape emerges. This one is wild and very beautiful. In winter, there is exciting downhill skiing among the snow gums

and peaks at village resorts such as Mount Buller and Falls Creek (see pp452–3). In summer, walk among the wildflowers in Alpine National Park, hike to the summit of Mount Feathertop, or try a rafting expedition down rivers such as the mighty Snowy.

To the east of Melbourne are the magnificent beaches of the Gippsland region. Favourite attractions here include Phillip Island with its fairy penguins, and Wilsons Promontory National Park with its wildlife, granite outcrops and pristine waters. Near the regional centres of Sale and Bairnsdale lie the Gippsland Lakes, Australia's largest inland waterway and an angler's paradise. Beyond, stretching to the New South Wales border, is Croajingolong National Park and 200 km (125 miles) of deserted coastline.

Canoeing down the Kiewa River near Beechworth in Eastern Victoria

◀ Snow daisies on Mount Hotham, in the Alpine National Park

Exploring Eastern Victoria

Excellent highways give access to the most popular tourist attractions and towns of Eastern Victoria. The Dandenong Ranges, Yarra Valley and Phillip Island are within an easy day trip from Melbourne; the region's coastline, which includes Gippsland Lakes, around Lakes Entrance, Wilsons Promontory and Croajingolong National Park, is further to the south and east. The mountains, ski resorts and inland farm valleys are better accessed from the northeast of the state. While most of the major sights can be reached by road, some areas of the Gippsland forests and the Victorian Alps must be explored in 4WD vehicles.

The 19th-century post office in Beechworth

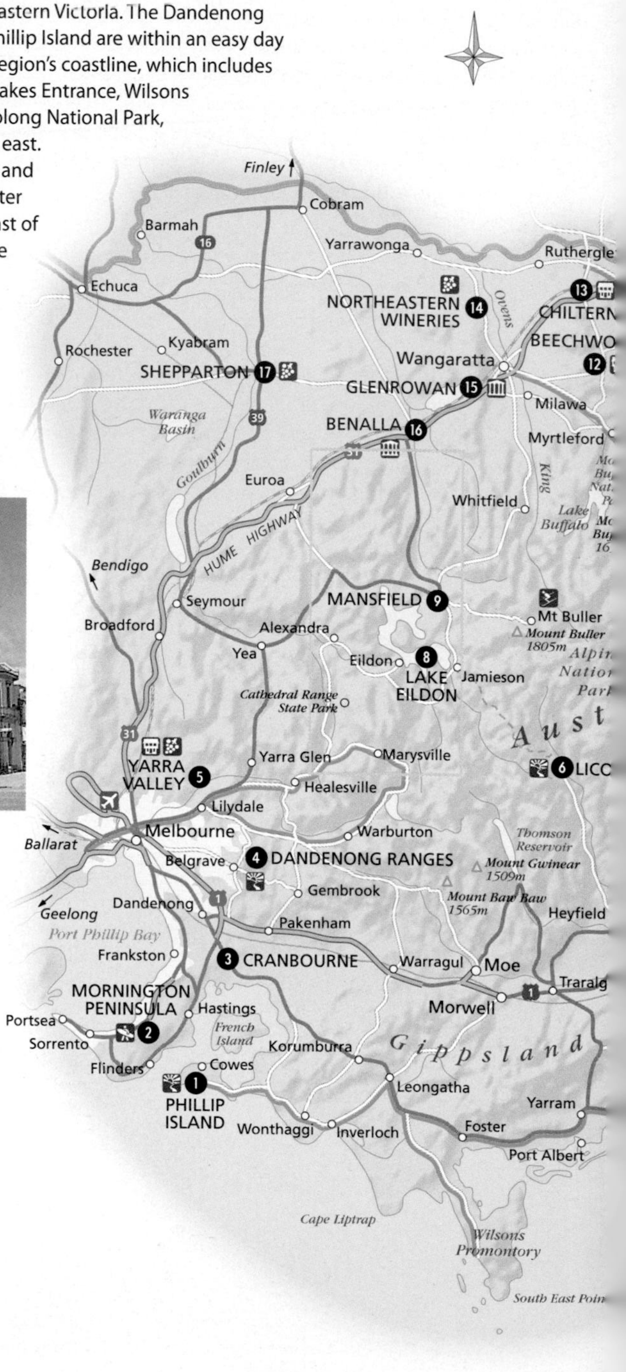

0 km   25
0 miles   25

Key

— Highway
— Major road
··· Minor road
-- Track
— Scenic route
···· Main railway
— Minor railway
— State border
△ Summit

For additional map symbols see back flap

Sights at a Glance

1. Phillip Island
2. Mornington Peninsula
3. Royal Botanical Gardens, Cranbourne
4. Dandenong Ranges
5. Yarra Valley
6. Licola
7. Buchan Caves
8. Lake Eildon
9. Mansfield
10. Mount Beauty
11. Bright
12. Beechworth
13. Chiltern
14. Northeastern Wineries
15. Glenrowan
16. Benalla
17. Shepparton

Upper Murray Valley in the heart of northeastern Victoria

Getting Around

There are regular train services to the Dandenongs and the Gippsland Lakes. Bus tours can be arranged to Phillip Island and the Yarra Valley, while regular buses run in winter to the ski resorts. However, the best way of exploring is by car. The Hume Hwy provides access to the northeast, the Princes Hwy to the Gippsland Lakes and the South Gippsland Hwy to Phillip Island and Wilsons Promontory.

Lake Eildon at the gateway to the Victorian Alps

❶ Phillip Island

🚌 Cowes. ⛴ Cowes. ℹ Newhaven
(03) 5956 7447. **Open** 9am–5pm daily;
summer hols: 9am–6pm daily.
🅆 visitphillipisland.com

The penguin parade on Phillip
Island is an extraordinary
natural spectacle. Every evening
at sunset at all times of the year,
hundreds of little penguins
come ashore at Summerland
Beach and waddle across the
sand to their burrows in the
spinifex tussocks (spiky clumps
of grass), just as their ancestors
have been doing for generations. Once ashore, the small
penguins spend their time in
the dunes preening themselves
and, in summer, feeding their
hungry chicks.

At Seal Rocks, off the rugged
cliffs at the western end of the
island, is Australia's largest
colony of fur seals. Approximately 16,000 of these seals
can be seen playing in the surf,
resting in the sun or feeding
their pups on the rocks. Tourists
can watch them from the cliff
top or on an organized boat
trip. There is also a large koala
colony on Phillip Island.

Cape Woolamai, with its red
cliffs and wild ocean seas, has
good walking trails, excellent
bird-watching opportunities
and some great surfing. The
peaceful town of Cowes is
ideal for swimming, relaxing
and dining.

The island gets very crowded
during car and motorcycle race
events so you need to reserve
accommodation
at these times.

Fairy penguins making their way up the sand dunes
of Phillip Island

Rock pools at Sorrento on the Mornington Peninsula

❷ Mornington Peninsula

🚉 Frankston. 🚌 to most peninsula
towns. ⛴ Stony Point, Sorrento.
ℹ Dromana (03) 5987 3078
🅆 visitmorningtonpeninsula.org

Only an hour's drive from
Melbourne, on the east side of
Port Phillip Bay, the Mornington
Peninsula is the city's summer
and weekend getaway. From
Frankston down to Portsea
near its tip, the area is ideal
for relaxing beach holidays.
The sandy beaches facing the
bay are sheltered and calm,
perfect for windsurfing, sailing
or paddling, while the rugged
coast fronting the Bass Strait
has rocky reefs, rock pools
and surf beaches.

Arthur's Seat, a high, bush
ridge offers views of the
peninsula. The surrounding
Red Hill wineries are fast
gaining a reputation for their
fine Chardonnays and Pinot
Noirs. Sip a glass of one of
these wines in the historic
village of Sorrento or take
a ferry trip across the
narrow and
treacherous Rip
to the beautiful
19th-century town
of Queenscliff
(see p430).
Running the length
of the peninsula,
the Mornington
Peninsula National
Park has lovely
walking tracks.
Point Nepean,
formerly a

quarantine station and defence
post, is now part of the national
park. The beach at the tip of The
Heads and Cheviot Beach, where
Prime Minister Harold Holt
disappeared while surfing in
1967, are both beautiful spots.

Environs
The village of Flinders is a
peaceful, chic seaside resort,
while Portsea is the summer
playground of Melbourne's rich
and famous. The atmosphere
at the remote French Island, a
short ferry trip from Crib Point,
is unique, with no electricity or
telephones. The island also
teems with wildlife, including
rare potoroo.

❸ Royal Botanic Gardens, Cranbourne

Off South Gippsland Hwy, 1000
Ballarto Rd. **Tel** (03) 5990 2200.
🚉 Cranbourne. 🚌 Cranbourne.
Open 9am–5pm daily. **Closed** 25
Dec, days of total fire ban. ♿ ▯
🅆 rbg.vic.gov.au/visit-cranbourne

The Royal Botanic Gardens
in Melbourne are the city's
pride and joy (see pp402–3), but
they have not concentrated
exclusively on native flora. The
Cranbourne Botanic Gardens
fill that niche. Amid the lakes,
hills and dunes of this bushland
park, banksias, wattles, grevilleas,
casuarinas, eucalypts and pink
heath bloom, while wrens,
honeyeaters, galahs, rosellas,
cockatoos and parrots nestle
among the gardens' trees.

❹ Dandenong Ranges

🚉 Ferntree Gully & Belgrave. 🚌 to most towns. 𝒊 Upper Ferntree Gully (03) 8739 8000. **Open** 9am–5pm daily. 🆆 **experiencethedandenongs. com.au**

Since the mid-19th century, the Dandenong Ranges, to the east of Melbourne, have been a popular weekend retreat for city residents. The cool of the mountain ash forests, lush fern gullies and bubbling creeks provide a welcome relief from the bayside heat.

The great gardens of the Dandenongs, many of which once belonged to the mansions of wealthy families, are magnificent for walks and picnics. Particularly popular is the Alfred Nicholas Memorial Garden at Sherbrooke with its oaks, elms, silver birches and Japanese maples around a boating lake. Flowers are the obvious attraction of the National Rhododendron Gardens at Olinda and Tesselaar's Tulip Farm at Silvan. A steam train, Puffing Billy, runs several times daily from Belgrave through 24 km (15 miles) of gullies and forests to Emerald Lake and on to Gembrook.

The superb lyrebird makes its home in the Dandenongs, particularly in Sherbrooke Forest. The 7-km (4-mile) Eastern Sherbrooke Lyrebird Circuit Walk through mountain ash offers a chance to glimpse these beautiful but shy birds.

Domaine Chandon vineyard in the Yarra Valley

Another tranquil walk is the 11-km (6-mile) path from Sassafras to Emerald.

Healesville Sanctuary, with its 30 ha (75 acres) of natural bushland, remains the best place to see indigenous Australian animals in relatively relaxed captivity. Highlights of any visit are the sightings of rare species such as platypuses, marsupials and birds of prey. This is a popular place to bring children who want to learn about Australian wildlife.

Further east are the Steavenson Falls and also nearby are the mountains of the Cathedral Ranges and the snow fields and trails of Lake Mountain (*see pp452–3*).

🏞 **Healesville Sanctuary**
Badger Creek Rd, Healesville.
Tel (03) 5957 2800. **Open** 9am–5pm daily. 🅿 ♿ 🆆 **zoo.org.au**

Sparkling wine of the Yarra Valley

❺ Yarra Valley

🚉 Lilydale. 🚌 Healesville service. 𝒊 Healesville (03) 5962 2600.

The beautiful Yarra Valley, located at the foot of the Dandenong Ranges, is home to some of Australia's best cool-climate wineries (*see pp382–3*). They are known for their *Méthode Champenoise* sparkling wines, Chardonnays and Pinot Noirs. Most of the wineries are open daily for wine tastings. Several also have restaurants, serving food to accompany their fine wines.

Just past the bush town of Yarra Glen is the historic Gulf Station. Owned by the National Trust, it provides an authentic glimpse of farming life at the end of the 19th century.

The famous Puffing Billy steam train, making its way through the Dandenong Ranges

The Gippsland Coastline

The beautiful coastline of Gippsland is equal to any natural wonder of the world. Approximately 400 km (250 miles) of deserted beaches, inlets and coves are largely protected by national park status. There is the largest inland lake system in Australia, Gippsland Lakes, the pristine sands of Ninety Mile Beach and rare natural features such as the Mitchell River silt jetties. Birds, fish, seals and penguins abound in the area. With little commercial development, the coastline is a popular location with anglers, sailors, divers, swimmers and campers.

③ **Woodside Beach**
This easily accessible white sandy beach is popular with families, sunbathers and surfers. The area behind the beach benefits from many well-signposted bushwalks.

⑥ **Gippsland Lakes**
The lagoons, backwaters, islands and lakes of this region make up Australia's biggest inland waterway. Lakeside settlements are home to large sailing and fishing fleets.

Port Albert, the oldest port in Gippsland, was used by thousands of gold diggers heading for the Omeo and Walhalla gold fields in the 1850s. Quaint buildings with shady verandas line its streets, and it is home to the oldest pub in the state.

⑤ ★ **Letts Beach**
This sandy beach benefits from the ocean on one side and beautiful lakes on the other. Part of the Lakes National Park, the beach is home to the endangered fairy tern.

② **Corner Inlet**
This small inlet protects some of the world's most southerly mangroves and seagrass beds, as well as rare birds such as the red-necked stint.

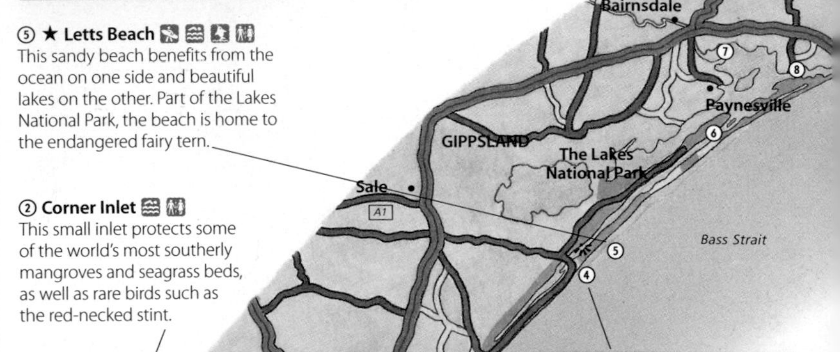

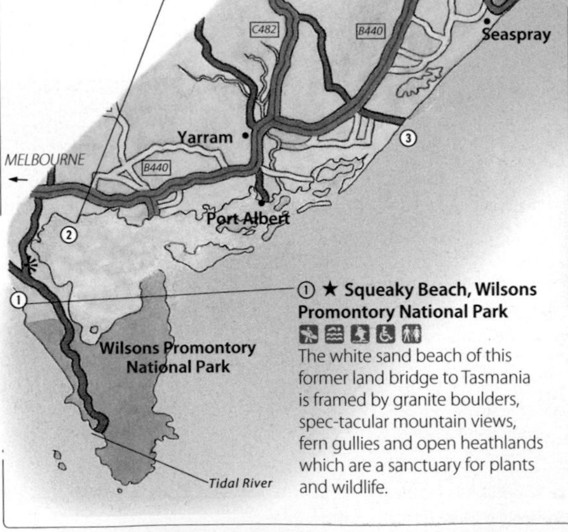

① ★ **Squeaky Beach, Wilsons Promontory National Park**
The white sand beach of this former land bridge to Tasmania is framed by granite boulders, spec-tacular mountain views, fern gullies and open heathlands which are a sanctuary for plants and wildlife.

④ ★ **Golden Beach**
The calm waters of this stretch of ocean make it a popular destination for water sports enthusiasts. Fishing and sailing are two of the regular activities available in the area.

Bairnsdale
Paynesville
GIPPSLAND
The Lakes
National Park
Sale
Bass Strait
Seaspray
Yarram
MELBOURNE
Port Albert
Wilsons Promontory
National Park
Tidal River

Bairnsdale is one of the major towns of the Gippsland region, together with its neighbour, Sale. St Mary's Church, in the centre of the town, has distinctive Italianate-style painted walls and ceilings, as well as beautiful carved statuary set in its exterior walls.

⑫ ★ Gipsy Point, Mallacoota Inlet 🏕️ 🚻 🚶
This idyllic spot within a pleasant holiday region is ideal for summer picnics. Bird-watching and bushwalking are popular local activities.

Locator Map

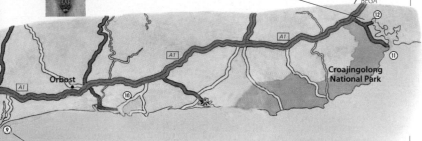

Croajingolong National Park

Orbost

Lakes Entrance

⑨ ★ Lakes Entrance 🏕️ 🚻 🚶
Lakes Entrance is the only entrance from the Gippsland Lakes to the sea, through the treacherous Bar. This major fishing port is also well equipped with motels, museums and theme parks for children

⑦ Eagle Point 🏕️ 🚻 🚶
Silt banks from the Mitchell River stretch 8 km out into Lake King from Eagle Point. The silt banks are second only in length to those of the Mississippi River.

⑧ Metung 🏕️ 🚻 🚶
This pretty boating and holiday region, popular with campers, benefits from hot mineral pools.

⑩ Marlo 🏕️ 🚻 🚶
Located at the mouth of the great Snowy River, Marlo is a popular holiday destination, particularly with avid local anglers. Nearby is the large town of Orbost, the centre of East Gippsland's extensive timber industry.

⑪ Mallacoota 🏕️ 🚻 🚶
This remote fishing village is extremely popular with both Victorian and overseas tourists. It is set on an inland estuary of the Bass Strait, ideal for canoeing, fishing and sailing.

Croajingolong National Park is a magnificent stretch of rugged and coastal wilderness, classified as a World Biosphere Reserve. Captain Cook caught his first sight of Australia in 1770 at Point Hicks.

0 kilometres	25
0 miles	25

Key

🚧 Freeway
— Major road
= = = Minor road
〰️ River

⑥ Licola

🏠 20. 🚌 Heyfield. 🅸 Licola Wilderness Village, Jamieson Rd (03) 5148 8/91. 🆆 **licola.org.au**

Licola is a tiny village perched on the edge of Victoria's mountain wilderness. North of Heyfield and Glenmaggie, follow the Macalister River Valley north to Licola. The 147-km (90-mile) journey from Licola to Jamieson, along unsealed roads, takes in the magnificent scenery of Victoria's highest peaks. Only 20 km (12 miles) from Licola is Mount Tamboritha and the start of the popular Lake Tarli Karng bushwalk in the Alpine National Park, also a good base for those keen to explore the surrounding country. The village store has information.

Licola is entirely owned by the Lions Club of Victoria (the only privately owned town in the state). The club has developed the Lions Wilderness Village, which provides camp sites and a range of activities for young people.

Farmland near the tiny mountain village of Licola

⑦ Buchan Caves

Buchan Caves Reserve, Buchan. **Tel** (03) 5155 9203 or 13 19 63. **Open** daily except 25 Dec. 🅲 daily 🆆 **parkweb.vic.gov.au**

Some of the most spectacular limestone formations in Australia can be found at Buchan Caves. Two of the finest are Fairy Cave and Royal Cave, within Buchan Caves Reserve. Both caves are lit and have walkways; guided tours are conducted throughout the day, alternating between the two caves. Dating back 300–400 million years, the caves and

their awe-inspiring stalactites and stalagmites were made by ancient rivers coursing and seeping through the limestone rock. Royal Cave also has colourful calcite-rimmed pools. Entry to the reserve, where there are picnic facilities and a spring-fed pool suitable for swimming, is free. There are also camp sites and walking trails, while the nearby township of Buchan offers other accommodation. The reserve is a wildlife refuge to native animals such as kangaroos, possums, bellbirds and lyrebirds.

⑧ Lake Eildon

🚌 Eildon. 🅸 Eildon Visitors' Information Centre, Main St, Eildon. 🆆 **lakeeildon.com**

Lake Eildon, the catchment for five major rivers, including the Goulburn River, is a vast irrigation reserve that turns into a recreational haven in summer. Surrounded by the Great Dividing Range and Fraser and Eildon national parks, the lake is a good location for water-skiing, houseboat holidays, horse-riding, fishing and hiking. Kangaroos, koalas and rosellas abound around the lake, and trout and Murray cod are common in the Upper Goulburn River and in the lake. Canoeing on the Goulburn River is also a popular activity.

Limestone formations at Buchan Caves

A variety of accommodation is available, from rustic cabins and camp sites in Fraser National Park to luxurious five-star lodges and guesthouses.

⑨ Mansfield

🏠 2,500. 🚌 🅸 Visitors' Information Centre, 175 High St, Mansfield (03) 5775 7000. 🆆 **mansfieldmtbuller. com.au**

Mansfield, a country town surrounded by mountains, is the southwest entry point to Victoria's alpine country. A memorial in the main street of Mansfield, just near to the 1920s cinema, commemorates the death of three troopers shot by the infamous Ned Kelly and his gang at nearby Stringybark Creek in 1878 – the crime for which he was

Blue waters of Lake Eildon, backed by the Howqua Mountain Ranges

For hotels and restaurants in this area see pp495–6 and pp531–3

Classic 19th-century architecture in the rural town of Mansfield

hung in Melbourne in 1880 (see p398).

The scenery of Mansfield became well known as the location for the 1981 film *The Man from Snowy River*, which was based on the poet "Banjo" Paterson's legendary ballad of the same name (see p39). Many local horsemen rode in the film. Activities include woodchopping, whipcracking, haystacking and bushcraft, as well as displays of the cattle mens' horse-riding abilities.

Environs

The excellent downhill slopes of the Mount Buller ski resort (see pp452–3) are less than one hour's drive from Mansfield. Mount Stirling (see pp452–3) offers year-round activities, such as mountain bike riding (see p538).

⑩ Mount Beauty

🏔 2,300. 🚌 ℹ️ 31 Bogong High Plains Rd, Mt Beauty (03) 5755 0596. 🌐 mtbeauty.com

The town of Mount Beauty was first built to house workers on the Kiewa hydro-electricity scheme in the 1940s. It has since developed into a good base for exploring the beauty of the Kiewa Valley, with its tumbling river and dairy farms. Also nearby is the wilderness of the Bogong High Plains and the Alpine National Park (see pp452–3), with their walks, wildflowers and snow gums.

Within the national park, Mount Bogong, Victoria's highest mountain, rises an impressive 1,986 m (6,516 ft) above the

town. The sealed mountain road to Falls Creek (see pp452–3) is one of the main access routes to the region's ski slopes in winter. In summer, Rocky Valley Dam near Falls Creek is a popular rowing and high-altitude athletics training camp. There are beautiful bushwalks, and at the top of the High Plains, there are opportunities for fishing, mountain biking, horse-riding and hang-gliding.

⑪ Bright

🏔 2,500. 🚌 ℹ️ 76a Gavan St (03) 5755 2275. 🌐 brightvictoria. com.au

Bright is a picturesque mountain town near the head of the Ovens River Valley, with the towering rocky cliffs of Mount Buffalo (see pp452–3)

to the west and the peak of the state's second highest mountain, Mount Feathertop, to its south. The trees along Bright's main street flame into spectacular colours of red, gold, copper and brown for its Autumn Festival in April and May (see p46). In winter, the town turns into a gateway to the snow fields, with the resorts of Mount Hotham and Falls Creek in the Victorian Alps close by (see pp452–3). In summer, swimming and fly-fishing for trout in the Ovens River are popular activities.

The spectacular **Mount Buffalo National Park** is also popular all year round; visitors can camp amid the snow gums by Lake Catani and walk its flower-flecked mountain pastures and peaks, fish for trout, hang-glide off the granite tors over the Ovens Valley or rock climb the imposing sheer cliffs. During the winter, Mount Buffalo is a great place for cross-country skiing and snow play. A range of walking trails are available with wonderful views of Buckland Valley. Other activities on offer include canoeing, caving, horse-riding and paragliding.

🏕 **Mount Buffalo National Park**
Mount Buffalo Rd. **Tel** 13 19 63. 🅿️ ♿ some areas.

Buffalo River meandering through Mount Buffalo National Park

Skiing in the Victorian Alps

Australia offers fantastic skiing opportunities that rival the best in the world. Most of the resorts fall within Alpine National Park *(see pp444–5)*, and are open for business from June to late September. Given that the season is so short, conditions can be variable. Mount Buller, Falls Creek and Mount Hotham are the main resort villages, and the whole region is very fashionable. There are chic lounge bars, top-end lodges and fine dining prepared by some of Melbourne's best chefs. Pistes are not as long as those in Europe and the USA, but the views of the High Plains are an unmissable experience.

Mount Buffalo 🎿 🎿
These less-crowded slopes are popular with beginners, intermediates and cross-country skiers.

Mount Stirling Entry to Mount Buller includes free cross-country skiing on Mount Stirling's groomed trails.

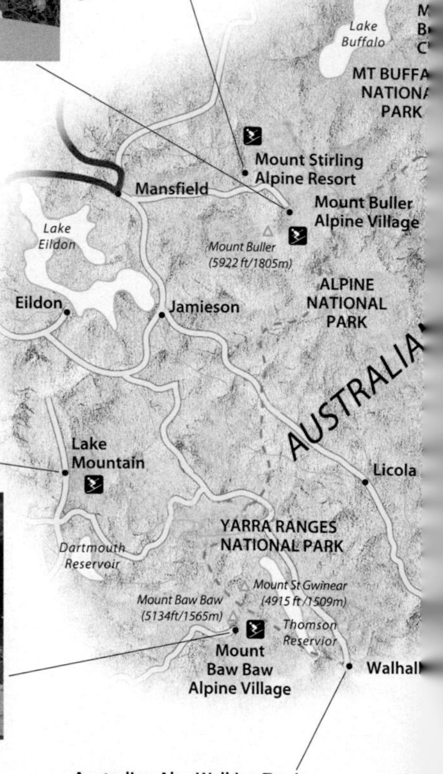

Mount Buller 🎿 🎿 🎿
This is the most accessible of the major resorts, and hence the busiest and trendiest. Slopes suit beginners through to advanced skiers, with 80 km (48 miles) of groomed trails and a 405-m (1,300 ft)-vertical drop. The entrance car park at Mirimbah is 16 km (10 miles) from the village; there is a free shuttle bus for daytrippers.

Lake Mountain This resort is ideal for cross-country skiing. Most runs are for beginners to intermediates. There is no on-mountain accommodation. Nearby Mount Donna Buang is fine for snowmen and toboggan runs.

Mount Baw Baw 🎿 🎿
The closest downhill ski resort to Melbourne is an excellent option for beginners, families and skiers on a budget. Nearby Mount St Gwinear offers superb cross-country skiing but no on-mountain accommodation.

Australian Alps Walking Track
The 655-km (393-mile) Australian Alps Walking Track runs from historic Walhalla north-east to the Brindabella Ranges outside Canberra.

Map labels:

Mount Buffalo (5558 ft/1695m)

Lake Buffalo

MT BUFFALO NATIONAL PARK

Mansfield

Mount Stirling Alpine Resort

Mount Buller Alpine Village

Lake Eildon

Mount Buller (5922 ft/1805m)

Eildon

Jamieson

ALPINE NATIONAL PARK

AUSTRALIA

Lake Mountain

Licola

YARRA RANGES NATIONAL PARK

Dartmouth Reservoir

Mount St Gwinear (4915 ft /1509m)

Mount Baw Baw (5134ft/1565m)

Thomson Reservoir

Mount Baw Baw Alpine Village

Walhalla

Falls Creek 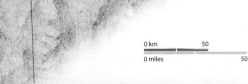 Australia's only real ski-in ski-out resort village is popular with cross-country and advanced skiers. It also offers the country's longest green run and plenty of options for freestylers. The inner-city nightlife suits an extended stay.

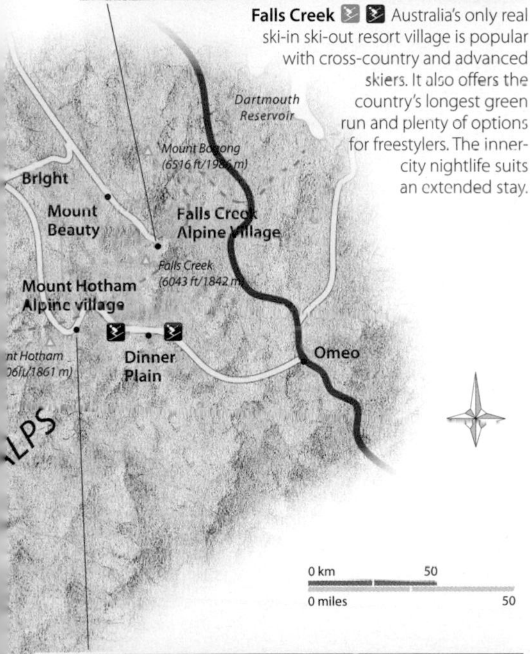

(Map)
- Dartmouth Reservoir
- Mount Bogong (6516 ft/1986 m)
- Bright
- Mount Beauty
- Falls Creek Alpine Village
- Falls Creek (6043 ft/1842 m)
- Mount Hotham Alpine village
- nt Hotham 061t/1861 m)
- Dinner Plain
- Omeo
- LPS

| 0 km | | 50 |
| 0 miles | | 50 |

Advice for Skiers

Costs
Entry fees are about A$30 per car per day. Lifts cost about A$100 per day per adult.

Transport and Equipment Hire
Roads are sealed to all resorts except Dinner Plain, Mount Baw Baw and Mount Stirling By law, vehicles must carry chains. Equipment can be hired from the resorts listed here. Coaches run from Melbourne to every resort except Mount Baw Baw. Aircraft and helicopters from Melbourne and Sydney fly to Mount Hotham and Mount Buller. A helicopter shuttle flies between Mount Hotham and Falls Creek.

Ski Resorts

Dinner Plain
W dinnerplain.com
Tel (03) 5159 6451 or 1800 670 019 (toll free).

Falls Creek
W fallscreek.com.au
Tel (03) 5758 1202.

Lake Mountain
W lakemountainresort.com.au
Tel (03) 5957 7222.

Mount Baw Baw
W mountbawbaw.com au
Tel (03) 5165 1136.

Mount Buller
W mtbuller.com.au
Tel (03) 5777 6077.

Mount Hotham
W mthotham.com.au
Tel (03) 5759 4444.

Mount Stirling
W mtstirling.com.au
Tel (03) 5777 6077.

For hotels in the area, see pp495–6.

Key
- △ Peak
-  Resort
- ▬ Major road
- ═ Minor road
- - - Walking track
- Beginner
- Intermediate
- Advanced

Mount Hotham
Featuring mostly challenging terrain, this area best suits intermediate to more advanced skiers. The resort has definitely gone more up-market in recent years. There is an airstrip 20 km (12 miles) from the village. Nearby Dinner Plain is popular with cross-country skiers.

Typical 19th-century honey granite building in Beechworth

⑫ Beechworth

🏠 3,500. 🚌 ℹ️ Town Hall, Ford St (03) 5728 8064.
🌐 **beechworth.com**

Beautifully sited in the foothills of the Victorian Alps, Beechworth was the centre of the great Ovens gold fields during the 1850s and 1860s *(see pp58–9)*. At the height of its boom, the town had a population of 42,000 and 61 hotels.

Today, visiting Beechworth is like stepping back in time. One of the state's best-preserved gold rush towns, it contains more than 30 19th-century buildings now classified by the National Trust. Its tree-lined streets feature granite banks and a courthouse, hotels with wide verandas and dignified brick buildings on either side. The majority of these are still in daily use, modern life continuing within edifices of

a bygone era. Many of the old buildings are now restaurants, and bed-and-breakfasts. Dine in the stately old bank which is now the Provenance restaurant *(see p532)*, stand in the dock of the courthouse where Ned Kelly was finally committed for his trial in Melbourne *(see p398)* and marvel at the old channel blasted through the granite to create a flow of water in which miners panned for gold.

The evocative Chinese cemetery is also worth a visit as a poignant reminder of the hundreds of Chinese who worked and died on the gold fields *(see pp58–9)*.

⑬ Chiltern

🏠 1,500. 🚉 ℹ️ 30 Main St (03) 5726 1611. 🌐 **chilternvic.com**

This sleepy village was once a booming gold-mining town with 14 suburbs. Only 1 km (half a mile) off the Hume Highway, halfway between the major towns of Wangaratta and Wodonga, today its colonial architecture and quiet atmosphere, as yet unspoiled by large numbers of tourists, make a visit to this pleasant town a worthwhile experience.

Chiltern has three National Trust properties: Dow's Pharmacy; the Federal Standard newspaper office; and Lakeview House. The last is the former

home of Henry Handel Richardson, the pen name of Ethel Richardson *(see p39)*, who wrote *The Getting of Wisdom* . Chiltern was her childhood home. The house, on Lake Alexander, has been restored with period furniture, and gives an insight into the life of the wealthy at the turn of the 20th century.

An unusual sight is the **Grapevine** museum. This shows the oldest and largest grapevine in the southern hemisphere – it once covered Chiltern's Star Hotel in its entirety.

For opening hours and other information on these attractions, check with the tourist information office in the town.

Lakeview House in Chiltern

⑭ Northeastern Wineries

🚉 Wangaratta & Rutherglen.
🚌 Wangaratta & Rutherglen.
ℹ️ Rutherglen (02) 6033 6300; Wangaratta (03) 5721 5711.
Campbells Winery: **Tel** (03) 6033 6000. **Open** 9am–5pm Mon–Sat, 10am–5pm Sun. **Closed** Good Fri, 25 Dec.
Chambers Rosewood Winery: **Tel** (02) 6032 8641. **Open** 9am–5pm Mon–Sat, 10am–5pm Sun & public hols. **Closed** Good Fri, 25 Dec.
Brown Bros: **Tel** (03) 5720 5500. **Open** 9am–5pm daily. **Closed** Good Fri, 25 Dec.
🌐 **brownbrothers.com.au**

The Northeastern area of Victoria is famous throughout the world for its vineyards and wineries *(see pp382–3)*. In a region that now spreads south to encompass the King and Ovens valleys around Glenrowan, Milawa, Everton, Rutherglen and Whitfield, the wines produced can vary in style enormously, depending on the elevation and microclimate of each vineyard.

Rutherglen is best known for its full-bodied "Rutherglen Reds",

Rows of grapevines in one of northeastern Victoria's many vineyards

Elegant Benalla Art Gallery on the shores of Lake Benalla

such as Cabernet Sauvignons from 100-year-old wineries including Campbells and Chambers. The Muscats, Tokays and ports from both Rutherglen and Glenrowan are even more internationally renowned, with Bullers, Morris and Bailey's among the best. Rutherglen itself is a graceful town lined with antiques shops, and a selection of hotels and restaurants.

The grapes grown in the cool-climate region around Whitfield and Milawa make for crisp whites and lighter, softer reds. One of the more popular wineries in Northeastern Victoria is Brown Brothers at Milawa. The winery is open daily for both wine tasting and sales at the cellar door, and its excellent restaurant specializes in local delicacies from the region, including particularly good trout, cheese, honey and lamb. While at Milawa, visits to the Milawa Cheese Factory and Milawa Mustards are recommended.

⑮ Glenrowan

🏠 1,000. 🚌 🚉 Wangaratta.
ℹ️ Glenrowan Tourist Centre, 41 Gladstone St (03) 5766 2367.
🌐 glenrowantouristcentre.com.au

Glenrowan was the site of the last stand by Australia's most notorious bushranger, Ned Kelly, and his gang (see p398). In a shoot-out with police in 1880, on Siege Street near the town's railway station, Kelly was finally captured after more than two years on the run. During this time he had earned almost hero status among Victoria's bush poor, particularly its many Irish Catholic farming families, as a Robin Hood-type character. Kelly knew the country around Glenrowan, especially the lovely Warby Ranges, in great detail and often used Mount Glenrowan, west of town, as a lookout. Kelly was later hanged at Melbourne Gaol.

Today Glenrowan thrives on its Kelly history as a tourist attraction. A giant iron effigy of the bushranger greets visitors at the entrance to the town and there are various displays, museums and re-enactments depicting the full Kelly story, including his last defeat.

Iron effigy of Ned Kelly

⑯ Benalla

🏠 8,500. 🚉 🚉 🚌 ℹ️ The Creators' Gallery, 14 Mair St (03) 5762 1749.
🌐 benalla.vic.gov.au

The rural town of Benalla is where Ned Kelly grew up and first appeared in court at the age of 15. Today it is most famous for its art gallery, built over Lake Benalla, which contains a fine collection of contemporary and Australian art. A Rose Festival is held in its magnificent rose gardens each November.

The town is also known as the Australian "capital" of gliding, with excellent air thermals rising from both the hot plains and nearby mountains.

⑰ Shepparton

🏠 30,000. 🚉 🚌 🚉 🚌 ℹ️ Greater Shepparton Visitors' Centre, 33 Nixon St 1800 808 839. 🌐 discover shepparton.com.au

The modern city of Shepparton, at the heart of the fertile Goulburn River Valley, is often called the "fruit bowl of Australia". The vast irrigation plains around the town support Victoria's most productive pear, peach, apricot, apple, plum, cherry and kiwi fruit farms. A summer visit of the town's biggest fruit cannery, SPC, when fruit is being harvested, reveals a hive of activity.

The area's sunny climate is also ideal for grapes. The two well-known wineries of Mitchelton and Tahbilk Wines, 50 km (30 miles) south of town, are both open for tours and tastings (see pp382–3).

Harvesting fruit in Shepparton's orchards

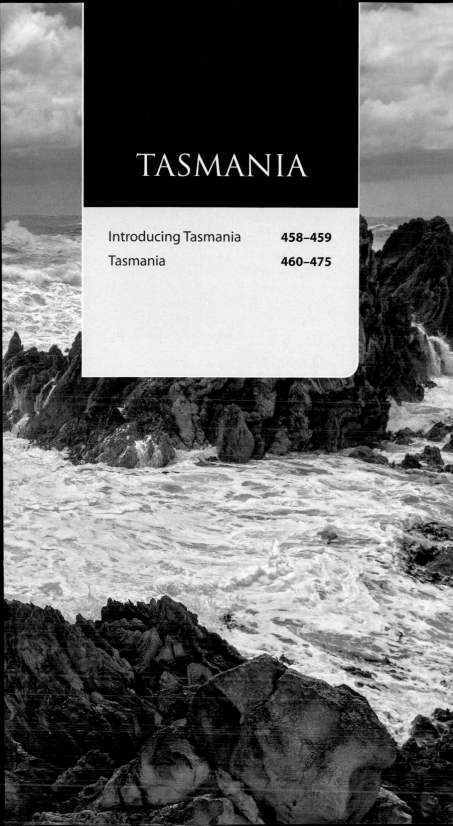

TASMANIA

Tasmania's Wildlife and Wilderness

Tasmania's landscape varies dramatically within its small area. Parts of Tasmania are often compared to the green pastures of England; however, the west of the state is wild and untamed. Inland there are glacial mountains and wild rivers, the habitat of flora and fauna unique to the island. More than 20 per cent of the island is now designated as a World Heritage Area (see pp30–31).

Russell Falls at Mount Field National Park

Mountain Wilderness

Inland southwest Tasmania is dominated by its glacial mountain landscape, including the beautiful Cradle Mountain – the natural symbol of the state. To the east of Cradle Mountain is the Walls of Jerusalem National Park, an isolated area of five rocky mountains. To the south is Mount Field National Park, a beautiful alpine area of glacial tarns and eucalypt forests, popular with skiers in the winter months.

Deciduous beech (Nothofagus gunnii) is the only such native beech in Australia. The spectacular golden colours of its leaves fill the mountain areas during the autumn.

Cradle Mountain, looking down over a glacial lake

The Bennett's wallaby (Macropus rufogriseus) is native to Tasmania's mountain regions. A shy animal, it is most likely to be spotted at either dawn or dusk.

Coastal Wilderness

The climate of Tasmania's eastern coastline is often balmy and sustains a strong fishing industry. The western coast, however, bears the full brunt of the Roaring Forties winds, whipped up across the vast expanses of ocean between the island state and the nearest land in South America. As a result, the landscape is lined with rocky beaches and raging waters, the scene of many shipwrecks during Tasmania's history.

The Tasmanian devil (Sarcophilus harrisii) is noisy, potentially vicious and one of only three marsupial carnivores that inhabit the island.

Banksia comes in many varieties in Tasmania, including Banksia serrata and Banksia marginata. It is distinctive for its seed pods.

Rugged coastline of the Tasman Peninsula

◀ Wild coastline at Rupert Point, in the Tarkine Wilderness

Calm area of Franklin Lower Gordon Wild River

River Wilderness

The southwest of Tasmania is well known for its wild rivers, particularly among avid whitewater rafters. The greatest wild river is the 120-km (75-mile) Franklin River, protected within Franklin-Gordon Wild Rivers National Park by its World Heritage status. This is the only undammed wild river left in Australia, and despite its sometimes calm moments it often rages fiercely through gorges, rainforests and heathland.

Huon pine (*Lagarostrobus franklinii*) is found in the southwest and in the south along the Franklin-Gordon River. It is prized for its ability to withstand rot. Some examples are more than 2,000 years old.

Brown trout (*Salmo trutta*), an introduced species, is abundant in the wild rivers and lakes of Tasmania, and a popular catch with fly-fishers.

The eastern quoll (*Dasyurus viverrinus*) thrives in Tasmania, where there are no predatory foxes and forests are in abundance.

Preserving Tasmania's Wilderness

An inhospitable climate, rugged landforms and the impenetrable scrub are among the factors that have preserved such a large proportion of Tasmania as wilderness. Although there is a long history of human habitation in what is now the World Heritage Area (Aboriginal sites date back 35,000 years), the population has always been small. The first real human threat occurred in the late 1960s when the Tasmanian government's hydroelectricity programme drowned Lake Pedder despite conservationists' protests. A proposal two decades later to dam a section of the Franklin River was defeated when the federal government intervened. The latest threat to the landscape is tourism. While many places of beauty are able to withstand visitors, others are not and people are discouraged from visiting these areas.

Dam protests were common occurrences in Tasmania during the 1980s, when conservationists protested against the damming of the Franklin River. The *No Dams* sticker became a national symbol of protest.

Protest badges

TASMANIA

Human habitation of Tasmania dates back 35,000 years, when Aborigines first reached the area. At this time it was linked to continental Australia, but waters rose to form the Bass Strait at the end of the Ice Age, 12,000 years ago. Dutch explorer Abel Tasman set foot on the island in 1642 and inspired its modern name. He originally called it Van Diemen's Land, after the governor of the Dutch East Indies.

Belying its small size, Tasmania has a remarkably diverse landscape that contains glacial mountains, dense forests and rolling green hills. Its wilderness is one of only three large temperate forests in the southern hemisphere; it is also home to many plants and animals unique to the island, including a ferocious marsupial, the Tasmanian devil. Tasmanians are fiercely proud of their landscape and the island saw the rise of the world's first Green political party, the "Tasmanian Greens". One-fifth of Tasmania is protected as a World Heritage Area (see pp30–31).

The Tasmanian Aboriginal population was almost wiped out with the arrival of Europeans in the 19th century, however more than 4,000 people claim Aboriginality in Tasmania today. Evidence of their link with the landscape has survived in numerous cave paintings. Many Aboriginal sites remain sacred and closed to visitors, but a few, such as the cliffs around Woolnorth, display this indigenous art for all to see.

The island's early European history has also been well preserved in its many 19th-century buildings. The first real settlement was at the waterfront site of Hobart in 1804, now Tasmania's capital and Australia's second-oldest city. From here, European settlement spread throughout the state, with the development of farms and villages, built and worked by convict labour.

Today, Tasmania is a haven for wildlife lovers, hikers and fly-fishermen, who come to experience the island's many national parks and forests. The towns scattered throughout the state, such as Richmond and Launceston, with their rich colonial histories, are well worth a visit, and make excellent bases from which to explore the surrounding wilderness.

The historic port area of Battery Point in Hobart

◀ Coastline at Boulder Point, part of Mount William National Park

Exploring Tasmania

Part, and yet not a part, of Australia, Tasmania's distinctive landscape, climate and culture are largely due to its 300-km (185-mile) distance from the mainland. The isolation has left a legacy of unique flora and fauna, fresh air, an abundance of water and a relaxed lifestyle. More than 27 per cent of Tasmania's land surface is given over to agriculture, with the emphasis on wine and fine foods. The state also benefits from vast expanses of open space, since approximately 40 per cent of Tasmanians live in the capital, Hobart. Tasmania, therefore, offers the perfect opportunity for a relaxing holiday in tranquil surroundings.

Nelson Falls in Franklin-Gordon Wild Rivers National Park

Yachts in Constitution Dock, Hobart

Three Hummock Island

Hunter Island

17 WOOLNORTH

15 STANLEY

Smithton

Marrawah   Trowutta   Wynyard

Arthur   BURNIE **14**   Penguin

Temma   DEVONPORT

Gunns Plains

Sandy Cape   Waratah   Sheffield

Savage River

Corinna   Cradle Valley   Lie

Pieman River State Reserve   **18**
Rosebery   CRADLE MOUNTAIN
Zeehan   LAKE ST CLAIR   Walls
                 NATIONAL   Jerusa
Southern Ocean   PARK   Natio
                                         Par
Queenstown   Lake St Clair

Strahan   Derwent Bridge

MACQUARIE HARBOUR **19**   **20**
                                FRANKLIN-
                                GORDON
                                WILD RIVERS
                                NATIONAL PARK
                                         Lal
                                         Go

Strathgordon

Lake Pedder

South We
Nationa
Park

King Island

0 km   15

0 miles   15

Cape Wickham

Egg Lagoon

Yambacoona

16
KING ISLAND

Naracoopa

Currie

Grassy

Stokes Point

Key

— Major road

--- Minor road

— Scenic route

For additional map symbols *see back flap*

Getting Around

Within this small, compact island, traffic is rarely a problem, and any visitor can journey across the diverse landscape with little difficulty. While all major cities and towns are linked by fast highways and major roads, some of the most splendid mountain, lake, coastal and rural scenery lies off the key routes, along the many alternative and easily accessible country roads. A car is recommended, but coach services run between most towns and to some of the state's natural attractions.

Sights at a Glance

1. Hobart pp464–5
2. Richmond
3. New Norfolk
4. Bothwell
5. Oatlands
6. Freycinet National Park
7. Bicheno
8. Ross
9. Ben Lomond National Park
10. Launceston
11. Flinders Island
12. Hadspen
13. Devonport
14. Burnie
15. Stanley
16. King Island
17. Woolnorth
18. Cradle Mountain Lake St Clair National Park
19. Macquarie Harbour
20. Franklin-Gordon Wild Rivers National Park
21. Mount Field National Park
22. Bruny Island
23. Port Arthur pp474–5

Wineglass Bay in Freycinet National Park

❶ Hobart

Spread over seven hills between the banks of the Derwent River and the summit of Mount Wellington, Australia's second oldest city has an incredible waterfront location, similar to that of her "big sister", Sydney. Hobart began life on the waterfront and the maritime atmosphere is still an important aspect of the city. From Old Wharf, where the first arrivals settled, round to the fishing village of Battery Point, the area known as Sullivans Cove is still the hub of this cosmopolitan city. It is the centre of attention in late December every year as the finish line of the famous Sydney to Hobart yacht race.

Hobart and its docks nestled on the Derwent River

🏛 Narryna Heritage Museum
103 Hampden Rd, Battery Point. **Tel** (03) 6234 2791. **Open** 10am–4pm Tue–Sun. **Closed** July (two wks), Good Fri, 25 Apr, 25 Dec. 🅦 narryna.com.au

Located in an elegant 1836 Georgian house called Narryna, in Battery Point, this is the oldest folk museum in Australia. Beautiful grounds make a fine backdrop for an impressive collection of early Tasmanian pioneering relics.

🏛 Battery Point
This maritime village grew up on the hilly promontory adjacent to the early settlement and wharves. The site was originally home to a gun battery, positioned to ward off potential enemy invasions. The old guardhouse, built in 1818, now lies within a leafy park, just a few minutes' walk from Hampden Road with its antiques shops, art galleries, tea-rooms and restaurants.

Battery Point retains a strong sense of history, with its narrow gas-lit streets lined with tiny fishermen's and workers' houses, cottage gardens and colonial mansions and pubs.

Hobart Historic Walks depart daily at 10am from the Visitors' Centre located on Davey and Elizabeth streets.

🏛 Salamanca Place
Once the site of early colonial industries, from jam-making to metal foundry and flour milling, this graceful row of sandstone warehouses at Salamanca Place is now the heart of Hobart's lively atmosphere and creative spirit.

Mount Wellington towers above the buildings lining the waterfront, which have been converted into art galleries, antique stores and antiquarian book shops. The Salamanca Arts Centre houses artists' studios, theatres and galleries. The area also has some of the city's best pubs, cafés and restaurants (see pp534–5). The Salamanca Market is held every Saturday morning.

🏛 Castray Esplanade
Castray Esplanade was originally planned in the 19th century as a riverside walking track and it still provides the most pleasurable short stroll within the city. En route are the old colonial Commissariat Stores. These have been beautifully renovated for inner-city living, architects' offices and art galleries, focussing on Tasmanian arts and crafts.

🏛 Parliament House
Salamanca Place. **Tel** (03) 6212 2200. **Open** Mon–Fri. **Closed** public hols. ♿ 🚗 10am & 2pm non-sitting days.

One of the oldest civic buildings in Hobart, designed by John Lee Archer and built by convicts between 1835 and 1841. Partly open to the public.

🏛 Maritime Museum of Tasmania
Cnr Davey & Argyle sts. **Tel** (03) 6234 1427. **Open** 9am–5pm daily. **Closed** Good Fri, 25 Dec. 🚗 ♿ 🅦 maritimetas.org

Steeped in seafaring history, the museum is housed in the Carnegie Building, the former Hobart Public Library. It contains a fascinating collection of old relics, manuscripts, and voyage documents, as well as an important photographic collection which records Tasmania's maritime history.

Bustling Saturday market in Salamanca Place

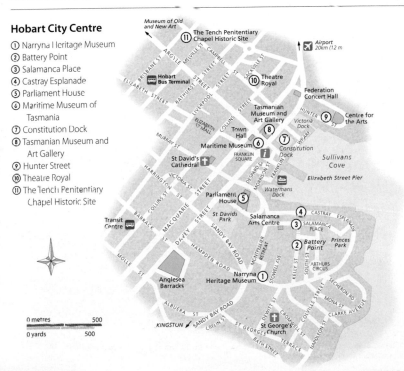 Constitution Dock

Davey St.

The main anchorage for fishing boats and yachts also serves as the finish line of the annual Sydney to Hobart Yacht Race. This famous race attracts an international field of competitors (see p45).

Constitution Dock borders the city and the old slum district of Wapping, which has now been redeveloped. Many of the old warehouses have been restored to include restaurants and cafés. One houses the idiosyncratic restaurant, the Drunken Admiral.

Tasmanian Museum and Art Gallery

40 Macquarie St. **Tel** (03) 6211 4134. **Open** 10am–4pm Tue–Sun. **Closed** Good Fri, 25 Apr (until 12:30pm), 25 Dec. **tmag.tas.gov.au**

This 1863 building, designed by the city's best-known colonial architect, Henry Hunter, is now home to a fine collection of prints and paintings of Tasmania, Aboriginal artifacts, and botanical displays.

Hunter Street

Once joined to Hobart Town by a sandbar and known as Hunter Island, this historic harbour-side locale is an art and culture precinct. It is lined with colonial warehouses and was once the site of the Jones & Co. IXL jam factory. The heart of this redevelopment is the award winning Henry Jones Art Hotel (see p497).

Theatre Royal

29 Campbell St. **Tel** (03) 6233 2299. Auditorium: **Open** Mon–Sat. **Closed** public hols. for shows only. **theatreroyal.com.au**

Built in 1837, this is the oldest theatre in Australia, and one of the most charming in the world. Almost gutted by fire in the 1960s, the ornate decor has since been restored.

The Tench Penitentiary Chapel Historic Site

Cnr Brisbane & Campbell sts. **Tel** (03) 6231 0911. **Open** 10am–7:30pm daily. **Closed** Good Fri, 25 Dec. obligatory, by appt 10am, 11:30am, 1pm, 2:30pm.

VISITORS' CHECKLIST

Practical Information
Hobart. 195,000. 20 Davey St (03) 6238 4222. Sydney–Hobart Yacht Race (26–29 Dec). **discovertasmania.com.au**

Transport
20 km (12 miles) NE of the city. Red Line Coaches, Transit Centre, 199 Collins St.

In colonial days, courts and prison chapels were often next to each other, making the dispensing of swift judgment convenient. The complex also exhibits solitary confinement cells and an execution yard.

Museum of Old and New Art (MONA)

655 Main Rd, Berriedale. **Tel** (03) 6277 9900. **Open** 10am–6pm Wed–Mon. **mona.net.au**

Carved out of a sandstone cliff, this museum houses an eclectic collection that ranges from ancient Egyptian mummies to some of the world's most unusual contemporary art.

Hobart City Centre

0 metres 500
0 yards 500

For keys to symbols see back flap

Hop farm on the Derwent River in New Norfolk

❷ Richmond

🏠 880. 🚌 ℹ️ Old Hobart Town, Bridge St (03) 6260 2502.
W richmondvillage.com.au

In the heart of the countryside, 26 km (16 miles) from Hobart, lies the quaint village of Richmond. This was the first area granted to free settlers from England for farming, and at its centre they established a township reminiscent of their homeland. Richmond now includes some of Australia's oldest colonial architecture. Most of the buildings were constructed by convicts, including the sandstone bridge built in 1823, the gaol of 1825 and the Roman Catholic Church of 1834.

Today, Richmond is a lively centre for rural artists and artisans. On the main street, between the old general store and post office, they occupy many of the historic homes.

❸ New Norfolk

🏠 5,200. 🚌 ℹ️ Circle St (03) 6261 3700. **W newnorfolk.org**

From Hobart, the Derwent River heads north, then veers west through the Derwent River Valley. The hop farms and oast houses along the willow-lined river are testimony to the area's history of brewing.

At the centre of the valley, 38 km (24 miles) from Hobart, is the town of New Norfolk. Many of the first settlers in the region abandoned the colonial settlement of Norfolk Island to come here, hence the name. One of Tasmania's classified historic towns, it contains many interesting buildings, such as the Bush Inn of 1815, which claims to be one of Australia's oldest licensed pubs.

Typical 19th-century building in Bothwell

❹ Bothwell

🏠 400. 🚌 ℹ️ Australasian Golf Museum, Market Place (03) 6259 4033.
W ausgolfmuseum.com

Nestled in the Clyde River Valley, Bothwell's wide streets are set along a river of the same name, formerly known as the "Fat Doe" river after a town in Scotland. The area's names were assigned by early Scottish settlers, who arrived from Hobart Town in 1817 with their families and 18-l (5-gal) kegs of rum loaded on bullock wagons.

The town's heritage is now preserved with some 50 National Trust buildings dating from the 1820s, including the Castle Hotel, the Masonic Hall (now

Richmond Bridge, constructed with local sandstone

For hotels and restaurants in this area see pp496–7 and pp533–5

an art gallery), Bothwell Grange Guest House and the Old Schoolhouse, now home to the Australasian Golf Museum. The stone heads above the door of the Presbyterian St Luke's Church depict a Celtic god and goddess. Even the town's golf course has a claim on history as the oldest in Australia, as it was laid out in the 1820s.

The town lies at the centre of the historic sheep-farming district of Bothwell, stretching along Lakes Hwy from the southern midlands to the famous trout fishing area of the Great Lakes. It is also the gateway to the ruggedly beautiful Central Plateau Conservation Area – a tableland which rises abruptly from the surrounding flat countryside to an average height of 600 m (nearly 2,000 ft).

❺ Oatlands

🗺 550. 🚍 ℹ️ Heritage Highway Visitor Centre, 1 Mill Lane (03) 6254 1212.

Oatlands was one of a string of military stations established in 1813 during the construction of the old Midlands Hwy by convict chain gangs. Colonial Governor Lachlan Macquarie ordered the building of the road in 1811, to connect the southern settlement of Hobart (see pp464–5) with the northern settlement of Launceston (see p468). During a later trip, he chose locations for the townships en route, naming them after places in the British Isles. The road ran through the area

Distinctive façade of the 1837 Callington Flour Mill, in Oatlands

Coles Bay, backed by the Hazards Mountains, Freycinet Peninsula

of Tasmania corresponding in name and geography to that of the British Midlands region, giving it its original name, but since the 1990s it has been dubbed the Heritage Hwy.

Oatlands soon became one of the colonial coaching stops for early travellers. Today, it has the richest endowment of Georgian buildings in the country, mostly made of local sandstone, including the 1829 courthouse and St Peter's Church (1838). As a result, the township is classified by the National Trust. Its most distinctive building, the Callington Flour Mill, still operates today with tours on the hour between 10am–3pm daily.

❻ Freycinet National Park

🚍 from Bicheno. ℹ️ Visitors' Centre (03) 6256 7000. **Open** Nov–Apr: 8am–5pm daily; May–Oct: 9am–4pm daily. **Closed** 25 Dec. 🌐 **parks.tas. gov.au**

The Freycinet Peninsula on the east coast of Tasmania is a long, narrow neck of land jutting south, dominated by the granite peaks of the Hazards Mountain Range. Named after an early French maritime explorer, the peninsula consists of ocean beaches on its eastern rim and secluded coves and inlets to the west. The fishing village of Coles Bay lies in the largest cove, backed by the Hazards.

Freycinet National Park on the tip of the peninsula is crisscrossed with walking tracks along beaches, over mountains,

around headlands and across lagoons. The most popular walk is Wineglass Bay – a short, steep trip up and over the saddle of the mountains. The blue waters of the bay are cupped against a crescent of golden sand, which inspired the name.

The drive up the east coast is a highlight of Tasmania. There are superb ocean views and marshlands inhabited by black swans. Small towns such as Orford and Swansea are good for overnight stays.

❼ Bicheno

🗺 640. 🚍 ℹ️ 41B Foster St (03) 6375 1500.

Together with Coles Bay, Bicheno is the holiday centre of Tasmania's east coast. In summer, the bay is very popular due to its sheltered location, which means temperatures are always a few degrees warmer than elsewhere in the state.

The area also includes Tasmania's smallest national park, the 16,080 ha (39,700 acre) Douglas Apsley National Park. It contains the state's largest dry sclerophyll forest, patches of rainforest, river gorges, waterfalls and spectacular views along the coast. This varied landscape can be taken in along a three-day north to south walking track through the park. The north of the park is only accessible by 4WD. Other attractions in the area include the Apsley Gorge Winery and a 3-km long penguin breeding colony.

Man-O-Ross Hotel at the Four Corners of Ross crossroads

❽ Ross

🏠 275. 🚌 ℹ️ Tasmanian Wool Centre, Church St (03) 6381 5466. 🌐 **taswoolcentre.com.au**

Set on the banks of the Macquarie River, Ross, like Oatlands (see p467), was once a military station and coaching stop along the Midlands Hwy. It lies at the heart of the richest sheep farming district in Tasmania, internationally recognized for its fine merino wool. Some of the large rural homesteads in the area have remained within the same families since the 1820s when the village was settled.

The town's most famous sight is Ross Bridge, built by convict labour and opened in 1836. It features 186 unique carvings by convict sculptor Daniel Herbert, who was given a Queen's Pardon for his intricate work. The town centres on its historic crossroads, the Four Corners of Ross: "Temptation, Damnation, Salvation and Recreation". These are represented respectively on each corner by the Man-O-Ross Hotel, the jail, the church and the town hall.

❾ Ben Lomond National Park

🚌 when ski slopes are open. ℹ️ National Parks & Wildlife Service, 167 Westbury Rd Prospect, Launceston (03) 6777 2179. 🎿

In the hinterlands between the Midlands and the east coast, 50 km (30 miles) southeast of Launceston, Ben Lomond is the highest mountain in northern Tasmania and home to one of the state's two main ski slopes. The 16,000-ha (40,000-acre) national park surrounding the mountain covers an alpine plateau of barren and dramatic scenery, with views

Man O'Ross hotel sign

stretching over the northeast of the state. The vegetation includes alpine daisies and carnivorous sundew plants. The park is also home to wallabies, wombats and possums. From Conara Junction on the Heritage Hwy, take the Esk Main Road east before turning off towards Ben Lomond National Park.

The mountain's foothills have been devastated by decades of mining and forestry, and many of the townships, such as Rossarden and Avoca, have since suffered an economic decline. The road through the South Esk Valley along the Esk River loops back to the valley's main centre of Fingal. From here, you can continue through the small township of St Marys before joining the Tasman Hwy and travelling up the east coast.

❿ Launceston

🏠 71,400. ✈️ 🚌 Georgetown 🚢 to Devonport, then bus (summer only). ℹ️ Travel & Information Centre, 69–72 Cameron St 1800 651 827.

In colonial days, the coach ride between Tasmania's capital, Hobart, and the township of Launceston took a full day, but today the 200-km (125-mile) route is flat and direct. Nestling in the Tamar River Valley, Launceston was settled in 1804 and is Australia's third-oldest city. It has a charming ambience of old buildings, parks, gardens, riverside walks, craft galleries and hilly streets lined with

Alpine plateau in Ben Lomond National Park, backed by Ben Lomond Mountain

For hotels and restaurants in this area see pp496–7 and pp533–5

Heritage buildings in central Launceston

weatherboard houses. The **Queen Victoria Museum and Art Gallery** has the country's largest provincial display of colonial art, along with an impressive modern collection. It also shows Aboriginal and convict relics, and has displays on minerals, flora and fauna of the region.

Cataract Gorge Reserve is alive with birds, wallabies, pademelons, potoroos and bandicoots, only a 15-minute walk from the city centre. A chairlift, believed to have the longest central span in the world, provides a striking aerial overview.

In nearby Underwood is the award-winning **Treetops Adventure**, which combines the tranquillity of the forest with adrenalin-fueled canopy tours. These take place in all weathers, and there is also a night-time ride. Visitors enjoy a unique view of the beautiful forest environment from above.

🎦 **Queen Victoria Museum and Art Gallery**
Museum: 2 Wellington St, Royal Pk, Launceston; Gallery: 2 Invermay Rd, Inveresk. **Tel** (03) 6323 3777. **Open** 10am–4pm daily. **Closed** Good Fri, 25 Dec. 🚻 ⓦ qvmag.tas.gov.au

🌳 **Treetops Adventure**
66 Hollybank Road, off the Launceston–Lilydale Rd, Underwood. **Tel** (03) 6395 1390. **Open** daily. 🅿
ⓦ treetopsadventure.com.au

Environs

In the 1830s, the Norfolk Plains was a farmland district owned mainly by wealthy settlers who had been enticed to the area by land grants. The small town of **Longford**, with its historic inns and churches, is still the centre of a rich agricultural district. It also has the greatest concentration of colonial mansions in the state. Many, such as Woolmers and Brickendon, are open for public tours.

Cape Barren geese in the Patriarch Sanctuary on Cape Barren Island

⓫ Flinders Island

🛫 from Launceston, Melbourne. 🚌 from Bridport. 🚢 Flinders Island Tourism (03) 6359 5002.

On the northeastern tip of Tasmania, in the waters of the Bass Strait, Flinders Island is the largest within the Furneaux Island Group. These 50 or so dots in the ocean are all that remains of the land bridge which once spanned the strait to the continental mainland (see pp26–7).

Flinders Island was also the destination for the last surviving 133 Tasmanian Aborigines. With the consent of the British administration, the Reverend George Augustus Robinson brought all 133 of them here in the 1830s. His aim was to "save" them from extinction by civilizing them according to European traditions and converting them to Christianity. In 1847, however, greatly diminished by disease and despair, the 47 survivors were transferred to Oyster Cove, a sacred Aboriginal site south of Hobart, and the plan was deemed a failure. Within a few years, all full-blooded Tasmanian Aborigines had died.

Much of Flinders is now preserved as a natural reserve, including Strzelecki National Park, which is particularly popular with hikers. Off the island's south coast is Cape Barren Island, home to the Patriarch Sanctuary, a protected geese reserve.

Flinders Island can be reached by air from Launceston and Melbourne. There is also a leisurely ferry trip aboard the *Matthew Flinders* from Launceston and the small coastal town of Bridport.

Entally House in Hadspen

⓬ Hadspen

🏠 1,900. 🚌 ℹ️ Travel & Information Centre, cnr St John & Cimitiere sts, Launceston 1800 651 827.

Heading west along the Bass Highway, a string of historic towns pepper the countryside from Longford through to Deloraine, surrounded by the Great Western Tiers Mountains. The tiny town of Hadspen is a picturesque strip of Georgian cottages and buildings which include an old 1845 coaching house.

The town is also home to one of Tasmania's most famous historic homes open to the public. Built in 1819 on the bank of the South Esk River, the **Entally House**, with its gracious veranda, has its own chapel, stables, horse-drawn carriages and 19th-century furnishings.

Period furniture in Entally House

🏠 **Entally House**
782 Meander Valley Rd, via Hadspen. **Tel** (03) 6393 6201. **Open** 10am–4pm daily. **Closed** Good Fri, 25 Apr, 24–26 Dec, 1 Jan, Jun–Aug. 🅿️ ♿
🌐 **entally.com.au**

⓭ Devonport

🏠 22,500. ✈️ 🚌 🚌 ⛴️ ℹ️ Devonport Visitor Centre, 92 Formby Rd (03) 6424 4466.

Named after the county of Devon in England, the state's third-largest city is strategically sited as a river and sea port. It lies at the junction of the Mersey River and the Bass Strait, on the north coast.

The dramatic rocky headland of Mersey Bluff is 1 km (half a mile) from the city centre, linked by a coastal reserve and parklands. Here, Aboriginal rock paintings and carvings can be seen on a short, self-guided walk from near the lighthouse. The walk route circles around the former Tiagarra Aboriginal Cultural Centre and Museum, which is no longer open to the public.

From Devonport, the overnight car and passenger ferry *Spirit of Tasmania* sails to the Port of Melbourne on the mainland several times each week. With a local airport, Devonport is also an excellent starting point for touring northern Tasmania. Heading northwest, the old coast road offers unsurpassed views of the Bass Strait.

⓮ Burnie

🏠 16,000. ➡️ 🚌 🚌 ℹ️ 2 Bass Highway (03) 6430 5831.

Further along the northern coast from Devonport is Tasmania's fourth-largest city, founded in 1829. Along its main streets are many attractive 19th-century buildings decorated with wrought ironwork. Previously, Burnie's prosperity centred on a thriving wood-pulping industry. One of the state's main enterprises, Associated Pulp and Paper Mills, established in 1938, was sited here. Today the city has shed its industrial character,

although some industry survives, notably the Lactos company, which has won many awards for its French- and Swiss-style cheeses. The sampling room has tastings and a café. Burnie also has a number of gardens, including Fern Glade, where platypuses are often seen feeding at dusk and dawn. Situated on Emu Bay, the area's natural attractions include forest reserves, fossil cliffs, waterfalls and canyons and panoramic ocean views from nearby Round Hill.

"The Nut" chairlift in Stanley

⓯ Stanley

🏠 470. 🚌 ℹ️ Stanley Visitors Centre, 45 Main Rd (03) 6458 1330.

The rocky promontory of Circular Head, known locally as "the Nut", rises 152 m (500 ft) above sea level and looms over the fishing village of Stanley. A chairlift up the rock face offers striking views of the area.

Stanley's quiet main street runs towards the wharf, lined with fishermen's cottages and many bluestone buildings dating from the 1840s. Stanley also contains numerous top-quality bed-and-breakfasts and eateries serving fresh, local seafood *(see p535)*.

Nearby, **Highfield House** was the original headquarters of the Van Diemen's Land Company, a London-based agricultural holding set up in 1825.

The home and grounds of its colonial overseer are now open for public tours.

🏠 **Highfield House**
Green Hills Rd, via Stanley. **Tel** (03) 6458 1100. **Open** Sep–May: 10am–4pm daily. **Closed** Jun–Aug: weekends. 🖼

⑯ King Island

✈ ℹ Tasmanian Travel and Information Centre, cnr Davey & Elizabeth sts, Hobart (03) 6238 4222.

Lying off the northwestern coast of Tasmania in the Bass Strait, King Island is a popular location for wildlife lovers. Muttonbirds and elephant seals are among the unusual attractions.

Divers also frequent the island, fascinated by the ship-wrecks that lie nearby. The island is also noted for its cheese, beef and seafood.

⑰ Woolnorth

Via Smithton. ℹ Tasmanian Travel and Information Centre, cnr Davey & Elizabeth sts, Hobart (03) 6238 4222. 📷 obligatory.

The huge sheep, cattle and dairy farming property on the outskirts of Smithton is the only remaining land holding of the Van Diemen's Land Company. The last four Tasmanian tigers held in captivity were caught in the bush backing on to Wool-north in 1908. Day-long tours

Elephant seal bull on King Island – males can weigh up to 3 tonnes

of the property, booked in advance, include a lunch of local beef fillet and a trip to Cape Grim, known for the cleanest air in the world.

⑱ Cradle Mountain Lake St Clair National Park

🏕 Cradle Mountain, Lake St Clair. ℹ Cradle Mountain (03) 6492 1110 (shuttle from gate is every 20 mins in summer, infrequent at other times). Lake St Clair (03) 6289 1172. 🖼 ♿

The distinctive jagged peaks of Cradle Mountain are now recognized as an international symbol of the state's natural environment. The second-highest mountain in Tasmania reaches 1,560 m (5,100 ft) at the northern end of the 161,000-ha (400,000-acre) national park. The park then stretches 80 km (50 miles) south to the shores

of Lake St Clair, the deepest freshwater lake in Australia.

In 1922, the area became a national park, founded by Austrian nature enthusiast Gustav Weindorfer. His memory lives on in his forest home Waldheim Chalet, now a heritage lodge in Weindorfer's Forest. Nearby at Ronny Creek is the registration point for the celebrated Overland Track, which traverses the park through scenery ranging from rainforest, alpine moors, buttongrass plains and waterfall valleys. Walking the track takes an average of six days, stopping overnight in tents or huts. At the halfway mark is Mount Ossa, the state's highest peak at 1,617 m (5,300 ft). In May, the park is ablaze with the autumn colours of Tasmania's deciduous beech *Nothofagus gunnii*, commonly known as "Fagus" *(see p458)*.

Dove Lake backed by the jagged peaks of Cradle Mountain

Boats sailing on the deceptively calm waters of Macquarie Harbour

⑲ Macquarie Harbour

Strahan. *i* The Esplanade, Strahan (03) 6472 6800 or 1800 352 200.

Off the wild, western coast of Tasmania there is nothing but vast stretches of ocean until the southern tip of Argentina, on the other side of the globe. The region bears the full brunt of the "Roaring Forties" – the name given to the tremendous winds that whip southwesterly off the Southern Ocean.

In this hostile environment, Tasmania's Aborigines survived for thousands of years before European convicts were sent here in the 1820s and took over the land. Their harsh and isolated settlement was a penal station on Sarah Island, situated in the middle of Macquarie Harbour.

The name of the harbour's mouth, "Hell's Gates", reflects conditions endured by both seamen and convicts – shipwrecks, drownings, suicides and murders all occurred here. Abandoned in 1833 for the "model prison" of Port Arthur *(see pp474–5)*, Sarah Island and its penal settlement ruins can be viewed on a guided boat tour available from the fishing port of Strahan.

Strahan grew up around an early timber industry supported by convict labour. It became well-known in the early 1980s when protesters from across Australia came to Strahan to fight government plans to flood the wild and beautiful Franklin River for a hydroelectric scheme. A fascinating exhibition at the visitor centre in Strahan charts the drama of Australia's most famous environmental protest.

Strahan today is one of Tasmania's loveliest towns, with its old timber buildings, scenic port and natural backdrop of fretted mountains and dense bushland. The town's newest attraction is a restored 1896 railway, which travels 35 km (22 miles) across rivers and mountains to the old mining settlement at Queenstown.

⑳ Franklin-Gordon Wild Rivers National Park

Strahan. *i* The Esplanade, Strahan (03) 6472 6800.
W parks.tas.gov.au

One of Australia's great wild river systems flows through southwest Tasmania. This spectacular region consists of high ranges and deep gorges. The Franklin-Gordon Wild Rivers National Park extends southeast from Macquarie Harbour and is one of four national parks in the western part of Tasmania that make up the Tasmanian Wilderness World Heritage Area *(see pp30–31)*. The park takes its name from the Franklin and Gordon rivers, both of which were saved by conservationists in 1983.

Within the park's 442,000 ha (1,090,000 acres) are vast tracts of cool temperate rainforest, as well as waterfalls and dolerite- and quartzite-capped mountains. The flora within the park is as varied as the landscape, with impenetrable horizontal scrub, lichen-coated trees, pandani plants and the endemic conifers, King William, celery top and Huon pines. The easiest way into this largely trackless wilderness is via a boat cruise from Strahan. Visitors can disembark and take a short walk to see a 2,000-year-old Huon pine. The park also contains the rugged peak of

Imposing Frenchmans Cap looming over the Franklin-Gordon Wild Rivers National Park

Idyllic, deserted beach on the rugged Bruny Island

Frenchmans Cap, accessible to experienced bushwalkers. The Franklin River is also renowned for its rapids.

The Wild Way, linking Hobart with the west coast, runs through the park. Sections of the river and forest can be reached from the main road along short tracks. Longer walks into the heart of the park require a higher level of survival skills and equipment.

Russell Falls in Mount Field National Park

㉑ Mount Field National Park

ℹ️ Lake Dobson Rd, at entrance to the Park, (03) 6288 1149.

Little more than 70 km (45 miles) from Hobart along the Maydena Road, Mount Field National Park's proximity and beauty make it a popular location with nature-loving tourists. As a day trip from Hobart, it offers easy access to a diversity of Tasmanian

vegetation and wildlife along well-maintained walking tracks.

The most popular walk is also the shortest: the 10-minute trail to Russell Falls starts out from just within the park's entrance through a temperate rainforest environment. Lake Dobson car park is 15 km (9 miles) from the park's entrance up a steep gravel path. This is the beginning of several other walks.

The 10-km (6 mile) walk to Tarn Shelf is a bushwalker's paradise, especially in autumn, when the glacial lakes, mountains and valleys are spectacularly highlighted by the red-orange hues of the deciduous beech trees. Longer trails lead up to the higher peaks of Mount Field West and Mount Mawson, southern Tasmania's premier ski slope.

Truganini, the Bruny Island Aborigine

㉒ Bruny Island

Travel by car only – no public transport or taxis on Bruny Island. ℹ️ Bruny D'Entrecasteaux Visitors' Centre, Ferry Road (inside Mermaid Café), Kettering (03) 6267 4494.

On Hobart's back doorstep, yet a world away in landscape and atmosphere, the Huon Valley and D'Entrecasteaux Channel can be enjoyed over several

hours or days. In total, the trip south from Hobart, through the town of Huonville, the Hartz Mountains and Southport, the southernmost town in the country, is only 100 km (60 miles). On the other side of the channel are the orchards, craft outlets and vineyards around Cygnet.

The attractive marina of Kettering, just 40 minutes' drive from Hobart, is the departure point for a regular ferry service to Bruny Island.

The name Bruny Island actually applies to two islands joined by a narrow neck. The south island townships of Adventure Bay and Alonnah are only a half-hour drive from the ferry terminal in the north. Once home to a thriving colonial whaling industry, Bruny Island is now a haven for bird-watchers, boaters, swimmers and camel riders along its sheltered bays, beaches and lagoons.

Unfortunately, Bruny Island also has a sadder side to its history. Truganini, of the Wuenonne people of Bruny Island, is said to have been one of Tasmania's last full-blooded Aborigines. It was also from the aptly named Missionary Bay on the island that Reverend Robinson began his ill-fated campaign to round up the indigenous inhabitants of Tasmania for incarceration (see p469).

㉓ Port Arthur

Port Arthur was established in 1830 as a timber station and a prison settlement for repeat offenders. While transportation to the island colony from the mainland ceased in 1853, the prison remained in operation until 1877, by which time some 12,000 men had passed through what was commonly regarded as the harshest institution of its kind in the British Empire. Punishments included incarceration in the Separate Prison, a building set apart from the main penitentiary, where inmates were subjected to sensory deprivation and extreme isolation in the belief that such methods promoted "moral reform". Between 1979 and 1986, a conservation project was undertaken to restore the prison ruins. The 40-ha (100-acre) site is now Tasmania's most popular tourist attraction.

Commandant's House
One of the first houses at Port Arthur, this cottage has now been restored and furnished in early 19th-century style.

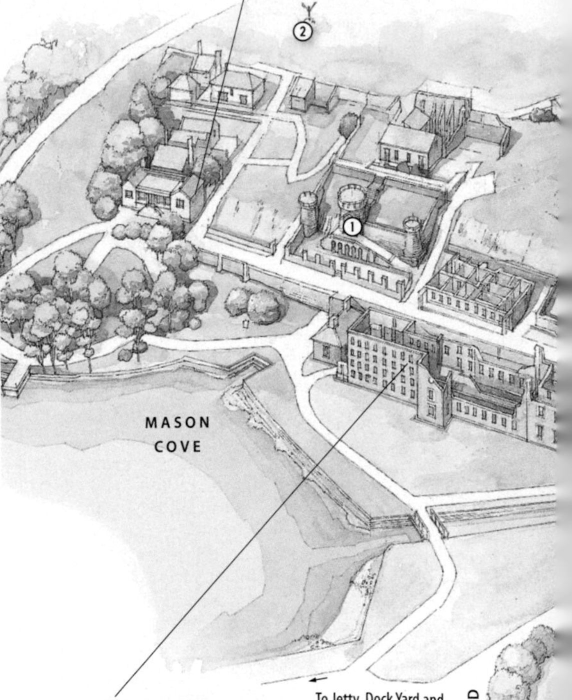

KEY

① **The Guard Tower** was constructed in 1835 in order to prevent escapes from the settlement and pilfering from the Commissariat Store, which the tower overlooked.

② **The Semaphore** was a series of flat, mounted planks that could be arranged in different configurations, in order to send messages to Hobart and across the peninsula.

③ **The Paupers' Mess** was the dining area for poor ex-convicts.

④ **Museum and café**

⑤ **The Separate Prison** was influenced by Pentonville Prison in London. Completed in 1854, the prison was thought to provide "humane" punishment. Convicts lived in 50 separate cells in silence and anonymity, referred to by number not by name.

⑥ **Trentham Cottage** was owned by the Trentham family who lived in Port Arthur after the site closed. The refurbished interior is decorated with early 20th-century furnishings.

⑦ **Government Cottage** was built in 1853 and was used by visiting dignitaries and government officials.

MASON COVE

To Jetty, Dock Yard and Isle of the Dead Cemetery

JETTY ROAD

★ Penitentiary
This building was thought to be the largest in Australia at the time of its construction in 1844. Originally a flour mill, it was converted into a penitentiary in the 1850s and housed almost 500 prisoners in dormitories and cells.

Hospital
This sandstone building was completed in 1842 with four wards of 18 beds each. The basement housed the kitchen with its own oven, and a morgue, known as the "dead room".

VISITORS' CHECKLIST

Practical Information
Hwy A9.
Tel 1800 659 101 or (03) 6251 2310.
[W] **portarthur.org.au**
Open 8:30am–dusk daily.

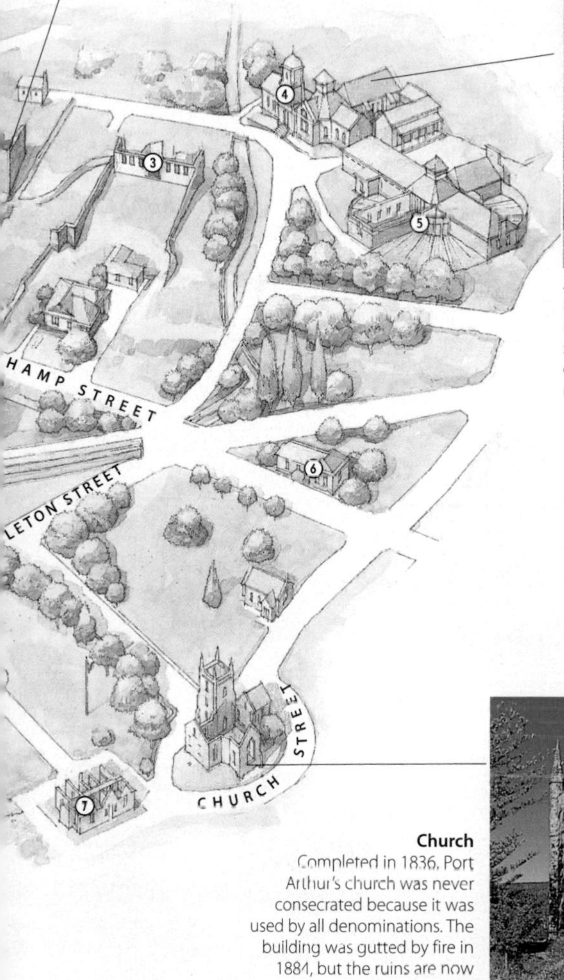

Asylum
By 1872, Port Arthur's asylum housed more than 100 mentally ill or senile convicts. When the settlement closed, it became the town hall, but now serves as a museum and café.

| 0 metres | 50 |
| 0 yards | 50 |

HAMP STREET

LETON STREET

CHURCH STREET

Church
Completed in 1836, Port Arthur's church was never consecrated because it was used by all denominations. The building was gutted by fire in 1884, but the ruins are now fully preserved.

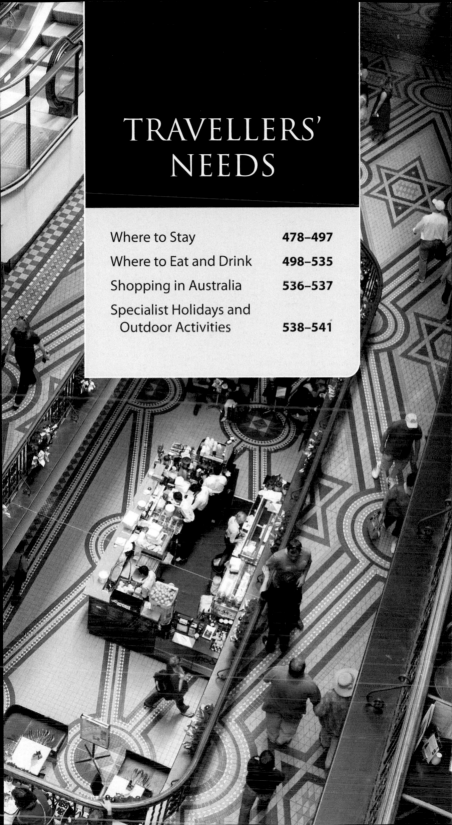

TRAVELLERS' NEEDS

WHERE TO STAY

The wide range of places to stay in Australia is a reflection of the country's size and diversity, as well as its position as a major tourist destination. There are tropical island resorts, luxury and boutique city hotels, ski lodges, converted shearers' quarters on vast sheep stations, colonial cottage bed and breakfasts, self catering apartments, youth hostels, houseboats and, of course, all the usual international chains. Visitors will find accommodation options to suit every need and budget – from simple beds for the night to glitzy all-inclusive holiday resorts.

The superb harbour-front location of the Park Hyatt Sydney hotel *(see p482)*

Gradings and Facilities

State motoring organizations, some state and regional tourism bodies, and the **STAR Ratings** scheme rank hotels with one to five stars as a useful indicator of standards and facilities. **Ecotourism Australia** runs a certification scheme for environmentally friendly properties.

In city hotels, resorts and motels, air-conditioning in the summer and heating in the winter are almost always provided. Other standard features include tea- and coffee-making facilities, televisions, radios, refrigerators and ensuite shower rooms; bathtubs are less common. A room for two may have either a double bed or twin beds. Luxury accommodation often features on-site swimming pools, exercise facilities, and a bar or restaurant.

Prices

Prices for accommodation vary according to the location and the facilities on offer. The presidential suite in a luxury city or resort hotel may have a four-figure daily rate, while a night in a backpacker hostel will generally cost less than A$35 for a bed in a shared room or A$70 for a private room. Budget motels and the majority of B&Bs operate within the A$80–A$180 range. Prices may increase slightly during peak seasons and come down during the low season. Tipping is not expected and is discretionary.

Bookings

Pressure on room availability can be high, especially in the capital cities and the coastal destinations in Queensland. For school holidays and major cultural and sporting events *(see pp44–7)*, it is advisable to book well in advance.

Local and state tourist offices can help with or even make bookings. Major airlines, agents and operators also often have discounted packages on offer *(see pp554–7)*.

Children

Travelling with children is relatively easy throughout the country. Most forms of accommodation will provide a small bed or cot in family rooms, often at no extra charge; enquire about any special rates in advance. Many hotels also

Impressive manicured gardens of Canberra's Hyatt Hotel *(see p485)*

The pool terrace at the Coral Sea Resort in Airlie Beach *(see p487)*

offer baby-sitting services. However, be aware that some of the country house hotels are strictly child-free zones.

Disabled Travellers

Australian building codes now stipulate that any new buildings or renovations must provide facilities for the disabled. It is always advisable, however, to check in advance.

Luxury Hotels and Resorts

In the state capitals, well-known international names – **Hyatt**, **Hilton**, **InterContinental**, **Four Seasons**, **Sheraton** and **Westin** – stand side by side with local institutions such as The Hotel Windsor in Melbourne *(see p493)*. Major beach destinations abound with luxury resorts.

Chain Hotels

Australia's chain hotels and motels offer reliable and comfortable, if occasionally bland, accommodation. Some of the best-known chains are **Choice Hotels**, **Metro Hotels**, **Best Western**, **Travelodge**, **Country Comfort** and **Accor**.

Country House Hotels

Ranging from elegant mansions to simple cottages, country house hotels can be found throughout the country. They offer the comforts of home and a more rustic experience than chain hotels.

Among the best country houses are those found in the wine regions *(see pp40–41)*, around the old gold fields *(see pp58–9)* and in Tasmania *(see pp456–75)*. Eco lodges offering

a close-to-nature experience can be found in beautiful wilderness areas, including islands and coastal forests.

Leather armchairs in the Globe bar at the Langham Sydney hotel *(see p482)*

Backpacker Hotels and Youth Hostels

Despite their budget prices and basic facilities, most accommodation options for young backpackers are clean and comfortable, though standards can vary widely in different areas. The internationally renowned **Youth Hostel Association (YHA)** caters for all ages and covers all the major cities, ski resorts and many of the national parks. There are also numerous independent hostels. The backpacker scene changes quickly, so ask other travellers for recommendations.

While it is necessary to book at some hostels, others offer beds on a first-come-first-served basis. Apartments, rooms and dormitories are all available. Note that dormitories may sometimes be mixed sex, so check in advance, if needed.

Funky, contemporary balcony suite at the Tolarno Hotel in St Kilda, Melbourne *(see p494)*

"The Grand" ballroom in the Hotel Windsor, Melbourne *(see p493)*

Boutique Hotels and B&Bs

In Australia, the term "boutique" is used rather loosely to describe a small hotel or motel. The best offer luxury accommodation and an intimate atmosphere.

Australian bed and breakfasts (B&Bs), many housed in heritage-listed premises, also tend to be of a high standard. They offer personalized accommodation and the best way to experience traditional Australian life. Many have only one or two guestrooms and offer all the comforts of home.

Self-catering Apartments

Self-catering apartments usually come with full kitchen and laundry facilities. Within cities, some apartments also cater for business travellers. Prices are generally on a par with the major chain motels.

Pub Accommodation

In Australia, "hotel" is the historic term for a pub (originally known as public houses). Many pubs still offer bed-and-breakfast accommodation. The quality can vary and they can be noisy, but they are usually good value for money.

Farm Stays and Houseboats

Many sheep and cattle stations welcome visitors for farm stays, offering a unique perspective on rural Australian life. Many are near major cities, while others are in the vast Outback *(see pp32–3)*. Accommodation may be in traditional shearers' or cattle herders' quarters, or within the homestead itself. A stay usually includes the opportunity to be involved in the working life of the station. Ask state tourist offices for details.

Another interesting and more relaxing holiday option is to rent a houseboat on the vast Murray River, which crosses from New South Wales and Victoria to South Australia. An international driving licence is the only requirement to be your own riverboat captain.

Camping and Caravan Parks

Camping and caravan sites are found throughout the country, most of them dotted along the vast coastline and in the inland national parks. They offer a cheap and idyllic way of enjoying the natural beauty and wildlife of Australia. Many camp sites don't insist on advance bookings, but some require a permit. Holiday parks often have on-site vans and cabins for rent at relatively low prices, athough there are increasingly high end offerings too. Facilities usually include laundry and shower blocks and a small general store for provisions.

Comfortable room at Glen Isla House on Phillip Island *(see p496)*

A permanent tent in Wilpena Pound Resort, Wilpena *(see p492)*

Recommended Hotels

The hotel listings in this book offer a selection of recommended places to stay throughout the country across a range of budgets. Divided into 17 geographical areas corresponding to the chapters in this guide, the entries are then organized by town and price. Hotels listed as Value for Money are places that offer more than

would usually be expected for the price – whether that's luxury toiletries, free airport transfers, Wi-Fi access or a convenient central location. Places listed as "Rural" are hotels, lodges, cottages and camps that are found in farmland, wilderness or the Outback. "Beach and Coast" accommodation have an enviable position near the sea. "Character" hotels are usually

smaller guesthouses with additional charm and a friendly welcome; some are housed in a heritage building. Entries highlighted as "DK Choice" offer something extra special, whether that's a stunning location, notable history, excellent facilities and service, or a combination of factors. Whatever the reason, each one offers a memorable stay.

DIRECTORY

Grading and Facilities

Ecotourism Australia
W ecotourism.org.au

STAR Ratings
W starratings.com.au

Luxury Hotels and Resorts

Four Seasons
Tel 1800 222 200
or (02) 9250 3100 (Sydney).
W fourseasons.com

Hilton
Tel 1800 024 766.
W hilton.com

Hyatt
Tel 131 234.
W hyatt.com

InterContinental
Tel 138 388.
W ihg.com

Sheraton
Tel 1800 073 535.
W starwoodhotels.com

Westin
Tel 1800 656 535.
W starwoodhotels.com

Chain Hotels

Accor Hotels
Tel 1300 656 565.
W accorhotels.com.au

Best Western
Tel 131 779.
W bestwestern.com.au

Choice Hotels
Tel 132 400.
W choicehotels.com

Country Comfort Hotels
Tel 1300 272 132. W silver
needlehotels.com

Metro Hotels
Tel 1800 004 321.
W metrohotels.com.au

Travelodge
Tel 1300 886 886.
W tfehotels.com

Backpacker Hotels and Youth Hostels

Youth Hostel Association (YHA)
Tel (02) 9261 1111
or 9218 9090.
W yha.com.au

Tourist Offices

Australian Capital Tourism
333 Northbourne Ave,
Braddon, Canberra, ACT.
Tel (02) 6205 0666.
W visitcanberra.com.au

South Australian Tourism Commission
108 North Terrace,
Adelaide, SA.
Tel 1300 764 227.
W southaustralia.com

Tourism Australia
Sydney: Tel (02) 9360
1111. W australia.com
UK: Australia House,
6th Floor, Melbourne
Place, The Strand,
London WC2B 4LG.
Tel (020) 7438 4600.
USA: 6100 Center Dr,
Los Angeles, CA 90045.
Tel (310) 695 3200.

Tourism NSW
55 Harrington St,
Sydney, NSW.
Tel (02) 8273 0000.
W visitnsw.com

Tourism Queensland
Level 10, 30 Makerston St,
Brisbane, QLD 4000.
Tel (07) 3535 3535.
W queensland.com

Tourism Tasmania
22 Elizabeth St, Hobart,
Tasmania. Tel (03) 6230
8235/ 6115 5334 or 1800
990 440.
W discovertasmania.
com.au

Tourism Top End
Cnr Smith and Bennett
sts, Darwin, NT.
Tel 1300 138 886 or
(08) 8980 6000.
W tourismtopend.
com.au

Tourism Victoria
2 Swanston St,
Melbourne, VIC.
Tel (03) 9653 9777.
W visitvictoria.com

Tourism Western Australia
2 Mill St,
Perth, WA 6000.
Tel 1300 361 351
or (08) 9483 1111.
W westernaustralia.com.au

Places to Stay

Sydney

The Rocks and Circular Quay

Lord Nelson Brewery Hotel $$
Character
19 Kent St, NSW 2000
Tel *(02) 9251 4044* **Map** 1 A2
W lordnelsonbrewery.com
The top floor of this convivial pub offers simple but cosy bedrooms with stone walls.

Sydney Harbour YHA $$
Hostel
110 Cumberland St, NSW 2000
Tel *(02) 8272 0900* **Map** 1 B2
W yha.com.au
Modern and comfortable hostel. The multishare or double rooms all have ensuites. A roof terrace provides top-dollar harbour views for a reasonable price.

The Langham Sydney $$$
Luxury
89–113 Kent St, NSW 2000
Tel *(02) 8248 5220* **Map** 1 A2
W sydney.langhamhotels.com.au
This celebrated top-of-the-range hotel is tastefully furnished with antiques and fine artworks.

Old Sydney Holiday Inn $$$
Luxury
55 George St, NSW 2000
Tel *(02) 9252 0524* **Map** 1 B2
W ihg.com
Small enough to provide personal attention. Good amenities and a spectacular view from the rooftop.

Park Hyatt Sydney $$$
Luxury
7 Hickson Rd, NSW 2000
Tel *(02) 9256 1234* **Map** 1 B1
W sydney.park.hyatt.com
Top class hotel decorated with contemporary Australian art. Boasts Opera House views from many rooms.

Pier One Sydney Harbour $$$
Luxury
11 Hickson Rd, Walsh Bay, NSW 2000
Tel *(02) 8298 9999* **Map** 1 B1
W pieronesydneyharbour.com.au
Housed in a heritage building on a 1912 finger wharf, this hotel has crisp, sleek decor in neutral shades.

Shangri-La Sydney $$$
Luxury
176 Cumberland St, NSW 2000
Tel *(02) 9250 6000* **Map** 1 A3
W shangri-la.com
All the luxury and style one can expect from this brand.

City Centre and Darling Harbour

Railway Square YHA $$
Character
8–10 Lee St, NSW 2000
Tel *(02) 9281 9666* **Map** 4 E5
W yha.com.au
Unique hostel adjoining Central Station. Guests can sleep in a converted railway carriage and chill in the great spa pool.

Y Hotel Hyde Park $$
Value for Money
5–11 Wentworth Ave, NSW 2000
Tel *(02) 9264 2451* **Map** 4 F3
W yhotel.com.au
Modest but stylishly decorated hotel. Shared kitchen and laundry. Breakfast is included in the price.

The Darling $$$
Luxury
80 Pyrmont St, NSW 2009
Tel *(02) 9777 9000* **Map** 3 B1
W thedarling.com.au
Located within the Star Casino complex. The upscale rooms all have floor-to-ceiling windows.

DK Choice

Establishment Hotel $$$
Boutique
5 Bridge Ln, NSW 2000
Tel *(02) 9240 3100* **Map** 1 B3
W merivale.com.au
Historic character meets contemporary style and elegance at this hip celebrity favourite. Rooms and suites boast marble or stone bathrooms, and either a lively or a tranquil colour scheme. Some of the city's best places to eat and drink can be found downstairs. Soundproofing ensures a peaceful stay.

Hilton Sydney $$$
Luxury
488 George St, NSW 2000
Tel *(02) 9266 2000* **Map** 1 B5
W hiltonsydney.com.au
A reliable choice with high standards. Quality furnishings and a fantastic health club.

Meriton World Tower $$$
Self-catering
91–95 Liverpool St, NSW 2000
Tel *(02) 8263 7500* **Map** 4 E3
W meritonapartments.com.au
Smart, serviced two- or three-bed apartments in Sydney's tallest residential building. Dazzling views.

Novotel Sydney on Darling Harbour $$$
Luxury
100 Murray St, NSW 2009
Tel *(02) 9934 0000* **Map** 3 C2
W noveldarlingharbour.com.au
This towering modern structure is a family-friendly luxury hotel. Outdoor tennis court and pool.

Sheraton on the Park $$$
Luxury
161 Elizabeth St, NSW 2000
Tel *(02) 9286 6000* **Map** 1 B5
W sheratonontheparksydney.com
From the entrance to the plush rooms, this hotel offers a deluxe stay. Helpful, 24-hour service.

Sofitel Sydney Wentworth $$$
Luxury
61–101 Phillip St, NSW 2000
Tel *(02) 9228 9188* **Map** 1 B4
W sofitelsydney.com.au
This hotel brilliantly blends 21st-century design with heritage-listed features. A true five-star experience.

The Westin $$$
Luxury
1 Martin Place, NSW 2000
Tel *(02) 8223 1111* **Map** 1 B4
W westinsydney.com
A marble-floored lobby sets the scene for this luxurious retreat. Many rooms have superb views.

Breathtaking views over Sydney harbour from the restaurant at Shangri-La Sydney

The York by Swiss-Belhotel **$$$**
Self-catering
5 York St, NSW 2000
Tel *(02) 9210 5000*   **Map** 1 A3
W theyorkapartments.com.au
Smart, fully equipped apartments, varying in size from studios to two-bedroom penthouses. Babysitting available.

Botanic Gardens and The Domain

Sir Stamford at Circular Quay **$$$**
Luxury
93 Macquarie St, NSW 2000
Tel *(02) 9252 4600*   **Map** 1 C3
W stamford.com.au/sscq
Elegant place decorated with beautiful antiques and fine art.

Kings Cross, Darlinghurst and Paddington

Arts Hotel **$$**
Value for Money
21 Oxford St, NSW 2021
Tel *(02) 9361 0211*   **Map** 5 B3
W artshotel.com.au
Basic but convenient. Pay a little extra for a room overlooking the courtyard garden.

Victoria Court Hotel **$$**
Boutique
122 Victoria St, Potts Point, 2011
Tel *(02) 9357 3200*   **Map** 5 B2
W victoriacourt.com.au
Centrally located hotel housed in a historic building. Charming Victorian-style rooms; most have marble fireplaces.

Blue Sydney **$$$**
Luxury
6 Cowper Wharf Rd, Woolloomooloo, NSW 2011
Tel *(02) 9331 9000*   **Map** 2 E4
W bluehotel.com.au
A glamorous place, with luxurious loft rooms and a fabulous cocktail bar. Minimalist, urban-industrial decor.

Hughenden Boutique Hotel **$$$**
Boutique
14 Queen St, Woollahra, NSW 2025
Tel *(02) 9363 4863*   **Map** 6 E4
W thehughendenhotel.com.au
Rambling 19th-century building comfortably furnished to retain a Victorian feel. Dogs welcome.

Medusa **$$$**
Boutique
267 Darlinghurst Rd, NSW 2010
Tel *(02) 9331 1000*   **Map** 5 B1
W medusa.com.au
A brightly coloured Modernist hotel with great amenities and artistic touches in each room.

The beautiful pool area at The Byron at Byron, Byron Bay

Simpsons of Potts Point **$$$**
Character
8 Challis Ave, Potts Point, 2011
Tel *(02) 9356 2199*   **Map** 2 E4
W simpsonshotel.com
Charming B&B built in 1892 as a family residence. Breakfast served in a glass-roofed conservatory.

Further Afield

BONDI BEACH: Ravesi's **$$$**
Boutique
118 Campbell Parade, NSW 2026
Tel *(02) 9365 4422*
W ravesis.com.au
A beach-watching spot with show-stopping views of Bondi and a popular restaurant. Some rooms have private balconies.

BONDI JUNCTION: Meriton Bondi Junction **$$**
Self-catering
97 Grafton St, NSW 2022
Tel *(02) 8305 7600 or 131 672*
W meritonapartments.com.au
Tower-block complex of spacious apartments with one to three bedrooms. Fine views.

COOGEE: Dive Hotel **$$**
Boutique
234 Arden St, NSW 2034
Tel *(02) 9665 5538*
W divehotel.com.au
A great alternative to Coogee's hostels, with designer bathrooms and a sleek colour scheme.

DOUBLE BAY: The Savoy Hotel Double Bay **$$**
Value for Money
41–45 Knox St, NSW 2028
Tel *(02) 9326 1411*
W savoyhotel.com.au
Well-established hotel offering personal service in a tranquil environment. Great location.

MANLY: Novotel Sydney Manly Pacific **$$$**
Beach
55 North Steyne, NSW 2095
Tel *(02) 9977 7666*
W novotelmanlypacific.com.au
Right on the beach, and boasting unbeatable views. Light, spacious rooms with balconies.

SURRY HILLS: Adina Apartment Hotel Sydney, Crown Street **$$**
Self-catering
359 Crown St, NSW 2010
Tel *(02) 8302 1000*
W tfehotels.com
Spacious one- and two-bedroom apartments with full-size kitchens and splashes of colour.

The Blue Mountains and Beyond

BALLINA: Ballina Heritage Inn **$$**
Motel
229 River St, NSW 2478
Tel *(02) 6686 0505*
W ballinaheritageinn.com.au
Comfortable motel that prides itself on service. Saltwater pool. Babysitting available.

DK Choice

BYRON BAY: The Byron at Byron **$$$**
Luxury
77–97 Broken Head Rd, NSW 2481
Tel *(02) 6639 2000 or 1300 554 362*
W thebyronatbyron.com.au
Beautiful resort set in a fragrant grove of eucalyptus and palm trees. Stay in contemporary suites filled with luxury touches. Start the day with yoga by the gorgeous pool, enjoy a spa treatment or wander through the trees to the beach.

BYRON BAY: The Oasis Resort **$$$**
Self-catering
24 Scott St, NSW 2481
Tel *(02) 6685 7390 or 1800 336 129*
W byronoasis.com.au
Spacious two-bedroom apartments and "treetop houses". Close to the beach, with a pool fringed by tropical greenery.

COFFS HARBOUR: BreakFree Aanuka Beach Resort **$$$**
Beach
11 Firman Dr, NSW 2450
Tel *(02) 6652 7555 or 1800 783 552*
W breakfreeaanukabeachresort.com.au
Beachfront resort with rooms and self-catering apartments. The café and restaurant have ocean views and live entertainment.

For more information on types of hotels *see page 481*

Safari-style tent at Paperbark Camp, Jervis Bay

GOSFORD: Terrigal Pacific Motel & Apartments $$
Self-catering
224 Terrigal Dr, NSW 2260
Tel (02) 4385 1555
W terrigalaccommodation.com
Spacious apartments with balconies overlooking lush gardens. Close to the beach.

HUNTER VALLEY: Hunter Valley YHA $
Hostel
100 Wine Country Dr, Nulkaba, NSW 2325
Tel (02) 4991 3278
W yha.com.au
Low-key hostel in a timber cabin. Offers Wine Country tours and bike hire. Great service.

HUNTER VALLEY: Hunter Valley Resort $$$
Luxury
Cnr Hermitage Rd & Mistletoe Ln, Pokolbin, NSW 2320
Tel (02) 4998 7777
W hunterresort.com.au
Pleasant rooms and cottages located in a Shiraz vineyard. Plenty of on-site activities.

KATOOMBA: Lilianfels Resort and Spa $$$
Luxury
Lilianfels Ave, NSW 2780
Tel (02) 4780 1200
W lilianfels.com.au
Historic country house amid English-style gardens. Idyllic spa, great food and stunning scenery.

KATOOMBA: The Mountain Heritage Hotel & Spa Retreat $$$
Character
Cnr Apex & Lovel sts, NSW 2780
Tel (02) 4782 2155
W mountainheritage.com.au
Classic country house hotel. Relax in the gardens or curl up by a log fire in the snug lounge.

LITHGOW: Eagle View Escape $$
Luxury
271 Sandalls Dr, Rydal via Lake Lyell, NSW 2790
Tel (02) 6355 6311 or 1300 851 829
W eagleview.com.au
Perfect for a romantic getaway. Stay in either a suite or cabin at this lush 100-acre property.

MUDGEE: Cobb & Co Court Boutique Hotel $$
Boutique
97 Market St, NSW 2850
Tel (02) 6372 7245
W cobbandcocourt.com.au
Delightful small hotel close to many wineries. Good restaurant.

NEWCASTLE: Crowne Plaza $$$
Luxury
Cnr Merewether St & Wharf Rd, NSW 2300
Tel (02) 4907 5000
W ihg.com
Excellent harbourfront hotel right on the foreshore promenade. Modern faciltes and a large pool.

PORT STEPHENS: Wanderers Retreat $$
Rural
7 Koala Place, One Mile Beach, NSW 2316
Tel (02) 4982 1702
W wanderersretreat.com
Eco-friendly cabins and tree houses in quiet bushland, home to koalas. Short stroll to the beach.

TAMWORTH: Plumes on the Green $$
Guesthouse
25 The Ringers Rd, NSW 2340
Tel (02) 6762 1140
W plumesonthegreen.com.au
Popular with birdwatchers and golfers, Plumes prides itself on its sophisticated atmosphere.

WAGGA WAGGA: Mercure Wagga Wagga $$
Value for Money
1 Morgan St, NSW 2650
Tel (02) 6939 7200
W accorhotels.com
Comfortable hotel, with modern facilities and two pools.

The South Coast and Snowy Mountains

BATEMANS BAY: Lincoln Downs Hotel $$
Value for Money
Princes Hwy, NSW 2536
Tel (02) 4478 9200
W lincolndowns.com.au
A peaceful coastal resort set in an English country-style garden. Ornamental lake and tennis court.

BOWRAL: Milton Park Country House Hotel $$$
Luxury
Horderns Rd, NSW 2576
Tel (02) 4861 8100
W milton-park.com.au
A fine example of Federation Arts and Crafts architecture. Great day spa and parkland views.

BUNDANOON: Tree Tops Guesthouse $$
Boutique
101 Railway Ave, NSW 2578
Tel (02) 4883 6372
W treetopsguesthouse.com.au
Quiet Edwardian house featuring four-poster beds and log fires.

CHARLOTTES PASS: Kosciuszko Chalet Hotel $$$
Ski Resort
Kosciuszko Rd, NSW 2624
Tel 1800 026 369
W charlottepass.com.au
Built in the 1930s, this ski-in, ski-out hotel offers peace and quiet.

COOMA: Kinross Inn $$
Motel
15 Sharp St, NSW 2630
Tel (02) 6452 3577
W kinrossinn.com.au
Popular motel, an hour from the ski slopes. Good facilities.

GOULBURN: Pelican Sheep Station $
Rural
Braidwood Rd, NSW 2580
Tel (02) 4821 4668
W pelicansheepstation.com.au
Experience rural life at this family-owned sheep station. Camps, bunkhouses and cabins.

DK Choice

JERVIS BAY: Paperbark Camp $$$
Rural
571 Woollamia Rd, Woollamia, NSW 2540
Tel (02) 4441 6066
W paperbarkcamp.com.au
Stay in luxurious, safari-style tents tucked in a grove of mature gum trees at this peaceful, eco-friendly bush lodge. The treetop dining room serves imaginative cuisine based on local produce. Watch possums, sugar gliders and birds from the veranda.

MERIMBULA: Albacore Apartments $$$
Self-catering
Market St, NSW 2548
Tel (02) 6495 3187
W albacore.com.au
Five-storey block of smartly furnished apartments with lake views.

NAROOMA: Mystery Bay Cottages $$
Self-catering
121 Mystery Bay Rd, NSW 2546
Tel *(02) 4473 7431*
w mysterybaycottages.com.au
Two-bedroom cottages in a peaceful location. Light and airy, with log fires.

NOWRA: Shoalhaven Lodge $$
Self-catering
480 Longreach Rd, NSW 2541
Tel *(02) 4422 6686*
w shoalhavenlodge.com.au
Chalet-style lodges and suites in peaceful farmland surroundings.

PERISHER VALLEY: Marritz Alpine $$$
Ski Lodge
Kosciuszko Rd, NSW 2624
Tel *1800 767 756*
w marritzalpine.com.au
Quaint ski lodge with an elegant indoor heated pool and access to Australia's largest alpine facilities.

TATHRA: Tathra Beach House $$
Self-catering
57 Andy Poole Dr, NSW 2550
Tel *(02) 6499 9900*
w tathrabeachhouse.com.au
Unpretentious complex of apartments sleeping up to seven. Great location near the surf beach.

THREDBO: Thredbo Alpine Hotel $$$
Ski Resort
Friday Dr, NSW 2625
Tel *(02) 6459 4200*
w thredbo.com.au
A favourite with skiers since it is close to the ski lift. Cheaper and quieter in the summer. Facilities include tennis and golf.

TILBA: The Two Story Bed & Breakfast $$
Character
Bate St, NSW 2546
Tel *(02) 4473 7290*
w tilbatwostory.com
A lovingly restored former post office close to craft shops and bushwalks. Pleasantly chintzy.

WOLLONGONG: Novotel Wollongong Northbeach $$$
Coast
2–14 Cliff Rd, NSW 2500
Tel *(02) 4224 3111*
w novotelnorthbeach.com.au
Peaceful hotel between the ocean and the mountains.

Canberra and ACT

CANBERRA: The Brassey of Canberra $$
Value for Money
Belmore Gardens & Macquarie St, Barton, ACT 2600
Tel *(02) 6273 3766 or 1800 659 191*
w brassey.net.au
Comfortable hotel in a tree-lined suburb. Traditional atmosphere.

CANBERRA: Canberra City YHA $$
Hostel
7 Akuna St, ACT 2601
Tel *(02) 6248 9155*
w yha.com.au
Friendly hostel close to the bus terminal. Good terrace views.

CANBERRA: Crowne Plaza Canberra $$
Luxury
1 Binara St, ACT 2601
Tel *(02) 6247 8999*
w crowneplazacanberra.com.au
Modern, centrally located hotel with spa, gym and kids' facilities.

CANBERRA: Novotel Canberra $$
Value for Money
65 Northbourne Ave, ACT 2600
Tel *(02) 6245 5000*
w novotelcanberra.com.au
Well-located hotel with indoor heated pool, gym and spa facilities.

CANBERRA: Peppers Gallery Hotel $$
Boutique
15 Edinburgh Ave, ACT 2601
Tel *(02) 6175 2222*
w peppers.com.au/gallery
A strikingly stylish hotel with contemporary furniture and art.

CANBERRA: QT Canberra $$
Value for Money
1 London Circuit, ACT 2600
Tel *(02) 6247 6244*
w qtcanberra.com.au
Designer guest rooms boasting wonderful views over Lake Burley Griffin.

CANBERRA: University House $$
Value for Money
Cnr Balmain & Liversidge sts, ACT 2601
Tel *(02) 6125 5276*
w anu.edu.au/unihouse
Peaceful place in the gardens of the Australian National University. Spacious rooms and apartments.

CANBERRA: Hotel Kurrajong $$$
Character
8 National Circuit, Barton, ACT 2604
Tel *(02) 6234 4444*
w hotelkurrajong.com.au
Unpretentious hotel in a heritage Art Deco building. Conference facilities, bar and restaurant.

DK Choice

CANBERRA: Hotel Realm $$$
Luxury
18 National Circuit, Barton, ACT 2600
Tel *(02) 6163 1888*
w hotelrealm.com.au
Relaxed for a five-star, this beautifully designed hotel has striking decor. Apple gadgets, coffee machines and luxury bathroom goodies easily make this the coolest high-end hotel in the capital. The business centre is open round the clock.

CANBERRA: Hyatt Hotel Canberra $$$
Luxury
Commonwealth Ave, Yarralumla, ACT 2600
Tel *(02) 6270 1234*
w canberra.park.hyatt.com
Sophisticated heritage Art Deco hotel surrounded by manicured gardens. Rooms feature Italian black marble bathrooms. Impressive fitness centre.

MACGREGOR: Ginninderry Park $$
Rural
468 Parkwood Road, ACT 2615
Tel *(02) 0400 546 464*
w ginninderry.com.au
Beautiful guesthouse on a working farm, with gardens to enjoy and pastoral views framed by the distant Brindabella Ranges. Generous breakfasts.

Spacious, premier room at Peppers Gallery Hotel, Canberra

For more information on types of hotels *see page 481*

Brisbane

CITY CENTRE: Brisbane City YHA $
Hostel
392 Upper Roma St, QLD 4000
Tel *(07) 3236 1004*
w yha.com.au
Award-winning hostel with bright, modern rooms. Good kitchen facilities and a rooftop pool.

CITY CENTRE: Eton House $
Guesthouse
436 Upper Roma St, QLD 4000
Tel *(07) 3236 0115*
w babs.com.au
Stay in a relaxed, heritage-listed Queenslander built in 1877. Shared kitchen, lounge and courtyard.

CITY CENTRE: George Williams Hotel $$
Value for Money
317 George St, QLD 4000
Tel *(07) 3308 0700*
w hgw.com.au
Simple but decent rooms in a great location. Restaurant on site.

CITY CENTRE: Hotel Ibis $$
Value for Money
27 Turbot St, QLD 4000
Tel *(07) 3237 2333*
w ibis.com
Surprisingly stylish for the price, with useful extras such as laundry and babysitting.

CITY CENTRE: Brisbane Marriott Hotel $$$
Luxury
515 Queen St, QLD 4000
Tel *(07) 3303 8000*
w marriott.com.au
Elegant decor, a luxury spa and panoramic views.

Contemporary conference room at Spicers Balfour Hotel, Brisbane

CITY CENTRE: Hilton Brisbane Hotel $$$
Luxury
190 Elizabeth St, QLD 4000
Tel *(07) 3234 2000*
w brisbane.hilton.com
Dramatic atrium, pool, quality fittings and excellent views at this beautiful 20th-century hotel .

CITY CENTRE: The Inchcolm Hotel $$$
Boutique
73 Wickham Terrace, QLD 4000
Tel *(07) 3226 8888*
w inchcolm.com.au
A heritage hotel with modern furnishings amid original features such as shutters and oak panelling.

DK Choice

CITY CENTRE: Spicers Balfour Hotel $$$
Luxury
37 Balfour St, QLD 4005
Tel *(07) 3358 8888*
w spicersretreats.com
Housed in a traditional Queenslander building, Spicers Balfour has contemporary decor in rich jewel tones. Gorgeous bed linen, Bose stereos and a good library. Enjoy views of the Story Bridge over fabulous cocktails and pre-dinner canapés in the rooftop bar.

FORTITUDE VALLEY: TRYP Fortitude Valley Hotel $$
Boutique
14–20 Constance St, QLD 4006
Tel *(07) 3319 7888*
w trypbrisbane.com
Stylish rooms with playful artwork. Ultra-modern furnishings.

FORTITUDE VALLEY: Emporium Hotel $$$
Boutique
1000 Ann St, QLD 4006
Tel *(07) 3253 6999*
w emporiumhotel.com.au
Up-market urban hotel with a rooftop pool. Fantastic cocktail bar.

KANGAROO POINT: The Point $$
Value for Money
21 Lambert St, QLD 4169
Tel *(07) 3240 0888*
w thepointbrisbane.com.au
Good facilities and stunning views from the upper floors.

NEW FARM: Bowen Terrace $$
Value for Money
365 Bowen Terrace, QLD 4005
Tel *(07) 3254 0458*
w bowenterrace.com.au
Friendly and welcoming place in a quiet residential area. Simple shared and private rooms.

PADDINGTON: Fern Cottage B&B $$
Character
89 Fernberg Rd, QLD 4064
Tel *(07) 3511 6685*
w ferncottage.net
Enchanting, refurbished 1930s Queenslander with immaculate rooms. Beautiful courtyard garden.

PADDINGTON: Lucerne on Fernberg $$
Value for Money
23 Fernberg Rd, QLD 4064
Tel *(07) 3369 6686*
w lucerne.net.au
Two well-appointed cottages nestled in lovely gardens.

SPRING HILL: Metro Hotel Tower Mill $$
Value for Money
239 Wickham Terrace, QLD 4000
Tel *(07) 3832 1421*
w metrohotels.com.au
Located in a cylindrical tower block, there are panoramic views from the upper floors. Rooms are simple; some have balconies.

SPRING HILL: Hotel Watermark $$$
Luxury
551 Wickham Terrace, QLD 4000
Tel *(07) 3058 9333*
w watermarkhotelbrisbane.com.au
Spacious, comfortable rooms overlooking Spring Hill or the Roma Street Parkland.

SPRING HILL: Punthill Brisbane $$$
Luxury
40 Astor Terrace, QLD 4000
Tel *(07) 3055 5777*
w punthill.com.au
Smart studio and one-bedroom apartments. Great contemporary decor. Laundry facilities and bike hire available.

WEST END: Franklin Villa $$$
Boutique
35 Brighton Rd, QLD 4101
Tel *(07) 3255 0889*
w franklinvilla.com.au
Splendid rooms in a beautifully restored mansion. The verandas afford sweeping views of the city skyline.

South of Townsville

AGNES WATERS: Mango Tree Motel $$
Beach
7 Agnes St, QLD 4677
Tel *(07) 4974 9132*
w mangotreemotel.com.au
Budget motel close to the main surf beach. Popular shops, cafés and restaurants are all nearby.

Guests relaxing in one of the pool bars, Kingfisher Bay Resort, Fraser Island

AIRLIE BEACH: Coral Sea Resort $$$
Coast
25 Oceanview Ave, QLD 4802
Tel *(07) 4964 1300*
W coralsearesort.com
Relaxed resort with nautically themed decor. Spectacular ocean views from the pool terrace.

CARNARVON NATIONAL PARK: Carnarvon Gorge Wilderness Lodge $$
Rural
4043 O'Briens Rd, QLD 4702
Tel *(07) 4984 4503 or 1800 644 150*
W carnarvon-gorge.com
Stay in an inviting, airy cabin nestled in woodland. Good spot for walks and birdwatching.

FRASER ISLAND: Eurong Beach Resort $$
Rural
Fraser Island, QLD 4655
Tel *(07) 4120 1600*
W eurong.com
Simple but comfortable resort in the World Heritage wilderness. Close to the rainforest and lakes. Access by 4WD only.

DK Choice

FRASER ISLAND: Kingfisher Bay Resort $$$
Rural
Fraser Island, QLD 4655
Tel *(07) 4120 3333*
W kingfisherbay.com
An award-winning eco-lodge with lovely grounds, a good restaurant and lots of activities on offer. Surrounded by unspoilt coastal dunes and forest, it is satisfyingly remote, but easy to reach. Rooms and villas available.

GLADSTONE: Auckland Hill Bed and Breakfast $$
Boutique
15 Yarroon St, QLD 4680
Tel *(07) 4972 4907*
W ahbb.com.au
Delightful guesthouse. Relax on the large deck with a seafood or cheese platter (on request).

GOLD COAST: Palazzo Versace $$$
Luxury
Sea World Dr, Main Beach, QLD 4217
Tel *(07) 5509 8000*
W palazzoversace.com.au
Sensual and opulent hotel with spectacularly decorated interiors, rich fabrics and grand vistas. Features a lavish pool, gym and spa.

GOLD COAST: Q1 Resort and Spa $$$
Luxury
Hamilton Ave, Surfers Paradise, QLD 4217
Tel *(07) 5630 4500*
W q1.com.au
Gleaming luxury suites and apartments in a striking skyscraper that is the tallest building in the southern hemisphere.

GOLD COAST: Sheraton Mirage Resort & Spa $$$
Luxury
71 Sea World Dr, Main Beach, QLD 4217
Tel *(07) 5577 0000*
W sheratonmiragegoldcoast.com
Sleek yet tasteful, this oceanfront resort is set amid scenic lagoons and tropical gardens.

HERVEY BAY: The Bay B&B $$
B&B
180 Cypress St, Urangan, QLD 4655
Tel *(07) 4125 6919*
W baybedandbreakfast.com.au
Set in an idyllic tropical garden. Shady terraces and a heated swimming pool.

HERVEY BAY: Mantra Hervey Bay $$
Value for Money
Buccaneer Dr, Urangan, QLD 4655
Tel *(07) 4197 8200*
W mantraherveybay.com.au
Pleasant resort on the marina with impressive views from the balconies. Handy for whale-watching trips.

LADY ELLIOT ISLAND: Lady Elliot Island Resort $$$
Rural
QLD 4216
Tel *(07) 5536 3644*
W ladyelliot.com.au
Unique, eco-friendly island retreat located in an important marine wildlife habitat.

LAMINGTON NATIONAL PARK: Binna Burra Mountain Lodge $$
Rural
QLD 4211
Tel *(07) 5533 3622*
W binnaburralodge.com.au
Rustic eco-tourism retreat with simple rooms in a rainforest.

LAMINGTON NATIONAL PARK: O'Reilly's Rainforest Retreat $$$
Rural
QLD 4275
Tel *(07) 5544 0644*
W oreillys.com.au
Escape to this beautiful setting with modern comforts in the heart of the park.

MACKAY: Cape Hillsborough Nature Resort $
Rural
51 Risley Parade, Cape Hillsborough, QLD 4740
Tel *(07) 4959 0152*
W capehillsboroughresort.com.au
Camp or stay in a room or cabin surrounded by a coastal reserve. Ideal for relaxing, hiking and kangaroo-watching.

MAGNETIC ISLAND: Sails on Horseshoe $$
Self-catering
13–15 Pacific Dr, Horseshoe Bay, QLD 4819
Tel *(07) 4778 5117*
W sailsonhorseshoe.com.au
Modern two-bedroom and studio apartments close to the beach. Free use of kayaks and bikes.

NOOSA: Halse Lodge YHA $
Hostel
2 Halse Ln, Noosa Heads, QLD 4567
Tel *(07) 5447 3377*
W halselodge.com.au
This 1880s guesthouse is one of Australia's most atmospheric hostels. Relaxed café-restaurant.

NOOSA: Sheraton Noosa Resort & Spa $$$
Luxury
14–16 Hastings St, Noosa Heads, QLD 4567
Tel *(07) 5449 4888*
W sheraton.com/noosa
In a fashionable location, with spacious rooms, superb beds and the best breakfast in town.

NORTH STRADBROKE ISLAND: Straddie Views B&B $$
Beach
26 Cumming Parade, Point Lookout, QLD 4183
Tel *(07) 3409 8875*
W stradbrokeisland.com
Airy seaside B&B where guests are welcomed with home-made biscuits and a decanter of port.

For more information on types of hotels *see page 481*

Spacious lounge of an Estate Suite at the Spicers Clovelly Estate, Sunshine Coast

ROCKHAMPTON:
Myella Farm Stay $$
Rural
Myella Baralaba, QLD 4702
Tel *(07) 4998 1290*
W myella.com
Authentic Queensland holiday experience on a cattle station. Learn to milk cows and horse-ride.

SUNSHINE COAST:
The Arabella Guesthouse $$
B&B
297 Mooloolaba Rd, QLD 4556
Tel *(07) 5478 1339*
W arabellaguesthouse.com.au
Welcoming guesthouse located in a quaint village. Enjoy breakfast on the deck overlooking the ocean.

SUNSHINE COAST:
Spicers Clovelly Estate $$$
Luxury
68 Balmoral Rd, Montville, QLD 4560
Tel *(07) 5452 1111 or 1300 252 380*
W spicersretreats.com
Elegant country house hotel with fine dining and sweeping gardens.

TOOWOOMBA: Vacy Hall $$
Guesthouse
135 Russell St, QLD 4350
Tel *(07) 4639 2055*
W vacyhall.com.au
Heritage luxury in the heart of Toowoomba. Gourmet breakfasts.

TOWNSVILLE: Seagulls Resort $$
Value for Money
74 The Esplanade, Belgian Gardens, QLD 4810
Tel *(07) 4721 3111*
W seagulls.com.au
Set in tropical landscaped gardens. Offers a range of holiday facilities.

WHITSUNDAY ISLANDS:
Qualia $$$
Luxury
Hamilton Island, QLD 4803
Tel *1300 780 959*
W qualia.com.au
Plush resort on the northernmost tip of Hamilton Island. Splendid views of the Coral Sea. Offers a pool, gym and spa facilities.

Northern Queensland and the Outback

CAIRNS: Ellis Beach Oceanfront Bungalows $$
Beach
Captain Cook Hwy, Ellis Beach, QLD 4879
Tel *(07) 4055 3538 or 1800 637 036*
W ellisbeach.com
Bungalows and cabins that sleep up to four people in an idyllic and unspoilt setting. Gorgeous sea views. Look out for dolphins.

CAIRNS: The Hotel Cairns $$
Character
Cnr Abbott & Florence sts, QLD 4870
Tel *(07) 4051 6188*
W thehotelcairns.com
Queenslander-style property with white shutters, latticework and verandas. Free use of cars.

CAIRNS: Novotel Cairns Oasis Resort $$
Design
122 Lake St, QLD 4870
Tel *(07) 4080 1888*
W novotelcairnsresort.com.au
Good-value suites with Jacuzzis. Balconies overlook the tropical gardens, mountains or the pool.

CAIRNS: Pullman Reef Hotel Casino $$$
Character
35–41 Wharf St, QLD 4870
Tel *(07) 4030 8888*
W reefcasino.com.au
Smart, stylish rooms with plantation shutters. See lots of animals, including a crocodile, in the rainforest dome on the roof.

COOKTOWN: The Sovereign Resort Hotel $$
Character
128 Charlotte St, QLD 4895
Tel *(07) 4043 0500*
W sovereign-resort.com.au
Combination of traditional Queensland pub and modern resort, with beautiful rooms.

DAINTREE:
Daintree Riverview $$
Rural
Stewart St, QLD 4873
Tel *(07) 0409 627 434*
W daintreeriverview.com
Cabins and a camping ground overlooking the Daintree River.

KARUMBA: The End of the Road Motel $$
Self-catering
26 Palmer St, QLD 4891
Tel *(07) 4745 9599*
W endoftheroadmotel.com.au
Comfortable self-contained apartments. Right on the beach.

LONGREACH:
Albert Park Motor Inn $$
Motel
Sir Hudson Fysh Dr, QLD 4730
Tel *(07) 4658 2411*
W longreachaccommodation.com
Standard motel close to all major attractions and the airport.

MOSSMAN: Marae B&B $$
Rural
Lot 1, Chook's Ridge, off Ponzo Rd, Shannonvale, QLD
Tel *(07) 4098 4900*
W marae.com.au
A glamorous secluded retreat in the bush, with only two rooms. Wallabies graze in the garden.

MOSSMAN: Silky Oaks Lodge and Healing Waters Spa $$$
Luxury
Finlayvale Rd, QLD 4873
Tel *(07) 4098 1666*
W silkyoakslodge.com.au
Luxury treehouses situated in the rainforest, all with private hammocks. Great spa.

MOUNT ISA: Isa Hotel $$
Boutique
11 Miles St, QLD 4825
Tel *(07) 4749 8888*
W redearth-hotel.com.au
Modern, clean and comfortable choice in the heart of town.

PALM COVE: Pullman Palm Cove Sea Temple Resort & Spa $$$
Luxury
5 Triton St, QLD 4879
Tel *(07) 4059 8600 or 1800 010 241*
W pullmanhotels.com
Choice of studios, apartments and penthouses. Private plunge pools, rooftop terraces and a spa.

PORT DOUGLAS:
Port O'Call Eco Lodge $$
Hostel
Cnr Port St & Craven Close, QLD 4877
Tel *(07) 4099 5422 or 1800 892 800*
W portocall.com.au
Popular, modest lodge with a four-green-star rating for sustainability.

DK Choice

UNDARA VOLCANIC NATIONAL PARK: Undara Experience Lava Lodge $$
Rural
Savannah Way, QLD 4871
Tel *(07) 4097 1900 or 1800 990 992*
W undara.com.au
Set in the national park's amazing surroundings, with its ancient lava tubes and wildlife. Accommodation ranges from restored railway carriages to a luxury tent village, cabins and a camping ground. Start the day with a bush breakfast.

WINTON: Boulder Opal Motor Inn $$
Motel
16 Elderslie St, QLD 4735
Tel *(07) 4657 1211*
W boulderopalmotorinn.com.au
Comfortable motel with queen, single and two-bedroom choices. Good Outback-themed bistro.

Darwin and the Top End

DARWIN: Palms City Resort $$
Value for Money
64 Esplanade, NT 0800
Tel *(08) 8982 9200*
W palmscityresort.com
Surrounded by tropical gardens, this charming resort offers simple, self-contained rooms and villas.

DARWIN: Vibe Hotel Darwin Waterfront $$
Design
7 Kitchener Dr, NT 0800
Tel *(08) 8982 9998*
W vibehotels.com.au
Casual, bright and fun, with spacious rooms. Overlooks the swimming lagoon at Stokes Wharf.

Safari bungalow interior, Bamurru Plains, Mary River

DARWIN: SKYCITY Darwin $$$
Luxury
Gilruth Ave, NT 0801
Tel *(08) 8943 8888*
W skycitydarwin.com.au
Darwin's only five-star beachfront resort offers everything from standard rooms to luxury villas.

JABIRU: Gagudju Crocodile Holiday Inn $$
Luxury
1 Flinders St, NT 0886
Tel *(08) 8979 9000*
W gagudju-dreaming.com
A 110-room hotel built in the shape of a giant crocodile. A comfortable choice near Kakadu.

JIM JIM: Gagudju Lodge Cooinda $$
Rural
Kakadu Hwy, NT 0886
Tel *(08) 8979 1500*
W gagudjulodgecooinda.com.au
Comfortable lodge with spacious rooms. Convenient access to Kakadu National Park.

DK Choice

MARY RIVER: Bamurru Plains $$$
Rural
Harold Knowles Rd, Humpty Doo, NT 0836
Tel *1300 790 561*
W bamurruplains.com
Bamurru offers luxury bungalows set on the edge of the Mary River floodplain, with bathrooms, handmade furniture and fine linens. River cruises, nature walks, fishing, helicopter trips and 4WD safaris are offered. Air-conditioning on request. A truly memorable eco-adventure.

The Red Centre

ALICE SPRINGS: Alice Springs YHA $
Hostel
Cnr Parsons St & Leichhardt Terrace, NT 0870
Tel *(08) 8952 8855*
W yha.com.au
Award-winning hostel set around a historic outdoor movie theatre. Free nightly shows.

ALICE SPRINGS: Aurora Alice Springs $$
Value for Money
Leichhardt Terrace, NT 0870
Tel *(08) 8950 6666*
W auroraresorts.com.au
The town's most centrally located hotel with a riverside entrance. One-hour free Wi-Fi for guests.

ALICE SPRINGS: DoubleTree by Hilton $$
Luxury
82 Barrett Dr, NT 0870
Tel *(08) 8950 8000*
W doubletree3.hilton.com
High-end resort with mountain views from every room, but still within walking distance of town.

ALICE SPRINGS: Quest Alice Springs $$
Self-catering
9–10 South Terrace, NT 0870
Tel *(08) 8959 0000*
W questapartments.com.au
Stylish, spacious apartments perfectly suited to both business and leisure travellers.

ERLDUNDA: Desert Oaks Resort $$
Value for Money
Cnr Stuart & Lasseters hwys, NT 0872
Tel *(08) 8956 0984*
W desertoaksresort.com
No-frills roadhouse 250 km (155 miles) from Uluru National Park. Good base for exploring the natural sights of the Red Centre.

KINGS CANYON: Kings Canyon Resort Hotel $$$
Rural
Luritja Rd, Watarrka National Park, NT 872
Tel *(08) 8956 7442*
W kingscanyonresort.com.au
Comfortable retreat after a day of hiking. Stay in one of the spa rooms for complete indulgence.

YULARA: Outback Pioneer Hotel & Lodge $$
Hostel
Yulara Dr, NT 872
Tel *(02) 8296 8010*
W ayersrockresort.com.au/outback
Clean and basic. Some rooms have shared bathrooms. The communal BBQ area lends a friendly vibe.

YULARA: Desert Gardens Hotel $$$
Value for Money
Yulara Dr, NT 872
Tel *(02) 8296 8010*
W ayersrockresort.com.au/desert
Stroll in the gardens, sip cocktails by the pool and join in the free daily activities with the local Anangu people.

YULARA: Emu Walk Apartments $$$
Self-catering
Yulara Dr, NT 872
Tel *(02) 8296 8010*
W ayersrockresort.com.au/emu
Spacious apartments with well-equipped kitchens. Ideal for families and groups.

For more information on types of hotels *see page 481*

DK Choice

YULARA: Longitude 131 $$$
Luxury
Yulara Dr, NT 872
Tel *(02) 9918 4355*
W longitude131.com.au
The 15 secluded, elevated tents at Longitude 131 have magical views of Uluru, comfortable beds and ensuite bathrooms. Luxury in the wilderness in the truest sense of the word. Price includes airport transfers, and all meals and drinks.

Perth and the Southwest

ALBANY: The Beach House at Bayside $$$
Boutique
33 Barry Ct, Albany, WA 6330
Tel *(08) 9844 8844*
W thebeachhouseatbayside.com.au
Elegant country hotel with plush furnishings and warm service.

BUNBURY:
Bunbury Backpackers $
Hostel
16 Clifton St, WA 6230
Tel *1800 039 032*
W bunburybackpackers.com.au
Friendly hostel a short walk from the city and beach. Dorm-style rooms, plus singles and doubles.

BUSSELTON: The Sebel Busselton $$$
Self-catering
553 Bussell Hwy, WA 6280
Tel *(08) 9754 9800*
W thesebel.com
Good leisure facilities. The Margaret River wineries, beaches and restaurants are all nearby.

Outdoor pool amid lush green lawns at Windmills Break, Yallingup

DK Choice

FREMANTLE:
Be Fremantle $$$
Self-catering
43 Mews Rd, WA 6160
Tel *(08) 9430 3888*
W befremantle.com.au
In a prime spot overlooking bustling Fremantle harbour, these modern, tasteful apartments offer spectacular views of the ocean. Choose from one-, two- and three-bedroom apartments.

HYDEN: Wave Rock Motel $$
Motel
2 Lynch St, WA 6359
Tel *(08) 9880 5052*
W waverock.com.au
Comfortable motel with a spa, solar-heated pool, two restaurants and two bar areas.

KALGOORLIE: Rydges Kalgoorlie Resort and Spa $$$
Luxury
21 Davidson St, WA 6430
Tel *(08) 9080 0800*
W rydges.com/kalgoorlie
An oasis in the desert offering a day spa and spacious rooms with dream beds. Golf course nearby.

MARGARET RIVER: Pullman Resort Bunker Bay $$$
Luxury
42 Bunker Bay Rd, Naturaliste, WA 6281
Tel *(08) 9756 9100*
W pullmanhotels.com
Villa-style bungalows nestled on the beachfront. Close to the wineries.

PEMBERTON: Old Picture Theatre Holiday Apartments $$
Character
Cnr Ellis & Guppy sts, WA 6260
Tel *(08) 9776 1513*
W oldpicturetheatre.com.au
Unique accommodation in a converted 1929 movie theatre. Period fittings, modern amenities.

PERTH: Travelodge $$
Value for Money
417 Hay St, WA 6000
Tel *(08) 9238 1888*
W tfehotels.com
Bright rooms. Convenient downtown location. Free city buses.

PERTH: Adina Apartment Hotel $$$
Self-catering
33 Mounts Bay Rd, WA 6000
Tel *(08) 9217 8000*
W tfehotels.com
Well-equipped apartments in a central location. Good amenities.

PERTH: Fraser Suites $$$
Self-catering
10 Adelaide Terrace, WA 6004
Tel *(08) 9261 0000*
W frasershospitality.com
Executive accommodation in a 19-storey tower. Elegant open living areas and chic bathrooms.

ROTTNEST ISLAND:
Hotel Rottnest $$$
Beach
Bedford Ave, WA 6161
Tel *(08) 9292 5011*
W hotelrottnest.com.au
The island's only resort on the beach. Choose between bayside and garden courtyard rooms.

YALLINGUP: Cape Lodge $$$
Luxury
3341 Caves Rd, WA 6282
Tel *(08) 9755 6311*
W capelodge.com.au
Secluded lodge in distinctive Cape Dutch style. Excellent restaurant offering fine local food and wine.

YALLINGUP:
Seashells Yallingup $$$
Self-catering
Yallingup Beach Rd, WA 6282
Tel *(08) 9750 1500*
W seashells.com.au
Luxuriously furnished Art-Deco style apartments set in pretty gardens. Restaurant and bar next door.

YALLINGUP:
Windmills Break $$$
Boutique
2024 Caves Rd, WA 6282
Tel *(08) 9755 2341*
W windmillsbreak.com.au
Beautiful rooms with leather seats. Surrounded by lush grounds. Ideal for a romantic retreat.

YORK: Settlers House $$
Character
125 Avon Terrace, WA 6302
Tel *(08) 9641 1884*
W settlershouseyork.com.au
This modern motel with a colonial façade is located in the middle of the historic town of York. Close to nearby attractions.

North of Perth and the Kimberley

BROOME: Cable Beach Club Resort & Spa $$$
Luxury
Cable Beach Rd, WA 6725
Tel *(08) 9192 0400*
W cablebeachclub.com
Asian serenity and Colonial indulgence meet in this tropical haven overlooking Cable Beach.

BROOME: Oaks Cable Beach Sanctuary $$$
Beach
1 Lullfitz Dr, WA 6726
Tel *(08) 9192 8088*
W oakshotelsresorts.com
Range of self-contained options, including three-bedroom villas with private plunge pools.

BROOME: Pinctada McAlpine House $$$
Boutique
55 Herbert St, WA 6725
Tel *(08) 9192 0588*
W pinctada.com.au
Beautifully renovated 1910 pearler's home set in tropical gardens with exotic birds. Tranquil and private.

CAPE RANGE NATIONAL PARK: Sal Salis Ningaloo Reef $$$
Rural
Yardie Creek Rd, WA 6707
Tel *(02) 9571 6399*
W salsalis.com.au
Barefoot luxury abounds at this safari camp hidden in sand dunes, just metres from a pristine beach.

DAMPIER: Cygnet Bay Pearl Farm $$$
Rural
Cape Leveque Rd, WA 6725
Tel *(08) 9192 4283*
W cygnetbaypearls.com.au
This operational pearl farm offers stays in safari tents, historic pearlers' cottages and divers' quarters. Ideal for groups.

KUNUNURRA: Kununurra Country Club Resort $$
Value for Money
47 Coolibah Dr, WA 6743
Tel *(08) 9168 1024*
W kununurracountryclub.com.au
A sanctuary to return to after exploring Kimberley. Modern rooms and beautiful grounds.

DK Choice

NEW NORCIA: Monastery Guesthouse $
Character
Great Northern Hwy, WA 6509
Tel *(08) 9654 8002*
W newnorcia.wa.edu.au
A special and unusual experience, where guests can seek quiet contemplation, learn about the workings of the monastery and use it as a base to explore the town. Home-style meals and simply furnished rooms, most with ensuites. Guests are invited to dine with the monks. Payment is by donation only – A$80 recommended.

Stylish lounge room in a guest suite at The Louise in the Barossa

SHARK BAY: Monkey Mia Dolphin Resort $$$
Beach
1 Monkey Mia Rd, Denham, WA 6537
Tel *(08) 9948 1320*
W monkeymia.com.au
Offers a range of accommodation. Good facilities include an artesian spring hot tub. Dolphins visit the beach daily.

Adelaide and the Southeast

ADELAIDE: Adelaide Central YHA $
Hostel
135 Waymouth St, SA 5000
Tel *(08) 8414 3010*
W yha.com.au/adelaide
Big, friendly place close to the city's nightlife. Rooms for couples, families and solo travellers.

ADELAIDE: Adina Apartment Hotel Adelaide Treasury $$
Character
2 Flinders St, SA 5000
Tel *(08) 8112 0000*
W adinahotels.com.au
Old-world elegance in the old State Treasury building, converted into spacious and convenient self-contained apartments.

ADELAIDE: Majestic Roof Garden Hotel $$
Luxury
55 Frome St, SA 5000
Tel *(08) 8100 4400*
W majestichotels.com.au
Comfortable, quiet and airy rooms in a prime location near Rundle Mall. Rooftop views.

ADELAIDE: Stamford Grand Hotel $$$
Luxury
Moseley Sq, Glenelg, SA 5045
Tel *(08) 8376 1222*
W stamford.com.au/sga
Up-market hotel in the popular beachside suburb of Glenelg. Good dining and resort facilities.

THE BAROSSA: Abbotsford Country House $$$
Luxury
219 Yaldara Dr, Lyndoch, SA 5351
Tel *(08) 8524 4662*
W abbotsfordhouse.com
Rural retreat set on picturesque farmland with sweeping views.

THE BAROSSA: Collingrove Homestead $$$
Character
Angaston Rd, Angaston, SA 5353
Tel *(08) 8564 2061*
W collingrovehomestead.com.au
The former servants' quarters in this grand old home are now elegant guest rooms.

THE BAROSSA: The Kirche @ Charles Melton Wines $$$
Self-catering
Krondorf Rd, Tanunda, SA 5253
Tel *(08) 8563 3606*
W thekirche.com.au
Two rooms, a living area and a stunning kitchen in a renovated church. Great vineyard setting.

DK Choice

THE BAROSSA: The Louise $$$
Luxury
Cnr Seppeltsfield & Stonewell rds, Marananga, SA 5352
Tel *(08) 8562 2722*
W thelouise.com.au
Nestled among the Barossa vineyards, this tranquil boutique hotel offers the perfect retreat, with stylish suites, spa tubs and outdoor rain showers. The kitchen garden provides ingredients for the award-winning restaurant.

KANGAROO ISLAND: Southern Ocean Lodge $$$
Luxury
Hanson Bay, SA 5223
Tel *(02) 9918 4355*
W southernoceanlodge.com.au
Exclusive cliff-top lodge with dramatic ocean views. Dinner and wine are included in the tariff.

For more information on types of hotels *see page 481*

McLAREN VALE: McLaren Vale Studio Apartments $$$
Self-catering
222 Main St, SA 5171
Tel *(08) 8323 9536*
W mvsa.com.au
Bright, modern apartments, each themed around a different wine. Great beds and a spa bath.

McLAREN VALE: Serafino $$$
Value for Money
39 Kangarilla Rd, SA 5171
Tel *(08) 8323 8911*
W serafinomclarenvale.com.au
Spacious, comfortable rooms in a peaceful park-like setting.

MOUNT GAMBIER: Lakes Resort $$$
Value for Money
17 Lakes Terrace W, SA 5290
Tel *(08) 8725 5755*
W lakesresort.com.au
Set on the edge of a crater lake. Lovely city views. Quiet location.

MOUNT GAMBIER: Precinct on Jardine $$$
Self-catering
2 Jardine St, SA 5290
Tel *0438 224 626*
W precinctonjardine.com.au
Classy, fully furnished apartments designed to complement their heritage surroundings.

PENOLA: Must @ Coonawarra $$
Self-catering
126 Church St, SA 5277
Tel *(08) 8737 3444*
W mustatcoonawarra.com.au
Self-contained luxury apartments with contemporary decor.

PORT ELLIOT: Port Elliot Beach House YHA $$
Hostel
13 The Strand, SA 5212
Tel *(08) 8554 1885*
W yha.com.au
Affordable and comfortable dorms, double and family rooms in a stunning historic building.

ROBE: Robe House $$
Character
1A Hagen St, SA 5276
Tel *(08) 8768 2770*
W robehouse.com.au
Four apartments with high-vaulted ceilings in a charming 1847 sandstone building.

STIRLING: Thorngrove Manor Hotel $$$
Luxury
2 Glenside Ln, SA 5152
Tel *(08) 8339 6748*
W thorngrove.com.au
Flamboyant, castle-inspired suites offering outstanding amenities and absolute privacy.

VICTOR HARBOR: The Bluff Resort Apartments $$$
Luxury
123 Franklin Parade, Encounter Bay, SA 5211
Tel *(08) 8552 1200*
W bluffresort.com.au
Stylish, self-contained apartments with splendid ocean views.

The Yorke and Eyre Peninsulas and South Australian Outback

DK Choice

ARKAROOLA: Arkaroola Wilderness Sanctuary $$
Rural
Umberatana Rd, SA 5732
Tel *(08) 8648 4848*
W arkaroola.com.au
The family-run Arkaroola is a good base for exploring the spectacular Flinders Ranges. The resort has accommodation to suit all budgets, from camping to motel and self-contained apartments. Do not miss the Ridgetop tour's breathtaking 360-degree panorama.

CLARE VALLEY: Burra Heritage Cottages $$
Character
8–18 Truro St, Burra, SA 5417
Tel *(08) 8892 2461*
W burraheritagecottages.com.au
Built in 1856, these bluestone cottages all have open fires.

CLARE VALLEY: Clare Country Club $$
Value for Money
White Hut Rd, Clare, SA 5453
Tel *(08) 8842 1060*
W countryclubs.com.au/clare
Attractive resort offering well-appointed rooms with spa baths.

CLARE VALLEY: Clare Valley Motel $$
Character
74A Main North Rd, Mintaro, SA 5453
Tel *(08) 8842 2799*
W clarevalleymotel.com.au
Centrally located accommodation surrounded by scenic gardens.

COOBER PEDY: Desert Cave Hotel $$
Character
Hutchison St, SA 5723
Tel *(08) 8672 5688*
W desertcave.com.au
Sleep snug in one of the fantastic subterranean rooms here.

PORT HUGHES: The Lighthouse Port Hughes $$$
Character
42B Dowling Dr, SA 5554
Tel *0415 056 611*
W lighthouseporthughes.com.au
Well-appointed holiday home that can accommodate up to 12 guests. Ideal for families.

PORT LINCOLN: Port Lincoln YHA $
Hostel
24–26 London St, SA 5606
Tel *(08) 8682 3605*
W yha.com.au
Bright, ultra-modern hostel. Outdoor barbecue.

PORT LINCOLN: Port Lincoln Hotel $$
Beach
1 Lincoln Hwy, SA 5606
Tel *1300 766 100*
W portlincolnhotel.com.au
Deluxe spa suites and rooms with balconies overlooking beautiful Boston Bay.

WILPENA: Wilpena Pound Resort $$$
Rural
Hawker–Wilpena Rd, SA 5434
Tel *(08) 8648 0004*
W wilpenapound.com.au
An oasis in Flinders Ranges, this resort offers a range of rooms.

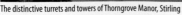

The distinctive turrets and towers of Thorngrove Manor, Stirling

Key to Price Guide *see page 482*

Façade of Hotel Windsor, one of Melbourne's grandest hotels

Melbourne

ALBERT PARK: Pullman Melbourne Albert Park $$
Luxury
65 Queens Rd, VIC 3004
Tel *(03) 9529 4300* **Map** 3 B5
W pullmanalbertpark.com.au
Smart business and leisure hotel with views of the city's Formula 1 Grand Prix track and golf course.

CARLTON: Carlton Terrace $$
Boutique
196 Drummond St, VIC 3053
Tel *(03) 9662 2735* **Map** 1 C1
W carltonterrace.com.au
Elegant mini apartments in a restored 19th-century house on a quiet tree-lined street.

**CARLTON:
Downtowner on Lygon** $$$
Value for Money
66 Lygon St, VIC 3053
Tel *(03) 9663 5555* **Map** 1 C1
W downtowner.com.au
Simple, good-quality rooms and serviced apartments aimed at sports fans and business travellers.

**CITY CENTRE:
Greenhouse Backpacker** $
Hostel
228 Flinders Ln, VIC 3000
Tel *(03) 9639 6400* **Map** 1 C4
W greenhousebackpacker.com.au
Appealing budget choice with well-sized rooms and dormitories. Pancakes on Sunday mornings.

**CITY CENTRE:
Quest Gordon Place** $$
Self-catering
24 Little Bourke St, VIC 3000
Tel *(03) 9663 2888* **Map** 1 D2
W questgordonplace.com.au
Compact but appealing serviced apartments in an attractive brick building with a gym and pool.

CITY CENTRE: Rendezvous Hotel Melbourne $$
Luxury
328 Flinders Street, VIC 3000
Tel *(03) 9250 1888* **Map** 1 C4
W tfehotels.com
Contemporary design and historic elegance combine here.

**CITY CENTRE:
Sofitel Melbourne on Collins** $$
Value for Money
25 Collins St, VIC 3000
Tel *(03) 9653 0000* **Map** 2 D3
W sofitel.com
Great comfort, facilities and service for the price. Huge windows with panoramic views.

CITY CENTRE: Victoria Hotel $$
Value for Money
215 Little Collins St, VIC 3000
Tel *(03) 9669 0000* **Map** 1 C3
W victoriahotel.com.au
Trusted landmark hotel with no-fuss hospitality. Close to theatres, restaurants and boutiques.

**CITY CENTRE:
The Crossley Hotel** $$$
Boutique
51 Little Bourke St, VIC 3000
Tel *(03) 9639 1639* **Map** 2 D2
W crossleyhotel.com.au
Crisp, clean rooms in a great location. Friendly service.

**CITY CENTRE:
The Grand Hotel Melbourne** $$$
Self-catering
33 Spencer St, VIC 3000
Tel *(03) 9611 4567* **Map** 1 B4
W grandhotelmelbourne.com.au
Serviced apartments in a heritage building. Elegant styling.

CITY CENTRE: Grand Hyatt $$$
Luxury
123 Collins St, VIC 3000
Tel *(03) 9657 1234* **Map** 2 D3
W melbourne.grand.hyatt.com
Five-star hotel designed to impress. Marble bathrooms and a large fitness centre.

CITY CENTRE: Hotel Causeway $$$
Boutique
275 Little Collins St, VIC 3000
Tel *(03) 9660 8888* **Map** 1 C3
W causeway.com.au
Basic rooms in a 1920s Art Deco building. Rooftop terrace, gym and steam room.

CITY CENTRE: Hotel Lindrum $$$
Boutique
26 Flinders St, VIC 3000
Tel *(03) 9668 1111* **Map** 2 D3
W hotellindrum.com.au
This chic place, in a heritage build-ing, has striking photography on the walls. Cosy and comfortable.

**CITY CENTRE:
The Hotel Windsor** $$$
Character
111 Spring St, VIC 3000
Tel *(03) 9633 6000* **Map** 2 D2
W thehotelwindsor.com.au
Grand Victorian hotel, built in the Gold Rush era. Five-star luxury.

CITY CENTRE: Jasper Hotel $$$
Boutique
489 Elizabeth St, VIC 3000
Tel *(03) 8327 2777* **Map** 1 B2
W jasperhotel.com.au
Sleek hotel with funky lighting and first-rate service. Rooms and suites available.

**CITY CENTRE:
Mantra on the Park** $$$
Self-catering
333 Exhibition St, VIC 3000
Tel *(03) 9668 2500* **Map** 2 D2
W mantra.com.au
Spacious apartments sleeping up to six. Crisp, contemporary style.

**CITY CENTRE:
Rydges Melbourne** $$$
Luxury
186 Exhibition St, VIC 3000
Tel *(03) 9662 0511* **Map** 2 D2
W rydges.com/melbourne
Stylish hotel in a large block opposite Her Majesty's Theatre. Top-quality beds and finishes.

**CITY CENTRE:
Stamford Plaza Melbourne** $$$
Luxury
111 Little Collins St, VIC 3000
Tel *(03) 9659 1000* **Map** 2 D3
W stamford.com.au/spm
Plush one- or two-bedroom suites with stylish touches.

**CITY CENTRE:
The Westin Melbourne** $$$
Luxury
205 Collins St, VIC 3000
Tel *(03) 9635 2222* **Map** 1 C3
W starwoodhotels.com/westin
Large, chic rooms. Some have balconies and offer magnificent views of the city.

FITZROY: Metropole Hotel Apartments $$$
Self-catering
44 Brunswick St, VIC 3065
Tel *(03) 9411 8100* **Map** 2 E1
W metropole.org
Peaceful accommodation within easy reach of the city.

FITZROY: The Nunnery $$$
Character
116 Nicholson St, VIC 3065
Tel *(03) 9419 8637* **Map** 2 D1
W nunnery.com.au
A former convent with elegant Georgian features. Guesthouse rooms or dorms with bunk beds.

For more information on types of hotels *see page 481*

FITZROY: Quest Royal Gardens Apartments $$$
Self-catering
8 Royal Ln, VIC 3065
Tel *(03) 9419 9888* **Map** 2 D1
W questapartments.com.au/royalgardens
Modern apartments. Pool and barbecue in the shared garden.

RICHMOND:
Amora Hotel Riverwalk $$
Value for Money
649 Bridge Rd, VIC 3121
Tel *(03) 9246 1200*
W melbourne.amorahotels.com
Pleasant apartments or clean, modern rooms with lovely views.

RICHMOND:
Richmond Hill Hotel $$
Character
353 Church St, VIC 3121
Tel *(03) 9428 6501* **Map** 4 E2
W richmondhillhotel.com.au
Housed in a beautiful heritage-listed Victorian terrace. Choice of basic or more elegant rooms.

SOUTH YARRA:
Hotel Claremont $
Character
189 Toorak Rd, VIC 3141
Tel *(03) 9826 8000*
W hotelclaremont.com
Friendly and popular budget hotel with comfortable double or family rooms and dorm bunks.

SOUTH YARRA:
The Como Melbourne $$
Luxury
630 Chapel St, VIC 3141
Tel *(03) 9825 2222* **Map** 4 E5
W accorhotels.com
Stylish pad with a bar favoured by celebrities. Cool, minimal design with colourful accents.

SOUTHBANK:
Crown Promenade Hotel $$$
Luxury
8 Whiteman St, VIC 3006
Tel *(03) 9292 6688* **Map** 1 C5
W crownhotels.com.au
Contemporary hotel with first-class leisure facilities, such as a sauna, steam rooms and a pool.

SOUTHBANK: Langham Hotel $$$
Luxury
1 Southgate Ave, VIC 3006
Tel *(03) 8696 8888* **Map** 1 C4
W melbourne.langhamhotels.com.au
Luxury at its best, with chandeliers, sweeping staircases and marble bathrooms. Superb facilities.

ST KILDA: Base Backpackers $
Hostel
17 Carlisle St, VIC 3182
Tel *(03) 8598 6200* **Map** 5 C5
W stayatbase.com
Budget hostel with a modern vibe. Has a women-only level.

ST KILDA: 28 Mary Street $$
Boutique
28 Mary St, VIC 3182 Map 5 B4
W bandmelbourne.com.au
Gorgeous, arty B&B in a Victorian house with ornate period features.

DK Choice

ST KILDA: The Prince $$$
Boutique
2 Acland St, VIC 3182
Tel *(03) 9536 1111* **Map** 5 B5
W theprince.com.au
Slick minimalist design and understated luxury hide behind the Art Deco façade of this hotel. Rooms are tastefully decorated and good value. Spend a relaxing day at the spa before enjoying dinner at the celebrated restaurant, Circa.

ST KILDA: Tolarno Hotel $$$
Boutique
42 Fitzroy St, VIC 3182
Tel *(03) 9537 0200* **Map** 5 B4
W hoteltolarno.com.au
Style-driven boutique hotel with bold contemporary design.

ST KILDA ROAD PRECINCT:
The Hotel Charsfield $$$
Boutique
478 St Kilda Rd, VIC 3004
Tel *(03) 9866 5511* **Map** 5 B1
W charsfield.com
Heritage-listed, Victorian-era mansion with tastefully decorated rooms. Facials, spa

and massages are some of the treats on offer.

ST KILDA ROAD PRECINCT:
Royce Hotel $$$
Boutique
379 St Kilda Rd, VIC 3004
Tel *(03) 9677 9900* **Map** 3 B4
W roycehotels.com.au
Chic, designer hotel with a ballroom and glamorous bar.

Western Victoria

AIREYS INLET:
Airey's Inlet Getaway Resort $$
Value for Money
2 Barton Court, VIC 3221
Tel *(03) 5289 7021*
W aireysinletgetaway.com.au
Fantastic leisure facilities, gardens and proximity to the ocean make this a popular resort.

APOLLO BAY: Chris's Beacon Point Restaurant & Villas $$$
Luxury
280 Skenes Creek Rd, VIC 3233
Tel *(03) 5237 6411*
W chriss.com.au
Well-equipped villas high above town. Floor-to-ceiling windows with stunning views.

BALLARAT:
Comfort Inn Sovereign Hill $$$
Character
41 Magpie St, VIC 3350
Tel *(03) 5337 1199*
W sovereignhill.com.au
Accommodations here range from up-market suites to bunk room units. Close to Sovereign Hill.

BENDIGO: Hotel Shamrock $$
Character
Cnr Pall Mall & Williamson St, VIC 3550
Tel *(03) 5443 0333*
W hotelshamrock.com.au
Elegant, affordable rooms in one of Bendigo's best hotels. A fixture on the social scene since 1854.

CASTLEMAINE:
Castlemaine Colonial Motel $$
Character
252 Barker St, VIC 3450
Tel *(03) 5472 4000*
W castlemainemotel.com.au
Luxury rooms and apartments in a renovated 19th-century building.

CASTLEMAINE: The Empyre $$$
Boutique
68 Mostyn St, VIC 3450
Tel *(03) 5472 5166*
W empyre.com.au
Painstakingly restored beautiful suites with antique furnishings, stately beds, chandeliers and leadlight windows.

Deluxe courtyard room, Amora Hotel, Richmond

Key to Price Guide *see page 482*

DAYLESFORD: Lake House $$$
Luxury
King St, VIC 3460
Tel *(03) 5348 3329*
W lakehouse.com.au
An all-round experience with an award-winning restaurant, a spa, deluxe suites and country gardens.

ECHUCA: Cock 'n' Bull $$$
Character
17–21 Warren St, VIC 3564
Tel *(03) 5480 6988*
W cocknbullechuca.com
Tastefully restored heritage home with luxury suites and a courtyard.

GEELONG:
Hotel Novotel Geelong $$
Value for Money
10–14 Eastern Beach Rd, VIC 3220
Tel *(03) 5223 1377*
W novotel.com
Located on the waterfront, with great views of the bay. Also close to the central business district.

GELLIBRAND:
Otways Tourist Park $$
Value for Money
25 Main Rd, VIC 3239
Tel *(03) 5235 8357*
W otwaystouristpark.com
Well-run park close to the beaches. Self-contained apartments and camping facilities.

HALLS GAP:
Grampians YHA Eco-Hostel $
Hostel
Grampians Rd, VIC 3381
Tel *(03) 5356 4544*
W yha.com.au
Eco-hostel with solar electricity, reverse cycle fans, waste-water and rainwater management.

HALLS GAP: Aurora Cottages $$$
Rural
300 Tunnel Rd, Pomonal, VIC 3381
Tel *0433 131 054*
W auroracottages.com.au
Private sanctuary in the bush with lovely cottages and the resident wildlife for company.

DK Choice

HEPBURN SPRINGS: Peppers Mineral Springs Hotel $$$
Luxury
124 Main Rd, VIC 3461
Tel *(03) 5348 2202*
W mineralspringshotel.com.au
Relaxing and romantic, this 1930s guesthouse has been transformed into a deluxe retreat retaining its Art Deco character. It fits in wonderfully with the surrounding landscape. Enjoy a roaring fire, an outstanding restaurant and a day spa.

LORNE: Mantra $$$
Luxury
Mountjoy Parade, VIC 3232
Tel *(03) 5228 9777*
W mantralorne.com.au
The only hotel in Lorne directly on the beachfront. Excellent leisure facilities and beautiful landscaped gardens.

MALDON: Miners Cottages $$$
Character
41 Main Street, VIC 3463
Tel *(04) 1354 1941*
W heritagecottages.com.au
Comfortable, self-contained private cottages with quality linen and full kitchens.

MILDURA: Quality Mildura Grand Hotel $$
Value for Money
Seventh St, VIC 3500
Tel *(03) 5023 0511*
W qualityhotelmilduragrand.com.au
Variety of accommodation choices. Home to the award-winning Cellars restaurant.

PORT FAIRY: Oscars Waterfront Boutique Hotel $$$
Boutique
41B Gipps St, VIC 3284
Tel *(03) 5568 3022*
W oscarswaterfront.com
Overlooking the marina, the stylish riverfront rooms have comfortable king-sized beds. Just a short stroll to the beach.

TORQUAY:
Peppers The Sands Resort $$$
Luxury
2 Sands Blvd, VIC 3228
Tel *(03) 5264 3333*
W peppers.com.au
Perched on a headland with spectacular views. Excellent golf course and heated indoor pool.

Eastern Victoria

BAIRNSDALE:
Comfort Inn Riversleigh $$
Rural
1 Nicholson St, VIC 3875
Tel *(03) 5152 6966*
W riversleigh.com.au
Victorian property with ornate balconies, comfortable rooms and fine views of the Mitchell River.

BEECHWORTH:
Barwood House $$
Character
15B Loch St, VIC 3747
Tel *0409 284 110*
W barwoodhouse.com.au
Elegant Victorian country house offering well-appointed rooms with modern furnishings.

Entrance to Peppers Mineral Springs Retreat, Hepburn Springs

BRIGHT: Ashwood Cottages $$
Self-catering
22A Ashwood Ave, VIC 3741
Tel *(03) 5755 1081*
W ashwoodcottages.com.au
Charming one-bedroom cottages with wood-burning stoves. Peaceful green surrounds.

DINNER PLAIN: Peppers Rundells Alpine Lodge $$$
Rural
Big Muster Dr, VIC 3898
Tel *(03) 5159 6422*
W rundells.com.au
Rustic, cosy lodge. Provides ski equipment in the winter and tennis and mountain biking in the summer. Open from March to September.

FALLS CREEK:
The Falls Creek Hotel $$$
Ski Lodge
23 Falls Creek Rd, VIC 3699
Tel *(03) 5758 3282*
W fallscreekhotel.com.au
Ski-in, ski-out chalet-style hotel open from June onwards. All rooms have slope views.

GIPPSLAND LAKES:
The Moorings at Metung $$
Self-catering
44 Metung Rd, VIC 3904
Tel *(03) 5156 2750*
W themoorings.com.au
Spacious waterfront apartments with one to three bedrooms and good facilities.

KING VALLEY: Casa Luna $$
Rural
1569 Boggy Creek Rd, Myrrhee, VIC 3732
Tel *(03) 5729 7650*
W casaluna.com.au
Stylish and tranquil retreat. King suites have private balconies and queen suites have walk-in showers. Gourmet getaway featuring Italian-style cuisine.

For more information on types of hotels *see page 481*

LAKES ENTRANCE: Comfort Inn & Suites Emmanuel $
Value for Money
151 Esplanade, VIC 3909
Tel *(03) 5155 1444*
w choicehotels.com.au
With rooms, apartments, a barbecue area and a playground, this is a good option for families.

**MANSFIELD:
Mansfield Valley Motor Inn** $$
Value for Money
Cnr Elvins St & Maroondah Hwy, VIC 3722
Tel *(03) 5775 1300*
w mansfieldvalley.com.au
Simple rooms and apartments with views of Mount Buller. Big gardens with a barbecue area.

MANSFIELD: The Riverhouse at Howqua Dale $$
Luxury
85 Howqua River Rd, VIC 3722
Tel *(03) 5777 3503*
w theinspiredtraveller.com.au
This country house set among beautiful riverside gardens offers privacy and comfort. Self-catering or B&B. Tennis court on site.

**MORNINGTON PENINSULA:
Mount Martha B&B By the Sea** $$
B&B
539 The Esplanade, Mount Martha, VIC 3934
Tel *(03) 5974 1019*
w mountmarthabandb
bythesea.com.au
Well-furnished, luxury rooms with splendid ocean or garden views.

**MORNINGTON PENINSULA:
Bayplay Adventure Lodge** $$$
Hostel
46 Canterbury Jetty Rd, Blairgowrie, VIC 3942
Tel *(03) 5984 0888*
w bayplay.com.au
Simple rooms and good facilities. Perfect for group getaways.

Glen Isla House surrounded by heritage gardens, Phillip Island

**MOUNT BAW BAW:
Kelly's Lodge** $$$
Rural
11 Frosti Ln, VIC 3068
Tel *(03) 5165 1129*
w kellyslodge.com.au
Intimate alpine lodge very close to the ski lift and toboggan run. Big summer discounts.

**MOUNT BULLER:
Mount Buller Chalet** $$$
Rural
207 Summit Rd, VIC 3723
Tel *(03) 5777 6566*
w mtbullerchalet.com.au
A winter-only luxury retreat with first-class fitness facilities, including sauna, gym and squash court.

**MOUNT HOTHAM:
Snowbird Inn** $$
Rural
Great Alpine Rd, VIC 3741
Tel *(03) 5759 3503*
w snowbirdinn.com.au
This central, no-frills lodge near the ski lift offers backpacker-style rooms. There is a bistro and café.

DK Choice

NARBETHONG: Woodlands Rainforest Retreat $$$
Rural
137 Manby Rd, VIC 3778
Tel *(03) 5963 7150*
w woodlandscottages.com.au
Built using local beech and mountain ash, each of the four cottages in this beautiful woodland property is perfectly secluded for a romantic escape. Watch or hear cockatoos, parrots, wallabies and wombats from the balcony. Savour the chef-prepared dinners for two.

**PHILLIP ISLAND:
Glen Isla House** $$$
Luxury
230–232 Church St, Cowes, VIC 3923
Tel *(03) 5952 1882*
w glenisla.com
Award-winning hotel in a heritage property with a homely atmosphere. Set amid lush gardens with 100-year-old oak trees. Close to the beach.

PHILLIP ISLAND: Phillip Island Retreat and Cottages $$$
Self-catering
183–189 Justice Rd, Cowes, VIC 3922
Tel *(04) 0094 0301*
w phillipislandretreatand
cottages.com.au
A four-bedroom house and many one-bedroom cottages on an attractive property. Sustainably designed and surrounded by fragrant eucalyptus trees.

POREPUNKAH: Buffalo Motel & Country Retreat $$
Value for Money
6774 Great Alpine Rd, VIC 3740
Tel *(03) 5756 2242*
w buffalomotelretreat.com.au
Modest and relaxed family retreat with comfortable, warm rooms. Close to the Rail Trail bike track.

**WALHALLA:
Windsor House B&B** $$
Character
12 Right Hand Branch Rd, VIC 3825
Tel *(03) 5165 6237*
w windsorhouse.com.au
Heritage property with period features dating back to the 1890s.

**WILSONS PROMONTORY:
Tidal River Cabins** $$
Rural
National Parks Service, Tidal River, VIC 3690
Tel *(03) 5680 9555*
w parkweb.vic.gov.au
National Park camps, eco-friendly cabins and luxury safari-style tents. Open from February to November. Book well ahead.

YARRA VALLEY: Sanctuary House Resort Motel $$
Value for Money
326 Badger Creek Rd, Healesville, VIC 3777
Tel *(03) 5962 5148*
w sanctuaryhouse.com.au
Surrounded by native bush, this is a resort-style motel offering good family facilities.

Tasmania

BURNIE: Glen Osborne House $$
Character
9 Aileen Crescent, TAS 7320
Tel *(03) 6431 9866*
w glenosbornehouse.com.au
This ornate two-storey mansion houses an elegant B&B furnished with antiques and fireplaces.

COLES BAY: Freycinet Lodge $$$
Rural
Freycinet National Park, TAS 7215
Tel *(03) 6256 7222*
w freycinetlodge.com.au
Eco-friendly lodge with one- and two-room cabins set in bushland. Some balconies have sea views.

COLES BAY: Saffire Freycinet $$$
Luxury
2532 Coles Bay Rd, TAS 7215
Tel *(03) 6256 7888*
w saffire-freycinet.com.au
Award-winning contemporary luxury suites that complement the natural coastal bush setting. Views of Great Oyster Bay.

CRADLE MOUNTAIN: Cradle Mountain Lodge $$$
Rural
4038 Cradle Mountain Rd, TAS 7306
Tel *(03) 6492 2100*
W cradlemountainlodge.com.au
Award-winning lodge in a rainforest setting. Don't miss the fantastic Waldheim Alpine Spa.

HOBART: The Shipwright's Arms $
Value for Money
29 Trumpeter St, Battery Pt, TAS 7004
Tel *(03) 6223 5551*
W shipwrightsarms.com.au
A traditional English-style pub in the quaint village setting of Battery Point. Comfortable rooms.

**HOBART:
Customs House Hotel** $$
Character
1 Murray St, TAS 7000
Tel *(03) 6234 6645*
W customshousehotel.com
Possibly the best value in town, with large Colonial-style rooms and a historic sandstone pub.

HOBART: Wrest Point $$
Luxury
410 Sandy Bay Rd, TAS 7005
Tel *(03) 6221 1888*
W wrestpoint.com.au
Casino-hotel complex with plush, spacious rooms and an iconic revolving restaurant.

DK Choice

HOBART: The Henry Jones Art Hotel $$$
Luxury
22 Hunter St, TAS 7000
Tel *(03) 6210 7700*
W thehenryjones.com
This hotel is located in a former jam factory on the harbourfront. The individually designed guest rooms, erected around a magnificent glass atrium, reflect Australia's early trade with China and India. The walls display art by emerging local artists.

HOBART: The Islington $$$
Luxury
321 Davey St, TAS 7000
Tel *(03) 6220 2123*
W islingtonhotel.com
Lavish and tasteful historic home looking out on to Mt Wellington. King-sized beds, large bathtubs and a choice of sitting rooms.

HOBART: Macquarie Manor $$$
Character
172 Macquarie St, TAS 7000
Tel *(03) 6224 4999*
W macmanor.com.au
Classic 19th-century Colonial-style manor house. Quiet and

Luxury furnishings of a garden room at the Islington hotel, Hobart

centrally located, with elegant furnishings. Modern facilities.

**HOBART:
The MONA Pavilions** $$$
Luxury
655 Main Rd, Berriedale, TAS 7011
Tel *(03) 6277 9900*
W mona.net.au
State-of-the-art pavilions on the banks of the Derwent River. Part of the MONA complex.

LAUNCESTON: Country Club Resort & Villas $$
Rural
Country Club Ave, TAS 7250
Tel *(03) 6335 5777*
W countryclubtasmania.com.au
Spacious rooms and villas in a sprawling setting. Lots of activities, from golf to horse riding. Wallabies graze in the grounds.

LAUNCESTON: Quamby Estate $$
Luxury
1145 Westwood Rd, TAS 7292
Tel *(03) 6392 2135*
W quambyestate.com.au
Extensive estate with a genteel country atmosphere. Large, individually designed rooms.

**LAUNCESTON:
Peppers Seaport Hotel** $$$
Character
28 Seaport Blvd, TAS 7250
Tel *(03) 6345 3333*
W peppers.com.au
Built in the shape of a ship and located in a former dock, this smart hotel has contemporary rooms, each with a kitchenette.

**LAUNCESTON:
York Mansions** $$$
Character
9–11 York St, TAS 7250
Tel *(03) 6334 2933*
W yorkmansions.com.au
Airy two-room apartments built within a National Trust classified mansion house. Some are furnished with antiques.

**PORT ARTHUR:
Stewarts Bay Lodge** $$
Rural
6955 Arthur Hwy, TAS 7182
Tel *(03) 6250 2888*
W stewartsbaylodge.com.au
One-, two- or three-bedroom log cabins in the bush, all with decks overlooking the water. Close to the Port Arthur Historic Site.

ROSS: Man-o-Ross Hotel $
Character
35 Church St, TAS
Tel *(03) 6381 5445*
W manoross.com
Sandstone pub with Colonial-style rooms, in the heart of a picturesque village.

STANLEY: Old Cable Station $$
Character
435 Green Hills Rd, TAS 7331
Tel *(03) 6458 1312*
W oldcablestation.com.au
This 1930s telecommunications station on the remote northwest coast is now a stylish B&B with self-contained suites.

STRAHAN: Risby Cove $$
Rural
The Esplanade, TAS 7468
Tel *(03) 6471 7572*
W risbycove.com.au
Luxury waterfront motel overlooking a private marina. Studio, one- and two-room suites Superb restaurant and art gallery.

One of the impressive hi-tech MONA pavilions, Hobart

For more information on types of hotels *see page 481*

WHERE TO EAT AND DRINK

Australia has developed a strong culinary identity. Modern Australian (or Mod Oz, as it is more commonly known) cuisine is a fresh, inventive style that gives local ingredients, particularly seafood and beef, a Mediterranean or Asian twist. Australia also has a wealth of ethnic restaurants, reflecting the country's multicultural population. Native Australian food is increasingly popular, as some chefs begin to embrace meats such as kangaroo and emu, and native fruits and vegetables. The best restaurants offer a superb selection of local wines or beers *(see pp502–3)*.

Picturesque outside terrace at Lavandula La Trattoria *(see p531)*

Types of Restaurants

All major Australian cities have a wide variety of formal and informal restaurants, bistros, cafés and pubs offering everything from haute cuisine to quick snacks. Many have outdoor tables for alfresco dining. Outside the main cities, some restaurants, particularly at wineries and high-end resorts, are destinations in themselves.

Prices vary widely but tend to be slightly lower when compared to places in Europe and the United States. As a general guideline, the bill at a showcase restaurant in Melbourne or Sydney featuring a celebrity chef will be at least A$150 per head, including a shared bottle of wine. At a BYO (Bring Your Own) or an unpretentious Asian or Italian restaurant, it may be A$30–50 per head. A meal at a pub, café or snack bar should generally cost no more than A$20–40 per head, if you include the price of a drink.

Eating Hours and Reservations

Most restaurants serve lunch between noon and 3pm. Dinner tends to be served from 6:30 to 10:30pm, but budget and ethnic eateries often close earlier. Some bistros and cafés stay open from breakfast time until late at night. Restaurants in hotels are usually open daily, but other eateries may close one day a week, usually Mondays. For fashionable, high-end restaurants, booking in advance by phone or email is highly recommended.

Paying and Tipping

Most Australian restaurants accept major credit cards, but in cafés and pubs a minimum amount may apply for card payments. A 10 per cent Goods and Services Tax (GST) is included in all restaurant bills in Australia. Tipping is discretionary and not compulsory. In a restaurant, adding 10 per cent of the total bill to the credit card transaction, or leaving the same in cash on the table when leaving, is generally appropriate.

Children

Most restaurateurs will allow admission to children as long as they are well behaved. Many restaurants also provide high chairs and a children's menu. The best budget options for families are local sports club bistros, pub bistros, hamburger chains or one of the many no-fuss Italian or Asian eateries.

Wheelchair Access

Spurred by legislation in the various states, most restaurants now provide special wheelchair access and toilet facilities for the disabled. However, it is still advisable to check the facilities available in advance.

Vegetarians

It is rare for a restaurant not to feature at least one dish for vegetarians; a variety of choices is the norm, particularly in regions where there is an abundance of home-grown produce. There are also specialist vegetarian restaurants and cafés in the major cities.

Alfresco dining at Skillogalee Wines in the Clare Valley *(see p525)*

Doyles on the Beach in Watsons Bay, Sydney *(see p507)*

In the event of any special dietary requirements, it is recommended to call the restaurant in advance; this is especially pertinent for eateries in rural areas.

Ravesi's on Bondi Beach, one of many great eateries at the famous beach *(see p507)*

Alcohol and Other Drinks

If a restaurant is described as licensed, it refers to its licence to sell alcohol on its premises. Australian wine lists are outstanding and generally highlight the wines of the particular state or district *(see pp40–41)*. Wine is sold by the bottle, carafe or glass. There is usually a good choice of beers, ales, ciders and spirits as well.

BYO restaurants, which are not licensed to sell alcohol, are extremely popular. These offer diners the opportunity to bring the wines they wish to drink with their meal. Beer, however, may not be permitted. A minimal corkage fee is usually charged.

Tap water is safe, though many people prefer to drink bottled still or sparkling water. It is illegal for restaurants to charge for tap water, but bottled water can be expensive. Fresh fruit juices and Italian-style coffee are also very popular *(see pp502–3)*.

Dress

The phrase "smart casual" sums up the Australian approach to eating out. Dress codes are virtually non-existent, although a handful of the more up market restaurants may ask men to wear a tie in the evenings.

Most places, including beachside cafés, frown on beachwear, so remember to carry something to cover up.

Smoking

Smoking is banned inside all restaurants, cafés and pubs, but it is permitted in limited designated outside areas.

Recommended Restaurants

The restaurants recommended on the following pages are among the best in their categories, whether serving haute cuisine or pub meals.

The list includes a range of eateries that offer everything from Modern Australian dishes, such as fresh fish with Oriental spices, to pub classics, such as pies and burgers (more popularly known as counter meals), as well as excellent

options for coffee and cake. In international cuisine, there are Italian classics such as pizza and pasta, Chinese banquets of meat or seafood with rice or noodles, and Japanese-style sushi to choose from. Some top-end restaurants offer degustation or tasting menus – a succession of tiny, delicious courses. Other culinary trends are afternoon tea – a selection of savouries and cakes or scones, served with speciality tea or coffee and "share plates" designed for diners to share a variety of dishes.

Restaurants which are labelled as "DK Choice" are distinctive and highly acclaimed options. Many of these are award-winning, special-occasion restaurants that offer something truly unique.

Stunning views of the Opera House from the Dining Room, Sydney *(see p504)*

The Flavours of Australia

Modern Australian cuisine has been evolving from traditional British since World War II. An influx of people from Italy, Greece, Turkey, Lebanon, Thailand, China, Malaysia, Indonesia and Vietnam (to name but a few) have contributed influences to what is now known as Mod-Oz cuisine. However, a lot of Aussies will still sit down to a Sunday roast and swelter over turkey on a midsummer Christmas day. Dramatically varying climates over such a large country mean an abundance and diversity of local produce, so it's no surprise that some of the world's best chefs hail from this rich and exciting culinary playground.

Wattleseed, pepperberry and lemon myrtle

Chef filleting snapper, one of Australia's finest fish

Native Ingredients

There are many native foods in Australia that have been used by Aborigines for thousands of years, and which are now becoming widely popular. Quandong, munthari, bush tomato, wild limes and rosellas are native fruits with distinctive colours, flavours and textures, while warrigal greens are a spinach-like herb. All of them are still primarily wild-harvested by Aboriginal communities. Although native Australians never used seasonings in their campfire cooking, modern Australians have discovered the exciting flavours of such indigenous herbs and spices as lemon myrtle, wattleseed, mountain pepperleaf, pepperberry, forest berry and akudjura. Native meats such as kangaroo and emu are also being used more frequently, although don't expect to see witchity grubs on many menus. These native meats sit alongside a vast and impressive array of beef, lamb and, of course, seafood. Fish native to Australia include barramundi, trevally and blue-eye trevalla. The popular native shellfish, yabbies and Moreton Bay bugs, are similar to, but smaller than, lobster. Also worth a mention is the lovely fragrant honey produced out of native Australian forests.

Samphire Snapper Lobster Oysters
Scallops Red mullet
Selection of seafood to be found in the oceans around Australia

Australian Dishes and Specialities

Anzac biscuits

Australians love a barbecue, as a social and culinary hub, and you will find a wide variety of meats and cuisines on the grill. Major cities offer a huge choice of foods, from high end French-style fare to fish and chips or cheap and cheerful noodle bars. Melbourne, in particular, has a strong Greek and Italian influence and prides itself on a vibrant café culture, serving unbeatable coffee. Meat pies are a staple in the Aussie diet with the annual Meat Pie Competition attracting great interest, and you will see pies inspired by different cuisines such as Thai, Indian and Moroccan.

For those with a sweet tooth, pumpkin scones are a traditional Australian favourite, alongside passionfruit tart, Lamingtons, Pavlova, and oat and coconut Anzac biscuits.

Kangaroo pizza The Italian classic is given a modern Australian spin with the addition of seared lean fillet of kangaroo.

Vegetable stall at Queen Victoria Market, Melbourne *(see p390)*

The World on a Plate

Having one of the most eclectic populations on earth means great things for food (or "tucker"). Australians are as happy exporting their wealth of homegrown produce as they are embracing international cuisine.

Farming plays a very important role in Australia, the world's largest producer of beef. The lush pastures on the coast are particularly good for farming, and the milk-fed lamb from New South Wales is as wonderful as the brie produced in South Australia. King Island, between Victoria and Tasmania in the Bass Strait, is dedicated to dairy produce; farmers sell their amazing cheese and creams all around the country. Alongside the rapidly growing wine industry is olive oil and balsamic vinegar production, examples of which are found at the cellar door of many vineyards.

Australia has one of the most diverse marine faunas in the world, due to its range of

Wooden crate of sweet, juicy apples from Tasmania

habitats, from the warm tropical northern waters to the sub-Antarctic Tasman sea, as well as its geographical isolation. A total of 600 marine and freshwater species are caught in Australian waters, providing chefs with plenty of inspiration.

Every kind of fruit and vegetable is produced in Australia. Pineapples and mangoes are widely grown in Queensland, apples in Victoria, strawberries in New South Wales and rambutans in the Northern Territory. Exotic and notoriously hard to farm, truffles have been cultivated in several states, highlighting just how versatile Australia's land is.

Food on the Run

Sushi Major cities are dotted with tiny counters offering fresh sushi to grab on the go.

Juice bars This booming industry is found on most city streets, serving delicious, cool blends of fruit.

Milk bars As well as milk-shakes, ice creams and salads, these sell a wide range of deep-fried foods.

Coffee & cake Little cafés everywhere also sell Italian-style cakes and pastries.

Pubs Most pubs serve a decent steak sandwich.

Pies An Aussie institution, pies are readily available. Look out for gourmet versions.

Grilled barramundi Served on ginger and bok choy risotto, this is a great mix of local seafood and Asian flavours.

Prawn laksa This spicy coconut noodle soup can be found all over the country in noodle bars, cafés and pubs.

Lamingtons These little Victoria sponge cakes are coated in chocolate icing and shredded coconut.

What to Drink in Australia

Australia has one of the world's finest cuisines and part of its enjoyment is the marriage of the country's wine with great food. Australians have a very relaxed attitude to food and wine mixes, so red wine with fish and a cold, dry Riesling as an aperitif can easily be the order of the day. Also, many of the restuarants in the wine regions offer exclusive brands, or offer rare wines so these are worth seeking out. It is estimated that

there are 10,000 different Australian wines on the market at any one time. Australians also enjoy some of the best value wine in the world (see pp40–41). Australians also love their beer, with a wide range of choices available. While the health-conscious can choose from a variety of bottled waters and select-your-own, freshly-squeezed fruit juices. Imported wines, beers and spirits are also readily available.

Domaine Chandon in the Yarra Valley (see p447) in Eastern Victoria

Sparkling Wine

Australia is justly famous for its sparkling wines, from Yalumba's Angas Brut to Seppelts Salinger. Most recently, Tasmania has showed considerable promise in producing some high quality sparkling wines, particularly Pirie from Pipers Brook. However, the real hidden gems are the sparkling red wines – the best are made using the French Méthode Champenois, matured over a number of years and helped by a small drop of vintage port. The best producers of red sparkling wines are Rockford and Seppelts. These sparkling wines are available throughout the country from "bottle shops".

Angus Brut premium

White Wine

Rhine Riesling   Botrytis Semillon

The revolution in wine making in the 1970s firmly established dry wines made from international grape varieties on the Australian table. Chardonnay, Sauvignon Blanc, and more recently Viognier and Pinot Gris are all popular. However, there has also been a renaissance and growing appreciation for Riesling, Marsanne and Semillon, which age very gracefully. Australia's other great wines are their fortified and desert wines. Australian winemakers use botrytis cinera, or noble rot, to make luscious dessert wines such as De Bortoli's "Noble One".

Some of the vines in Australia are the oldest in the world

Grape Type	Best Regions	Best Producers
Chardonnay	Geelong, Beechworth (VIC)	Bannockburn, Giaconda, Stonier
	Hunter Valley (NSW)	Lakes Folly, Rosemount, Tyrrell's
	Margaret River (WA)	Leeuwin Estate, Pierro, Cullen
	The Barossa (SA)	Penfolds, Mountadam
Semillon	Hunter Valley (NSW)	Brokenwood, McWilliams, Tyrrell
	The Barossa (SA)	Peter Lehmann, Willows, Penfolds
	Margaret River (WA)	Moss Wood, Voyager, Evans & Tate
Riesling	Clare Valley and Adelaide Hills (SA)	Grosset, Pikes, Petaluma, Mitchells
	The Barossa (SA)	Richmond Grove, Leo Buring, Yalumba
	Tasmania (TAS)	Piper's Brook
Marsanne	Goulburn Valley (VIC)	Chateau Tahbilk, Mitchelton

Red Wine

Australia's benchmark red is Penfold's Grange, the creation of the late vintner Max Schubert in the 1950s and 1960s. Due to his work, Shiraz has established itself as Australia's premium red variety. However, there is also plenty of diversity with the acknowledged quality of Cabernet Sauvignon produced in the Coonawarra. Recently, there has also been a re-appraisal of traditional "old vine" Grenache and Mourvedre varieties in the Barossa and McLaren Vale.

Vineyards of Leeuwin Estate, Margaret River

Shiraz   Pinot Noir

Grape Type	Best Regions	Best Producers
Shiraz	Hunter Valley (NSW)	Brokenwood, Lindmans, Tyrrells
	Great Western, Sunbury (VIC)	Bests, Seppelts, Craiglee
	The Barossa (SA)	Henschke, Penfolds, Rockford, Torbreck
	McLaren Vale (SA)	Hardys, Coriole, Chapel Hill
	Margaret River, Great Southern (WA)	Cape Mentelle, Plantagenet
Cabernet Sauvignon	Margaret River (WA)	Cape Mentelle, Cullen, Moss Wood
	Coonawarra (SA)	Wynns, Lindemans, Bowen Estate
	The Barossa, Adelaide Hills (SA)	Penfolds, Henschke, Petaluma
	Yarra Valley, Great Western (VIC)	Yarra Yering, Yerinberg, Bests
Merlot	Yarra Valley, Great Western (VIC)	Bests, Yara Yering
	Adelaide Hills, Clare Valley (SA)	Petaluma, Pikes
Pinot Noir	Yarra Valley (VIC)	Coldstream Hills, Tarrawarra
	Gippsland, Geelong (VIC)	Bass Philip, Bannockburn, Shadowfax

Beer

Most Australian beer is vat fermented real ale or lager, both consumed chilled. Full-strength beer has an alcohol content of around 4.8 per cent, mid-strength beers have around 3.5 per cent, while "light" beers have less than 3 per cent. Traditionally heat sterilized, cold filtration is now becoming increasingly popular. Among the hundreds of fine lagers and stouts are James Boag and Cascade from Tasmania, XXXX Gold from Queensland, Fosters and VB from Victoria, Toohey's New from New South Wales and Cooper's Sparkling Ale from South Australia. Aficionados of real ale should seek out a pub brewery. Beer is ordered by glass size: a schooner is a 426 ml (15 fl oz) glass and a middy is 284 ml (10 fl oz) in NSW, though glass sizes can vary.

VB (Victoria   Cascade Premium
Bitter) Beer   Lager

Spirits

Australian distillers produce fine dark and white rums from Queensland's sugar cane plantations (see p250). Notable labels include Bundaberg, from the town of that name, and Beenleigh. Australia's grape vintage is also the basis of good-value domestic brandies. Popular labels are St Agnes and McWilliams.

Bundaberg rum

Other Drinks

With a climate ranging from tropical to alpine, Australia has year round fresh fruit for juicing. Its apples are also used to make cider. Scores of still and sparkling mineral and other bottled waters now supply an annual market of nearly 200 million litres. Hepburn Spa, Deep Spring and Mount Franklin have national distribution. Coffee, prepared in a wide variety of ways, is another immensely popular drink with Australians.

White coffee

Pear and kiwi   Banana   Strawberry
frappé   smoothie   juice

Caffe latte

Where to Eat and Drink

Sydney

The Rocks and Circular Quay

Vintage Café on the Rocks $
Mediterranean   **Map** 1 B2
Shop R2, 3 Nurses Walk,
NSW 2000
Tel *(02) 9252 2055*
Tucked away in a cobbled court-
yard, this is a great little place
for a breakfast omelette, tapas
or a plate of paella accompanied
by a glass of sangria.

Heritage $$
Belgian   **Map** 1 B3
135 Harrington St, NSW 2000
Tel *(02) 8488 2460*
Lively bar and restaurant with a
good selection of Belgian beers
on tap. Try the mussels, cooked
one of eight ways and served
in a pot.

MCA Café $$
Modern Australian   **Map** 1 B2
Museum of Contemporary Art,
140 George St, NSW 2000
Tel *(02) 9250 8443*
Sydney favourites such as
pan-fried kingfish, risotto, and
twice-baked cheese soufflé.
Fabulous harbour views from
the terrace.

Aria $$$
Modern Australian   **Map** 1 C2
1 Macquarie Street, East Circular
Quay, NSW 2000
Tel *(02) 9240 2255*
Striking harbour views and
imaginative fine dining in this
elegant space close to the Opera
House. Extensive international
wine list.

Café Sydney $$$
Modern Australian   **Map** 1 B3
Level 5, Customs House, 31 Alfred St,
NSW 2000
Tel *(02) 9251 8683*   **Closed** *Sat lunch*
Buzzing restaurant in the historic
Customs House. A tandoor oven,
wood-fired grill, rotisserie and
wok turn out a variety of food.

The Dining Room $$$
Modern Australian   **Map** 1 B1
Park Hyatt Sydney, 7 Hickson Rd,
NSW 2000
Tel *(02) 9256 1234*
A stylish spot with incredible views
of the Sydney Opera House.
Guests can enjoy elegant food
while watching the ferries pass by.

DK Choice

Est $$$
Modern Australian   **Map** 1 B3
Level 1, Establishment,
252 George St, NSW 2000
Tel *(02) 9240 3000*   **Closed** *Sun*
With highly imaginative food,
a superb wine list and top-
notch service, this fine-dining
restaurant keeps hauling in the
awards. Head chef Peter Doyle
is considered one of the
founding fathers of Modern
Australian cuisine. His tasting
menus offer diners a series of
key dishes, matched with wines.

Quay $$$
Modern Australian   **Map** 1 B2
Upper Level, Overseas Passenger
Terminal, NSW 2000
Tel *(02) 9251 5600*
Spectacular views and food to
match. Star chef Peter Gilmore
combines fresh ingredients in
surprising ways.

Price Guide

Prices are based on a three-course meal
per person, with half a bottle of house
wine and service charges.

$	up to A$50
$$	A$50 to A$90
$$$	over A$90

Rockpool $$$
Modern Australian   **Map** 1 B3
11 Bridge St, NSW 2000
Tel *(02) 9252 1888*   **Closed** *Sun*
Celebrity chef Neil Perry uses
European and Asian influences
to create elaborate dishes with
beautiful textures and flavours.

Sailors' Thai $$$
Thai   **Map** 1 B3
106 George St, NSW 2000
Tel *(02) 9251 2466*   **Closed** *Sun;*
lunch (except Fri)
Complex, sophisticated food
prepared with superb, top-
quality ingredients. There is
a relaxed canteen upstairs.

Yoshii $$$
Japanese   **Map** 1 A3
115 Harrington St, NSW 2000
Tel *(02) 9247 2566*   **Closed** *Sun*
One of Sydney's top sushi chefs,
Ryuichi Yoshii serves dinner
in the *kaiseki* style, with a
series of small dishes to warm
the stomach.

City Centre and Darling Harbour

Bodhi in the Park $
Chinese   **Map** 1 C5
Cook & Phillip Park, 2–4 College St,
NSW 2000
Tel *(02) 9360 2523*   **Closed** *Mon*
A wonderful place for lunch or
dinner in warm weather, when
seating is under the fig trees.
Superb organic vegan *yum cha*.

Chat Thai $
Thai   **Map** 4 E4
20 Campbell St, Haymarket, NSW 2000
Tel *(02) 9211 1808*
Trendy Thai eatery serving tangy
and authentic dishes. Groovy
decor and youthful staff. Often
busy, so be prepared to wait.

Din Tai Fung $
Chinese   **Map** 4 E3
Level 1, World Square, 644 George St,
NSW 2000
Tel *(02) 9264 6010*
Delicious Chinese food, including
gorgeous dumplings, wonton
soup and steamed buns. Be
sure not to miss the mango
ice cream.

Impressive view of Sydney Opera House from The Dining Room, Sydney

Madame Nhu $
Vietnamese **Map** 4 E2
Shop 5, The Galeries, 500 George St, NSW 2000
Tel *(02) 9283 3355*
Great place to sample fresh, flavourful Vietnamese street food. Choose from the traditional *pho* (noodle soup), or stir fries.

Mamak $
Malaysian **Map** 4 D4
15 Goulburn St, NSW 2000
Tel *(02) 9211 1668*
Popular restaurant offering tasty, traditional fare served on low tables with wooden stools. Fans queue round the block.

Mother Chu's Vegetarian Kitchen $
Vegetarian **Map** 4 E3
367 Pitt St, NSW 2000
Tel *(02) 9283 2828* **Closed** *Sun*
Cheerful canteen-style restaurant serving hearty stir-fries and curries that blend the flavours of Taiwan, China and Japan.

Café del Mar $$
Seafood **Map** 4 D2
The Roof Terrace, Cockle Bay Wharf, 201 Sussex St, NSW 2000
Tel *(02) 9267 6700*
Eat fresh, local seafood right by the water. The graphic dining room decor and harbour views are spectacular.

Diethnes $$
Greek **Map** 1 B5
336 Pitt St, NSW 2000
Tel *(02) 9267 8956* **Closed** *Sun*
A Sydney institution, with kitsch decor and hearty meals. Serves traditional Greek dishes such as *tzatziki* and *spanakopita*.

Zaaffran $$
Indian **Map** 3 C2
Level 2, 10 Darling Drive, 345 Harbour-side Shopping Centre, NSW 2000
Tel *(02) 9211 8900*
This restaurant is a haven for vegetarians, but the lamb shank stew and chicken biryani are superb too. Outdoor seating.

Golden Century $$$
Seafood/Chinese **Map** 4 E4
393–399 Sussex St, NSW 2000
Tel *(02) 9212 3901*
Huge menu of Cantonese seafood dishes. Specialities include deep-fried mud crab and steamed baby abalone.

Marigold $$$
Chinese **Map** 4 E3
683 George St, NSW 2000
Tel *(02) 9281 3388*
Classic *yum cha* restaurant, with waiters pushing laden trolleys.

A selction of tasty Chinese dishes at Bodhi in the Park, Sydney

Go for the Cantonese seafood or the roast suckling pig. Diners pick their fish from a tank.

DK Choice

Momofuku Seiobo $$$
Modern Asian **Map** 3 B1
The Star, Level G, 80 Pyrmont St, NSW 2009
Tel *(02) 9777 9000* **Closed** *Sun; Mon–Fri lunch*
An attention-grabbing open kitchen makes a night out at this much-lauded restaurant a theatrical experience. The chefs are a cool, well-groomed crowd with fast fingers. The food is imaginative and innovative. Do not miss the stuffed steamed buns, which chef David Chang has turned into an art form. Book in advance.

Pendolino $$$
Italian **Map** 4 E2
Shop 100, Level 2, The Strand Arcade, 412–414 George St, NSW 2000
Tel *(02) 9231 6117* **Closed** *Sun*
Elegant and romantic restaurant with an award-winning menu and attentive service. The artfully pres-ented dishes burst with flavour.

An intimate dining area at the Spice Temple restuarant, Sydney

Spice Temple $$$
Chinese **Map** 4 F1
10 Bligh St, NSW 2000
Tel *(02) 8078 1888* **Closed** *Sun*
Modern Chinese restaurant, softly lit by lanterns. Chillies feature in many forms – dried, fresh, salted, pickled, brined and fermented.

Tetsuya's $$$
Japanese **Map** 4 E3
529 Kent St, NSW 2000
Tel *(02) 9267 2900* **Closed** *Sun & Mon*
Revered as one of Australia's best restaurants. Menus fuse Japanese flavours with French technique. Book well in advance.

Botanic Gardens and The Domain

Botanic Gardens Restaurant $$
Modern Australian **Map** 2 D4
Royal Botanic Gardens, Mrs Macquaries Rd, NSW 2000
Tel *(02) 9241 2419* **Closed** *dinner*
Set among lush greenery, this excellent-value lunch venue opens on to a terrace, letting in the sounds of the gardens.

Chiswick at the Gallery $$
Modern Australian **Map** 2 D4
The Art Gallery of New South Wales, Art Gallery Rd, NSW 2000
Tel *(02) 9225 1819* **Closed** *dinner*
Discuss the latest exhibition over lunch in the gallery's contem-porary dining room. The menu at the more casual café is great for children.

The Pavilion $$
Modern Australian **Map** 2 D4
1 Art Gallery Rd, NSW 2000
Tel *(02) 9232 1322* **Closed** *Mon*
This is the ideal spot to enjoy a decadent breakfast, an elaborate lunch or a delicious afternoon treat. Serene and enchanting ambience.

For more information on types of restaurants *see page 498*

The elegant dining room at the Buon Ricordo, Paddington

Kings Cross, Darlinghurst and Paddington

Bill and Toni's $
Italian   **Map** 5 A1
74 Stanley St, NSW 2010
Tel *(02) 9360 4702*
A Sydney stalwart offering home-style Italian cooking, Bill and Toni's is much loved for its old-fashioned feel.

Gelato Messina $
Ice Cream   **Map** 5 B2
Shop 1, 241 Victoria St, NSW 2010
Tel *(02) 8354 1223*
Rightly popular, this *gelateria* produces scrumptious ice cream in imaginative flavours such as tiramisu, salted caramel with white chocolate, or pear and rhubarb. Choice of sorbets also available.

Govinda's $
Vegetarian   **Map** 5 B1
112 Darlinghurst Rd, NSW 2010
Tel *(02) 9380 5155* **Closed** *Mon & Tue*
Much-loved restaurant where locals pile up a plate of delicious curries from the all-you-can-eat buffet. Movie room upstairs.

Paddington Inn $
International   **Map** 6 D4
338 Oxford St, NSW 2021
Tel *(02) 9380 5913*
Popular pub that is especially busy on weekend afternoons, when hip locals meet over beers and tapas-style plates or pub classics such as bangers and mash.

The Fish Shop $$
Seafood   **Map** 2 E4
22 Challis Ave, Potts Point, NSW 2011
Tel *(02) 9326 9000* **Closed** *Sun dinner*
Enjoy locally caught and freshly prepared seafood at this casual, nautical-themed restaurant. Try the fisherman's basket or the fish burger. The whitewashed interior is decked up with fishing gear.

Fu Manchu $$
Chinese   **Map** 5 B2
229 Darlinghurst Rd, NSW 2010
Tel *(02) 9360 9424* **Closed** *Mon–Sat lunch*
This sleek spot is always crowded with *yum cha* enthusiasts on Saturdays and Sundays. Sample the gorgeous dumplings and prawn sesame rye toast.

Mahjong Room $$
Chinese   **Map** 5 A2
312 Crown St, NSW 2010
Tel *(02) 9361 3985* **Closed** *Sun*
Delicious Cantonese food served on *mah jong* tables. Drop in at lunchtime on Friday or Saturday to learn this Chinese game.

Buon Ricordo $$$
Italian   **Map** 5 C2
108 Boundary St, NSW 2021
Tel *(02) 9360 6729* **Closed** *Sun & Mon*
Off-duty chefs love this restaurant with a Neapolitan and Roman menu. The signature dish is fettuccine with Parmesan cheese, cream and truffled egg.

Guillaume $$$
French   **Map** 6 E3
92 Hargrave St, NSW 2025
Tel *(02) 9302 5222* **Closed** *Sun & Mon; Tue–Thu lunch*
Renowned chef Guillaume Brahimi assures patrons a fine dining experience at this elegant restaurant. The artfully presented dishes are prepared with impeccable attention to detail.

Lucio's $$$
Italian   **Map** 6 D3
47 Windsor St, NSW 2021
Tel *(02) 9380 5996* **Closed** *Sun & Mon*
This art-lovers' eatery is adorned with works by contemporary Australian artists, such as John Olsen, John Coburn and Tim Storrier. On the menu is expertly cooked, seasonal food.

Otto $$$
Italian   **Map** 2 D4
Area 8, 6 Cowper Wharf Rd, NSW 2011
Tel *(02) 9368 7488*
Upbeat, modern Italian restaurant offering fabulously colourful dishes in relaxed and attractive surroundings. Sample wines from Australia, New Zealand, Italy and France.

Pinbone $$$
Modern Australian   **Map** 6 D4
3 Jersey Rd, NSW 2025
Tel *(02) 9328 1600* **Closed** *lunch; Sun–Tue dinner*
Inventive, interestingly named dishes is what attracts guests to this contemporary restaurant. Sunday brunch is less quirky than dinner but still spectacular.

Further Afield

BONDI BEACH:
Bondi Trattoria $$
Modern Australian
34 Campbell Parade, NSW 2026
Tel *(02) 9365 4303*
A café by day and a restaurant at night. Join the locals for superb views of the beach from every table. Try the buttermilk pancakes with blueberry compote for breakfast, or angel hair pasta with raw tuna for dinner.

BONDI BEACH:
Hurricane's Grill $$
Grill
130 Roscoe St, NSW 2026
Tel *(02) 9130 7101*
Juicy steaks, burgers, chicken, ribs and vegetarian dishes are basted in South African sauces before being grilled to perfection at this upbeat restaurant and bar.

The trendy bar area at Hurricane's Grill, Bondi beach

BONDI BEACH:
Icebergs Dining Room $$$
Italian
1 Notts Ave, NSW 2026
Tel *(02) 9365 9000* **Closed** *Mon*
One of Bondi's swishest restaurants. A palette of ocean blues, giant chandeliers and silk cushions create a glamorous beach feel.

BONDI BEACH: Ravesi's on
Bondi Beach $$$
International
118 Campbell Parade, NSW 2026
Tel *(02) 9365 4422* **Closed** *Sun dinner*
Exciting dishes with multicultural influences. Dine inside or out on the terrace, and take in the buzz of the beach.

BONDI BEACH: Sean's
Panorama $$$
Modern Australian
270 Campbell Parade, NSW 2026
Tel *(02) 9365 4924* **Closed** *Mon & Tue*
Intimate restaurant serving rustic seasonal dishes. Menu changes daily. Attentive, friendly staff and a pleasant beachside location.

MANLY: The Manly Wharf
Hotel $$
Seafood
Manly Wharf, 21 East Esplanade, NSW 2095
Tel *(02) 9977 1266*
Zoom across from Sydney's central business district by boat to soak up Manly's relaxed vibe and tuck into fresh calamari. Locals come here to enjoy drinks on sunny afternoons.

ROSE BAY: Catalina $$$
Modern Australian
1 Sunderland Ave, Lyne Park, NSW 2029
Tel *(02) 9371 0555* **Closed** *Sun dinner*
A lovely spot for an alfresco lunch, this award-winning eatery resembles a docked ship. Fresh food with Mediterranean and Asian influences.

SURRY HILLS:
Bourke St Bakery $
Café
633 Bourke St, NSW 2010
Tel *(02) 9699 1011*
Tremendously popular for its artisan bread and handmade pies, tarts and pastries. Be prepared to wait for a table.

SURRY HILLS: Café Mint $
Middle Eastern
579 Crown St, NSW 2010
Tel *(02) 9319 0848* **Closed** *Mon; Sun dinner*
This tiny café serves excellent coffee and fabulous-value food. Sample the *mezze* plate for a rainbow of dips and pickles. It can be crowded.

SURRY HILLS: Longrain
Restaurant & Bar $$$
Thai **Map** 4 F4
85 Commonwealth St, NSW 2010
Tel *(02) 9280 2888* **Closed** *Sat–Thu lunch*
Modern Asian dining serving great hot, sour, salty and sweet dishes to combine and share. Offers cocktail-mixing classes.

SURRY HILLS: Porteño $$$
Argentinian
358 Cleveland St, NSW 2010
Tel *(02) 8399 1440* **Closed** *Sun & Mon*
One of the coolest places to eat in town, Porteño pays homage to South American cuisine by grilling succulent meats over a fire pit. The 8-hour slow-roasted pork with crisp crackling is superb.

SURRY HILLS: Toko
Restaurant & Bar $$$
Japanese
490 Crown St, NSW 2010
Tel *(02) 9357 6100* **Closed** *Sun; Sat & Mon lunch*
Informal *izakaya*-style dining inspired by Japanese sake bars. Toko serves a large range of tasty little courses.

SURRY HILLS: The Winery $$$
Modern Australian
285A Crown St, NSW 2010
Tel *(02) 8070 2424*
Fun wine bar and restaurant that can often get rowdy. Posh bar snacks and juicy steaks served on a board with chips.

WATSONS BAY:
Doyles on the Beach $$$
Seafood **Map** 1 C2
11 Marine Parade, NSW 2030
Tel *(02) 9337 2007*
Head out to Doyles for tasty fish and chips by the harbour. The barramundi and lobster are pricey but worth every cent.

The Blue Mountains and Beyond

BELLINGEN: Oak Street
Food & Wine $$
Modern Australian
2 Oak St, NSW 2454
Tel *(02) 6655 9000* **Closed** *Sun–Tue*
Award-winning restaurant with an understated feel. Treats from chef Ray Urquhart include flower-pot bread with roast garlic oil.

BROKEN HILL: The Silly Goat $
Modern Australian
360 Argent St, NSW 2080
Tel *(08) 8088 4774* **Closed** *dinner*
A bustling café as well as a breakfast and lunch spot serving a good range of freshly prepared dishes. Great coffee, organic juices and shakes.

BYRON BAY: Fishmonger's $
Seafood
Bay Lane, NSW 2010
Tel *(02) 6680 8080*
Sample fresh seafood, hand-cut chips and vegetable tempura at this cult café and takeaway.

BYRON BAY: St. Elmo $$
Mediterranean
22 Fletcher St, NSW 2481
Tel *(02) 6680 7426* **Closed** *lunch*
Urban eating space that is both chic and relaxed. Serves Spanish-style tapas to share.

BYRON BAY:
Byron Beach Café $$$
Modern Australian
Clarke's Beach, Lawson St, NSW 2481
Tel *(02) 6685 8400*
Quality café fare in a busy, bright and breezy setting with fabulous ocean views. Also offers takeaways to enjoy on the beach.

Excellent view of Bondi Beach from the outdoor terrace of Ravesi's on Bondi Beach

For more information on types of restaurants *see page 498*

Delicious honey-glazed duck with fennel, mandarin and chestnuts, Subo, Newcastle

COFFS HARBOUR: Shearwater $$
Modern Australian
321 Harbour Drive, NSW 2450
Tel *(02) 6651 6053* **Closed** *Sun–Tue dinner*
Dine right beside the water at this pleasant restaurant on Coffs Creek. Local seafood gets top billing, followed by meat dishes.

COFFS HARBOUR: Y-Knot Bistro $$
International
30 Marina Drive, NSW 2450
Tel *(02) 6651 1741*
An airy, easy-going coastal eatery. The brunch is especially popular with local yacht owners, beach fans and families.

GOSFORD: Caroline Bay Brasserie $$
International
36 Webb St, NSW 2250
Tel *(02) 4324 8099* **Closed** *dinner*
Set in Japanese-style gardens that are often used for weddings and special occasions. Crowd-pleasing menu of salads, quiches and grills.

HUNTER VALLEY: The Servants Quarters Tea Rooms $
Café
175 Swan St, Morpeth, NSW 2321
Tel *(02) 4934 1857*
Enjoy breakfast, morning tea or lunch inside this quaint café or out in the garden. Home-made scones with jam and fresh cream are irresistible.

HUNTER VALLEY: Matilda Bay Brewhouse & Dining $$
Italian
Hunter Resort, 917 Hermitage Rd, Pokolbin, NSW 2320
Tel *(02) 4998 7777* **Closed** *Mon & Tue; Wed, Thu & Sun dinner*
Relax over pizza, pasta and a glass of great wine; or a selection of 12 craft brews including tasting notes for each.

HUNTER VALLEY: Chez Pok $$$
French
Peppers Guesthouse, Ekerts Rd, Pokolbin, NSW 2320
Tel *(02) 4993 8999* **Closed** *Mon–Thu lunch*
The menu, inspired by rustic French cuisine, features goat's cheese soufflé and charcuterie. Romantic for dinner *à deux*.

HUNTER VALLEY: Esca Bimbadgen $$$
Winery Restaurant
Bimbadgen Estate, 790 McDonald's Rd, Pokolbin, NSW 2320
Tel *(02) 4998 4666* **Closed** *Sun–Tue dinner*
The menu suggests a wine to match every dish. Finish with a scrumptious dessert tasting plate paired with Botrytis Semillon.

HUNTER VALLEY: Leaves and Fishes $$$
Modern Australian
737 Lovedale Rd, Lovedale, Pokolbin, NSW 2320
Tel *(02) 4930 7400*
Sample sublime, healthy dishes out of first-class ingredients, particularly seafood.

DK Choice

HUNTER VALLEY: Muse Restaurant & Café $$$
Winery Restaurant
Hungerford Hill Wines, 1 Broke Rd, Pokolbin, NSW 2320
Tel *(02) 4998 6777* **Closed** *Mon–Fri lunch; Sun–Tue dinner*
With dramatic architecture, green surroundings and impeccable food and wine, Muse sets the bar for Australian winery restaurants. The emphasis here is on craftsmanship: everything – from the bread, pasta and gnocchi to the pastries and ice creams – is lovingly handmade.

KATOOMBA: The Yellow Deli Café $
214 Katoomba St, NSW 2780
Tel *(02) 4782 9744* **Closed** *Fri dinner; Sat*
Unique café run by a Messianic Christian community. Quirky, rustic interior and wonderfully wholesome fare, such as soup and healthy treats.

KATOOMBA: Darley's $$$
Modern Australian
Lilianfels, Lilianfels Ave, NSW 2780
Tel *(02) 4780 1200* **Closed** *Sun & Mon; lunch*
Polished restaurant in a beautiful 19th-century retreat house with open fireplaces. Well known for venison. It also has an enviable wine list.

KATOOMBA: The Rooster $$$
French
48 Merriwa St, NSW 2780
Tel *(02) 4782 1206* **Closed** *Mon–Fri lunch*
Sit near the fireplace in this gorgeous Federation-style guesthouse and enjoy delicious food paired with the perfect wine.

KINGSCLIFF: Fins $$$
Seafood
5–6 Bells Blvd, Salt Village, NSW 2487
Tel *(02) 6674 4833* **Closed** *Mon–Thu lunch*
At Fins, only the freshest produce is used, often from the chef's own garden. The fish is line-caught wherever possible, sometimes only hours before the meal.

LAKE MACQUARIE: Milano's on the Lake $$$
International
89 Soldiers Rd, Pelican, NSW 2281
Tel *(02) 4972 0550* **Closed** *Mon–Tue; Sun dinner*
Attractive marina restaurant. The veranda hangs over the water and is a great place to relax at sunset with a drink and a dozen oysters.

LENNOX HEAD: Mi Thai $
Thai
2/76 Ballina St, NSW 2478
Tel *(02) 6687 5820*
Local surfers love the food at this intimate restaurant. Modern and classic Asian cuisine, including mouth-watering *choo chee* curry, made with coconut milk.

LEURA: Silk's Brasserie $$$
International
128 The Mall, NSW 2780
Tel *(02) 4784 2534*
Family-friendly fine-dining place that gives colouring pencils to children to keep them busy. Book ahead.

MEGALONG VALLEY:
Megalong Valley Tea Rooms $
Café
Megalong Rd, NSW 2785
Tel *(02) 4787 9181*
Watch kangaroos graze nearby
while tucking into apple pie
or scones with cream at this
long-established family-run
tea-room.

NEWCASTLE:
Customs House Hotel $$
International
1 Bond St, NSW 2300
Tel *(02) 4925 2585* **Closed** *Sun dinner*
Good, flavoursome food and
reasonably priced drinks in
unfussy surroundings. The
menu is inspired by French
brasserie fare.

NEWCASTLE: Scratchleys on
The Wharf $$
Modern Australian
200 Wharf Rd, NSW 2300
Tel *(02) 4929 1111*
An eco-friendly restaurant
housed in an energy-efficient
pavilion that perches over
the harbour. Particularly good
for fish.

NEWCASTLE: Subo $$$
Modern Australian
551D Hunter St, NSW 2300
Tel *(02) 4023 4048* **Closed** *Mon &*
Tue; lunch
A husband-and-wife team
produce imaginative, aromatic
and textured dishes. The five-
course degustation menu is
highly recommended. Warm and
knowledgeable staff.

PORT MACQUARIE:
The Stunned Mullet $$$
Modern Australian
12 William St, NSW 2444
Tel *(02) 6584 7757*
Easy-going restaurant. Inventive
combinations include prawns
with shiitake mushrooms and
oat flakes, and baby squid with
green papaya.

PORT STEPHENS: Watercress $$
Modern Australian
16 Stockton St, Nelson Bay, NSW 2315
Tel *(02) 4984 2211* **Closed** *Sun &*
Mon; lunch
Enjoy top-notch, visually exciting
haute cuisine in a relaxed setting.
Ingredients include fresh seafood,
meat, game, herbs and fruit.

PORT STEPHENS: The Point $$$
International
Soldiers Point Marina, Sunset
Boulevard, Soldiers Point, NSW 2317
Tel *(02) 4984 7111*
Waterfront restaurant offering the
freshest catch such as Tasmanian
salmon and Red Emperor, along
with meat dishes and salads.

WAGGA WAGGA:
Indian Tavern Tandoori $
Indian
81 Peter St, NSW 2650
Tel *(02) 6921 3121*
Cuisine from across India, ranging
in spiciness from super hot to
mild. The butter chicken with
cashew nut butter is a favourite.

The South Coast and Snowy Mountains

BATEMANS BAY: On the Pier $$
Seafood
Old Punt Rd, NSW 2536
Tel *(02) 4472 6405* **Closed** *Mon–*
Thu lunch, Tue & Wed dinner; mid-
Jun–end-Jul
Seafood with great bay views.
Four seasonal menus, plus daily
specials served in a heritage
former punt house on the river.

BERMAGUI: Il Passaggio $$
Italian
Shop 5, Level 1, Fishermen's Wharf,
NSW 2546
Tel *(02) 6493 5753* **Closed** *Mon &*
Tue; Wed & Thu lunch; Sun dinner
Highly rated Italian food. Enjoy
the fabulous *antipasti*, thin-crust
pizzas and succulent pasta dishes.

BERRIMA: Eschalot $$$
Modern Australian
24 Old Hume Hwy, NSW 2577
Tel *(02) 4877 1977* **Closed** *Mon &*
Tue; Wed lunch & Sun dinner
Eschalot presents a contemporary
take on regional European
cuisine in an elegant heritage
building from the 1840s.
Enjoy pre-dinner drinks by
the open fire.

BERRY:
Berry Sourdough Café $$
Café
23 Prince Alfred St, NSW 2535
Tel *(02) 4464 1617* **Closed** *Mon &*
Tue; dinner
Sample organic sourdough
bread, cakes and savouries from
the owners' own bakery. Light
meals and good coffee as well.

BERRY: Silos Estate $$$
Winery Restaurant
Silos Estate, B640 Princes Hwy,
NSW 2535
Tel *(02) 4448 6082* **Closed** *Mon–Wed*
Taking its name from the estate's
old grain stores, Silos Estate
serves a select menu of superb
Middle Eastern, Asian and
Modern Australian fare. The wine
list contains fine local wines,
including some of Silos' own.

DK Choice

BOWRAL: Biota Dining $$$
Modern Australian
Kangaloon Rd, NSW 2576
Tel *(02) 4862 2005* **Closed** *Tue–*
Thu lunch
This excellent restaurant loves
to experiment. The interesting
menu may feature blackened
forest mushrooms with
chlorophyll, pine seeds and
yogurt made with goat's
milk, or mulloway with sweet
carrid shrimps and sea lettuce.
Top-quality ingredients, many
coming straight from the
kitchen garden.

Relaxing outdoor seating area at Customs House Hotel, Newcastle

For more information on types of restaurants see page 498

BOWRAL:
Hordern's Restaurant $$$
Modern Australian
Milton Park Country House Hotel,
Hordern's Rd, NSW 2576
Tel *(02) 4861 1522*
Elegant country hotel with two
dining rooms, high-backed chairs,
sumptuous fabrics and garden
views. Contemporary menu with
European and Asian influences.

EDEN: Sprout $
Café
134 Imlay St, NSW 2551
Tel *(02) 6496 1511*
Appealing, community-focused,
eco-friendly produce store
and café. Breakfast includes
BLT (bacon, lettuce, tomato)
sandwich with organic avocado
on toasted panini. Tasty lunch
specials, too.

GOULBURN: Fireside Inn $$
Modern Australian
23 Market St, NSW 2580
Tel *(02) 4821 2727* **Closed** *Sun & Mon*
True to its name, this landmark
mock-Tudor restaurant has a
large, open fire to welcome
guests in the winter months.
Serves hearty seasonal fare.

JERVIS BAY: Supply $
Café
Shop 1, 54 Owen St, Huskisson,
NSW 2540
Tel *(02) 4441 5815* **Closed** *dinner*
Airy café and deli in a sunny
location with sparkling bay views.
Good coffee, tasty breakfasts and
fresh, flavoursome lunches.

JERVIS BAY: The Gunyah
at Paperbark Camp $$$
Modern Australian
571 Woollamia Rd, Woollamia,
NSW 2540
Tel *(02) 4441 7299* **Closed** *early Jun–*
end Aug
Architect-designed treetop
dining room in serene bushland.
Dishes based on local produce
include kangaroo fillet, local fish
and seasonal berries.

Duck confit dish at The Gunyah at Paperbark
Camp, Jervis Bay

KIAMA: Hanoi on Manning $$
Vietnamese
10 Manning St, NSW 2533
Tel *(02) 4232 3315* **Closed** *Tue*
Welcoming restaurant with good
vegetarian and vegan options.
Popular with Sydneysiders who
visit the coast at weekends.

MERIMBULA:
Zanzibar Café $$$
Modern Australian
Cnr Main & Market sts, NSW 2548
Tel *(02) 6495 3636* **Closed** *Sun &*
Mon dinner; Sat–Wed lunch
A cut above most regional
restaurants, with carefully
presented seasonal cuisine from
a chef who has worked in some
of Australia's best kitchens.

MITTAGONG: Esco Pazzo $$
Italian
84 Main St, NSW 2575
Tel *(02) 4872 2400* **Closed** *Mon*
Italian-born chef Emilio Picchio
serves up stone-fired pizzas, fresh
pastas and authentic seafood
and meat dishes.

MOLLYMOOK: Bannister's
Pool and Cocktail Bar $$
Seafood
191 Michell Parade, NSW 2539
Tel *(02) 4455 3044* **Closed** *lunch*
Delicious and affordable light
fare, pizzas and desserts served

nightly (from 5pm) in a casual,
airy and stylish poolside-bar
setting with ocean views.

NAROOMA: Quarterdeck $
Seafood
Riverside Drive, NSW 2546
Tel *(02) 4476 2723* **Closed** *Tue & Wed*
Popular, child-friendly café
overlooking Wagonga Inlet.
Seafood favourites include
fish 'n' chips, salt-and-chilli squid,
bouillabaisse, tapas and local
Narooma oysters.

THREDBO: Cuisine on
Lake Crackenback $$$
Modern Australian
Lake Crackenback Resort,
1650 Alpine Way, NSW 2627
Tel *(02) 6451 3000*
Focuses on local produce such
as smoked mountain trout and
poached rabbit. Special kids'
menu. Reservations essential.

THREDBO: Jean-Michel
at The Knickerbocker $$$
European
Riverside Cabins, Diggings Terrace,
NSW 2625
Tel *(02) 6457 6844* **Closed** *Mon & Tue*
A French-inspired menu and an
award-winning wine list. Relaxed
atmosphere and stunning river
and mountain views.

WOLLONGONG:
Diggies $
Modern Australian
1 Cliff Rd, North Beach, NSW 2500
Tel *(02) 4226 2688* **Closed** *dinner*
Housed in a small, hip beach
shack this place serves
scrumptious breakfasts and
brunches with awesome views.

WOLLONGONG:
Caveau $$$
French
122–124 Keira St, NSW 2500
Tel *(02) 4226 4855* **Closed** *Sun & Mon*
Modern French restaurant and
cookery school led by master
chef Peter Sheppard. The seasonal
menu changes monthly.

Canberra and ACT

CANBERRA:
Ethiopia Down Under $
Ethiopian
Shop 1, 70 Hodgson Crescent,
Pearce, ACT 2607
Tel *(02) 6286 1659* **Closed** *Sun; lunch*
An unpretentious place to try
Ethiopia's staple, *injera* (pancake),
served with dollops of spicy
sauces. To round off the
experience there's an ice cream
made with Ethiopian coffee.

Light and airy dinning area at Cuisine on Lake Crakenback, Thredbo

CANBERRA:
The Porkbarrel $
International
King George Terrace, Parkes,
ACT 2600
Tel *(02) 6273 1455*
This lovely café in the National
Rose Gardens serves a selection
of casual dining options from big
breakfasts to pizzas.

CANBERRA: Portrait Café $
Café
National Portrait Gallery,
King Edward St, ACT 2600
Tel *(02) 6102 7162*   **Closed** *dinner*
For a break during a visit to the
National Portrait Gallery, head
to the back of the building and
enjoy delicious tea or a seasonal
lunch with a glass of wine.

CANBERRA: Timmy's Kitchen $
Chinese/Malaysian
Manuka Village, Furneaux St,
Manuka, ACT 2603
Tel *(02) 6295 6537*   **Closed** *Mon*
This popular restaurant offers
cheap, speedy and good food.
The Malaysian items, including the
curry *laksas*, are recommended.

CANBERRA:
Benchmark Wine Bar $$
European
65 Northbourne Ave, ACT 2600
Tel *(02) 6262 6522*   **Closed** *Sat*
lunch; Sun
Over 100 wines by the glass and
another 600 bottles to choose
from. Great food and friendly
service in a lively atmosphere.

CANBERRA: The Chairman
and Yip $$
Chinese
108 Bunda St, Civic, ACT 2601
Tel *(02) 6248 7109*   **Closed** *Sun &*
Mon; Sat lunch
Creative Asian restaurant that
combines Cantonese and Western
flavours to produce contemporary
dishes. Has been popular ever
since it opened in the early 1990s.

CANBERRA: Italian and Sons $$
Italian
7 Lonsdale St, Braddon, ACT 2612
Tel *(02) 6162 4888*   **Closed** *Sun; Sat*
& Mon lunch
Styled after a traditional Roman
trattoria. Good renditions
of regional classics such as
charcuterie, pasta dishes and
pizzas, as well as daily specials.

CANBERRA: Morks $$
Thai
Unit 3, 37 Kesteven St, Florey, ACT 2615
Tel *(02) 6259 0112*   **Closed** *Sun*
dinner; Mon
One of Canberra's best
contemporary Thai restaurants

Outdoor seating in a peaceful lakeside setting at The Boat House by the Lake, Canberra

offers traditional banquets and
a tasting menu in a simple,
uncluttered space with plain
wooden furniture.

CANBERRA: Pistachio Dining
at Torrens $$
Modern Australian
3A Torrens Place, Torrens, ACT 2607
Tel *(02) 6286 2966*   **Closed** *Sun &*
Mon; lunch (except Fri)
The menu at this Woden Valley
restaurant features flavour-
packed dishes such as roast pork
tenderloin with baby beetroot,
and Tasmanian salmon pie with
garlic potato purée.

CANBERRA: The Artisan $$$
French
16 Iluka St, Narrabundah, ACT 2604
Tel *(02) 6232 6482* **Closed** *Sun & Mon*
A modern, minimalist bistro
with imaginative food served by
cheerful staff. The degustation
menu with matching wines is
worth trying.

CANBERRA: Aubergine $$$
European
18 Barker St, Griffith, ACT 2603
Tel *(02) 6260 8666*   **Closed** *Sun*
The inventive menu at Aubergine
may feature veal tartare with
bitter cocoa and quail egg, or
ribeye with smoked potato
and bone-marrow vinaigrette.
Impressive wine list.

CANBERRA: The Boat House
by the Lake $$$
Modern Australian
Grevillea Park, Menindee Drive,
Barton, ACT 2600
Tel *(02) 6273 5500* **Closed** *Sun; lunch*
Quality creative fare in a serene
location with views over Lake
Burley Griffin. Try the blue
cheesecake for dessert. In good
weather, ask for a table on the
deck. Bookings are essential.

DK Choice

CANBERRA: Courgette $$$
European
54 Marcus Clarke St, ACT 2601
Tel *(02) 6247 4042*   **Closed** *Sat*
lunch; Sun
Courgette has been showered
with praise by critics, locals
and visitors alike. Owner James
Mussillon trained under chef
Marco Pierre White. His culinary
creations are elegant but
uncomplicated, and the decor
reflects this. Exceptionally
good-value three-course lunch
and four-course dinner menus.

CANBERRA: Rubicon $$$
European
6A Barker St, Griffith, ACT 2603
Tel *(02) 6295 9919*   **Closed** *Sat*
lunch; Sun
White tablecloths and candlelight
in understated surroundings set
the scene for one of Canberra's
most pleasant dining experiences.
Excellent vegetarian options.

CANBERRA:
Sage Dining Rooms $$$
International
Gorman House Arts Centre,
Batman St, Braddon, ACT 2612
Tel *(02) 6249 6050* **Closed** *Sun & Mon*
Fine-dining venue with a
buzzing, yet discreet atmosphere.
Every plate is a delicate and
delicious work of art. Book ahead.

CANBERRA: Water's Edge $$$
European
40 Parkes Place, Parkes, ACT 2600
Tel *(02) 6273 5066* **Closed** *Mon & Tue*
Sweeping views across Lake Burley
Griffin, fine cuisine and excellent
service guarantee a memorable
meal at this stylish restaurant.
Treat yourself to the delightful
passion fruit soufflé for dessert.

Wonderful view of the Story Bridge from the atmospheric terrace at Customs House, Brisbane

Brisbane

ALBION:
Breakfast Creek Hotel $$
Grill
2 Kingsford Smith Drive, QLD 4010
Tel *(07) 3262 5988*
An iconic pub that has been a Queensland favourite since 1889. Noted for its steaks – guests can choose theirs before it is cooked.

CAMP HILL:
Restaurant Rapide $$$
Modern Australian
4 Martha St, QLD 4152
Tel *(07) 3843 5755* **Closed** *Sun & Mon*
Small bistro with a monthly menu that may include Tasmanian salmon with seasonal vegetables or roasted wagyu bavette.

CITY CENTRE: Esq $$
Modern Australian/Korean
145 Eagle St, QLD 4000
Tel *(07) 3220 2123* **Closed** *Sun & Mon; Sat lunch*
The little brother of Esquire, Brisbane's much-lauded fine-dining restaurant, Esq is a superb charcoal grill in fashionably simple and casual surroundings.

CITY CENTRE: Cha Cha Char $$$
Grill
Shop 3, 1 Eagle St, Eagle St Pier, QLD 4000
Tel *(07) 3211 9944* **Closed** *Sat; Sun lunch*
A favourite of local and visiting businessmen, this wood-fired steak restaurant specializes in grain-fed wagyu and mayura beef.

CITY CENTRE:
Customs House $$$
Modern Australian
399 Queen St, QLD 4001
Tel *(07) 3365 8921* **Closed** *Mon dinner*
Heritage icon standing grandly on the riverbank. Dine inside or on the terrace with views of the Story Bridge. Quality fare and friendly, professional service.

CITY CENTRE: E'cco Bistro $$$
Modern Australian
100 Boundary & Adelaide sts, QLD 4000
Tel *(07) 3831 8344* **Closed** *Sun & Mon*
Philip Johnson's award-winning bistro is simple and welcoming. The menu is based on fresh seasonal ingredients. Vegetarian and vegan options available.

DK Choice

CITY CENTRE: Esquire $$$
Modern Australian
145 Eagle St, QLD 4000
Tel *(07) 3220 2123* **Closed** *Sun & Mon; Sat lunch*
Brisbane's most imaginative and highly awarded restaurant has been turning many heads. Esquire features cool, cutting-edge cuisine and stripped-down decor. The degustation menu changes every day and features hand-picked seasonal ingredients. Guests are served either seven or 15 delicious little courses that are expertly prepared and elegantly presented.

CITY CENTRE:
Fix Restaurant $$$
Modern Australian
40 Edward St, Port Office Hotel, QLD 4000
Tel *(07) 3210 6016* **Closed** *Sat lunch; Sun*
In an 1880s heritage building, Fix has many classic options, from bar snacks and wood-fired pizza to Moreton Bay bugs (local lobster).

CITY CENTRE: Il Centro
Restaurant and Bar $$$
Italian
Eagle St Pier, 1 Eagle St, QLD 4000
Tel *(07) 3221 6090* **Closed** *Sat lunch*
Modern Italian fare, but with flavours unique to Queensland: fresh seafood, prime cuts of meat, tropical fruit, seasonal vegetables and delicate garden herbs.

CITY CENTRE: Moda $$$
Mediterranean
12 Edward St, QLD 4000
Tel *(07) 3221 7655* **Closed** *Sun; lunch (except Thu & Fri)*
Enjoy fine cuisine in an elegant setting. The house special is the Pica Pica lunch: five small Spanish-inspired dishes with coffee and sweet treats.

CITY CENTRE:
Restaurant Two $$$
Modern Australian
2 Edward St, QLD 4000
Tel *(07) 3210 0600* **Closed** *Sun & Mon*
Long-serving restaurant in the heritage-listed Old Mineral House, overlooking the Botanic Gardens. Refined, fine-flavoured menu, plus a satisfying wine list.

CITY CENTRE: Saké $$$
Japanese
Level 1, 45 Eagle St Pier, QLD 4000
Tel *(07) 3015 0557*
Lively, colourful little sushi joint with a fantastic reputation. Grab a table, or sit at the bar to watch the chefs in action.

CITY CENTRE: Urbane $$$
Modern Australian
181 Mary St, QLD 4000
Tel *(07) 3229 2271* **Closed** *Sun & Thu; lunch*
A critics' favourite, Urbane offers five- and nine-course menus in a relaxed and hip contemporary setting. Impressive wine list. Vegetarians catered for.

FORTITUDE VALLEY:
Asian Fusion $
Asian
149 Wickham St, QLD 4006
Tel *(07) 3852 1144* **Closed** *Tue lunch*
Delicious and Chinese and Vietnamese dishes. Fabulous Peking duck, Mongolian tofu and roll-your-own rice-paper rolls.

Chic interior of Il Centro Restaurant and Bar, Brisbane

Key to Price Guide *see page 504*

Sweet dessert pizza with berries and mascarpone, Beccofino, Teneriffe

FORTITUDE VALLEY:
Campos Coffee $
Café
11 Wandoo St, QLD 4006
Tel *(07) 3252 3612*
The flagship branch of this speciality coffee chain. Also offers "cupping" (coffee tasting) sessions on weekends.

FORTITUDE VALLEY:
Chouquette $
Café/French
19 Barker St, QLD 4005
Tel *(07) 3358 6336* **Closed** *Mon & Tue*
Friendly, French-speaking staff are on hand to serve café crème and scrumptious gâteau in this authentic *boulangerie* (bakery).

FORTITUDE VALLEY:
Pig 'n' Whistle $$
Pub
446 Brunswick St, QLD 4006
Tel *(07) 3852 6420*
Steak, seafood and British pub classics such as beef and Guinness pie and Lincolnshire sausage to be washed down with craft beers. Dozens of TVs to watch live sports while dining.

FORTITUDE VALLEY: Tartufo $$
Italian
1000 Ann St, QLD 4006
Tel *(07) 3852 1500*
This stylish place serves classic Italian dishes inspired by the chef's home town of Naples. It also has a pizzeria and a wine bar with a good menu of bar snacks.

FORTITUDE VALLEY:
Wagaya $$
Japanese
Level 1, TCB Centre, 315 Brunswick St, QLD 4006
Tel *(07) 3252 8888*
Fun bistro with accessible *izakaya*-style dining, the Japanese answer to tapas. A menu highlight is the pork *gyoza* with hints of ginger and herbs.

NEW FARM: Cirque $
Café
618 Brunswick St, QLD 4005
Tel *(07) 3254 0479* **Closed** *dinner*
Popular breakfast or brunch spot, especially at weekends, with excellent espresso and legendary eggs Benedict. Delicious lunches, too.

NEW FARM: Majo's $$
Italian
695 Brunswick St, QLD 4005
Tel *(07) 3254 0275*
Family-friendly restaurant serving some of the best pizzas in Brisbane, plus an assortment of delicious home-style Italian dishes to choose from. Good list of Italian wines and beers.

NEW FARM:
The Purple Olive $$
Modern Australian
79 James St, QLD 4005
Tel *(07) 3254 0097* **Closed** *Mon*
This popular spot is styled like a classic European restaurant. Authentic Mediterranean flavours are adapted to modern Australian tastes.

PADDINGTON:
Montrachet $$$
French
224 Given Terrace, QLD 4064
Tel *(07) 3367 0030* **Closed** *Sat & Sun*
Waving the flag for traditional French cuisine, this delightful, intimate restaurant is the creation of French-Australian chef Thierry Galichet.

SOUTH BRISBANE:
Bamboo Basket $
Chinese
Shop 1003-4, 199 Grey St, QLD 4101
Tel *(07) 3844 0088*
Succulent noodles and fresh *xiao long baos* (steamed dumplings, literally "little dragon buns") are the best things to order at this busy eatery.

SOUTH BRISBANE: GOMA
Restaurant $$
Modern Australian
Stanley St, QLD 4101
Tel *(07) 3842 9916* **Closed** *Mon & Tue; dinner (except Fri)*
Sophisticated alfresco seating makes this an elegant spot for lunch before, after or during a visit to Brisbane's world-class GOMA complex.

TENERIFFE: Beccofino $$
Italian
10 Vernon Terrace, QLD 4005
Tel *(07) 3666 0207* **Closed** *Mon, Tue & Wed lunch*
Enjoy excellent food in a contemporary café-restaurant. The scarlet signage and seating make it impossible to miss. Pizzas are the specialty here.

TOOWONG: 85 Miskin St $$$
Modern Australian
85 Miskin St, QLD 4066
Tel *(07) 3371 4558* **Closed** *Mon; Tue lunch*
Housed in an old cottage with minimalist interiors. Serves innovative contemporary cuisine in a relaxed atmosphere.

WEST END: The Gunshop Café $
Café/Modern Australian
53 Mollison St, QLD 4101
Tel *(07) 3844 2241* **Closed** *Sun– Thu dinner*
This delightful, award-winning spot, dotted with quirky artworks, is always buzzing. They also serve superbly flavoursome main meals.

WEST END: Little Greek Taverna $
Greek
Shop 5, 1 Browning St, QLD 4101
Tel *(07) 3255 2215* **Closed** *Mon*
Family-run restaurant with a bright, airy feel. Offers scrumptious Greek salads with fat olives and tasty dips, plus classics such as *souvlaki* skewers.

For more information on types of restaurants *see page 498*

WEST END: Mondo Organics $$$
Modern Australian
166 Hardgrave Rd, QLD 4101
Tel *(07) 3844 1132* **Closed** *Mon &
Tue; Wed & Thu lunch; Sun dinner*
This inspiring modern eatery only
uses the finest natural, organic
ingredients. A firm favourite with
Brisbane's health conscious and
environmentally aware.

WEST END: Tukka $$$
Native Australian
145B Boundary St, QLD 4101
Tel *(07) 3846 6333* **Closed** *Sat dinner*
Produces delicious meals from
native ingredients such as smoked
kangaroo, redclaw yabbies and
anisata leaves (from a rainforest
tree). Refreshingly original.

WOOLLOONGABBA:
Green Papaya $$
Balinese/Thai
898 Stanley St East, QLD 4169
Tel *(07) 3891 5000* **Closed** *Mon*
Unpretentious restaurant. Sample
delicately flavoured soups, curries
and seafood dishes garnished
with fresh vegetables and spicy
sauces. Cooking lessons available.

South of Townsville

AIRLIE BEACH: Mr Bones $
Pizzeria
263 Shute Harbour Rd, QLD 4802
Tel *(04) 1301 7331* **Closed** *Sun & Mon*
Breezy café-restaurant famous for
its pizzas. It also serves breakfast,
light bites and daily specials.

BUNDABERG: Indulge $
Café/Modern Australian
80 Bourbong St, QLD 4670
Tel *(07) 4154 2344* **Closed** *Sun*
Burgers, salads and sandwiches
on sourdough or Turkish bread,
plus luscious breakfasts. The focus
is on local, seasonal produce.

Arty, quirky interior of Black Coffee Lyrics,
Gold Coast

Vanitas restaurant overlooking the lagoon pool at Palazzo Versace hotel *(see p487)*, Gold Coast

GLADSTONE: Chattin Café $$
Café
Shop 5/100 Goondoon St, QLD 4680
Tel *(07) 4972 8377* **Closed** *Sun*
Breakfast options range from
multigrain toast to more
indulgent doughnuts with jam
and cream. Light lunches, too.

GOLD COAST:
Black Coffee Lyrics $$
Café/Bistro
*Shop 41, 3131 Surfers Paradise Blvd,
Surfers Paradise, QLD 4217*
Tel *(04) 0218 9437* **Closed** *Mon*
Hip little restaurant and bar that
offers fine dining in a casual, laid-
back atmosphere. Functions as
a café on weekends.

GOLD COAST:
Burleigh Bluff Café $$
Café
*The Old Burleigh Theatre Arcade,
66 Goodwin Terrace, Burleigh Heads,
QLD 4220*
Tel *(07) 5576 6333*
Lively at breakfast time, sunny
for lunch and beautiful at
sundown, this café is a favourite
for its reasonably priced food
and friendly service. Close to
the beach.

GOLD COAST: Stingray $$
American
*7 Staghorn Ave, Surfers Paradise,
QLD 4217*
Tel *(07) 5584 1200*
Lively, sophisticated and fun,
with super-cool retro decor.
Perfect place to share cocktails
or cold beers and mini-bites.

GOLD COAST: Bazaar $$$
International
*7 Staghorn Ave, Surfers Paradise,
QLD 4217*
Tel *(07) 5584 1200*
Buffet dining with a global twist:
for a set price, guests can sample
a dizzying array of dishes inspired
by global culinary specialities.

GOLD COAST: Rock Salt
Modern Dining $$$
Modern Australian
*Shop 12, The Aria Building,
Albert Ave, Broadbeach, QLD 4218*
Tel *(07) 5570 6076* **Closed** *Mon*
Award-winning restaurant with
a smart-casual feel. The chef
prepares wonderful dishes from
oysters, scallops, line-caught fish
and organic vegetables.

GOLD COAST: Vanitas $$$
Modern Australian
*94 Seaworld Drive, Main Beach,
QLD 4217*
Tel *(07) 5509 8000* **Closed** *Sun & Mon*
Elegant and tasteful hotel-
restaurant with original art and
fine-quality furnishings. The food
and wine list are equally superb.

MOUNT MEE: Birches $$
Modern Australian
1350 Mount Mee Rd, QLD 4521
Tel *(07) 5498 2244* **Closed** *Mon & Tue*
Birches offers a range of fare,
including gluten-free and
vegetarian options. Welcoming
country atmosphere.

NOOSA: Organika $
Café
*Shop 2, 3 Gibson Rd, Noosaville,
QLD 4566*
Tel *(07) 5442 4973* **Closed** *dinner*
Purveyor of all things fresh and
fragrant, this organic produce
store has a deck for guests to
bite into something savoury
and sip a first-class coffee.

NOOSA: Thomas Corner
Eatery $$
Modern Australian
*1/201 Gympie Terrace, Noosaville,
QLD 4566*
Tel *(07) 5470 2224* **Closed** *Sun dinner*
This superb casual eatery has a
chic urban-beach vibe. It is owned
by David Rayner, one of the chefs
to seal Noosa's reputation as a
food lovers' paradise.

**NOOSA: Berardo's Bistro
on the Beach** $$$
Modern Australian
*Noosa Beachfront on the Beach
Resort, 49 Hastings St,
Noosa Heads, QLD 4567*
Tel *(07) 5448 0888*
Healthy or decadent breakfasts
and fresh, flavourful lunches and
dinners are accompanied by the
relaxing sound of the ocean
waves. Good coffee and tasty
sweet and savoury muffins as well.

NOOSA: Wasabi $$$
Japanese
*2 Quamby Place, Noosa Sound,
QLD 4567*
Tel *(07) 5449 2443*   **Closed** *Mon &
Tue; Fri & Sun lunch*
Situated on the waterfront, with
lovely sunset views over the
Noosa River. Come here to indulge
in excellent flavoursome food.
There is a fashionable dining
room, plus a *tatami* room that
seats 20 diners in traditional style.

DK Choice

**NORTH TAMBORINE:
Songbirds Rainforest
Retreat** $$$
Modern Australian
*Lot 10, Tamborine Mountain Rd,
QLD 4272*
Tel *(07) 5545 2563*   **Closed** *Mon
& Tue*
This multiple award-winning
hinterland hotel-restaurant
offers organic fine dining in a
beautiful, tranquil rainforest
setting. The ambience is smart
yet relaxed. The well-presented,
delicious food is carefully
matched with local and
imported wines. Parrots, whip
birds, lorikeets and lyrebirds all
make their presence heard in
the leafy surroundings.

**ROCKHAMPTON:
The Coffee House** $$
Café/Bistro
51 William St, QLD 4700
Tel *(07) 4927 5722* **Closed** *Sun dinner*
Tidy and compact café-restaurant
with a bistro-style menu featuring
beef from the local area. Gluten-
free meals for the health-minded.

**SUNSHINE COAST:
The Curry Bowl** $
Indian
*7/115 Point Cartwright Drive,
Buddina, QLD 4575*
Tel *(07) 5478 0800* **Closed** *Mon; lunch*
Sunshine Coast curry house with
a reputation for friendly service
and tasty, fresh ingredients. Great
samosas (stuffed fried pastry)
and *naan* bread.

**TOOWOOMBA:
Veraison** $$
Modern Australian
205 Margaret St, QLD 4350
Tel *(07) 4638 5909* **Closed** *Sun & Mon*
Highly respected for its expert
cooking and wine list, Veraison
occasionally hosts speciality
wine dinners, showcasing
vintages that have caught the
sommelier's imagination.

**TOWNSVILLE:
Watermark** $$
Modern Australian
72–74 The Strand, QLD 4810
Tel *(07) 4724 4281*
Waterfront restaurant with a
sleek, stylish vibe and modern
Queensland cuisine. The terrace,
under a striking glass canopy, is
great for cocktails or dinner on a
warm evening.

**YANDINA:
Spirit House** $$$
Asian
20 Ninderry Rd, QLD 4561
Tel *(07) 5446 8994*   **Closed** *Sun–
Tue dinner*
Tropical garden restaurant and
cooking school. Sample Asian-
style stir-fries and curries to the
sound of birds, wind chimes and
water features. Advisable to book
in advance.

Northern Queensland
and the Outback

CAIRNS: Cruze $
Café
105 Grafton St, QLD 4870
Tel *(07) 4051 1444*   **Closed** *Sun*
Relish fresh coffee prepared by
a team that know their coffee
beans perfectly. Choose from
a wide variety of beans and
brewing styles, plus tasty treats
to accompany the drinks.

Bright and colourful building of Ochre
Restaurant, Cairns

**CAIRNS: Barnacle Bill's
Seafood Inn** $$
Seafood
103 The Esplanade, QLD 4870
Tel *(07) 4051 2241*
An established local favourite,
with a menu offering fresh
oysters, mussels, scallops,
calamari, prawns, lobster and
fish. The house speciality is a hot
and spicy seafood jambalaya.

CAIRNS: Donnini $$
Italian
*Hilton Cairns, 34 The Esplanade,
QLD 4870*
Tel *(07) 4050 2020*
Savour traditional Italian delights
such as handmade pastas, pizzas
and salads, all made from fresh,
local produce. Friendly staff.

CAIRNS: L'Unico Trattoria $$
Italian
*75 Vasey Esplanade, Trinity Beach,
QLD 4879*
Tel *(07) 4057 8855*
Smart but relaxed place making
good use of local ingredients.
Try the angel hair pasta with
Moreton Bay lobster. Pizzas have
unusual toppings. Buzzing vibe.

**CAIRNS:
Mondo Café Bar & Grill** $$
Cafe
34 The Esplanade, QLD 4870
Tel *(07) 4052 6780*
Outdoor café under the shade
of a giant poinciana tree. Light
meals, burgers, salads and snacks
with an international flavour.
Great for a casual drink, too.

CAIRNS: Ochre Restaurant $$
Native Australian
43 Shields St, QLD 4870
Tel *(07) 4051 0100*   **Closed** *Sat &
Sun lunch*
Interesting food, with an
emphasis on Australian bush fare.
The menu features game (emu,
crocodile and kangaroo), seafood
and fruits such as quandong.

**CAIRNS:
Perrotta's at the Gallery** $$
International
Abbott & Shields sts, QLD 4870
Tel *(07) 4031 5899*
Popular local haunt, crowded at
breakfast and particularly busy at
weekends. Casual café food with
a tropical twist and good coffee.

CHARLEVILLE: Heinemann's $
Café
84 Alfred St, QLD 4470
Tel *(07) 4654 3991*
This small bakery and café is a
great place to fuel up for the day
with fresh, tasty pies and sweet
baked goods.

CLONCURRY: The Gidgee Inn Bar & Grill $$
Modern Australian
Matilda Hwy, QLD 4824
Tel *(07) 4742 1599* **Closed** *Sun*
The menu at this à la carte restaurant features seafood from the Gulf of Carpentaria and beef from the surrounding region. Choose from oysters, prawns and barramundi, or succulent steaks.

DAINTREE:
Tea House Restaurant $
Native Australian
3225 Mossman Daintree Rd, QLD 4873
Tel *(07) 4098 6161* **Closed** *dinner*
Lovely spot in a breathtaking rainforest setting. Serves delectable food featuring local produce and tropical fruits.

KARUMBA: Sunset Tavern $$
Modern Australian
The Esplanade, QLD
Tel *(07) 4745 9183*
The signature seafood platter is piled with local fish and mud crabs. Excellent Gulf prawn. Good steaks, pizzas and pastas, too.

LONGREACH: Oasis Restaurant $$
Modern Australian
Albert Park Motor Inn, Sir Hudson Fysh Drive, QLD 4730
Tel *(07) 4658 2411* **Closed** *lunch; Sun dinner*
Steak, grilled chicken and pork, as well as seafood dishes feature on the menu here. Generous servings at reasonable prices.

MAREEBA: Skybury Coffee $
Café
136 Ivicevic Rd, QLD 4880
Tel *(07) 4093 2190* **Closed** *dinner; Sat & Sun*
Set in a coffee plantation, this casual restaurant spills on to an elevated deck. It offers a range of light meals, cakes and coffee.

MOSSMAN: Mojos Bar & Grill $$
International
41 Front St, QLD 4873
Tel *(07) 4098 1202* **Closed** *Sat lunch; Sun*
Casual but classy restaurant. The signature Surf & Turf dish is char-grilled sirloin with salt-and-pepper squid and garlic aïoli. Try one of the seafood *antipasti* platters.

PALM COVE:
Vivo Bar & Grill $$
International
49 Williams Esplanade, QLD 4879
Tel *(07) 4059 0944*
Colonial-style restaurant with a wide veranda. Choose from a tapas menu or a range of dishes featuring seafood and local produce with a tropical twist.

PALM COVE: Beach Almond $$$
Modern Asian/Seafood
145 Williams Esplanade, QLD 4879
Tel *(07) 4059 1908*
Relax in the huge veranda that overlooks the sea at this former beach shack, while enjoying fresh seafood prepared with vibrant Asian colours and flavours.

DK Choice

PALM COVE: NuNu $$$
International
123 Williams Esplanade, 1 Veivers Rd, QLD 4879
Tel *(07) 4059 1880*
The award-winning NuNu features an interesting and innovative menu with Asian and Mediterranean influences. It offers simply prepared dishes alongside more elaborate specialities. The Queensland mud crab will have guests talking about it long after their meal is over. The beachfront atmosphere is casual, and the staff friendly.

PORT DOUGLAS:
Port O Call Bistro $
Café
Port St, QLD 4877
Tel *(07) 4099 5422* **Closed** *Jan– end-Mar*
Hearty servings of simple, delicious food such as burgers, stir-fries, steaks, pasta and curry dishes are on offer at this café. Blackboard specials include local seafood. Friendly service in an casual atmosphere.

PORT DOUGLAS: On the Inlet $$
Seafood
3 Inlet St, QLD 4877
Tel *(07) 4099 5255*
Built out over the water, this is a great spot at sunset. Choose the mud crab or lobster from the live seafood tank.

PORT DOUGLAS:
Salsa Bar & Grill $$
Modern Australian
26 Wharf St, QLD 4877
Tel *(07) 4099 4922*
Trendy place, visited by everyone from presidents to pop stars. Terrific food, great prices and lively service. Leave room for the delectable desserts.

PORT DOUGLAS: Zinc $$
Modern Australian
Shop 3, 53–61 Macrossan St, QLD 4877
Tel *(07) 4099 6260*
Delicious creative food, service with a smile and a children's menu keep patrons coming back. Check out the cutting-edge restrooms, with floor-to-ceiling aquariums.

PORT DOUGLAS: Harrisons $$$
International
22 Wharf St, QLD 4877
Tel *(07) 4099 4011*
Northern Queensland's sole Michelin-starred chef, Spencer Patrick creates sensational dishes such as a slow-braised ox cheek with a red wine sauce.

PORT DOUGLAS: Nautilus $$$
International
17 Murphy St, QLD 4877
Tel *(07) 4099 5330*
A Port Douglas institution since the 1950s. Dine within a romantic rainforest oasis, right in the heart of town. Expensive, but a great experience. No children under 8 years.

WINTON: North Gregory Hotel $
Modern Australian
67 Elderslie St, QLD 4735
Tel *(07) 4657 0647*
A refurbished historic pub famed for hosting the first performance of "Waltzing Matilda" in 1895. Good pub fare.

Tables situated in a beautiful rainforest setting at Nautilus restaurant, Port Douglas

YUNGABURRA:
Eden House Restaurant $$
Modern Australian
20 Gillies Hwy, QLD 4884
Tel *(07) 4095 2387* **Closed** *Mon & Tue; Wed–Sat lunch*
Fine dining in a heritage building nestled in elegant, tropical surrounds. The sophisticated country menu features local produce.

Darwin and the Top End

DALY WATERS:
Daly Waters Historic Pub $$
Steaks/Seafood
Stuart St, NT 0852
Tel *(08) 8975 9927*
Iconic pub serving burgers, steaks and fresh, wild-caught barramundi with hot crusty damper bread (traditional Australian soda bread).

DARWIN: The Deck Bar $
Bistro
22 Mitchell St, NT 0800
Tel *(08) 8942 3001*
A cut above the usual corner pub, with a modern menu and creative food. Grand view of the impressive Colonial-style Parliament House.

DARWIN: Jetty & The Fish $
Seafood
260 Casuarina Drive, Nightcliff, NT 0810
Tel *(04) 2449 4057* **Closed** *Mon–Thu*
Fish is the focus at this food truck that offers everything from fish and chips to fish tacos, calamari and fish nuggets to take away.

DARWIN: Shenannigans Restaurant & Bar $
Native Australian
69 Mitchell St, NT 0800
Tel *(08) 8981 2100*
A large menu of pub favourites, including some inspired by the Northern Territory, such as the platter of crocodile sausage, kangaroo loin, buffalo sausage and barramundi.

DARWIN: Crustaceans on the Wharf $$
Seafood
Stokes Hill Wharf, NT 0800
Tel *(08) 8981 8658* **Closed** *lunch*
Set on a pier where dolphins can sometimes be seen playing in the water. The menu showcases Australian seafood at its best.

DARWIN: Ducks Nuts Bar & Grill $$
Bistro
76 Mitchell St, NT 0800
Tel *(08) 8942 2122*
Something to suit all tastes – salads, burgers, steaks, seafood,

An assortment of delectable dishes on offer at Moorish Café, Darwin

curries and lamb shanks, as well as excellent coffee. Try the popular slow roasted beef cheeks.

DARWIN: Essence $$
Grill
Rydges Darwin Airport Resort, 1 Henry Wrigley Drive, Marrara, NT 0812
Tel *(08) 8920 3333*
The eclectic menu takes a little bit of Asia and Europe and gives it a local twist. Wonderful tropical ambience. Near the airport.

DK Choice

DARWIN: Hanuman $$
Asian
Holiday Inn Esplanade, 93 Mitchell St, NT 0800
Tel *(08) 8941 3500* **Closed** *Sat & Sun lunch*
Offering some of the Territory's best Asian food, Hanuman draws on Thai, Malaysian and Indian cuisines for its innovative menu. The skillfully prepared dishes are served against a stylish backdrop, but prices are reasonable and the atmosphere relaxed. Try the signature dish: oysters with lemongrass, chilli and coriander.

DARWIN: Il Lido $$
Italian
Wharf One, 19 Kitchener Drive, NT 0800
Tel *(08) 8941 0900*
Linger over a drink, tapas or Italian food at this polished restaurant with terraces overlooking the waterfront and wave pool.

DARWIN: Moorish Café $$
International
37 Knuckey St, NT 0800
Tel *(08) 8981 0010* **Closed** *Sun*
A Darwin favourite, with dishes inspired by the flavours of Spain, the Mediterranean and Northern Africa. Tropical cocktails and great coffee, too.

DARWIN: Viva la Vida $$
Tapas
48 50 Smith St Mall, NT 0800
Tel *(08) 8942 0544* **Closed** *Sun*
Funky bar with vast menu of tapas, including local buffalo milk cheese. Great drinks list, with around 50 wines by the glass.

DARWIN: Cove $$$
Seafood
Skycity Darwin, Gilruth Ave, The Gardens, NT 0800
Tel *(08) 8943 8940* **Closed** *Mon & Tue, Wed Fri lunch*
Heaven for seafood lovers. The selection of modern and classic dishes highlight fresh Australian seafood and local produce.

DARWIN: Evoo $$$
Fine Dining
Skycity Darwin, Gilruth Ave, The Gardens, NT 0800
Tel *(08) 8943 8940* **Closed** *Sun & Mon; lunch*
For an extravagant night out, enjoy first-class dining at Evoo and watch the sun set over Mindil Beach.

DARWIN: Pee Wee's at the Point $$$
Modern Australian
Alec Fong Lim Drive, East Point Reserve, Fanny Bay, NT 0801
Tel *(08) 8981 6868* **Closed** *lunch; Nov–Apr: Sun & Mon*
An enticing setting – most tables have views over the water. The menu reflects the Top End's multicultural flavour. Specialities include banana prawns and buffalo cheese.

JABIRU: Escarpment $$
Modern Australian
Gagudju Crocodile Holiday Inn, Flinders St, NT 0886
Tel *(08) 8979 9013*
After exploring Kakadu National Park, unwind in Jabiru's best restaurant. The barramundi is a speciality.

For more information on types of restaurants *see page 498*

KATHERINE: Big Fig $
Bistro
20 Shadforth Rd, NT 0850
Tel *(08) 9872 3311*
Nestled amid the trees in a
caravan park, Big Fig dishes up
good-value, home-style meals
and sweet treats. Friendly service.

KATHERINE:
The Finch Cafe $
Café
Katherine Terrace, NT 0850
Tel *(08) 8972 1990*   **Closed** *Mon*
Fresh food, good coffee and a
lively atmosphere makes this
eatery a good choice, particularly
for healthy breakfasts.

KATHERINE: Savannah Bar &
Restaurant $$
Bistro
Knott's Crossing Resort, cnr Giles &
Cameron sts, NT 0850
Tel *(08) 8972 2511*   **Closed** *dinner*
Serving a colourful, affordable
menu that highlights the tastes
and produce of the Top End. Go
for the roast pork, steaks, or salads.

MATARANKA: Katherine
Country Club $
Bistro
40 Pearce St (off Victoria Hwy),
NT 0850
Tel *(08) 8972 1276*
Basic bistro fare with limited
choice served in a casual setting.
Welcoming atmosphere.

The Red Centre

ALICE SPRINGS:
Epilogue Lounge $
Tapas
1/58 Todd St, NT 0870
Tel *(08) 8953 4206*   **Closed** *Tue*
Popular spot with relaxing
alfresco seating on the rooftop.
Good coffee and tapas menu.
Casual ambience.

ALICE SPRINGS:
Loco Burrito $
Mexican
Shop 10, 74 Todd St, NT 0870
Tel *(08) 8953 0518*   **Closed** *Sun*
A go-to place for a quick, hearty
lunch. Choose from a wide range
of burrito fillings on the menu, or
build your own. The pulled pork
is a favourite.

ALICE SPRINGS: Page 27 $
Café
3 Fan Arcade, NT 0870
Tel *(08) 8952 0191*   **Closed** *dinner*
Great café and an ideal pit stop
for breakfast or lunch. Enjoy
freshly prepared juices, coffees
and tasty, filling food.

Stunning scenery surrounds the dining area at Under a Desert Moon, Kings Canyon

ALICE SPRINGS: Hanuman $$
Asian
DoubleTree by Hilton Hotel,
82 Barrett Drive, NT 0870
Tel *(08) 8950 8000*   **Closed** *Sat &*
Sun lunch
Elaborate Thai artifacts greet
diners at this stylish restaurant.
The menu is an innovative fusion
of Thai and Indian.

ALICE SPRINGS:
Monte's Lounge $$
International
95 Todd St, NT 0870
Tel *(08) 8952 4336*   **Closed** *Mon & Tue*
Part restaurant, part cabaret venue.
A fun place to have dinner while
enjoying music and dance perfor-
mances. Extensive menu: pizzas,
steaks, curries and seafood.

ALICE SPRINGS:
Overlanders Steakhouse $$
Steak
72 Hartley St, NT 0870
Tel *(08) 8952 2159*
Serious meat, including huge
steaks, camel and kangaroo.
World-class wine cellar. Cricket
memorabilia on the walls.

ALICE SPRINGS: Sporties $$
Bistro
Ansett Building, 58 Todd Mall,
NT 0870
Tel *(08) 8953 0935*
A favourite with locals, this
restaurant-style pub is decked
out in sporting paraphernalia.
Light meals, pasta, meat and
vegetarian dishes in big portions.

ALICE SPRINGS:
Red Ochre Grill $$$
Native Australian
11 Leichhardt Terrace, NT 0870
Tel *(08) 8952 9614*
Seafood and native game take
on the flavours of the Australian
bush. Panoramic images by
photographer Ken Duncan
decorate the walls.

KINGS CANYON:
Desert Oaks Bistro $$
Bistro
Kings Canyon Resort, Luritja Rd,
Watarrka National Park
Tel *(08) 8956 7442*
Light meals and snacks during
the day and an evening à la carte
menu of steak, chicken and
seafood, all served in a relaxed
Outback setting.

KINGS CANYON: Outback
BBQ & Grill $$
Bistro
Kings Canyon Resort, Luritja Rd,
Watarrka National Park
Tel *(08) 8956 7442*   **Closed** *Nov–Mar*
Enjoy a true Aussie experience
on an Outback veranda. This
casual bar and grill offers barbe-
cued fare, salads and vegetables.

KINGS CANYON:
Under a Desert Moon $$$
Modern Australian
Kings Canyon Resort, Luritja Rd,
Watarrka National Park
Tel *(08) 8956 7442*   **Closed** *Nov–Mar;*
Tue, Thu & Sun
Dine under the stars in this
intimate venue where places
are limited to 16 people. Begin
with a glass of bubbly around the
campfire before indulging in a
four-course menu of fine food.

TENNANT CREEK: Woks Up $$
Chinese
108 Patterson St, NT 0860
Tel *(08) 8962 3888*
Generous portions of Chinese
dishes with some Malaysian influences. Quick service.

YULARA: Bough House
Restaurant $$
Native Australian
Outback Pioneer Hotel, Yulara Drive,
NT 0870
Tel *(02) 8296 8010*
Buffalo, wallaby, kangaroo and
crocodile all feature in the buffet

that brings the spirit of the Outback to the table of this family-friendly restaurant.

YULARA: Ilkari Restaurant $$
International
Sails in the Desert Hotel,
Yulara Drive, NT 0870
Tel *(02) 8296 8010*
Indigenous flavours add a local touch to an eclectic international menu of roasts, grills, pasta dishes and Asian specialities.

YULARA: Arnguli Grill $$$
Brasserie
Desert Gardens Hotel, Yulara Drive,
NT 0870
Tel *(02) 8957 7714*
Delectable food – the highlight being steaks cooked to perfection – along with lovely decor and good service make this pleasant restaurant a go-to place in Yulara.

YULARA:
Sounds of Silence $$$
Modern Australian
Ayers Rock Resort, Yulara Drive,
NT 0870
Tel *(02) 8296 8010*
Listen to the sound of the didgeridoo as the sun sets, enjoy a buffet of bush tucker-inspired dishes, and finish the evening with a round of storytelling and star-gazing.

DK Choice

YULARA: Tali Wiru $$$
Modern Australian
Ayers Rock Resort, Yulara Drive,
NT 0870
Tel *(02) 8296 8010* **Closed** *Nov–Mar*
Much more than just a dining experience, Tali Wiru offers a memorable night under the stars, limited to just 20 people. As the sun sets on Uluru, guests enjoy a four-course dinner with premium wines and soak up the spirituality of the indigenous people and their connection to the land.

Perth and the Southwest

ALBANY: Due South $$
Pub
6 Toll Place, WA 6330
Tel *(08) 9841 8526*
This waterfront restaurant offers fantastic views of Albany and King George Sound. The menu includes regular pub favourites and a choice of drinks.

COWARAMUP: Vasse Felix $$
Winery Restaurant
Cnr Tom Cullity Dr & Caves Rd,
WA 6284
Tel *(08) 9756 5050* **Closed** *dinner;*
public hols
The beautiful setting of vineyards and bush is surpassed only by the food, which incorporates local produce in a superb array of flavourful contemporary dishes.

DARLINGTON:
Darlington Estate Winery $$
Winery Restaurant
1495 Nelson Rd, WA 6070
Tel *(08) 9299 6268* **Closed** *Mon–Wed*
Located 25 minutes from Perth's CBD, this place delivers picturesque views over the bush land. The seasonal menu has low-fat, gluten-free and vegetarian options.

FREMANTLE: Gino's Cafe
& Trattoria $$
Italian
1–5 South Terrace, WA 6160
Tel *(08) 9336 1464*
Located at Fremantle's famous Cappuccino Strip, this café is a great place to unwind while enjoying coffee or chilli mussels – the house favourite.

FREMANTLE: Little Creatures
Brewery $$
Tapas
40 Mews Rd, WA 6160
Tel *(08) 6215 1000*
Order some tapas dishes and a glass of Little Creatures Pale Ale, then kick back and relax in this busy brewery-café. Try the signature kangaroo skewers.

GRACETOWN: Sunsets Café
Gracetown $$
Fusion
4 Bayview Drive, WA 6284
Tel *(08) 9755 9271* **Closed** *Jun–Aug*
This cosy café and restaurant has an Austrian-influenced menu and serves a range of breakfasts, burgers, soups and muffins.

JARRAHDALE:
Millbrook Winery $$
Winery Restaurant
Old Chestnut Lane, WA 6124
Tel *(08) 9525 5796* **Closed** *Mon & Tue*
Spectacular forest setting with sweeping views. Seasonal menu prepared using local produce and vegetables picked daily from the restaurant's kitchen garden.

MANDURAH: The Bridge Garden
Bar & Restaurant $$
Bistro
Cnr Mandurah Terrace & Pinjarra Rd,
WA 6210
Tel *(08) 9535 1004*
Located in one of the city's most historic buildings. Guests enjoy fresh local ingredients in a lovely waterside setting.

MANDURAH: M on the Point $$
Modern Australian
1 Marco Polo Drive, WA 6210
Tel *(08) 9534 9899*
Modern gastropub with an easy-going vibe and water views. Extensive menu with burgers and pizzas, as well as hearty dishes.

MANJIMUP:
The Truffle Kitchen $$
Modern Australian
The Truffle & Wine Co, 490 Seven
Day Rd, WA 6258
Tel *(08) 9777 2474* **Closed** *dinner;*
Mon–Wed lunch
The menu and chalkboard specials highlight seasonal local produce. Excellent truffles in season. Local wines to match.

MARGARET RIVER: Cullen
Restaurant $$
Winery Restaurant
4323 Caves Rd, WA 6280
Tel *(08) 9755 5656* **Closed** *dinner*
Sophisticated dishes made with fresh, organic ingredients, many of them sourced from the winery's own garden.

Spectacular setting looking out to Uluru at Tali Wiru, Yulara

For more information on types of restaurants *see page 498*

MARGARET RIVER:
Muster Bar and Grill $$
Bistro
107 Bussell Hwy, WA 6285
Tel *(08) 9758 8877* **Closed** *public hols*
Detailed attention goes into the
menu here, emphasising organic
produce and aged beef. Diners
eat at a communal table. Well-
thought-out wine list.

MARGARET RIVER: Xanadu $$
Modern Australian
Boodjidup Rd, WA 6285
Tel *(08) 9295 9500* **Closed** *Tue &
Wed; dinner*
A lovely place to linger over a
sophisticated lunch of Middle
Eastern-inspired dishes, including
some great vegetarian options.

MARGARET RIVER:
Leeuwin Estate Winery $$$
Modern Australian
Stevens Rd, WA 6285
Tel *(08) 9759 0000* **Closed** *dinner
(except Sat)*
One of Margaret River's finest
restaurants, serving outstanding
food and wine in a peaceful,
picturesque setting.

MUNDARING:
Little Caesars Pizza $
Pizzeria
7125 Great Eastern Hwy, WA 6073
Tel *(08) 9295 6611* **Closed** *Tue; lunch
(except Sun)*
Creativity and the use of top-
quality ingredients have won this
pizza company a string of awards.
Don't miss the dessert pizzas.

PEMBERTON:
Foragers Field Kitchen $$
Modern Australian
*Cnr Roberts & Pemberton Northcliffe
rds, WA 6260*
Tel *(08) 9776 1580* **Closed** *Sun–
Thu; lunch*
Cooking school offering a
unique dining experience at

long tables. The seasonal menu
relies on ingredients grown
locally and on site.

PERTH: The Byrneleigh Hotel $
Modern Australian
*156 Hampden Rd, Nedlands,
WA 6009*
Tel *(08) 6161 2722*
Good-value dining at this trendy
local pub. Specials are also
available several nights a week.

DK Choice

PERTH: Greenhouse $
Australian
100 St Georges Terrace, WA 6000
Tel *(08) 9481 8333* **Closed** *Sun*
The menus at this eco-friendly
venue are always interesting.
There is a thoughtful and
sometimes playful use of
seasonal, local ingredients,
served in quirky surrounds.
Here recycling is chic; chairs
are made from road signs and
water poured from old
milk bottles.

PERTH:
Peninsula Tea Gardens $
Tearoom
*Peninsula Farm Tranby House, 2A
Johnson Rd, Maylands, WA 6051*
Tel *(08) 9272 8894*
Tranby House is a lovely spot
to enjoy afternoon tea with
tranquil views of the river.

PERTH:
The Bird Cage Restaurant $$
Asian
Level 1, 140 William St, WA 6000
Tel *(08) 9226 0259* **Closed** *Sun & Mon*
Cool restaurant and bar in The
Aviary, which offers an Asian-
inspired menu and bird's-eye
views. Dishes are designed to be
shared to encourage guests to
explore different flavours.

Contemporary decor at The Byrneleigh
Hotel eatery, Perth

PERTH: Divido $$
Modern Italian
*170 Scarborough Beach Rd,
Mt Hawthorn, WA 6050*
Tel *(08) 9443 7373* **Closed** *Sun; lunch*
A casual Italian eating and
drinking experience in an
intimate, cosy venue. Highly
experienced chef.

PERTH: The George $$
Modern Australian
216 St Georges Terrace, WA 6000
Tel *(08) 6161 6662* **Closed** *Sun
(except afternoon tea)*
A sophisticated venue open
for breakfasts, leisurely lunches,
dinners and drinks. Afternoon
teas on offer at weekends.

PERTH: La Vie $$
Fine Dining
*Crown Perth, Great Eastern Hwy,
Burswood, WA 6100*
Tel *(08) 9362 7777* **Closed** *Sun; lunch*
Enjoy a stunning array of delicate
canapés, including oysters and
caviar. There is an opulent lounge
serving the finest champagne,
cocktails and spirits.

PERTH: Meeka Restaurant $$
International
361 Rokeby Rd, Subiaco, WA 6008
Tel *(08) 9381 1800* **Closed** *Sun &
Mon; lunch*
Head chef Leah Clarke dishes up
a wonderful menu of contem-
porary Australian delights infused
with a Middle Eastern twist. Don't
miss their delicious desserts.

PERTH: Must Wine Bar $$
Modern Australian/Wine Bar
519 Beaufort St, Highgate, WA 6003
Tel *(08) 9328 8255*
Food and wine aficionados flock
to this little slice of France. Great
bistro fare, cool ambience and
more than 500 wines.

Foragers Field Kitchen nestled in the forest, Pemberton

Key to Price Guide *see page 504*

PERTH: Pata Negra $$
Spanish
26 Stirling Hwy, Nedlands, WA 6009
Tel *(08) 9389 5517* **Closed** *Sun & Mon; lunch (except Fri); Fri dinner*
Tapas bar with home-made charcuterie, flavourful vegetable dishes, the signature cuttlefish paella and a nine-course degustation menu.

PERTH: St Michael 6003 $$
Modern Australian
483 Beaufort St, Highgate, WA 6003
Tel *(08) 9328 1177* **Closed** *Mon & Tue; lunch*
Inventive small plates prepared using local ingredients. Degustation menu on offer for dinner. Exceptional service.

PERTH: Balthazar $$$
Modern Australian
6 The Esplanade, WA 6000
Tel *(08) 9421 1206* **Closed** *Sat lunch; Sun*
Busy spot inside a heritage building. Creative and seasonal menu offering oysters, snapper, emu and duck, all cooked to perfection. A 400-strong wine list.

PERTH: C Restaurant $$$
Fine Dining
Level 33, 44 St Georges Terrace, WA 6000
Tel *(08) 9220 8333*
Enjoy stunning city and river views from this revolving restaurant. The sophisticated menu matches the prime location. Elegant afternoon tea, too.

PERTH: Fraser's Restaurant $$$
Modern Australian
Fraser's Ave, King's Park, West Perth, WA 6005
Tel *(08) 9481 7100*
Informal yet refined, with views of the city and Swan River. The menu changes regularly and draws on European and Asian flavours and quality local fare.

PERTH: Restaurant Amuse $$$
Modern Australian
64 Bronte St, East Perth, WA 6004
Tel *(08) 9325 4900* **Closed** *Sun & Mon; lunch*
A special-occasion restaurant whose degustation menu is a delight. The food is pure artistry.

SWAN VALLEY: Elmars in the Valley $$$
German
8731 West Swan Rd, Henley Brook, WA 6055
Tel *(08) 9296 6354* **Closed** *Mon & Tue*
Great dining venue in the valley offering German-flavoured dishes. Don't forget to sample their locally brewed beers.

Expertly prepared dish from the "Trust the chef" menu at Knee Deep in Margaret River

WALPOLE: Slow Food Café $$
Winery Restaurant
Old Kent River Winery, South Coast Hwy, Kentdale, WA 6397
Tel *(08) 9840 8136* **Closed** *Mon & Tue; dinner*
A pleasant stop after the treetop walk. Home-grown menu based around marron, a local crustacean, and lamb reared on the property.

WILYABRUP: Flutes $$
Winery Restaurant
Brookland Valley Wines, 4070 Caves Rd, WA 6280
Tel *(08) 9755 6250* **Closed** *Tue & Wed (in winter); dinner*
Sample the chef's fine cooking in a magical setting overlooking the Wilyabrup Brook. Great local wines.

WILYABRUP: Knee Deep Wines in Margaret River $$
Winery Restaurant
160 Johnson Rd, WA 6280
Tel *(08) 9755 6776* **Closed** *dinner*
Fine seasonal food befitting the beautiful vineyard setting. The "Trust the chef" degustation menus add a fun element.

YALLINGUP: Cape Lodge $$$
Fine Dining
3341 Caves Rd, WA 6282
Tel *(08) 9755 6311* **Closed** *lunch; Mon dinner (Jun–Aug)*
Boutique hotel offering cooking classes, a superb cellar and fine food featuring local ingredients. The menu changes daily.

North of Perth and the Kimberley

BROOME: 1861 Restaurant & Bar $$
Modern Australian
Oaks Broome, 99 Robinson St, WA 6725
Tel *(08) 9192 9500* **Closed** *lunch (except Sun)*
Indulge in gourmet pizzas, barramundi, Kimberley ribeye and porterhouse steak.

BROOME: The Aarli $$
Modern Australian
Cnr Frederick & Hamersley sts, WA 6725
Tel *(08) 9192 5529*
Asian-inspired restaurant with all-day dining. Signature dishes include jungle curry, crispy pork hock and coconut battered threadfin salmon.

BROOME: Cables Restaurant & Bar $$
International
Oaks Cable Beach Sanctuary, 1 Lullfitz Drive, WA 6726
Tel *(08) 9192 8088*
Stunning pool views. Enjoy a choice of light or hearty breakfasts. In the evening, mains include seafood, prime beef and pasta dishes.

BROOME: The Mango Place $$
Modern Australian
Lot 4, 120 Kanagae Drive, 12 Mile, Kanagae Estate, WA 6725
Tel *(08) 9192 5462*
Sample mango wine and relax in the shade with beef and mango pie or a slice of mango liqueur cake. Wood-fired pizzas on Friday and Sunday (Apr–Jan).

BROOME: Matso's Broome Brewery $$
Modern Australian
60 Hamersley St, WA 6725
Tel *(08) 9193 5811*
Try the mango-flavoured beer at this microbrewery. The menu changes seasonally.

BROOME: Zanders at Cable Beach $$
Modern Australian
Cable Beach Rd, WA 6726
Tel *(08) 9193 5090*
This relaxed, child-friendly beach-front haven offers a contemporary menu with culinary influences from all over the world. Lively atmosphere and friendly service.

DK Choice

BROOME: Club Restaurant $$$
Italian
Cable Beach Club Resort, 1 Cable Beach Rd, WA 6725
Tel *(08) 9192 0411* **Closed** *Sun & Mon; lunch*
This award-winning restaurant serves local dishes such as Harvey grain-fed beef, pearl meat and barramundi with a tropical twist. Enjoy exquisite food and wine under the stars or inside, among extraordinary artworks by the likes of Elizabeth Durack and Sir Sydney Nolan.

CARNARVON: Water's Edge $$
Seafood
Carnarvon Hotel, 121–125 Olivia Terrace, WA 6701
Tel *(08) 9941 1181* **Closed** *Sun Tue*
Watch the glorious sunset while enjoying a quick snack or gourmet fare such as seared scallops, fresh crabs, prawns or fish from Shark Bay.

CARNARVON: The Good Paddock Restaurant $$$
International
The Gascoyne Hotel, 57 Olivia Terrace, WA 6701
Tel *(08) 9941 1412*
A delightfully relaxing spot. Various specials are available on different nights, with an emphasis on local seafood and produce. Eight beers on tap.

CORAL BAY: Fins Café $$
International
Peoples Park Shopping Village, Robinson St, WA 6701
Tel *(08) 9942 5900*
The eclectic menu highlights local seafood; try the Cajun soft-shell crab. Good Mediterranean dishes and curries as well.

DENHAM:
The Old Pearler Restaurant $$
Modern Australian
71 Knight Terrace, WA 6537
Tel *(08) 9948 1373*
Full of character, the Old Pearler is the world's only restaurant built entirely of coquina shells. Seafood is a speciality here.

ECO BEACH:
Jack's Bar & Restaurant $$
Modern Australian
Thangoo Station/Lot323 Great Northern Hwy, WA 6725
Tel *(08) 9193 8015*
Situated on Aboriginal land, this eco-friendly place offers great ocean views. The focus is on natural flavours, and much of the food is home-grown. The seasonal menu is simply delicious.

Bistro Dom, a popular restaurant in Adelaide

EXMOUTH:
Mantaray's Restaurant $$
Brasserie
Novotel Ningaloo Resort, Madaffari Drive, WA 6707
Tel *(08) 9949 0000*
A relaxed ambience with great gulf views. The varied menu includes risotto, pasta dishes, meat and seafood.

KALBARRI:
Finlay's Fresh Fish $
Seafood
24 Magee Crescent, WA 6536
Tel *(08) 9937 1260* **Closed** *Mon; lunch*
No-frills BYO eatery in a tin shed where guests can actually sing for their supper and gain a free meal. Wonderfully fresh seafood, as well as barbecued steaks and chicken, burgers. Good value for money.

KARRATHA:
Blanche Bar $$
Modern Australian/Mediterranean
Pelago Centre, cnr Warambie Rd & Sharpe Ave, WA 6714
Tel *(08) 9185 6667*
Great wine and cocktail list, boutique beers and ciders, tapas and mains. Go for the Surf & Turf – barramundi with seared lamb cutlets and cider jus.

ONSLOW: Nikki's Licensed Restaurant $$
Modern Australian
17 First Ave, WA 6710
Tel *(08) 9184 6121* **Closed** *Sun dinner; Mon*
An unexpected find at the end of a long road, Nikki's is popular for its delicious steak and seafood dishes. The salt-and-pepper squid is a local favourite.

POINT SAMSON:
Tata's Restaurant $$$
International
56 Samson Rd, WA 6720
Tel *(08) 9187 1052*
Premium fresh seafood, prime beef and free-range chicken feature in an internationally inspired menu. Tata's offers one of the region's finest food and wine experiences.

PORT HEDLAND:
Silver Star Café $$
Café
12a Edgar St, WA 6721
Tel *(04) 1114 3663* **Closed** *dinner (except Fri & Sat)*
The Sundowner, a 1930s railway dining car, gets a new lease of life as a quirky BYO café. Daytime meals and a set evening menu of tapas on Friday and Saturday.

SHARK BAY:
Boughshed Restaurant $$
Modern Australian
Monkey Mia Dolphin Resort, Monkey Mia, WA 6537
Tel *(08) 9948 1171*
Dine within metres of the ocean. Dinner includes fresh local seafood, beef and vegetarian fare. Coffee and snacks all day.

Adelaide and the South East

ADELAIDE: Bar 9 $
Australian
96 Glen Osmond Rd, Parkside, SA 5063
A local favourite, Bar 9 is a go-to place for good-value, healthy breakfasts (served till 2pm). Don't forget to try their famous coffee.

ADELAIDE: Ying Chow $
Asian
114 Gouger St, SA 5000
Tel *(08) 8221 7998* **Closed** *Fri lunch*
Although loud and with little atmosphere, this popular eatery has a loyal following. Try the tea-smoked duck and shallot pancakes.

Devilled lamb cutlets with crushed potato and mustard seed salad, Blanche Bar, Karratha

Key to Price Guide *see page 504*

ADELAIDE: Bistro Dom $$
French
24 Waymouth St, SA 5000
Tel (08) 8231 7000
Choose from French-inspired
bistro fare such as duck,
charcuterie and frites.
Imaginative desserts and an
extensive wine list.

**ADELAIDE:
Jolleys Boathouse** $$
Modern Australian
1 Jolleys Lane, SA 5000
Tel (08) 8223 2891   **Closed** Mon–
Thu lunch
An elegant space by the river
with alfresco dining in summer
and a fire in winter. Asian and
Middle Eastern flavours feature
on the seasonal menu.

**ADELAIDE:
Kenji Modern Japanese** $$
Japanese
Shop 5, 242 Hutt St, SA 5000
Tel (08) 8232 0944 **Closed** Sun; lunch
Behind an unassuming shopfront,
this compact restaurant delivers
creative East-meets-West dishes
with a Japanese touch. Try the
signature slow-cooked pork belly.

**ADELAIDE:
The Pot Food & Wine** $$
Bistro
160 King William Rd, Hyde Park,
SA 5061
Tel (08) 8373 2044   **Closed** Mon
Laid-back, unpretentious spot to
enjoy appetizing small plates of
top-quality food. The extensive
wine list covers about 300 labels.

ADELAIDE: The Unley $$
Modern Australian
27 Unley Rd, Parkside, SA 5063
Tel (08) 8271 5544
Sophisticated bar and restaurant
with modern interiors. It has an
outdoor rooftop and lounge
areas. Well-chosen list of wines.

ADELAIDE: Auge $$$
Italian
22 Grote St, SA 5000
Tel (08) 8410 9332   **Closed** Sun;
lunch (except Fri)
Fine food and wine with an
Italian accent, served in elegant
surroundings. Classic dishes and
modern interpretations. Fixed
price Friday and Saturday nights.

ADELAIDE: Celsius $$$
Modern Australian
95–97 Gouger St, SA 5000
Tel (08) 8231 6023   **Closed** Sun &
Mon; lunch (except Fri)
Top-quality meat and home-
grown produce combine to form
creative and beautifully presented
food in this dimly lit space.

ADELAIDE: Chianti Classico $$$
Italian
160 Hutt St, SA 5000
Tel (08) 8232 7955
This long-established and highly
regarded Italian diner delivers
the classics with precision. Try
the slow-cooked rabbit or the
pappardelle with duck.

ADELAIDE: Orana $$$
Modern Australian
285 Rundle St, SA 5000
Tel (08) 8232 3444
This place offers an innovative
touch to contemporary
Australian cuisine. The menu
makes good use of indigenous
produce. Impressive selection
of wines.

**ADELAIDE:
Press Food and Wine** $$$
Modern Australian
40 Waymouth St, SA 5000
Tel (08) 8211 8048   **Closed** Sun
A popular and trendy downstairs
area, plus a more formal section
upstairs. Good food and an
extensive wine list. The tasting
menu is a highlight.

**THE BAROSSA:
1918 Bistro & Grill** $$
Modern Australian
94 Murray St, Tanunda, SA 5352
Tel (08) 8563 0405
A gorgeous 1918 stone villa is
the setting for an Australian
menu with a touch of Asia.
Dine in the beautiful garden.

**THE BAROSSA:
FermentAsian** $$
Asian
90 Murray St, Tanunda, SA 5352
Tel (08) 8563 0765   **Closed** Mon &
Tue; Wed lunch & Sun dinner
This award-winning restaurant
brings a fresh Asian touch to
the European-focused Barossa

Casual outdoor seating at the Appellation at The Louise, The Barossa

wine region with dishes such
as red duck curry with lychee
and pineapple.

**THE BAROSSA:
The Lord Lyndoch** $$
Bistro
23 Barossa Valley Way, Lyndoch,
SA 5351
Tel (08) 8524 5440
Quaint, old-world eatery with a
somewhat retro menu that
delivers highly praised food.
Cape Grim steak is a favourite.
Generous portions.

**THE BAROSSA:
Taste Eden Valley** $$
Australian
6 Washington St, Angaston, SA 5353
Tel (08) 8564 2435
Housed in a historic building.
Great opportunity to taste
award-winning, boutique wines
made in the valley. Helpful and
knowledgeable staff.

**THE BAROSSA:
Appellation at The Louise** $$$
Modern Australian
Cnr Seppeltsfield & Stonewall rds,
Marananga, SA 5355
Tel (08) 8562 4144   **Closed** lunch
This boutique hotel offers
five-star dining with ingredients
from its kitchen garden and
bespoke producers. Helicopter
transfer can be arranged
from Adelaide.

**THE BAROSSA:
Hentley Farm** $$$
Winery Restaurant
Cnr Gerald Roberts & Jenke rds,
Seppeltsfield, SA 5355
Tel (08) 8562 8427   **Closed** Mon–
Wed; Thu, Fri & Sun dinner
Brilliant food presented in the
restored stables of an 1840s
homestead, now a boutique
cellar door.

For more information on types of restaurants see page 498

THE BAROSSA:
Jacob's Restaurant $$$
Winery Restaurant
Jacob's Creek, Barossa Valley Way,
Rowland Flat, SA 5352
Tel *(08) 8521 3000*   **Closed** *dinner*
The contemporary menu is
designed by one of the state's
leading chefs. A great spot to
dine while experiencing some of
Australia's wine-making history.

BRIDGEWATER: Petaluma's
Bridgewater Mill $$$
Modern Australian
386 Mount Barker Rd, SA 5155
Tel *(08) 8339 9200*   **Closed** *dinner*
Housed in a historic 1860s flour
mill. Sample elegant food with a
distinctive European edge, such
as seared venison with glazed
pear and black pudding.

COONAWARRA: Fodder $$
Café
5 Memorial Drive, SA 5263
Tel *(08) 8736 3170*   **Closed** *Tue &*
Wed; dinner
Organic produce – mainly from
the Fodder garden – is used
here. There is a great selection
of wood-fired pizzas. Book ahead.

COONAWARRA:
Upstairs at Hollick $$
Winery Restaurant
Cnr Riddoch Hwy & Ravenswood Ln,
SA 5263
Tel *(08) 8737 2318*   **Closed** *Mon &*
Tue; dinner (except Sat)
Sublime food and wine served in
quiet and relaxing surroundings.
The full-length windows afford
great views of the vineyard.

GUMERACHA:
Chain of Ponds Balcony Café $$
Winery Restaurant
198C Torrens Valley, SA 5233
Tel *(08) 8389 1415*   **Closed** *Tue–Thu;*
dinner
Sit on the balcony with a glass of
wine and feast on country-style
pies, cheese and regional platters.

HAHNDORF:
Chocolate @ No 5 $
Café
5 Main St, SA 5245
Tel *(08) 8388 1835*   **Closed** *Mon &*
Tue; dinner
Popular café to indulge in
scrumptious sweet treats,
including waffles, chocolate
brownies and caramel slices.

HAHNDORF: Sikko's
Pannekoeken Huis $
Dessert
Shop 3, 13–15 Mount Barker Rd,
SA 5245
Tel *(08) 8388 7428*   **Closed** *dinner*
Savour tasty pancakes from all
over the world at this delightful
restaurant. *Poffertjes* (small, fluffy
Dutch pancakes) with butter and
icing are must-tries.

HAHNDORF:
The Lane Vineyard $$
Winery Restaurant
Ravenswood Lane, SA 5245
Tel *(08) 8388 1250*   **Closed** *dinner*
Exquisite food served in a
beautiful setting overlooking the
vineyard and hills beyond. There
is a wood fire in winter and alfresco
dining in the summer months.

KINGSTON-ON-MURRAY:
Banrock Station $$
Modern Australian
Holmes Rd, SA 5331
Tel *(08) 8583 0299*   **Closed** *dinner*
Native Australian ingredients –
wattleseed, pepperleaf, lemon
myrtle – take centre stage here.
Sit on the deck and enjoy grazing
platters, pizzas or hearty mains.

McLAREN VALE:
The Barn Bistro $$
Modern Australian
252 Main Rd, SA 5171
Tel *(08) 8323 8618*
Renowned for its high-quality
food, ambience and good service.
Guests can choose a bottle from
the walk-in wine cellar.

Pleasant outdoor terrace at Chocolate @
No 5, Hahndorf

McLAREN VALE:
Coterie Restaurant $$
Winery Restaurant
Woodstock Wine Estate, Douglas
Gully Rd, McLaren Flat, SA 5171
Tel *(08) 8383 0156*   **Closed** *Wed;*
dinner (except Fri)
Sample the regional platter or
choose from the à la carte menu
at this lovely restaurant nestled in
the bush. There is an impressive
list of wines made at the family-
owned winery.

DK Choice

McLAREN VALE:
d'Arry's Verandah $$$
Winery Restaurant
d'Arenberg Winery, Osborn Rd,
SA 5171
Tel *(08) 8329 4848*   **Closed** *dinner*
There are few better ways
to spend an afternoon than
dining on the veranda
looking out over undulating
vineyards and the distant
hills. The postcard view at
d'Arry's Verandah provides
a perfect backdrop for the
signature dish of lobster
medallion with prawn and
lobster ravioli, and desserts
such as passion fruit soufflé
or the wonderfully soft-centred
chocolate pudding.

McLAREN VALE:
The Kitchen Door $$$
Modern Australian
Penny's Hill Winery, 281 Main Rd,
SA 5171
Tel *(08) 8557 0840* Closed *Tue & Wed*
Diners look out to vineyards and
grazing sheep at this restaurant
of the renowned Penny's Hill
Winery. Tasting menu of four
courses matched or unmatched
with wine, as well as an à la carte
selection of more substantial
seasonal dishes. Book in advance.

A beautifully presented entrée platter at Coterie Restaurant, McLaren Vale

Key to Price Guide *see page 504*

McLAREN VALE:
Serafino $$$
Winery Restaurant
Kangarilla Rd, SA 5171
Tel *(08) 8323 0157* **Closed** *Thu–Sat lunch*
Located near a tranquil lake, surrounded by 200-year-old gum trees. A great place to relax and enjoy dishes including the superb chargrilled beef fillet.

NORTON SUMMIT:
The Scenic Hotel $$
Modern Australian
Old Norton Summit Rd, SA 5136
Tel *(08) 8390 1705*
Dine on the deck in summer and by open fires in winter. Blackboard specials change nearly every day. The wine list focuses on the Adelaide Hills. Breathtaking views.

OVERLAND CORNER:
Overland Corner Hotel $
Modern Australian
Old Coach Rd, SA 5345
Tel *(08) 8588 7021*
Built in 1859, this National Trust-owned hotel takes guests back in time. The restaurant serves hearty, wholesome food, including beautifully cooked root and beef.

PENOLA: Pipers of Penola $$
Modern Australian
58 Riddoch St, SA 5277
Tel *(08) 8737 3999* **Closed** *Sun & Mon*
In a lovely old building that once served as a church. Stylish yet casual restaurant showcasing top-quality regional produce.

PORT WILLUNGA:
Star of Greece $$
Modern Australian
1 Esplanade, SA 5173
Tel *(08) 8557 7420* **Closed** *Mon & Tue; dinner (except Fri & Sat)*
Beach-house vibe, with amazing ocean views. Fresh seafood and local produce are presented with flair. Excellent wine list.

STIRLING:
Organic Market & Café $
Café
5 Druid Ave, SA 5152
Tel *(08) 8339 4835* **Closed** *dinner*
This organic grocer-cum-café serves simple, wholesome food including *antipasti*, soups, salads, focaccias, bruschetta, curries and cakes. Good coffee, too.

STIRLING: Locavore $$
Modern Australian
49 Mount Barker Rd, SA 5152
Tel *(08) 8339 4416* **Closed** *Mon; Sun dinner*
The food, wherever possible, is sourced from within a 160-km (100-mile) radius of this Adelaide

The pretty patio area at Reilly's Cellar Door and Restaurant, Clare Valley

Hills eatery. The wine list is from the region as well. The tapas platter is great for sharing and includes dishes such as pork and almond terrine.

WILLUNGA: Fino $$
Modern Australian
8 Hill St, SA 5712
Tel *(08) 8556 4488* **Closed** *Mon; dinner (except Fri & Sat)*
Mediterranean decor, a superb wine list and a menu that focuses on local produce. One of the country's best regional restaurants.

WILLUNGA: Russell's Pizza $$
Pizzeria
13 High St, SA 5712
Tel *(08) 8556 2571* **Closed** *Sun–Wed*
Rustic decor with old wooden tables and stone floors. Thin-crust pizzas have toppings such as slow-cooked lamb, fresh seafood and roasted vegetables.

The Yorke and Eyre Peninsulas and South Australian Outback

CLARE VALLEY: Mr. Mick $
Tapas
7 Dominic St, SA 5453
Tel *(08) 8842 2555* **Closed** *dinner (except Fri)*
Enjoy tapas-style dining in a casual atmosphere at this award-winning restaurant. The wine cellar offers tasting notes for a range of wines crafted in-house.

CLARE VALLEY: Artisans Table $$
Modern Australian
Wendouree Rd, SA 5453
Tel *(08) 8842 1796* **Closed** *Mon & Tue, Sun dinner*
In a picturesque country setting, the chef offers a diverse menu of meticulously crafted food inspired by and featuring Mediterranean and North African flavours.

CLARE VALLEY: Reilly's Cellar Door and Restaurant $$
Australian
Cnr Hill St & Leasingham Rd, Mintaro, SA 5415
Tel *(08) 8843 9013* **Closed** *dinner*
Dine in a heritage-listed stone cottage. Daily specials feature fresh local produce. Leave some room for the home-made cakes and desserts.

CLARE VALLEY:
Skillogalee Wines $$
Winery Restaurant
Trevarrick Rd, via Clare, Sevenhill, SA 5453
Tel *(08) 8843 4311* **Closed** *dinner*
This charming 1850s cottage serves a contemporary Australian menu to match the wines on offer. Dine on the veranda or under the olive tree.

COFFIN BAY: 1802 Oyster Bar + Bistro $$
Seafood
61 Esplanade, SA 5607
Tel *(08) 8685 4626*
Relish local oysters caught straight from the bay, cooked and served at your table. Outdoor seating available.

COOBER PEDY: Tom & Mary's Greek Taverna $$
Greek
2 Hutchison St, SA 5723
Tel *(08) 8672 5622* **Closed** *lunch*
An Outback gem, this busy diner evokes the flavours of Greece with dishes such as *moussaka*, *gyro*, Greek salads and seafood. Try the popular Saganaki prawns.

COOBER PEDY: Umberto's $$
International
Desert Cave Hotel, 20 Hutchison St, SA 5723
Tel *(08) 8672 5688* **Closed** *lunch*
Mediterranean pasta, fish and chicken dishes are served in a relaxed setting with desert views. The Essential Tastes of the Outback platter is an excellent choice.

For more information on types of restaurants *see page 498*

Simple interior of Marion Bay Tavern, Marion Bay

HAWKER: The Woolshed Restaurant $$$
Native Australian
Rawnsley Park Station, Wilpena Rd, SA 5434
Tel *(08) 8648 0126*
Sit inside a renovated authentic woolshed or dine on the outdoor deck with views across Rawnsley Bluff. Try the famous "Lamb on a Spit" evenings during May and June.

MARION BAY: Marion Bay Tavern $$
Bistro
Section 90/Stenhouse Bay Rd, SA 5575
Tel *(08) 8854 4141*
Corrugated iron and old jetty pylons lend this bistro a rustic beachside vibe. Wood-fired pizzas and innovative seafood dishes.

MOONTA BAY: Coffee Barn Gelateria $
Café
Warren St, SA 5558
Tel *(08) 8825 2315* **Closed** *Mon–Thu*
Unpretentious café set on 11 ha (27 acres) of historical mining country. Try the tasty pancakes and home-made gelato. Relaxed atmosphere and friendly service.

PARACHILNA: Prairie Hotel $$
Native Australian
High St, SA 5730
Tel *(08) 8648 4844*
Outback pub renowned for its creative use of native and feral (wild plant) ingredients. There are plenty of choices for the less adventurous, too.

PORT LINCOLN: The Rogue & Rascal $
Café
62 Tasman Terrace, SA 5606
Tel *(04) 6761 1086*
A perfect spot to enjoy a light lunch followed by great coffee, or sip on a glass of whiskey or wine after dinner.

DK Choice

PORT LINCOLN: Del Giorno's Café Restaurant $$
Seafood
80 Tasman Terrace, SA 5606
Tel *(08) 8683 0577*
Port Lincoln offers some of South Australia's finest seafood. For the best of the catch, visit Del Giorno's, where Kinkawooka mussels, King George whiting, Arno Bay kingfish and southern bluefin tuna feature regularly. The extensive menu draws on local produce, including beef and lamb, served in friendly, comfortable surroundings.

WALLAROO: Prince Edward Hotel $
Modern Australian
32 Hughes St, SA 5556
Tel *(08) 8823 2579*
Value-for-money pub food at this local favourite. Salad bar, veggie options and great seafood platters. The fish 'n' chips features the prized King George whiting.

WAROOKA: Inland Sea $$
Seafood
12918 Yorke Hwy, SA 5577
Tel *(08) 8854 5499* **Closed** *Mon & Tue*
The perfect setting for a casual dinner. Dine inside or alfresco in the courtyard. Signature dishes may include a seafood platter or the classic reef and beef.

WHYALLA: Watersedge Restaurant $$
Modern Australian
12 Watson Terrace, SA 5600
Tel *(08) 8645 8877* **Closed** *lunch (except Fri)*
Dedicated owners are committed to taking this restaurant to new heights. Local ingredients star in dishes such as panko crumbed King George whiting and the signature dessert Eton Mess.

Melbourne

CARLTON: Abla's $$
Lebanese
109 Elgin St, VIC 3053
Tel *(03) 9347 0006* **Closed** *Sun*
Melbourne's love affair with Lebanese and Middle Eastern cuisine was kindled by Abla Amad's hearty, tangy classics. Try the chicken rice pilaf with almonds and pine nuts.

CARLTON: Brunetti $$
Italian
380 Lygon St, VIC 3053
Tel *(03) 9347 9281*
Classy café and restaurant with outdoor seating. Wonderful cakes, pastries and ice cream. Fill up on delicious regional Italian cuisine.

CARLTON: Hotel Lincoln $$
Modern Australian **Map** 1 C1
91 Cardigan St, VIC 3053
Tel *(03) 9347 4666*
This revamped pub aims high, with quality fare such as wagyu fillet, roast Tasmanian salmon and confit belly of free-range pork.

CARLTON: Shakahari $$
Vegetarian
201–203 Faraday St, VIC 3053
Tel *(03) 9347 3848* **Closed** *Sun lunch*
Fresh, light, inventive food at reasonable prices. Start with the house specialty – avocado wedges and red capsicums served with a coriander purée.

CENTRAL MELBOURNE: Grill'd $
Modern Australian **Map** 1 C2
222 Lonsdale St, QV Centre, VIC 3000
Tel *(03) 9663 0399*
This growing burger chain uses quality ingredients and a flame grill for healthy scrumptiousness. Vegetarian options available too. Friendly service.

DK Choice

CENTRAL MELBOURNE:
Hardware Société $
Café **Map** 1 B3
120 Hardware St, VIC 3000
Tel *(03) 9078 5992*
Located at the heart of
Melbourne, this popular café
is an ideal place to enjoy a
hearty breakfast or lunch. Try
the baked eggs with chorizo
sausage, piquillo peppers and
queso de cabra (goat cheese),
or some of their delicious
sweet treats along with a cup
of coffee. The contemporary
dining area has a large
communal table.

CENTRAL MELBOURNE:
Pellegrini's Espresso Bar $
Café **Map** 2 D2
66 Bourke St, VIC 3000
Tel *(03) 9662 1885*
Lively eatery that has been a
Melbourne icon for decades.
Simple pasta dishes. Quick service.

CENTRAL MELBOURNE:
Becco $$
Italian **Map** 2 D2
11–25 Crossley St, VIC 3000
Tel *(03) 9663 3000* **Closed** *Sun & Mon*
An inspiring and innovative
Italian bistro. Dishes include
barramundi with *caponata
fregola* (an aubergine dish), crispy
saltbush and *verjuice* (sour juice).

CENTRAL MELBOURNE:
Chin Chin $$
Southeast Asian **Map** 2 D3
125 Flinders Lane, VIC 3004
Tel *(03) 8663 2000*
A place based on the concept
of shared eating. If deciding on
any particular dish proves tricky,
simply tell the waiter "feed me",
and you will receive up to six
of their most popular dishes of
the day. All-Australian wine list.
No bookings.

CENTRAL MELBOURNE:
Cookie $$
Thai **Map** 1 C2
252 Swanston St, VIC 3000
Tel *(03) 9663 7660*
An unusual combination of beer
hall and Thai restaurant. The
kitsch decor and lively atmo-
sphere attract a large, arty crowd.

CENTRAL MELBOURNE:
Cumulus Inc $$
International **Map** 2 D3
45 Flinders Lane, VIC 3000
Tel *(03) 9650 1445*
Good design, fine wine and great,
unpretentious food at
this popular restaurant

CENTRAL MELBOURNE:
Grossi Florentino $$
Italian **Map** 2 D2
80 Bourke St, VIC 3000
Tel *(03) 9662 1811* **Closed** *Sun*
Three eateries on three levels: a
casual Tuscan grill, sumptuous
fine dining in the *fin-de-siècle*
Mural Room, and light bites in
the cellar bar.

CENTRAL MELBOURNE:
Il Solito Posto $$
Italian **Map** 2 D3
Basement, 113 Collins St, VIC 3000
Tel *(03) 9654 4466* **Closed** *Sun*
A welcoming basement *trattoria*
with well-stocked shelves of
both local and Italian wines and
a delectable menu of regional
Italian specialities, such as squid
ink linguini and pumpkin risotto.

CENTRAL MELBOURNE:
Mamasita $$
Mexican **Map** 2 D3
Level 1, 11 Collins St, VIC 3000
Tel *(03) 9650 3821*
This upbeat restaurant champions
authentic Mexican food with its
flavoursome dishes including
chicken *tostaditas* and corn
with chipotle mayo. Be prepared
to queue.

CENTRAL MELBOURNE:
MoVida $$
Spanish **Map** 2 D3
1 Hosier Lane, VIC 3000
Tel *(03) 9663 3038*
Australia's finest proponent of
modern Spanish tapas. Daily
specials, along with a list of
small dishes. Book ahead.

CENTRAL MELBOURNE:
Yu-u $$
Japanese **Map** 2 D3
137 Flinders Lane, VIC 3000
Tel *(03) 9639 7073* **Closed** *Sat & Sun*
This eccentric little restaurant
serves good, reasonably priced
Japanese classics. Advisable to
book ahead.

CENTRAL MELBOURNE:
The European $$$
European **Map** 2 D2
161 Spring St, VIC 3000
Tel *(03) 9654 0811*
Smart place attracting politicians
and the pre-theatre crowd.
Styled like an old-school bistro,
with superb wines from France,
Italy, Germany and Spain.

CENTRAL MELBOURNE:
Ezard $$$
Modern Australian **Map** 2 D3
187 Flinders Lane, VIC 3000
Tel *(03) 9639 6811* **Closed** *Sat
lunch & Sun*
Renowned chef Teage Ezard
explores the complexities of
contemporary Australian
cuisine in an ultra-modern,
lively setting.

CENTRAL MELBOURNE:
Flower Drum $$$
Chinese **Map** 2 D2
17 Market Lane, VIC 3000
Tel *(03) 9662 3655* **Closed** *Sun lunch*
Considered by many the best
Cantonese restaurant in the
whole of Australia. Flower
Drum attracts celebrities but
remains accommodating
and relaxed.

CENTRAL MELBOURNE:
Hanabishi $$$
Japanese **Map** 1 B3
187 King St, VIC 3000
Tel *(03) 9670 1167* **Closed** *Sat & Sun*
Often voted Melbourne's best
Japanese restaurant, this is an
excellent place for sashimi,
steaming hotpots and melt-in-
your-mouth tempura.

CENTRAL MELBOURNE:
Pei Modern $$$
Modern Australian **Map** 2 D3
Collins Place, 45 Collins St, VIC 3000
Tel *(03) 9654 8545* **Closed** *Sat & Sun*
Celebrated chef Mark Best's
eatery serves natural-flavoured
dishes. Sleek café decor.

The sleek interior of the popular Cumulus Inc restaurant in Melbourne

For more information on types of restaurants *see page 498*

DK Choice

CENTRAL MELBOURNE:
Vue de Monde $$$
Modern Australian **Map** 1 R4
Level 55, Rialto, 525 Collins St, VIC 3000
Tel *(03) 9691 3888* **Closed** *Mon & Sat lunch, Sun dinner*
Eating at Vue de Monde is a beautiful, delicious experience. Exciting, award-winning fine cuisine is served in a striking, modern interior. The wagyu beef, the beef cheek and the marron with brown butter and pork floss are sensational. The owner, acclaimed Australian chef Shannon Bennett, aims to make this Australia's most sustainable restaurant and uses organic, small-farm produce and cutting-edge eco-technology.

COLLINGWOOD:
Huxtaburger $
American **Map** 2 F1
106 Smith St, VIC 3066
Tel *(03) 9417 6328*
Superb beef or tofu burgers with crinkle-cut chips. Delicious extras include bacon, beetroot, jalapeños and sesame soy mayo.

COLLINGWOOD:
Jim's Greek Tavern $$
Greek
32 Johnston St, VIC 3066
Tel *(03) 9419 3827* **Closed** *lunch*
One of the best tavernas in the city, Jim's Greek is a favourite among Melbourne's large Greek community. Generous and flavourful seafood platters.

FITZROY:
Babka Bakery Café $
Eastern European
358 Brunswick St, VIC 3000
Tel *(03) 9416 0091* **Closed** *Mon*
Small, casual café. Light meals, many with a Russian flavour, include meat pies and salads. Guests can dine outdoors in fine weather.

FITZROY: Moroccan Soup Bar $
Moroccan
183 St Georges Rd, VIC 3068
Tel *(03) 9482 4240* **Closed** *Mon; lunch*
This bohemian café does great things with chickpeas, lentils, couscous and yogurt. Vegetarian food, enticingly presented.

FITZROY: Charcoal Lane $$
Native Australian **Map** 2 E1
136 Gertrude St, VIC 3065
Tel *(03) 9418 3400* **Closed** *Sun & Mon*
This imaginative restaurant serving food based on Aboriginal ingredients and recipes provides work experience to disadvantaged young people. Minimalist decor.

FITZROY: Ladro $$
Italian
224 Gertrude St, VIC 3065
Tel *(03) 9415 7575* **Closed** *lunch weekdays*
Award-winning restaurant with roasts, the best crispy wood-fired pizzas in town and a reasonably priced wine list. Hugely popular.

FITZROY:
Little Creatures Dining Hall $$
Bistro
222 Brunswick St, VIC 3065
Tel *(03) 9417 5500*
Created by a brewery with a cult following. Cool, urban beer hall with decent pub food, including oysters, pizzas, seafood and steaks.

FITZROY: Mario's $$
Italian
303 Brunswick St, VIC 3065
Tel *(03) 9417 3343*
A cool retro vibe and classic café food – *antipasti* and pasta dishes – make this bustling joint a favourite with the local arty crowd.

FITZROY:
RST Seafood Restaurant $$
Seafood
5 Rae St, VIC 3065
Tel *(03) 9489 1974* **Closed** *Sun & Mon*
Snug but light and airy seafood restaurant. The fish is delivered

daily and filleted on the premises. Superb mixed platters. Casual interiors and attentive staff.

FITZROY: Vegie Bar $$
Vegetarian
380 Brunswick St, VIC 3065
Tel *(03) 9417 6935*
Fun, community-spirited place. Generous portions of healthy vegetarian fare ensure an enthusiastic following. Vegan and gluten-free dishes available.

FITZROY: Cutler & Co $$$
Modern Australian **Map** 2 E1
55–57 Gertrude St, VIC 3065
Tel *(03) 9419 4888* **Closed** *Mon–Thu dinner*
Converted metalworks with a gritty, urban feel. In an interesting contrast, the food is deliciously delicate, scattered with tiny flowers and leaves.

RICHMOND: Richmond Hill Café and Larder $$
Café **Map** 4 D2
48–50 Bridge Rd, VIC 3121
Tel *(03) 9421 2808* **Closed** *dinner*
This light and airy venue serves great coffee and light meals in a characterful 1860s building. The cheeses are to die for.

RIPPON LEA: Attica $$$
Modern Australian
74 Glen Eira Rd, VIC 3185
Tel *(03) 9530 0111* **Closed** *Sun & Mon; lunch*
The chef at this restaurant loves to experiment with unusual ingredients and off-the-wall techniques. Five- or eight-course menus only.

SOUTHBANK: Persimmon $$
Modern Australian **Map** 2 D4
Ground Level, NGV International, 180 St Kilda Rd, VIC 3004
Tel *(03) 8620 2434* **Closed** *Tue*
Lunch at Melbourne's finest gallery restaurant is a treat whether you're attending an art exhibition or not. Garden views add to the serene experience.

Chefs working to create exquisite dishes at the stylish Vue de Monde, Melbourne

Key to Price Guide *see page 504*

The cheerful, wood-furnished interiors of Donovans, St Kilda

SOUTHBANK: Saké
Japanese   **$$**   Map 2 D4
Hammer Hall, Arts Centre Melbourne, 100 St Kilda Rd, VIC 3004
Tel *(03) 8687 0775*
Perfect choice for a pre- or post-theatre meal. New-style and classic Japanese cuisine served at the sushi bar or at the intimate booths.

SOUTHBANK:
Rockpool Bar & Grill   **$$$**
Grill   Map 1 B5
Crown Complex, 8 Whiteman St, VIC 3006
Tel *(03) 8648 1900*   **Closed** *Sat lunch*
Rockpool Bar & Grill has an uncompromising eye for the very best cuts of meat. Succulent wagyu burgers and steaks. Crisp, business-like decor.

SOUTH MELBOURNE:
Hercules Morse   **$$**
Modern Australian
283 Clarendon St, VIC 3205
Tel *(03) 9690 9402*   **Closed** *Mon*
Centrally located, this modern restaurant serves an array of delectable meals. Relaxed and comfortable ambience. A must-visit place.

SOUTH MELBOURNE:
O'Connell's   **$$**
Modern Australian
407 Coventry St, VIC 3205
Tel *(03) 9699 9600*
Convivial, gentrified corner pub featuring an extensive international wine list and plenty of craft beers on tap. The menu has a broad range of gastropub classics.

SOUTH MELBOURNE:
Pony Fish Island   **$$**
Pub   Map 1 C4
Southgate Pedestrian Bridge, VIC 3006
Located at the heart of Yarra river, this bar-restaurant is accessible only via stairs on the pedestrian bridge. Take in a spectacular view of Melbourne while enjoying a light lunch or cocktails.

SOUTH YARRA:
Caffé Sienna Ristorante   **$$**
Italian   Map 6 E1
Shop 2, 402 Chapel St, VIC 3142
Tel *(03) 9827 1353*
Contemporary, yet relaxed spot that is a celebrity favourite. Come for coffee and cocktails, or for light meals, cakes and tasty desserts.

SOUTH YARRA:
Caffe e Cucina   **$$$**
Italian   Map 4 E5
581 Chapel St, VIC 3141
Tel *(03) 9827 4139*
Bustling café-restaurant, with style and attitude aplenty, serves excellent traditional italian fare. A perennial favourite with Melbourne's people-watchers and younger celebrities. Intimate atmosphere and attentive service.

SOUTH YARRA:
France-Soir   **$$$**
French   Map 4 D5
11 Toorak Rd, VIC 3141
Tel *(03) 9866 8569*
Energetic bistro serving *plats de résistance* such as *filet de boeuf béarnaise* (beef steak with Béarnaise sauce) and *poisson du jour* (catch of the day). It is also said to make Melbourne's best crème brûlée.

ST KILDA: Cicciolina   **$$$**
Italian
130 Acland St, VIC 3182
Tel *(03) 9525 3333*
Earthy, full-bodied comfort food is the order of the day at this simple restaurant. Jammed with small tables and often full. Extensive wine list.

ST KILDA: Circa   **$$$**
Modern Asian   Map 5 B5
The Prince, 2 Acland St, VIC 3182
Tel *(03) 9536 1122*
Subtle yet unexpected combinations define this modern eatery. The setting is low-key but highly stylish. Service is unobtrusive.

ST KILDA: Donovans   **$$$**
Modern Australian
40 Jacka Boulevard, VIC 3182
Tel *(03) 9534 8221*
Set in a former foreshore bathing house, this unique restaurant has the feel of a large family beach house. Finely rendered seafood and meat dishes.

WINDSOR: Journeyman   **$$**
Café   Map 6 F2
169 Chapel St, VIC 3181
Tel *(03) 9521 4884*
This local favourite is perfect for breakfasts. Serves world-class coffee. Don't miss the signature avocado hummus toast. Excellent service.

Western Victoria

AIREYS INLET:
A La Grecque   **$$$**
Greek
60 Great Ocean Rd, VIC 3231
Tel *(03) 5209 6922*   **Closed** *Mon & Tue in off season; late Apr–beg Aug*
Run by a family who have produced a cookbook, this place is known worldwide for its Greek-inspired cuisine. Good selection of *mezze* and beautifully cooked seafood.

APOLLO BAY: La Bimba   **$$**
Moroccan
125 Great Ocean Rd, VIC 3233
Tel *(03) 5237 7411*
Service can vary, but the food always hits the spot with Middle Eastern and Asian influences. Tiled balcony tables and wall hangings add an exotic touch. Go for the seafood platter for two.

APOLLO BAY: Chris's Beacon Point Restaurant   **$$$**
European
280 Skenes Creek Rd, VIC 3233
Tel *(03) 5237 6411*   **Closed** *Mon–Fri lunch*
This much-lauded clifftop restaurant offers a modern Mediterranean-inspired menu. Seafood is a specialty here, as are the chef's popular Greek style dishes. Dine while enjoying jaw-dropping views of the coastline.

BALLARAT: Kambei Japanese Restaurant $$$
Japanese
501 Main Rd, VIC 3350
Tel *(03) 5331 1468*   **Closed** *Mon; Tue–Thu lunch*
Relax and enjoy some of the best Japanese food Ballarat has to offer. The dishes are prepared from freshest ingredients.

BENDIGO: Mr. Beebe's $$
Modern Australian
17 View Point, VIC 3550
Tel *(03) 5441 5557*
Delicious food with an extensive drinks menu. Order from the chef's tasting menu for a multi-course delight.

BENDIGO: Bouchon $$$
French
61 High St, VIC 3550
Tel *(03) 5444 5272* **Closed** *Sun & Mon*
A little slice of France. Well-priced, beautifully cooked food includes snails, charcuterie, confit duck and other classics with a local twist.

BIRREGURRA: The Meating Place Café $$
Modern Australian
43 Main St, VIC 5422
Tel *(03) 5236 2611* **Closed** *lunch Mon–Fri; dinner*
Boutique chic meets old-world charm at this butcher's shop, provedore, wine merchant and café. Weekend brunch and lunch; only drinks and cakes Tue–Sun.

BIRREGURRA: Brae $$$
Modern Australian
4285 Cape Otway Rd, VIC 5422
Tel *(03) 5236 2226* **Closed** *Tue & Wed; Thu–Sat lunch; Fri–Mon dinner*
This modern restaurant offers a seasonally changing menu that uses the highest quality local produce, most of it grown in the restaurant's organic, on-site garden.

Sophisticated interior of the Royal Mail Hotel restaurant, Dunkeld

Situated on the pier, Baveras in Geelong has wonderful water and city skyline views

DAYLESFORD: Cliffy's $
Café
30 Raglan St, VIC 3460
Tel *(03) 5348 3279* **Closed** *dinner*
Part café, part general store, this quirky place is like stepping into the past. The menu changes daily based on what farmers bring in.

DAYLESFORD: Farmers Arms $$
Modern Australian
1 East St, VIC 3460
Tel *(03) 5348 2091*
This charming pub dating back to 1857 serves fresh food from a great menu. No bookings.

DAYLESFORD: Sault $$
International
2349 Ballan-Daylesford Rd, VIC 3460
Tel *(03) 5348 6555* **Closed** *Mon & Tue*
French-style country house restaurant overlooking fields of lavender. Blending contemporary Australian and Spanish cuisine, the menu offers a selection of tapas and other savoury items.

DAYLESFORD: Kazuki's $$$
International
1 Camp St, VIC 3460
Tel *(03) 5348 1218* **Closed** *Tue & Wed; Thu lunch*
The owner-chef Kazuki Tsuya efficiently blends Japanese and modern Australian flavours to create an unforgettable experience for patrons. The dishes use only the best local produce.

DAYLESFORD: Lake House $$$
Modern Australian
4 King St, VIC 3460
Tel *(03) 5348 3329*
Fine country dining with a seasonal, cutting-edge slant is available here. The chef works tirelessly to support small local suppliers.

DK Choice

DUNKELD: Royal Mail Hotel $$$
Modern Australian
Royal Mail Hotel, 98 Parker St (Glenelg Hwy), VIC 3294
Tel *(03) 5577 2241*
A gastronomic destination, this country hotel in the shadow of the Grampians has won every award under the sun for its world-class food. The chef prepares two menus every day based on produce from his garden, local artisan producers and the wild.

GEELONG: Baveras $$$
Modern Australian
Cunningham Pier, 10 Western Beach, Foreshore Rd, VIC 3220
Tel *(03) 5222 6377* **Closed** *Sun dinner*
A glorious location on the pier and superb food to match the stunning views. Breakfast is a treat too, with good coffee and perfectly scrambled eggs.

HEPBURN SPRINGS: The Argus Dining Room $$$
Australian
Peppers Mineral Springs Retreat, 124 Main Rd, VIC 3461
Tel *(03) 5348 4199*
This elegant restaurant in an original Art Deco dining room focuses on fresh, seasonal, locally grown food. Indulge in the five- or seven-course degustation menu.

KYNETON: La Bonta $$$
Italian
12–14 Piper St, VIC 3444
Tel *(03) 5422 3683* **Closed** *Mon & Tue; Sun dinner*
Tim Austin, the owner-chef, draws on traditional Italian recipes and adds his modern spin. Wonderful service.

LORNE: Cuda Bar $$
Modern Australian
82 Mountjoy Pde, VIC 3232
Tel *(03) 5289 5006*
Enjoy picturesque views of Louttit Bay while savouring contemporary delights. Friendly ambience.

MACEDON:
Sitka Foodstore and Café $
Café
23 Victoria St, VIC 3440
Tel *(03) 5426 3304* **Closed** *Mon & Tue; dinner*
Inviting café with home-made and local specialities. Tempting deli items and gourmet foods to take home, too.

MILDURA: Jim McDougall in Stefano's Cellar $$$
Modern Australian
Quality Mildura Grand Hotel, cnr Seventh St & Langtree Ave, VIC 3502
Tel *(03) 5022 0881* **Closed** *Sun & Mon; lunch*
Located in the original hotel cellars. Expect a magical evening orchestrated by Jim McDougall, one of the upcoming names in Australian gastronomy. Menu changes daily.

MILDURA:
Spanish Bar and Grill $$$
Steakhouse
Quality Mildura Grand Hotel, cnr Seventh St & Langtree Ave, VIC 3502
Tel *(03) 5021 2377*
Exceptionally good steaks, local ingredients and superb cooking. There is nothing Spanish about this place – the name is simply a tribute to its forerunner.

MOONAMBEL: Warrenmang Vineyard Resort $$$
Modern Australian
188 Mountain Creek Rd, VIC 3478
Tel *(03) 5467 2233* **Closed** *Mon; Sun dinner*
European-style hospitality and fine food. Local yabbies, berries, cheese, rabbit and trout can often be found on the menu. Lodging options in cottages as well.

PORT FAIRY: Merrijig Inn $$$
Modern Australian
1 Campbell St, VIC 3284
Tel *(03) 5568 2324* **Closed** *Tue & Wed; lunch*
Lots of charm in the dining room of Victoria's oldest inn. The menu (written daily) features the area's best produce. Excellent wine list.

QUEENSCLIFF: Vue Grand $$$
Modern Australian
46 Hesse St, VIC 3225
Tel *(03) 5258 1544* **Closed** *Sun–Tue; lunch*
Step back into a bygone era at this hotel, where you can dine in a chandelier-lit room as a grand piano plays in the background. Light, modern food on the menu.

SHEPHERDS FLAT: Lavandula La Trattoria $$
Italian
350 Hepburn–Newstead Rd, VIC 3461
Tel *(03) 5476 4393* **Closed** *Wed & Thu (Mon–Thu in winter); dinner*
Indulge in lavender scones and tea or enjoy a Mediterranean-style lunch. Dine inside the warm café or alfresco, overlooking the lavender fields.

TIMBOON: Timboon Railway Shed Distillery $$
Modern Australian
Bailey St, VIC 3268
Tel *(03) 5598 3555*
This old railway shed-cum-micro-distillery demonstrates a deep commitment to locally grown produce. Casual café fare, plus Friday pizza evenings and Saturday night dinners.

TRENTHAM: Du Fermier $$
French
42 High St, VIC 3458
Tel *(03) 5424 1634* **Closed** *Mon–Wed; dinner (except Fri & Sat)*
Annie Smithers' delightful restaurant serves rustic French fare. The menu changes weekly featuring ingredients from the restaurant's garden and the best poultry and meat from the region.

WOODEND: Colenso $$
Modern European
Cnr Old Bakery Ln & Anslow St, VIC 3442
Tel *(03) 5427 2007* **Closed** *Sun*
Enjoy good coffee and casual food by day, and choose from a more sophisticated set menu on Saturday nights. Works by local artists add to the atmosphere.

Eastern Victoria

AVENEL: Bank Street Woodfired Pizzas and Gardens $$
Pizzeria
5 Bank St, VIC 3664
Tel *(03) 5796 2522* **Closed** *Mon–Thu*
Laid-back weekend eatery in a former bank with dark-wood fittings. Creates imaginative pizzas in a wood-fired oven. The "Smooshed Potato" pizza won't disappoint. Eat inside or in the garden.

AVENEL: Fowles $$
Winery Restaurant
1175 Lambing Gully Rd (cnr Hume Freeway & Lambing Gully Rd), VIC 3664
Tel *(03) 5796 2150* **Closed** *dinner*
Fowles is a welcome pit stop while exploring the wineries of the region. Offers *antipasti*, charcuterie and other European dishes, especially game.

BEECHWORTH:
Bridge Road Brewers $$
Brewery/Pizzeria
Old Coach House, Brewers Lane, Ford St, VIC 3747
Tel *(03) 5728 2703* **Closed** *Mon–Thu dinner*
Gourmet pizzas made by an Austrian chef who adds Bavarian wheat beer to the dough mix. The food is perfectly matched with Bridge Road's hand-crafted ales.

BEECHWORTH: The Press Room Wine Bar $$
Spanish
37 Camp St, VIC 3747
Tel *(03) 5728 2360* **Closed** *Mon & Tue; lunch*
Offers a range of tapas, local wines, craft beer and cocktails. Don't miss the delectable churros (fried dough pastry). Book ahead.

The restored historic stone building at Lavandula La Trattoria, Shepherds Flat

For more information on types of restaurants *see page 498*

Spacious, modern interior of Ten Minutes by Tractor, Mornington Peninsula

BEECHWORTH: Provenance $$$
Modern Australian
86 Ford St, VIC 3747
Tel *(03) 5728 1786*
Highly acclaimed restaurant in a stately 1856 bank building with a shady courtyard. The old gold vault is now a cellar, stocked with fine Australian wines.

BRIGHT: Coral Lee $
Café
8 Barnard St, VIC 3741
Tel *(03) 5755 5113*
This friendly little café is a great lunch spot. House specialities include a twice-baked cheese soufflé, spicy sausages and beetroot tart. Great retro feel.

BRIGHT: Simone's $$$
Italian
98 Gavan St, VIC 3741
Tel *(03) 5755 2266*
Located in a renovated heritage building. Signature dishes include Umbrian-style home-made pasta, rabbit, duck and Welsh black beef, enhanced by local produce such as wild spinach.

BRUTHEN: Bullant Brewery $$
Brewery/International
46 Main St, VIC 3885
Tel *(03) 5157 5307*
Cheerful contemporary café decked out in timber and corrugated iron. Serves tasty bites such as cheese, rustic chips and pizza to accompany the beers brewed on site.

DINNER PLAIN: Graze $$$
Bistro
Rundells Alpine Lodge,
Big Muster Dr, VIC 3898
Tel *(03) 5159 6422*
Appealing à la carte and tasting menus. After dinner, relax by the fire with a warming glass of schnapps from the Wildbrumby distillery in the Snowy Mountains.

DANDENONG RANGES: Café de Beaumarchais $
Café/French
Shop 1, 372 Mt Dandenong Tourist Rd, Sassafras, VIC 3787
Tel *(03) 9755 1100*
The dark, elegant decor lends a Baroque edge to this inviting café. Fresh salads, filled baguettes and a wonderful selection of cakes on offer. Try the pistachio and orange cake or indulge in a rich chocolate brownie served with cream. Wonderful coffee.

DANDENONG RANGES: The General Food Store $$
Café
377 Belgrave Gembrook Rd, Emerald, VIC 3782
Tel *(03) 5968 3580*
One of the best places in the area for coffee or a cooked breakfast. Good lunches and cakes, too. Monthly dinners are held to celebrate the season's harvest. Friendly staff.

FALLS CREEK: Astra Lodge $$
Modern Australian
5 Sitzmark St, VIC 3699
Tel *(03) 5758 3496*
Beautifully designed ski lodge with a restaurant that uses locally grown ingredients, such as bush tomatoes and wild berries, to create delicious dishes.

LAKES ENTRANCE: Kalimna Hotel $$
Greek
1 Hotel Rd, Kalimna, VIC 3909
Tel *(03) 5155 1202*
Sleek restaurant specializing in authentic Greek food. Try *tzatziki* (yogurt and cucumber), taramasalata (roe) and *melitzanosalata* (aubergine) dips, grilled octopus and fried fish.

MILAWA: Milawa Cheese Factory Restaurant $$
Winery Restaurant
17 Milawa–Bobinawarrah Rd, VIC 36/8
Tel *(03) 5727 3589*
Amazing bread and handmade cheese are just two of the highlights served in this bright, simple café. Pizzas and simple bistro fare are also available. Cheese tastings on request.

MILAWA: Patricia's Table Restaurant $$$
Modern Australian/French
Brown Brothers Winery, 239 Bobinawarrah Rd, VIC 3678
Tel *(03) 5720 5540*
Every dish at this family-owned restaurant is designed to complement Brown Brothers' own wine. First-rate local trout, lamb and venison on the menu. Booking is essential.

MORNINGTON: Counting House $$
Modern Australian
787 Esplanade, VIC 3931
Tel *(03) 5975 2055*
Originally built in 1912 to be a bank, this beautiful historic building provides the perfect setting to relish contemporary Australian cuisine with a hint of French influence.

MORNINGTON PENINSULA: Montalto Vineyard and Grove $$
Winery Restaurant
33 Shoreham Rd, Red Hill, VIC 3937
Tel *(03) 5989 8412*
Contemporary architecture with French-inspired cuisine and views over the olive grove, vineyard and gardens. This is a picturesque spot for a picnic, too.

MORNINGTON PENINSULA: Ten Minutes by Tractor $$$
Winery Restaurant
1333 Mornington Flinders Rd, Main Ridge, Red Hill, VIC 3928
Tel *(03) 5989 6080*
Remarkable wine list with around 400 options from all over the world. The food is accomplished Modern Australian.

NOOJEE: The Toolshed $$
Bistro
The Outpost Retreat, 38 Loch Valley Rd, VIC 3833
Tel *(03) 5628 9669*
Noojee's landmark watering hole has an appealingly rustic feel and fare to match. The lamb pot roast and hand-crumbed chicken parmigiana are always popular.

Elegant dining area looking out over the gardens at Eleonore's, Yarra Valley

OXLEY: King River Café $$
Modern Australian
1143 Snow Rd, VIC 3678
Tel *(03) 5727 3461*
Housed in the town's charming 1860s post office and general store. The menu favours King Valley wines and produce, and delivers ever-changing flavours. Make sure you save room for the tangy lemon tart

PHILLIP ISLAND:
Rusty Water Brewery $$
Brewery
1821 Phillip Island Rd, Cowes, VIC 3922
Tel *(03) 5952 1666*
Down-to-earth place with delicious hand-crafted ales and good local food such as pies and fish 'n' chips. Gluten-free and vegetarian options are available. Live jazz or folk music every Friday evening.

WARRAGUL:
Wild Dog $$
Winery Restaurant
Warragul–Korumburra Rd, VIC 3820
Tel *(03) 5623 2211*
Housed in a striking building with a large open deck surrounded by lawns. Offers pizza, charcuterie, sliders and multi-course set meals. A good place for an enjoyable lunch.

YARRA VALLEY:
Innocent Bystander $$
Winery Restaurant
336 Maroondah Hwy, Healesville, VIC 3777
Tel *(03) 5962 6111*
Winery restaurant in an urban setting. The in-house staff create wood-fired pizzas, bake artisan bread and brew great coffee.

YARRA VALLEY: Quince Dining $$
Modern Australian
Healesville Hotel, 256 Maroondah Hwy, Healesville, VIC 3777
Tel *(03) 5962 4002*
Laid-back eatery in a smart country pub offering quality local produce. Buxton salmon, Yarra Valley cheeses and home-grown herbs and salad greens.

DK Choice

YARRA VALLEY: Eleonore's $$$
Modern Australian
Chateau Yering, 42 Melba Hwy, Yering, VIC 3770
Tel *(03) 9237 3333*
Superb dining in a 19th-century house. The dining room has white linen, upholstered chairs and large sash windows with views of lawns and trees. Award-winning executive chef, Mathew MaCartney creates delicious contemporary menus inspired by the changing seasons. Impeccable service.

YARRA VALLEY: Locale $$$
Winery Restaurant
De Bortoli, Pinnacle Lane, Dixons Creek, VIC 3775
Tel *(03) 5965 2271*
The De Bortoli family are wine-making legends. The North Italian menu boasts scrumptious suckling pig served with savoy cabbage and champagne vinaigrette.

Tasmania

BARRINGTON:
Glencoe Rural Retreat $$
French
1468 Sheffield Rd, TAS 7306
Tel *(03) 6492 3267*   **Closed** *Mon & Tue lunch*
A little slice of rural France in Tasmania, with a café open to the public by day.

CAMBRIDGE: Barilla Bay $$
Seafood
1388 Tasman Hwy, TAS 7170
Tel *(03) 6248 5454*   **Closed** *Sun–Thu dinner*
Located near Hobart Airport, this restaurant overlooks an oyster farm. Select the "Shucking Awesome" platter – 30 cooked, natural oysters with a variety of toppings.

CAMPBELL TOWN: Zeps Café $
Café
92–94 High St, TAS 7210
Tel *(03) 6381 1344*
Convenient stop on the highway. All-day breakfasts, pizzas, panini and pasta dishes, along with good coffee, pastries and cakes.

CRADLE MOUNTAIN:
Highland Restaurant $$$
Modern Australian
Peppers Cradle Mountain Lodge, 4038 Cradle Mountain Rd, TAS 7306
Tel *(03) 6492 1303*   **Closed** *lunch*
Be pampered with fine Tasmanian food and wine at this spot in one of Australia's most scenic locations. The salmon fillet with squid and prawn ravioli is a winner.

CYGNET: Lotus Eaters Café $
Café
10 Mary St, TAS 7112
Tel *(03) 6295 1996*   **Closed** *Tue & Wed; dinner*
Rustic and informal café. Pies, curries, gourmet pizzas, soups and vegetarian dishes, all made from scratch using local produce.

CYGNET: School House Coffee Shop $
Café
23 Mary St, TAS 7112
Tel *(03) 6295 1206*   **Closed** *Sat; dinner*
Good coffee and delectable home-made pies served in a cosy little space. The curried scallop pie is a crowd favourite. Welcoming service.

Homely dining room at Glencoe Rural Retreat, Barrington

For more information on types of restaurants *see page 498*

ELIZABETH TOWN: Christmas Hills Raspberry Farm $
Café
9 Christmas Hills Rd, TAS 7304
Tel *(03) 6362 2186* **Closed** *dinner*
Savour fresh raspberries by the bowlful (in season, Dec–May) or enjoy the berries in cakes, ice creams, muffins, desserts, jams and wine at this busy farm restaurant.

GEORGE TOWN:
Cove Restaurant and Bar $$
Modern Australian
Peppers York Cove, 2 Ferry Blvd, TAS 7253
Tel *(03) 6382 9990* **Closed** *Mon lunch & Sun dinner*
Bright, contemporary interior with stunning river views. The menu plays homage to the finest local ingredients.Try the salmon or the confit duck terrine. Sample the region's award-winning wines.

HOBART: Fish Frenzy $
Seafood
Shop 1, Elizabeth St Pier, TAS 7000
Tel *(03) 6231 2134*
There is a great vibe at this waterfront eatery where the fish is served simply in big paper cones. Grilled seafood, oysters, scallops and seafood chowder also tempt. No bookings.

HOBART: Maldini's Café Restaurant $$
Italian
47 Salamanca Place, TAS 7000
Tel *(03) 6223 4460*
Relaxed dining, either in a historic warehouse or on the esplanade. Watch the passing parade over a light lunch or delicious Italian meal, or simply a coffee or drink.

HOBART:
Prossers on the Beach $$
Seafood
19 Beach Rd, Long Point, Sandy Bay, TAS 7005
Tel *(03) 6225 2276* **Closed** *Mon & Tue lunch, Sun dinner*
A relaxed seaside vibe and an international menu. The owners source fresh food directly from local fishermen. Tanks with live crayfish and abalone.

HOBART:
Ristorante Da Angelo $$
Italian
47 Hampden Rd, Battery Point, TAS 7004
Tel *(03) 6223 7011* **Closed** *Sat–Thu lunch*
A Hobart institution, this popular Italian restaurant has a cheerful feel and a loyal following. Traditional pizzas and desserts, and fresh home-made pasta.

HOBART: Smolt $$
Tapas
2 Salamanca Square, TAS 7000
Tel *(03) 6224 2554*
A cool, modern, light-filled space serving good, simple food. Gourmet pizzas, pastas, tapas, sea-food and meat dishes. The salmon tasting plate is a good choice.

HOBART:
Tavern 42 Degress South $$
Modern Australian
Elizabeth St Pier, Elizabeth St, TAS 7000
Tel *(03) 6224 7742*
Kick back and watch the boats sail by this cool, casual venue offering reasonably priced bistro fare and an extensive list of more than 200 wines.

HOBART: Franklin $$$
Modern Australian
28 Argyle St, TAS 7000
Tel *(03) 6234 3375* **Closed** *Sun*
Housed in a renovated Ford showroom, Franklin features a minimalist concrete interior with an open kitchen. The menu highlights include Tasmanian produce, particularly seafood and whole wood-roasted pigeon.

HOBART: Islington $$$
Fine Dining
321 Davey St, TAS 7000
Tel *(03) 6220 2123*
The small, stylish menu befits this sophisticated boutique hotel in a Regency-style building. Mountain views and fine wine cellar. Dining only for in-house guests.

HOBART: Lebrina $$$
European
155 New Town Rd, New Town, TAS 7008
Tel *(03) 6228 7775* **Closed** *Sun & Monday; lunch*
Set in an elegant and charming 1840s cottage decorated with antiques and modern art. Sublime dishes created with European techniques are served with carefully chosen wines.

HOBART: Monty's on Montpelier $$$
Fine Dining
37 Montpelier Retreat, Battery Point, TAS 7004
Tel *(03) 6223 2511* **Closed** *Sun & Mon; lunch*
Inviting atmosphere in a stylishly decorated cottage. Sample innovative and exciting food. Superb wine list and Hobart's most extensive cheese list.

Modern, trendy decor at the Islington, Hobart

The contemporary exterior of The Source, Hobart

HOBART: The Point Revolving Restaurant $$$
International
410 Sandy Bay Rd, Sandy Bay, TAS 7005
Tel 1800 030 611 Closed Sun & Mon; lunch (except Fri)
Revolving 17th-floor restaurant with spectacular views. Dine on French-inspired cuisine with a local twist. Braised wagyu beef and the orange créme Brûlée are both superb. Book in advance.

HOBART: The Source $$$
Fine Dining
655 Main Rd, Berriedale, TAS 7011
Tel (03) 6277 9904 Closed Tue; Sun & Mon dinner
Part of MONA, the island's art museum. There is a modern, edgy feel to both the food and the surroundings at this light-filled dining room. The three-course degustation menu won't disappoint.

LATROBE: House of Anvers $
Chocolate Café
9025 Bass Hwy, TAS 7307
Tel (03) 6426 2958 Closed dinner
All chocolate dreams come true at this café and chocolate-making facility. Indulge in chocolates, hot cocoa and chocolate desserts. Light meals as well.

DK Choice

LAUNCESTON:
Black Cow Bistro $$$
Steakhouse
70 George St, TAS 7250
Tel (03) 6331 9333 Closed lunch
This up-market offshoot of Launceston's acclaimed Stillwater is located in a lovely Art Deco building that was once a butcher's shop, now smartly attired with white tablecloths and a warm ambience. An ode to beef, this steakhouse sources the best dry-aged, grass-fed, free-range steak from around Tasmania. The menu also includes herb baked salmon. The service is excellent.

LAUNCESTON: Josef Chromy $$$
Modern Australian
370 Relbia Rd, Relbia, TAS 7258
Tel (03) 6335 8700 Closed dinner (except Fri & Sat)
Pretty gardens and manicured vineyards provide a seductive backdrop for fine food made with top-quality local produce such as Flinders Island lamb and East Coast oysters.

LAUNCESTON: Stillwater River Café $$$
Modern Australian
Ritchies Mill, 2 Bridge Rd, TAS 7250
Tel (03) 6331 4153 Closed Sun & Mon dinner
In a charming old wooden building overlooking the Tamar River, Stillwater celebrates Tasmanian produce in beautifully executed dishes. The six-course degustation menu is a triumph.

RANELAGH: Home Hill Winery Restaurant $$
Modern Australian
38 Nairn Rd, TAS 7109
Tel (03) 6264 1200 Closed dinner (except Fri & Sat)
This attractive restaurant serves classy regional food. Southern rock lobster, Tasmanian salmon and a game pie of wallaby, venison and hare all appear on the menu.

SHEFFIELD: T's Chinese Restaurant $$
Chinese
83 Main St, TAS 7306
Tel (03) 6491 2244
Owned by the Zhao family, who grow their produce and rear their own cows and lamb for meat. The food is a cut above the rest.

STANLEY: Old Cable Station Colonial Retreat $$
Modern Australian
435 Greenhills Rd, TAS 7331
Tel (03) 6458 1312
Enjoy a Slow Food experience. Dishes are cooked in a wood-fired oven using superb local fare. Signature crayfish dish.

STRAHAN: Risby Cove $$
Bistro
The Esplanade, TAS 7468
Tel (03) 6471 7572 Closed lunch
Waterfront eco-tourism centre highly regarded for its food and wine. Take in the west coast sunset and bask in the peaceful setting while enjoying scrumptious dishes.

WOODBRIDGE: Peppermint Bay Bar Dining & Terrace Bistro $$
Modern Australian
3435 Channel Hwy, TAS 7162
Tel (03) 6267 4088
Cruise from Hobart or drive the scenic route to this relaxed establishment in a striking building with breathtaking water views. Choose from a range of light meals featuring local produce, freshly baked goods and Tasmanian wines.

The shop at House of Anvers in Latrobe where guests can buy chocolate treats to take home

For more information on types of restaurants see page 498

SHOPPING IN AUSTRALIA

Australia has much to offer the visiting shopper beyond the standard tourist fare of koala bear purses and plastic boomerangs. The tourist shops can be worth exploring, because stock can be of a high standard and include goods not available in other countries. In each state capital, especially Sydney *(see pp136–9)* and Melbourne *(see pp410–13)*, there are precincts and open-air markets with a range of shops, stalls and cafés to explore. Wine and gourmet food products are a major attraction, and a wide range of reasonably priced world-class goods is available. Australian contemporary design has a refreshing irreverence for convention – look out for homewares and fashion in the inner-city precincts. In country areas, items made by local craftspeople make good buys. Australia has a 10 per cent goods and services tax (GST) on the cost of most manufactured items (included in displayed prices).

Browsers at a stall in Mindil Beach Sunset Markets, Darwin *(see p276)*

Shopping Hours

Standard weekday opening times are 9am–5:30pm, Monday to Friday. Late night shopping is usually available on Thursdays or Fridays, when stores stay open until 9pm. Weekend hours vary greatly. Deregulation has meant that many stores, particularly in city locations, open on both Saturday and Sunday. In most country areas, however, stores will open only until 1pm on Saturday. A few supermarkets in city and suburban areas operate 24 hours. Bookshops and other specialist shops stay open late – until around 10pm – in downtown areas.

How to Pay

Major credit cards are accepted by most stores, sometimes with a minimum purchase limit and or a credit card surcharge, between 1.5 and 3 per cent. Identification, such as a valid passport or driver's licence, is required when using traveller's cheques. Personal cheques may be accepted at the majority of larger stores, with identification, but a telephone check on your account may be made. Payment by cash is the preferred method for traders and may help to negotiate a lower price for your goods.

Rights and Refunds

The laws on consumer rights in Australia vary slightly from state to state. If you have a complaint or query, look under "Consumer" in the government section at the front of the White Pages telephone directory or online. If the goods purchased are defective in any way, customers are entitled to a full refund. If you decide you don't like an item, try to get a refund, but you will probably have to settle for a credit note or exchange. As a general rule, the larger stores are more lenient – you can always ask to speak to a manager or customer relations officer if you are unhappy with the service you receive.

Essentially Australian

Aboriginal or indigenous art is available for purchase from community-owned or managed galleries in the Northern Territory and good specialist galleries in the cities. Take the time to discuss the work with the painter or gallery staff: spiritual and cultural meanings are inextricably linked with aesthetic properties, and the painting or artifact that you choose will be all the more valuable with a little knowledge. These artworks are by their nature expensive, so do not be beguiled by cheaper imitations.

Australia produces 95 per cent of the world's opals. Their quality

Shoppers in London Court, Perth's Tudor-style street *(see p309)*.

An arts and crafts stall in one of Australia's many markets

the city centre and suburbia. These precincts represent some of the best and most interesting shopping in the country. Young designer outlets, specialist book stores, craft studios and galleries sit next to food stores, cafés, restaurants and bars. Some of these precincts are decidedly up-market, while others relish their bohemian roots. There is nearly always a strong mix of cultural influences – Jewish, Italian, Lebanese, Vietnamese, for example – depending on the area and the city. Ask at tourist information centres for the best precincts in each city.

varies greatly, so when considering a purchase a little research will go a long way. Opals are widely available at duty-free stores. Many other places will deduct the luxury excise tax from the price if you produce your passport.

Outback clothing is a specialist industry in Australia. Look for Akubra hats, boots by RM Williams and Driza-bone overcoats in camping and army stores. Surf clothing has become highly desirable among tourists, as it can be cheaper to buy in Australia than abroad. Board shorts and bikinis are popular purchases.

fruits. Melbourne's Queen Victoria Market (see p390) and the Adelaide Central Market (see p350) are particularly good and well worth visiting. Community markets, such as those in Paddington, Sydney (see p128), and Salamanca Place, Hobart (see p464), offer an interesting and eclectic range of locally designed clothing and crafts. In a class of their own, the Mindil Beach Sunset Markets in Darwin combine eating, shopping and entertainment in a spectacular tropical setting (see p276).

Herbal infusions on sale in Brisbane's Chinatown (see p231)

Out of Town

Shopping in Australian country areas can be a mixed experience. In some areas the range of standard items is limited and prices can be much higher than you would expect to pay in the city. However, there are always unexpected surprises such as dusty second-hand shops with rare knick knacks at absurdly low prices and small craft outlets and galleries with unusual items that make great gifts.

Department Stores

Department stores occupy the up-market end of the chain-store scale and sell quality merchandise. They include names such as Myer and David Jones (see p410) and some of the top stores are sumptuously decorated. Local and overseas designer fashions, top-brand cosmetics and all manner of household goods and furnishings can be purchased. These stores are competitive and will often match prices on identical items found at more down-market stores. Their shopper facilities and standards for customer service are excellent.

Fresh fish on display at Wollongong Fish Market (see p190)

Markets

Most Australian cities have a large central produce market and a range of small community markets that operate at the weekend. The bustling city food markets are as sensational for their vibrant multicultural atmosphere as they are for the extraordinary range of fresh, cheap produce available. Look out for local specialities such as cheeses, olives and unusual

Shopping Precincts

Because the city centres have been colonized by the retail giants in Australia, many small and interesting shops have moved out to the lively precincts that lie somewhere between

The attractive tiled interior of a shopping arcade in Adelaide

SPECIALIST HOLIDAYS AND OUTDOOR ACTIVITIES

To make the most of a trip to a country as vast and geographically diverse as Australia, a specialist holiday is an excellent idea. Whether you're pursuing an interest, acquiring a new skill or learning about the environment, such holidays can be very rewarding experiences. There is a wide range of specialist operators to choose from. If travelling to Australia from abroad, the best starting points are the local Tourism Australia offices or your local travel agent. Once in the country, the state tourism associations *(see p547)* can offer expert advice, make bookings with reputable companies and contact local activity associations for information.

Bushwalking in Namadgi National Park in the ACT *(see p211)*

Bushwalking

National Parks are without doubt the best places for bushwalking in Australia. Not only do they preserve the best of the country's natural heritage, but they also offer expert advice and well-marked trails for bushwalkers. These parks are state-managed and each state has a central information service. Look under "National Parks" in the government listings at the front of the telephone directory.

Equipment, including backpacks, boots and tents, is available for hire from camping stores in city and country areas. Joining up with a tour is a good alternative for those planning long bushwalking trips, as tour members will benefit from a guide's expertise on local flora and fauna, and access to remote wilderness areas. Exceptional bushwalking regions in Australia include Cradle Mountain in Tasmania *(see p471)*, the MacDonnell Ranges in the Northern Territory *(see p288)* and the Blue Mountains in New South Wales *(see pp172–5)*.

Cycling

With its vast stretches of near-empty roads, many of them without a hill in sight, it is no wonder that Australia is becoming increasingly popular as a long-distance cycling destination. Visitors can bring their own bicycles, but are advised to check first whether this is acceptable with the airlines. Trains and buses will usually carry bikes provided they are dismantled. To hire a bike in Australia, look under "Bicycles" in the Yellow Pages or search online. Bike helmets are a legal requirement throughout Australia and can be bought cheaply or hired.

Many cyclists spend several days on the road camping along the way, while others will arrange an itinerary that allows them to stop for the comfort of a bed and meal in a town. The wine-growing areas of South Australia *(see pp342–3)*, the Great Ocean Road in Victoria *(see pp432–3)* and almost anywhere in Tasmania *(see pp460–75)* are terrific cycling destinations.

Bicycling associations in Australia also arrange regular cycling tours that anyone can join. These include accommodation, food and vehicle back-up; most of the organizations are non-profit-making, so the costs are generally low. Contact **Bicycle New South Wales** for a catalogue specializing in Australian cycling publications. They will also provide information on their sister associations in other states.

Cycling around Canberra's lake *(see pp198–9)*

Adventure Sports

Appropriate training is a component of adventure sports in Australia, so novices are always welcome alongside more expert adventurers. Contact specialist tour operators or national associations *(see p541)* for information about anything from a one-day class to a two-week tour.

Abseiling, canyoning, rock climbing and caving are all popular in Australia, which has some fantastic natural landscapes ideally suited to these pursuits. The Blue Mountains are something of a mecca for enthusiasts of all the above. Naracoorte in South Australia *(see p359)* is a great location for caving, while the Grampians National Park in Victoria *(see p431)* attracts a large share of abseilers and climbers.

Climbing on Wilsons Promontory in Victoria *(see p448)*

Golf

There are more than 1,500 golf courses in Australia and 1,580 golf clubs. Many clubs have affiliations with clubs overseas and offer reciprocal membership rights, so check with your own club. There are also public municipal golf courses in many towns.

Australian courses are of a high standard, and Melbourne is home to two of the top 30 courses in the world, the Royal Melbourne and Kingston Heath. A round of golf will cost anything from A\$20–\$250. The **Australian Golf Union** has a handbook that lists all of the golf courses in Australia.

Camel trekking along Cable Beach, Broome *(see p334)*

Aboriginal Heritage Tours

Aboriginal heritage tours can range from a visit to an Aboriginal art gallery to days spent with an Aboriginal guide touring Arnhem Land or Kakadu National Park in the Northern Territory *(see pp280–81)*. With the highest percentage of Aboriginal land and people in the country, the Northern Territory has the greatest number of activities, but there are sights and operators all over Australia. The focus of activities varies and may encompass a number of themes, including traditional bush food, hunting, rock art and Aboriginal culture.

Perhaps the best aspect of many of these tours is the chance to see the remarkable Australian landscape from a different perspective; Aboriginal spirituality is closely linked with the land. In addition, some tours will journey to Australia's most remote areas and travel through Aboriginal lands that are usually closed to all but members of the local Aboriginal communities.

Camel Trekking

Camels have been an invaluable form of transport in Australia's Outback since Afghan-run camel trains were used to carry goods across the Australian desert from the 1840s until the coming of the railway. Joining a camel trek today is still an adventure, and activities range from a one-hour jaunt to a two-week trek. Food and accommodation (usually camping) are provided by tour operators. Alice Springs *(see pp286–7)* is the most popular starting point, but tours are available country-wide.

Aerial Tours

Aerial Tours can provide an exhilarating overview of an area and are a good option for time-restricted travellers who want to see some of the more far-flung attractions. Aerial safaris, stopping at major sights, are popular in the Outback. For charter flights to Australia's furthest flung territory, a section of Antarctica, contact **Croydon Travel**.

Seaplane moored at Rose Bay in Sydney, ready for a scenic flight

Fishing

Australia has around four million fishing enthusiasts and, given the country's natural advantages, it's not difficult to see why. Vast oceans, a 12,000-km (7,500-mile) shoreline and a large inland river system, all combined with a terrific climate, make Australia a haven for local and visiting anglers alike.

Fishing for barramundi in the remote inland waters of the Northern Territory and game fishing off Australia's tropical coastline for species such as black marlin and yellowfin tuna are among the world's best fishing experiences. You will need to join a charter as these activities require a great deal of local expertise. Most operators will provide equipment.

The inland waters of Tasmania are famed for their excellent trout fishing prospects. The estuaries and beaches in the southern states, such as the Fleurieu Peninsula in South Australia (see pp354–5), are full of species such as bream, salmon and flathead. Small boats are readily available for hire and fishing tackle can be bought and occasionally hired at most popular fishing destinations. Each state has a government department with a special fisheries section. Staff provide excellent information on locations, restrictions, safety issues and obtaining fishing licences. Check the weather forecast and heed warnings about dangerous spots, particularly rock platforms.

Ecotourism

This tourism concept has its roots in activities as old as bird watching and wildflower identification. It incorporates many of the activities mentioned in this section, but is generally distinguished by its emphasis on issues concerning the appreciation and conservation of the natural heritage. Given

Canoeing on the Roper River in the Northern Territory (see pp272–3)

Mural advertising water-based recreational activities

Australia's enormous natural bounty, it is hardly surprising that the market is now flooded with operators offering an astonishing range of nature-based activities. These encompass wildlife watching (including whales, birds and dolphins), nature walks, and trekking and rafting expeditions to remote wilderness areas. Visitors can also stay at resorts which are operated along strictly "green" guidelines. These are eco-friendly and are usually located within some of the most environmentally valuable regions in the country. The **Ecotourism Association of Australia** can provide information on tour operators and publications.

Water Sports

Australia is one of the world's great diving destinations, and the Great Barrier Reef is the centre of most of the diving activity (see pp216–21). Visitors can combine a holiday on the reef with a few days of diving instruction from one of the many excellent schools in the area. There are opportunities for diving all around Australia, however, and other popular locations include Rottnest Island (see pp312–13) and Esperance (see p323) in Western Australia

and the beautiful World Heritage Area of Lord Howe Island off the coast of New South Wales.

Canoeing in Australia can mean a quiet paddle in a hire-boat on a city lake, or an exciting adventure in a kayak on the high seas. It is a reasonably priced sport and is widely available throughout the country. Popular spots include the Murray River (see p359), Sydney Harbour (see pp148–9) and the rivers of national parks nationwide.

Whitewater rafting is another favourite sport in this land of outdoor enthusiasts and there are many opportunities for people of all abilities to have a go. The inexperienced can try a day with an instructor on an easy run; the confident can tackle a two-week tour on the rafter's mecca, the Franklin-Gordon River system in Tasmania (see p472).

Sailing in Gippsland Lakes Coastal Park, Eastern Victoria (see p448)

Long stretches of unspoilt coastline, remote bays and harbours, tropical reefs and uninhabited islands make Australia an excellent destination for sailing enthusiasts. Skippered cruises are the most usual kind of holiday, but some visitors will want to hire a vessel and set off for themselves – a practice known as bareboating. To do this you will need to prove to the operator that you are an experienced sailor. It is difficult to beat the tropical splendours of the Whitsunday Islands in Queensland *(see p250)* as a location. Other popular sailing areas include Pittwater in New South Wales and Queensland's Gold Coast *(see pp242–3)*.

Australia is also world-renowned for its abundance of outstanding surfing beaches. For more information about the country's best places to surf, *see pages 42–3*.

Skiing

The Ski season in Australia extends from June to September. Downhill skiing is restricted to the Victorian Alps *(see p450–53)*, the New South Wales mountains and two small resorts in Tasmania *(see p473)*. The ski villages have excellent facilities, but the fields can get crowded during school holidays and long weekends, and prices for ski-lifts and equipment hire can be high.

Upland areas around these resorts are superb for cross-country skiing. Traversing gentle slopes and rounded peaks,

Skiing Eagle Ridge on Mount Hotham in the Victoria Alps

skiers will be treated to glimpses of Australia's rare alpine flora and fauna, and spectacular sweeping scenery.

Spectator Sports

Most sports enthusiasts will enjoy taking in a fixture during their trip, while a few visitors come to Australia especially for a sporting event, such as yacht races, cricket or tennis events. Early booking is advisable as competition for tickets can be fierce. Regular highlights include the Australian Tennis Open, Melbourne Cup and the Formula 1 Grand Prix, all Melbourne events, and international Test cricket and the Australian Open golf that moves each year *(see pp44–7)*. Rugby League and Australian Rules football are the most popular spectator sports. The finals are the main event, but excitement is high at almost any match.

DIRECTORY

Clubs and Associations

Australian Golf Union
95 Coventry St, South Melbourne, VIC 3205. **Tel** (03) 9626 5050.
W golf.org.au

Australian Parachute Federation
Unit 3, 2994 Logan Road, Underwood, QLD 4119. **Tel** (07) 3457 0100. W apf.asn.au

Australian Yachting Federation
22 Atchison St, St Leonards, NSW 2065. **Tel** (02) 8424 7400.
W yachting.org.au

Bicycle New South Wales
1st Floor, Heritage Building A, 1 Herb Elliott Ave, Sydney Olympic Park, Homebush Bay, NSW 2127. **Tel** (02) 9704 0800.
W bicyclensw.org.au

Ecotourism Association of Australia
Tel (07) 3252 1530.
W ecotourism.org.au

Gliding Federation of Australia
C4/1–13 The Gateway, Broadmeadows, VIC, 3047. **Tel** (03) 9359 1613. W gfa.org.au

New South Wales Snow Sports Association
PO Box 934, Jindabyne, NSW 2627. **Tel** 0402 123 796.
W nswsnowsports.com.au

Skiing Australia
1 Cobden St, South Melbourne, VIC 3205. **Tel** (04) 2863 6516.
W ski.com.au

Tour Operators

Adventure Associates
Level 8, 309 Pitt St, Sydney.
Tel (02) 4758 9922.
W adventureassociates.com

Croydon Travel
34 Main St, Croydon, VIC 3136. **Tel** (03) 9725 8555.
W croydontravel.com.au

STA Travel
Tel 134 782.
W statravel.com.au

World Expeditions
Level 5, 71 York St, Sydney, NSW 2000. **Tel** 1300 720 000.
W worldexpeditions.com.au

AFL Australian Rules football grand final in Melbourne

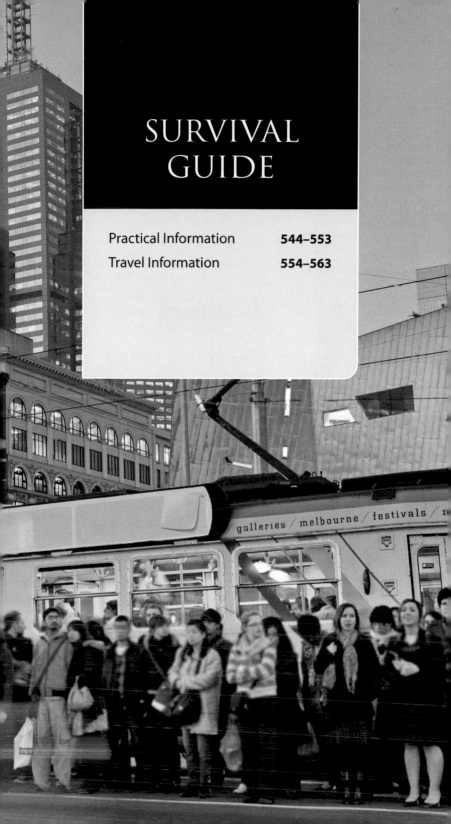

SURVIVAL GUIDE

galleries / melbourne / festivals /

PRACTICAL INFORMATION

Australia continues to surge ahead as a major tourist destination, and facilities for travellers have kept pace with this rapid development. Visitors should encounter few problems in this safe and friendly destination. Accommodation and restaurants *(see pp478–535)* are of international standard, public transport is readily available *(see pp556–63)* and tourist information centres are everywhere. The following pages contain useful information for all visitors. Personal Security and Health *(see pp548–9)* details a number of recommended precautions, Banking and Local Currency *(see pp550–51)* answers all essential financial queries, and Communication and Media *(see pp552–3)* describes Australia's telephone, Internet and postal services.

Skiers enjoying the slopes at Falls Creek in Eastern Victoria *(see p453)*

When to Go

The northern half of the country lies in a tropical zone and is subject to "wet" and "dry" seasons *(see pp48–9)*. The dry season falls between May and October, and is regarded as the best time to visit this area. During the wet season, conditions are hot and humid, and many areas are inaccessible because of flooding. For those with an interest in wildlife, however, there are areas such as Kakadu National Park *(see pp280–81)* which are particularly spectacular at this time of year.

The southern half of the continent is temperate and the seasons are the exact opposite to those in Europe and North America. Victoria and Tasmania can be a little cloudy and wet in winter, but they are very colourful and quite balmy in autumn. The vast southern coastline is a popular touring destination during the summer months – the climate is warm, with a gentle breeze. Avoid the Outback areas during the summer, however, as the temperatures can be extreme.

The popular ski season is between June and September and takes place in both the New South Wales Snowy Mountains *(see p191)* and the Victoria Alps *(see pp452–3)*. In the states of South Australia and Western Australia, there are spectacular wild flower displays between September and December.

Entry Requirements

Visitors to Australia must have a passport valid for longer than the intended period of stay. All visitors, except New Zealand passport holders, must also have a visa issued before arrival. For stays of up to three months the easiest option for most is to get an Electronic Travel Authority (ETA), or an eVisitors, depending on the country of origin. Neither requires a stamp in your passport or has a visa application charge. They can be obtained from travel agents, airlines (usually when you book your flight) or can be applied for online at the **Department of Immigration** website *(see p547)*. Always check the latest entry requirements with the Australian embassy in your country before leaving.

For stays of three to six months, a tourist visa may be applied for in person at the Australian Embassy or by post. Visitors will be asked for proof of a return ticket and of sufficient funds for the duration of their stay. Some visitors, including British nationals, between the ages of 18 and 30 may apply for a 12-month working holiday visa.

Tourist Information

Tourism Australia is the central tourism body, but each state and territory has its own tourism authority. Travel centres in the capital cities provide abundant information and these are often the best places to seek advice on specialist tours and to make bookings. Information booths can also be found at airports, tourist sites and in shopping centres.

Smaller towns often have tourist offices located in general stores, galleries or petrol stations – look for the blue and

Visitor information kiosk and booking centre

◀ Bustling Federation Square in Melbourne, with the city skyline in the background

The platform and view of Sydney Harbour at Circular Quay station, accessible to disabled travellers

white information symbol. In remoter areas, national park visitors' centres will provide useful information on bushwalks and the local terrain.

Opening Hours and Admission Prices

Most major tourist sites are open seven days a week, but it is always advisable to check first. However, many places are closed on Good Friday and Christmas Day. In smaller places, galleries and other sites are often closed during the early part of the week. Admission prices are generally moderate and, in some cases, admission is free. Exceptions are major touring exhibitions, zoos, theme parks and specialist attractions such as Sovereign Hill in Ballarat (see p437). Make the most of weekdays – locals will be competing for viewing space at weekends.

Aquarium sign in Queensland

Etiquette

While Australian society is generally laid-back, there are a few unwritten rules which visitors should follow.

Australians drive on the left and, generally, walk on the left-hand side of a path. They stand on the left of a busy escalator to allow others to pass. Eating and drinking is frowned upon while on public transport, in taxis and also in many shops and galleries.

Dress codes are casual, particularly in summer when the weather can get very hot, but some bars and restaurants may require men to wear shirts and place a ban on jeans and sports shoes.

Topless bathing is accepted in designated areas on some beaches, but it is advisable to see what the locals are doing. While a tiny bikini may go unnoticed on the beach, it is considered polite to cover up when sitting in a café or restaurant.

Continental table manners apply in restaurants. Placing your knife and fork together on the plate indicates to wait staff that you have finished your meal. Tipping is optional; however, 10 to 15 per cent of the final bill for good service in a restaurant is customary, as is rounding up to the nearest dollar for taxi drivers, porters and bar tenders.

Smoking is prohibited in all public buildings, on public transport, in taxis, stores, sports grounds, cafés, and restaurants. Depending on the state, smoking is also banned to a lesser or greater extent in pubs and nightclubs, with many providing an outdoor smoking area. Ask about smoking policies when booking hotels.

To avoid causing offence, always ask before taking someone's photograph, especially if the person is an Aboriginal Australian. If taking photographs for commercial purposes, permission is required before photographing on private land.

Disabled Travellers

Disabled travellers can generally expect the best in Australia in terms of facilities. Many hotels, restaurants, tourist sites, cinemas, theatres, airports and shopping centres have wheelchair facilities, and guide dogs for the blind are always welcomed.

Traditionally, public transport is a problem for wheelchair users, although most states are now making their systems more accessible to disabled travellers. Contact the transport authority state by state for more detailed information. Tourist information centres and council offices can provide maps that show sites with wheelchair access.

One of the most useful organizations for disabled travellers is the **National Information Communication Awareness Network (NICAN)** in Canberra. This nationwide database provides information on disabled facilities in different parts of the country and, if they don't have the appropriate information at hand, they will do their best to seek it out. They also have details of many publications written for disabled travellers in Australia.

One particularly good publication is *Easy Access Australia*, written specifically for people with mobility problems. The **Information on Disability and Education Awareness (IDEAS)** website has an extensive listing of disability-friendly accommodation in its travel section.

Mother and child feeding some of Australia's famous marsupials

Travelling with Children

Australia is an ideal destination for children. Most hotels welcome children as guests and can usually provide cots, highchairs and, in some cases, babysitting. However, some of the smaller bed-and-breakfast places advertise themselves as child-free zones.

Restaurants are also generally welcoming to children and offer children's portions, although it is advisable to check first with the more up-market establishments. City department stores and most major tourist sites have feeding and nappy-changing rooms as standard features. Parents travelling with young children are also encouraged by a range of discounts on air, coach, train and boat travel *(see pp554–63)*.

National laws governing the restraint of children in cars were introduced in 2009. These stipulate that children under the age of seven must be restrained in an appropriate infant seat and must not travel in the front seat of a car. As many cars do not have these restraints as standard fixtures, it is essential that prior arrangements be made.

Car hire firms will generally supply car restraints for a small extra charge. **Gillespie's Hire and Sales Service** leases restraints, push-chairs, baby carriers and travel cots. It is illegal to leave children unattended in a car.

Two informative websites filled with great destinations, attractions and other child-friendly information are **BYO Kids** and **Holidays with Kids**. Both offer useful tips even if you don't book through them.

Student Travellers

The International Student Identity Card (ISIC) is available to all students worldwide in full-time study. The ISIC card should be purchased in the student's own country at a Student and Youth Travel office or online from the Student Travel Association (STA) website (www.statravel.com).

Card-holders are entitled to substantial discounts on overseas air travel *(see pp554–7)*, national train and bus services *(see pp558–9)*, as well as discounts on admission to theatres, galleries, museums and other establishments.

Gay and Lesbian Travellers

Within inner city areas, the gay and lesbian scene is accepted but you may still find homophobic attitudes across much of Australia. Legality and age of consent for homosexual sex varies according to state laws, ranging from 16 to 21 years in Western Australia. More information can be found on the **Gay and Lesbian Rights Lobby (GLR)** website.

The **Gay and Lesbian Tourism Association (GALTA)** is a not-for-profit organization promoting and listing tolerant businesses for travellers.

Free magazines designed for the gay and lesbian market are available in all major cities. Look out for the lesbian magazine *Cherrie* and the gay monthly, *AXN*.

Budget Travel

Accommodation is more expensive in inner city and tourist areas than in outlying suburbs and country towns. Staying outside the cities and using public transport to get in is a good, cheap option.

Petrol is more expensive in rural areas and varies from state to state; Queensland is always the cheapest. Eating out tends to be cheaper outside cities where good-value hearty meals are served at local cafés. Groceries, on the other hand, are more expensive in smaller towns.

Australian Time Zones

Australia is divided into three separate time zones: Western Standard Time, Central Standard Time and Eastern Standard Time. Eastern Australia is two hours ahead of Western Australia; Central Australia is one-and-a-half hours ahead. Daylight saving is observed in New South Wales, the ACT, Victoria and South Australia, from October to March, which adds an hour to the time differences.

City and State	Hours + GMT
Adelaide (SA)	+9.5
Brisbane (QLD)	+10
Canberra (ACT)	+10
Darwin (NT)	+9.5
Hobart (TAS)	+10
Melbourne (VIC)	+10
Perth (WA)	+8
Sydney (NSW)	+10

Electrical Appliances

Australia's electrical current is 240–250 volts AC. Electrical plugs have either two or three pins. Most good hotels will provide 110-volt shaver sockets and hair dryers, but a flat, two- or three-pin adaptor will be necessary for other appliances. Buy these from electrical stores.

Responsible Travel

There is an annual nationwide environmental event known as "Clean Up Australia Day", when volunteers help to clear local areas of rubbish. Most councils across Australia also run recycling schemes, and encourage the separation of recyclable materials from general rubbish. However, discarded spring water bottles have become a huge environmental problem, and many councils now supply refilling stations, such as the one at Bondi Beach, to encourage people to reuse their bottles. Drought is an ongoing issue, with government

Collection point encouraging people to recycle cans

campaigns encouraging very careful use of water as well as mandatory water restrictions.

Respect Australia's wonderfully diverse ecosystem. When bushwalking keep to marked tracks or boardwalks. This is particularly important in coastal areas, where the regeneration of sand dunes is necessary to prevent beaches from being washed away.

Local farmers' markets are increasingly popular across the country and allow visitors to support the local economy and sample organic produce. Contact the **Australian Farmers' Markets Association (AFMA)** for details of local markets.

Most shops offer plastic bags but shoppers tend to reject them in favour of reusable green fabric shopping bags.

Look for the **Green STAR** accreditation when booking accommodation – this indicates properties that are energy efficient, minimize waste and take steps to prevent excessive water use.

Conversion Chart

Imperial to Metric
1 inch = 2.54 centimetres
1 foot = 30 centimetres
1 mile = 1.6 kilometres
1 ounce = 28 grams
1 pound = 454 grams
1 pint = 0.6 litres
1 gallon = 4.6 litres

Metric to Imperial
1 centimetre = 0.4 inches
1 metre = 3 feet, 3 inches
1 kilometre = 0.6 miles
1 gram = 0.04 ounces
1 kilogram = 2.2 pounds
1 litre = 1.8 pints

DIRECTORY

Immigration

Department of Immigration
3 Lonsdale St, Braddon, ACT 2612.
Tel 131 881.
Ⓦ immi.gov.au

Disabled Travellers

Easy Access Australia
Ⓦ easyaccessaustralia.com.au

Ideas
Tel 1800 029 904.
Ⓦ ideas.org.au

Nican
48 Brookes St, Mitchell, ACT 2911. **Tel** 1800 806 769. Ⓦ nican.com.au

Travelling with Children

BYO Kids
Ⓦ byokids.com.au

Gillespie's Hire & Sales Service
13 Elizabeth St, Artarmon, NSW 2064. **Tel** (02) 9411 2180. Ⓦ ghss.com.au

Holidays with Kids
Ⓦ holidayswithkids.com.au

Gay and Lesbian Travellers

Gay and Lesbian Rights Lobby
Ⓦ glrl.org.au

Gay and Lesbian Tourism Association
Ⓦ galta.com.au

Tourism Australia Offices

Australia
Ⓦ australia.com

United Kingdom
Australia House, 6th Floor, Melbourne Place, The Strand, London WC2B 4LG.
Tel (020) 7438 4600.

USA and Canada
6100 Center Drive, Suite 1150, Los Angeles, CA 90045.
Tel (310) 695 3200.

State Tourist Offices

ACT
330 Northbourne Ave, Dickson, ACT 2602.
Tel (02) 6205 0666.
Ⓦ visitcanberra.com.au

New South Wales
Cnr Argyle & Playfair sts, The Rocks, NSW 2000.
Tel (02) 8273 0000.
Ⓦ visitnsw.com.au

Northern Territory
Cnr Smith & Bennett sts, Darwin, NT 0800.
Tel 1300 138 886 or (08) 8980 6000. also at: 67 Stuart Hwy, Alice Springs, NT 0870.
Tel (08) 8951 8471.
Ⓦ tourismtopend.com.au

Queensland
The Mall, Brisbane, QLD 4001. **Tel** (07) 3006 6200. also at: Cairns Information Centre, 51 The Esplanade, Cairns, QLD 4870.
Tel (07) 3535 3535.
Ⓦ queensland.com

South Australia
18 King William St, Adelaide, SA 5000.
Tel 1300 655 276.
Ⓦ southaustralia.com

Tasmania
20 Davey St, Hobart, TAS 7000. **Tel** (03) 6230 8235.
Ⓦ discovertasmania.com.au

Tourism Australia
Ⓦ tourism.australia.com

Victoria
Federation Square, cnr Swanston & Flinders sts, Melbourne, VIC 3000.
Tel (03) 9653 9777.
Ⓦ visitvictoria.com

Western Australia
2 Mill St, Perth, WA 6000.
Tel (08) 9483 1111.
Ⓦ westernaustralia.com

Responsible Travel

AFMA
Tel (02) 9360 9380.
Ⓦ farmersmarkets.org.au

Green STAR
Ⓦ starratings.com.au

Personal Security and Health

Australia has a low crime rate and is generally regarded as a safe tourist destination. There is a strong police presence in all the state capitals, and even small towns will have at least one officer. In terms of climate and environment, however, Australia is a tough country, and visitors must observe safety procedures whether travelling to remote areas or merely planning a day at the beach. If you get into trouble, contact one of the national emergency numbers or helplines in the directory opposite.

Police vehicle

Fire engine

Intensive care ambulance

What to be Aware of

Leave valuables and important documents in your hotel safe, and don't carry large sums of cash with you. Traveller's cheques are generally regarded as the safest way to carry large sums of money. It is also worth photocopying vital documents in case of loss or theft.

Be on guard against pickpockets in places where big crowds gather. Prime areas for petty theft are tourist attractions, shopping centres, beaches, markets, sporting venues and on peak-hour public transport.

Never carry your wallet in an outside pocket where it is an easy target for a thief. Wear shoulder bags and cameras with the strap across your body and with any clasps fastened. If you have a car, always try to park in well-lit, reasonably busy streets. Lock the vehicle securely and don't leave any valuables or property visible that might attract a thief.

Personal Safety

There are few, if any, off-limit areas in Australian cities. Red-light districts may be a little seedy, but the fact that they are often busy and well policed probably makes them safer than the average suburban street at night.

Avoid poorly lit areas and parks at night. Buses (and trams in Melbourne) are regarded as a safe means of travel at night. However, when travelling by train it is worth remembering that many stations are not staffed after hours, particularly in suburban areas. Travel in the train carriage nearest the driver or in those marked as being safe for night travel. Taxis are a safe and efficient way of getting around late at night. Hitchhiking is not advisable, and is illegal in some states (see p562).

Country towns can shut down fairly early in Australia, which

is often a surprise to many visitors. It is advisable to reach a destination before nightfall and avoid wandering around looking for accommodation or a meal after dark. The majority of places are friendly to travellers but in remote areas visitors do stand out and as such are potential targets if a threat exists.

Women Travellers

It is safe for women, generally speaking, to travel throughout Australia, although all the usual rules about personal safety apply. Drink "spiking" sometimes happens, so don't leave drinks unattended and only accept drinks from people you know. Sexual harassment of women can occur; if possible, ignoring it is the best course of action.

Medical Matters

Australia's medical services are among the best in the world. Under reciprocal arrangements visitors from the UK, New Zealand, Malta, Italy, Finland, Sweden and Holland are entitled to free hospital and medical treatment provided by Australia's national insurance scheme, Medicare. Medicare does not, however, cover dental work, so dental insurance is worth considering. Visitors from countries other than those mentioned will face prohibitive

Park ranger

Policeman

Fire officer

medical bills if uninsured. Arrangements for adequate medical cover should be made before leaving home.

Dial 000 in any part of the country for ambulance assistance. Most public hospitals have a casualty department. For less urgent treatment, queues can be very long. There are 24-hour medical centres in the major cities, and doctors in or near most towns. Look in the local Yellow Pages under "Medical Practitioners".

There are dental hospitals in the state capitals providing emergency treatment. Call the **Australian Dental Association** for emergency advice and a list of dentists in your area.

Pharmacies

Pharmacies (or chemist shops as they are known in Australia) are plentiful in cities and suburbs, but can be thin on the ground in remote areas. Unrestricted drugs such as painkillers and other goods such as cosmetics, toiletries, suncreams and baby products are standard stock items. Most pharmacies will provide free advice on minor ailments, but foreign prescriptions can only be met if endorsed by a local medical practitioner.

Hotel staff and hospitals will direct you to after-hours pharmacies in major cities.

Environmental Hazards

Paid lifeguards dressed in blue and white, and/or volunteer lifesavers in red and yellow, patrol many beaches in populated areas. Safe swimming areas are indicated by red and yellow flags during spring and summer. However, there are vast stretches of unpatrolled beaches in Australia and many of these are subject to dangerous rips. Rips can often be identified as a darker and calmer stretch of water between the breaking waves. Do not falsely equate calmer water with safe swimming. Certain rips can be so strong that even wading

Surf lifesaving sign indicating a dangerous undertow or "rip"

can pose a threat. Follow local advice and, if in any doubt, do not swim. You should never swim alone.

Even in well-trodden areas of the Australian bush, hikers can lose their way. Always inform someone of your route. Staff at national parks can offer expert advice along with maps, and will keep a note of your intended trip. Take a basic first-aid kit, food and water, and extra clothing. In many regions, temperatures plummet when the sun sets.

Australia shelters some of the most venomous creatures on earth. Basic precautions such as good boots and a wary eye are necessary. Snake-bite victims should be kept calm while emergency help is sought. Try to identify the creature by size and colour so that the appropriate anti-venom can be administered.

Crocodiles are fascinating but dangerous creatures. In the northern regions, heed the warning signs and make enquiries if you intend to swim in remote, unpatrolled areas. Box jellyfish patrol tropical waters between October and May and their sting is deadly. Again, observe the signs.

Bush fires are a fact of life in Australia. When planning a camping trip, ring the **NSW Rural Fire Service** to check on restrictions. Total fire bans are not uncommon during warm, dry seasons when use of electric and gas barbeques are restricted and many national parks are

Tasmania parks logo

closed to the public. Avoid high-risk areas and dial 000 if in immediate danger from fire.

Protecting Your Skin

Australia has the highest rate of skin cancer in the world, caused by the harmful effects of ultraviolet radiation. The risk of skin damage is high, even on cloudy days. Always use a good SPF 30+ sunscreen and cover up by wearing sun protective clothing, a hat and sunglasses. Keep in the shade if possible, especially between 10am and 2pm. The **Cancer Council of Australia** website has more information, and check UV alerts in daily newspapers or at the Bureau of Meteorology (www. bom.gov.au).

Banking and Local Currency

Branches of national, state and some foreign banks can be found in the central business districts of Australia's state capitals. Suburban shopping centres and country towns will often have at least one branch of a major Australian bank. If travelling to remote areas, find out what banking facilities are available in advance. Banks generally offer the best exchange rates; money can also be changed at bureaux de change, large department stores and hotels. There is no limit to the amount of personal funds that can be taken in or out of Australia, although cash amounts of A$10,000 or more must be declared to customs on arrival or prior to departure.

Using electronic transfer (EFTPOS) to pay for goods

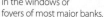
High street bank logos

Banking

Banks are usually open 9:30am–4pm Monday–Thursday and until 5pm on Fridays. Some branches are also open to midday on Saturdays. Major city banks open 8:30am–5pm on weekdays. Outside banking hours, many transactions can be handled through automatic teller machines (ATMs). Exchange rates are displayed in the windows or foyers of most major banks.

Automatic cash dispenser

Traveller's Cheques

Australian dollar traveller's cheques issued by major names such as Thomas Cook and American Express are usually accepted (with a passport) in large shops. You may have problems, however, cashing these in smaller outlets. Banks are the best places to cash traveller's cheques, as their fees are lower. Foreign currency cheques can be cashed at all major banks, bureaux de change and established hotels in the main cities.

Credit Cards

All well-known international credit cards are widely accepted in Australia. Major credit cards such as VISA, MasterCard, Diners Club and American Express can be used to book and pay for hotel rooms, airline tickets, car hire, tours and tickets. However, some companies, such as travel agencies, charge a fee of 1–3 per cent of the total purchase price for using them. Credit cards are accepted in most restaurants and shops. Check first, though, as many places don't accept American Express or Diners Club due to the large commissions they charge and smaller places may impose a minimum charge. You can also use credit cards in ATMs to withdraw cash. You should carry some emergency cash, however, if travelling to remote areas, particularly the Outback. Credit cards may not be accepted at small stores and cafés, and alternatives, such as a 24-hour ATM, may not be available.

Automatic Teller Machines and Electronic Transfer

Automatic teller machines (ATMs) can be found in most banks, as well as in shopping and tourist areas. In most cases it is possible to access foreign accounts from ATMs by using a linked debit card. Ask your bank about making your card valid for this kind of use.

An appropriate debit card will also give you access to EFTPOS (Electronic Funds Transfer at Point Of Sale). Pay for goods using a card, and funds are automatically debited from your chosen bank account. In many stores customers will also be able to withdraw cash, providing a purchase has been made. This "cash-back" facility is useful if the town you are in doesn't have an appropriate ATM.

Bureaux de Change

Australian cities and larger towns, particularly those popular with tourists, have many bureaux de change. These are usually open Monday to Saturday from 9am to 5:30pm. Some branches also operate on Sundays.

While the opening hours of bureaux de change make them a convenient alternative to a bank, their commissions and fees are generally higher. Post offices will also often change foreign money.

DIRECTORY

Foreign Currency Exchange

American Express
Tel 1300 132 639.
W americanexpress.com.au

Commonwealth Bank
Tel 13 22 21.
W commbank.com.au

Travelex
Tel 1800 400 039.
W travelex.com.au

Westpac
Tel 13 20 32. W westpac.com.au

Local Currency

The Australian currency is the Australian dollar (A$), which breaks down into 100 cents (c). The decimal currency system now in place has been in operation since 1966.

Single cents may still be used for some prices, but as the Australian 1c and 2c coins are no longer in circulation, the total amount to be paid will be rounded up or down to the nearest five cents.

It can be difficult to change A$50 and A$100 notes, so avoid using them in smaller shops and cafés and when paying for taxi fares. If you do not have change, tell the taxi driver before you start your journey to avoid any misunderstandings. Otherwise, when you arrive at your destination, you may have to find change at the nearest shop or ATM.

To improve security, as well as increase their lifespan, all Australian bank notes have now been plasticized.

Bank Notes

Australian bank notes are produced in denominations of A$5, A$10, A$20, A$50 and A$100. All bank notes are made of plastic. Paper notes have been phased out and are no longer legal tender.

A$100 note

A$50 note

A$20 note

A$5 note

A$10 note

5 cents (5c)

10 cents (10c)

20 cents (20c)

50 cents (50c)

1 dollar (A$1)

2 dollars (A$2)

Coins

Coins currently in use in Australia are 5c, 10c, 20c, 50c, A$1 and A$2. There are several different 20c, 50c and A$1 coins in circulation; all are the same size and shape, but have different commemorative images on the face. The 10c and 20c coins are useful for local telephone calls (see pp552–3).

Communication and Media

Communications systems in Australia are fast, modern, efficient and of international standard. The majority of Australians have mobile phones and home Internet connections, and Internet cafés and Wi-Fi areas are also widely available in cities and large towns.

Postal services within Australia are usually next day delivery in the same city and international mail can take less than a week. Online versions of Australian national newspapers are regularly updated with domestic and international news, while the standard of Australia's television and radio broadcasting is generally considered to be high.

Telstra public telephone booths at Bondi Junction, Sydney

Public Telephones

Payphones can be found on main streets throughout Australia's cities and towns. Most accept both coins and phone-cards, although some operate solely on phonecards and major credit cards. Phonecards can be bought from selected news-agents and news kiosks, and from other outlets with the blue and orange Telstra sign.

Although slightly varied in shape and colour, all public telephones have a hand-held receiver and a 12-button key pad, as well as clear instructions on their use (in English only), a list of useful phone numbers and copies of telephone directories.

Payphone Charges

Local calls are untimed and cost 50 cents. Depending on where you are, "local" means the city and its suburbs, or outside the city, a defined country region. **Telstra** can provide information on exact costs. Dial freephone 1800 113 011 for an estimate of the cost of long-distance and international calls.

Credit card phones have a A$1.20 minimum fee. Long-distance calls are less expensive if you dial without the help of an operator. The cheapest method of calling long distance is by using a prepaid phonecard; they can reduce the rate of international calls to about 5 cents per minute. Check the different kinds

available to find one that suits your needs. Prepaid phonecards can be bought at newsagents, local shops, post offices and other retail outlets.

Telephone Directories

Each city and region in Australia has two telephone directories: the **White Pages** and the **Yellow Pages.** The White Pages lists private and business numbers in alphabetical order. It also has a guide to emergency services and government departments. The Yellow Pages lists businesses under relevant headings such as Dentists, Car Hire and so on. Both are available online.

Mobile Phones

Short-term mobile phone rentals are available for visitors, but if your phone is compatible it may be cheaper to bring it with you and buy a local Sim card once you have arrived. This way you can also avoid paying the high cost of international fees on incoming calls to your mobile.

Optus, Telstra, Virgin and **Vodafone** are the main mobile phone service providers. They differ significantly in the coverage and costs they offer, so it is worth looking into each one to find the best deal.

While international texting is relatively cheap, international calls are very expensive from mobile phones in Australia, so using a prepaid phonecard may be a better option if you need to make a lot of

Reaching the Right Number

- To ring Australia from the UK dial **0061**, then the area code, then the local number.
- To ring Australia from the USA or Canada dial **011 61**, then the area code, then the local number.
- For long-distance direct-dial calls outside your local area code, but within Australia (STD calls), dial the appropriate area code, then the number.
- For international direct-dial calls (IDD calls) from a fixed phone line in Australia: dial **0011**, followed by the country code (USA and Canada: 1; UK: 44; Republic of Ireland: 353; New Zealand: 64, South Africa: 27), then the city or area code (omit initial 0) and then the local number.

- Directory information with automatic connection (incurs an additional charge) to local and national destinations: dial **12455**.
- Local and national directory enquiries: dial **1223**.
- Reverse charge or third-party charge calls: dial **12550** or **1800 738 3773**.
- National and international operator assisted calls: dial **1234** or **12550**.
- National and international call-cost enquiries: dial **1800 113 011**.
- Numbers beginning with **1 800** are toll-free numbers.
- Numbers beginning with **13** are charged at the local call rate from anywhere in Australia.
- Numbers beginning with **04** are mobiles.
- See also Emergency Services, *p549.*

Standard and express postboxes

international calls. Making calls while driving is illegal and carries a stiff fine. Many places in remote Australia are not on the mobile network.

Internet

Internet cafés provide relatively cheap Internet and email access and are widely spread throughout tourist areas. Public libraries also provide Internet access, although terminals may need to be booked in advance.

Wireless local area network (Wi-Fi), which allows you to connect to the Internet using your own laptop in a "hotspot", is becoming increasingly common in Australia. Many hotels provide a Wi-Fi service but may charge a premium for it. Lists of free Wi-Fi hotspots are available at www. freewifi.com.au and www. wififreespot.com.

For a cheap alternative to long-distance phone calls download a VoIP (Voice Over Internet Protocol) on to your laptop before travelling. The most popular one is Skype and many Internet cafés already have this installed on their machines.

Postal Services

Post offices are open 9am–5pm weekdays and some are open on Saturday mornings. Most offer a wide range of services including poste restante and fax services. In country towns, the local general store often doubles as the post office. Most newsagents also sell stamps.

All standard domestic mail is first class. Post boxes for standard mail are red and can be found on most street corners. Express Post, for which you need to buy the special yellow and white envelopes sold in post offices, guarantees faster, often next-day, delivery within Australia. Postboxes for Express Post are yellow. Post offices also offer international courier services.

Newspapers, Television and Radio

Australia has two national newspapers, *The Australian*, a well-respected broadsheet with excellent national and overseas news coverage, and the *Australian Financial Review*, which largely reports on international business and monetary matters. *Time* magazine is Australia's leading weekly international news magazine, though many stories are taken from the American version of the magazine. All major foreign newspapers and magazines are readily available in cities and large towns. Each state capital also has its own broadsheet and tabloid newspaper.

The Australian Broadcasting Corporation (ABC) is a state-owned nationwide television

and radio broadcaster which provides excellent news and current affairs coverage, children's programmes and high-quality local and international drama. In addition, the corporation has its own local and national AM and FM radio stations which offer a wide range of services, including news, arts commentary, modern and classical music, women's programmes and an acclaimed nationwide channel for the under 30s called Triple J. SBS (Special Broadcasting Service) is Australia's other state-run television and radio network and caters to Australia's many cultures with foreign language programmes. There are also three commercial television networks, Channels 7, 9 and 10, all of which offer a range of soap operas, sports, news, game shows and other light entertainment on three channels each.

In all state capitals there is an enormous variety of local FM and AM radio stations. Details of current programming are available in local newspapers. Of interest also are the community radio stations which cater to local cultural and social interests.

ABC⑩
Australian
Broadcasting
Corporation

Logo for the
ABC network

Illuminated sign at a local Internet café

TRAVEL INFORMATION

While some visitors to Australia may choose to arrive by sea, the vast majority arrive by air. Once here, flying between locations is also the most popular form of long-distance travel, but there are some other choices, all of which offer the chance to see something of the country along the way. The national rail network links all major cities, while coach routes provide regular services to most provincial and country areas. If you have the time, driving in Australia is an excellent option. Boat travel is best if you want to visit Australia's islands, principally Tasmania, but regular services run to other island destinations such as Rottnest Island off the coast of Western Australia *(see pp312–13)*.

Green Travel

Given the location and sheer size of the country, and unless you have unlimited time, it is difficult to travel to and within Australia without using environmentally unfriendly, long-haul flights. A journey of four hours by plane can take three days by train and, in most cases, a flight is the cheaper option. However, if you can spare the time and money, there are some spectacular long-distance train routes through the country where, especially with the speciality "luxury" operators *(see pp558–9)* the journey can become a worthwhile part of your holiday.

If you plan to hire a car, the Australian government produces a **Green Vehicle Guide** which rates cars according to their carbon emissions and allows useful comparisons between vehicles. Within cities public transport is relatively cheap and efficient, and has the advantage of avoiding costly parking at each destination.

Arriving by Air

Australia is served by around 50 international airlines. The Australian airline **Qantas** has a worldwide network and offers the most flights in and out of Australia every week. Qantas is also one of the main domestic carriers in Australia *(see p556)*. **Air New Zealand**, Qantas and **United Airlines** have regular flights from the US, with a range of stopovers. The large Asian and European carriers, **British Airways, Emirates, Singapore Airlines, Cathay Pacific** and **Japan Airlines**, also offer a variety of different routes and stopovers on the Europe–Asia–Australia run. Canadian travellers can fly direct using **Air Canada**.

International Flights

Flights between Australia and Europe take upwards of 22 hours, and with delays you may be in transit for more than 30 hours. A stopover in Asia is worth considering, especially if travelling with children, as is one in Hawaii or the Pacific islands for visitors from the US. Also, consider arranging flights so that they account for international time differences. Arriving in the afternoon, spending the rest of the day awake, then going to sleep in accordance with local time is a recommended way to help counteract jet lag.

Australia has several international air terminals so visitors can choose different arrival and departure points. Sydney and Melbourne have major airports servicing flights from all over the world. Sydney's Kingsford Smith Airport is the busiest and can be congested. Melbourne Tullamarine Airport is consistently voted one of the world's best airports by travellers. Hobart has flights from New Zealand in the summer months, while Adelaide has direct flights to Singapore and flights to Europe via Sydney or Melbourne. Visitors to the west coast can arrive in Perth from Africa, Asia and the UK. Darwin, Brisbane and Cairns mostly service Asia, but there are a few possibilities for connections from Europe.

Air Fares

Flights to Australia can be expensive, especially during December, the peak season. January to April is slightly cheaper. During the off-peak

International Qantas flight arriving in Sydney

Singapore Airlines 747 taking off at Perth Airport

season, airlines offer Apex fares that are often 30–40 per cent below economy fares *(see p556)*. Many stipulate arrival and departure times and carry cancellation penalties. Round-the-world fares are good value and increasingly popular.

Check with discount travel agents if you can fly at short notice, as they regularly receive unsold tickets from the airlines. In these cases, flexibility isn't usually a feature. Departure Tax is now included in the price of a ticket out of Australia.

On Arrival

Just before setting down in Australia you will be given customs documents to fill in. On arrival you will be asked to present your documents, including passport, at the Entry Control Point. You can then collect your baggage and, if you have nothing to declare, proceed straight into the main

area of the airport. Note that Australia has strict quarantine laws. Food, plants and wooden items must be declared at quarantine. Sniffer dogs are common and your bags may be X-rayed on arrival to check for banned goods. Most items will be allowed but there are stiff penalties for non-disclosure.

Larger airports such as Melbourne and Sydney have better services, but most have good shopping, postal and medical facilities. You can hire cars and change money at all airports. Taxis and buses are available for transport into city centres.

Arrangements for domestic flight connections are usually made when purchasing your original ticket. Airline staff will advise you how to proceed. In Melbourne's main airport, the domestic and international services are in the same terminal but in many places

DIRECTORY

Airline Carriers

Air New Zealand
Tel 132 476.
W airnewzealand.com.au

British Airways
Tel 1300 767 177. W ba.com

Air Canada
Tel 1300 655 767.
W aircanada.com

Cathay Pacific
Tel 131 747. W cathaypacific.com

Emirates
Tel 1300 303 777.
W emirates.com

Japan Airlines
Tel 1800 802 228. W au.jal.com

Jetstar
Tel 131 538.

Qantas
Tel 13 13 13. W qantas.com.au

Singapore Airlines
Tel 131 011. W singaporeair.com

United Airlines
Tel 131 777.
W unitedairlines.com

Virgin Australia
Tel 136 789.

Green Travel

Green Vehicle Guide
W greenvehicleguide.gov.au

the terminals are separate and distances can be long – 10 km (6 miles) in the case of Perth. Free shuttle buses transfer passengers between terminals.

Airport	Information	Distance from City	Taxi Fare to City	Bus Transfer to City
Sydney	(02) 9667 9111 W sydneyairport.com.au	9 km (6 miles)	A$40	30 mins
Melbourne	(03) 9297 1600 W melbourneairport.com.au	22 km (14 miles)	A$55	30–40 mins
Brisbane	(07) 3406 3000 W bne.com.au	15 km (9 miles)	A$40	30 mins
Cairns	(07) 4080 6703 W cairnsairport.com	6 km (4 miles)	A$30	10 mins
Perth	(08) 9478 8888 W perthairport.com	15 km (9 miles)	A$50	25 mins
Adelaide	(00) 0308 9211 W adelaideairport.com.au	6 km (4 miles)	A$25	20 mins
Darwin	(08) 8920 1811 W ntapl.com.au	6 km (4 miles)	A$30	15 mins
Hobart	(03) 6216 1600 W hobartairpt.com.au	22 km (14 miles)	A$40	20–30 mins

Domestic Air Travel

Air travel accounts for a large proportion of long- distance journeys in Australia and is by far the most practical way of taking in a country of this size, particularly for those with time constraints. The main domestic air carriers in Australia, **Qantas**, **Virgin Australia** and **Jetstar**, concentrate on the high-volume interstate routes, while a host of small operators including Regional Express (Rex) handle air travel within states and to remote locations. Fares can be expensive, but with the range of discounts available in a deregulated and competitive industry it is unlikely you will ever have to pay the full fare, providing you plan your trips in advance. Speciality aerial tours of distant or hard-to-reach places are also available *(see p539)*.

Domestic flight operated by Virgin Australia

normally expensive. When buying these passes before your trip, you are sometimes required to pay half the cost before leaving home and half when booking the flights. In these cases, avoid buying too many flights in case your plans change. The passes offer greater convenience than return flights and are usually fairly flexible, but restrictions do apply, so check when booking.

Other Budget Fares

The cheapest domestic flights are available from the budget, no-frills airline services of **Jetstar**, a subsidiary of Qantas, Virgin Australia and Tigerair, which is part owned by Virgin Australia. The best deals are found by booking direct with them online, but flights can be cancelled at short notice if they are not full.

Watch out for "super" deals, when airlines flood the market with sales of cheap seats, including "light fares", for which passengers are only allowed carry-on luggage. However, such deals offer little or no flexibility so make sure you understand the strict conditions and cancella-tions policies before booking.

Tiny domestic terminal in Birdsville, Queensland

Air Routes and Airlines

Australia's air network is vast, but reasonably streamlined, so arranging flights to even the most remote spots should never be a problem. It is possible to fly direct between most major destinations such as Sydney–Darwin or Melbourne–Perth. However, if you are travelling to smaller centres, you will invariably have to fly first to the capital city in the state before then taking another flight on to your final destination.

The small airlines that cover out-of-the-way routes are generally affiliated with **Qantas** or **Virgin Australia**, which means bookings can be made through Qantas' or Virgin's centralized booking services.

Discounts for Overseas Visitors

Discounted domestic air travel is often offered as part of an international package, so check with your travel agent about booking domestic trips before

leaving home. Once you are in Australia, Qantas offers immediate discounts on domestic flights to overseas travellers, which range from 25–40 per cent; proof of overseas residence is required when booking these tickets.

Various air passes are available from Qantas which allow you to make a number of single flights for a set price. You can then move from leg to leg around the country rather than having to make return flights, which are

Plane on the harbourside runway, Hamilton Island *(see p221)*

Fly-drive Deals

A great way to see Australia is to fly to a destination and then continue on by car. To make things more convenient, arrangements can be made for different pick-up and drop-off points for hire vehicles. For example, you could pick up a car in Sydney, drive to Brisbane and drop off the car, fly to Alice Springs and then pick up another car there.

Virgin Australia and Qantas both have deals with the major car hire companies, and they offer discounts to passengers who are travelling on those airlines (see p560).

Baggage Restrictions

Baggage restrictions vary considerably on domestic flights and depend on the type of ticket you have booked. Jetstar's cheapest fare class does not allow for any checked-in baggage at all; the next fare class allows for 20 kg (45 pounds) of baggage but an additional fee of A$70 is charged for baggage if booked at the airport; and the standard fare allows for 20 kg (45 pounds) at no additional cost. Virgin Australia's fares follow a similar structure, allowing 23 kg (50 pounds) but at an additional charge applies if booked at the airport; and their full-price fare allows 23 kg (50 pounds) with no fee. Regardless of the fare, Qantas domestic flights allow 20 kg (45 pounds) for checked-in baggage.

Additional baggage fees are charged for any excess baggage; bear in mind also that airlines do not guarantee that additional baggage beyond the normal allowance will be carried. Carry-on luggage weight allowances vary between 7 kg (15.5 pounds) and 10 kg (22 pounds), depending on the airline.

QANTAS

Qantas logo

Checking In

Airlines request that you check in at least 30 minutes before your flight time, and many now offer online seat allocation up to two days before a flight. Check online to ensure that the flight is on time, and be sure to alight at the right terminal – some domestic and international terminals are at separate locations.

DIRECTORY

Domestic Airlines

Jetstar
Tel 131 538.
W jetstar.com.au

Qantas
Tel 131 313.
W qantas.com.au

Virgin Australia
Tel 136 789 or
(61 7) 3295 2296.
W virginaustralia.com

Principal Domestic Air Routes

Domestic flights cover vast distances. Sydney to Perth, for example, is 3,400 km (2,225 miles) and a flight of 5 hours; the 2,600-km (1,615-mile) flight from Adelaide to Darwin is 3.5 hours.

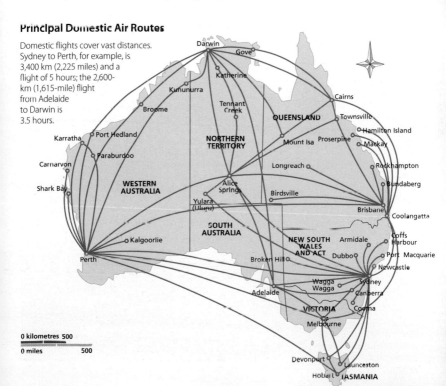

Travelling by Train and Coach

Australia offers some of the most spectacular train journeys in the world. The vast and diverse continent offers rail travel across red deserts as well as through beautiful rainforests and spectacular coastal scenery; often the journey is as much about enjoying the view as arriving at a destination. However, the train network is not comprehensive – with its small population, Australia has never been able to support an extensive system of long-haul railways. Train journeys are useful for quick trips away from city centres, and regular services link the cities of the east coast. Coaches fill any gaps in overland travel, servicing major centres and remote outposts.

A railway journey across the Australian desert

The Australian Rail Network

The Australian railway system is run by a complex group of several private and state-owned companies. The major tourist-orientated operators, including Countrylink, Great Southern Rail and Traveltrain, have formed an alliance called **Rail Australia**. You can get information and book tickets via the Rail Australia website.

Due to the advent of cheap flights, train travel is no longer cheaper than flying, and journey times are long. The Sydney–Brisbane trip takes 13.5 hours and Sydney–Melbourne takes 10.5 hours.

State governments accept responsibility for providing access to most areas. Queensland has increased its rail services of late, most of which are aimed at the tourist market. Increasingly, however, state-run coach services have replaced under-used railway journeys and, where there is no rail network, such as in Tasmania,

there will be an efficient, cheap coach network instead.

Speciality Trips

The chance to take in some of the country's extraordinary landscapes is what makes rail journeys in Australia so special. Standards are high, often with a level of luxury reminiscent of the grand old days of rail travel.

The Indian Pacific route takes three days to cover the 4,352 km (2,700 miles) from Sydney to Perth. The 478-km (300-mile) crossing of the Nullarbor Plain (see p323) is on the world's

longest length of straight railway track. The fabled Ghan railway runs between Adelaide and Darwin. A museum in Alice Springs recounts its history (see p287). The 2,979-km (1,852-mile) trip offers amazing scenery and takes two days.

Two different services run the 1,681 km (1,045 miles) between Brisbane and Cairns: the Sunlander and the Tilt Train. Another Queensland journey is aboard the Gulflander, a 152-km (95-mile) trip through some of Australia's most remote country.

The Overland (Melbourne–Adelaide) and the fast XPT (express passenger trains) services (Brisbane–Sydney–Melbourne) have a rather more utilitarian approach to train travel.

Travel Classes

There are three types of travel available on most interstate trains. Overnight services, such as Melbourne–Adelaide, offer first-class sleeper, first-class sit-up and economy sit-up. In addition, the Indian Pacific, the Ghan and various Queensland trains offer economy sleepers. All long-distance trains have dining facilities. First-class travel includes meals in the ticket price.

Motorail means you can travel with your car. The service is expensive, however, and you are better off hiring a car at your destination.

Tickets and Bookings

Bookings for rail travel can be made with travel agents and at railway stations or via the Rail

Mass Transit Railway Station in Perth

Greyhound coach station in Sydney

DIRECTORY

Rail Companies

Rail Australia
Tel 132 147.
W railaustralia.com.au

Coach Companies

Greyhound Australia
Tel 1300 473 946.
W greyhound.com.au

Premier Motor Service
Tel 133 410.
W premierms.com.au

Australia website. A choice of seven passes offer international travellers unlimited rail travel within either a three or six month period. The Backtracker Rail Pass allows between 14 days and six months of unlimited economy class trips between Melbourne, Sydney and Brisbane, while the Austrail Flexi-Pass offers either 15 or 22 days of travel over a six-month period.

Standard rail fares can be high, but there is a good range of discounts available for advance bookings.

Coach Travel

Coach travel is cheap, efficient and generally safe. The two main operators are **Greyhound Australia** and **Premier Motor Service**. The latter only operates on the east coast.

There are a range of passes that reduce the cost of any extended travel. The Greyhound Kilometre Pass gives you 12 months to use a pool of kilometres; Mini Traveller Passes provide travel between two popular destinations in the one direction; and Micro Passes allow you to travel between two popular destinations with a

limited number of stops. They are valid for 10–14 days depending on the route. However, bear in mind that this kind of travel involves many days on the road, and nights spent sleeping upright.

There are a range of other companies operating locally – good for trips to particular sights or national parks. Tourist information bodies (see p547) in each state will give advice on services and routes.

Australia's Principal Rail and Coach Routes

In Australia, travel by both rail and coach routes can be easily combined to reach any desired destination.

Key

— Principal rail route

— Principal coach route

0 kilometres 500

0 miles 500

Travelling by Car and Four-Wheel Drive

It is well worth considering hiring a car when visiting Australia. Other modes of transport will get you around the cities and from one country town to another, but, once you arrive in a rural area or a small town, you may find it impossible to explore the area other than on foot or with a tour. Australia offers the motorist the chance to meander through areas such as the vineyard regions of South Australia *(see pp342–3)*, the Southern Highlands of New South Wales *(see pp190–91)* and the Great Ocean Road of Victoria *(see pp432–3)*, as well as the experience of Outback travel on near-empty roads.

Driving through the Outback desert in Australia's Red Centre

Driving Licences

Pro ... g your driving licence is in Eng sh and you have proof that you are a tourist, there is no need for an additional permit when driving in Australia. If the licence is not in English, you must carry a translation. It is a legal requirement that you have your licence with you at all times when driving.

Car Hire

Rental cars are available just about anywhere in Australia. They can be picked up at the airport on arrival, or arrangements can be made for delivery to your hotel. The big car rental firms **Avis**, **Budget**, **Hertz** and **Thrifty** have nationwide networks *(see p562)* – an advantage if you are considering making several different trips across the continent. Check with your travel agent before leaving home about discounts or special fly-drive offers.

Rates vary from around A$55 a day for a small car to A$100 a day for larger vehicles. It is invariably more expensive to hire a 4WD vehicle; rates average out at around A$120 and are more costly in remote areas where the demand is high. You can reduce daily rates by hiring over longer periods (usually three days and over), or if you accept a limited kilometre/mileage deal. These deals usually give you the first 100 km (60 miles) a day as part of the daily charge, and a per kilometre rate after that. This is worth considering for inner-city driving, but not good value beyond the city limits where distances add up very quickly. The smaller local operators offer very competitive rates,

sometimes as low as A$25 a day, but read the small print carefully. Often, the quote does not include the extras that the larger companies consider standard. If travelling with children, make sure the car is equipped with restraints according to Australian laws *(see p546)*. A Global Positioning System (GPS) can also be hired for around A$11 per day or A$60 per week.

Credit cards are the preferred method of payment when hiring a car. If paying with cash you will usually be required to pay the full cost of the rental, plus a deposit.

Insurance

For peace of mind it is a good idea to have comprehensive insurance when hiring a car. "Third party fire and theft" insurance is standard and included in the cost of the hire, as is insurance against accidental damage to the hire car. However, you will have to pay extra to reduce the excess payment. From upwards of A$7 a day, you can bring the excess down from around A$2,000 to a more comfortable A$100. This option is usually only offered by the larger car hire companies.

Personal accident plans are also available, but they may not be necessary, depending on the cover offered with your own travel insurance. Four-wheel drive vehicles attract an excess rate of around A$4,000. For A$20 a day this can be reduced to a A$1,000, but never lower. Car hire companies will not offer insurance on any off-road driving, regardless of the vehicle

Car and van rental company in Sydney

A Caltex Woolworths petrol station in Sydney

type. Higher rates of insurance apply to drivers under the age of 25. Car hire in Australia is often not available to drivers under the age of 21.

Petrol

Petrol is relatively cheap in urban areas compared to prices in Europe (though this may change), but in remote regions of the country prices rise considerably. Prices also vary according to the day of the week and it is a good idea to watch the prices and fill up on days they are lower. Fuel is dispensed by the litre and can be purchased in regular unleaded, premium unleaded, diesel and LPG (liquid petroleum gas) grades. Most petrol stations are self-service and most accept major credit cards and have an EFTPOS facility (see p550).

Rules of the Road

Australians drive on the left and give way to the right in all circumstances unless otherwise indicated. Drivers must also give way to emergency vehicles – if possible, pull over to the side of the road when you hear a siren. The speed limit is 40–60 km/h (25–37 mph) in cities, towns and suburban areas and 100–110 km/h (62–68 mph) on major highways. The wearing of seat belts is compulsory for drivers and passengers. Baby capsules and child restraints must be used for all children up to the

age of ten. It is illegal to drive a vehicle while using a hand-held mobile phone. This includes when the vehicle is stopped at traffic lights or in heavy traffic. Drink-driving laws are strictly enforced in Australia. The legal blood alcohol limit is 0.05 per cent. Should you be involved in an accident while over the alcohol limit, your vehicle insurance may be invalidated. Police in country areas are just as vigilant as their counterparts in the city, and it is not unusual to see a random breath-test taking place on an otherwise deserted road.

Any accident involving injury in Australia must be reported to the police within 24 hours. In Western Australia all accidents must be reported and in other states it is advisable to do so if there is considerable property damage. Always get insurance details and a name, licence number and residential address from the other motorist.

The city of Melbourne has two road laws worth noting. First, motorists must stop behind a stationary tram to allow passengers to alight. Second, at certain city intersections motorists intending to turn right must pull over to the left (see pp416–17). Called hook turns, they are designed to prevent traffic queuing across tram tracks.

Road rules are governed by the relevant state authority. Each has a website with traffic reports, highway conditions, road closures and webcams.

Road Conditions

Stretches of multi-lane highways are found on most major routes, with the majority of other routes covered by two-lane highways. All are generally well sealed and signposted. Unsealed dirt roads exist in country regions, but are rarely the only means of getting to a destination. Tollways are restricted to areas in the

Beware of kangaroos sign

NEXT 5 km

immediate vicinity of the large cities, such as the Western Motorway that covers part of the Sydney–Blue Mountains route. Melbourne has an intricate tollway system. Some tollways, tunnels and bridges, including Sydney Harbour Bridge, are now cashless and require payment by card or an electronic tag.

Service stations are plentiful along all the well-travelled routes, but are few and far between in the Outback. A particularly Australian and very dangerous road hazard is the prevalence of wildlife crossing country highways. At night danger increases when the nocturnal mammals, such as kangaroos and wallabies, are more active.

Roadside Assistance

Car hire companies look after breakdowns of their rental cars and, if necessary, arrange for vehicle replacements. State-based motoring organizations provide roadside assistance for members around the country (see p562). They also sell maps and guides in their central branches, and are a great source of information on road rules and conditions, and Outback driving. Members of motoring organizations in Great Britain, Canada and the US usually have reciprocal membership rights with Australian organizations.

Royal Automobile Association vehicle in Adelaide

South approach to the Harbour Bridge in Sydney

Inner-city Driving

If you are planning to drive within any city, a good street directory will be essential. If possible, avoid peak-hour traffic (7:30–9:30am and 4:30–7:30pm). Traffic reports are broadcast on radio stations. The larger the city, the more difficult it will be to park in the city centre. Parking restrictions are clearly signposted and usually specify an hour or two of metered parking. Carry coins for the meters, although most now take credit card payments. Many cities have clearly signposted clearway and bus zones that apply at certain times and parked vehicles will be towed away during the specified times; telephone the local traffic authority or the police to find out where your vehicle has been impounded. Car parks are also found in city centres and shopping centres and are signposted with a large white P in a blue rectangle.

Outback Driving

For any Outback travel, first check your route to see if a 4WD is required. Although some

Outback areas now have roads of a high enough standard to carry conventional cars, a 4WD is essential in wild and remote areas. Motoring organizations and tourist information centres can provide information about this.

A number of basic safety points should be observed. Plan your route and carry up-to-date maps. If you are travelling between remote destinations, inform the local police of your departure and expected arrival times. Check road conditions before you start and carry food and water. Find out where you can get petrol and carry extra supplies if necessary. If you break down, remain with your vehicle – if you fail to arrive at the expected time, a search party will be sent out.

The **Royal Flying Doctor Service of Australia (RFDS)** offers safety advice. You can also hire radio sets with an emergency call button to the RFDS from **BTW Communications**.

Observe important guidelines to protect the land. Native flora and fauna should not be damaged. Stick to vehicle tracks, carry a stove and fuel to avoid lighting fires, and don't leave rubbish. Be aware of Aboriginal boundaries and national parks, and leave gates as you find them: either open or shut.

Hitchhiking

It is not considered safe to hitch-hike in Australia. In Queensland and Victoria it is illegal; their laws do not allow obstructing traffic from the roadside. Elsewhere, pedestrians are not allowed on motorways or freeways but are permitted on highways and other roads where they can find rides.

DIRECTORY

Car Hire Companies

Avis
Tel 136 333. W avis.com.au

Budget
Tel 13 27 27. W budget.com.au

Hertz
Tel 133 039. W hertz.com.au

Thrifty
Tel 1300 367 227.
W thrifty.com.au

State Road Departments

Roads and Maritime Services, NSW
Tel 132 213. W rms.nsw.gov.au

VicRoads, Victoria
Tel 131 171.
W vicroads.vic.gov.au

Motoring Organizations

National Roadside Assistance
Australia-wide breakdown service. Tel 131 111

New South Wales and ACT
National Road and Motorist's Association (NRMA). Tel 131 122.
W mynrma.com.au

Northern Territory
Automobile Association of NT Inc (AANT). Tel (08) 8925 5901.
W aant.com.au

Queensland
Royal Automobile Club of Queensland (RACQ). Tel 13 19 05.
W racq.com.au

South Australia
Royal Automobile Association of SA Inc (RAA). Tel (08) 8202 4600.
W raa.com.au

Tasmania
Royal Automobile Club of Tasmania (RACT). Tel 132 722.
W ract.com.au

Victoria
Royal Automobile Club of Victoria (RACV). Tel 13 11 11 or (03) 8792 4006. W racv.com.au

Western Australia
Royal Automobile Club of WA Inc (RACWA). Tel 13 17 03. W rac.com.au

Outback Driving

BTW Communications
Tel (02) 6884 5237. W btw.com.au

Royal Flying Doctor Service of Australia
Tel (08) 8238 3333.
W flyingdoctor.net

Driving a 4WD along the Gibb River Road in the Kimberley

Travelling by Ferry and Cruise Boat

The cruise market has boomed in Australia in recent years. Domestic cruises up the east coast from Sydney to Queensland, and internationally to Pacific Islands, Southeast Asia and New Zealand are popular. Elsewhere ferries run between the mainland and island destinations such as Rottnest Island, Western Australia *(see pp312–13)*, and Fraser Island, off the Queensland coast *(see p246)*. Large cruise ships concentrate on the local Pacific area and in most cases sail in and out of Sydney.

Passenger ships berthed at Circular Quay, Sydney *(see pp78–89)*

Arriving by Boat

There is probably no better way of arriving in Australia than to sail into Sydney Harbour aboard a cruise ship. Cruising is expensive, however, and the services to Australia are limited. To sail to Australia from the US or Europe, you may have to wait for the next world cruise on **P&O** or **Cunard Line** vessels. Another option is to fly to an Asian city such as Hong Kong and join up with **Princess Cruises**. Sydney is the main port of call for most cruise ships, and there are two passenger terminals, one in the heart of the city and another at White Bay.

Ferries to Tasmania

The *Spirit of Tasmania* takes just over 14 hours to cross the Bass Strait from Melbourne to Tasmania. It runs at 8pm, Monday to Saturday during winter and nightly during summer, departing from Port Melbourne and Devonport. The ship has every level of accommodation ranging from reclining cruise seats and backpacker berths to fully equipped suites. There are restaurants, shops, and entertainment for children. The price is fair, considering the experience – a double cabin will cost around A$500 return for a couple in off-peak season, less if there is a special offer.

Island Cruises and Ferries

A **Sealink** ferry departs from Cape Jervis, south of Adelaide, for Kangaroo Island *(see p358)*. In Western Australia, **Rottnest Express** runs regular ferries to Rottnest Island from Perth. There are many services between the mainland and the Barrier Reef islands *(see p220)*. A boat also runs between Seisia, Cape York, and Thursday Island, *(see p256)*. Check the **Great Barrier Reef Marine Park Authority** website for a list of certified operators.

DIRECTORY

Shipping Companies

Cunard Line
Sydney. **Tel** 132 441.
W **cunardline.com.au**
Southampton, UK.
Tel (0845) 678 0013.

P&O
Sydney. **Tel** 132 494.
W **pocruises.com.au**
Southampton, UK.
Tel (0843) 374 0111.

Princess Cruises
Sydney. **Tel** 13 24 88.
W **princess.com**

Sealink
Kangaroo Island.
Tel 131 301, (08) 8202 8688.
W **sealink.com.au**

Spirit of Tasmania
Devonport. **Tel** 1800 634 906.
W **spiritoftasmania.com.au**

Tourist Information

Great Barrier Reef Marine Park Authority
W **gbrmpa.gov.au**

Rottnest Express
W **rottnestexpress.com.au**

Rivers and Harbours

Hiring a houseboat is an excellent way of seeing some of Australia's spectacular river scenery. Popular spots include the Hawkesbury River, New South Wales, and the Murray River which runs through New South Wales, Victoria and South Australia. There are tours of Darwin and Sydney harbours, and cruises of the Swan River in Perth and the Yarra River in Melbourne. State tourist authorities can provide details *(see p547)*.

Taking the ferry to Rottnest Island *(see pp312–13)*

General Index

Museum; *Spirit of Tasmania*; Supreme Court (Melbourne); Tandanya National Aboriginal Cultural Institute Inc; Victoria Arts Centre Trust; WA Maritime Museum; and all the other sights too numerous to thank individually.

Picture Credits
Key: a - above; b - below/bottom; c - centre; f - far; r - right; t - top.

The publisher would like to thank the following individuals, companies and picture libraries for their kind permission to reproduce their photographs:

123RF.com: Mykhaylo Palinchak 194. **ABC pool:** 75tl; **Alamy Images:** aeropix 238; Bill Bachman 392bl, 411tl; The Art Archive 8-9; Martin Berry 561tl; David Bigwood 186; CulturalEyes - AusGS2; Foodpix 500cl; Andrew Holt 242bl; LEDPIX 545t; Chris McLennan 250tl; Ball Miwako 547tc; Robert Mora 103cr; National Geographic Image Collection 169cb; Martin Norris 126bc; Radius Images 362; RosalreneBetancourt 4 237bl; Matt Smith 235br; Richard Sowersby 560br; Dave Stamboulis 302; Doug Stely 501tl, 501tl; Steve Vidler 212–3; David Wall 410cla; Rob Walls 120, 501c; John White Photos 264clb; Bosiljka Zutich 108; **Allsport:** 541bl; **Amora Hotel Riverwalk:** 494bl; **Appellation at The Louise:** 523tr; **AQWA – The Aquarium of Western Australia:** 310tr; **Ardea London Ltd:** © D Parer & E Parer Cook 220tr; © Francois Gohier 471tr; Jean-Marc La Roque 452cla; Peter Steyn 17ca; © Ron and Valerie Taylor 220cla; **Art Gallery of NSW:** *Amitabha Buddha*, 105 x 88 x 65cm 117cl; © Ms Stephenson-Meere 1996, *Australian Beach Pattern* 1940, Charles Meere (1890–1961) oil on canvas, 91.5 x 122cm, 69tl; *Bridge Pattern*, Harold Cazneaux (1070–1953), gelatin silver photography, 29.6 x 21.4cm, gift of the Cazneaux family, 1975, 76bc(d); *Banks of the Marne*, Paul Cézanne (1839-1906), oil on canvas, 65 x 81.3cm 115tl; © Art Gallery of NSW *Sofala* 1947 Russell Drysdale (1912-81), oil on canvas on hardboard, 71.7 x 93.1cm 114clb; *Mars and the Vestal Virgin* 1638, Jacques Blanchard oil on canvas, 130 x 110cm 114cr; © Tiwi Design *Executive* 1996, *Pukumani Grave Posts, Melville Island* 1958, various artists, natural pigments on wood, 165.1 x 29.2cm, gift of Dr Stuart Scougall 1959, 114cl; *Natives on the Ouse River, Van Diemen's Land* 1838, John Glover oil on canvas, 78 x 115cm 115crb; Art Gallery of NSW Foundation purchase 1990, *A Pair of Tomb Guardian Figures*, late 6th century AD Early, Unknown (China), sculpture earthenware with traces of red and orange pigment, 93 x 82cm, Art Gallery of NSW Foundation Purchase 1990 115cra; *The Golden Fleece – Shearing at Newstead* 1894, Tom Roberts, oil on canvas 104 x 158.7cm 115b; *Three Bathers* 1913, Ernst Ludwig Kirchner oil on canvas, 197.5 x 147.5cm 116tr; *Curve of the Bridge* 1928–1929, Grace Cossington Smith © Estate of Grace Cossington Smith oil on cardboard, 110.5 x 82.5cm 116cla; © Wendy Whitely 1996, *The Balcony 2* 1975, Brett Whitely (1939–92), oil on canvas, 203.5 x 364.5cm 116bl; © **Associated Press, London:** 63tl; **Auscape International:** 43cr; © Kathie Atkinson 30clb; © Nicholas Birks 348bl; © Donna Browning 272br; © John Cancalosi 29clb, 249bl; © Kevin Deacon 29cr; © Jean-Paul Ferrero 27bl, 28tr, 30cla, 163crb, 165cra, 241tr, 246cl, 265tc, 267tr, 292cla, 459tl/crb; © Jeff & Sandra Foott 29br; © Brett Gregory 172bl, 458bl; © Dennis

Harding 31bc; © Andrew Henley 44cra; © Matt Jones 281cra/bc; © Mike Langford 31crb; © Wayne Lawler 165crb; © Geoffrey Lea 461b; © Darren Leal 28br, 247tl, 248tr, 249cr; © Reg Morrison 28cb, 246cr, 458tr, 459cl; © Jean-Marc La Roque 22t, 28cr, 31cr, 32–3c, 185tr, 242cla, 243cb, 265br, 284cl, 380tr, 381tr/cb, 389cla, 430cr, 432tr/cl, 434tl, 544cla; © Jamie Plaza Van Roon 28bl, 29cl, 165tl/cb; © Becca Saunders 29cb, 220–21; **Australian Broadcasting Corporation:** 553crb; **Australian Capital Territory Museums and Galleries:** 21cla; **Australian Museum, Sydney:** www.austmus.gov.au: 34cla, 98cla, 98clb, 99cra, 99crb; Nature Focus/John N Cornish; Stuart Humpries 69bl; **Australian Picture Library:** 22c, 24b, 162bl; Adelaide Freelance 371bl; John Baker 24b, 25tr, 175tr, 182cb, 419br, 435t, 445tr; JP & ES Baker 164bl, 475cra; John Carnemolla 19t, 33crb, 42cl, 43cra, 45tr 146b, 162cla, 188tr, 215tl, 266tr, 268cl, 338cb, 355tl, 369t, 370bl, 376cl, 556br; Sean Davey 42–3c; R. Eastwood 474tr; Flying Photos 546tl; Evan Gillis 371tr; Owen Hughes 257b; S & B Kendrick 339bc, 358tr; Craig La Motte 215br; Michael Lees 431b; Lightstorm 192bl, 364bc, 365cla; Johnathan Marks 189cr, 432crb; Aureo Martelli 173cra; Leo Meier 31tr, 254cl, 256tr, 267clb; PhotoIndex 261br; Fritz Prenzel 432br, 446bl; Peter Solness 42tr; Oliver Strewe 36cl, 37tr; Neale Winter 372bc; Gerry Withom 173tl; Australian Reptile Park: 176bl; **Australian War Memorial:** 205c.

Bill Bachman: 30tr, 32cl, 35c, 37tl, 47tl/b, 169b, 171tr, 249br, 260b, 278tl, 279cr/bl, 280bl, 291b, 300bl, 339crb, 450tr; **Bamurru Plains Hotel:** 489bl; **Greg Barrett:** 143bc; **Bartel Photo Library:** 175b; **Baveras Brasserie:** 530tr; **Beccofino Restaurant:** 513t; **Beringer Blass Wine Estates:** 342br; 361cr; **Best's Wines:** 382ca; © Mervyn Bishop: 63cb; **Bistro Dom:** 522tc; **Black Coffee Lyrics:** 514bl; **The Boat House by the Lake.** 511t; **Bodhi Restaurant.** 505ti, **Botanic Gardens Trust, Sydney:** 110bc; 110cla; **Bridgeclimb Sydney:** 85tl; **Bridgeman Art Library London/ New York:** *Bush Plum Dreaming* 1991 (acrylic) by Clifford Possum Tjapaltjarri (b.c.1932), Corbally Stourton Contemporary Art, London © Aboriginal Artists Agency Ltd 37cra; *Men's Dreaming* 1990 (acrylic) by Clifford Possum Tjapaltjarri (b.c.1932), Corbally Stourton Contemporary Art, London © Aboriginal Artists Agency Ltd 34tr; *Kelly In Spring*, 1956 (ripolin on board) by Sidney Nolan (1917–92), Arts Council, London © Lady Mary Nolan 38bl; National Maritime Museum, London 53clb(d); British Museum 55cra; Mitchell Library, State Library of NSW 58tr/bl, 59tl; National Library of Australia 54tr(d), 57tl, cb, 58–9c; *Bush Tucker Dreaming*, 1991 (acrylic) by Gladys Napanangka (b.c.1920) Corbally Stourton Contemporary Art, London, © Aboriginal Artists Agency Ltd 267cr; *The Ashes*, 1883 (The Urn) Marylebone Cricket Club, London, 440bc; **Courtesy of Brisbane Marketing:** 223b, 226tr; 236cr; **Britstock-IFA/Gottschalk:** 264ca; **Buon Ricordo Restaurant:** 506tl; **The Byrneleigh:** 520tr; **The byron at byron:** 483tc.

Canberra Deep Space Communication Complex: D. Paterson 210bl; **Canberra Tourism:** 195b, 538cla; **Centrepoint Management:** 95br; **Cephas Picture Library:** Andy Christodolo 167tl, 342clb, 343c, 382cl; Chris Davis 338cla; Mick Rock 23tr, 40cl, 41cr, 167cr, 178tr/cla, 343c, 345b, 360cla, 361tr, 383tl; **Chocolate @ No 5:** 524tr; **Peter Clarke:** 406br; **Bruce Coleman Ltd:** John Cancalosi 73b;

Acknowledgments

Dorling Kindersley would like to thank the following people whose contributions and assistance have made the preparation of this book possible.

Consultant
Helen Duffy is an editor and writer. Since 1992 she has managed and contributed to a range of tourist publications.

Main Contributors
Louise Bostock Lang has worked on a number of Dorling Kindersley Travel Guides.
Jan Bowen is a travel broadcaster and writer. Her travel books include *The Queensland Experience*.
Paul Kloeden lives in Adelaide. A freelance writer and historian, his work ranges from travel articles to government-sponsored heritage surveys.
Jacinta le Plaistrier is a Melbourne-based journalist, poet and librettist.
Sue Neales is a multi-award winning Australian journalist. Her travel articles have appeared in major Australian newspapers and magazines.
Ingrid Ohlsson is a Melbourne-based writer who has contributed to many travel publications.
Tamara Thiessen is a Tasmanian freelance travel writer and photographer.

Additional Contributors
Tony Baker, Libby Lester.

Additional Photography
Simon Blackall, Terry Carter, DK Studio, Geoff Dunn, Jean-Paul Ferrero, Esther Labi, Jean-Marc La Roque, Michael Nicholson, Ian O'Leary, Rob Reichenfeld, William Shaw Carol Wiley, Alan Williams.

Cartography
Lovell Johns Ltd, Oxford, UK; ERA-Maptec Ltd, Dublin, Ireland.

Additional Illustrations
Rockit Design.

Indexer
Hilary Bird.

Senior Revisions Editor
Esther Labi.

Design and Editorial
Duncan Baird Limited
Picture Research: Victoria Peel.
DTP Designer: Rhona Green.
Dorling Kindersley Limited
Senior Managing Editor: Vivien Crump.
Managing Editor: Helen Partington.
Project Editor: Rosalyn Thiro.
Deputy Art Director: Gillian Allan.
Art Editor: Stephen Bere.
Map Co-ordinators: Emily Green, David Pugh.
Production: David Proffit.

Revisions Team
Ross Adams, Emma Anacootee, Iasneet Arora, Rosemary Bailey, Lydia Baillie, Chloe Baker, Kate Berens, Emily Bieber, Uma Bhattacharya, Hanna Bolus, Debbie Brand, Sue Callister, Wendy Canning, Divya Chowfin, Louise Cocks, Sherry Collins, Laura Cook, Lucinda Cooke, Bronwen Davies, Surya Deogun, Stephanie Driver, Angus Duncan, Jonathan Elphick, Mariana Evmolpidou, Emer FitzGerald, Fay Franklin, Anna Freiberger, Camilla Gersh, Emma Gregg, Alex Guyver, Vinod Harish, Shobhna Iyer, Gail Jones, Bharti Karakoti, Christine Keilty, Sumita Khatwani, Esther Labi, Maite Lantaron, Stefan Laszczuk, Jude Ledger, Maria Leonardis, Jason Little, Siobhan Mackay, Nicola Malone, Nicolette Martin, Alison McGill, Ciaran McIntyre, Claudine Meissner, Sam Merrell, Jason Mitchell, John Miles, Tania Monkton, Casper Morris, Lee Mylne, Claire Naylor, George Nimmo, Scarlett O'Hara, Ryan Paine, Elizabeth Pallot, Michael Palmer, Catherine Palmi, Manisha Patel, Sangita Patel, Alok Pathak, Susie Peachey, Marianne Petrou, Giles Pickard, Adrian Potts, Rachel Power, Rada Radojicic, Garry Ramler, Marisa Renzullo, Louise Roberts, Ellen Root, Lamya Sadi, Christine Salins, Sands Publishing Solutions, Mark Sayers, Shailesh Sharma, Azeem Siddiqui, Kunal Singh, Rituraj Singh, Beverly Smart, Deborah Soden, Jaynan Spengler, Naomi Stallard, Domenic Stanton, Stuti Tiwari Bhatia, Adrian Tristram, Diana Tucker, Lynda Tyson, Conrad Van Dyke, Nikhil Verma, Ros Walford, Dora Whitaker, Kim Wildman, Carol Wiley, Steve Womersley, Ed Wright.

Special Assistance
Sue Bickers, Perth; Craig Ebbett, Perth; Peter Edge, Met. Office, London; Chrissie Goldrick, The Image Library, State Library of NSW; Cathy Goodwin, Queensland Art Gallery; Megan Howat, International Media & Trade Visits Coordinator, WA Tourist Commission; John Hunter and Fiona Marr, CALM, Perth; Vere Kenny, Auscape International; Selena MacLaren, SOCOG; Greg Miles, Kakadu National Park; Ian Miller, Auslig; Gary Newton, Perth; Murray Robbins, Perth; Ron Ryan, Coo-ee Historical Picture Library; Craig Sambell and Jill Jones, GBRMPA; Norma Scott, Australian Picture Library; Andrew Watts, QASCO; and all state tourist authorities and national park services.

Photography Permissions
Dorling Kindersley would like to thank the following for their kind assistance and permission to photograph at their establishments: Art Gallery of WA; Australian Museum; National Gallery of Australia; Australian War Memorial; Ayers House; Department of Conservation and Land Management (WA); Department of Environment and Natural Resources (Adelaide); Department of Environment (Queensland); Government House (Melbourne); Hermannsburg Historic Precinct; Jondaryan Woolshed Historical Museum; Museum and Art Gallery of NT; Museum of WA; National Gallery of Victoria; National Maritime Museum; National Museum of Australia; National Parks and Wildlife Services (all states); National Trust of Australia (all states); Parliament House (Melbourne); Port Arthur Historic Site; Powerhouse Museum; Rottnest Island Authority; Royal Flying Doctor Service of NT; Shrine of Remembrance Trustees (Victoria); South Australian

Ochre Restaurant: 515bc; Photography courtesy of the Olympic Co-ordination Authority: Photo: Karl Carlstrom 151clb; © Open Spaces Photography: Photo: Andrew Barnes 443b; Photo: Glen Tempest 539cl, 541tc; © Outback Photographics, NT: Steve Strike 1994 292tr; Steve Strike 1995 293cla; Oxford Scientific Films: © Mantis Wildlife Films 298cl; © Babs & Bert Wells 298clb.

Palazzo Versace: 514tr; Paperbark Camp: 484tl, 510tc; Park Hyatt Sydney: 478cl, 499br, 504bl; Kay Parkin: 340br; Parliament House: The Hon Max Willis, RFD, ED, LLB, MLC, President, Legislative Council, Parliament of NSW. The Hon J Murray, MP, Speaker, Legislative Assembly, Parliament of NSW. Artist's original sketch of the historical painting in oils by Algernon Talmage, RA, The Founding of Australia. Kindly loaned to the Parliament of NSW by Mr Arthur Chard of Adelaide, 86tl; Peppers Mineral Springs Retreat: 495tr; Photo Index: 297cr, 298tr/bl/br, 298–9c, 312tr, 314bc, 317cr, 323tr/c/bl; Photolibrary: Geoff Higgins 452tr; Rob Jung 450clb; David Messent 563cla; Photolibrary.com: 164cla; © Phototone Colonial Library: 59br; Pictor International: 222, 358bl; Planet Earth Pictures: © Gary Bell 218tr/b, 219c.; © Daryl Torkler 149br; © Norbert Wu 367br; © Polygram/Pictorial Press: 33tr; Powerhouse Museum Reproduced courtesy of the Trustees of the Museum of Applied Arts and Sciences, Sydney: 61bl, 106clb, 106tr, 106bc, Marinco Kojdanovski 68br, 106clb; Jean-Francis Lanzarone 106cla; © Susanna Price: 431tr.

Qantas: 60br, 557cla; Collection of The Queensland Art Gallery: R Godfrey Rivers, Under the Jacaranda, 1903, oil on canvas, 233c; Russell Drysdale, Bushfire 1944, oil and ink on canvas on composition board, 62 × 77cm, Gift of Capt Neil McEacharn through CL Harden 1954, 232cl; © Succession Picasso/DACS London 2011, Pablo Picasso, La Belle Hollandaise 1905, gouache on cardboard mounted on wood, 77 × 66.3cm, purchased 1959 with funds donated by Major Harold de Vahl Rubin, 232clb; Rupert Bunny, Bathers 1906, oil on canvas, 229.2 × 250cm, purchased 1988, 232tr; © Queensland Ballet: 233crb; John Oxley Library, State Library of Queensland: 246br; Queensland Travel and Tourist Corporation: 214bc.

Ravesi's on Bondi Beach: 499cl, 507br; Reilly's Cellar Door and Restaurant: 525tr; The Rocks Discovery Museum: 81tl; Royal Flying Doctor Service: 287tl; Royal Mail Hotel Restaurant: 530bl.

Sand Hills Vineyard: 166cra; Science Centre (Brisbane): 226clb; Shangri-La Sydney: 482br; © Skyscans/ Photographer: David Hancock 277crb, 269c/bl; Southcorp

Wines Europe: 166tl, 503tr; Southlight Photo Agency: © Milton Wordley 339cr, 342tr, 343br; Spectrum Colour Library: 32bl, 34br, 45crb, 243cr, 290–91c, 339tl, 373b, 588t; Stan Squire 367tr; Spice Temple Restaurant: 505bc; Spicers Balfour Hotel: 486bl; Spicers Clovelly Estate: 488tl; St Mary's Cathedral Appeal: 307cra; © Tony Stone Images: 322bl; Gary John Norman 43tl; Fritz Prenzel 26–7c, 235tl; Robin Smith 46br, 171br, 187b; Oliver Strewe 28crb; Penny Tweedie 35bl; Ken Wilson 62bc; Story Bridge Adventure Club: Story Bridge Adventure Club 234tl; Charles Stuart University Winery: 166bc; Subo: Josh Vincent Photography 508tl; Superstock: Age Fotostock 282; Dean Fox 90; Sydney & Bondi Explorer: 133br; Sydney Harbour Foreshore Authority: 100bc, 101bl; Sydney Jewish Museum: 69br; Sydney Opera House Trust: 88tr/cla, 89tl/crb/bl; Photography courtesy of the Sydney Organizing Committee for The Olympic Games (SOCOG): 151tl; Sydney Theatre: 142cla.

The Tahbilk Group: Four Sisters 382br; Tall Wiru Restaurant: 519br; State Library of Tasmania: 55tr; Ten Minutes by Tractor: 532; Tenterfield District & Visitors' Information: 163tr; Suzie Thomas Publishing: Thomas O'Flynn bc; Thorngrove Manor Hotel: 492bl; Tolarno Hotel: 479bl; Courtesy of Tourism New South Wales: Phase IX 164tr; Tourism Victoria: 409tr; Trip & Artdirectors Photographic Library: Eric Smith 33bl, 451br; D Silvestris 354bl; Virgin Australia: 556tr; Visions of Victoria: Peter Dunphy 410br, 417bc; Tim Webster 411c; Visit Alexandrina: 357c; Vue de Monde: 528b; Courtesy of Watermark Press (Sydney): 61tr; Whiteman Park: 311b; © Wildlight Photo Agency: Ellen Camm 163tl; Carolyn Jones, 377cra; Tom Keating 301cr/crb; Mark Lang 180t; Philip Quirk 23bl, 25bl, 43bl, 185bl; Sean Santos 184bc; Grenville Turner 183cr, 301tl/br; Wilpena Pound Resort: 481t; The Windsor Melbourne: 493tl; World Pictures: 26tr, 27tl, 204cr, 221bl, 254bl, 255tl, 305cra, 444cl; Yalumba Wine Co.: 502cra; Zefa: 26cl, 481t.

Front Endpaper: Alamy Images: aeropix Rt; David Bigwood Rcrb; Radius Images Lcl; Dave Stamboulis Ltl. Corbis: Frans Lanting Ltc; Stephane Lemaire Lb; Steve Parish Rtl. Dreamstime: John Casey Rtr; Darren Falkenberg Lbl; Radmurphy Lbc. Getty Images: Pete Atkinson Rtc; Alex Hare Rcr; Daniel Osterkamp Rcl; David Wall Photo Rbr; Peter Walton Photography Lbr, Rbl. Superstock: Age Fotostock Ltr.

Jacket
Front and Spine - Alamy Images: Doug Armand. All other images © Dorling Kindersley. For further information see: www.dkimages.com

Special Editions of DK Travel Guides

DK Travel Guides can be purchased in bulk quantities at discounted prices for use in promotions or as premiums. We are also able to offer special editions and personalized jackets, corporate imprints, and excerpts from all of our books, tailored specifically to meet your own needs.

To find out more, please contact:
(in the United States) specialsales@dk.com
(in the UK) travelguides@uk.dk.com
(in Canada) wspecialmarkets@dk.com
(in Australia) penguincorporatesales@ penguinrandomhouse.com.au

Alain Compost 341tl; Francisco Futil 72tr; Hans Reinhard 340bc; Rod Williams 341bl; **Colorific:** 35tr; Bill Angove 267bl, 297bc; Bill Bachman 261tl, 363b; Penny Tweedie 269tr, 271b; **Coo-Ee Historical Picture Library:** 36–7c, 37br, 39cr, 53tl, 54bc, 55cb, 56crb, 60cr, 61clb, 437cra, 438br, 459bl, 473c; **Coral Sea Resort:** 479t;**Corbis:** Free Agents Limited 453bc; JAI/Walter Bibikow 93crb; Michael Kai 45cl; Frans Lanting 324; Stephane Lemaire 384; Steve Parish 270; Lothar Schulz 262–3; **Sylvia Cordaiy Photo Library Ltd:** © John Farmer 338bl; Nick Rains 300cl, 373tr; **Coterie Restaurant:** 524bl; **Cuisine on Lake Crackenback:** 510bl; **Cumulus Inc Restaurant:** 527br; **Customs House Brisbane:** 512tl; **Customs House Hotel:** 509b.

Rupert Dean: 40br, 360clb/bc, 361cb, 383bl, 502cla, 502crb; **Diamant Hotel:** 485bl; **Dixon Galleries, State Library of NSW:** 84tr; © **Domaine Chandon, Australia:** 447c; © **Ken Done:** 38cr; **Donovans:** 529tl; **Dreamstime.com:** Arnab & Manisha Maity 401tl; Gordin Bell 385b; John Casey 222; Sam D'cruz 560cla; Darren Falkenberg 344; Markus Gann 15t; Anton Harder 297tr; Hotshotsworldwide 2–3; Debra James 21b; Katerinasamsonova 17bl; Lev Kropotov 101tc; Shariff Che Lah 476–7; Lucidwaters 239b; George Mdivanian 20; OnAir2 78; Radmurphy 426; Travelling-light 296clb; Verdelho 14b; Vselenka 44br; Robert Winslow 12tl; © **DW Stock Picture Library:** 192tr; P Brunotte 561br; **Eleonore's:** 533tl; **Environmental Protection Agency, Queensland:** 244cla; Gollings Photography 386tr; **Fairfax Photo Library:** 62clb/bl, 85crb, 150 cla, 177br(d), 276br; Ken James 143tr; McNeil 124clb; **Falls Creek Alpine Resort:** 453tl; **Falls Wines:** 166cla; **Foragers Field Kitchen:** 520bl; **Forest of Tranquility – Australian Rainforest Sanctuary:** 176cr; **Fotolia:** akjswift 329tr; Nadja 10bl; Stevofarrugia84 11cl.

Getty Images: 44cl, 150bl, 460; AFP 46tl; AFP/Stringer 553bl; Artie Photography 294–5; Pete Atkinson 252; Scott E Barbour: 542–3; Tom Cockrem 400tl; Stuart Hannagan 374–5; Alex Hare 168; Daniel Osterkamp 64–5; Peter Parks 401br; David Wall Photo 160–61; Peter Walton Photography 442;, 456–7 John White Photos 336–7; David Woolley 550tr; **Glencoe Rural Retreat:** 533br; **Glen Isla House:** 480b, 496bl; **Gorge Wildlife Park:** 356cr/bl; **Government House Perth:** 306clb; **Ronald Grant Archive:** Buena Vista 25cl; Universal 39bl; © **Great Barrier Reef Marine Park Authority:** 219tr, 221tc/cr; Photo: S Browne 219bl; Photo: W Craik 216bl; Photo: N Collins 216cla; Photo: L Zell 217bl, 218cla; **Great Southern Rail:** Steve Strike 558cla; **The GreenRoom:** 517br;

Robert Harding Picture Library: 294–5, 379tl, 587t; © Nick Servian 344, 562tl; **C Moore Hardy:** 142br; **Hood Collection, State Library of NSW:** 85bl; **Horizon:** © Andris Apse 283b; **House of Anvers:** 535br; **Hurricane's Grill Bondi Beach:** 506br; **Hutchison Library:** © R. Ian Lloyd 542–3; © Sarah Murray 558br.

Il Centro Restaurant: 512br; **Images Colour Library:** 30b, 215cla, 291t, 293br; **The Image Library, State Library of NSW:** 38tl, 40bl, 52tc/clb, 53c, 56bla, 59crb, 62tc, 353br; **Islington Hotel:** 497tr, 534b; **iStockphoto.com:** John Kirk 214cl; **Ali Kayn:** 396cla; © **Dr Ruth Kerr** (Commissariat Stores,

Brisbane): 226bl; **Kingfisher Bay Resort:** 487tl; **Knee Deep in Margaret River:** Jenny Clark 521tr.

Frank Lane Picture Library – Images of Nature: 28clb, 219br; © Tom & Pam Gardner 29bc, 341clb; © David Hosking 29tr, 341tr/clb; © E & D Hosking 341crb, 459cra/cb; © M Hollings 340crb; © Gerard Lacz 165br; © Martin Withers 172cla, 340clb; **Langham Sydney Hotel:** 479cr; **Lavandula La Trattoria:** 498tl, 531br; **Lion Nathan:** 342ca; **Lochman Transparencies:** © Bill Belson 327cr; © Wade Hughes 300t; © Jiri Lochman 311tr, 312cla; © Marie Lochman 296ca, 313tl; © Len Stewart 307br; **Lonely Planet Images:** Glenn Beanland 392tr; **The Louise:** 491tr.

Marion Bay Tavern: 526tl; **Lindsay May Pr:** 342cl; **Merlin Entertainments Group Australia:** 102b; © Greg Miles (Environmental Media): 280br; © **Mirror Australian Telegraph Publications:** 62cr; **Mitchell Library, State Library of NSW:** 52bl; 54–5c, 56b, 85cra, 112c, 113tr; **The MONA Pavillions:** 497br, 535tl; **Moorish Cafe:** 517cr; **Mount Baw Baw Alpine Resort:** James Lauritz 452bl; **Multiplex Property Services:** 102tr; **Museum of Contemporary Art, Sydney:** 68cla, 80bl; Alex Davies 82br.

Collection of The National Gallery of Australia, Canberra: Clarice Beckett, *Sandringham Beach,* c.1933 206crb; Tom Roberts, *In a corner in a Macintyre* 1895, oil on canvas, 73.4 x 88.0cm, 206cl; Margaret Preston; ADAGP, Paris and DACS, London 2011; Aristide Maillol, *The Mountain (La Montagne)* 1937, lead, 167,4 (h) x 193.0 (w) x 82.3 (d)cm 206bl; © ARS, NY and DACS, London 2011, Jackson Pollock, *Blue Poles* 1952, oil enamel and aluminium paint on canvas, 212.0 x 489.0cm, 207tl; © Bula'bula Arts, Ramininging Artists, Ramininging, Central Arnhem Land, NT, *The Aboriginal Memorial* 1998, natural pigments on wood: an installation of 200 hollow log coffins, height 40.0 to 327.0cm, purchased with the assistance of funds from gallery admission charges and commissioned in 1987, 207cr; **National Gallery of Victoria, Melbourne:** 404cla; **National Library of Australia:** 39tl, 50, 53bc (original in possession of the WA Museum), 56ca, 57cra 59cra, 60tl, 201br; Rex nan Kivell Collection 53crb/br, 55crb; ES Theodore, Campaign Director, ALP State of NSW, Trades Hall 60clb; **National Maritime Museum, Sydney:** 55tl, 101cra, 105cra, 105tl, bc; **Nature Focus:** H & J Bestel 458cl; Rob Blakers 458br; John Fields 72bl; Dave Watts 458cr; Babs & Bert Wells 291cra; © Australian Museum 34cla, 36tr, **National Museum of Australia:** 208crb; © Australia-China Friendship Society, *The Harvest of Endurance Scroll.* The scroll is of 18 segments, ink and colour on paper, mounted on silk and paper 209t, *Untitled* by Charlie Alyungurra, 1970 pigment on composite board 209cra, *The Mermaid Coffin* by Gaynor Peaty, 209br; **National Trust of Australia:** © Christopher Groenhout 408cl, 409tl/bc; **Natural History Photographic Agency:** © A.N.T 28cl, 165cr, 217tl, 299bl/br, 340tr/cra, 458ca/cb, 462tr; © Patrick Faggot 252; © Pavel German 290tl; © Martin Harvey 29ca; © Ralph & Daphne Keller 298cb; **Nautilus Restaurant:** 516bl; **Peter Newark's Historical Pictures:** 33cr, 54clb; **Tourism NSW:** 182cla/c; **Northern Territory Library:** 268–9c, 269crb; Percy Brown Collection 268br; N Gleeson Collection 268tr; **Nucolorvue Productions Pty Ltd:** 57br.

Sydney Transport Map

Key

- ▢ Major sight
- 🚉 Sydney Trains station
- 🚉 Main railway station
- 🚈 Light rail station
- ⛴ Ferry boarding point
- --- Ferry route
- ━ Sydney Explorer
- ━ Bondi Explorer
- ━ Bus route

Terminal ❶ Circular Quay

309, 310 – Port Botany
373, 374 – Coogee
380 – Watson's Bay (via Bondi)
389 – Bondi
392 – Little Bay
394, L94 – La Perouse
396, 397 – Maroubra
422 – Kogarah
    (via Newtown & Tempe)
423 – Kingsgrove (via Newtown)
426 – Dulwich Hill (via Newtown)
428 – Canterbury (via Newtown)
520 – Parramatta

Terminal ❷ Gresham/Pitt/Spring St

311 – Railway Square
    (via Elizabeth Bay)
391 – La Perouse & Port Botany

Terminal ❸ Millers Point
(Argyle St)/Walsh Bay

339 – Clovelly
431 – Glebe
433 – Balmain (via Glebe)

Terminal ❹ Wynyard
(Carrington St)

247 – Taronga Zoo

Terminal ❺ Queen Victoria
Building (York Street)

442 – Balmain East (Darling St Wharf)

Terminal ❻ Railway Square

311 – Gresham/Pitt/Spring St
    (via Elizabeth Bay)
372 – Coogee
378 – Bronte
393 – La Perouse
395 – Maroubra Beach
L88 – Avalon
L90 – Palm Beach

Terminal ❼ King Street Wharf

412 – Campsie (via Dulwich Hill)
Terminal Woolloomooloo
441 – Birchgrove

0 metres   500
0 yards   500

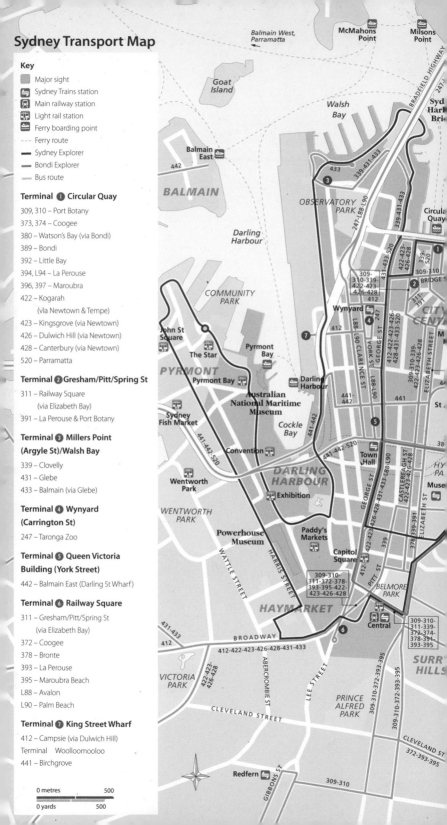